THE HISTORY OF WALES

GENERAL EDITOR
GLANMOR WILLIAMS

RENEWAL
AND REFORMATION
WALES
*c.*1415–1642

BY

GLANMOR WILLIAMS

Oxford   New York
OXFORD UNIVERSITY PRESS
1993

Oxford University Press, Walton Street, Oxford OX2 6DP

Oxford New York Toronto
Delhi Bombay Calcutta Madras Karachi
Kuala Lumpur Singapore Hong Kong Tokyo
Nairobi Dar es Salaam Cape Town
Melbourne Auckland Madrid
and associated companies in
Berlin Ibadan

Oxford is a trade mark of Oxford University Press

First published 1987 as Recovery, Reorientation and Reformation: Wales, c.1415–1642
First issued as an Oxford University Press paperback 1993

British Library Cataloguing in Publication Data
Data available

Library of Congress Cataloging in Publication Data
Williams, Glanmor.
[Recovery, reorientation, and Reformation]
Renewal and Reformation : Wales c. 1415–1642 / Glanmor Williams.
p. cm.—(The History of Wales ; 3)
Originally published: Recovery, reorientation, and Reformation : Wales,
1415–1642. Oxford : Clarendon Press ; [Cardiff] ; University of Wales Press, 1987.
Includes bibliographical references and index.
1. Wales—History—To 1536. 2. Renaissance—Wales.
3. Reformation—Wales. 4. Wales—History. I. Title. II. Series: History of Wales ; v. 3.
942.9—dc20 [DA715.W536 1993] 92-28333
ISBN 0-19-285277-9

Printed and bound in Great Britain by
Biddles Ltd, Guildford and King's Lynn

TO
MY WIFE AND FAMILY

PREFACE

In 1919, when W. Llewelyn Williams, last of the Liberal–progressive interpreters of the history of early–modern Wales, published his vigorously argued and influential book, *The Making of Modern Wales*, no shadow of doubt crossed his mind that Henry VIII's reign was the great watershed of Welsh history; the line of demarcation between medieval and modern Wales. Nor, in an equally, if not more, seminal short study of Welsh literature published some years later, *Braslun o Hanes Llenyddiaeth Gymraeg*, did Saunders Lewis, though writing from an almost diametrically different and strongly nationalist standpoint, have any uncertainty about the significance of the Henrician epoch. For Williams, Henry was an autocrat but a benevolent one, who broke the shackles of papal dominion, freed Wales from the outworn vestiges of medieval servitude and lawlessness, gave it a liberal constitution, and set it on the road to enlightenment and progress. Saunders Lewis, on the contrary, viewed Henry as a Machiavellian tyrant, embodying the imperialist instincts of the English state, who finally snuffed out what remained of Welsh independence, brought to an end the golden epoch of cultural autonomy, literary achievement, and deep religious faith, and fatally lured the Welsh ruling class into an era of swift anglicization and subservience to English masters.

Both have had followers; Saunders Lewis many more than Llewelyn Williams. There was, and indeed still is, much to be said for the concept of a fateful break with the past, whether regarded as an act of emancipation or of oppression. Henry's Act of Union, 1536–43, cleared away much of the debris of medieval political and legal systems, merged Wales wholly with England, made the Welsh full citizens of the realm, imposed on them uniform law and administration based on English custom and practice, and entrusted authority within the shires and hundreds to the local gentry—on condition that for all official purposes they spoke only English. His reign also introduced the first instalment of sweeping modifications of the medieval Church, shattering papal authority and cutting England and Wales off from western Christendom, dissolving the houses of religion and establishing himself as Supreme Head of a national church co-terminous with the boundaries of his realm. These were drastic and long-lasting changes. For good and ill, in politics, law, administration, religion, and culture, Wales would never be the same again.

In the past half-century or so, historians have come to attach less weight to political changes and have given greater attention to social and economic conditions. In the light of this gradual shift of emphasis it may well seem to our generation that the significance of the Tudor changes has been over-estimated. The hundred years which preceded Henry's reign and the hundred years which followed it had a great deal more in common than is often supposed. Fifteenth-century Wales, though turbulent and disordered, was not the theatre of anarchy and lawlessness that has usually been depicted. There was a greater measure of security, recovery, and prosperity than has frequently been realized. Nor did 'instant' peace and order follow magically in the immediate wake of the Act of Union. Resort to force and violence was commonplace a hundred years later; and for many of the population the years between c.1585 and 1642 were economically much grimmer than most of the fifteenth century had been. Yet, economically and socially, the two centuries between 1415 and 1642 were, throughout, very similar in the basic conditions of getting and spending and of relationships between the varying social degrees. Not until the coming of the Industrial Revolution was there any fundamental change in this respect.

These earlier two centuries constituted the age of the dominance of the squires. So much so that I was sorely tempted to entitle this volume with yet another variant of a flippant formula, widely and popularly applied with considerable effect, and call this book, 'Gentry Rules OK'. Throughout the fifteenth century they had been taking advantage of the many opportunities on offer to build up their estates, possessions, and standing, had asserted their supremacy in town and countryside, and, by playing a bold and active role in local and wider politics and government, had made their position acceptable, indispensable even, to the King and his government. So that the Act of Union, when it came, did not do much more than give *de jure* validation to a situation which had long existed *de facto*. Those families and individuals who had previously ruled the roost in practice, as deputies to royal officials and Marcher lords, or even occasionally in their own right, now continued to do so on an official footing as sheriffs and justices of the peace. That was why, perhaps, there was so little comment from contemporary Welshmen on legislation which seems to loom so large to historians. National politics and national issues could mean surprisingly little to the men of this age, except in so far as they affected their own positions locally. Their rivalries in the fifteenth and sixteenth centuries were pursued for local stakes, for what John Wynn described as the 'sovereignty of the countryside'. Even with the advent of the Civil Wars in 1642, what concerned them most was how far could adverse consequences be avoided, or at least minimized, for their own county and district.

The Reformation, too, may have made less difference in practice than we often suppose. Worship and belief were far more a matter of habit and custom than intellectual and spiritual conviction. Most men and women continued to be 'collective Christians', depending on the clergy to undertake on their behalf whatever was necessary in the way of ritual to protect them against the Evil One and his minions. Only a minority conceived of religion as necessitating on their part a profound individual and inward responsibility for their relationship with God and their diurnal behaviour and conduct. Down to the reign of Charles I—and beyond— earnest Protestant reformers like Vicar Prichard inveighed against the religious ignorance and apathy of the mass of the population, how slow it was to change, and how attached to its former superstitious beliefs and practices. True, the gentry had readily accepted an erastian monarch's supremacy as head of the Church and welcomed the additional control over its jurisdiction and property which the Reformation had brought them. But they could not separate the question of authority in the Church from that of authority in the State and in society. What really mattered to them, and what they were prepared to make considerable sacrifices for, was the security of the political and social order from threats internal and external. Its stability was guaranteed in their eyes by the successful liaison between royal jurisdiction and their own pre-eminence in the locality. The Reformation as a body of doctrine and belief could not come of age for most people until the eighteenth century had made many of them literate.

Important cultural changes there undoubtedly were; chief among them the decline of the old poetic order and the spread of an English-language, printed-book culture. These have often been explained, a little simplistically perhaps, as the outcome of the 'language clause' of the Act of Union. But the process can now be seen as altogether more subtle and complex; one which is still not fully explained, but which calls for a much wider and deeper social explanation than it has usually received. Moreover, it calls also for an interpretation of the remarkably energetic response which the crisis of the language and the literature evoked from a minority of Welsh scholars and intellectuals. This was far from achieving all they would have wished, but it was by no means an unqualified failure.

As for the mass of the peasant population—small farmers and labourers—all these changes made singularly little difference to their hard-working, humdrum existence. Essentially, throughout these two centuries, we are still in the midst of an under-developed, pre-industrial farming society, which was tightly constrained by the facts of physical structure and climate and would not be fundamentally changed until the coming of the Industrial Revolution. It was still a society dominated by the landowning gentry. It was profoundly affected by the state of the harvest, the growth in population, and the inflation of prices. It was these long-term secular changes which had the profoundest impact on their lives and not the effects of political, religious, and cultural modifications, however significant these may have been in upper-class existence. Nothing has impressed me more deeply than the courage and tenacity with which the ordinary man and woman faced the adversities and tribulations which so often afflicted them and have frequently gone almost unchronicled.

In the end I settled for a title which seemed to me to sum up, in so far as that can be done in four words, the main trends of the period: Recovery, Reorientation, and Reformation. The economic and social recovery from the suffocating disasters of the aftermath of the Glyndŵr Rebellion was quite remarkable and characterizes the fifteenth century more than any other feature of its history. The reorientation of Welsh life was undertaken by the Tudors not merely in political and legal terms but also on the basis of the change of attitude on the part of their Welsh subjects who, as I try to show, believed in the 'Welshness' of the dynasty because they were genuinely proud of it and, more importantly, because they believed it to be in their interests to do so. The Reformation, however slow its initial progress may have been, in the long run brought about far-reaching changes, not simply in the organization of the Church and religious belief but also had profound significance for the language, culture, and national sentiment of Wales. More than anything else, it kept Wales Welsh.

I have tried to give a rounded and comprehensive picture of the whole of Welsh society and not just its upper classes during this period, even though the materials available for studying the latter are so much fuller. Inadequate as the end-product may be, I am still as utterly convinced as I was when this series was first mooted that the time is ripe for a large-scale series on the history of Wales and that the attempt should be made in this generation. If proof of that were needed, it was surely abundantly furnished by Dr Kenneth Morgan in his magisterial volume for this series—which gave his fellow-contributors so much delight and also such a headache in having to follow in his steps! I am not unaware of how thin and inadequate the straw has been for making the bricks at many crucial points, or how much more work in depth is called for. But I thought it best to give as wide a conspectus as I could, even though the detailed research is lacking for many aspects of the history of the period. I have depended heavily on the native literature. Difficult and in some respects unsatisfactory as it may be as an historical source, it is nevertheless much the most important Welsh voice that has come down to us for many topics. It was deeply loved and respected by most of the Welsh of the period. For that reason alone it deserves to be taken seriously into account by historians.

Completing the book has taken me much longer than I had originally hoped. While I held the Chair of History at University College, Swansea, I found my time and energies increasingly mortgaged to other matters— necessary but distracting. Only when I took early retirement was I able to get down to the task in all seriousness. I have to thank Mr Ivon Asquith of the Oxford University Press and Mr John Rhys for the University of Wales Press for being so patient and long-suffering with me. I am deeply grateful to the staff of the Oxford University Press for the immense care and trouble they have taken in seeing the volume through the press. I should also like to thank the staffs of the Public Record Office, British Library, National Library of Wales, and the Library of University College, Swansea, for all their help over many years. My friend and colleague, Mr Guy Lewis of University College, Swansea, was kind enough to draw the maps so clearly for me. Many friends have helped me enormously, more than they probably realize, not only by their published and unpublished work, but also by taking the time and trouble to discuss problems with me. I have to thank generations of students at University College, Swansea, for contributing so much by their discussion, questions, and essays to my understanding of a subject I purported to teach them. I should also like warmly to thank Dr F. G. Cowley, Professor R. R. Davies, Professor R. A. Griffiths, Dr G. H. Jenkins, Dr Gareth E. Jones, Dr K. O. Morgan, Dr P. T. J. Morgan, Mr Richard Welchman, Professor J. Gwynn Williams, and Professor J. E. Caerwyn Williams for all their help and kindness. To one friend above all others I owe a particular debt of gratitude. Professor Ieuan Gwynedd Jones has discussed with me endlessly the problems of Welsh history—to my immense advantage. He has also had more confidence in my ability to write the book than I had, and on more than one occasion when my morale flagged badly his enthusiasm revived it. I have left until the last my deepest debt—to my wife. We celebrated this year forty years of extremely happy married life; in all that time she has been an unfailing source of help, encouragement, and inspiration to me. I dedicate the book to her and our family as an inadequate token of all that I owe them.

GLANMOR WILLIAMS

Swansea
June 1986

The book has been retitled *Renewal and Reformation: Wales c. 1415–1642* for this paperback edition.

May 1992

CONTENTS

MAPS

ABBREVIATIONS

Note that full details of titles abbreviated in the following list will be found in the Bibliography at the end of the volume.

AAST	Anglesey Antiquarian Society Transactions
Add. MSS	Additional Manuscripts (British Library)
Agrarian Hist.	*The Agrarian History of England and Wales*
APC	*Acts of the Privy Council*
Arch. Camb.	*Archaeologia Cambrensis*
BBCS	*Bulletin of the Board of Celtic Studies*
BIHR	*Bulletin of the Institute of Historical Research*
BL	British Library
Cardiff Recs	*Records of the County Borough of Cardiff*
Carew MSS	*Calendar of the Carew Manuscripts*
Cath. Rec. Soc.	Catholic Record Society
CLNW	*Calendar of Letters relating to North Wales*
CLP	*Clenennau Letters and Papers*
C.Pap.L.	*Calendar of Papal Letters*
C.Pat.R.	*Calendar of the Patent Rolls*
CSP Dom.	*Calendar of State Papers Domestic*
CSP Ireland	*Calendar of State Papers Ireland*
CSP Span.	*Calendar of State Papers Spanish*
CSP Ven.	*Calendar of State Papers Venetian*
CWP	*Calendar of Wynn Papers*
D. ab E.	*Gwaith Dafydd ab Edmwnd*
DL	Duchy of Lancaster
D.Ll.F.	*Gwaith Dafydd Llwyd o Fathafarn*
DN	*The Poetical Works of Dafydd Nanmor*
DWB	*Dictionary of Welsh Biography*
EHR	*English Historical Review*
FHSP	*Flintshire Historical Society Publications*
GCH	*Glamorgan County History*
GG	*Gwaith Guto'r Glyn*
GO	*L'Œuvre poétique de Gutun Owain*
GPC	*Geiriadur Prifysgol Cymru*
GRO	Glamorgan Record Office
Hall	*The Union of the Two Noble and Illustre Famelies York and Lancaster*
H.C.Ll.	*Gwaith Huw Cae Llwyd ac Eraill*
HG	*Hen Gwndidau, Carolau a Chywyddau*
HGF	*History of the Gwydir Family*
HMC	Historical Manuscripts Commission

HS	*Gwaith Hywel Swrdwal a'i Fab Ieuan*
HWL	Parry, *History of Welsh Literature*
ID	*Casgliad o Waith Ieuan Deulwyn*
IGE	*Cywyddau Iolo Goch ac Eraill*
JMHRS	*Journal of the Merioneth Historical and Record Society*
JHSCW	*Journal of the Historical Society of the Church in Wales*
L. and P.	*Letters and Papers, Foreign and Domestic, of the Reign of Henry VIII*
Leland	*Leland's Itinerary in Wales*
LGC¹	*Gwaith Lewys Glyn Cothi* (1837)
LGC²	*Gwaith Lewys Glyn Cothi* (1953)
LGC³	*Lewys Glyn Cothi (Detholiad)*
LM	*Gwaith Lewys Môn*
Mont. Colls.	*Montgomeryshire Collections*
NLW	National Library of Wales
NLWJ	*National Library of Wales Journal*
OBWV	*The Oxford Book of Welsh Verse in English*
Owen	Owen, *Description of Penbrokshire*
Pembs. Hist.	*The Pembrokeshire Historian*
PRO	Public Record Office
RBRR	*Gwaith Rhys Brydydd a Rhisiart ap Rhys*
RCAHM	Royal Commission on Ancient and Historical Monuments (Wales)
RHS	Royal Historical Society
Rot. Parl.	*Rotuli Parliamentorum*
RS	Rolls Series
SP	State Papers
ST	*Gwaith Siôn Tudur*
STAC	Star Chamber Proceedings
SWMRS	South Wales and Monmouthshire Record Society
TA	*Gwaith Tudur Aled*
TDHS	*Transactions of the Denbighshire Historical Society*
THSC	*Transactions of the Historical Society of Caernarfonshire*
TP	*Gwaith Tudur Penllyn*
Trans. Cymm.	*Transactions of the Cymmrodorion Society*
TRHS	*Transactions of the Royal Historical Society*
Treatises	Penry, *Three Treatises concerning Wales*
WHR	*Welsh Historical Review*
W.Ll.	*Barddoniaeth Wiliam Llŷn*
WWR	Evans, *Wales and the Wars of the Roses*
YB	*Ysgrifau Beirniadol*
Y Cymmr.	*Y Cymmrodor*

PART I

REBELLION AND RECOVERY
THE TWILIGHT OF MEDIEVAL WALES
1415–1536

CHAPTER I

THE GLYNDŴR REBELLION AND ITS AFTERMATH

CLOSE on two hundred years after Owain Glyndŵr's Rebellion had been suppressed, David Powel, an eminent Tudor historian of Wales, in his *Historie of Cambria* (1584) dismissed Owain's title to the Principality of Wales as 'altogether frivolous' and his attempt to establish it as a 'fool's paradise'.[1] That was the wisdom of sixteenth-century hindsight not late fourteenth-century politics. Over-ambitious Owain's ultimate intention may have been and for his miscalculation he and his countrymen paid a fearful price. Yet, in originally resorting to armed force to put pressure on King, Marcher Lord, and English officials, he could well have had in mind many precedents for such attempts on the part of upper-class Welsh leaders like himself—some successful, many others disastrous, in their outcome. Ever since Edward I's conquest of Wales in 1282–3 there had been a series of rebellions, riots, and the threat of them. The names of notable Welsh rebels like Rhys ap Maredudd (1287), Madog ap Llywelyn (1295), Llywelyn Bren (1316), 'Wyrion Eden' (1345 and other occasions), and Owain Lawgoch (1372) can hardly have been unfamiliar to Glyndŵr. Moreover, in the 1390s, the decade before he took up arms, law and order had been unmistakably deteriorating in Wales and dissatisfaction growing among the population there. Nor had he any reason to suppose that taking the law into his own hands, even if unsuccessful, would necessarily lead to humiliation and permanent exclusion from royal favour. His own influential kinsmen, the Tudor brothers Rhys and Gwilym ap Tudur—*ben ymwanwyr Môn* [chief fighters of Anglesey]—and their ancestors had long been adepts at applying armed pressure at critical junctures and yet retaining their influence and their offices. Conceivably it was they who injected the bacillus of armed uprising into Glyndŵr's thinking as he attempted to win redress against Lord Grey of Ruthin and in 1400 flattered his hopes of being recognized as 'Prince of Wales'. Whether, at the outset, Owain seriously proposed to set himself up as prince of an independent or quasi-autonomous regime must be considered doubtful.

Whatever Owain's intentions may have been when he raised rebellion in September 1400, there was no mistaking the scale of his initial defeat at Henry IV's hands in the campaign that followed. Once the King had

---

[1] David Powel, *Historie of Cambria*, ed. W. Wynne (London, 1697), pp. 315–22.

administered that crushing military rebuke, had he then been able to
handle Owain, his Tudor kinsmen, and the other rebels in conciliatory
fashion, the whole uprising might have been snuffed out at birth. But the
panicky and vindictive attitude shown by the Parliaments of 1401 and 1402
in imposing stringent legislation against the Welsh, the so-called 'Lancastrian
penal code', ensured that Welsh opposition would continue and become
inflamed. Even with the rebels' military successes of 1402–3, however, it
was by no means clear that Owain was seeking to re-establish an
independent Welsh principality. In 1401 he had seemingly dropped the title
of Prince of Wales, and his relations with Mortimer and the Percies in 1403
could be regarded in the light of a dangerous feudal conspiracy to
overthrow Henry IV, replace him with a Mortimer, and establish a regime
from which Owain and his Welsh confederates could hope to benefit. It
was still not necessarily a national rebellion. Not until 1404 did his larger
intentions become fully evident. At this point, his military success had
been encouraging enough and the measure of support for him in Wales
sufficiently enthusiastic for him to have himself crowned Prince of Wales in
the presence of envoys from Scotland, France, and Spain. Significantly, he
assumed the arms of the former princes of Wales, the four lions of
Gwynedd, in place of the single lion rampant of Powys, and set up his own
court at Harlech Castle. He unveiled plans for an autonomous state with its
own appropriate institutions and personnel, summoned a parliament to
meet at Harlech, and entered into an alliance with the king of France,
Henry IV's principal enemy. There was more to follow. In 1406 Owain
agreed to transfer his allegiance to the Avignon pope, Benedict XIII, and
adumbrated far-reaching proposals for a church independent of the
authority of Canterbury and the founding of two university institutions in
Wales.

Yet, even as these grandiose schemes for new power structures were
being sketched out on the policy drawing-board of the new Cymric
principality, the military props which alone could ensure their being given
substance were being steadily knocked away. In 1405 the first major set-
backs in the field began and, from 1406 onwards, Owain's power visibly
waned, as that of his adversaries no less obviously waxed. The latter year
witnessed large-scale loss of territory in Flintshire and Anglesey in north
Wales, while, in the south, Glamorgan, Gower, Ystrad Tywi, and much of
Ceredigion slipped from his grasp. The icy talons of the winter of 1407–8,
the coldest in living memory, pierced deep and damagingly into the rebel
cause. The two castles that were the twin poles of Owain's military and
territorial power were probably lost in the summer of 1408—Aberystwyth
certainly, and Harlech could not have held out later than early 1409.
Thereafter, Owain was obliged to surrender all pretensions of being an
independent ruling prince. He was once more the hunted outlaw, the

guerrilla leader on the run. Not that his resistance was completely at an end! As late as 1410 came his last desperate major effort: a great raid on the Shropshire border, only to encounter humiliating defeat and the loss of some of his best remaining captains. Following this débâcle, he made 'no great attack until he disappeared'.[2] A handful of rebels continued to cling to him, and his reputation was fearsome enough to cause the King to draft many soldiers into Wales to keep a watchful eye on him. A plot of 1415 still envisaged his being brought back to co-operate with the Lollard, Sir John Oldcastle; but a Welsh chronicle records that in that very year he went into hiding and adds, 'Very many say that he died; the seers maintain he did not'.[3] His eventual fate and the date of his death, even, are enveloped in mystery. The most recent studies have only been able to come to the tentative conclusion that he may have died in 1415. Like the comet of 1402, which had excited so many euphoric Welsh expectations, Owain had streamed luminously through the political firmament and had finally vanished without trace.

Just how many of those who supported him at one time or another shared his visions of an independent state it is difficult to tell. While there was an overflow of furious anti-English feeling and plenty of vague aspirations for a future Welsh victory over the ancient enemy, more constructive ambitions for the setting up of an autonomous Welsh polity were in short supply. They may have been shared by no more than a handful of the more intelligent, educated, and enterprising laymen, clerics, and lawyers in Owain's entourage. That many among those on whom he depended most heavily for military leadership and support were hard-bitten men, little given to sentiment or idealism, there can be no question. Some, like Henry Don of Kidwelly, after serving a term of imprisonment for their part in the Rebellion, remained unchastened by their experiences and rode as rough-shod and assertively over lesser men after the Rebellion was over as before. Many of the rebels were actuated by the normal motives of that form of 'bastard feudalism' that bound them to their *uchelwyr* chiefs and employers: they fought chiefly, if not wholly, for their own profit and survival. Not a few of them had anyway made peace with the King in the course of the Rebellion and subsequently held office for him in Wales and fought for him in France. A man like William Gruffydd of Penrhyn contrived to make his own and his family's fortunes by such tactics. It seems impossible now to discover what aspirations had prompted those ordinary Welshmen—peasants, labourers, and others—to give Owain their support, beyond an understandably pressing desire to rid themselves of their desperate economic and social burdens and improve their daily lot. There were, of course, some eminent Welshmen, like David

[2] J. E. Lloyd, *Owen Glendower* (Oxford, 1931), p. 54.
[3] Lloyd, *Glendower*, p. 154.

Gam or David Holbeach, who had never shown the slightest sympathy for the rebel leader and who rejoiced in his defeat. As for the English minority in Wales, they must have been unfeignedly relieved when the greatest menace to their position of privilege and superiority disappeared from the scene.

However many or few had been stirred by Owain's resplendent dreams of a revived principality and for whatever reasons they had responded, his defeat appeared to be the death-blow to any pretensions for an independent regime in Wales. For the rest of the fifteenth century no more would-be princes of Wales emerged to kindle ambitions for a *Wallia Rediviva*. True, there were plenty of men eager to seize power and turn to their own advantage any Welsh patriotism that was going; but they made no secret of their willingness to manœuvre within the existing framework of English politics. They were mobilized in support of a Lancastrian or Yorkist leader: a Jasper Tudor, William Herbert, or even Edward IV by virtue of his descent from Llywelyn the Great's daughter, Gwladus Ddu. By 1484–5, admittedly, much of what might be described as the 'professional patriotism' of the poets and their enthusiasm for a 'son of prophecy' [*mab darogan*], on which Glyndŵr himself had depended a great deal, had been concentrated on Henry Tudor. Yet even Henry's uncle and chief mentor, Jasper Tudor, had until 1471 been wholly loyal to the Lancastrian dynasty and only after the death of Henry VI and his heir did he see his nephew as a possible contender for the throne. In Jasper's eyes, Henry may well have appeared first and foremost as the best Lancastrian candidate for king and only secondly as a descendant of old British Cadwaladr, admirably fitted to attract Welsh support. It was as a claimant to the throne of England most likely to advance their interest, not as an independent ruler of Wales, that Henry's Welsh supporters also saw him.

Nevertheless, the Welsh patriotic fervour and its complementary bitter antagonism to things and persons English, which the Rebellion had raised to fever heat, did not disappear and were easily reawakened in the generations that followed. Many of Owain's former partisans and their kinsmen, for a generation and more after the Rebellion was over, continued to take their vengeance on those who had stood by the Crown, laying waste their lands, attacking their persons, and bringing all kinds of accusations against them. None of the later poets, the authentic inciters and interpreters of Welsh emotional attitudes, reproached Owain for his failure, devastating though its consequences had been for Wales. On the contrary, a number of them saw in him the very pattern of their hopes and desires. 'The poets in their eulogies of prospective leaders always saw with the inward eye the shape of Owain Glyndŵr.'[4] Moreover, that prophetic

---

[4] E. D. Jones in *Wales through the Ages*, ed. A. J. Roderick (Llandybïe, 1959), p. 185.

poetry, which for centuries had foretold that a prince descended of the blood of Cadwaladr, last King of the Britons, would appear to lead his people to victory over the Saxons, was given a new lease of life in the fifteenth century. Well aware of the rhetorical exaggeration that was the hallmark of this and other poetry, few of its hearers expected the literal fulfilment of forecasts of resounding victory which would reinstate the Welsh as rulers of the whole island of Britain. For many Welshmen, all the same, that poetry at the heart of it continued to reaffirm two essential beliefs which they resolutely refused to relinquish: that the Welsh were sprung from one of the oldest and most illustrious peoples in Europe and as such were entitled to honourable treatment; and secondly, having been betrayed, cheated, and suppressed regularly by the English, that their best hope of obtaining justice was from a leader born of their own people. Welsh monks, like poets ancient guardians of such aspirations, were also on occasion alleged to be harbouring and fostering notions of this kind. Mathew ap Llywelyn Ddu, canon of Talyllychau (Talley), was thus accused in 1427; and an unnamed monk of Whitland, mother house of the native strain of Cistercians, was charged with having narrated Welsh chronicles and traditions and stirring up the people to rebellion in 1443.

Closely allied to the prophetic theme was the poets' ineradicable instinct during the course of the wars between Lancaster and York to look upon the battles not as so many faction fights between rival sets of contenders for power in English politics but rather as further episodes in the age-old contentions between Welsh and English. Their attitude emerges plainly enough in the verse of some of the greatest poets of the fifteenth century. Lewys Glyn Cothi was a poet of Lancastrian sympathies, who depended largely on Lancastrian patrons. Yet he showed himself little concerned with factional loyalties and was preoccupied much more intensely with Welsh hatred of the English and with keeping a memory of Glyndŵr vividly in mind. When a great company of Welsh Yorkists were killed at the battle of Edgecote in 1468, this Lancastrian poet took no delight at all in a Yorkist defeat; he was overwhelmed with grief at the loss of so many gallant Welshmen slaughtered by Saxons. In similar vein, his fellow Lancastrian, Dafydd Llwyd o Fathafarn, vented not only his anguish at the death of William Herbert and his contingent but also his fury at the 'children of Alice' (the English) who had brought it about. Guto'r Glyn, on the other hand, had been an ardent Yorkist who probably served Edward IV as a soldier. He could, nevertheless, enter a strong plea for mercy for the Welsh Lancastrians at Harlech who had finally had to yield to Yorkist William Herbert after a long and desperate siege. When Herbert himself was killed, it was the spilling of Welsh blood that Guto lamented in agonized and extravagant tones:

> Ef a'm llas i a'm nasiwn
> Yn awr y llas yr iarll hwn.[5]

[He killed me and my nation who now killed this earl.]

Throughout the civil wars the poets consistently appealed to Welsh leaders to transmute these conflicts between Lancaster and York into a crusade to champion Welsh interests and enlarge them, in defiance of the wishes of the English if need be. In one of the most celebrated passages of fifteenth-century poetry, Guto'r Glyn issued a stirring appeal to William Herbert to unify the whole of Wales under his authority.

> Dwg Forgannwg a Gwynedd,
> Gwna'n un o Gonwy i Nedd;
> O digia Lloegr a'i dugiaid,
> Cymru a dry yn dy raid.[6]

[Bring Wales from Glamorgan to Gwynedd under thy sway; unite it all from Conwy to Neath. If England and her dukes are offended, Wales will rally to thy cause.]

The incipient patriotism observable in countries like England, France, Scotland, Bohemia, and Hungary, could also be seen fermenting in Wales; much of it negative in character and vented in hatred of the traditional enemy.

In the climate of opinion thus being expressed and stimulated it was inevitable that prejudice against one another, on the part of the English and Welsh, should remain intense. As that prince of Tudor antiquaries, George Owen of Henllys, was to record over a century later, 'there grew about the time [the early fifteenth century] deadly hatred between them [the Welsh] and the English nation, insomuch that the name of a Welshman was odious to the Englishman, and the name of Englishman woeful to the Welshman'.[7] On the other side, the dire warning to his fellow-countrymen uttered by the author of *The Libel of English Policy* is so well-known as to have become almost hackneyed, but has still not lost its power to convey its author's sense of dread of the Welsh:

> Beware of Wales, Christ Jesus must us keep
> That it make not our child's child to weep,
> Nor us also, if it go his way
> By unawareness; since that many a day
> Men have befeared of her rebellion.
> Look well about, for, God wot, we have need.[8]

In much of the contemporary Welsh poetry the themes of hatred and mistrust of Englishmen throbbed with relentless persistence and, on occasion, were expressed with raw and undisguised virulence. Tudur

---

[5] *GG*, p. 144.   [6] *GG*, p. 131.   [7] Owen, III, 37.
[8] T. Wright (ed.), *Political Songs and Poems* . . . (RS, 2 vols. 1859–61), II, 190.

Penllyn, friend and admirer of those Welsh outlaws who set English authority at naught, sang with rabid anti-English exultation of 'Rheinallt of the Tower's' feats against the men of Chester: 'a bloody sword to the whole world was he', whose fearsome weapon had been wielded under the protection of one who might be considered an unlikely mentor—'the Holy Virgin of Mold'.[9] Crucial events, like the hanging of Sir Gruffydd Fychan in 1447 or the death of so many Yorkists at Edgecote in 1468, served only to confirm the deeply ingrained animus of the Welsh against what they believed to be the habitual treachery of the English. 'Alas for us poor wretches, the remnants of Troy'—a reference to the firmly held belief that the ancient Britons were the descendants of Brutus and the Trojans who had first founded the kingdom of Britain—'did we not know the treachery of the English these endless centuries?', expostulated the poet Dafydd Llwyd.[10] Not until the emergence of Henry Tudor as a contender for the throne in 1483–4 did Dafydd and many other poets espy a real possibility of turning the tables. Luckily for the Tudors, many of these emotions converged in a tide of support for them at the end of the century: hopes of being able to win the Crown within the existing context of English political life and at the same time of fulfilling those hoary prophecies of enthroning a descendant of Cadwaladr, together with the long-delayed triumph of the Welsh and the humiliation of the English.

Yet the temptation to overstate these feelings of resentment against the English and longing for Welsh vengeance against them is one that must be resisted. Admittedly, the passions aroused by the Rebellion, the vendettas it spawned, and the penal legislation it provoked, had all engendered a more intense anti-English prejudice, which could always be invoked and incited into outbursts of wrathful indignation when occasion demanded. It might make excellent propaganda for a faction leader to induce a poet to stir the blood of his less sophisticated followers by appeals to their gut reaction of hatred of the English, when a call to support a Yorkist or Lancastrian claimant might have fallen distinctly flat. Such bitterness against the ancestral enemy had always lain near the surface and never took much to rouse it. But its significance has to be kept in perspective; for the truth was that it had never hindered for long a degree of co-operation between Welsh and English which, in the light of the immemorial enmity between the two peoples, might have seemed wholly surprising. For, at least a century before the Glyndŵr Rebellion broke out, leading Welsh families in the Principality had found ways of accommodating themselves to English rule and making themselves acceptable to the King as office-holders; even essential to him if his administration in Wales was to work at all. The careers of Glyndŵr's ancestors, and his own activities before 1400,

---

[9] *TP*, p. 3.   [10] *D.Ll.F.*, p. 121.

fit this well-established model of adjustment and co-operation embarrassingly neatly. Nor did the traumas of the Rebellion do more than interrupt the pattern for most of the leading families; they certainly did not break it. When the rising was all over, even before it had ended in many instances, the old familiar story of Welshmen holding office, intriguing boldly in English politics, fighting in English armies abroad and at home, intermarrying with English families, carrying on trade, and migrating to English towns was resumed (see below, pp. 27–9). The era of the Wars of the Roses and the events that led up to them 'produced more remarkable examples of Welsh local boys who made good than any other period'.[11]

Nothing had fuelled Welsh acrimony against the privileges accorded to the English in Wales, and the natives' own subordinate position as colonized subjects, more than the reinforced statement by the legislation enacted in 1401–2 of their existing position of inferiority. Such restrictions had originally been imposed on them by Edward I, probably as the result of the violent Welsh uprising of Madog ap Llywelyn (1294–5), and these were given statutory form by Parliament in 1401–2. Their general tenor was to prevent Welshmen from acquiring land or property or office in English border boroughs or in English towns in Wales; to ensure that Englishmen in Wales were tried by other Englishmen in courts of justice; that castles were securely guarded; that Welshmen were not allowed to fortify their houses, congregate in any number, or carry arms to places of assembly; that bards and other 'vagabonds' were restrained; and that English people marrying Welsh spouses should lose their privileges. It seems very likely that there was never any intention of literally enforcing these measures at all times. They were, essentially, an emergency measure, not to say an act of desperation, designed to allay the hysterical fears aroused in the English by the Rebellion. So intense was English alarm in 1401, if we are to believe Adam of Usk, that the destruction of the Welsh tongue had been decreed by the English and would have been insisted upon had not God 'mercifully ordained the recall of this decree at the prayer and cry of the oppressed'.[12] If these measures were intended to dragoon the Welsh into obedience they met with scant success. It may, indeed, be the promulgation of these edicts that had the effect of provoking many Welsh *uchelwyr* to resort to arms. In the crisis of the next few years, with English officials in Wales like John Fairford calling on Henry IV to 'ordain a final destruction of all the false nation of the Welsh'[13] and the latter reportedly seeking to destroy the English tongue and proclaim Owain as rightful King of England and Prince

[11] G. Roberts, *Aspects of Welsh History* (Cardiff, 1969), p. 316.
[12] Adam of Usk, *Chronicon Ade de Usk*, ed. E. M. Thompson (London, 1904), p. 6.
[13] F. C. Hingeston (ed.), *Royal and Historical Letters during the Reign of Henry IV* (RS, 1860), I, 142.

of Wales, it could have seemed, to panic-stricken members of Parliament and English burgesses, that such draconian Acts were justified. Nor did the suppression of the Rebellion ease the fears of the privileged minority. Round about 1429 there was presented to Parliament a petition requesting that there be reaffirmed all the statutes passed against the Welsh, who bore 'ancient malice and enmity towards the English in Wales'.[14] The statutes were confirmed in 1431, again in 1433, once more in 1444, and with even greater severity in 1447.

There can be no denying the understandable ambition of English burgesses and tenants to maintain a constitutional position of security and superiority which conferred upon them valuable rights. Equally, we can appreciate why the Welsh, even if the Rebellion had failed, were no more willing than before to be excluded from such privileges. Some of the wealthier and more enterprising among them, therefore, sought to enter the promised land through the side door of denizen rights, which King and Parliament might be induced to confer upon them. Some, such as David ap Thomas of Cardiganshire, loyally devoted to Henry V, or Rhys ap Madog, attendant upon the duke of Bedford and a soldier of some prowess, received their denizen rights as a reward for service. Others, like Rhys ap Thomas of Cardiganshire or Gruffydd ap Nicholas of Carmarthenshire, were ambitious up-and-coming politicians. Hugh Bennaythe of Pembroke claimed to have served the King and the duke of Gloucester in their Chanceries of South Wales since he was twelve years of age. William Gruffydd of Penrhyn not only claimed that he was a loyal servant of the King but also made the groundless assertion that he had 'been born, engendered and descended for the most part wholly from the English race'.[15] It may have been such claims that led the 'English people in Wales' to petition the King and Parliament in wildly exaggerated terms that Welshmen accorded denizen rights had 'so oppressed the English in boroughs, towns and districts that they were entirely destroyed'. They viewed with even greater consternation those Welshmen who infiltrated into the towns in spite of legislation to the contrary and claimed to be 'English by nature and condition, whereas they be in fact true Welshmen at heart and of lineage'.[16]

The protesting English burgesses were trying in vain to push back the incoming tide. Welshmen continued to covet the rights enjoyed by Englishmen as they had done for a long time. They badly wanted to buy land in the boroughs, to hold influential and lucrative office, to enjoy equal judicial rights, to be able to marry English wives, whenever that seemed possible, and, above all perhaps, to be free from commercial and feudal

---

[14] William Rees (ed.), *Calendar of Ancient Petitions relating to Wales* (Cardiff, 1975), p. 38.
[15] Rees, *Ancient Petitions*, p. 15.   [16] Rees, *Ancient Petitions*, pp. 328–9.

tolls. To acquire these privileges they had already laid hands on office and entered towns in the fourteenth century. Many of the Marcher boroughs were noticeably less exclusive than the garrison boroughs of the Principality. At Holt, in 1391, 37 out of 78 families (47 per cent) were Welsh and, as late as 1459, there were still 23 Welsh families there in a sharply reduced population. Ruthin has been described as a genuine Anglo-Welsh community before, during, and after the Rebellion. Brecon may have tightened up its charter against Welshmen in 1411 but that did not prevent it from including them in growing numbers among its burgesses in the fifteenth century. Even in the two 'capitals' of the Principality, Caernarfon and Carmarthen, Welshmen had not been unknown before the Rebellion. Two eminent Welshmen, Hwlcyn Llwyd of Glynllifon and Ieuan ap Maredudd of Cefn-y-fan, had died defending Caernarfon, the very bastion of military power and colonial administration, against Welsh attack. During those 'brooding years' after the Rebellion had run its course, English burgesses would vouch for Welsh office-holders and would, in turn, accept sureties of Welsh and English on their own account. In spite of the most strenuous efforts by the royal authorities in the course of the Rebellion, they had been quite unable to stop the indispensable and, no doubt, highly profitable wartime trade between towns like Chester, Oswestry, Shrewsbury, and Bristol and the Welsh rebels when Glyndŵr was at his most menacing. As late as 1413, one Eneas Telyssor was alleged by a jury of former rebels to have carried provisions from Chester to the insurgents for the previous six years. Once the insurgency was over, there was no stopping the flow of trade between the Welsh and the emporia of the March—Chester, Oswestry, Shrewsbury, Ludlow, Hereford, Gloucester, and Bristol—not to mention smaller centres. Many permanent Welsh migrants followed the trade and settled in these towns.

The two-way traffic between Welsh and English did not end with commercial relations. Marriages between families belonging to the two peoples had long been common enough. Beginning with Llywelyn the Great, members of Welsh princely houses, down to Owain Glyndŵr himself, had often found English brides for themselves. Families not all that far below them in the social scale, like the Boldes, Hollands, and Spencers of Caernarfon, Gruffydds of Penrhyn, Hanmers, Thelwalls, Salusburys, Herberts, Vaughans, and Stradlings, all continued the tradition of inter-marriage (see below, pp. 94-5).

It also took more than a parliamentary act or a royal ordinance to exclude Welshmen from holding office. David Holbeach, a Welshman who was steward of the town and lordship of Oswestry, remained in office throughout the Rebellion and suffered severe losses at the hands of the insurgents. But he survived, prospered, and became MP for Shrewsbury in 1413 and 1417. Gwilym ap Gruffydd of Penrhyn had initially supported his kinsman, Glyndŵr, but late in 1405 made his peace with the King. Subsequently, Fortune and the Crown favoured this astute operator to such an extent that he acquired most of the lands of his Tudor cousins. He married as his second wife an English woman, Janet, daughter of Sir William Stanley of Cheshire, and his descendants were conspicuous as Chamberlains of North Wales. Similarly, John Llwyd was a Carmarthen merchant who became embroiled in the Glyndŵr Rising and was imprisoned in Carmarthen Castle between 1409 and 1411. By 1413, none the less, he had been able to gain royal favour and in 1415 went overseas in the King's retinue. These were only a few among many Welshmen who refused to allow themselves to be deterred or held back by formal restrictions. They were, it is true, excluded from the highest offices—those of justice or chamberlain—though increasingly they were to act as deputies for these eminent personages, who were often absentees. At a lower level in the administration, as *rhaglaw*, *rhingyll*, or beadle in the Principality, or as bailiff or steward in the Marches, they were to prove as indispensable as ever.

In spite of the many exceptions in practice, the restrictive legislation nevertheless remained on the statute book and was deeply resented. It could always be enforced or reaffirmed if necessity or expediency demanded. Two clear examples of invoking the statutes for partisan ends are the actions taken against Robert Trefor and John Scudamore. At some point between 1425 and 1432 the burgesses of the town of Holt presented a hotly worded and virulently anti-Welsh petition to their lady, Joan de Beauchamp, against the proposal to appoint Robert Trefor of Trefalun, grandson of Glyndŵr's sister, Lowri, as receiver of Bromfield and Yale, on the grounds that, as a man of Welsh descent, his loyalty could not be depended upon. Another of Owain's relatives, his son-in-law, John Scudamore, was similarly treated. Scudamore was a man who may secretly have received on his father-in-law's behalf large sums of money from England, but he might have been thought to have long outlived his earlier associations with the rebels by 1433. In that same year, however, he had the fact of his Welsh marriage flung in his teeth by Edmund Beaufort and was dismissed from office under the statute of 1402. Both these instances may have been blatant examples of acting upon the letter of the law in order to secure malicious personal ends by the instigators; but they showed that, while the statutes remained theoretically in force, there could be no security that they might not be put into operation when occasion served. They were more than paper tigers; they could sometimes be given real teeth. That was why they may have been detested by the Welsh and why they were later to loom large in the writings of those Tudor commentators who commended the policies of the dynasty so ardently. David Powel thought these laws were 'more heathen than Christian', and George Owen, severest of all their critics, delivered his strictures on 'laws made by King Henry IV most unnaturally against Welshmen, not only for their punishment but also to deprive them of all liberty and freedom'.[17] The very existence of these statutes served as a perpetual reminder to the Welsh of their position of inferiority and insecurity.

These penal statutes were without doubt a contributory factor to the perceptible rise in crime and violence during the Rebellion and long afterwards. There was certainly greater lawlessness in a border English county like Shropshire, and doubtless, if the records had survived more fully for Wales, would have been equally demonstrable there also. An indication of the disturbed state of affairs comes in a Duchy of Lancaster record for 1413. An assize roll of the sessions in eyre held in the Welsh lordships of the duchy may well point to the kind of breaches of the peace that were current in many parts of Wales. The most serious indictment in the record concerned a riot of July 1413, in the course of which it was alleged that a gang of twenty armed men had sought to kill the king's steward and had broken into the gaol of Ogmore Castle to rescue an imprisoned Welsh felon. Certainly, robbery and violence were said to have been rife at this time, and complainants to Parliament attributed much of the disorder to the practice so prevalent in the Marches of Wales of lawbreakers migrating from one lordship to another and becoming advowry tenants in the lordship whither they went. For a generation or more after 1415, those who had been loyal to the Crown during the Glyndŵr Rebellion petitioned Parliament on the grounds that they were the victims of persecution and ill-treatment at the hands of Glyndŵr's former partisans and their families. As late as 1427, protests were aired in Parliament on this score; particularly as a result of the 'patriots'' use of the old Welsh legal practice of *rhaith* (the oath of 300 men) to cause vexation and losses to the 'loyalists'.

The most destructive and long-lasting effects of the Rebellion, experienced in the border districts of England as well as in Wales, were its appalling economic and social consequences. For centuries, men recalled them with horror and dismay. John Leland, the 'King's antiquary', making his rounds of Wales in Henry VIII's reign, recorded ruin after ruin said to have been 'defaced in Henry the Fourth's days by Owen Glendower'.[18] In Elizabethan times, Thomas Churchyard still shuddered as he remembered how

> Owen Glendower set bloody broils abroach,
> Full many a town was spoiled and put to sack
> And clear consumed to countries' foul reproach,
> Great castles razed, fair buildings burnt to dust.[19]

[17] Owen, iii, 35–6.   [18] Leland, *passim*.
[19] T. Churchyard, *The Worthiness of Wales* (London, 1587; repr., 1876), p. 2.

As a result, 'the spoil and desolation in Wales was greater and more general than upon any or all the wars going before, for despair extinguishing the sense of preservation subjected all to fire and sword, whereof in most of the towns there remain the marks to this day', so a seventeenth-century chronicler averred.[20] In 1620 the jurors of Bromfield and Yale were firmly convinced that the economic decline of their lordship was to be attributed to the 'great mortality and plagues which in former times had been in the reign of Edward the Third and also the Rebellion of Owen Glindwr and troubles that thereupon ensued'.[21] Such was the grim and sorry reckoning that posterity set at the Welsh rebel leader's door!

We must allow for a natural and persistent human tendency to blame seismic and spectacular disorders like the Black Death and the Glyndŵr Revolt for most if not all the ills that flesh is heir to and to be unaware of the slower and more imperceptible workings of less obviously impressive economic forces—especially in an age when the findings of the 'gloomy science' were still unknown. Even so, there was, and indeed still is, good reason why the impact of the Rebellion should thus be remembered. It had been preceded by a whole century of economic difficulties, set-backs, and upheavals of diverse kinds. As early as 1300, Wales, like much of Europe, was probably seriously over-populated, the most recent demographic studies have suggested. That being so, the adverse changes of climate which appear to have overtaken Europe in the fourteenth century became all the more disruptive in their effects. They made an already less than favourable cool and damp Welsh climate even more uncongenial, reduced a short growing season, and added to the burdens of wresting a living from a land, much of which consisted of grudging upland soil. To compound these difficulties had come the widespread famines of 1315–18, the first of many, which having initially raised prices served in the longer run only to reduce them and depress demand. The outbreak of the Hundred Years War in 1337 quickly led to heavy taxation, currency shortages, and enforced devaluation, all of which had baneful effects on economic life. Even more shattering was the impact of the Black Death (1348–50) and subsequent visitations of epidemic disease until the end of the century and after. The incidence of the Black Death was uneven and it may have more lightly affected parts of upland Wales with its thinly scattered settlements than it did the densely populated lowlands and estuaries; but its overall effect was markedly to reduce the population. In spite of initial recovery it led, long-term, to a further fall in demand for agricultural products and a contraction of economic activity in town and country. Reduced rent-rolls gave rise to heavy administrative and financial pressures on the part of King and Marcher lords alike for the payment of tolls, taxes, and levies

[20] NLW, Llanstephan MS 154, fo. 33.
[21] R. R. Davies, *Lordship and Society in the Marches of Wales* (Oxford, 1978), p. 425.

which had to be shouldered in full by communities that were already grievously reduced in numbers and resources. Adjusting to the changed economic situation was a slow and painful process, though there is little doubt that it was the fortunate, well-placed few who gained, or at least managed best. The heavier burden which the Welsh were called upon to bear was partly economic and partly administrative. Both of these aspects were associated in the popular mind with the privileged position enjoyed by the English in Wales: a superiority resented as much, if not more, by the well-to-do among the Welsh as by the poor.

The Glyndŵr Rebellion brought long years of warfare which, from an economic point of view, was a much greater evil than plague. War, unlike pestilence, destroyed capital on a greater scale than people, and in existing medieval societies capital was already in short supply in relation to population. Those who survived the conflict found themselves living in abjectly miserable conditions. When the Rebellion had broken out, few if any could have realized how bitter and protracted resistance to the Crown would prove to be. Unlike most of the uprisings of the period which were over in a matter of months, if not weeks, Glyndŵr's Revolt dragged on for ten years and was not finally extinguished for another decade. It broke out in 1400 and, though the main hostilities were over by 1409, Glyndŵr himself and a small band of loyal supporters were active until 1412–13, and his son did not finally give in until 1420, after a last desperate bid to enlist Scottish support. Besides, it was not just a rebellion; it had all the ingredients of racial conflict and unleashed those elements of fury and vindictiveness, hitherto barely repressed. Given the nature of the opposition they faced, the Welsh rebels were obliged, as many other outnumbered and under-armed guerrillas have been, to resort to 'scorched-earth' tactics, 'so as to bring all things to waste that the English should not find strength nor resting-place in the country'.[22] The castles, towns, and Englishries in Wales and the border, those bastions of foreign overlordship, were attacked by Glyndŵr 'like a second Assyrian', harrying town and countryside with 'fire and sword . . . carrying off the spoil of the land and especially the cattle to the mountains of Snowdonia'. Royal troops repaid the rebels in the same coin. Adam of Usk was as severe in his comments on Henry IV's methods as on Owain's: he describes how, in 1402, with Owain and his 'poor wretches keeping close [i.e., hidden] in their caves and woods the King laid waste the land and returned victoriously with a countless spoil of cattle'.[23] Nor was his son, the future Henry V, any more tender. In 1403 he burnt the rebel leader's home at Sycharth and told with unconcealed pride and delight how he had proceeded to the vale of Edeirnion and there 'laid waste a fine and populous country'.[24] Injecting additional inflammation

[22] *HGF*, p. 53.   [23] Adam of Usk, *Chronicon*, p. 247.
[24] A. G. Bradley, *Owen Glyndwr* (London, 1902), p. 188.

and devastation were those internal tensions within Wales which fed the flames of war. Not only were most of the English burgesses and tenants of Wales opposed to Owain Glyndŵr and obliged to suffer heavy losses, like that Thomas Dyer of Carmarthen reputed to have lost £1,000, but a number of individuals and families of Welsh origin also remained loyal to the Crown or Marcher lords. If Henry IV savaged the Welsh Cistercian abbey of Strata Florida, Glyndŵr and his men were guilty of inflicting the same rapine on the White Monks of Cwm-hir. The Welsh origins of the inhabitants of the boroughs of Pwllheli and Nefyn did not spare them from wholesale destruction by the Welsh, nor had the rebels any compunction about burning the houses of the Welsh loyalist, Ieuan ap Maredudd, at Cefn-y-fan and Cesailgyfarch. David Gam, a Welshman born, conspired dangerously against Owain; and Hywel Selau, Owain's own cousin, was traditionally said to have tried to kill him. Both parties to the struggle looked upon war as a trade, calculated destruction as an integral part of its methods, and pillage and plunder as its profits.

All parts of Wales experienced the ravages caused by the Rebellion and the efforts to suppress it. Successive campaigns waged between 1400 and 1408 by Henry IV and the Prince of Wales, not always strikingly successful in their outcome, were mounted by large, costly, and powerfully equipped contingents. They carried war and devastation to the remoter corners of the land. Being as heedless of the consequences of their actions on friend as on foe as armies usually are in these circumstances, the royal troops had nearly as destructive an effect on lordships through which they passed as on the rebels, or so the inhabitants of Whittington testified when they addressed a petition complaining of the great loss and injury they had suffered at the hands of English troops as the latter passed through the lordship on their way to Wales. Though Hugh Morton, prior of Ewenni, was a prominent royal agent engaged in suppressing the rebels, his house suffered as badly from the attentions of royal troops as from their enemies. Owain and his men, for their part, had been active in all regions, switching their attacks rapidly and unpredictably from one part of Wales to another. Nor had they spared the border shires of England; their attacks on Herefordshire having reduced that county at one point to near-panic and the danger of widespread flight. Little wonder that many parts of Wales and the Marches, in desperate efforts to fend off the destructive attention of the rebels, had endeavoured to buy peace. In 1404 the people of Shropshire were urgently pressing the Council to allow them to make terms with Owain and pay him to leave them alone. Edward Charlton of Powys negotiated a similar compact and so, possibly, did the inhabitants of the lordship of Ruthin and the clergy and people of Pembrokeshire. The men of the hill country of Brecon, hedging their bets, agreed to submit to the King if he could defeat Owain but otherwise to remain loyal to the rebels.

The cynical Thomas Barneby, king's Chamberlain of North Wales, true to form, exacted his price from both sides, cheerfully profiting from each.

The warfare not only disastrously injured all districts of Wales; it also had dire consequences for all strata of the population: Welsh and English, townsmen and countryfolk, *uchelwr* and bondman, artisan and labourer, layman and cleric. It was, however, the poorer elements who were hardest hit, as always in times of conflict and crisis. Upper-class *uchelwyr* might have their estates forfeited and be forced to go on the run; but they had their *plaid* [retinue] to defend them, had more resources to call upon, and found it easier to withdraw to safer districts. Some of them were able to come to the king's peace and pick up the threads of something like their normal existence once more. Merchants might suffer crippling losses in the short term, but they had the influence to plead for compensation and could recover much more quickly. It was the humbler freemen, and, above all, the unprivileged bondmen and labourers, who had least to fall back on and most to suffer in face of the attacking forces of either side, or if they took flight to new and unfamiliar surroundings. Knowing how marginal their existence must always have been, one is left wondering how many of them managed to survive in a war-torn countryside after the appalling hardships of the winter of 1407–8. It comes as no surprise to learn of whole areas left deserted and desolate (see below, pp. 22–3).

When the Rebellion was at its height, economic life was so disrupted and the administration of county and lordship so paralysed that, in many districts, no revenues could be raised or courts conducted. For the county of Flint no ministers' accounts exist at all for the years from 1403 to 1405, and when records do resurface they reveal widespread ruination, with some whole townships completely devoid of tenants. At the opposite end of Wales, in Carmarthenshire and Cardiganshire, ministers' accounts are wanting for an even longer period, from 1401 onwards. Those for Carmarthenshire reappear fairly fully by 1409, though decayed rents for devastated lands and tenements reported in them were cripplingly heavy. The position in Cardiganshire, which had been more solidly in support of the rebels, was distinctly worse. True, the borough of Cardigan returned its accounts, though reporting that no fairs had been held and rents had had to be respited for five years; but the southern commotes of the county were not brought back under control before 1409 and the northern ones not until 1413, when most of the rents could still not be collected.

Nor were the Marches in markedly better state. There, the insurgents had systematically destroyed the assets of the manors: buildings were set on fire, ironwork removed, timber felled, meadows ravaged, and livestock rustled or slaughtered. Tenants were killed or driven away and tenements wasted, with the result that the total of decayed rents rose to far higher levels than even after the Black Death. Mills, presumably on account not only of their indispensable function in maintaining economic life but also of their extreme unpopularity as symbols of seigneurial jurisdiction, were singled out for special destructive attention. Brass and iron fittings were removed and millstones shattered to such an extent that it took decades to repair some, while a few were left permanently in ruins. As early as 1401 the rents of the lordship of Presteigne had fallen to £3. 7s. 'because the tenements were destroyed and burnt by rebels'.[25] In 1403 the auditors of the Duchy of Lancaster reported that no revenue at all was received nor any accounts rendered from the lordships of Brecon, Kidwelly, Carnwyllion, Iscennen, and Ogmore; and the same was true of the lordships of Gwynllŵg and Mathern that year. The nearby lordship of Gower was later reported as being worth only £100, half of its earlier value, allegedly because both halves of it, Gower Anglicana and Gower Wallicana, were in great part destroyed by Welsh rebels. The large and valuable lordship of Glamorgan, valued at £300 per annum in 1375, was, in 1408, rented at only about £100, rising for two years to £200, and afterwards for seven years at £266. 17s. 4d.; in short, ten years after the collapse of the Rebellion, a 10 per cent drop in income was expected. Further west, in 1409, two-thirds of the lordship of Llandovery were said to have been destroyed or burnt by rebels and the same fate had befallen the lordship of Cemaes. As a result of the Rebellion, it seems almost certain that the economic life of Wales and its population had reached a lower ebb than at any other point in the Middle Ages.

Castles and towns were inevitably the main targets of the insurgents. In Principality, March, and Borderland they represented the outward tokens and principal focuses of alien rule and privilege, with something of the order of ten to fifteen per cent of the population living in them.[26] In so far as concentrations of wealth could be said to have existed, they were found chiefly in the towns, which were also the main agents of social change, directed primarily in the English interest. 'For that they [the towns] stood for the King of England' it was on their inhabitants' heads that the Welsh rebels poured out the vials of their wrath. Out of the hundred or so towns of every size existing in Wales at this time, more than forty of them, at least, including nearly all the more important ones, suffered serious damage; not to mention the havoc inflicted over the border in England. Many of the towns lay in the shadow of great stone castles; powerfully constructed, well-manned, and strongly defended, with some twenty-two of them in south Wales and the March having artillery at their disposal. Often victualled and reinforced from the sea or by water, they were all the more difficult to reduce because the Welsh usually lacked sea-power.

---

[25] William Rees, *South Wales and the March, 1284–1415* (Oxford, 1924), p. 277.
[26] Ian Soulsby, *The Towns of Medieval Wales* (Chichester, 1983); R. A. Griffiths (ed.), *Boroughs of Medieval Wales* (Cardiff, 1978).

Some, like Caernarfon and Flint, stubbornly resisted prolonged sieges; or, like Brecon and Haverfordwest, were too powerful to be seriously threatened. But other notable strongholds were forced to succumb to rebel pressure. The two most celebrated captures were those of Aberystwyth, which suffered two successive sieges—the one by the Welsh and the other by the English—and Harlech, which for about four or five years was Glyndŵr's capital, though that had not prevented the town from being earlier destroyed by the Welsh and its burgesses suffering heavy losses at their hands. Some of the castles had provided shelter and refuge for the townspeople when their town was assailed. At Flint the burgesses 'dared not linger outside the castle',[27] and those of Kidwelly, whose town was razed, were equally dependent on their castle for protection.

Powerful castles, however, could not always save towns from frightful damage. Conwy had perhaps the most impressive Edwardian castle anywhere in Wales and massive fortified walls; yet when that superb fortress was captured, as the result of a spectacularly daring and well-planned raid in 1401, Conwy suffered worse in the process than almost any other town in Wales, with damage calculated (exaggeratedly no doubt!) at the enormous total of £16,000—nearly eight times that of Caernarfon or Beaumaris. The town of Rhuddlan, also the site of another forbidding Edwardian fastness, was completely burnt and destroyed; and, thirty-five years later, some sixty of its burgages were reported as still unrepaired. Many other castellated towns also suffered serious damage: Cardiff, Cricieth, Montgomery, Newcastle Emlyn, Newport, New Radnor, Presteigne, Swansea, Usk, and Welshpool, to name only some of the more important. Town walls and other fortifications were formidable enough to keep the rebels out at Pembroke, Tenby, and Caernarfon, though the suburbs of the last-named were burnt to the ground in the course of Welsh attacks. Other towns, like Brecon, Beaumaris, or Ruthin, having supped their fill of the horror of rebel onslaughts, learnt the lesson of the need for town defences somewhat late in the day. But many of the non-garrison boroughs, with neither castle, nor town walls, nor garrison to protect them, were subjected to the full and unbridled force of the rebels' anger. Overton's burgesses abandoned their town and, a century later, only twenty houses survived there. The little town of Holt shared Overton's fate and never really recovered. As late as 1472 and 1479, it was described as having houses which had been destroyed by rebels and were still not repaired because of the absence of tenants and the poverty of the townspeople. It was not only the English burgesses of these Flintshire boroughs whose way of life was largely destroyed; the Welsh burgesses of the little towns of Gwynedd fared no better. Lying open and undefended, boroughs like Pwllheli,

[27] I. C. Messham, 'The County of Flint and the Rebellion of Owain Glyndwr . . . ', *FHSP*, XIX (1961), 21–31.

Nefyn, or Llanrwst were also easy and tempting options for rebel hostility on account of the alien influences which radiated from them. The entire township of Pwllheli was recorded as destroyed and laid waste; and, if Sir John Wynn is to be believed, green grass grew on what had been Llanrwst's market-place and deer frequented its churchyard.[28]

Most of the English settlements and manors of the lowlands inflamed the rebels' spleen as readily as did the towns and served to focus their onslaughts. The inhabitants of such places, having no castle or town wall to defend them, were perhaps more defenceless than the urban burgesses. All the available evidence points to their having had to endure disastrous losses. When the ministers' accounts for Flintshire make their hesitant reappearance in 1406, they reveal widespread damage and depopulation, especially in the English townships and manorial settlements. Down in south Wales, the Duchy of Lancaster manor of Ogmore, which had yielded £382 in revenue in 1382, was laid waste and made no return between 1402 and 1405. In 1406, allowing for respites, it produced no more than £13. 18s. 7d. and, in spite of some recovery, was worth only £100 in 1413. The manor of Lake (Bronllys) could be let for only about half of its former revenue because its buildings were totally destroyed and no one could be found to farm it for a larger sum. In 1409 and 1410, the manors of Llantrisant (Usk) and Caerleon were described as being of little value, with the former alleged to be seriously lacking in tenants (the term may well have included sub-tenants) because of the burning and devastation of tenements in the course of the Rebellion. Further west, at Carmarthen, Glyndŵr had not only burnt the town, hanged 50 men and destroyed records—there were few things that gave rebels profounder satisfaction than obliterating all written memorials of their hated debts and obligations!— but had also wrought havoc on the defenceless demesne of the borough at Llan-llwch, which was alleged to have been totally destroyed in the course of the blitzkrieg of 1402 and 1405. For many years after the Rebellion, lords were unable to levy a large proportion of the rents that should have been due to them. As late as 1428 in the large lordship of Ogmore, for example, more than half the tenant land was unoccupied; and Ogmore is unlikely to have been alone in that respect. Lords were obliged to accept whatever terms they could negotiate for the lease of their lands and other assets. 'For many decades' there were few signs of recovery and a 'period of stagnation ensued', by comparison with which the 'years following the Black Death seem almost progressive'.[29] As if their cup of woe were not already running over with the destruction, disruption, and shortages caused by the uprising, to add to their miseries the unfortunate inhabitants had to endure outbreaks of pestilence. As high-born a lady as the countess

[28] *HGF*, p. 52.   [29] Rees, *South Wales*, p. 280.

of March, insulated we might suppose from most of the tribulations besetting lesser mortals, bemoaned dejectedly, 'now the pestilence is so severe and cruel where we are that I am much afraid to die in great debt' and added that her enemies would come to no agreement to allow her to withdraw until the mortality was past.[30]

The Welsh population, on its side, had been obliged to suffer possibly a more insupportable burden. The large and formidably equipped armies of Henry IV and his son were old hands at the nihilist techniques of those *chevauchées* perfected by long practice in France. Traversing the Welsh countryside, they ravaged unmercifully with fire, sword, and pillage. The plight of the hapless populace is not difficult to imagine. Faced on the one hand by the prospect of unrelenting retribution from royal troops and on the other by the iron-fisted pressure brought to bear on lesser men by those upper-class leaders who formed the tough core of Owain Glyndŵr's support, ordinary men were reportedly very willing to opt out of the Rebellion, if only they could be guaranteed reliable protection. Such, at least was Reynald of Bayldon's opinion when he wrote to his royal master:

I have heard myself many of the gentlemen and commons of Merioneth and Caernarvonshire swear that all men of the foresaid shires, except four or five gentlemen and a few vagabonds, would fain come to peace, so that Englishmen were left in the country to help keep them from misdoers.[31]

Admittedly, we may have here the exaggerated optimism of a royal agent anxious to present a favourable report; but the essential point he made in his letter seemed to be borne out in 1406 when the men of Anglesey yielded to the Crown. The unrestrained pillaging of the whole island in 1405, by an army from Ireland, was the final disaster that broke the backbone of Anglesey's resistance. By 1406, food shortages, war-weariness, sapped morale, recognition of the daunting cost of continued opposition, and a resigned acceptance of the need to come to terms, were characteristic of widespread areas of Wales once enthusiastically in arms for Owain, though there were many who still rejected any suggestion of surrender.

The price which support for the Rebellion had exacted from former insurgents soon became apparent in the returns being made by the Crown's ministers. In Flintshire, many lands were unoccupied because their Welsh tenants had fled to what they considered to be safer areas and had still not returned by 1411. Similar conditions prevailed in large parts of Cardiganshire until as late as 1413. In Eifionydd, in 1407–8, no revenue was being received and, in 1409–10, it was reported that no one was living there because of the Rebellion. The bond vills of Caernarfonshire and Merioneth, already subject to alarming periodic flights of serfs in the

---

[30] Hingeston, *Roy. and Hist. Letters*, I, 299–302.
[31] G. Williams, *Owen Glendower* (Oxford, 1966), pp. 49–50.

fourteenth century, were particularly hard hit. The Rebellion had caused many tenants from those counties to flee their homes, and in 1413 the lord of Powys, the earls of March and Arundel, and the Chamberlain of South Wales were ordered to ensure the return from their own territories of those refugees who had escaped there from the Principality of North Wales. The effect on the bondmen had been abnormally severe. The unfree vills of Talybont and Ystumanner in Merioneth, which had sustained upwards of 150 families in 1292–3, were said to be completely depopulated, and for the commotes of Ardudwy and Penllyn there is ample evidence of deserted holdings. The bond tenants of the unfree townships of Gest and Botewin in Caernarfonshire had disappeared and for much of the fifteenth century their lands lay derelict. In 1417 a memorandum on the governance of the Principality of North Wales, submitted to the King's Council, urged that the lords of the March be required to send back the bondmen of North Wales to the three north-western counties; but, as late as the reign of Henry VII, the descendants of those missing bondmen were still being sought.

It has, of course, to be recognized that long before 1400 bondmen, labourers, and others had been on the move, secretly or openly. It may well be that one of the effects of the Rebellion had been to facilitate, amid all the upheaval and confusion, their migration in much larger numbers to what they hoped might be safer quarters and the prospect of a better livelihood. Moreover, the Welsh economy was in the main a pastoral one and the peasants' few livestock and meagre farm and household possessions could be moved without too much trouble to a new district—they were, after all, already familiar enough with moving their herds the much shorter distances to summer homes and pastures (see below, pp. 60–61). But even the animals, not to mention human beings, needed corn to keep them going over the winter months and that provender was not easily obtained by small peasant proprietors and cottagers, bond or free, even if the burgesses of Chester and other towns showed the middle-man's customary eagerness to continue trading with the Welsh when the war was in full swing. Nor do we know how much pressure Glyndŵr and his associates imposed on those who chose to stay, in order to make them render support in cash or kind, though it is difficult not to suppose that one of the chief purposes for which he summoned those four men from every commote to his Parliament at Machynlleth in 1404 was to provide him with the wherewithal to prosecute his struggle. Indeed, one of the unanswered, and probably unanswerable, mysteries of the Rebellion is just how did Owain and his men provide themselves with the resources to continue their resistance. It is tempting to speculate what degree of continuity in financial and administrative matters was provided in their own areas, and on what terms, by the large number of ex-Crown servants who switched their allegiance to the insurgent leader. Nor can we assess with any degree of certainty just how crushing a weight and diversity of human suffering lay behind those terse entries of 'decayed rents' and enormous debts and arrears that were dutifully inscribed in ministers' accounts. Possibly the experience, in our own century, of hard-pressed rebels and guerrillas and the luckless populace ground between the upper millstone of official retribution and the nether millstone of insurgent pressure may supply us with some uncomfortably disturbing clues.

After the Rebellion had been put down, attempts were regularly made by the Crown, from 1411 onwards, to recover the arrears owing to it by imposing heavy fines on the communities concerned, including impositions for possible breach of statutes. Heavy demands of this nature were made to run concurrently during the reigns of Henry V and VI, being levied in instalments by specially approved collectors. In practice, however, it proved impossible to recover more than a fraction of the fines or the current rents that were owing. Further impositions were nevertheless added to the already overloaded backs of the king's subjects in Wales by attempts to raise money by means of subsidies in 1417, 1430, and other years.

Laymen were not the only ones obliged to shoulder the ruinous pressures exerted as a result of the Rebellion. The distinguished Elizabethan bishop of St Davids, Richard Davies, gave a harrowing account of how the Revolt had permanently mutilated religious and cultural life in Wales. In his *Letter to the Welsh People*, with which he prefaced the first Welsh New Testament of 1567, he wrote:

What destruction of books Wales suffered as a result of the war of Owain Glyndŵr may easily be understood from the townships, bishops' houses, monasteries, and churches that were burnt throughout all Wales at that time. What a pitiable condition for a people to be despoiled and robbed of the light they had and to be left like blind men to journey and travel through the wilderness of this world.

Davies was justified in drawing attention to the despoliation the Church had undergone. It was a more tempting and vulnerable target than almost any and an institution which, at its topmost levels, had become increasingly associated with the Crown and the English overlords. In consequence, it inevitably awakened the vengeful and plundering instincts of the rebels. In the early stages of the rising, Glyndŵr had laid a heavy hand on the diocese of St Asaph, whose bishop, John Trefor, was at that time a leading royal servant. Trefor's cathedral, his episcopal palaces, and the houses of his canons were burnt. So, too, were the cathedral and canons' dwellings at Bangor. Llandaff cathedral was spared but the churches of this, the most anglicized diocese in Wales, were ruthlessly assailed. In all the dioceses many parish churches were left ruined and partly desolate, and, early in Henry VI's reign, so reduced was the condition of the clergy that the Crown had to recognize that there was not the slightest hope of collecting subsidies which had been due a dozen years earlier.

Monasteries, owners of some of the largest and richest estates in Wales, as was to be expected, were calamitously affected. The houses of south and east Wales, many of which had generally been Norman or English in outlook and sympathy, were all badly injured. A tiny Benedictine nunnery at Usk had by 1405 become so ruined by 'wars, fires and plunderings' that it was feared the nuns would have to disperse; but the 'greater part' of even the largest and wealthiest abbey in Wales, Tintern, had also been wasted by the Rebellion. Houses more sympathetic to the Welsh cause, like Talyllychau (Talley) had been 'despoiled, burned and almost destroyed' by 'frequent incursions of men-at-arms on both sides',[32] while Margam, in 1412, was said to be utterly destroyed, with its monks and abbot dispersed and wandering about like so many vagabonds. The poverty and misfortunes of the Church lasted well into the fifteenth century. In 1428, the bishop of Llandaff claimed that his church was in danger of total desolation on account of the Rebellion and pestilences. Throughout the first half of the century, monasteries like Carmarthen, Talyllychau, Whitland, Conwy, and Cymer were plagued by acute economic difficulties, compounded in some instances by poor management. Many parish churches had to seek a grant of papally issued indulgences in order to repair their finances, while, as late as 1453, the bishop of Bangor and his officers could not afford to pay the fees due on the occasion of his consecration.

The quality of ecclesiastical control and discipline spiralled sharply downwards during these years. When the Rebellion was at its height the chaotic conditions prevailing in Wales must have made it extremely difficult to maintain anything like intact the machinery earlier devised by the Church to supervise dioceses, rural deaneries, parishes, or religious houses. Restoring harmonious relations after the Rising was over proved a slow and arduous task. The wedge between the bishops and many other non-Welsh members of the hierarchy, on the one side, and the Welsh clergy and lay population, on the other, already inserted well before 1400, had been driven deeper by the Rebellion itself and also by the Anglophobia which widely prevailed after it was over. The non-Welsh majority among the higher clergy became unwilling to spend any length of time in Wales—not that they had sojourned there for long, even before 1400! They can hardly be blamed for their reluctance to dwell among a population which so disliked them, but their regular and prolonged absences could only have been to the detriment of the Church. Monastic

---

[32] *C.Pap.L.*, VI, 230–1.

visitors were just as hesitant to venture into any encounters with the 'fierce and fickle Welsh', as one of them described the native population. Cistercian discipline, which should have been applied to the largest and best-known houses in Wales, had never fully recovered from the breakdown brought about by the Great Schism and the severance of links with Cîteaux, and much of the jurisdiction which should have been exercised by the Order itself was usurped by the Crown. Not until the latter half of the fifteenth century would the Church and its clergy, secular and monastic, be seen to have restored a measure of discipline.

In the prevailing conditions of tumult and confusion during and after the Rebellion, there is some evidence of the existence, if not of Lollard sympathizers, at least of a state of affairs of which Lollards could hope to take advantage. The Welsh Lollard from Herefordshire, Walter Brut, who had championed his views articulately and effectively in the presence of the bishop of Hereford in 1393, had taken up arms in support of Glyndŵr. Disturbed conditions in Cardiganshire in 1413 had led to the suspicion that the Lollard leader, Sir John Oldcastle, and his adherents, were planning to seize the castle at Cardigan. A project for confederation between Glyndŵr and Oldcastle was mooted in 1415 but came to nothing. Two years later, Oldcastle himself and other leading Lollards, including the much-feared Thomas Payn, a Welshman from Glamorgan and Oldcastle's chief councillor, retired to the Marches of Wales. This move may have been prompted less by the strength of Lollard sympathizers there than by the fact that it was a lawless region which might well offer Oldcastle, one of its native sons, a suitable place in which to take refuge. Of serious Lollard activity continuing in fifteenth-century Wales almost no evidence has survived.

More apparent and widespread than any willingness to embrace Lollard doctrines was an evident tendency towards contrition and self-criticism expressed in religious terms, as were most contemporary political and social reactions. Much of the poetry associated with the name of Siôn Cent (*flor.* 1400–30) was written in this vein. Though such verse cannot always be safely attributed to that poet himself, it attained considerable popularity in Wales. Its themes, strongly characteristic of the asceticism of medieval religious thought and literature, had to some extent been voiced before the Rebellion—the failure of mankind to recognize how brief life was, how transitory its delights, and how vain and unenduring the worldly riches and pleasures which men coveted (see below, pp. 128–9). But, following the Rebellion, they attained a much greater vogue and a more compelling relevance. Siôn Cent, and others like him, preached a stark and austere puritan message of penitence, renunciation of earthly gratifications, and reconciliation with God. It may well have been a note fittingly attuned to the temper of the age. Many believed that they had failed and were being

punished on account of their sins; their over-weening ambition had
provoked condign punishment; and their only hope of salvation lay in
treading the path of repentance. The resonant overtones of the poetry, so
familiar in medieval sermons from which most of the poets' material was
drawn, of redressing the balance between the mighty and the oppressed,
offered a crumb of melancholy comfort in the aftermath of defeat. It could
also be significant that this kind of gloomy, remorseful, and self-chiding
poetry appears to dominate bardic output to a considerable extent in the
generation immediately following the Rebellion, as though it seemed to
give tongue to a mood widely common among those who commissioned the
verse at this time—laymen and clerics. Was it, perhaps, provoked in large
measure by the dire adversities which Glyndŵr's Rising and his defeat
brought in their immediate aftermath?

Acknowledging, as we must, the grave and lasting damage which the
Rebellion inflicted, it is essential, nevertheless, that we keep it in
perspective and guard against overemphasizing the catastrophic outcome
to the point of ignoring the possibilities for recovery which lay latent within
Wales. Painful, debilitating, and long-lasting as the devastation was, there
can be no mistaking the tendency for contemporaries and later generations
to overstate the extent and the permanence of the damage caused. It was
often in their own interest to do so. Ministers and officials found it an
advantage to be able to blame the Rebellion, and not their own
shortcomings and miscalculations, for their failure to collect all the
revenues due to Crown or Marcher lord. The same tactics also suited
burgesses of towns and others who wished to conceal from their overlords
the profits accruing from increased prosperity, or tenants who had no mind
to pay an increased rent for lands to which they were not always legally
entitled. Arrears originally caused by the Rebellion became frozen in the
form of convenient clichés regularly repeated in stultified accounts of the
period. Fifteenth-century men and women, however, must be given more
credit for having been sufficiently resilient and able to recover from these
disasters than has often been allowed them. They were accustomed to a
dangerous and precarious existence in which the hazards of nature and
accidental fires, no less than the premeditated damage and conflagrations
of war, banditry, and rebellion, were not uncommon. Their homes and
out-buildings were, for the most part, relatively flimsy structures of timber
and thatch, easily burnt, but without too much difficulty reconstructed.
The town of Ruthin was reported to have been razed in 1400 and to have
suffered damage to the extent of £2,100; but, its 'powers of recovery were
very considerable and the borough must have risen from the ashes like a
phoenix, or else the accounts of destruction were wantonly exaggerated at

different times'.[33] What was true of Ruthin could equally have held good for other towns and lordships like Brecon, Cardiff, Oswestry, and Denbigh. If, again, we inspect a very different kind of record, the episcopal registers of St Davids, which survive from 1397 down until 1410, years when the Rebellion was at its height, we find these records showing little sign of a complete breakdown in the continuity of worship or administration. Neither do those of the diocese of Bangor for 1408–17. The phlegmatic conventionality of the ecclesiastical archive ought not to be overemphasized; but, equally, if on this evidence it might never be suspected that an insurgency of volcanic proportions had irrupted, it would hardly be less difficult, on the basis of the record of destruction, to explain how survival and recovery were ever possible.

Obviously not all parts of Wales were equally affected by the tide of adversity and ravage. Places like Tenby and Pembroke escaped completely the effects of direct assault. Not surprisingly, they participated in profitable ventures associated with the increasing trade of fifteenth-century Bristol. They were joined in those enterprises, however, by other south Wales ports like Haverfordwest, Carmarthen, Kidwelly, Swansea, Cardiff, Newport, Usk, and Chepstow, which had been fiercely attacked by the rebels. Sailors from south Wales were well-known figures on Bristol's busy and prosperous 'Welsh Back' and a growing colony of merchants with Welsh names were nearly as numerous as the English traders within the city. Welshmen were also found—in much smaller numbers, naturally—in other cross-Channel ports like Bridgwater or Barnstaple. Moreover, the major commodities of the thriving trade from these south Wales ports—cloth, wool, and hides—were strongly indicative of the gradual recovery of inland districts also. Rehabilitation of the north Wales ports was slower; but they, too, were as closely meshed into Chester's commercial orbit as were those of south Wales into Bristol's. Conwy, for instance, in spite of widespread damage in the town, had recovered much of its prosperity by Henry V's reign; though that was not achieved at Beaumaris and Pwllheli until Henry VI's time. Cricieth Castle may never have been rebuilt but the town was resettled within a generation. Inland centres of trade and market towns like Brecon, Denbigh, or Oswestry, all of which were undoubtedly thriving during the first half of the fifteenth century, could hardly have flourished unless the countryside which they served had regained some, at least, of its lost prosperity. Monmouth, too, with its 201 burgesses in 1441 was not far short of the 266 which it recorded in 1610. Even in the bond vills of Caernarfonshire, which might be considered to have been among the worst sufferers of all, wide differences in the incidence of destruction and poverty have been discovered.

---

[33] R. I. Jack, 'Owain Glyn Dŵr and the Lordship of Ruthin', *WHR*, II (1964–5), 320.

One of the main reasons why some of the most damaging consequences of the Rebellion may have been avoided, or at least contained within bounds, was the nature of the agreements which many districts concluded with Glyndŵr. A number of such truces are known to have been agreed to at various times (see above, p. 17). As late as 1409, when the rebels were well past the peak of their strength and when terrifying rumours coming out of Wales must have lost their power to alarm, Henry IV felt it to be necessary to issue a sharp reprimand to four of the leading lords of north-east Wales—the earl of Arundel, Lord Grey of Ruthin, Charlton of Powys, and Richard Lestrange of Knockin—for having allowed their officers in Wales, on their own authority, to conclude agreements of neutrality with Owain Glyndŵr. Such concordats were understandably a source of profound irritation to the King; but they may have led in these lordships and elsewhere to a greater degree of uninterrupted continuity and tacit co-operation between Welsh and English than might have been supposed. Their long-term effects of limiting damage and aiding recovery may, paradoxically enough, have been of benefit to the Crown.

Nor can there be any question that, once the Rising was over, Henry IV and Henry V, especially, were willing to restore Welshmen, including most of those who had rebelled against them, to their possessions and their offices. What other alternative had they if they were not to see their territories deserted or peopled by openly hostile outlaws? It might be feasible to encourage well-heeled and venturesome migrants from Cheshire to snap up lucrative bargains and opportunities in the town of Caernarfon, where the majority of the population was English; but there was little chance of repeating such tactics in, say, the depths of rural Merioneth or Cardigan. Adventurers were not to be attracted to Wales in large numbers as they were to fifteenth-century Normandy. So unpromising was the outlook for such recruitment in Wales that the Crown had no choice but to allow rebels to be restored to their former lands. The appalling weakness of local government in Wales made it all the more imperative that native gentlemen had to be given a chance of office, which they were quick to seize. Hugh Burgh, lord of Mawddwy since 1414, had no alternative but to follow the royal example and allow the sons of known partisans peaceably to inherit their father's lands and positions. In the lordship of Newport the willingness of Ieuan ap Jenkin Kemys to throw in his lot with Glyndŵr was not sufficient to prevent his sons from being taken into the service of the house of Stafford during the second quarter of the fifteenth century.

The most consequential effect of Glyndŵr's Rebellion, however, was the way in which it drastically speeded up changes that had long been in progress. The disruption, slaughter, shortages, and disease which it brought in its train had the effect of reducing still further a population that had already fallen in numbers even before 1400. In the confusion and turmoil which it created, many serfs and free tenants fled from their former homes. Whole communities, savagely reduced in numbers and resources, found it well-nigh impossible to meet the communal dues that were expected of them. To the traditional institutions of an earlier Wales—the *gwely*, *gafael*, and manor—already in marked decline before 1400, the Rebellion effectively gave the *coup de grâce*. Land became available in large quantities for lease or purchase by the ambitious and enterprising who were in a position to take advantage of the new openings; conditions created a buyer's market, which provided an admirable opportunity for some. They included not just the families of incipient gentry, some of whom had been active in the process of acquiring embryonic estates in the fourteenth century; not only the prosperous bourgeoisie who wasted no opportunity of buying up valuable land in the vicinity of towns; but also many substantial and wide-awake freeholders or tenants, later to be recognized as yeomen. They, too, seized the chances of adding to their holdings, consolidating them, and finding sub-tenants or employing labourers. The economic and social face of Wales was changing rapidly and coming to bear an increasing resemblance to that of England.

CHAPTER 2

PRINCIPALITY AND MARCH: GOVERNMENT AND LAW

EVER since the twelfth century Wales had been divided into two parts. In the more mountainous regions of the north and the south-west, the native princes of Gwynedd, Powys, and Deheubarth had managed, with varying degrees of success, to retain a large measure of independence *vis-à-vis* the kings of England. Between the territories acknowledging the allegiance of the Welsh rulers and the kingdom of England lay the lordships of the March (from the French *marche*, 'frontier'), carved out as a result of the restless initiative of the first generations of tough and venturesome Norman lords who had encroached upon Welsh lands from their bases along the English border. The March swung in a rough arc from Chester south to Chepstow and thence west to Pembroke, covering a large part of southern and eastern Wales (see Map 1). In 1282–3 Edward I had dealt the final blow to the military and political independence of Wales by defeating the last princes of Gwynedd, Llywelyn ap Gruffydd, and his brother, Dafydd. The former had been killed in December 1282 and the latter was executed in the summer of 1283. The rule of their house had been extinguished for ever. By the settlement which followed in the Statute of Rhuddlan of 1284, Edward annexed most of Gwynedd, and the Principality of Wales became one of the feudal demesnes of the Crown. Effectively, Edward had confirmed the duality of rule and administration which existed in Wales. From 1284 to 1536 there was no single political unit recognized as 'Wales'. The country was divided between the Principality and the March, the latter comprising a number of individual jurisdictions and lordships, within which the King's writ did not run.

The Principality during this period was a dual entity, consisting of the three north-western shires of Anglesey, Caernarfon, and Merioneth and the two south-western shires of Carmarthen and Cardigan. The remaining north-eastern shire of Flint, consisting of the former Welsh lands of Tegeingl and Maelor Saesneg, which Edward, Prince of Wales, acquired in 1301 in his other capacity as earl of Chester, was placed under the Justice of Chester. Thereafter, it became the normal practice for the king of England to constitute his eldest son prince of Wales and to confer rule over the Principality upon him. During the fifteenth and sixteenth centuries there were six such princes: Henry (afterwards Henry V), son of Henry IV, 1399–1413; Edward, son of Henry VI, 1454–71; Edward, son of Edward

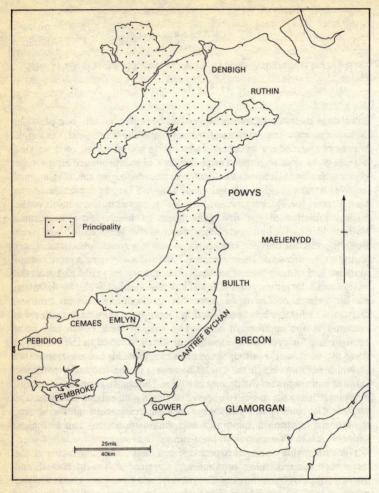

DENBIGH

RUTHIN

POWYS

MAELIENYDD

·Principality

BUILTH

CEMAES EMLYN

CANTREF BYCHAN

PEBIDIOG

BRECON

PEMBROKE

GOWER GLAMORGAN

25mls
40km

MAP I Principality and March

IV, 1471–83; Edward, son of Richard III, 1483–4; Arthur, son of Henry VII, 1489–1502; and Henry (later Henry VIII), son of Henry VII, 1503–9. These princes ordinarily had their own Councils and Households to assist and advise them in ruling their territories. Though there might be long intervals between some of the Princes, the Principality continued to exist.

The three shires of Anglesey, Caernarfon, and Merioneth had been carved out of the heartland of the former Welsh principality of Gwynedd, west of the River Conwy and north of the River Dyfi. For judicial, administrative, and financial purposes the three were grouped together and placed under the authority of the Justice and Chamberlain of North Wales, with a Chancery and Exchequer sited at Caernarfon. The Justice was the chief judicial officer within the area and was, to all intents and purposes, the King's viceroy in North Wales. He visited various centres periodically and there held his court, which became known as the justice's sessions. The Chamberlain was the principal financial officer of the Crown in North Wales and was authorized to collect the King's revenues, pay fees and wages to the officials, and expend money on local needs. Each of the principal castles erected or modified by Edward in the region—Caernarfon, Conwy, Beaumaris, Harlech, and Cricieth—had its own constable, who was entrusted with important military responsibilities. He was also ex-officio mayor of the borough which adjoined the castle and was planted with non-Welsh officials, traders, and craftsmen. These towns were endowed with about 5,000 acres of high-quality agricultural land each, and all trade was concentrated within them. Within each shire the usual offices of sheriff and coroner were instituted, and the commote officials accounted to them and they, in turn, to the Chamberlain. A sheriff in North Wales was in much the same position as a feudal bailiff or steward and was deputed to run the administration of the county in all its aspects. He was answerable to none but the King and the two principal officers of the Principality. The coroner's duty was to hold the pleas of the Crown. Each county had its county court, the judicial and administrative organ of the shire, held by the sheriff once a month and in a fixed place, and at which all the freeholders were suitors. The sheriff also held his tourn once a year. All the most important officials appointed to the major posts of Justice and Chamberlain, in the period following the Conquest, were Englishmen, and so were most of the sheriffs and coroners. At a lower level, many of the previous native administrative and judicial arrangements were retained. The existing Welsh unit, the commote, was treated as though it were the equivalent of the English hundred and kept its courts and its officials. These officers, the *rhaglaw* and the *rhingyll*, were drawn from the leading members of the local Welsh gentry, who were eager to hold office under the Crown and thereby to consolidate and extend their influence within their own districts. These shires were not, however, subject to English common law; neither had they the right of appeal to courts in England, nor were they represented in the English Parliament.

In the two south-western shires, usually referred to as the 'Principality of South Wales' in contra-distinction to the 'Principality of North Wales', the position was broadly similar to that pertaining in the north-west. Royal rule, however, had been established in these two counties earlier than in the north, and the nucleus of shire administration had been in being in each for a generation before 1284. The sole reference to them in the Statute of Rhuddlan, therefore, was briefly to ordain that there should be 'a Sheriff of Carmarthen with its cantreds and commotes and ancient metes and bounds. A Sheriff of Cardigan and Llanbadarn . . . There shall be coroners in those counties and bailiffs of commotes as before.'[1] In 1287, following the suppression of the rebellion of Rhys ap Maredudd, a scion of the princes of Deheubarth, a large area of the territory formerly ruled over by him was added to the shire. It included the castle of Dryslwyn, the commotes of Catheiniog, Caeo, Mabelfyw, Mabedrud, and half the commote of Mallaen Iscoed, all in the north of the county. Even so, the county boundaries then only included within them about half the area of the historic county of Carmarthenshire, which came to an end in 1974. As far as Cardiganshire was concerned, a good deal of confusion and controversy existed in the fourteenth century as to where its courts should be housed. Not until 1395 was it laid down once and for all that the courts of great sessions and petty sessions and the county court of the shire were to be held at Cardigan.

The Justice and the Chamberlain were the two principal officers in the south as in the north, though it has been pointed out that because the Principality was more important to the Crown as a source of revenue than anything else, the Chamberlain was its key officer in spite of the greater authority and prestige attaching to the office of justiciar. Although Carmarthen and Cardigan each had a Chancery and Exchequer, fees and annuities seem to have been paid only at Carmarthen. The sheriff's function in the southern counties was decidedly more limited than in the north. He did not hold the county court nor the tourn in the south, nor did he control the local officials in the commote. The highest court was that of Great Sessions, which tried cases of homicide, rape, and arson and was held by the Justice. A lesser court, known as Petty Sessions, held by the deputy to the Justice, came into being to assist the more august assembly. There was also an English county court and a Welsh county court in Carmarthenshire. The choice of personnel was dictated by very much the same considerations as in the north. The leading officials were Englishmen, while many of the lesser men were drawn from among the most prominent of the local gentry.

The most significant legal changes were those effected in the criminal law, whereby Edward abolished the previously prevailing Welsh law and replaced it with English law and its procedures. The Statute of Rhuddlan declared that 'in thefts, larcenies, burnings, murders, manslaughters and

---

[1] I. Bowen, *The Statutes of Wales* (London, 1908), p. 3.

manifest and notorious robberies . . . we will that they shall use the laws of England'. The community as a whole, not the kindred as under Welsh law, was made responsible for crime. The sheriff and the coroner became 'the keystones of the system' and the part to be played by the 'jury of presentment and the tourn and by the customs of appeal, hue and cry, indictment and outlawry was carefully laid down'.[2] Punishment for conviction of felony in the Justice's court was invariably death. In civil matters, however, the Welsh were allowed to retain their own law for real and personal actions, though Edward took care to explain in great detail and precision alternative English processes in such issues as trespass and debt, contract, covenant, and dower, which became increasingly popular among Welsh litigants as time went on. Welsh land law, in relation to partible succession and equal inheritance among all heirs, was allowed to continue, though illegitimate sons were no longer permitted a share and, in the event of failure of male heirs, daughters were to be allowed to obtain a portion. From early on, it became possible for freemen to pay for permission to obtain villein land and, on occasion, villeins were allowed to purchase land from freemen. But, in proceedings relating to land, an innovation of major importance was the introduction of writs such as those of Novel Disseisin and Mort d'Ancestor. In spite of the changes introduced by the Statute of Rhuddlan, it is clear that some of the provisions of Welsh law survived in the Principality long after 1284.

Alongside the Principality, the March continued in existence. It included some districts, like Clun or Oswestry or Archenfield, which were to be incoporated into England at the time of the Act of Union in 1536. Following Edward's conquest of Wales, although the King showed himself prepared to take a firm line with some of the leading Marcher lords, he had far too much need of his great magnates to contemplate any major reduction in their status and privileges. In fact, he was perfectly prepared to constitute additional lordships to reward those whom he favoured. The former Welsh lands of the *Perfeddwlad* [middle country], so bitterly contested between Welsh and English in their long struggle, were now divided up into new lordships. Out of the former Welsh lands known as Rhos and Rhufoniog was created the lordship of Denbigh which was given to the de Lacy earl of Lincoln. Similarly, the lordships of Ruthin (formerly Dyffryn Clwyd), Bromfield and Yale, and Chirk were carved out for the Greys, the Fitzwarins, and Roger Mortimer respectively. Although all these lordships were brought into being by royal charter there was no significant difference between the constitutional position of their lords and that enjoyed by the lords of those domains originally won by the sword. All were accorded almost identical autonomous privileges.

[2] R. R. Davies, 'The Survival of the Bloodfeud in Medieval Wales', *History*, LIV (1969), 338–57, at 339–40.

Seven of the Marcher lordships of north-east Wales, which had previously been part of Llywelyn's principality, were held 'in chief of the Prince of Wales as of his principality', whereas the older Marcher lordships were held 'in chief as of the Crown'. Edward's reign witnessed the virtual completion of the March and the confirmation of the division between it and the Principality. True, there was to be one important new Marcher lordship created by Edward IV in 1465, that of Raglan, brought into being as a mark of special favour for William Herbert, with an impressive list of rights and liberties to put it on much the same footing as the other lordships. In general, though, the situation of the 45 or so lordships in being at the end of the thirteenth century remained almost unaltered until the Act of Union, though actual possession of them changed hands a number of times.

Within the boundaries of each lordship its Marcher lord retained his regalian rights and exercised almost complete autonomy. He ruled like a miniature king, and two of the larger lordships, Pembroke and Glamorgan, were counties palatine having their own county courts, complete with sheriff and coroner, which entertained pleas of the crown, pleas by writ, and all the ordinary business of county courts, on the model of English shires. Each lord enjoyed such prerogatives as the right to maintain his own troops, his own *caput* [capital], and his own law. In his courts he had powers of life and death, with no right of appeal to courts in England. He could levy taxes, mint coins, and create boroughs. As late as 1394, 1442, and 1496, the lords of Ruthin, for instance, reissued charters to their borough of Ruthin—a source of privilege to the burgesses but also one of considerable profit to their lords. It was a truism that the King's writ did not run in the March. There were occasions when the King could interfere, nevertheless: on the death of a lord without heirs or with an heir under age, or if a lord were convicted of felony or treason, or if he abandoned his territory in time of war. Moreover, Marcher lords, being ordinarily major possessors of land in England, knew well how much indirect influence the King could exert in their midst. By 1390, nine of the seventeen English earls and dukes had a major stake in the March and were under no illusions about how much their ability to acquire lordships there or to marry wealthy heiresses depended on royal favour. With the rapid reversals of political and military fortunes in the middle of the fifteenth century, the lottery of the processes by which lordships were won and lost came to depend even more heavily on royal goodwill.

The problems of the management of these lordships were those to be found in running any scattered and widely dispersed estates. They were compounded in the Marches by the geographical situation of these lordships on the periphery of the lord's English holdings and by the problems within the March of a conquered Welsh population, with its unfamiliar social framework, the survival of many of its own laws, and the existence of its distinctive language and culture. To assist him in the administration of his lordship each lord ordinarily had his own council, drawn in the main from his retainers among the English or Marcher gentry, lawyers, and auditors. Some of the larger lordships even had their own Chanceries and Exchequers. The three main officers who exercised jurisdiction over the whole lordship were, usually, the constable, steward, and receiver; offices from which the local Welsh families would normally be debarred. Judicial lordship was much more important and much more lucrative for the lord in the March than in England. It implied not only the maintenance of law and order and the punishment of crime—after a fashion—but also was the means of enforcing lordship over men and land. Most lordships were divided into two parts: the Englishry and the Welshry. The former normally covered the more favoured low-lying areas, below the 600ft. or even 400ft. contour, while the latter usually embraced the upland area of the lordship. Each moiety of the lordship had its own separate officials and its own courts.

The laws and customs of the March consisted of a body of unwritten, customary laws; shaped by the will of the lord, the precedents of the court, and the collective memory of the inhabitants. These laws were by no means static or inflexible. They were always liable to be modified at the dictates of the lords, who reserved to themselves the right to 'declare, to add to or to reduce the . . . laws, customs, and services of their lordship', though they could do so usually only as a result of a working compromise with the wishes of their tenants. These laws differed in detail not only from one lordship to another but also within a single lordship, as between its English and Welsh inhabitants, its free and unfree tenants, and its burgesses and countryfolk. Nevertheless, there were certain common characteristics shared by the law of all the lordships. In the first place, this law offered much freer scope for the survival and even the efflorescence of feudal concepts than did the law in England. Again, Welsh law and custom were also widely invoked within the Marcher lordships, as we shall see. At the same time, and not surprisingly in view of the close connections between the March and England, Marcher law borrowed heavily from English common law and continued to do so to such an extent that, by the fifteenth century, common law had become completely victorious in the south-eastern March. The essence of Marcher law was that it was one of amalgamation not separate development. English inhabitants were not slow to seize upon the advantage to themselves of Welsh procedures, such as *prid* (see below, p. 81), any more than the Welsh were reluctant to embrace English law and custom whenever they believed themselves liable to gain from doing so. As for the lords and their officers, they were only too determined to preserve what seem to have been antiquated and outmoded usages or to introduce new ones as long as they could exact financial advantage to themselves from doing so.[3]

One of the more interesting features of the legal scene in the Principality and the March was the willingness of the Crown and the Marcher lords to allow the provisions and the practice of Welsh law to be applied, if it appeared to be in their interest—usually financial—to do so. That there was a persistent desire on the part of some of their Welsh subjects during the fourteenth and fifteenth centuries to invoke the law of Hywel Dda there can be no doubt. Even in the sphere of criminal law, where Edward I had so stringently prohibited the continued use of Welsh law, the practice of *galanas*, or the redeeming of a homicide by a money payment, remained a recognized action at law and still survived in some cases, most notably in the lordship of Clun. Welsh customs persisted even more frequently in cases of theft, where compurgators, drawn in specified proportions from relatives on the side of the father and mother of the man accused (*rhaith*), could swear to his innocence. Still more common was the practice of paying *amobr*, the fee due under Welsh law for the marriage of a woman, or for a sexual offence. A number of Welsh civil actions were also proceeded with; at least eight cases for debt, two for trespass, and one for pledge were prosecuted between 1440 and 1450 in the single commote of Llannerch in Dyffryn Clwyd. But the most common of all were cases relating to land law. Welsh law concerning land survived most strongly in south-west Wales in Ceredigion and Ystrad Tywi, where actions relating to land disputes were heard in accordance with the practices of Welsh law right up to the Act of Union. In many of the Marcher lordships, too, cases relating to *prid* or Welsh mortgage were not uncommon, and those in respect of *cynnwys*, the right of illegitimate sons to succeed to land in return for the payment of a fee, were certainly known in the Principality, Chirk, and Denbigh. Welsh actions of various kinds were common enough for the King to find it necessary to employ a pleader or attorney 'in the laws of Hywel Dda' in the Southern Principality during the early part of the fifteenth century, though 'the combination of an attorney in English and Welsh law in 1436 suggests that Welsh law was experiencing something of a decline'.[4] On the other hand, as late as 1521 John Walbeef, deputy steward and receiver of Brecon, was referred to with manifest respect by the King's surveyors as a 'sad and an honest ancient personage . . . practised both in the laws of England and Wales'.[5] Yet traditional Welsh practice, even in the realm of land law, was fighting a losing battle in the century before the Act of Union. Many of the more ambitious and thrusting Welsh landowners were

---

[3] R. R. Davies, 'The Law of the March', *WHR*, v (1970), 1–30.
[4] R. A. Griffiths, *The Principality of South Wales in the Later Middle Ages* (Cardiff, 1972), p. 34.
[5] T. B. Pugh, *The Marcher Lordships of South Wales, 1415–1536* (Cardiff, 1963), p. 249.

openly adopting English methods of conveyancing, including entail. A 'cursory examination' of Ruthin court rolls tended to show that at least nine out of ten cases were decided by a verdict of a jury. Overall, the conclusion was 'quite inescapable that the number of pleas by Welsh law was singularly exiguous in the court rolls'.[6]

NEW DEVELOPMENTS IN THE FIFTEENTH CENTURY

The historic problem of medieval Wales had been the fractionization of political power and it was one that was aggravated in the fifteenth century as the result of rebellion and civil war. In the first two decades of the century, the Glyndŵr Rebellion had had a disastrously adverse effect on the judicial and financial administration of the Principality and the March. The long years of warfare and upheaval had badly interrupted or even destroyed the exercise of royal and seigneurial authority, the continuation of administration, the holding of courts, and the collecting of revenues. The enactment of the statutes against the Welsh in 1401–2 imposed severe additional restraints on them and exacerbated their resentment against a regime which, even before the passage of the legislation, had been profoundly disliked. The Rebellion had left in its wake a blighting legacy of feuds, mistrust, and hatred in all parts of Wales. Much of this turmoil and disturbance, which was far from having been wholly quietened, was rekindled during the difficult years of mid century, from about 1440 to 1471, when the authority of the Crown was enfeebled and tension between the rival factions became more acute. The years from 1450 to 1464 and 1469 to 1471 were unusually troubled. In 1450 the parliamentary commons declared that the realm was beset by a wave of disorder greater than ever before. Seven years later, John Harding claimed that public order had

> exiled been away and foul overturned,
> in so far forth that north and south and west
> And east is now full little rest.

The roll of the Coventry Parliament in 1459 referred to the 'great and lamentable complaints of your true poor subjects universally throughout every part of your realm' about robberies, riots, and extortions, which forced them into payment of fines and ransoms.[7] For some years after 1471, when Edward IV seemed firmly established on the throne, there were gloomy complaints of the extremely disordered state of Wales.

The dislocation caused by the Glyndŵr Rebellion and these later turmoils of mid-century gravely disrupted the maintenance of judicial

[6] R. R. Davies, 'The Twilight of Welsh Law', *History*, LI (1966), 143–64.
[7] John Bellamy, *Crime and Public Order in England in the Later Middle Ages* (London, 1973), pp. 9–10.

authority and the levying of revenue from all sources in Principality and March. In the former, during the years from 1413 to 1416, sums of no more than about £306 gross (£167 net) for North Wales and £400 gross (£200 net) from South Wales were all that could be gathered in. The drop then experienced was catastrophic and the miserable sums collected represented hardly a tenth of those which had been forthcoming in the year 1376–7—some £3,000 net for North Wales and £1,680 net for the South. Although they subsequently improved to an average yearly figure of £1,300 (£900 net) in North Wales and £1,585 (£975 net) for South Wales during the reign of Henry VI, they still only amounted to about 40 per cent of what they had been a hundred years earlier. In mid-century the conflicts between Lancaster and York made the management of the Principality a complicated and often risky operation. In 1460, for example, Henry VI was obliged to grant the Prince of Wales 500 marks a year for life to compensate him for lands being unlawfully detained from him. Even the restoration of stability during the reign of Edward IV effected little or no improvement in the financial sphere. During that period, average annual receipts from North Wales were £1,000 (£250 net) and from South Wales £700 (£360 net).

In the March, income ordinarily accruing from the lordships during the fourteenth century had been potentially very valuable. At that time several lordships had been worth upwards of £500 a year and a few more than £1,000. The medium-sized lordships of Newport and Caus supplied more than one-third of the £1,724. 15s. 7¼d. which Thomas, earl of Stafford, received from his lands in 1390–1; much of this income being derived from judicial profits. The same source also accounted for nearly half of the income of Newport lordship in 1400–1 (£244 out of £537). But in the course of the Glyndŵr Rebellion no income was received from this latter lordship for several years. Later, during the minority of Humphrey, earl of Stafford, the situation had improved sufficiently for it to be farmed for £300 per annum; still well below its fourteenth-century value, though. In the Marcher lordships of the north, the economic consequences of the Rebellion and other crises had been very similar. In 1426 the revenues of the lordship of Denbigh were only about a half to two-thirds of what they had earlier been and were to go on slumping very alarmingly. The lordship of Newport provided further evidence in mid-century of continuing financial difficulties. In 1447–8 a *valor* of the lordship estimated its annual value as £491. 12s. 5¼d. and its clear yearly worth at £326. 3s. 8¾d.; but this estimate ignored the problem of arrears, which was becoming more acute at this time. The main reason for the fall in revenues was the reduction in the level of judicial profits, which slithered from £225 a year before the Glyndŵr Rebellion to £73. 8s. 5d. in 1444–5 and £50. 1s. 6d. in 1451–2. They continued to decline for the remainder of the fifteenth century, and by 1497–8 (an exceptionally bad year) were down to £4. 5s. 0d.

In addition to these ordinary sources of revenue, the Marcher lords had other more occasional ones which were peculiar to their Welsh lordships. They included *mises*, or payments made when a lord first took possession of his lordship (though they were also paid in the counties of Carmarthen and Cardigan); *donum*, a payment levied on miscellaneous occasions such as to redeem the Great Sessions, or buy a pardon, or gain a grant of new liberties; aids or subsidies; and other fines. They could be distinctly lucrative. For example, *mises* in the lordship of Glamorgan amounted to 1,000 marks paid over five years. Again, the *donum* of £251. 5s. 6d. paid to Richard, duke of York, in 1442–3 for his lordships of Builth, Radnor, Clifford, Glasbury, Dinas, and Ewias, was a handsome amount. But they could also be burdensome and increasingly unpopular, especially the tallage levied for the redeeming of the Great Sessions.

The last-named practice was a favourite device employed in lordships of the March, and also in the Principality of South Wales, in order to try to stabilize the income derived from the profits of justice. During the fourteenth century, itinerant justices had appeared in a number of lordships in south Wales to hold sessions in eyre on behalf of the lord, similar to those conducted in the Principality by the King's justices. These sessions were held at intervals of three to five years and were supposed to supplement the jurisdiction of the main court of the lordship held every few weeks. But, judging by the few surviving records of their activities, they were not very effective and by the fifteenth century were quite useless for their ostensible purpose, being by that time a transparent device to exact the fine that was intended to buy them off. Even before 1400 the practice of redeeming the sessions had begun. In the lordship of Brecon, large payments of *donum* were made in 1373 and 1397, almost certainly for buying off the sessions, and there were comparable payments in the lordship of Haverford in 1392 and the Duchy of Lancaster lordships in 1394–5. Following the disruption of the Glyndŵr Rebellion and offences committed by many Welshmen, large communal fines were paid by the inhabitants of Duchy of Lancaster lordships and, in 1418–19, Great Sessions were redeemed in the lordship of Brecon for 2,000 marks. The practice became widespread in the fifteenth century, when it is known to have occurred in the Buckingham lordships of Newport, Brecon, Hay, and Huntington, the Duchy of Lancaster lordships, and the lordships of Pembroke, Haverford, Usk, Caerleon, Chepstow, and Glamorgan. The lordship of Gower seems a rare exception in south Wales in having escaped. The tallages imposed for the privilege of redeeming the sessions were heavy. In Glamorgan, where sessions were held every seven years, the sum of 1,000 marks had to be paid within five years, and in Pembroke 300 marks had to be paid every three years. Sessions were also redeemed in the two counties of the southern Principality from early in Henry VI's reign onwards. Of the fifty-two sessions held in Carmarthen between 1422 and 1485, only twelve ran their full course; and in Cardiganshire only seven out of forty-seven known sessions proceeded without being brought to an early end by paying a fine. The amounts paid varied from 400 marks in Carmarthen and 300 marks in Cardigan, in 1430, to 600 marks and 400 marks, in 1432; though by Edward IV's reign they had returned to the more reasonable earlier levels. The practice did not extend to the Principality of North Wales nor to the northern lordships, with the exception of those of Denbigh and Bromfield and Yale.

The reasons for redeeming the sessions seem fairly clear. Justice in most parts of Wales had evidently become subordinate to securing a financial return. In the Principality, buying off the sessions provided the Crown with a steady and assured income, whereas collecting individual fines might have been very difficult. The freeholders on their side welcomed the move, at first anyway, because it spared them the possible expense and inconvenience of having to attend at sessions for perhaps as long as fifteen days at such awkward times as the harvest period, not to mention any financial penalties or exactions to which they might have been liable. In the lordships the reasons offered for buying off the courts were very much the same. At Newport, in 1432, the justices allowed the tenants to redeem the sessions for a fine of 1,000 marks, ostensibly on account of the 'good governance, goodwill, and tranquillity' of the lordship and because of the great poverty of the inhabitants. In 1476 the sessions at Newport were bought off for a fine of 650 marks and the tenants granted a general pardon. Recognizances for good behaviour were also taken at this time, probably because the Crown required them, since a few months earlier Edward IV had called a meeting of Marcher lords at Ludlow to discuss, with the Prince of Wales' Council, measures for the control of crime and the maintenance of order (see below, pp. 52–4).

By the beginning of the sixteenth century, however, resistance to the custom of redeeming the sessions had clearly emerged. In 1503 the tenants and residents of the lordship of Brecon, except the inhabitants of the borough of Brecon, offered a fine of 2,000 marks; but there were unequivocal signs that the inhabitants of the lordship were becoming increasingly reluctant to assume the heavy burden that such a fine imposed upon them. By 1518 disputes between the duke of Buckingham and his tenants in his lordships of Brecon and Hay were sufficiently serious to call for the intervention of the King's Council and were finally settled by a decree in Star Chamber. Following the execution of the duke in 1521, no attempt was made to hold Great Sessions in the lordship until 1524. A petition from the tenants in 1525 made it plain that although they were willing to redeem the sessions 'for that time only', they wished from henceforth never to be 'compelled by any means to redeem any sessions there, but that all murderers, felons and other offenders may be there duly punished, depressed, and corrected for their offences'. Already in 1526 it had come to be recognized that collection of fines of redemption was one of the main causes of disorder in the Marches and in that year the Council of the Princess Mary forbade the practice. A few years later, in 1532, the earl of Worcester came to an agreement with his men in the lordship of Gower that inhabitants and residents were only to attend on the first day of the sessions unless they were involved as parties to suits. Thereby he removed one of the principal reasons why they had previously been anxious to buy off the sessions. Finally, the Act of 1542 established the Court of Great Sessions as it survived until 1830.[8]

The difficulties described above, which were encountered in overseeing the judicial and financial arrangements of the Principality and the March, served only to encourage the persistent tendency towards absenteeism, on the part of the leading officials of the Principality and the lords of the March, which had become unmistakably apparent in the fourteenth century. From early on, the great officers of the Principality had frequently been Marcher lords or other major figures, whose interests and duties necessitated their presence on their own estates, at court, or with the King's armies overseas. Already in the fourteenth century, also, the Marcher lordships had become concentrated in the hands of a restricted circle of great English aristocrats, and this tendency became reinforced during the fifteenth century. Most of the lordships of the March over which they ruled were outlying members of wider English estates where the territorial wealth and political interests of the lords were centred. These *grands seigneurs* valued their Marcher lordships highly as major sources of men, money, and influence but only came to the Marches occasionally and then for very short spells. Humphrey, duke of Gloucester, was Justice of South Wales; he was also earl of Pembroke and held the lordships of Llanstephan, Tenby, and Cilgerran. Furthermore, he retained many Welshmen in his affinity. But clearly his interests at court and elsewhere left him almost no leisure for his Welsh possessions and offices. Similarly, Richard Nevill, the so-called 'king-maker', was also Justice of South Wales for about a year. He, too, came into possession of a number of lordships in south Wales and coveted others. But he, again, was far too heavily embroiled in the politico-military contentions of the age to spend much time in Wales. Henry, second duke of Buckingham, Justice of North and South Wales in 1483, and lord of Brecon, Newport, and other lordships, might come to Brecon in 1483 but largely for the purpose of raising troops against Richard III. Even Jasper Tudor, duke of Bedford, and Justice of

---

[8] Pugh, *Marcher Lordships*, p. 9.

South Wales, for all his assiduous nursing of Welsh contacts and his occasional descents on the Welsh coast, during his twenty years or more on the run from Yorkist power, and in spite of the handsome endowments of land with which his nephew rewarded him after 1485, was thereafter pleased to live almost exclusively on his English estates when not at court. The one great exception to this tendency was William Herbert, specially created a Marcher lord by Edward IV in 1463 (see below, pp. 193–4). Being that *rarissima avis*, a Welshman elevated to the ranks of the English peerage, he was content to make his family home, Raglan Castle, his main base. What was true, in general, of the Marcher lords was equally true of the leading figures in the royal administration of the Principality, who were, in any event, drawn from much the same exclusive group of magnates as the rulers of the March and who turned the office of Justice in Wales into a 'pawn in the game of political chance'.[9] These officers of the Principality were granted their positions of justice, chamberlain, and constable as non-resident sinecures in reward for their services to the King or as a result of the favour they enjoyed in his eyes. When Humphrey, duke of Gloucester, became Justice of South Wales in 1440, or Richard, duke of Gloucester, combined that office with that of chamberlain in 1470, or Henry, duke of Buckingham, became virtual dictator of Wales, combining all the great offices of north and south in his own person, no one expected any one of them to come in person to exercise that authority.

In the absence of these nominally commanding figures in Principality and March, power on the spot inevitably passed to their deputies and officials. Many of the latter were chosen from the ranks of neighbouring English gentlemen in favour with the grandees; but not a few were recruited from the local gentry. Some were drawn from settler families, like the Stradlings, St Johns, Pulestons, or Thelwalls. Others were of Welsh stock, like the Gruffydds of Penrhyn, who were trusted servants in the Principality of North Wales, or the Morgans of Tredegar, or the descendants of Einion Sais in Brecon, who had a long tradition of loyal service to successive Marcher lords. Patronage was extremely important to these families of the March, who had no alternative ladder of promotion. In the Principality counties of north and south Wales, many leading Welsh notabilities had long acquaintance with serving in county courts, hundred courts, juries, sheriff's tourn, and minor office. By the end of the fifteenth century, they had experience of presiding over those courts and were, *de facto*, exercising authority over the countryside. A handful among the Welsh gentry could even aspire to wield the highest power in their own right. William Herbert became a Marcher lord and also Justice of North and South Wales. Three generations of the Gruffydd family held sway as

[9] Griffiths, *Principality*, p. 33.

Chamberlains of North Wales. After his grandfather, Gruffydd ap Nicholas, had earlier been ruler of south-west Wales in all but name, Rhys ap Thomas became Chamberlain and, in due course, Justice of South Wales. Though gentle birth and local prestige, knowledge, and experience counted as significant qualifications to become chosen as officials, what mattered much more were adequate wealth and economic status and force of character.

The absence of those ostensibly charged with the responsibility of exercising authority and the consequent need to depute power to local men, with office often leased to them for long periods, rarely worked in the best interests of justice or effective administration. George Owen not unfairly referred to the most injurious jurisdiction exercised by 'bad, partial and covetous ministers'.[10] The men on the spot were chiefly concerned to advance their own interests and were not over-scrupulous about the methods they employed to do so. Contemporary criticism throughout the period was directed not so much at the machinery of the courts and administration as at the personnel responsible for them. It was the officers who were taxed with forging court rolls, embezzlement, extortion, and improper use of force for their own ends. When John Mowbray, earl marshal of England, acquired his lordship of Chepstow in 1413 he found a sorry situation there. It was not, as might have been expected, the consequences of the Glyndŵr Rebellion which were the principal cause of this but the malign outcome of a succession of minorities and the 'prolonged absence of a marcher lord of full age, able to take care of his own interests'.[11] When the Great Sessions were held in the lordship in 1415, fines of £132, £101, and £36 were imposed on three leading officials, Thomas Saunders (steward), John Hay (clerk of the courts), and John Don (bailiff of Chepstow), respectively, for a series of grave frauds and misdemeanours, including forgery of the court rolls. Yet none of these men seems to have been deprived of his office and all probably sued for pardon of at least some of the penalties. In mid-century Gruffydd ap Nicholas, 'the greatest rogue of his time in Wales', was nevertheless acting as deputy-justice and virtual ruler of south-west Wales. When Sir Robert Whitney was sent from Westminster to deal with him, he was 'seduced by drink', robbed of his commission, and returned to Westminster humiliated by Gruffydd.[12]

Nor were conditions any better in North Wales. Gruffydd Vaughan of Corsygedol and his wife, Maud, petitioners against Sir Richard Croft, himself one of the most prominent members of the prince's council, late in Edward IV's reign described the officers of the March as owing him 'such right great and special favour' that the petitioners 'could not in any wise

[10] W. Ll. Williams, *The Making of Modern Wales* (London, 1919), p. 41.
[11] Pugh, *Marcher Lordships*, p. 9.   [12] Griffiths, *Principality*, p. 31.

have any sufficient council learned in all those parts that would be against the said Sir Richard in that matter'.[13] This was an all-too-common complaint in the Principality and the March. In Chirkland and Oswestry the two rival families, the Kyffins and the Trevors, were contending for the sovereignty of the country and 'had their alliance, partisans and friends in all countries round thereabouts, to whom as the manner of that time was they sent all such of their followers as committed murder or manslaughter, which were safely kept as very precious jewels and they received the like from their friends'. The result was that it 'was impossible . . . to have judicial proceeding against them'.[14] Every office in the northern Principality had its price and, not unexpectedly, there was a long tradition of force and extortion on the part of office-holders to recover their outlay.

On the very eve of the Act of Union, we find in the lordship of Gower that the conduct of its steward, Sir George Herbert, was thoroughly deplorable. An agreement of 1532 to regulate abuses there suggests that, as steward of the lordship, Herbert must have borne considerable responsibility for them himself. Worst of all, however, was his cold-blooded resort to judicial murder when, having extorted from a young man a false confession of stealing sheep from his father, Herbert had him hanged in spite of explicit instructions from the Council in the Marches that he should do nothing until it had further considered the matter.

In these circumstances it is not surprising that there should be a high incidence of lawlessness and disorder in fifteenth-century Wales. Everywhere in the kingdom, at this period, the maintenance of justice and good order was at a low ebb. The key governmental problem in England and Wales was that of public order. Success in coping with it depended largely on the strength of the monarchy and partly on the quality of local officials. For much of the reign of Henry VI, the monarchy was enfeebled and a prey to faction and, in consequence, local justice and order sadly deteriorated. Men sought to gain their ends in lawcourts by the favour of those responsible for holding them, by offering gifts or rewards, or by abuse of friendship. Law and lawcourts were notoriously corrupt; money could work the oracle to escape punishment from most crimes.

> In England, as all men wyten,
> Law, as best, is bought and sold;

even for murder,

> I shall fyndyn a man of law
> Will take my penny and let me go.[15]

---

[13] D. E. Lowe, 'The Council of the Prince of Wales . . . during the Reign of Edward IV', *BBCS*, xxvii (1977–8), 278–96.
[14] *HGF*, pp. 41–2.
[15] V. J. Scattergood, *Politics and Poetry in the Fifteenth Century* (London, 1971), p. 322.

If such methods failed lawbreakers, or were considered not to be worth trying, there remained the resort to force, or the threat of it, against justices, jurors, witnesses, or rival parties. Maintenance, or illegal support through dishonest means, as the result of obtaining the good offices of a man so powerful that no one would readily offend him, was widespread; and there was a great deal of the abuse of power which was never revealed in court at all. Armed conflict or the possibility of it were widely prevalent and so, too, were serious crimes such as homicide, larceny, assault, abduction, rape, arson, and highway robbery. The most common form of crime was theft, which accounted for about half the criminal offences heard in the courts; it sprang not only from greed but very often from dire poverty.

On top of all this, Wales had its own particular problems. There was no single overall judicial authority within the country, divided as it was between Principality and March. The March was further subdivided into a congeries of jurisdictions, each independent of the other, enabling offenders to escape from one lordship into another or into England. The lawbreakers who fled could place themselves under the protection of the lord by paying the *arddel* or avowry fine, or else they might be harboured by an official who benefited from rendering his favour in return for a financial consideration. Outlaws found refuge in this way, and other men were abducted and released on ransom. Men from the March committed offences in England and escaped unpunished. Cattle-stealing in the border areas was a very common form of theft and so, though to a lesser extent, was the stealing of horses, sheep, pigs, and geese. More heinous crimes were also prevalent. In 1456, one Walter Vaughan, a kinsman of Sir William Herbert (later earl of Pembroke), was murdered in Hereford. Herbert, accompanied by twenty-one other Welsh gentry, on 15 March took over the city and held it for two nights and a day. He and his company forced the justices to declare that John Glover and other tradesmen were responsible for Vaughan's death and had them summarily hanged. Conversely, English merchants were sometimes seized in the March and their goods distrained in compensation for some offence in which they had had no part. As late as 1528, tenants of the lordship of Brecon and the burgesses of the borough complained to the King that they were impoverished and revenue was being lost because justice was not kept there. An inquiry made before the Act of Union reported three main obstacles to maintaining law and order in the Marches of Wales: the stealing of cattle from one lordship to another; the difficulty of obtaining honest and impartial juries; and the practice of collecting *cymhorthau* (*commortha*). The last-named levies were taken 'if any gentleman or mischievous person do murder any man or be taken for a thief then he maketh his fine with the evil officers of the said lordship and then gathereth *cymhorthau* of the King's poor subjects to pay the fine'.[16]

Yet John Wynn's *History of the Gwydir Family*, or what we know of the misdemeanours of Gruffydd ap Nicholas and others like him, present a picture of the Principality, north and south, which suggests that the situation was little, if at all, better there. Wynn's account depicts a society riddled with feuds, conflict, lawlessness, and a readiness to resort to armed force. Moreover, men escaped from the Principality to the March, or from north to south Wales, with impunity, and without giving the impression that the possibility of being punished for their offences was greater in the one area than the other. Lawbreakers resisted hotly any attempt to bring them to court to answer for their crimes; and Evan ap Robert, taking law and punishment into his own hands, struck off the heads of two murderers. Ironically enough, in one case where Wynn suggested that offenders were very loth to face the dangerous journey to Caernarfon, when they eventually got there, it was their opponents who had brought them who were the more severely dealt with. At Ysbyty Ifan, Wynn recorded that a gang of desperadoes had abused the privilege of sanctuary to such an extent that the place became 'a receptacle of thieves and murderers, who being safely warranted there by law . . . no place within twenty miles about was safe from their incursions and robbery . . . they had to their backstay friends and receptors in all the county of Merioneth and Powys land'.[17]

As was to be expected in such disturbed conditions following the Glyndŵr Rebellion and during the civil wars, many men refused to surrender and took to a life of outlawry, or were placed outside the law as a result of their misdemeanours. Sir Gruffydd Fychan and his associates spent the three years from 1444 to 1447 as outlaws; and the poet Lewys Glyn Cothi also became an outlaw—on two occasions apparently. Given the heavily forested nature of much of the Welsh landscape and the morcellation of jurisdiction in the March, the outlaws' retreat to the woodlands was understandable. Outlawry was not intended principally as a form of punishment but as the ultimate means of forcing an offender to submit to the judicial process. But the procedure was singularly toothless in Wales and the Marches, where it appeared that men were so little troubled by it that they made no effort to secure its reversal. Later in the fifteenth century there was much less inclination to flee to the woods. Instead, men lay low at some distance from their homes, taking refuge with their friends, keeping hidden during the day, and at night venturing to the nearest tavern or winehouse, to 'make merry and to wench'.[18] So secure did many of them feel that they did not deign to buy a pardon, even when it might have been easily and cheaply acquired.

The most famous of the Welsh outlaws of the age was Dafydd ap

---

[16] William Rees, 'The Union of England and Wales', *Trans. Cymmr.*, 1937, p. 36.
[17] *HGF*, pp. 53–4.   [18] *HGF*, p. 41; cf. Bellamy, *Crime and Disorder*, p. 105.

Siancyn, a captain of the Lancastrian faction who was reputed to have kept the rock of Carreg y Walch for fifteen years. Like Robin Hood, he clad his followers in green and dispersed them hither and thither among his friends. So elusive were they that those who happened to catch sight of them took them for fairies! Though they must have seemed solid and substantial enough to the inhabitants of Evan ap Robert's house when they were assaulted furiously by them. Among Dafydd's exploits was his attack on Denbigh Castle when he killed the royal officials, Henry Heaton and Richard Pemberton. Himself a man of good birth [*o'r hynaif gorau'r hanwyd*], Dafydd ap Siancyn was warmly greeted by some of the poets, notably Tudur Penllyn and Ieuan ap Gruffydd Leiaf, not as an outlaw but as a hero defying his enemies; 'the tall Kai of the fresh saplings and the leaves', 'his castle the wild wood; the meadow oaks his towers'.[19] The poets were loud in their praise for him and other outlaws for their generosity to the weak and poor who sought their bounty at Rhyd Goch. The poets gave a stern warning, though, against the treachery of the English and the town burgesses. Much of this poetry, like the contemporary English references to Robin Hood, presents an idealized picture of the outlaw's life: free and undominated by authority, not a hunted criminal but an agent for moral good who righted society's wrongs.

Poets were themselves not unfamiliar with outlawry. *Cywyddau* by Lewys Glyn Cothi describe the days he spent on the run, with his lair in a hollow oak, though he made for his patron's home to obtain supper and a bed. He also recalls another occasion when he and Owain ap Gruffydd ap Nicholas were outlaws together in Gwynedd and when he depended on the latter for gold and wine to keep body and soul together. From another poet, Llywelyn ab y Moel, we derive illuminating glimpses of both sides to the outlaw's existence. He warmed to the praise of his hide-out in Coed y Graig Lwyd as a 'dark tent overhead' where he had saved his honour; this was no 'turf-topped villein's den', he assures us. But the life he described in another poem, 'Battle of Waun Gaseg', was very different. Here, his exploits were sadly lacking in heroism. He told with wry, mocking humour how, at the onset of the enemy, he and his fellows fled precipitately, 'their bloodless lances bright and clean'. As for the brave poet himself, he excelled only in running away faster than his comrades.[20] Doubtless Llywelyn's satire, just as typically as his praise, would have been overstated; yet there must have been more than a grain of truth in this picture of hard-pressed outlaws desperate in their efforts to escape from their pursuers.

That violence and disorder existed in the fifteenth century is unquestionable; but the extent and prevalence of it have often been seriously

[19] H. I. Bell, 'Translations from the *Cywyddwyr*', *Trans. Cymmr.*, 1940, p. 244.
[20] *OBWV*, pp. 59–60.

overemphasized. The turbulence of the fifteenth century was less bad than that of some earlier medieval centuries and certainly no worse than that of any century of the Middle Ages. Indeed, it was probably not more disordered on the whole than the sixteenth century. The impression of greater disruption is partly due to the better documentation which becomes available during the period, partly to the more vivid terms in which disorder is sometimes described, and partly to the increase in tension during relatively limited periods of civil strife and confusion. Moreover, men were still not accustomed to thinking of lawcourts as places where they could obtain impartial justice so much as instruments which they could manipulate in order to secure their own ends more successfully in their quarrels with others. While it is impossible to quantify precisely the degree of law-breaking, it would appear that Wales was no worse than other outlying parts of the realm, like the northern border, Yorkshire, or Devon and Cornwall. It did, it is true, have its own particular problems. The existence of Principality and March complicated the task of law enforcement. The embittered legacy of the Glyndŵr Rebellion, the absenteeism of great officials and Marcher lords, and the outbreaks of civil war all added to the difficulty of maintaining good order. Yet much of the evidence for the disorderly state of Wales has been drawn from Tudor sources: from the authors of the preambles to the statutes enacting the changes of the 1530s, or from later commentators like Rice Merrick, John Wynn, or George Owen. All of these subscribed to the notion of powerful and beneficent Tudor rulers bringing peace by their heroic exertions to a wildly disordered and divided Wales, whose ills had to be heavily exaggerated in order to highlight the healing skills of the royal physicians alleged to have performed the miracle cure.

Yet, when John Wynn was narrating some of the most furious and fiercely contested feuds, he could nevertheless not conceal the fact that the courts at Caernarfon were operating and were far from helpless in dealing with offenders. Other kinds of evidence from the fifteenth century itself present a much more stable and less turbulent scene. The life portrayed in the verse of some of the greatest poets of the age—Dafydd ab Edmwnd and Gutun Owain, for example—contains virtually no hint of conflict or struggle, but is one where enjoyment of the delights of love, nature, and pleasurable living wholly dominates. A large part of the work of even the most politically conscious poets, like Guto'r Glyn or Lewys Glyn Cothi, for much of the time suggests little stress or disorder but a great deal of leisured comfort, high spirits, and merriment. People of all ranks in society moved freely around the countryside, seemingly without let or hindrance. Poets, pilgrims, friars, students, drovers, tradesmen, craftsmen, harvest workers, and others went about their lawful business unimpeded for most of the time. Secular and ecclesiastical building, implying a settled and fairly prosperous society and involving considerable movement of craftsmen and materials, went on apace, especially during the latter half of the fifteenth century and the beginning of the sixteenth. The clear impression we derive, especially from the poetry, much the most abundant native source of information, is not primarily that of violence, disorder, and bloodshed— though they are certainly present—but rather of more peaceful society in which many enjoyed a relatively high standard of living and a reasonably secure existence.

Following the recovery of royal authority during the reigns of Edward IV and Henry VII, there is reliable evidence which tends to show that courts were being regularly held and justice dispensed. The plea rolls of Anglesey between 1509 and 1516 show that, although acts of violence were certainly committed and the courts were somewhat lacking in efficiency and vigour, there 'was no serious disorder. The machinery of the courts was kept running'.[21] The Justice of North Wales (or his deputy) held his sessions and the sheriffs their county courts and tourns. The stewards of ecclesiastical possessions, like those of the bishop of Bangor or the abbot of Conway, also brought offenders to stand trial in the justice's court. Even the representatives of the Order of St John of Jerusalem brought them from Ysbyty Ifan, once so notorious as a haunt of wrongdoers. A leading poet of the early sixteenth century, Tudur Aled, refers to a number of his patrons—Richard Herbert, Sir Thomas Salusbury, William Edwards of Chirk, Maredudd ab Ieuan, and others—as being active in their suppression of crime and disorder in various parts of north Wales.[22] Similarly, evidence from lordships such as those of Brecon, Hay, or Gower reveals that courts were regularly kept, although again not always as efficiently or energetically as might be desired. Nevertheless, the protest against the practice of redeeming the sessions in all three lordships shows the increasing awareness of the abuses arising from it and a determination to be shot of it. Moreover, the publication in recent years of the texts of accords, drawn up in the Welsh language and known as *cydfodau*, suggests that it was not at all unusual for provinces and lordships to agree among themselves in hammering out the settlement of differences or framing better regulations for the future.[23] Officials and inhabitants would assemble at accustomed places on the border of two jurisdictions, like Bwlchyroerddrws on the frontier between Powys and Meirionnydd, or at the place where conflict or disagreement had occurred.

---

[21] W. O. Williams, *Calendar of the Caernarvonshire Quarter Sessions Records* (Caernarfon, 1956), p. xxxi.

[22] *TA*, pp. lv–vii.

[23] J. B. Smith, 'Cydfodau o'r Bymthegfed Ganrif', *BBCS*, xxi (1966); cf. also *BBCS*, xxv (1973).

Nor was the King's government itself heedless of the difficulties arising in the March or unconcerned to grapple with them. At a number of points, attempts were made to tighten up administration and government in Wales, though complete success was far from being achieved. During Henry VI's reign there were abortive ventures to secure a better measure of order and good government, the most determined of them being the efforts of Richard, duke of York, to curb Gruffydd ap Nicholas's excesses during his short-lived term as Protector in 1454–5. Not until the 1470s, however, when Edward IV was firmly installed in power, could more ambitious steps be taken to try to produce the desired effect. In 1471 the young Prince of Wales was given a council of fifteen to manage his estates. Following bitter complaints in the Parliament of 1472, from representatives of the border counties, concerning the outrageous demeanour of Welshmen, and requests for a meeting with Marcher lords, Edward met the latter in 1473 and compelled them to enter into agreements to carry out their responsibilities. In the same year, the prince's council was increased to twenty-five and a separate household set up for him, with Lord Rivers and the bishop of Rochester in charge of it. They were given instructions to deal with specific disturbances but do not, at this time, seem to have been changed from a body responsible for managing estates into a court for administering the law. The prince now began to reside at Ludlow, the traditional headquarters of the former earldom of March, and it was only to be expected that his council should increasingly become the centre for the exercise of royal authority within the March. In 1476 important additional powers were accorded it by the grant of a commission of oyer and terminer within the Principality, Marches, and adjacent English shires; and in December 1477 the territories in the possession of the prince were enlarged. Some of the last bastions of the former Herbert influence were dismantled in 1479, when the second earl of Pembroke was removed from his offices of Justice and Chamberlain of South Wales.

It is evident that, during the last ten years of Edward IV's reign, the authority of the prince's council, often reinforced by that of the King's own council, permeated widely and effectually in Wales and the border areas. Its influence was sufficiently weighty for its disfavour not to be courted lightly. Not only did it exercise control from Ludlow but it also visited other centres like Shrewsbury and Coventry as well as local trouble-spots when necessary. In addition it maintained a 'council learned in the law' at Westminster. From 1473 onwards, it was responsible for trying to maintain a degree of law and order and co-ordinating justice as well as supervising estates. Some of its foremost members were placed on the commission of the peace in border counties and it took over the administration of Crown lordships like those of the Duchy of Lancaster, with which the prince had initially no concern. But David Powel, though acknowledging Edward IV's good intentions for the 'reformation of the estate of Wales', believed that the 'troubles and disquietness of his subjects' and the 'shortness of his time' 'sufficed him to do little or nothing in that behalf'.[24]

Not until 1489 did Henry VII revive the experiment. On 29 November in that year, his eldest son, Arthur, was created Prince of Wales and given a council. In that same year his chancellor, John Arundell, and others of his commissioners travelled to north Wales to levy a subsidy and provide for governance of the area. Further references to their activity exist for 1490.[25] In 1493, additional steps were taken when potential powers very similar to those of the earlier Yorkist prince were conferred upon him. He was empowered to appoint commissioners of oyer and terminer within the Principality, March, and border counties, and was given powers of array, examining liberties, and looking into the escape of criminals. Because the prince was so young, much of the practical exercise of his authority was delegated to Jasper Tudor. The prince was also entrusted with rule over a number of Marcher lordships, making him much the greatest territorial lord within the region and one who was in a position to oversee the functioning of justice, or at least to have it overseen in his name. The leading figures in the council at this time were John Alcock, bishop of Ely, and from 1494 onwards, William Smyth, bishop of Coventry and Lichfield, and later of Lincoln. Like its predecessor, the council functioned from Ludlow, but after the death of Prince Arthur in 1502, the King seemed to lose interest in the council and its functions are difficult to trace. It did not, however, go out of existence; it remained in being, moribund but capable of being effectively revived and galvanized into action.

Another indication of the determination of both Yorkist and Tudor rulers to exercise closer control over the conduct of their subjects in the March was the imposition by both Edward IV and Henry VII of a system of recognizances for good behaviour. In 1476, following Edward's conference with the Marcher lords, the inhabitants for the lordship of Newport were obliged to give assurances for their future law-abiding conduct on pain of the forfeiture of considerable sums if they defaulted. This has been interpreted as having originated in a demand by the King that they should enter into such obligations, and is unlikely to have been applied solely to the lordship of Newport. This precedent laid down by his predecessor was followed up by Henry VII, who found it a most useful device not merely for maintaining good order but also for frightening his subjects into parting with large sums of money. The texts of indentures which he entered into have survived and shed much light on his aims and methods. In his agreement of 1504, which he imposed on Edward Stafford, third duke of

[24] Williams, *Making Mod. Wales*, p. 43.
[25] J. B. Smith, 'Crown and Community in the Principality of North Wales in the Reign of Henry Tudor', *WHR*, III (1965-7), 145-71.

Buckingham, lord of Brecknock, Hay, and Newport, he committed the duke to 'put all manner of men under sufficient surety of their good abearing and their appearance in court.'[26]

These attempts, by means of councils set up for the princes and the imposition of recognizances for good behaviour, to curb some of the excesses and disorders caused by misrule in Wales and the March were neither wholly effective nor long-lasting. They depended too much on the somewhat fitful and short-lived interest shown by individual monarchs in the problem. Once that awareness faded, so, too, did the efficacy of the instruments they had devised to cope with it. Admittedly, the large territorial stake which the King had amassed by the end of the fifteenth century—far overshadowing that of any other proprietor there—and the prestige he enjoyed as sovereign gave him powerful levers in dealing with a now much-weakened Marcher aristocracy. But the truth was that, at best, he was not trying to do more than keep the existing arrangements running smoothly. Neither Edward IV nor Henry VII envisaged any attempt to get at the real roots of the difficulty: the morcellation of authority and the pursuit of private interests on the part of the lords and their officials. The situation was slowly becoming ripe for a radical solution. But it was to take a great politico-religious crisis in the 1530s and a decisive political architect to perceive the possibility of a root-and-branch amendment and to appreciate the need for implementing it.

[26] T. B. Pugh, 'The Indenture for the Marches', *EHR*, LXXI (1956), 436–41.

CHAPTER 3

GETTING AND SPENDING: THE WELSH ECONOMY

THE life of fifteenth-century Wales was that of an underdeveloped pre-industrial society. Very largely a self-sufficient economic entity—or, more accurately, perhaps, a loose bundle of mainly self-sufficient economic entities—it was based on peasant farming which had not changed in its essentials for centuries. Economic life depended on the basic resources of the land, primarily those of agriculture, supplemented to a lesser extent by woodlands and fisheries. Those same resources also sustained many of such industries as existed. Activities like the making of cloth, leather, and dairy products, or milling and brewing, obviously processed raw materials derived wholly or mainly from agriculture. Building, the making of wooden tools and utensils, charcoal burning and other timber-linked industries were tied to the exploitation of extensive woodland and forest; just as the salting of fish and the sun-drying of stockfish depended on the catches made along the sea-coast and in inland ponds and streams. Each rural neighbourhood had its own indispensable complement of craftsmen, such as blacksmiths, carpenters, millers, or weavers, nearly all of whom were part-time farmers as well and some of whom peddled their wares in the local market-towns. But many of the contemporary trades, crafts, and services were centred in the little towns, the largest of them no bigger than modern villages. The majority of the urban inhabitants were themselves partly engaged in agricultural pursuits in the arable fields, common pastures, woodlands, and wastes which surrounded them. Their towns were more important, however, as the locations of markets and fairs for the rural communities for some miles around. In addition, they were very often the ports and trading-centres, through which essential or luxury goods from outside were brought into the local economy.

What existed in the way of the exploitation of minerals and metals and the manufacturing or processing of goods from them was conducted on a small scale and, in almost every instance, intended chiefly as a useful increment to the income of the landed estates, great and small, where they were found. Nor should they be thought of as existing largely independently of the predominantly agricultural community. Industrial activity of this kind was usually seasonal and part-time, being geared to operate when demand for agricultural labour was slack. Those engaged in it were usually allowed smallholdings of land to work on their own account and limited rights of access to common pastures and woods. These industries, like contemporary agriculture itself at harvest, weeding-time, or other busy seasons, depended heavily for their labour force on the existence of large-scale under-employment or concealed unemployment among the population. There were many small peasants, cottars, and hired labourers, who could not contrive to obtain an adequate living from their own land or from working in agriculture only. To make ends meet they were perforce obliged to engage in such miscellaneous occupations as they could find at different times in the year and even in a variety of places. It was, for many, an economy of makeshifts, of 'bits and pieces', in which men, women, and children had to turn their hands to various tasks to make up the family livelihood. Though they showed dogged tenacity and great ingenuity, they might well, in lean seasons and bad years, be reduced to begging their bread from their more fortunate neighbours.

The economy showed a number of those symptoms of a pre-industrial regime nowadays associated with the countries of the 'Developing World'. The inescapable facts of geology and geography—soil, terrain, and climate—imposed on the economy severe limitations which could not be transcended. A relatively primitive agricultural and industrial technology, based on the muscle-power of man and beast, assisted marginally by power from wind, water, wood, charcoal, and coal, achieved only a low productivity and obliged the population to spend much more of its time and effort in extracting a far greater proportion of its needs from the soil than it does today. Agricultural conservatism, bred of ingrained habit, caution, and an inability to take risks, generally prevailed. There was no selection of seeds; crop rotation and farming implements were rudimentary; pesticides and weedkillers were unknown; and the main fertilizer, dung, was in short supply. Corn yields, at 3 or 4 to 1, were meagre; and it took one man five days to harvest an acre of corn. Farm animals were smaller, leaner, and less productive than their modern counterparts: the average cow was about one-quarter the weight of the contemporary animal and produced only one-sixth as much milk. Whereas in an advanced modern state every farm-worker is estimated to produce enough to feed twelve people, the fifteenth-century husbandman could only sustain 1½ persons by his efforts. Some of the extremes of wealth and poverty seen today in the Third World were equally apparent in the fifteenth century: the income of a grandee like Richard, duke of York, was about a thousand times or more that of a labourer. There were wide disparities between rich and poor in terms of accommodation, dress, and diet; a small, privileged fraction of the population commanded an overwhelmingly large proportion of its purchasing power and deployed it in buying luxury and exotic products.

It was an economy perched anxiously near the margin of subsistence. Always heavily dependent on the quality of the harvest in any given year, most of its members had few reserves with which to withstand the effects of a seasonal disaster like that of the year 1482, which experienced a sudden leap of 74 per cent in the price of corn. 'If the harvest fails in any year, then follow dire poverty, unrest and turbulence',[1] Ulrich von Hutten said of Germany, but his comment applied to every other European country as well. Yet it is also worth remembering that this was, for most people, a world unaccustomed to ease or luxury and one whose inhabitants were used to withstanding crushing misfortunes with the unsung courage and stoicism of peasant populations. Moreover, the century from c.1430 to 1530, in spite of all its drawbacks, may have been a relatively fortunate period in economic terms. For those who had survived earlier depopulation, warfare, and calamity, land for lease or purchase was far more readily available than it had been. Escape from unfree status, either by flight or by tacit or openly acknowledged manumission, was not all that difficult, and movement from one place to another relatively easy. Prices were stable, work was fairly plentiful, and wages were good—real wages in the building industry, for example, doubled during the century. Overall, the chances of advancement for those who were ambitious, enterprising, and unsqueamish were probably better than they had ever been. For those in a position to take advantage of it, this was an age of opportunity.

LIFE ON THE LAND (SEE MAP 2)

Agricultural activity, on which depended the overwhelming majority of the population of Wales, like other parts of Europe, was determined almost wholly by terrain and climate. Some 60 per cent of the total acreage of Wales lies over 500 feet above sea-level and more than a quarter of the whole above 1,000 feet. All the former counties of Wales, except Anglesey, Flint, Pembrokeshire, and Glamorgan, have land over 2,000 feet, while Brecon and Radnor have none below 100 feet. The depth and fertility of the soils vary markedly, in general in accordance with altitude; the shallowest and most barren naturally being found, for the most part, on the higher ground. A large proportion of the soils suffer from impeded drainage and are deficient in lime and phosphate. The weather is changeable and unreliable. Rainfall is high in incidence as well as amount, over most of the country, averaging about 40 inches (c.100 cm.) a year. Low amounts of sunshine mean that temperatures are generally cool, the growing season relatively restricted, and the prospects of ripening crops uncertain. Rivers flowing westward out of the central upland mass are mostly short with narrow valleys, although those flowing eastward and southward like the Dee, Severn, Wye, Usk, or Tywi, have longer valleys which broaden out where they meet the former Marcher lands.

[1] J. R. Hale, *Renaissance Europe, 1480–1520* (London, 1971), p. 211.

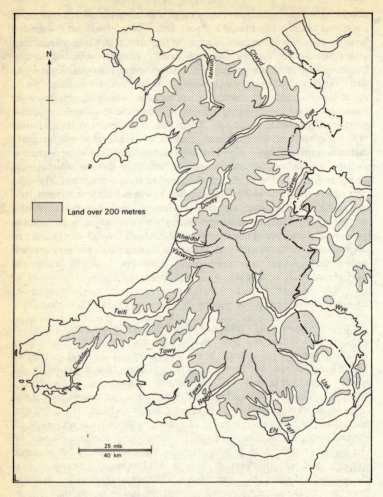

MAP 2 Wales: Physical Structure

The nature of the geography of Wales meant that the country was divided, broadly speaking, into two parts. The first consisted of a central upland mass, covering much of the area of the country; and the second of a series of narrow and somewhat restricted lowland zones along the coastline and also in some of the broader valleys like those of Clwyd or Tywi, or along the eastern border areas in the valleys of the Dee, Wye, or

Severn. Divisions which had originally been determined by geography were reinforced and, in some ways, complicated by earlier medieval history, when the Normans had brought large areas of the south and east under their control. Into the low-lying country of their conquests within the March—the Englishries lying below 600 feet or even the 400 feet contour line—they had introduced manorial practices and Anglo-Norman organization. But in much of the upland areas of those lordships—the Welshries above 400–600 feet—the communities had retained their own traditional agricultural methods and native laws. Tudor antiquarians, like George Owen of Pembrokeshire or Rice Merrick of Glamorgan, drew a sharp distinction between the mainly pastoral custom and practice in the north of their respective counties and the mixed farming of the southern regions. The same contrast between 'two landscapes, two cultures, and two peoples' in the lordship of Oswestry has likewise been emphasized by a modern writer.[2] Though it is certainly possible and necessary to differentiate in this way between the mainly pastoral activities of upland Wales and the greater emphasis on arable farming in the more low-lying areas, it has always to be remembered that such broad generalizations may conceal within them many variations in detail. Edeirnion in north Wales, for example, though geographically a part of the upland area, was always justifiably regarded in medieval times as an unusually prosperous region; while, in the same way, the parish of Llangynwyd, though technically a part of the *Blaenau* or uplands of Glamorgan, was so well situated as to become a rich parish and the cradle of the medieval literature of Morgannwg. Even within a limited area like an average parish, there were wide variations of location and fertility which could give rise to striking differences in output. Hence the care with which kin groups tried to divide the *rhandir*, or shared lands, between the heirs who took part in *cyfran*, or equal partition, in such a way that each would get a roughly equal share of the better soils and locations. The general nature of the topography of Wales meant that, as in most upland countries, there was a strong localism, reinforced by geographical isolation; an intense loyalty to the local community, customs, and manners, and an inherent suspicion of the outsider. In parts of the Marches, especially, there were long traditions of cattle-stealing, inter-lordship rivalries, and raiding, vendettas, and feuds between whole communities as well as families and individuals.

In most of upland Wales—within the Principality and the Marches—animal husbandry predominated. Animals were the fixed capital not only of agriculture but also of much of such contemporary industry, like cloth-making and tanning, as was practised as well. They were highly vulnerable to the epizöotic diseases, against which there was scant protection, as well

[2] Ll. B. Smith in Griffiths, *Boroughs Wales*, p. 221.

as to the losses caused by war, violence, and theft. The most important of
the livestock raised were cattle; and it is not a coincidence that they were
the beasts most highly valued in the native Welsh laws or that the Welsh
word for 'cattle'—*da*—stands also for 'goods' or 'wealth'. Cattle were
esteemed for their meat, milk, hides, and horn. They were also valued for
their dung and for their role as plough beasts, being steadier, stronger, and
cheaper to keep than horses, as well as being edible when too old to work.
The trade in store cattle with England, dating back maybe to pre-Norman
days, was growing steadily in importance in the later Middle Ages. Sheep,
though less important than cattle, in spite of the apparent suitability of
much of the countryside for rearing them, had become considerably more
significant in the fifteenth century. Earlier, the Cistercian monasteries in
south Wales, though not in the north, had blazed the trail as sheep-keepers
by introducing superior techniques of breeding sheep and selling their wool
in international markets. By the fourteenth and fifteenth centuries, the
shortage of manpower and the value of the wool-clip had provided strong
incentives for keeping sheep more widely. The high proportion of the value
of the tithe on wool in upland parishes like Dolgellau in Merioneth
(£8. 13s. 4d. out of £13. 6s. 8d.) or Llantrisant in Glamorgan (£10. 13s. 4d.
out of £14. 5s. 0d.)[3] gives a clear indication of the importance of sheep
there. They were most useful animals not only as a source of wool but also
of meat, milk, tallow, and dung.

Horses were greatly esteemed as noble animals fit for the more
prestigious occupations of war, hunting, and travel. The lovingly detailed
descriptions of them given by poets are reminiscent of the more ecstatic
advertisements of modern motor-car manufacturers.[4] But horses were also
used for such menial tasks as drawing the harrow and the dung-cart, even
though they were harnessed with more difficulty than oxen; and a good
pack-horse was valued at the relatively large sum of 10s. Herds of swine
were kept on the wastes and fattened on the pannage of woodlands in the
autumn. Goats were useful beasts on the rockier hills and mountains of
Wales, though their importance may have been overstated in the past. The
myriad troubles to which herding these cussed and obstreperous creatures
gave rise were amusingly detailed—and bewailed—in a wryly satirical
poem on the subject by Ieuan ap Huw Cae Llwyd.[5] Many farmers also kept
geese and other poultry, which were valuable enough to note a separate
mention in some of the returns of the *Valor Ecclesiasticus* in 1535,[6] e.g., in
some of the Monmouthshire parishes where they were rated as worth a few
shillings. There are a few instances in fifteenth-century poetry of a growing
interest in selective breeding, when the poets ask for gifts of animals in

---

[3] *Valor Ecclesiasticus* . . . (6 vols. London, 1810–34), IV, 348–9.
[4] E.g., Tudur Aled, *OBWV*, pp. 67–9.
[5] *H.C.Ll.*, pp. 119–20.   [6] *Val. Ecc.*, IV, 348–50.

their *cywyddau gofyn* [begging poems]. In addition to the frequent attention paid to those steeds sought from eminent horse-breeders such as Abbot Dafydd ab Owain, there are occasional references to bulls of exceptional merit, whose prowess as potential sires had been singled out. One Glamorgan poet, Deio ab Ieuan Ddu, went further in extolling the virtues of a specially chosen bull and heifer and looked forward to the day when they would produce calves of exceptional milk-yielding calibre.

In all the upland areas there would have been large acreages of rough upland pastures above 700 feet. The practice of transhumance, or seasonal movement of livestock, ensured that effective use was made of these resources at the appropriate season in the year. In the spring, traditionally at *Calan Mai* [May Day], after the ploughing and sowing were completed, the herds were driven up to the hill pastures so as to clear the meadows for hay and the arable for corn-growing. They were kept up there until *Calan Gaeaf* [1 November] on the *ffriddoedd* [upland pastures], where temporary summer dwellings [*hafodydd*, *hafotai*] were erected for the accommodation of the herds who looked after them. The great mountain pasture of Englefield in Flintshire, known as Mynydd Tegeingl, had livestock from a dozen parishes grazing there in the summer months. The cows, ewes, and goats were milked, and butter and cheese made from the milk. Place-names still reveal traces of these old medieval grazing practices. Names like *hafod* or *hafoty*, many of which became independent farmsteads from the sixteenth century onwards, are almost invariably found above a height of 600 to 700 feet, while the *hendre* [permanent home] names are found from 600 feet downwards. Similarly, the field names having clear and ancient links with arable farming, like *erw* [acre], *cyfer* [acre], or *dryll* [portion], may be found up to 500 or 600 feet; and hayland and pasture names, like *gweirglodd* [hayfield], *dôl* [meadow], and *morfa* [marsh], are associated with major valleys and coastal marshes. The larger landowners, like Cistercian monks or Marcher lords, had in the earlier Middle Ages successfully integrated the resources of uplands and lowlands in the management of their estates, having granges and manors in both hills and plains, between which they moved their stock in spring and autumn. But, with the break-up of older methods of estate management by the fifteenth century, it is not possible to tell how much of their earlier methods of interchange continued to take place.

It would, however, be a great mistake to overlook the key importance attached to the growing of limited quantities of corn in the upland areas of Wales. In all parts of the country, however unfavourable conditions might be, it was essential to grow a corn crop for consumption by humans and animals. In the light of the immense difficulties and heavy cost of transporting grain by land, especially in upland country, no district could afford to have to depend on outside sources for its corn. Crops had, therefore, to be grown at altitudes up to 1,000 feet, in adverse climate and poor soil. Quantitative evidence of the extent of corn-growing in Wales is scarce and nearly all of it dates from the 1530s, though there is little reason to believe that circumstances then reported had changed very dramatically over the previous fifty to hundred years; and, in so far as they had changed, more, not less, corn was probably being grown. A meticulously detailed analysis of the *Valor Ecclesiasticus* (1535) returns for the deanery of Abergavenny, one of only two or three deaneries, all concentrated in Gwent, for which comparable information is available, has shown how significant the corn crop was.[7] Even in the upland parishes of that deanery, like Llanfoist or Llanwenarth, it contributed 30 and 40 per cent respectively of the total value of the tithe. Evidence of the same kind, though less precise and detailed, shows similar conditions prevailing elsewhere in the diocese of Llandaff in typical upland parishes of Glamorgan. In the parish of Merthyr Tydfil the tithe of corn was worth £4. 6s. 8d. out of £20. 4s. 8d. (20 per cent) and at Gelli-gaer £5 out of £20. 17s. 0d. (25 per cent). More impressionistic, though not necessarily less valuable, testimony to the same effect is supplied by that experienced and widely travelled observer, John Leland. He described the Upper Taff valley, around Merthyr Tydfil, as a 'good valley for corn and grass' and the southernmost parts of Glyn Rhondda as 'meetly good for barley and oats'. In the lordships of Brecon and Llandovery he commented appreciatively that within the previous thirty years much greater quantities of barley had been grown, so that whereas they had once had to buy corn out of Herefordshire, 'they have enough for their own use and also to sell'. At the other end of Wales, in mountainous Caernarfonshire, he noted that in Llŷn and Eifionydd there was 'good corn', both 'by the shore and almost through upland', though in 'Eryri hills' there was 'very little corn, except oats in some places, and a little barley but scantly rye'.[8]

The corn crop chiefly grown in these upland areas, as Leland testified, was oats. Hardier, and more tolerant of acidic soils, lower temperatures, and higher rainfall than other corn crops, oats provided a valuable source of winter fodder for the livestock as well as for the making of that oatmeal bread eaten by almost all the inhabitants of Wales and praised for its excellent qualities by John Major in 1521. Smaller amounts of wheat, barley, and rye may also have been grown by the bigger farmers and those with better land; the wheat for breadcorn and the barley for malt. Leland was distinctly critical of what he regarded as Welsh farmers' indolence in the matter of corn-growing, censuring them for 'studying more to pasturage than tillage, as favourers of their consuete idleness'—though

---

[7] W. R. B. Robinson, 'The *Valor Ecclesiasticus* of 1535 as Evidence of Agrarian Output', *BIHR*, 56 (1983), 16–33.

[8] Leland, pp. 18, 22, 112–3, 81.

Italian observers were just as critical of Englishmen in this respect! But his own evidence shows that, in spite of the handicaps of climate and soil, farmers in all parts of Wales made strenuous efforts to cultivate such corn crops as they could. Evidence of their assiduity survives in narrow moorland valleys, where the remains of upland barns and cornmills still stand as testimony to their unending battle with a hostile climate and a grudging soil.

Comparatively little is known of the nature of the fields in which the corn crop was grown or the methods of cultivating it. The probability is that farmers followed those methods of infield–outfield production found in most highland areas. Because of the restricted size of the ground available, the corn was grown mainly in small infields lying near the homestead or hamlet. These were sometimes cultivated for the individual, more usually in common for the whole of the little township, with a good deal of co-operation in ploughing and other operations among all the inhabitants, kinsmen, and neighbours. The ground chosen for cultivation was enclosed and the animals folded on it during the months from mid-March to November, so as to fertilize it thoroughly before it was ploughed in preparation for sowing in the following March. This process went on annually until the soil was exhausted after a few years. Another method of preparing the soil for an arable crop was 'beating and burning' turf prior to the sowing of corn.

In the lowland areas of Wales, both those which had come under Norman influence and those of what had been *pura Wallia*, considerably greater emphasis was placed upon corn production in the mixed farming which prevailed there. In the low-lying parts of southern and eastern Wales—south Pembrokeshire, south Gower, the Vale of Glamorgan, the plain of Gwent, and the eastern fringes of Brecon and Radnor—survived the remains of a manorial organization. Here, in contrast to upland Wales, with its dispersed and thinly populated settlement patterns of hamlets and individual homesteads, were the small, compact Norman parishes with the nucleated villages common in a lowland economy. Around the villages lay the open fields, still largely unenclosed in the fifteenth century, capable of sustaining a relatively large population and geared to the effective production of corn. For these regions, the evidence of the *Valor Ecclesiasticus*, though late, brings out the significance of corn-growing. In the Vale of Glamorgan, that 'very principal good corn ground', as Leland described it, the most favoured parishes grew so much corn that out of the total value of tithes it might account for two-thirds in Gilestone (£4 out of £5. 18s. 0d.) or even three-quarters at Newton Nottage (£12. 13s. 4d. out of £17. 6s. 8d.). In the lowlands of neighbouring Gwent, equally high proportions were recorded in the parishes of Rockfield (75 per cent or £3. 6s. 8d. out of £4. 7s. 6d.) and Llanfihangel Lingoed (73 per cent or

£4. 1s. 4d. out of £5. 11s. 4d.).[9] No comparable figures exist for the parishes of south Pembrokeshire in the hundreds of Castlemartin and Dungleddy; but, in view of their remarkable reputation as corn-growing districts, it may reasonably be assumed that corn-growing was equally important there. Similarly, in north-eastern Wales, in highly favourable areas like the Vale of Clwyd and eastern border districts with easy access to Chester and bigger towns, large and flourishing corn crops were grown.

The *Valor Ecclesiasticus* provides fewer details about the actual corn crops grown, though it does reveal that in a Glamorgan parish like St Fagan's, wheat, oats, and barley were grown, on which tithes of £3. 10s. 0d., £3. 6s. 8d., and 15s. were paid respectively, while in more northerly Pentyrch, wheat brought in a tithe of 8s., rye 1s. 8d., barley 10s. 8d., and oats £2. 18s. 4d. Later evidence makes it plain that oats, wheat, and barley were the crops mainly cultivated—in that order, with rye a poor fourth.[10] To insure against the vagaries of climate and soil, farmers often seem to have played safe by sowing more than one sort of grain or a mixture like maslin (cereal with peas and/or beans). Hay was widely cultivated and was obtained mainly from permanent meadows. Gorse, too, was generally used to feed animals and, mixed with hay, straw, and bran, was used until the present century. Flax and hemp were commonly grown in the lowland areas, and linen made laboriously from the flax had become sufficiently usual for rags to be supplied in large quantities to paper-makers. The *Valor Ecclesiasticus* returns further reveal that apple and pear orchards were common in parts of Monmouthshire. Cider-making, which was a specialized production concentrated in south-eastern Wales in later centuries, may well have already been established there; the contemporary poets certainly enjoyed cider and referred appreciatively to it. Cornmills were universally established in considerable numbers in the low-lying counties, judging by the very large number of Monmouthshire parishes which explicitly recorded proceeds from the tithes on cornmills.

The farmers of lowland Wales also maintained large herds of livestock. Without the animals' dung, which was still the main fertilizer, intensive corn-growing would have been impossible and the soil would soon have lost its fertility—though in all those parishes which had access to the sea-coast, dung was supplemented by the use of seaweed and sand. From the large quantities of milk available, large amounts of butter and cheese were being made in some of the richer lowland areas of the south and they enjoyed a considerable reputation. But the breeding of cattle for sale in English markets had already assumed major importance and would grow to still greater proportions in the sixteenth and seventeenth centuries.

[9] *Val. Ecc.*, IV, 348–50.   [10] *GCH*, IV, 4.

In the first Welsh printed book, published in 1546 by Sir John Price of Brecon, the hints provided to help the farmers give us a broad indication of the nature of a Welsh husbandman's year in upland and lowland Wales alike. Sir John published careful instructions, presumably based on long practical experience, as to the routine to be followed in each month. He advised farmers when to prepare the soil, and recommended times at which to sow the most important crops (oats, peas, and beans in February and March; barley, flax, and hemp in April; and wheat and rye in May), and when to gather them in: haymaking in June and July, reaping wheat, oats, rye, and barley in August, September, and even October. He also counselled them to use the relatively slack month of November to fell ash trees for making the plough parts.[11] These ploughs, though they varied considerably in design, were well adapted to the essential task they had to perform. The poets, who had often closely observed the ploughmen at their work, praised them warmly for their skill and expertise in turning the soil, describing them as 'tailors of the headlands' [teilwriaid y talarau]. Ploughmen usually had a real affection for their oxen and were much concerned for their welfare. The poet Llawdden gives a graphic cameo of the way in which the plough-beasts were brought into the typical long house and there slept securely in close proximity to the ploughman and the geilwad [caller]. In addition to the plough, the other essential tools with which the farmer carried out his operations over the year were a mattock, spade, pike, flail, weeding tongs, harrow, and a cart or wain, many of which persisted in relatively simple forms down the twentieth century.

WOODLANDS AND FISHERIES

Besides the agricultural resources of the countryside, woodlands and forests contributed substantially to the economic life of the period.[12] Somewhere between ten and twenty per cent of the surface area of Wales was covered with trees, and most regions still had extensive timber resources. It was exceptional for Leland to have to observe that the district around Bangor-on-Dee or the vicinity of Cardiff had 'little wood'. More usual were his comments that there was 'marvellous good wood' south of Chirk or that the northern half of Miskin was nearly all 'hilly woods'.[13] All along the eastern borders from Flint to Monmouth, trees were thicker on the ground than humans or livestock. Place-names containing such elements as coed [woods], allt [wooded slope], gelli [grove], and tree-names like derw-en [oak(s)], gwern-en [alder(s)], and onn-en [ash] still survive in some profusion in areas where by today there may hardly be a

[11] [Sir John Price], Yny Lhyvyr Hwnn . . ., ed. J. H. Davies (Bangor, 1902).
[12] W. Linnard, Welsh Woods and Forests: History and Utilization (Cardiff, 1982).
[13] Leland, pp. 68, 19, 72, 16.

tree in sight. There were large forests like those of Snowdon or Glyn Cothi or Brecon—the last named bringing in an income of £109. 13s. 4d. in 1400. Originally established for hunting, exclusively by the King or the Marcher lords, the forests were ruled by their own laws and courts, which punished offenders severely.

Among the best and most carefully managed of the woods had been those belonging to the Cistercian monks, who had practised careful clearance, grazing, and assarting, and intelligent coppicing and felling, though by the fifteenth century most of the Cistercians' woodland reserves were leased out. Only at Grace Dieu monastery was there some evidence of a consistent policy of woodland management in the years before the Dissolution. During the fifteenth century, as a result of rebellion, war, depopulation, and the abandonment of poorer lands, whole areas may have become overgrown with scrub and secondary woodland. Sir John Wynn wrote graphically, though not without exaggeration, that in the fifteenth century, Caernarfonshire, Merioneth, and Denbigh seemed to be but one forest and wood, having few inhabitants. By Leland's time, however, much of western Wales, like Anglesey, Llŷn, or western Cardiganshire and Pembrokeshire, was largely denuded of trees, though its timber resources had always been much poorer than those of the east. It was Leland, too, who commented pointedly on the severe deterioration of the formerly handsome woods belonging to the abbey of Strata Florida. He identified as the main causes of decay the uncontrolled felling of timber, browsing by goats, deliberate clearances, large-scale grazing, peat-bog formation, and felling for lead-smelting. What had happened at Strata Florida as a result of loss of direct control by the monks and the leasing-out of their assets may well have occurred elsewhere also. One of the very few woods for which fifteenth- and early sixteenth-century records survive, however unsatisfactory they may be, was Machen Forest. If its fortunes were typical, the contribution of woodlands and the income being derived from them were falling off unmistakably. At Machen they declined from £19. 11s. 4d. in 1401 to a mere 14s. 0d. in 1522.[14] Already in 1500, a survey taken of them showed that they were in poor state, consisting mainly of overmature oaks, with few trees capable of producing worthwhile timber and little or no regeneration.

Nevertheless, woodlands remained an essential source of sustenance, employment, and income. The poet Lewys Glyn Cothi gave a lively impression of the enthusiasm with which the amenities and value of fine woods were esteemed when he complimented Rhys ap Dafydd of Blaen Tren on the excellence of his woods: the home of swarms of bees, deer, blackbirds, hawks, conies, squirrels, and other creatures. As a man who

[14] Pugh, *Marcher Lordships*, p. 170.

had, like many others of the time, spent some years of his life as an outlaw in the woods, Lewys had good cause to appreciate them. Hunting in them still provided food and sport, especially for the upper classes, who were fanatically addicted to the pastime, though more covertly for many lesser men as well. Hawks, one of the most valuable commodities produced in the forests, were particularly prized and sought after. The practice of agistment allowed large numbers of animals to be grazed within the forests and woods on payment of an appropriate rent. Herds of swine were fattened in autumn on acorns, hazel nuts, and beech mast, provided that the summer had not been so cold as to prevent mast from being produced. Large quantities of timber were needed for a variety of purposes, and the felling and carting of it provided employment for many at slack times in the agricultural year. Timber was also used on a big scale for building in castles, halls, houses, churches, and mills (with their carefully constructed wooden sluices, wheels, and other working-parts). It was needed, too, for making smaller utensils like buckets, barrels, bowls, and dishes, as well as for the hafts of tools. Clogs, worn by rich and poor alike, were fashioned from the alders growing in rich profusion in the damp valleys of Wales. Furthermore, most people depended very largely on fallen branches and dead wood, supplemented by furze, turf, and peat, for household fuel and for timber to build or repair dwellings, fences, and hedges. Wood, as the most common source of thermic energy in forges, furnaces, and smithies, was required in large quantities to be burnt into charcoal, so as to provide the fuel for smelting. Other major timber-linked activities were stripping oak bark for tanning, and the supply of wood ashes and dyer's ashes used in dyeing and soap-making.

Fisheries—off-shore and in lakes and rivers—added an important source of protein to food supplies. Coracle-fishing was centuries old by the fifteenth century and it still flourished along the estuaries of the rivers Dee, Severn, Usk, Wye, Monnow, Cleddau, and Conwy, from all of which it only disappeared during this century, as well as on the Teifi, Tywi, and Tâf, where coracles could be seen in living memory. John Leland, whose sharp eye rarely missed any economic potential that was worth exploiting, noted most active fishing-ports along the coast and the most rewarding rivers and lakes for trout and eels. Deep-sea fishing had not as yet been as intensively developed as it was to be in the sixteenth and later centuries; but already many of the inhabitants along the coastline of Pembrokeshire, Cardigan Bay, and Anglesey were engaged in part-time activity as summer fishermen. Owning part-shares in boats, they brought home sizeable catches of herrings from the Irish Sea to places like Beaumaris, Nefyn, Conwy, Pwllheli, Towyn, Aberystwyth, Tenby, Solfa, and Fishguard. Many of the fishing-rights were farmed out. Those of Beaumaris, at least, had attracted sailors from south Wales to poach seals there in 1466, and were sufficiently valuable by the end of the century to encourage Bishop Dean of Bangor to enter into litigation concerning them with his lessee, William Gruffydd.

Shellfish like mussels, cockles, and oysters were gathered at many points around the shores. Inland, most of the rivers and lakes were intensively fished and were straddled at the suitable points by weirs constructed of stone, timber, and wattle: the largest and best-known of them being that at Cilgerran, which had six traps. A warning against the manifold perils of monastic weirs was given to a salmon by the poet Gruffydd Llwyd; and with good reason, for the Cistercians had organized their fisheries, like their other resources, with exemplary skill and thoroughness. Nor were the more enterprising secular lords behindhand in this respect; they, too, had established highly successful and remunerative fisheries. Many of them, however, whether belonging to monks or laymen, were among the estate assets which had had to be leased out in the fifteenth century. Their value had frequently slumped dramatically by the end of that century because non-resident lords were not bringing close supervision to bear on their lessees. An interesting glimpse of the role that fisheries still occupied in the economic life of some parishes bordering on the sea or major rivers in Gwent is given by the *Valor Ecclesiasticus*, which records sums of up to 7s. or 8s. being paid in tithes on fisheries.

TOWNS (SEE MAP 3)

Just over a hundred towns of every kind have been identified in medieval Wales.[15] A number of them were so small and insignificant, like Adpar or Wiston or Painscastle, as hardly to warrant being categorized as towns at all and only about fifty towns with regular markets have been identified. The fewness of market-towns was hardly surprising, since it needed a relatively rich and prosperous surrounding arable agriculture or a highly developed industry to maintain a market of any size. Like nine out of ten of the ordinary English or European market-towns, none of the largest towns in Wales—Carmarthen, Wrexham, or Cardiff—was very big; and only Oswestry, largely Welsh by population if situated east of Offa's Dyke, numbered perhaps as many as 3,000 inhabitants. About 70 per cent of these Welsh towns were of alien foundation and had originally been established to tighten the Normans' grip on their conquests. The customary Norman creations of castle, borough, and priory, symbolizing the triple coercive forces of conquest—war, trade, and religion—still stood in many leading Welsh towns, as they had done for two centuries or more. In such circumstances it was to be expected that the majority of them should be

---

[15] Soulsby, *Medieval Towns, passim*.

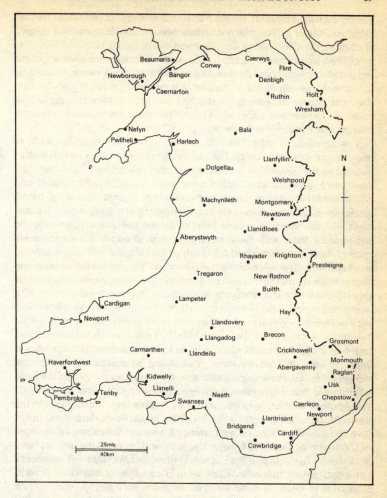

MAP 3 Main Market Towns

sited at strategic points on the estuaries along the coastline, or at major crossings and junctions inland. A number of them stood at the highest point which could be reached by ships or the lowest point at which a bridge could be thrown across. Though many of them housed castles intended as administrative as well as military focuses, the towns had had from the outset a major economic purpose as well and that had increased over the centuries. Much of the economic activity had been deliberately concentrated by king or Marcher lord in the towns and had been strictly prohibited from being conducted outside them. Towns were the nodal points on which the economic activity of the surrounding countryside, for a radius of anything up to twelve or fifteen miles, depending on population, was focused. What has been written of Oswestry as the 'link and hub', 'where the contrasts of race, geography, and environment were blended',[16] was *mutatis mutandis* true of many other Welsh towns.

Towndwellers remained closely associated with the agricultural life of the community around them. Like all medieval people, they had no wish to depend on the goodwill of others for their food, and so they cultivated their own town fields, grazed animals on town pastures and wastes, and maintained their own cornmills and woodlands. Within each town, barns, granaries, dairies, cowsheds, stables, gardens, and orchards were a familiar sight. All the same, the prime function of the towns was to provide the location for fairs and markets. Every town conducted a once-weekly market, and bigger towns like Brecon or Cardiff had two. Carmarthen's markets carried on a wholesale trade in bread, ale, fish, meat, cheese, and eggs, which traders then sold retail outside the walls, while Denbigh was described as a 'great market town, famous and much frequented with wares and people from all parts of north Wales'.[17] The average 'catchment area' served by a Welsh market-town was about 100,000 acres. Fairs for the sale of livestock, wool, cheese, and hides, on which much of the economic well-being of Wales depended, were held three or four times a year in some towns, as well as those still being organized by the bigger monasteries. To these fairs came also itinerant merchants and pedlars, offering for sale indispensable commodities like salt, iron, or tar, and luxuries such as wine, fine cloth, and pottery. As a rule, the fairs held in the towns of the south and east were, as would be expected, larger and richer than those of the north and west; some of the most flourishing being those of Carmarthen, Swansea, Cowbridge, Brecon, Hay (even though the town itself was badly decayed), Welshpool, Ruthin, and Wrexham. A number of the larger towns in south Wales were ports, closely linked to Bristol, emporium of the west, while those of the north were just as dependent on Chester. From both of these regional centres, a valuable inward and outward trade was conducted (see below, pp. 77–8).

Towns were also the main centres of crafts and services, even though most rural communities would have had their own blacksmiths and carpenters, who could turn their hands to making most things in iron and wood, and their own millers and weavers. Broadly speaking, the range of

---

[16] Smith in Griffiths, *Boroughs Wales*, p. 221.
[17] D. H. Owen in Griffiths, *Boroughs Wales*, p. 173.

crafts and services on offer varied widely in accordance with the size and prosperity of the individual town. In general, each offered three groups of crafts which catered at differing levels of price and sophistication for the three basic human needs of food, clothing, and shelter. Food trades were represented by millers, bakers, brewers, vintners, butchers, fishmongers, inn-keepers, and the like; the needs of the populace for clothing were met by weavers, fullers, tailors, hatters, shoemakers, tanners, glovers, and others; while carpenters, blacksmiths, masons, plumbers, tilers, glaziers, and comparable craftsmen coped with their building requirements. Organizations of craftsmen and merchants were slow to develop in the little Welsh towns; most of those engaged in trade were producers, craftsmen, and wholesale and retail traders all rolled into one.

Also concentrated in the towns were some small-scale industrial activities closely connected with raw materials produced in the course of agricultural activity. Particularly important was the processing of cloth and leather, deriving from the characteristic products of a mainly pastoral economy (see below, pp. 72–4). The specialized trades of milling corn and brewing ale were also extensively conducted in the towns. Building and repair work on castles and churches, too, called not only for the skilled services of masons but also for those of carpenters and joiners, and for the use of a good deal of timber—even as late as the sixteenth century. So, too, did the extensive reconstruction of damaged houses and the building of new ones after the devastation caused earlier by the Glyndŵr Rebellion. In seaport towns along the coast there was an added call for the services of many craftsmen in the construction of ships and boats.

As well as being focal points of economic activity, towns were the centres of royal administration within the Principality and seigneurial government in the Marches. Many of them were, additionally, important centres of religious worship, housing priories, friaries, hospitals, collegiate churches, and larger parish churches within, or just outside, their walls. As a result of these administrative and religious activities, they numbered among their inhabitants a population of professional and religious men: lawyers, notaries, clerks, scriveners, and messengers; monks, friars, clerics, chantry priests, musicians, teachers, sacristans, and the like. All these individuals, as well as their families and households in some cases, had to have their needs supplied. Moreover, people came to the town on administrative or legal business—often transacted on market-day. The churches, too, attracted many worshippers and pilgrims to their shrines, altars, images, and other attractions. Notabilities from the neighbourhood were usually buried in them with pomp, solemnity, and the distribution of alms. All these activities concerned with life and death attracted a number of participants and spectators and added much to the trade, business, and consequence of the town.

INDUSTRY AND TRADE

The two industries which engaged far more labour and contributed much more to contemporary economic life than any other were the making of cloth and leather goods. Each had been firmly established in the towns, though cloth-making had tended increasingly to migrate into the countryside. Cloth-making depended, for its supplies of wool, on the growing flocks of sheep reared on Welsh hills during the fifteenth century. Though a good deal of this wool was regarded as too coarse and rough to be woven into anything but inferior cloth, some of that produced along the eastern borders of Wales was of high quality and much esteemed. Large quantities of the Welsh wool-clip continued to be exported by land and sea, but a substantial amount was retained locally to be worked into cloth. It was collected, spun, and woven by small farmers and their families, including children who gathered and carded the wool. Crucial to the process of successful manufacture was the spread of the fulling mills in Wales. No fewer than 202 of them, at least, are known to have sprung up in all parts of Wales before 1547.[18] They were built and organized in the main by laymen and owed little or nothing to leadership and initiative by the Cistercians, in spite of their close connection with sheep-breeding and the sale of wool.

The main reasons put forward for the rise of the industry in parts of England are equally applicable to Wales. Here, too, there existed the custom of partible inheritance, a pastoral economy with a population pressing over-heavily on limited resources, and a working-unit made up of a family rather than a village. Again, the fulling mills, at which the cloth was pressed and cleaned, certainly needed, for their successful operation, adequate supplies of water, both for power to drive the mills and for use in the cleansing process; but that did not necessarily mean that they had to be sited on the banks of swiftly running streams, as is often thought. They were, in fact, widely distributed in all parts of Wales, though, with the exception of Denbighshire in the north, the heaviest concentration of them was in the south, in the former counties of Monmouthshire, Glamorgan, and Carmarthenshire. Far more of them were to be found in the March than in the Principality, and many owed much to the initiative of leading Marcher families, though they were also very attractive to local entrepreneurs. By the fifteenth century, most of them had been leased out. The craftsmen operating them, as well as their associates among the dyers and weavers, were usually farmers too. Ruthin seems to have been unique among Welsh towns in having a craft guild which successfully exploited the town's fairs in establishing a well-organized commercial enterprise. The complex interlocking of activities was carried out by fullers, weavers, and

[18] R. I. Jack, 'The Cloth Industry of Medieval Wales', *WHR*, x (1980–1), 443–60.

dyers, who were perfectly capable of carrying out the finishing processes themselves without having to send the cloth elsewhere for that to be done.

The markets for Welsh cloth at places like Ruthin and Oswestry were dominated by visiting mercers and clothiers. Large quantities were also disposed of at border towns such as Shrewsbury, Ludlow, and Bristol, where the quick tempers and broken accents of Welsh friezemen were well-known. A poem by Crowley refers to the Welsh cloth exported from Bristol:

> The fryses of Wales
> To Brystowe are brought;
> But before thei were woven
> In Wales thei are bought.[19]

Competition on the part of Welsh friezemen in Shrewsbury was so successful that there were demands from the Salopians for municipal protection against these interlopers. The existence of so vigorous and profitable a native cloth industry proved to be a potent stimulus to the raising of sheep by landowners and farmers in its vicinity. It has been described by the most recent student of the subject as 'outstandingly an organized and commercialized element in the economy of a country whose industrial development in the Middle Ages is too easily dismissed'.[20]

Second only in importance to the woollen industry was leather-making and the crafts associated with it, though considerably less is known about them than about cloth. The same general reasons adduced above for the rise of cloth-making held good, to a large extent, for the increase in leather-making. It flourished, also, in those over-peopled pastoral regions where calf-skins and sheepskins were amply available. Additionally, there were in Wales plentiful supplies of oak bark rich in tannin, the chemical agent which turns hides into leather. The bark was extensively harvested by casual labour from April to June, a relatively quiet season in agriculture. Local limestone was found in abundance in parts of the country, and tallow for dressing certain types of leather and clean water were accessible everywhere, though salt had to be imported from France or Spain. The outcome of this convergence of resources was that tanneries, representing a big investment in money and raw materials, were established in all the larger towns, where their owners were usually bracketed among the wealthier and more influential burgesses. Leather was used in a variety of ways: for boots, shoes, gloves, jerkins, and other items of clothing; and for saddles, horse-collars, and other equipment and furnishings. Small wonder that leather craftsmen—shoemakers, glovers, and saddlers—should have figured so largely among the trades represented

[19] W. A. Bebb, *Machlud yr Oesoedd Canol* (Swansea, 1951), p. 26.
[20] Jack, *WHR*, x, 460.

in most towns. As early as 1491, at least, and possibly earlier, corvisers and shoemakers were sufficiently numerous and influential in Ruthin to found their own craft guild. In Swansea, the leather industry was so important that, in a charter to the town agreed with Henry, earl of Worcester, in 1532, it was stipulated that all leather tanned in the town or brought in should be carefully examined, with provision for the forfeiture of any faulty leather and a stiff fine of 6s. 8d. for any defective hide.

Much of the exploitation of minerals and metals was conducted only on a very small scale and could be regarded as no more than an effort to make the most locally of such resources as were available. Such, clearly, was the motive underlying the abortive agreement arrived at between the duke of Buckingham and the German entrepreneur, Adrian Sprinker, in 1459, that the latter should work all the precious metals found in the duke's lordships. In metal-working, as in a number of other respects, the initiative had been taken by the Cistercians, ever alert to develop their resources and put them to profitable use. The monks of Neath and Margam in south Wales, of Strata Florida in mid-Wales, and Cymer in the north, had been the pioneers. Cymer had worked iron, Strata Florida lead, and Neath and Margam iron and coal. To encourage their workers, they had allowed them free pasture and access to the woodlands for timber. But by the fifteenth century these houses were largely content to lease their interests to lay entrepreneurs.

In the absence of advanced technological methods and knowledge, and in the light of the poor transport facilities available by land, coal could be worked on any scale only where seams outcropped near the surface and were sited conveniently near to water transport by sea or river. In north Wales it appears to have been mined in Flintshire, at Ewloe, Buckley, Mostyn, and Hope, and also in parts of Denbighshire. Much of the coal mined in Flintshire found a market among the flourishing merchants and craftsmen of Chester, whose handsome houses were equipped with stone chimneys so as to be able to burn it in their fires. Pack-horses transported the coal from Ewloe down to the shores of the Dee, whence it was shipped by boat along the estuary. Coal was taken from Mostyn to the castles and gentry houses along the coast of north Wales, from the mouth of the Dee to Anglesey. More activity took place at a number of points in the south Wales coalfield, notably at Llansamlet in the lordship of Cil-fai, where there had been comparatively large-scale workings first encouraged by the duke of Norfolk as lord of Cil-fai towards the end of the fourteenth century. Swansea and Neath seem to have been the main centres of coalmining in the south, though Leland refers to coal workings near Kidwelly, Tenby, and elsewhere in Carmarthenshire and Pembrokeshire. In some areas, digging for coal for personal use was regarded as one of the rights which manorial freeholders enjoyed. It was won either by excavation at the surface or by digging small, shallow 'bell-pits', but even at this early stage the inflow of water into the workings could be a serious problem. Demand for coal remained very restricted, however. Industrially little use was made of it, though blacksmiths used it extensively. Domestically there was still a lot of prejudice against it; Leland remarks with surprise that people in Carmarthenshire and Pembrokeshire should use it when there was plenty of wood available to them.

Lead and iron were needed in considerable quantities, for use in building castles and monasteries in particular, and workings for both metals had taken place sporadically at a number of places in north and south Wales from the thirteenth to the fifteenth centuries. It is worth noting that a survey of 1530 listed no fewer than thirty-three possible sites where lead, copper, and iron were to be found in Wales. The two principal locations for lead-working were Flintshire and Cardiganshire. Lead had already been mined extensively in Flintshire in the Middle Ages and, in the fifteenth century, its furnaces were well known to the poet Lewys Glyn Cothi and thoroughly disliked by him. The lead-bearing veins of Cardiganshire had also attracted a good deal of attention. Strata Florida had early taken an interest in prospecting for lead, and when Leland visited the area he found operations in progress at Briwnant. Smelting lead or iron had always necessitated extensive felling of timber and burning it as charcoal to obtain fuel for the furnaces and forges—a process later to cause great heartburning among the Welsh poets at the loss of woodland amenities. At Llantrisant, in 1531, accounts relating to smelting then in progress show that charcoal-burners considerably outnumbered the actual iron-ore miners. The work provided employment for a body of men during what would otherwise have been idle winter months, with more of them engaged in cutting and transporting timber than in burning it for charcoal. Leland had had sharp things to say about the effects of lead-smelting on reducing woodland resources; further large quantities of timber had been felled for use in the course of mining operations as roof and wall supports and for mine buildings, ramps, and sluices.

A limited amount of quarrying went on at this time. The excellence of Caernarfonshire slates as roofing material was recognized not only locally but also as far afield as Chester, many of whose buildings were roofed with them. In 1444 the trade in slates was sufficiently valuable for Huw Huws and Maredudd ap Thomas to pay the Crown a rent of £6. 13s. 4d. a year to quarry them. A poetic tribute to their hard-wearing qualities came from Guto'r Glyn, who testified in his poem 'To ask for slates' that though men might skilfully thatch roofs with straw, slate lasted far better.[21] Millstones were another much-prized commodity obtained from quarries in some

---

[21] *GG*, pp. 256–8.

parts of the country. The most famous were those of Anglesey, being quarried at Mathafarn Eithaf, Mathafarn Wion, and Penmon and exported far beyond the island. The once-profitable royal farm seems to have declined in the fifteenth century, probably at the expense of the rise of private quarries. But the fame of Anglesey's millstones was still sufficient for an early sixteenth-century poet to claim, with pardonable exaggeration, that they would 'shake a door through the confines of Hell'.[22] Trelleck in Monmouthshire and Hope in Flintshire were other good sources of these millstones so essential for an agricultural community, though by 1515 none of the valuable quarries of millstone, freestone, or limestone at Trelleck seems to have been producing any revenue for the lord.

There were also other local industrial activities, such as the making of pottery, the weaving of mats out of marram-grass, and the production of rabbit-skins, of which we know nothing more than that they existed. Potteries have been traced only in two or three limited regions: at Rumney Bridge near Cardiff and at Ewenni in south Wales; and near Buckley in the north-east. Much of the coarse earthenware produced at Buckley was sold locally at Hope, Flint, and Chester. Rush-mat making existed at Newborough in Anglesey until this century, and it was once common at Merthyr Mawr in Glamorgan.

Trade reflected the nature of economic production. The goods most in demand were those produced by Welsh agriculture: cattle, sheep, skins and hides, leather, wool, cloth, butter, and cheese. Cattle had, for centuries, been bred for sale and demand was stimulated in the fourteenth century by the need for meat to feed English armies fighting in the French wars and by added calls on the part of the Marcher lords. The needs of the armies continued from time to time in the fifteenth century; but as royal contracting declined, the trade passed into the hands of private merchants and was intended increasingly to meet the growing demands for domestic consumption of meat. Sold in local fairs, the cattle were driven overland into the English midlands to be fattened, along routes that were to be traditional for centuries, or were sent by water across the Severn and the Bristol Channel. The importance of this trade is indicated by the frequent concern expressed about thefts of cattle and violence offered to their drovers as they passed through the Marches or over the Severn ferries. Welsh mutton was consumed nearly as appreciatively as Welsh beef, and many sheep were likewise driven on the hoof into England. Guto'r Glyn, a man from upland Glyn Ceiriog and himself at one time a sheep-drover, sketched an amusing picture of the tribulations which befell him when he drove sheep on behalf of the parson of Corwen: savage dogs, treacherous streams, obstructive hedges, poor prices, disastrous losses, and unhappy

[22] *TA*, p. 467; *LM*, p. 67.

wanderings in the midlands and the north. There were, it seems, a number of these poet-drovers, of whom Tudur Penllyn was much the sharpest and most successful, being the owner of many sheep and full of the urge to become wealthy.[23]

In addition to the beasts themselves, their skins and wool were highly thought of and formed valuable items in the exports from ports of the south-west, like Cardigan, Haverfordwest, and Carmarthen, and from those of the south-east, such as Cardiff, Newport, and Chepstow. Much of the woollen cloth made in Wales found its way by land and water to the principal Marcher markets of Oswestry, Shrewsbury, and Bristol, whence some of it was dispatched abroad to Ireland and European countries like France, Spain, and Portugal. In 1494, sales of Welsh cloth in Bristol alone were worth £815, though there were also close contacts between the clothiers of south Wales and the smaller west-country ports of Bridgwater and Barnstaple. Other Welsh export commodities important since the thirteenth century were wood and fish. Smaller quantities of coal and iron found their way down to Chepstow from the Forest of Dean and were trans-shipped outwards from there, as well as from ports further west like Swansea, Neath, and Tenby. Slate and millstones were similarly shipped outwards from Beaumaris in Anglesey, mainly to Chester. Imports into Wales consisted mostly of those products that were either very scarce or unobtainable from native sources: corn or malt, salt, wine, oil, fruit, fine cloth, tar, and the like.

Some idea of how the traffic worked may be obtained from the trade of the port of Haverfordwest. Biggest market-town and busiest port in productive south Pembrokeshire, it was centrally placed for land transport; but even more important it was also situated at the head of the river navigation on the western Cleddau. It could be reached by ships of up to forty tons and all the barges that plied the waterways of Milford Haven in large numbers. It exported corn, cloth, wool, hides, and small amounts of coal; and received from Bristol and redistributed to south-western Wales a large proportion of its imports, mainly of luxury goods, while also taking in salt and wine direct from France. At the other end of the south Wales sea-coast, and one of the main outlets for the relatively rich plain of Gwent, was Newport, described in 1521 as a 'proper town and a goodly haven coming into it, well occupied with small quays, whereunto a very good ship may resort and have good harbour'.[24]

Overland trade was difficult because of the poor condition of the roads and tracks. A description of the funeral of Arthur, prince of Wales, in 1501, gives an idea of the bad state of roads in the Marches, one of the

[23] *GG*, pp. 84–6.
[24] M. Gray, 'The Dispersal of Crown Property in Monmouthshire, 1500–1603' (Ph.D. Thesis, Cardiff, 1985), p. 48.

more developed regions. Admittedly, the weather was very bad—'foul, cold, windy and rainy'—but the road between Ludlow and Bewdley was condemned as 'the worst way that I have seen; yea, and in some places they were fain to take oxen to draw the char, so ill was the way'.[25] Moreover, highway robberies of many different kinds were a very common form of crime in the fifteenth century. Yet, in spite of all these hazards, there may have been much more trade by land by means of trains of pack-horses than has often been supposed. Only thus, for example, could much of the Welsh cloth have been transported to its destination. But since it took about seventy pack-horses to carry the same load as a modern ten-ton lorry, most of the trade was carried by water because of its greater convenience and cheapness when bulky commodities had to be transported. Chester still dominated the trade of north Wales, even though the estuary of the Dee was tending to silt up. Bristol had no rival in the south, and innumerable ships and boats from ports all over south Wales, from Chepstow to Haverfordwest, tied up at the paved quay of its 'Welsh Back'. It also proved an irresistible magnet for the growing colony of Welsh merchants and apprentices—Vaughans, Goughs, Lloyds, ap Ryses, ap Meryks, and the rest—who came there to settle. One of them, Henry Vaughan, in the latter half of the fifteenth century was the most prominent of all Bristol merchants and had the singular honour of being the mayor of the city when his fellow-countryman, Henry VII, visited it in 1486. Nor were Welsh trading and Welsh ships confined to the waters of the Bristol Channel. Occasionally, larger vessels of from 60 to 120 tons had, since the fourteenth century, been sailing outwards to France, Italy, the Iberian Peninsula, and Ireland, and continued to do so in the fifteenth century.

CHANGES BETWEEN c. 1440 AND c. 1530

The fifteenth century and the early decades of the sixteenth were a time of major changes in the economic life of Wales. Gradually, there was a recovery from the baneful consequences of the earlier upheavals, which had left as their legacy depopulation, agricultural depression, and widespread devastation. Those who were able to survive these disasters, or were born after they had ended, found as the century wore on that much of the poor and marginal land, which had perforce been worked by an earlier, over-large population, pressing too heavily on inadequate resources, had gone out of cultivation. The Crown and the landlords, lay and clerical alike, had no choice but to abandon the less productive areas and concentrate on filling the better holdings. For the reduced numbers of would-be purchasers and lessees, there was considerably more land of

[25] Bebb, *Machlud*, p. 29.

better quality available to be taken up. The incomes of the estate-owners had in general fallen, mainly because of low rents, decreased numbers of tenants, and a dramatic fall in seigneurial revenues, the profits of courts, and the farms of mills, tolls, and other assets. Revenue in the lordship of Usk, for example, had dropped from £1,191 in 1330 to £467 in 1398, and it slumped still further in the fifteenth century. In the lordship of Newport, income fell by ten per cent between 1400 and 1447, while that from the lordship of Denbigh slipped catastrophically from £1,000 in 1400 to £50 in 1500. Lords were becoming poorly remunerated stockholders in the soil. The Bohuns were said to have been lax in the later fourteenth century; and that judgement was equally applicable to the earls of March, who were lords of Denbigh in the fifteenth century. But most of the lordships of the March had found their revenues dropping sharply, largely as a result of their officials' neglect and fraud, which inevitably crept in when absentee lords failed to exercise the necessary oversight. If a lord wanted his estate to flourish it was essential that he should be in a position to give it close personal supervision. It was only an occasional family among the lords of the March which managed to achieve this. Among them were the Grays of Ruthin, who were highly competent estate-managers and who had the good fortune, besides, not to have their administrative continuity broken by forfeiture or attainder.

Beneath the ranks of owners and lessees, the labourers who were available found that, in an age when labour was in short supply, their services could command relatively high wages in both town and country, and not until 1510 or thereabouts did 'real' wages appear to have turned downwards. Prices, too, were generally fairly stable. Evidence for the levels of wages and prices in Wales is admittedly not at all plentiful, but, such as it is, seems to show that there was little substantial difference between conditions in England and Wales at this period. Ranks of hired labourers were often swollen by the advent to their midst of erstwhile serfs or bondmen, or even small freeholders unable to maintain their former status. In spite of the political turbulence and upheavals of the latter half of the fifteenth century, it may reasonably be argued that it was, economically speaking, an age of opportunity and relative well-being for most groups in society. Not every year was as prosperous as another; not all regions nor all classes were equally favoured; and the differences between some areas and individuals and their less fortunate fellows were wide. The 'gross national product' may have been smaller in aggregate than it had been, but there were a good many fewer to share in it. Demand had increased and there was more flexibility in supplying it.

It was an age which witnessed a major redistribution of wealth, mainly, but by no means exclusively, in the interests of the more fortunate of the gentry and the better-off tenants. The overall evidence for this seems clear enough in a number of respects. There was a surge of development in activities in the cattle trade and the cloth trade, both responding vigorously to the demand for a higher standard of living, and relatively rapid recovery on the part of those towns that tended to benefit from such growth, especially along the southern coast and the eastern border. Again, nothing is more striking than the kind of society depicted in the contemporary Welsh poetry. Far from being an impoverished and woebegone community, it is one whose leading figures are comfortably enough placed to patronize poets generously, dispense hospitality lavishly, build themselves new houses, consume choice and even exotic foods and wines, wear fine clothes, surround themselves with rich possessions, and generally to enjoy life. The poetry indicates unmistakably that all the blessings of human existence—food and drink, love and nature, hunting and hawking, and craftsmanship in wood, steel, jewels, stone, and paint—were savoured with relish by contemporaries (see below, chapter 6). A still wider measure of prosperity was revealed in the religious life of the time. One of its most impressive features was the wholesale rebuilding, refurbishing, and beautifying of parish churches all over the country, to which many parishioners must have contributed in most instances. Similarly, there was an upsurge of popularity for pilgrimages, involving not only expensive journeys to the major shrines abroad but also more especially the frequent visits by a much wider and socially more mixed clientele of pilgrims to a whole series of newer shrines nearer home.

The processes of economic change had begun in the fourteenth century. Though most of the peasants had smallholdings of ten acres or less of arable land and there were many cottars and labourers who were either landless or virtually so, there had always been among them a handful of their fellows who held forty or fifty acres and towered above the rest. Not only did they own more land, but many also had more beasts; and the differences between these accretions of wealth and the average peasant stake were particularly noticeable in the lowland lordships of the March as compared with the upland districts. The greater amount of acquired land which became available in the later fourteenth century from assarts, escheats, and the leasing of demesnes and demesne resources like forests or mills, as opposed to hereditary land, which was more heavily protected by law and custom, provided all kinds of new opportunities for the enterprising and ambitious.

But the upheavals which had reached their climax in the course of the Glyndŵr Rebellion, in the first decade of the fifteenth century, greatly accelerated the process of the disintegration of both manorial and native economic institutions. As they broke up, the land market became much more fluid and offered even greater openings for the acquisition of land and income. For much of the earlier part of the century, rents were very low; between 1400 and 1470, for example, rents on the Duchy of Lancaster estates fell by about one-third. Early in Henry VI's reign, attempts were made to stabilize income in the lordship of Newport by long leases of demesne, in large and small packets of land, for twenty or thirty years, at a rent of only about three-quarters of earlier levels. All the great landowners were abandoning the direct exploitation of their estates to become collectors of rents, and in the process were relinquishing an important aspect of their lordship. Nor was it only demesne that was being leased; all their assets were being let to farm: land, pasture, waste, woodland, timber, fisheries, mills, mines, quarries, and anything else which could be rented out. Notable among the lessors were not only the Marcher lords but also the Cistercian monasteries, some of the biggest landowners in *pura Wallia*, whose lands had always been run on principles different from those embodied in native law. Hitherto, they had been among the foremost exponents of direct exploitation; from the Glyndŵr Rebellion onwards, though the tendency had begun much earlier, they had no alternative but to become *rentiers*. Again, a large amount of land accruing to the King, by escheat, as a result of rebellion, or by death, was re-let to men who had often had no previous connection with it and viewed it almost solely in the light of an investment from which they wanted to make a profit. In addition to leasing Crown land legally, some men—both big and small—took advantage of the prevailing uncertainties to encroach freely on royal possessions. Another means of extending holdings was through the Welsh device of *prid*, a kind of gage entered into for a four-year period and renewable regularly, which enabled the mortgagor and mortgagee to avoid the provisions of native law forbidding the alienation of hereditary freehold land. Although the practice was much older than the fifteenth century, *prid* became particularly widespread and prevalent at that time. Landowners found it an extremely useful instrument both to control land transactions and to raise income on their own account, by permitting its application only after the payment of a licence fee. But fifteenth-century records from Anglesey show that much land was alienated without resort to *prid* on payment of a fee. Furthermore, the normal processes of land acquisition by means of lease, exchange, and marriage had also been accelerated in so mobile a land market and were in full swing.

The recovery of town life was also contributing markedly to the kind of developments already discussed. Devastated by the Glyndŵr Rebellion as many of the towns had been and uneven though the course of their rehabilitation was, by the second half of the fifteenth century they had regained much of their former prosperity. There were wide differences between them in the pace and extent of their recovery. Holt's population, for instance, had dropped from about 1,000 in the early fourteenth century to some 300 in the mid-fifteenth, and Hay was described by Leland in the

1530s as badly decayed and almost deserted. But there is unmistakable evidence that the slowly growing trade was being channelled through the towns, damaged property was rebuilt or repaired, and population, though not back to the levels it had reached c.1300, nevertheless seems to have increased faster than that of the rural areas. Accounts relating to the towns seem to present a dismal picture of falling revenues; but these may not, in themselves, be evidence of economic decline so much as of activity escaping the vigilance of the lord and his servants, or at least of his officials' failure to exact the due share of income that should have been accruing from it. Lords, it is true, still retained a large measure of control over Welsh towns, which had always been too small and their overlords too powerful for the former to assert or to wish to assert their independence from the latter. Nevertheless, seigneurial hold over them, as over all estate resources, was decidedly slacker than it had earlier been. Absentee lords' interests in towns had been leased to men who had every reason not to wish to see their nominal masters exercise too close a supervision. The gentry of the countryside were not the only ones who had encroached illegally on rights not their own; their counterparts on the urban scene also had many interests they preferred to conceal from their lords. At Swansea, for example, accounts for 1449 appear to show clearly that the expansion of the cloth trade there, as evidenced by the marked increase in the number of fulling mills, was an aspect of the town's economic growth from which its lord was failing to recover his rightful revenues.

One of the features of fifteenth-century towns was the growing influx into them of Welsh inhabitants. The myth that the Welsh did not take kindly to an urban way of life dies hard, even though it has for some time been exploded by modern research. Welsh people had long been infiltrating into them and continued to do so in growing numbers during the fifteenth century. Guto'r Glyn was one of many who found the wealth, warmth, fine buildings, and conviviality of Oswestry, and other towns like it along the border, greatly to his liking. The Marcher towns had usually been more inclined to welcome Welsh settlers to their midst than the garrison boroughs of the north-west, and that continued to be true in the fifteenth century. Ruthin, Denbigh, Welshpool, Brecon, Newport, Cardiff, and Swansea, to mention but a few, had sizeable colonies of Welsh migrants within their walls, and still more in the 'suburbs' outside. Even those bastions of royal authority and control, like Carmarthen, Caernarfon, Conwy, or Beaumaris, found themselves being penetrated. At Aberystwyth and Newport, at least, we have evidence of bitter quarrels that ensued from Welsh attempts to control the destinies of those towns. Already, the processes of breaking down the barriers between town and country, and Welsh and English, which by the end of the sixteenth century would make the majority of the town populations Welsh by origin and would bring the towns themselves under the control of the gentry, were well under way.

Towns were closely associated with two of the most powerful solvents of the old order, from which many individuals from a variety of different social groups stood to benefit, namely the cloth and cattle trades. Long before 1500 these twin pillars of the Welsh rural economy were firmly in position. Prosperity during this period was linked much more closely with the production of meat, wool, and cloth than with that of corn.

Anxious to take advantage of all these new potential sources of wealth were a variety of go-ahead men: gentry, burgesses, clerics, and prosperous peasants. The gentry, of both native and 'settler' antecedents, were best placed to exploit the changing circumstances to their own benefit. Land was for them the foundation of wealth, status, and power. Lewys Glyn Cothi, addressing Llywelyn ap Rhys ap Siôn, constable of New Radnor, leaves us in no doubt of contemporary opinion that those who bought land became gentlemen and those who sold it sank quickly:

> A bryno tir â braint da,
> Yn ei ardal â'n wrda;
> A wertho tir wrth y tai,
> Efo weithian a fethai.[26]

[He who buys land with good privilege, becomes a gentleman in his district; he who sells land alongside the houses soon fails.]

Many of the gentry seized the chance of ingratiating themselves with the Crown or with absentee aristocrats in the March so as to hold office in Principality or March. It was only those already in a position of economic standing in their communities who were normally acceptable for holding office and being placed in a position of authority confirmed the influence they already enjoyed informally. The fees they received as office-holders were often less important than the additional prestige and power they acquired, which enabled them to advance their own economic interests and those of dependants or clients by way of annuities, leases, tenancies, marriages, and other advantages. Moreover, the holding of office often made them more credit-worthy and enabled them to raise money more easily for land purchase. So those fortunate families who managed to acquire office and land readily, married well, and did not have too many heirs to fragment the inheritance, and who had the advantages of ability, push, good health, and good luck were able to make rapid headway. Some families did extraordinarily well: the descendants of Dafydd Gam, including Herberts, Vaughans, and Games, the family of Dynevor, the Gruffydds of Penrhyn, and the Mostyns in the north-east, all built up highly successful accretions of land and power in four different regions of Wales—south-east, south-west, north-west, and north-east. Representatives

----

[26] *LGC*[1], p. 249.

of these families fought in the French wars and the civil broils at home, thereby greatly strengthening their connections with the Crown and the aristocracy. In the course of the faction fights they not only fought their political enemies but also, in the process, elbowed economic rivals out of their path.

By the beginning of the sixteenth century, the nuclei of a number of landed estates, large and middling, had come into being in all parts of Wales. The fortunes of only a few of the more favoured families can be noted here; but let us take, first of all, some examples from the relatively remote and poor counties of the north-west. In Merioneth, the family of Nannau, by careful leasing of land from the Cistercians of Cymer, judicious investment, and shrewd diplomacy, had not only kept their heads above water but had also consolidated their economic and social position in the midst of widespread poverty and depression, in a county hard hit by rebellion and civil war. So that, by the early sixteenth century, the poet Tudur Aled could refer in glowing terms to Huw Nannau's extensive holding of mountain land, woodland, cornland, and meadow, and his tenants as numerous as snowflakes in January.[27] In the same county by 1525, the Vaughans of Corsygedol, as a result of their diligence in pursuing their opportunities in the previous century, had accumulated an estate claiming to incorporate one hundred tenements, 3,000 acres of arable, 1,000 acres of meadow, 1,000 acres of woodland, 1,000 acres of underwood, 70 acres of turbary and marsh, together with fisheries in Ardudwy and Talybont. The rise of a number of comparable families in Anglesey, including the Bulkeleys and the Lewises of Prysaeddfed, and in Caernarfonshire, including the Glyns of Glynllifon, the Gruffydds of Penrhyn, the Wynns of Gwydir, and the Maurices of Clenennau, has been carefully traced. Such families had used all the devices of the period to come to the top: purchase of small freeholds—particularly those adjacent to their own holdings—leases, *prid*, entail, office-holding, marriages to heiresses, illegal encroachment on Crown lands, and the consolidation of a hamlet into a home farm.

In some of the more prosperous districts of the north-east, the same processes had been going at least as briskly and as successfully. The Salusburys, one of the most fortunate of all the families there, began as middling tenants of fourteenth-century Denbighland. Though most of the process of their estate-building is hidden from us, it is evident that by dint of application, enterprise, and well-judged marriages, by the end of the fifteenth century 'a considerable estate had been built up; for the family's wealth was then fully sufficient to sustain them in the rôle which favourable

---

[27] *TA*, p. lviii.

circumstances now enabled them to play'.[28] The Mostyns of Flintshire provide an extraordinary example of estate-building by patient accumulation of land, from the time of Iorwerth Ddu in the fourteenth century, and by spectacularly successful marriages, such as that of Ieuan Fychan, descendant of Iorwerth Ddu, to Angharad, daughter of Hywel ap Tudur, scion of another active line of land accumulators. Their son, Hywel ab Ieuan, and grandson, Richard ap Hywel, were both notable supporters of the house of Lancaster and close associates of Jasper Tudor.[29]

In the south there were equally notable instances of gentry advancement. Some were drawn from settler families, like the Stradlings of St Donat's or the Mansels of Gower; others were sprung from native stock, like the Morgans of Tredegar, the Matthews of Radyr, or the Dwns of Carmarthen-shire. All of these lines were just as keen to acquire land, office, and heiresses in order to extend and consolidate their estates.

In short, long before the even more dramatic changes of the sixteenth century, there were wide-awake and ambitious families in all parts of Wales already fully alert to the usual—and some more unusual—methods of estate-building and well-placed to take advantage of a fluid land market and the possibilities of redistributing landed wealth in their own favour. Not all of those families which flourished in the fifteenth century would enjoy continuing good fortune. Some would fail through lack of heirs; others from having too many heirs and their estates would be divided under the Welsh custom of *cyfran*, described by Sir John Wynn as 'the destruction of Wales', which made it easier for families to wane than wax. Some would not sustain into later generations the earlier qualities of drive and determination, and others would sink from sheer bad luck. But many of the most notable of these local dynasties were, by the beginning of the sixteenth century, poised for a run of success that would make their descendants economically and socially the most powerful figures in Wales for generations.

The people likely to benefit handsomely from the swiftly flowing currents of the cloth, cattle, and other trades were the affluent burgesses of the towns. Having ready cash to invest, they watched avidly for chances of entering the fluid land market. Even landowners as prominent as William Herbert, earl of Pembroke, might be greatly interested in commerce. He himself was described, at an early stage in his career, as a 'mere chapman' and all his life he remained keen to make money out of trade. The most notable and best-documented example of the successful merchant's business acumen when it came to acquiring land is that of Bartholomew Bolde, a burgess of Conwy. By a series of purchases and mortgages of

[28] W. J. Smith (ed.), *Calendar of Salusbury Correspondence, 1553–c.1700* (Cardiff, 1954), pp. 6–7.
[29] A. D. Carr, 'The Mostyn Family and Estate, 1200–1642' (PhD. Thesis, Bangor, 1976).

land, each rarely exceeding twelve acres in extent, he amassed an estate of sixty messuages, twenty-four tofts, two water mills, a fulling mill, 600 acres of arable land, 200 acres of meadow, forty acres of woodland, and 1,000 acres of pasture.[30] It was characteristic of contemporary attitudes among burgesses and gentry that each side was eager to avail itself of what the other had to offer and to be alert to the advantages to both that marriage alliances between them could confer. It, therefore, comes as no surprise to discover that this estate should have been bequeathed to one of Bolde's daughters, Alice, who had married William Bulkeley, junior, one of an up-and-coming gentry family of Anglesey. As well as a number of other burgesses from Conwy besides Bolde, families like the Forts of Llanstephan, the Kemyses of Newport, the Woodhalls of Holt, the Hollands of Abergele, and Spicers of Caernarfon, not to mention one-third of Ruthin's burgesses or many townsmen of Brecon, were engaged in comparable activity.

Another group to benefit from purchases and other acquisitions of land were some of the wealthier individuals among the clergy. They were usually descended from gentry families and inclined to share the attitude of their secular brothers towards possessions and their enlargement. Inheriting a sizeable patrimony as they often did, benefiting from tithes, Easter offerings, revenues from pilgrims, trading, and other income, they had the capital to spare for the accumulation of land and livestock. Siôn Mechain, parson of Llandrunio, Montgomeryshire, was a landowner, sheep-breeder and trader in a sufficiently profitable way to be a lavish patron of poets, described as one whose purse was never hidden. An even more remarkable example in the early sixteenth century was Robert ap Rhys, protégé of Wolsey and worthy emulator of his great master. He had amassed extensive lands by purchase and lease, sheep and cattle reputed to be worth more than 1,000 marks, and was said to be able to lay his hands on £2,000 and upwards in plate and ready cash. Being a cleric did not deter him from taking a wife and founding three of the more notable houses of gentry in north Wales.

Lesser men than all those so far described also availed themselves of the new possibilities on offer. When the great landowners found it necessary to lease their lands they were not at all loth, in innumerable instances, to enter into bargains with smaller freeholders or prospering tenants. In Caernarfonshire, many small freeholders managed to hold their ground in the fierce struggle for survival and even succeeded in adding to their existing holdings to emerge as yeoman-freeholders in the sixteenth century. A particularly striking example of the emergence of more substantial yeomen and leaseholding peasants has been traced in the

---

[30] T. Jones Pierce, *Medieval Welsh Society* (Cardiff, 1972), pp. 195–227.

lowland lordship of Ogmore in Glamorgan. An almost entirely new pattern of land distribution, accompanied by a veritable revolution in tenurial practice and social structure, occurred there in the fifteenth century. Not only was there a shift of population from the less fertile to the more productive areas within the lordship, but there was also a reallocation of land in favour of the larger farmer. As well as local gentry families, like the Matthews of Corntown and the Thomases of Brocastle, the bigger tenant farmers, like Howell Rawlyn, who merged three customary holdings into one, and David Gwyn Lougher, leaseholder of 128 acres of demesne, also benefited.[31] The gap between big farmers and smaller ones had widened, and the difference between free and bond tenants had virtually ceased to matter. In the lordship of Newport, too, in mid-fifteenth century there is clear evidence of small tenants being able to lease land for twenty or thirty years at twelve pence per acre instead of the former sixteen pence, in addition to the gains made by bigger men. What had also happened in the upland areas gives us ground for thinking that such developments were typical of south-east Wales generally.

In the same way, ministers' accounts and other documents relating to the monasteries at the time of their dissolution make it plain that their estates had been rented by many small or middling tenants as well as by more substantial figures. A large number of monastic tenants were either leaseholders or tenants-at-will, some of whom showed their eagerness both to extend their holdings and to safeguard their position by converting their tenancies-at-will into leaseholds.

The existence in fifteenth- and early sixteenth-century Glamorgan of a large number of substantial 'yeoman-type' houses provides further evidence of the emergence of a sizeable group of prosperous tenants, who might perhaps be designated 'yeomen', comparable to similar individuals who have been traced in Caernarfonshire and elsewhere in Wales. In spite of having to pay high wages to the labourers they had to employ and the static prices of agricultural production, they had clearly made a success of their operations.

Out of the debris of their former medieval structures, in Principality and March, were emerging the outlines of the more familiar pattern of landowner, tenant-farmer, and labourer. The change was far from complete and still had a considerable way to go. A large number of scattered *tyddynnod* [crofts] and communal strip fields still survived. Consolidation of holdings had not yet proceeded very far in many parts of the country—Leland told how Rowland Griffith of Anglesey informed him that 'in time of mind men used not in Tir Môn [i.e., Anglesey] to separate their ground but now still more and more . . . they divide their grounds

[31] *GCH*, III, Chap. 6.

after Devonshire fashion'.[32] Individual ownership of land was coming increasingly to the fore, and its proprietors would seek to mark, consolidate, and protect their holdings. Yet it should be emphasized that most of such estates—if that is not too grand a word to describe many of them—as had been accumulated were small and usually consisted of scattered portions. The same would be true of lesser men's holdings. The Welsh practice of *cyfran* had led to scattered distribution and morcellation, leaving farmers with widely dispersed quillets of land in what were still largely open arable fields of more than one township. Most of those who farmed the land, including the many small freeholders among them, remained medium to small peasants, with holdings ranging from 15–20 acres down to 4–5 acres of arable land. The smallest among them found it impossible to meet their family's needs from what their land was able to produce and had to take part in a wide range of multifarious economic activities as craftsmen or labourers to make ends meet.

That was even more true of the army of landless or virtually landless cottars and labourers, whose ranks were swollen as a result of the disappearance of the smallest holdings and their absorption by more prosperous tenants. Given the wide seasonal variations in the demand for labour during the agricultural year, they had no choice but to turn their hands to a variety of by-employments. Even at harvest time, the busiest season on the land when the demand for labour was at its most intense, numbers of them migrated temporarily to reap the earlier and more bountiful harvests along the border with England or in the lowland districts of Wales, before returning to garner the later and more meagre crops at home. Other harvests besides corn called for extra hands: oak bark for tanning, gathering fruit in the districts which had orchards, collecting fruits, berries, and nuts in the woodlands, shellfish or seaweed along the shore, or fishing at the appropriate season. Livestock needed additional care and attention at calving, lambing, shearing, and other busy seasons. Gathering and spinning wool, weaving cloth, and knitting; felling and carting timber, charcoal burning, cutting and gathering peat, turf, firewood, and gorse for fuel; helping to build ships, churches, mills, and houses; mining coal and metals; quarrying limestone, millstones, and slates; making cloth, leather, cheese, or butter; these and many other miscellaneous tasks made many demands for casual labour. It was an age which knew little of our notions of specialization or division of labour, or fixed hours of work, or restrictions on the employment of juveniles. Men, women, and children were prepared to fulfil a varied spectrum of functions and to work long hours with very little respite when necessary.

Hard though conditions were for the poorer groups, they were almost

---

[32] Leland, p. 90.

certainly nothing like as difficult as they would become in the following century when population pressures and inflation of prices increased acutely again. Labour was still scarce enough to command a reasonable wage, and prices were relatively stable until the first quarter of the sixteenth century. To describe the fifteenth century as a 'golden age' of labour is almost certainly to go further than the evidence warrants. Nevertheless, the descendants of the ordinary men and women who lived then might conceivably have looked back on it from mid-sixteenth century with wistful feelings of longing and regret.

CHAPTER 4

THE BONDS OF SOCIETY

POPULATION

THE demography of Wales in the later Middle Ages is shrouded in obscurity. Estimates of population everywhere in Europe during that period are difficult to arrive at; but in Wales the problem is made peculiarly intractable by the almost total lack of sources that might appropriately be used for the purpose of making even a rough approximation. Earlier calculations of a pre-plague population of 200,000 falling to 125,000 in 1377 are now viewed with considerable scepticism. A reasonable estimate for the population in 1536 is about 278,000; and another figure, based mainly on the lay subsidy returns of 1544, gives a total population of about 250,000.[1] So it might not be greatly wide of the mark to suggest a population for Wales in the 1530s of about a quarter of a million. Such a figure almost certainly represented a smaller total than had existed about 1300. It is true that the only two areas for which a reasonably dependable comparison can be made between 1300 and 1544 are Merioneth and Flint. Comparing estimates made for 1300 in these counties with later ones for Henry VIII's reign, we find that those for 1300 are considerably higher than those for 1544; though it is true that figures for Flint in 1300 are nearer those for 1544 than are the comparable figures for Merioneth.[2]

Some of the reasons for this drop in population were universally applicable in late medieval Europe; some were peculiar to Wales. The two most general and devastating causes were disease and war. The Black Death had hit Wales hard in 1348–50, though probably not as severely as those countries with dense urban and lowland concentrations of people. Plague had returned on a number of occasions in the fourteenth and fifteenth centuries. Contemporary observers were distressingly familiar with the ravages of the disease. One of Sir John Wynn's ancestors, Evan ap Robert, died in 1471 'in the flower of his age, being but one and thirty years old' from plague, which 'commonly followeth war and desolation'.[3]

---

[1] E. A. Wrigley and R. S. Schofield, *Population History of England* (Cambridge, 1981); D. Williams, 'A Note on the Population of Wales', *BBCS*, vii (1935–7), 359–63; L. Owen, 'The Population of Wales in the Sixteenth and Seventeenth Centuries', *Trans. Cymmr.*, 1959, pp. 99–113.
[2] K. Williams Jones, *The Merioneth Lay Subsidy Roll, 1292–3* (Cardiff, 1976), introd.
[3] *HGF*, p. 45.

Gruffydd ap Rhys, ancestor of the Mostyns, lost seven children in a week from plague; and a poet, Ieuan Gethin ab Ieuan ap Lleision, lost five and Gwilym ap Sefnyn ten. In 1478 Dafydd Nanmor attributed the onset of plague to the influence of the sinister planet, Saturn, and trembled aghast at the lethal trinity of epidemic, famine, and war that it brought about. As late as 1535, another poet, Gruffydd ab Ieuan ap Llywelyn Fychan, described plague as 'the arrow of death' [*Saeth y farwolaeth yw fo*]. Other fearsome diseases and epidemics, like typhus, smallpox, influenza, malaria, dysentery, leprosy, tuberculosis, scurvy, and rickets, were rife, and some of these were referred to by frightened contemporaries as 'plague' on account of the fearful harvest they reaped.[4]

The connection which Dafydd Nanmor and others saw between food shortages and a high incidence of death and illness was well founded. The dependence of society on the quality of the harvest has already been noted. Bad harvests were most often caused by inclement weather, to a lesser extent by plant and animal diseases, and, occasionally, by insect invasions. They could usually be expected once or twice a decade, and two bad harvests in succession always spelt disaster, with soaring prices, desperate shortages, and widespread famine. Any further adversities caused by the irruption of a public calamity, like war or plague, or a private misfortune, such as injury, illness, or premature death of the householder, could be catastrophic for whole families. In very wet years like 1437, 1439, or 1482, the harvest failed and many became desperately under-nourished and an easy prey to illness. But even in good harvest years, the food eaten was monotonous and seriously deficient in vitamins and protein. Much of it, too, was stale, decayed, or tainted; and water supplies were frequently polluted. The damp, draughty, squalid, overcrowded, and insanitary hovels in which many of the population lived, and their ragged, unwashed, and inadequate clothing rendered them all the more prone to pick up infection and spread it. Some parts of Wales, like Anglesey, were well supplied with doctors, although how far their limited knowledge of the nature, transmission, and treatment of disease allowed them to alleviate the suffering of even those who could afford to pay for a doctor's attentions is more open to question.

Nor was Dafydd Nanmor wrong to perceive war and disruption as having added immensely to the hazards faced by the populace. Thousands of Welshmen had been recruited to fight in the French wars, of whom a far greater proportion were killed by disease than battle. More devastating were the consequences of years of brutal conflict waged in the course of the Glyndŵr Rebellion. Its effects on people, livestock, and the fixed capital of industry and agriculture were destructive and long-lasting. Large numbers

[4] J. Cule (ed.), *Wales and Medicine* (London, 1975); G. P. Jones, *Newyn a Haint yng Nghymru* (Caernarfon, 1962).

were killed and others reduced to beggary. Collective depression lowered morale and many fled to areas regarded as safer, never to return. The general effect may have been to encourage even more of the population of Wales to migrate to the towns and rural areas of the Marches, which were not loth to recruit fresh blood so as to make good the drop in population caused by plague. In all the bigger towns along the border there were sizeable contingents of Welsh immigrants. Some of the later campaigns of the civil wars, too, though nothing like as destructive in their impact as the Glyndŵr Rebellion, were damaging enough and added to earlier devastation.

There were, therefore, many reasons why the level of fifteenth-century population should be low and should remain largely static. Yet, many of the conditions already referred to would have been largely applicable to earlier medieval centuries when population, nevertheless, increased markedly. Even the effects of plague, which did not start before 1348 and would go on recurring throughout the sixteenth century, when population did rise, would hardly seem enough in themselves to explain the failure of the population to recover more quickly in the fifteenth century. Such a phenomenon is all the more surprising at a time when, in terms of the land available and the levels of rents, wages, and prices, conditions were favourable and might have been expected to encourage people to marry early and rear large families. Their failure to do so on the expected scale has led some historians to postulate a widespread underlying lack of confidence and a psychological inclination to evade responsibilities. Some have even argued for the prevalence of primitive forms of family limitation by coitus interruptus and other practices; while others have drawn attention to the damaging effects on women's fertility of prolonged malnutrition and exposure to disease.[5]

Whatever the reasons may have been for its sluggish recovery, population did not begin to increase until well into the second half of the fifteenth century and then only very slowly. The low level of demand for land in mid-fifteenth century is still attributed to a falling or mainly static population. This low level of growth could hardly be attributed to the birth-rate, which was relatively buoyant at this time. In Europe overall, it averaged somewhere between 30–40 per 1,000 (as compared with 16.2 per 1,000 in the UK in 1970). But if the birth-rate was high, so was the death-rate. Even in a normal year it averaged 30–35 per 1,000 (as compared with 12.3 males and 11.2 females per 1,000 in the UK in 1970), while in a year of epidemic illness, acute dearth, or savage warfare, it might soar much higher. Infant mortality was of the order of anything up to 240 per 1,000 and child deaths were astronomically high, resulting in the loss during the first year of their lives of about half of the children born. The drudgery of

[5] J. D. Chambers, *Population, Economy and Society in Pre-industrial England* (Oxford, 1972); T. H. Hollingsworth, *Historical Demography* (London, 1969).

heavy manual labour prematurely aged most of the population, and life expectation was low: thirty-five years or less (as compared with 68.5 for males and 74.7 for females in the UK in 1970), though the rigours of the selection process meant that the tough who survived earlier mishaps could expect to live to a ripe old age.

In Europe nowadays, children from 0–14 years of age make up about 60–65 per cent of the dependent population; in the fifteenth century they represented about 90 per cent. Such a high proportion of dependent children created problems for society. Hence the many among them who may have died not only from disease or ignorance or unavoidable neglect but who may also have been exposed or abandoned by parents at their wits' end to know how to feed an extra hungry mouth. In these circumstances, with human life so precarious and family ties so uncertain and often of such short duration, it is difficult to produce evidence of affectionate family life or close bonding between parents and children. Children rarely appear in the art of the period and when they do are normally presented as miniature adults. Yet, on the few occasions when Welsh poets mention their children, they do so with what appears to be genuine and spontaneous affection. The most touching poem by far is Lewys Glyn Cothi's lament for his son, Siôn, which, if typical of other parents' emotions, reveals all too movingly how well they understood their children's winning ways and loved them with an intensity equal to that found in any modern affective family.[6] Nor does Ieuan Gethin grieve any the less in his elegy to his five sons and daughters, all carried off by the plague, nor Llywelyn ap Gutun in his lament for his children. Judging by this admittedly scanty testimony, family relationships may well have been warmer and more affectionate than is often supposed.

ENGLISH AND WELSH

The extended process by which Wales was conquered had lasted from the end of the eleventh century to 1282–3. In its train it had brought a considerable Anglo-Norman colonization, not only among the upper class of lords and knights but also among town burgesses and settlers of the Englishries. They had been accorded a privileged status, hotly resented by the Welsh, whose hostile reactions had found aggressive expression in the Glyndŵr Rebellion. Yet all they had served to bring about was the reinforcement of English superiority by Henry IV's anti-Welsh legislation. After 1415 the English inevitably sought to maintain their rights, pressing constant complaints against Welsh lawlessness and hostility and urging the government to reaffirm and enforce strictly anti-Welsh laws. Sharp

[6] Translation in A. Conran, *The Penguin Book of Welsh Verse* (London, 1967), pp. 185–6.

differences between Welsh and English were still obvious to George Owen late in Elizabeth's reign: 'these two nations keep each from dealings with the other, as mere strangers, so that the meaner sort of people will not nor doth not usually join together in marriage'.[7] The division had been even more pronounced a century and a half earlier. Fifteenth-century Welsh poets rarely missed a chance of venting their anti-English prejudices. Typical of the intense distaste felt for English burgesses was the outburst in an anonymous poem against the townsfolk of Flint, whose author in an angry leave-taking, vowed:

> I ne'er again will venture there.
> May death all further visits spare.[8]

Perhaps his hearers were not intended to take this poet's protestations too seriously, but in other bardic effusions much more envenomed and irreconcilable mutual antipathy than this was commonplace.

Nevertheless, in spite of all the rancour and prejudice that the two peoples cherished for one another, they were being thrown closer together in a number of ways. Whatever George Owen may have said about the reluctance of lower-class Welsh and English to marry, their social superiors were not deterred by any such inhibitions. Earlier Welsh leaders, including Glyndŵr, had established ample precedents for taking English wives. William Herbert married Anne Devereux, daughter of his staunch ally, Walter Devereux. The Stradlings intermarried with such notable Welsh families as the Herberts, Gruffydds of Penrhyn, and the line of Rhys ap Thomas. In north Wales the Pulestons, Conways of Bodryddan, Kynastons, and Hollands all forged marriage alliances with Welsh stock. Small wonder that, by the early sixteenth century, the poet Tudur Aled should ruefully have to admit that if he were to search too closely all the alien lineages now being intermingled with Welsh ones he might well find too many gaps in the pedigrees of proud strangers. Marriage was one of the most powerful agencies of cultural diffusion and closer unity; law was another. English law, particularly in matters of inheritance customs and procedures for buying and selling land, had an irresistible attraction for many ambitious, up-and-coming Welshmen, who were eagerly adopting its practices at the expense of their own native law. Such closer ties facilitated the interchange of culture and language between the Welsh and the English.

The Welsh were also finding their way into the towns in spite of prohibitory legislation. There, they often ensconced themselves in comfortably padded niches. Maredudd ab Ieuan ap Robert, sent to school at Caernarfon, 'fell in liking' with a young woman and married her. She was related to one Spicer, 'a landed man of some fifty pounds per annum', who 'had an office

---

[7] Owen, I, 39.   [8] *OBWV*, pp. 51–3.

in the Exchequer and dealt with trade of merchandise also, so he was a great wealthy man'.[9] In Ruthin, extensive intermarriage created such Anglo-Welsh families as the Thelwalls, Salusburys, Longfords, and Exmewes. In Oswestry, rural Welsh clans like the Cyffins, Trefors, and Blodwels had firmly established themselves. In south Wales, too, the same kind of immigration was taking place; to such an extent that Ieuan ap Huw Cae Llwyd could greet Brecon as the 'Constantinople' of the peoples of Wales, and in Swansea by 1543 half the names of its taxpayers were unmistakably Welsh.

Into the more fertile regions of the Englishries of the March and border areas of England, too, Welsh settlers had been moving, to fill some of the gaps left by plague and depopulation. A striking instance of this was the recymricization of the Vale of Glamorgan. This attractive lowland region, one of the most productive in Wales, had been seized in the early twelfth century by Norman invaders and turned into a land of knights' fees and manors, into which a large population of English-speaking settlers had been introduced. But by the second half of the fifteenth century it had been thickly enough peopled by a Welsh-speaking populace to cause many of its formerly English- or French-speaking families, including such notabilities as Stradlings, Malefants, Gamages, Turbervilles, Butlers, and others, to become so Welsh in speech and culture as to offer a warm welcome to Welsh poets, from Glamorgan and elsewhere, who regularly went on circuit through the gentry houses in the Vale. The leading poet, Iorwerth Fynglwyd, was born in St Bride's Major and the other significant figure, Lewis Morgannwg, lived in Cowbridge. Alongside the Welsh poetry emerged also a particularly robust and assured school of Welsh prose-writing. The population of the Vale had become largely Welsh-speaking again and would remain so until the eighteenth century.[10]

THE SOCIAL ORDER

The highest flights of the social order were occupied by the aristocracy. Strictly speaking, there were two sorts of aristocrats recognized in Wales: the native Welsh 'barons' and the English peerage. The former, descendants of Welsh princes though they were, counted for little. In Edeirnion and Dinmael they continued to cling to their titles and status as barons, but with every passing year their high-sounding pretensions became more hollow and meaningless. They figured from time to time as patrons of poets, but were obviously sinking into the ranks of the smaller squires; down-at-heel remnants of once-ruling stock, clinging to the fraying tatters of their sometime princely status. In Glyndŵr's lifetime a leading poet had

[9] *HGF*, p. 51.
[10] G. J. Williams, *Traddodiad Llenyddol Morgannwg* (Cardiff, 1948), Chap. 2.

commented acidly on the swelling impudence of those who had wealth but not high birth to commend them and the decline of those of princely birth who had once been mighty. The process intensified in the fifteenth century, when the only one among the formerly proud barons of Edeirnion who rated more than a passing mention was Dafydd ab Ieuan ab Einion, stalwart defender of Harlech, 1461–8.

The English aristocracy's standing was vastly superior to that of the Welsh 'barons'; but in their ranks, too, there had been great changes. Baronial families died out, on average, about every third generation, and power-shifts, as a result of war and faction, constantly reshuffled the cards of Marcher possessions. Some of the greatest families associated with the fourteenth-century March—Clares, Bohuns, and Despensers—were disappearing, and the celebrated FitzWarins died out in 1420. Even the most famous of the emergent families of that era, the Mortimers, had vanished by the 1420s. They were replaced by successors owing their elevation to marriage and/or royal support: Beauchamps, Mowbrays, Nevills, and Staffords, most of whom would be gone by 1536. Though, when the Marcher lordships were eventually done away with in 1536, there were still some considerable figures among their lords: the earl of Arundel, lord of Oswestry and Clun; the earl of Shrewsbury of Goodrich castle; and earl of Derby of Knockin, Ellesmere, and Hawarden; and Henry, Lord Stafford, of Hay and Caus. But they and their fifteenth-century predecessors had long since ceased to spend much of their time in the March.

In their absence, power on the spot passed to their deputies, drawn from the local notabilities. Some of them sprang from the border English gentry; many others from settler or native families in Wales. Though gentle birth counted as an important qualification when an official was chosen, what mattered much more was adequate wealth and economic standing. In this context, it is worth remembering that it was in the fifteenth century that the term 'gentleman' came increasingly to be applied to a person of social distinction who was not necessarily a nobleman. It was this which prompted the penetrating observation by K. B. McFarlane[11] that in the fifteenth century it was not a case of the 'rise of the gentry' so much as their 'fall' from the nobility. In an age of economic opportunity and social mobility, the new usage of the term spread, and many could aspire to regard themselves and be regarded by others as 'gentlemen', even though their wealth might originally have been acquired in trade or at the law as well as in land. But possession of land remained the ultimate accolade of gentility. By 1530, Garter King of Arms had concluded that in order to qualify for the right to bear a coat of arms, the distinguishing mark of gentlemanly status, a man ought to have a freehold income of at least £10 a

[11] K. B. McFarlane, *XIIe Congrès international des sciences historiques (1965)*, *Rapports*, I, 341.

year in land. Increasingly, the gentry of Wales had shown their desire to come within the scope of the College of Heralds and be recognized according to its criteria. In that same year of 1530, William Fellowe, Lancaster Herald, carried out a visitation in south Wales on behalf of the College of Heralds to record the arms of a number of families there.

Broadly speaking, there were two kinds of gentry recognized in Wales: the *advenae*, or settlers, and the native *bonheddig* or *uchelwr*. Some of the *advenae*, like the Stradlings or Wogans, had always been of upper-class status, more or less; but others, such as the Salusburys or Bulkeleys, were of humbler origin. What really counted by the fifteenth century, however, was not their origins but their ability to take advantage of opportunities open to thrusting individuals to acquire land, wealth, and office by war, service, marriage, enterprise, or any combination of them. In this way, they became established in their own and other men's eyes as 'gentlemen'. As they rose in society, they were quick to marry, whenever the alliance seemed favourable, with native Welsh families as well as with English ones; and the differences between them and the successful *uchelwyr* were becoming blurred to the point of extinction.

A large proportion of the native Welsh families—possibly as many as a half—claimed to be of free birth and belonging to the *bonedd*. The word *bonedd* derived from *bôn*, meaning a 'trunk' or 'stem', and signified those who could trace their birth from gentle stock. Those who made this claim believed themselves to be descended from those Trojans who came with Brutus to found an empire in Britain. It was an origin myth of extraordinary potency and seductiveness which still exercised an unusually powerful hold over the Welsh. The author of the *Description of England* (*c*.1480), like many other Englishmen, could not help being deeply impressed by it, too:

> So I take my tales
> And wend into Wales.
> To that noble brood
> Of Priamus' blood.
> Knowledge for to win
> Of great Jupiter's kin.[12]

Numbers of Welsh freemen, immensely proud of the alleged Trojan descent, were intensely interested in their own genealogies. Most of them looked back to some notable progenitor, from whom many stocks claimed to be descended: Rhirid Flaidd, Sandde Hardd, Elystan Glodrydd, Ednowain Bendew, Moreiddig, Iestyn ap Gwrgant, and the like.

Yet the truth was that, whatever their claims to ancient descent, with them, as with the *advenae*, what really mattered in practice was not their

---

[12] F. Jones, 'An Approach to Welsh Genealogy', *Trans. Cymmr.*, 1948, p. 362.

bloodline but what material gains they had been able to win for themselves in the fluid conditions of the fifteenth century. Sir John Wynn later recalled that many were 'brought to the estate of mean freeholders, and so having forgotten their descents and pedigrees are become as if they had never been'.[13] He attributed his own family's good fortune to 'God's mercy and goodness'; but, with all proper respect to the inscrutable workings of divine providence, we may be forgiven for seeing more than a modicum of human drive, ambition, and luck as accounting for the Wynns' success. Families needed determination and good fortune to catch the rising tide of economic opportunity and to circumvent the restrictions placed upon them by partible inheritance and by English law to prevent their rising in the world. The successful among them were as eager to secure land, wealth, and office as the *advenae* and as willing to intermarry advantageously. The offspring of such unions appreciated not only the material inheritance that resulted; they also set great store on the cultural inheritance which brought them into close contact with the Welsh poet-genealogists who were crucial in the creation and dissemination of the ideology which justified the gentry's economic and social dominance.

One thing which these emerging families, *advenae* and natives alike, intensely coveted was public and external attestation of their place in society, on grounds of birth and blood as well as wealth and office. They wanted to see their gentlemanly lineage, pedigrees, virtues, status, and supremacy recorded, proclaimed, and celebrated publicly in their halls when they gave feasts and entertained their guests—neighbours, followers, tenants, and dependants. They were keenly aware that, thus, they became heirs to an immemorial tradition of praise and recognition, by which heroes were applauded and immortalized. In Wales, the individuals consecrated by age-old custom to perform this task of public acclamation were the poets. They it was who did most to popularize genealogy and heraldry during the golden age of Welsh genealogy from 1450–1600, particularly during the fifteenth century, when the outstanding figure was the poet Gutun Owain. One of the three distinctive functions of a poet—*tri chof Ynys Prydain* [three records of the Isle of Britain]—was 'to keep the genealogies or descents of nobility, their division of lands and their arms'.[14] From this sprang the great flood of poems of praise to *uchelwr* patrons, with a heavy emphasis on their ancient descent, one of the most extravagant examples of which is Rhys Goch Eryri's poem to William Gruffydd, purporting to trace his descent all the way back to Brutus and thence, via Dardanus, Jupiter, and the patriarchs, to Adam! The same age also saw the careful compiling of genealogies and the copying of them into manuscripts. Now, too, were conjured up such beguiling genealogical

[13] *HGF*, p. 14.
[14] D. M. Lloyd (ed.), *A Book of Wales* (London, 1953), pp. 104–8.

myths as the 'five royal tribes', the 'fifteen noble tribes of Gwynedd', and the 'twelve knights of Glamorgan' intended to bolster pride in the glorious ancestors of the past.

The poets, of course, were not unaware of the racially mixed and sometimes suspect lineages of some of their patrons, but the deft footwork required of them in avoiding pitfalls and gaffes in the delicate task of praise was usually unerring. Some of their mentors were, on the face of it, rather improbable objects for a Welsh poet's encomiums. John Gray, lord of Powys, was patron to both Lewys Môn and Tudur Aled. Though their poems to him may sound somewhat incongruous to a twentieth-century ear, there is no reason to doubt that they were well enough received at the time. Similarly, in the county of Flint, which of all the regions of Wales had seen more intermarriage between Welsh and English gentry and probably had more Anglo-Welsh contacts of other kinds than almost any other part of Wales, there were at least three outstanding families of bardic patrons—Conways, Hanmers, and Pulestons. All of them had originally been settler families but now had strong infusions of Welsh blood in their veins, and poets regularly and gladly visited their halls. When, in some cases, a pedigree had gaps or was seriously lacking, poets and genealogists were usually helpful in 'co-operating' to make good the deficiencies or even to 'discover' august forebears for deserving patrons. Adam of Salzburg, a contemporary of William the Conqueror, was provided for the Salusburys, who first appear in the historical record as obscure yeomen in the mid-fourteenth century. The Herberts, too, were linked by the eye of genealogical faith, to Herbert, chamberlain to Henry I, as their illustrious ancestor.

The poets, however, felt happiest and most at their ease when they had the congenial task of praising the native gentry sprung on both sides from a long line of unmixed noble Welsh ancestors.

> Bonedd Gwynedd a genais,
> Blodau'r sir heb ledryw Sais.[15]

[I sang the praises of the *bonedd* of Gwynedd; flowers of the region with no admixture of Saxon blood.]

averred Tudur Aled, with more pride than strict accuracy. But we need not deny the poets and their patrons the pleasure that they must have derived from the recital of a long and honourable pedigree. John Wynn was not the only one who basked complacently in self-congratulation at the thought of what a 'great temporal blessing it is and a great heart's ease to a man to find that he is well descended and a greater grief it is for upstarts and gentlemen of the first head to look back into their descents being base in such sort'.[16] Happiest role of all for the poets was to be in a position to extol both a

---

[15] *TA*, p. liii.   [16] *HGF*, p. 37.

husband and wife descended from gentle families of long standing and thus to celebrate the uniting of two great stocks. The female lines were traced with as much care as the male descents, largely in order that fitting marriages could be contracted. Many of the poems which praise both husband and wife may well have been composed at the time of their marriage, or soon after, in order to emphasize what a worthy alliance had been entered into by both parties. Female successors were especially significant because it might be vitally important to show that the offspring of the marriage could claim descent on the distaff side from an ancient line that might otherwise have become extinct. Shrewdly contrived marriages of sons to such girls of good breeding and ample possessions were the basis on which the fortunes of many a successful Welsh house were at least partly founded—Mostyns, Gruffydds, Stradlings, Salusburys, Bulkeleys, and Herberts (aptly known as the 'Habsburgs of Wales') prominent among them.

When a poet set out to compose a joint panegyric to a married couple, his normal custom was to praise the husband's manly prowess, his wife's womanly virtues, each partner's illustrious descent, and the princely entertainment they both offered. On those rare occasions when they proved uncharacteristically ungenerous, both were stingingly taken to task, as with that hateful pair from Maelor, roundly chastised by Tudur Penllyn for deceitfully luring so many unsuspecting bards to their miserly household. In a much more typical poem to a husband and wife, Lewys Glyn Cothi went into raptures in his tributes to Dafydd ap Llywelyn ap Gwilym Llwyd and his wife, Lleucu. Lleucu had clearly made a deep and favourable impression on the poet, for when she died he went to the unusual length of composing two elegies for her. A single lament of this kind for husband or wife was common enough. Occasionally it is just possible to detect in them a note of deep personal loss which seems to go well beyond the conventional expressions of grief on the part of the bereaved partner. Though marriages of this period were essentially business contracts arranged by the kinsfolk of both partners in order to advance the social and material interests of the respective families, with little regard for personal feelings or sentiments of romantic love, a deep and genuine affection between a married couple often existed. Thus, when Tudur Aled says of the widow of one of his patrons, in a couplet which is, even by that great master's standards, profoundly moving, and one whose epigrammatic force and compassion defy adequate translation:

> Y gŵr marw, e' gar morwyn
> Ddaear dy fedd er dy fwyn.[17]

[Dead man, a lady loves the very soil of thy grave for thy sake]

[17] *TA*, p. 290.

it becomes impossible not to sense how grief-stricken the bereft woman appears to have been. Not that all marriages were so blissful or all partners so devoted. Poets often showed a scant disregard for the marital vows, and adultery on the part of men and women was far from unknown, however strictly a Welshman may have required his wife to be a wise and careful virgin before marriage.

The wives often seem to have been formidable ladies: fit companions for the doughty men of this warlike, touchy, easily provoked society, whose passions were at best only barely controlled. One of the most memorable of them comes startlingly alive in John Wynn's portrait of Evan ap Robert's wife who, though she was Howell ap Rees's sister, none the less identified herself completely with her husband in the feud which ensued between him and her brother. In her efforts to prevent Howell from setting upon her husband, she went to the extent of removing 'the *canllaw* or handstay of a footbridge' and 'with the same lets fly at her brother and if he had not avoided the blow she had struck him off his horse—*Furor arma ministrat*'. On another occasion she bestowed boiling wort liberally over the assailants of her husband's hall. Another lady of the same kidney was Ellen Gethin of Hergest, who killed a man for slaying her brother, or the mother of Hywel ap Madog, who swore upon his deathbed that his feud with John Owen 'should never be ended while his mother lived'.[18] Second-class citizens women may have been in the eyes of the law of Hywel Dda, but they could bear themselves with first-class spirit and courage when their blood was up.

Besides the more successful in the upper echelons of *uchelwyr*, there were many others in Wales who laid claim to gentle birth. Gerald of Wales had commented on the intense pride of all Welsh freemen in their genealogy; and 350 years later, Andrew Boorde (1542) could observe that they still 'set much store by their kindred and prophecies'.[19] A large part of the population consisted of freemen, who preserved a fierce pride in their gentility, even though partible inheritance and economic set-backs had eroded the worldly wealth of many of them. John Wynn recorded a telling anecdote of how his great-grandfather invited an eminent antiquary, Robin Iachwr, to present a nosegay to the 'best gent.' in the company, whereupon he gave it not to John Wynn's ancestor, as might have been expected, but to an obscure freeholder.[20] The economic and social status of this large body of minor gentry and lesser freeholders varied greatly. Some were still able to live and entertain like the greater gentry, though on a more modest scale. The celebrated family of Aberpergwm in the vale of Neath claimed to descend from the lords of Meisgyn and maintained a life-style appropriate to their dignity and honour. They welcomed to their hearth

---

[18] *HGF*, pp. 39, 55.   [19] Bebb, *Machlud*, p. 23.   [20] *HGF*, p. 36.

some of the most famous poets in Wales; no mere bucolic backwoods squirelings they, but men of taste and discernment, with a deep attachment to their native culture. There were a good many others like them all over Wales who delighted to receive poets—for reasons of social acclaim, perhaps, rather more than cultural delectation—and have their lineage proclaimed and their virtues applauded.

But, for all the plaudits of enthusiastic bards, it was becoming increasingly obvious that, however long and distinguished a man's ancestry might be, in practice money was talking decidedly louder than blood. Indeed, it always had done, but was now doing so more impudently and barefacedly than ever. In one of the most unorthodox but cleverest and most impenitently satirical poems of the age, Phylip Emlyn revealed the truth of the matter. Unashamedly drawing back the veils of conventional poetic fiction that shrouded the realities of the social scene, he disclosed how the possession of wealth and a full purse could quite transform a man's standing in the community and his future prospects in society. Wealth enabled any individual to acquire for himself not only many coveted material treasures—jewels, weapons, sacred relics, brilliant gems, heavy rings of gold, heaps of brooches, and fashionable clothes—but also a reputation for skill in learning, prowess in the military arts, and many a prosperous family to claim kinship with him. 'It is for my gold', explained the poet disarmingly, 'that I shall find the whole world sweet and kind. I shall be received by the whole of Wales, never neglected.'[21] More and more men were being obliged to realize, along with Phylip Emlyn, that it was wealth not descent that determined status in a changing world. When Leland came to Glamorgan in the 1530s he met one Leyshon, 'a gent. of ancient stock but now of mean lands'. In spite of Leyshon's proud boast that his family had been 'there in fame before the Conquest',[22] it was obvious that the family, on account of its reduced means, could no longer claim the status it had once enjoyed. John Wynn, too, put the position succinctly enough. God's work with families, he said, was like that of a man 'striking fire in a tinder box'; 'a number of sparkles of fire [were] raised. Whereof but one or two take fire, the rest vanish away.' 'Poverty soon forgets whence it be descended.'[23] It was wealth that kept the chosen few alight; many others had disappeared or dwindled into the ranks of insignificant peasants or labourers, their inheritance morcellated by gavelkind or reduced by other circumstances 'into so little parts'. What a life-saver Phylip Emlyn's bulging purse would have been for those who thus fell by the wayside!

[21] Bell, *Trans. Cymmr.*, 1940, pp. 237–9.
[22] Leland, p. 30.
[23] *HGF*, p. 32.

Successful burgesses had better reason than most to savour the salty tang of Phylip Emlyn's sardonic worldly wisdom. Those who made out well invariably wanted to invest a large part of their gains in land as the prime source of power, prestige, and profit. All aspired to rise to gentryhood or at least to marry their offspring into it. The wealth which Bartholomew Bolde had painstakingly accumulated was gratefully accepted by the Bulkeleys. William Mutton was a burgess of Rhuddlan in Henry IV's time; by Henry VIII's reign, his great-grandson, Peter Mutton, was installed in a fine house at Llannerch and had no hesitation about regarding himself as a gentleman. John Wynn's ancestor had been quick to snap up the wealthy Spicer's relative (above, pp. 94–5). William Kemys, younger son of a gentry family turned successful mercer at Newport, inherited the manors of his childless uncle John, and his descendants held them until 1611. No insuperable barriers existed between successful traders and ambitious landowners.

Flourishing lineal families like that of William Kemys were kept together—and sometimes broken up, too—by inheritance laws and customs. It has been estimated that, on average, something like one family in five would have no children and another one in five only daughters. But, in an age when families so frequently intermarried, when child mortality was high, deaths from plague and other diseases so common, and the toll of war and violence so grievous, daughters were much more likely than sons to survive. Hence the minute care shown by the families of bride and groom when surviving daughters were to be married, even though they could only inherit land other than 'family' land under Welsh law. It also explains the importance attached by poets to sons who outlived their parents. Lewys Glyn Cothi emphasized that leaders among men should leave successors worthy of them, as did such noble creatures of the animal world as eagles, lions, and stags; and Guto'r Glyn greeted five surviving sons as so many gleaming jewels. Such compliments may have had an element of consolation for the parents, and especially perhaps the sons, since the poets must have been all too uneasily aware that one of the key factors in ensuring the success of some families in the struggle for survival in their elevated status was the fewness of heirs who might partition the inheritance.

Among the majority of the population who either had no gentle blood of which to boast or had come down so far in the world as to be almost oblivious of it, there was at least one other status group, as opposed to the occupational groups—husbandmen, craftsmen, labourers etc.—to which most belonged. This consisted of the yeomen, a group emerging in fourteenth-century and, particularly, fifteenth-century Wales, though in palpably smaller numbers than in England. The Welsh term *iwmon* is first recorded in mid-fifteenth century, significantly enough in the work of

Hywel Swrdwal, a poet from the south-eastern borders,[24] where yeomen were likely to have appeared earlier and in greater numbers than elsewhere in Wales. But the term is far less commonly used than 'yeoman' in England, and it is clear that far fewer people in Wales thought of themselves as 'yeomen'. It is, in fact, very difficult to distinguish them from minor gentry and other freeholders. When, by the sixteenth century, surviving wills become more numerous, they often reveal that some of those categorized by themselves and their fellows as yeomen left more in the way of land and property than others styled as gentry. But from an economic standpoint, if not a social one, the yeomen were, broadly speaking, substantial farmers, either owning freehold land, leasing land, or holding a mixture of both, and working it profitably with the labour of the family, farm servants, and hired labour. This kind of farmer was found most usually in the former manorial lands along the southern lowlands and eastern borders. Ordinarily he farmed anything from 30–50 acres of arable land and possessed livestock to match. These yeomen and their households emerge more clearly in the light of the more voluminous sixteenth-century records.

Below them came the husbandmen: middling to small peasant farmers or craftsmen-cum-farmers. Some worked about 20 acres of arable, but the vast majority had only ten acres or less and possessed no more than a few livestock. In the upland districts, a number might still be freeholders, holding what little land remained within their possession from the free communities. Others would be small leaseholders, tenants-at-will or sub-tenants of bigger men. In the former manorial lands, a large number were holding copyholds in what had previously been villein land. Copyholders had taken advantage of the absence of so many lords in the fifteenth century and the glut of land to strengthen their position. They now enjoyed a much greater security of tenure and a relatively favourable position in the eyes of the law. Others, who had originally been newcomers, had managed in many areas to establish themselves as successful avowry tenants.

The position of bondmen in all this was decidedly confused. Bond status had been slow to change in Wales during the later fourteenth century, mainly because both the King and Marcher lords had done their best, for financial reasons, to resist any change in the status of their bond tenants. But the tumults of the Glyndŵr Rebellion had caused many of them to flee, and later in the fifteenth century others were burdened with such heavy exactions that many of them took flight or were crushed almost into extinction. The whole or large parts of former bond townships in the north-west lay deserted and in the March, by mid-fifteenth century, if not sooner, villeinage was extinct. Not all, however, were able to escape from serfdom;

---

[24] *GPC*, s.n. 'iwmon'.

in 1449, and again in 1456, records show bondmen and their posterity, goods, and services being hawked around like so many cattle. Others, in return for substantial concessions, chose to stay, and some throve prodigiously, like a bondman of the commote of Menai of 1481–2, whose goods and chattels fetched no less than £26. 18s. 4d. and who, like many successful bondmen, married a free woman. This example indicates how, by the end of the fifteenth century and beginning of the sixteenth, differences of status between freemen and bondmen had long been unrealistic. The distinction between them had been so far eroded that, in 1500, the tenants of the duke of Buckingham alleged that that there were no 'bondmen of blood' left in his Welsh lordships. The duke's officers were unconvinced and insisted that 'better search be made' in the records and with some success.[25] A few years later, in much of north-west Wales, Henry VII formally freed the remaining bondmen.

Of the life of these peasants, who made up the majority of the population but almost never figured in the literary records, we know almost nothing. Fortunately, we have in a late fourteenth-century poem by Iolo Goch, directed to *Y Llafurwr* (not 'labourer', as it is often translated, but 'husbandman' or 'ploughman'), a virtually unique but deeply sympathetic insight into the small farmer's hard life. He is portrayed as patient, hard-working, and pacific, in sharp contrast to the graspingly competitive and aggressive upper classes, at whose mercy he usually found himself. The peasant would

> Make and follow no war,
> He'll oppress no one for his goods;
> He's never brutal with us
> Nor will he pursue false claims.
> Suffering is his seemly way,
> Yet there's no life without him.[26]

This concept of the simple, god-fearing peasant, on whom the whole world ultimately depends, is widely found in European and English verse too.

Below the husbandmen in the social order came the farm servants and the hired labourers. They were found mainly in the lowlands where the bigger arable farms required more intensive labour than was ordinarily called for in the upland crofts, with their greater emphasis on pastoral farming. Farm servants, often unmarried men or women living in, usually did better than the labourers in terms of more regular employment and better meals. The hired labourers, having perhaps an acre or two of land or a garden, had a more insecure existence. They were much more at the mercy of the ups and downs of the labour market and obliged to cobble together a living by dint of more than one occupation.

[25] Gray, 'Dispersal Crown Property', p. 53.　　[26] *OBWV*, pp. 45–8.

Lowest of all came the poor. They were made up of the aged, sick and incapacitated, and young orphans. Pictures from the Europe of this period appear to show a great many crippled or disabled beggars. But a society with such a low average productivity could not afford to support many dependants. The old were forced to work as long as they could and the young to earn their keep as soon as they were able. The poor depended on such charitable institutions as existed—monastic houses, hospitals, and the local clergy—but looked chiefly to informal hand-outs of food, clothing, fuel, and other necessities on the part of their charitable and well-disposed neighbours. Much is made in the poetry of the goodwill of patrons and their wives. Nest Stradling of West Place near Llantwit Major sewed woollen gowns and mantles with her own hand for the sick and needy; and Tudur Aled asked of one of his patrons, 'was ever a maid born with nobler and more generous heart?'[27] Many a charitable man also had his good deeds recorded. Lewys Glyn Cothi told how one of his patrons had furnished every charity in his hall—to young and old, orphans, widows, cripples, and the sick. Such references were intended not only to acknowledge the generous patrons' charity but were also calculated to spur others into giving more readily. Not all, however, were as open-handed or as soft a touch. Siôn Cent, mordant as ever, ran his stern and caustic rule over his contemporaries and condemned them for failing to carry out the seven works of mercy enjoined on them by Christ to relieve poverty and suffering and warned them of the punishment that would befall them in the Last Judgement. In addition to the calls of the poor, whom they had always with them, the charity of the better-to-do was put under further pressure in the lean years when bad harvests, high prices, and famine reduced many to the ranks of the needy who would, in more normal seasons, never have been found there. At such desperate times, petty thefts of food, clothing, and necessities, always prevalent among the poor, multiplied enormously.

SOCIAL RELATIONSHIPS

The nature of medieval religious teaching and prevailing concepts about the state of society emphasized its hierarchical and static qualities. Social distinctions were believed to reflect the divine ordering of society which men must accept in humble and uncomplaining duty. In practice, however, things tended to be very different; society was distinctly more mobile and competitive than theory acknowledged. The ruling élite—the nobility—was divided within itself and its members jockeyed unceasingly for advantage. They may perhaps have been primarily concerned for their own standing within those lands over which they ruled, but that reputation

[27] *TA*, p. 165.

depended to a great extent on the kind of 'good lordship' they could offer
lesser men. 'Good lordship' was itself, in turn, determined in no small
measure by their relationship to the King and the main sources of profit
and power. The greatest rewards came from service to the King and from
royal favour. Under the feeble Henry VI the extreme susceptibility of the
Crown to pressure from favourites led to the growth of faction which
accentuated divisions among the nobility and increased their competitiveness.
In the absence of strong government and any kind of impartial police force,
men were obliged to look all the more to the ties of good lordship for their
own security and well-being. The late medieval 'bastard feudalism' was not
a recent corruption; ties of dependence had always existed. What the
circumstances of the fifteenth century did was to focus men's attention
more keenly upon them.

The bonds of clientage ramified downwards from the grandees through
the gentry to the smaller fry. Ordinary men had to attach themselves,
formally or informally, to a powerful local figure who could act as their
immediate patron and protector. He himself would, in turn, have to be
linked to the affinity of one of the great aristocrats. When the Imperial
Knight, Ulrich von Hutten, declared, 'I must attach myself to some prince
in the hope of protection. Otherwise everyone will look on me as fair
plunder',[28] he was doing no more than voice the concern of every
subordinate figure in Europe. The process in Wales is illuminated for us by
John Wynn. He described how a freeholder of Crug, three miles from
Caernarfon, attached himself to the family of Cesail Gyfarch, fifteen miles
away, 'so desirous men were in those days to have a patron that could
defend them from wrong, though they sought him never so far off'.[29] The
Vaughans of Cesail Gyfarch were themselves attached closely to Jasper
Tudor and his Lancastrian following.

In the process of maintaining these relationships, acts of gross violence
might be perpetrated, criminals protected, property forcibly seized,
pressure put on juries and officers, and the law disregarded; but if an
individual wished to safeguard his own interests and those of his family, he
had virtually no option but to play the game by the rules of the time. Only
as a member of a band of retainers, kinsmen, or clients could he find some
reassurance. If that entailed a clash with other rival groups of the same
kind he had little choice but to face up to the obligation. Once more, John
Wynn's invaluable flesh-and-blood insights bring the psychology of the age
to life. Speaking of its 'bloody and ireful quarrels', with the 'revenge of the
sword at such liberty as almost nothing was punished by law whatever
happened', he illustrates the point with many references to the feuds
between the Thelwalls and the family of Gruffydd Goch, the Cyffins and

[28] Hale, *Renaissance Europe*, p. 24.   [29] *HGF*, p. 50.

the Trevors, John Owen and Hywel ap Madog Vaughan, Hywel ap Rhys and Evan ap Robert, and William Gruffydd and John ap Maredudd. Many such quarrels had, at their root, what Wynn called contention for 'sovereignty of the countryside'.[30] While Wynn's narrative reveals the acceptable face of the fifteenth-century concept of loyalty and honour, it also shows, even more plainly, another darker and more sinister visage in its frequent accounts of treacherous and unbridled ambushes, assaults, killings, and burnings. 'In that wild world every man stood upon his guard and went not abroad but in sort and so armed as if he went to the field to encounter with his enemies.' He dared not go to church on a Sunday without leaving his house 'guarded with men and have the doors bolted and barred', 'such was the fury of the revengement of blood'.[31] No doubt there were long undisturbed periods when conditions were nothing like so tense or violent, but at times of crisis men certainly needed the kind of protection good lordship might be hoped to offer.

Bonds of kinship, like those of good lordship—and they often went together—were another of the essential ties of the age. Links of kinship often formed the basis of a claim to land as well of clientage. Marriages were normally arranged so as to bind two families closer together or to reinforce existing alliances. Men looked for favours and patronage at the hands of their influential kinsmen, who then expected loyalty in return. When William Herbert took the field at Edgecote in 1469 he had rallied a great army—one of the biggest forces raised in fifteenth-century Wales— consisting in large part of his numerous kinsmen and their followers to support his cause. Both Jasper and Henry Tudor played the card of kinsman loyalty equally effectively. When Henry came to claim the throne in 1485 he dispatched letters to his kinsfolk offering them rewards for their loyalty and indenting on their sense of solidarity with their kin. Motifs of such appeals to the ties of blood and kin constantly recur during the period. Not that the nexus of kinship always worked so harmoniously in practice. The Wars of the Roses made men more cautious and led them to calculate more nicely who was likely to win and what they might be induced to offer as the price of support rather than to rally instinctively to a kinsman. Quite apart from any disputes kindled by faction and war, there might be serious splits between kinsmen in ordinary circumstances. Such quarrels could be more than usually bloodthirsty, 'deadly feuds' more dangerous than civil war. Not surprisingly, Maredudd ab Ieuan ap Robert moved out of Eifionydd because, as he said, 'I must either kill my own kinsmen or be killed by them'.[32] It was the intensity of such divisions that led poets to attach key importance to the role, which they shared with priests, of being conciliators between kinsfolk. The most celebrated of all the poems of this kind was Tudor Aled's magisterial *cywydd* to reconcile Hwmffre ap Hywel ap Siencyn of Ynysmaengwyn and his kinsmen. Tudur urged them to remember the tragic futilities of past internecine differences, from which only the English had benefited at Welsh expense—a favourite touch.[33]

Finally, there was that sense of personal honour, so prevalent among all those of gentle birth, rich and poor alike. At its best it could be productive of a Spartan willingness to brave almost any odds and a refusal to be cowed in face of danger. The reaction is typified in John Wynn's account of the exploit of his ancestor, John ap Maredudd, with his *plaid* [following] of some one hundred gentlemen (most of them minor ones, of necessity in such a group). John ap Maredudd, an *uchelwr* in the characteristic fifteenth-century mould, was a born fighter and leader of men. Ambushed and outnumbered, he inspired his associates with a blood-warming speech, reminding them of the honour of their ancestors and concluding that 'it should never in time to come be reported that there was the place a hundred North Wales gentlemen had fled, but that there a hundred north Wales gentlemen were slain'.[34] But, at its worst, this kind of reaction could descend to a touchy and wafer-thin sensitivity to slight, genuine or imaginary, and a grossly inflated sense of what was due to one; as when an unfortunate parson of Llanfrothen was killed at the instigation of an envious woman because he had taken someone else's child to foster instead of her own. Throughout all the praise poetry there ran the insistent and recurrent appeal, explicit and implicit, to the patron's sense of honour and his inescapable duty to prove himself worthy of the stock whence he came and to do nothing that would shame himself, his lineage, or his people. The twin poles of the ideal were courage and generosity: fearlessness in the face of threat or enmity and willingness to overthrow the oppressor, coupled with an open-handed benevolence and a concern to uplift the poor and defenceless. In a characteristic phrase Tudur Penllyn saw William Gruffydd as

> Oen Duw fydd wrth un difalch;
> Arthur ofeg wrth ryfalch.[35]

[A lamb of God to the humble; an Arthur in addressing the overmighty.]

This theme which had rung down the centuries with resonant overtones from Scripture and unmistakable echoes of Virgil—*parcere subjectos et debellare superbos*—had been a central motif in Welsh poetry from its beginnings. But it may have gained a new relevance in the fifteenth century when it chimed in so harmoniously with contemporary concepts of praising individuals of courage and honour who were also good lords and protectors.

---

[33] *TA*, p. 268.   [34] *HGF*, p. 26.   [35] *TP*, p. 10.

Indeed, the repeated emphasis on the theme may have been needed because the ideal was so often breached in practice. Seen from the angle of the receiving end of strong men's oppressions, the picture was very different. Siôn Cent, odd man out among the poets, critic of the rising establishment and voice of its radical opposition, condemned the 'false pomp' of Welsh poets who disingenuously praised their patrons for their supposed courage and generosity but maintained a craven silence concerning the wrongs they had done. He himself, ever sharp-eyed for the ruthlessness of the powerful, was scathingly critical of their shameless ways with the weak and defenceless:

> To ask for a good farmhold
> On his lands is an offence;
> He gets a weak man under
> His thumb, and seizes his place,
> Takes his farm from one who's blind,
> And takes another's acres,
> Takes the grain under ashtrees,
> Takes an innocent man's hay.
> Collects two hundred cattle,
> Gets the goods, and jails the man.[36]

A generalized criticism from a prejudiced source, admittedly, but it was one that may have often have been valid in that acquisitive, no-holds-barred society.

THE MATERIAL STANDARD OF LIVING

In an ambitious, competitive society like this, where not a few were thriving, it was to be expected that men should grasp eagerly at the possibilities open to them of an improved standard of living. The three basic needs which all had to meet, though with widely differing degrees of success and comfort, were housing, food, and dress. There was a fourth, personal service, of which only the better-off could avail themselves. Shelter, sustenance, and clothing, however, involved major items of expenditure for everyone; but, though the wealthy spent extravagantly on them, the poor were often hard put to find enough even to spend on food. What Philippe Ariès has described as late medieval man's 'passionate love for this world' and his stubborn recalcitrance at the prospect of having to give up at death all the material blessings he had accumulated and to which he had become habituated, finds expression in the poetry of Siôn Cent, the most trenchant Welsh critic of this addiction to luxury and pleasure. In a well-known poem, he excoriated all those contemporaries who viewed

[36] *OBWV*, pp. 54–6.

'death not only as an end to being but also a separation from having'.[37] In a series of swift, incisive strokes, he graphically sketched the unattractive spectacle of the rich man's unwilling leave-taking, at death, of his newly enclosed hall and stately whitewashed mansion; sumptuous feasts, choice wines, and golden drinking-horns; his many guests, mistresses, officers, bards, harpists, and singers; his gold brooches, rings, jewels, and treasure; his well-stocked wardobe and expensive garments; and his costly steeds, hounds, and falcons.[38] Within the limits of this single poem were strikingly, if censoriously and exaggeratedly, delineated most of the objects of successful men's ambition, delight, indulgence, and expenditure. Though the verdict, like that of most medieval poetry, was delivered in moral and religious terms, much of the underlying criticism was essentially economic and social in character.

Men certainly spent freely on better housing. The two and and a half centuries from 1400 to 1650 constituted one of the great ages of Welsh vernacular architecture.[39] The emergence in the fifteenth century of literally scores, if not hundreds, of craftsman-built houses, identifiable by their cruck frames, half-timbering, and smoke-blackened roof-timbers, reveals the relative peace and prosperity of Wales, compared with contemporary Scotland or Ireland, and the rise of the wealthier gentry and farmers eager and able to acquire new houses during the period, especially within the eastern counties, which were markedly more flourishing than those of the west. It also proves the existence of a corps of skilled workmen, for it took a body of highly trained carpenters to erect these houses—permanent homes for many of the upper reaches of the population appearing for the first time in the Welsh countryside. A number of Welsh towns are known to have been rebuilt with half-timbered houses, too (Cardiff, Brecon Machynlleth, Dolgellau, Caernarfon, and Beaumaris among others)—though only Ruthin today substantially preserves the half-timbered look of a Welsh town. Some notable houses built at this time still exemplify the superb and ambitious craftsmanship responsible for them. Bryndraenog in Radnorshire is the largest surviving medieval house of its kind in Wales and remains today a prosperous farmhouse, standing virtually complete. Another fine house still to be seen is Tretower Court in Breconshire, home of Sir Roger Vaughan, who rebuilt and considerably enlarged the accommodation there between 1457 and 1470. Not a few houses have long been used as barns; but, even though sadly neglected, like Tŷ Mawr at Castell Caereinion, they continue to reveal their impressive size and accomplished workmanship. Poets were encouraged to

---

[37] P. Ariès, *The Hour of Our Death* (Peregrine Books, 1983), pp. 130–1, 138.
[38] *OBWV*, pp. 54–8.
[39] P. Smith, *Houses of the Welsh Countryside* (London, 1975); R. R. Davies *et al.* (eds.), *Welsh Society and Nationhood*, (Cardiff, 1984), p. 122–60.

praise them extravagantly; Guto'r Glyn, visiting Sir Richard Herbert's fine new house at Coldbrook, which still stands, though much-altered, at the foot of Skirrid Fach, likened it to Arthur's legendary hall, Ehangwen. Large numbers of such houses survive today in the eastern counties of Wales. Apart from being unmistakable symbols of new wealth and enhanced status, these houses provided their inhabitants with greater warmth, comfort, and privacy. Medieval people suffered much more than we do from the cold and were more than ordinarily appreciative of the welcome of blazing hearths in large, commodious halls. Guto'r Glyn's blood ran warm and fast as he remembered the blazing heath at Cwchwillan with its double source of heat—coal and wood. Dafydd Nanmor, too, lovingly recalled the warmth and comfort of that princely bed' of 'softest feathers' in which he'd slept snug in Dafydd ap Thomas's house.[40]

The ordinary farmer's house was very different and cannot have been much dissimilar to those simple constructions of twigs and mud, built with little cost or labour and sufficient to last a year, which Gerald of Wales described. About 1480 *The Description of England* commented that in Wales,

> Their houses been low withal
> And made of yerdes small

while Andrew Boorde about 1530 confirmed that their 'lodging was poor and bare'.[41] The poet Llawdden, it may be recalled, had spoken of the ploughman and his beasts sharing the same quarters; and another, Llywelyn ab y Moel, dismissed with contempt the villein's turf-topped den. The humbler ranks found their miserable homes difficult to heat, light, or ventilate. The poorer they were, the greater the squalor in which they were forced to eke out their overcrowded and comfortless existence. They stored within their houses such rotting vegetable remains as could be used to feed animals; outside stood heaps of dung, usually right up against the walls, which frequently polluted streams or wells. In the absence of any furniture or comfort to speak of, it was not surprising to find people seeking the consolations of the nearby tavern whenever they could afford them.

As far as diet was concerned, all classes in society for much of the time ate frugally and monotonously. It may well be the inadequacies of an unvaried diet, with its serious vitamin and other deficiencies, which, in some measure, accounted for the nervous restlessness, irascibility, and sudden outbursts of temper that characterized much of contemporary behaviour. Yet it also seems likely that, from time to time, all classes ate extremely well; the wealthy far more often and more lavishly than the

[40] *DN*, pp. 54–5.   [41] Jones, *Trans. Cymmr.*, 1948, p. 362.

poor, naturally enough. These bouts of gastronomic indulgence, which tend to figure so prominently in the literature, were given greater attention because of the contrast between them and the scarcity which so often prevailed. The poor spent up to 80 per cent of their income on food; but even then, in times of bad harvests and dearth, they could never be sure of getting enough to eat. Only the well-to-do could afford to buy and store food in sufficient quantity to ensure that they never went hungry.

A traditional social virtue on which Welsh *uchelwyr* had always prided themselves was *perchentyaeth*—the art and practice of managing estates and maintaining a bountiful hospitality. They liked to think of themselves as keeping up an open house without gatekeeper or lock on the door. There still survives in Peniarth MS 147 an old Welsh treatise detailing minutely the wide range of meats, fish, soups, vegetables, and sweets that were served in contemporary feasts. It describes what constituted each course, the times of year when main dishes were in season, and how to prepare and serve them. Nothing gave poets greater delight than tuning their lays to commend the lavish entertainment offered by a generous patron. They can still make a modern reader's mouth water by their description of the delicacies indulged in: white bread (not the inferior, coarse dark stuff made of oats or rye most people had to eat), plenty of roast meats and fish of different kinds, choice vegetables, exotic fruits like oranges and grapes, sugar and spices, and a bewildering array of imported wines to pour down thirsty throats, together with the native beer, cider, and metheglin. After being feasted at one hall, Tudur Penllyn exclaimed rapturously: 'a long night passes all too quickly here' [*Bernos yw hirnos yn hon*]; while Lewys Glyn Cothi concluded that he had in truth arrived in Paradise [*Yma'r ydwyf ym Mharadwys*].[42] Of all the poets Tudur Aled and Lewys Glyn Cothi were perhaps the keenest connoisseurs of food and wine, with the most fastidious and educated palates. Both loved to roll the names of these vintages trippingly off the tongue—wines from Rhine, Rhone, and Rochelle, or Bordeaux, Burgundy, and Bayonne. It was a point of honour with each of their patrons, undoubtedly, to seek to uphold his dignity with as lavish and prestigious a feast as he could muster, and there may have been keen competition among them to outrival one another, egged on enthusiastically by the bards.

These munificent junketings were reserved for particular seasons of the year and special occasions in a family's history. The great occasions of the Christian calendar—Christmas, Easter, and Whitsun—and the feast of the patron saint of the parish [*gŵyl mabsant*] were among the most important. Weddings and christenings were also the scenes of joyous celebrations. Funerals of the great were solemn ceremonies, with the corpse being

[42] Bebb, *Machlud*, pp. 43–4.

escorted to its last resting-place by a large cortège of mourners: relatives, friends, poets, dependants, and poor men; the pomp and display being commensurate with the deceased's rank and wealth. At all these major celebrations, poor and unfortunate men and women looked in hopeful anticipation of sharing in such remainders of food, alms, and clothing as they might be offered.

The lesser orders, like the wealthy, indulged themselves on seasonal and family occasions as and when they could. Langland, in *Piers Plowman*, recalled that English labourers insisted on having roast meat or baked fish, but he also told how Piers, more typically, in the lean days before harvest confessed that he was reduced to cheese, oatcake, and a loaf of beans and bran. For a great part of the time, it is safe to conclude, ordinary men's diet consisted very largely of oatmeal bread, cheese, and soups and gruels made from cereals and vegetables, with stocks having to be stretched as far as possible until the new harvest arrived. Meat, and even eggs, must have been rare luxuries.

Of the clothing worn by people in Wales at this time little is known. Siôn Cent gave those strongly suggestive hints of rich men's craving for fashionable raiment and expensive finery (above, pp. 110–11); and Tudur Aled speaks admiringly of luxurious materials like cambric, camlet, damask, ermine, fur, velvet, or miniver worn by his patrons.[43] All this suggests that in Wales, as elsewhere, those who could afford it were intent upon displaying wealth, power, and status by means of extravagant and fashionable costume. Much less is known of what ordinary men wore. English observers were struck by the scantiness of Welsh people's clothing. Bare-legged but

> clothed wonder well
> In a shirt and in a mantell

and a 'crisp breech', they ventured forth in wind, rain, and cold to 'fight, play, stand, sit, lie and sleep'.[44]

PASTIMES AND RECREATIONS

Of all the occupations that filled the lives of the upper classes and those most closely attached to their service, war and fighting took the place of honour. The values and attitudes of an earlier heroic age still tended to prevail; and preparation and training for combat continued to dominate the life of the *uchelwyr*. Of the twenty-four feats considered to be the hallmark of breeding, about half were intended to build up and maintain bodily strength, agility, and skill in the handling of weapons. Nothing gave

[43] *TA*, pp. lxiv–lxv.
[44] G. D. Owen, *Elizabethan Wales: the Social Scene* (Cardiff, 1962), pp. 42–4.

the poets greater pride and pleasure than to be able to refer in tones of admiration to the accomplishment of these feats by their patrons. To keep up their skills, gentlemen frequently arranged competitive matches [*chwaraefa gampau*]:

The fashion was in those days that the gentlemen and their retinues met commonly every day to shoot matches and try masteries . . . and there spent the day in shooting, wrestling, throwing the sledge and other acts of activity.[45]

The tournament and hunting, both closely related to warfare and preparations for it, were an obsession. The poet Rhys Goch Eryri greatly admired the skill of Robert ap Maredudd, a champion of the twenty-four traditional feats, at fighting with spears in mock warfare at the lists. Hunting and hawking were tremendously popular in the many districts still luxuriously wooded and abounding with deer and other game. Such pursuits were, for all practical purposes, the monopoly of the upper class. They had the abundant leisure to devote to them; and to be able to sustain the hunting expeditions, with the horses, dogs, and falcons needed, was another means of proclaiming their status in the community. The many request poems provide an unmistakable indication of the way in which war, tournament, and hunting absorbed upper-class interest. Of all the gifts solicited, the majority by far are those connected with war and hunting: steeds, bows, swords, bucklers, coats of mail, hounds, hawks, woodknives, and hunting-horns.

In spite of the emphasis placed by the tradition of the twenty-four feats on combativeness, strength, and agility, they also included a wide range of gentler and more civilized intellectual and artistic attainments such as poetry, heraldry, music, literacy in Welsh, and games demanding mental dexterity like chess. In one of the most interesting and original poems of the period, Ieuan ap Rhydderch, a gentleman-poet of Cardiganshire, recounts his prowess at the physical achievements of muscular strength and co-ordination and with the art of hunting game—and ladies! But his main concern is to inform us, not without a little pardonable conceit, of his wide-ranging education, his cultural and intellectual attainment, and his skill at games likes chess and backgammon. He was, no doubt, a more than averagely bright and learned member of the gentry, but by no means unique. Guto'r Glyn praised one of his patrons for his knowledge of dialectic, law, languages, metre, grammar, astronomy, music, and Welsh prosody. Music and literature were clearly very popular among the *uchelwyr*. Among the most attractive tableaux presented to us is one of Lewys Glyn Cothi and his patron, Wiliam Siôn, reading and studying together history and literature, and another of Guto'r Glyn and Rhys of

Glyn Neath avidly poring over manuscripts. Another poet recounts the many kinds of musicians and entertainers wending their way to his patron's hall (below, pp. 163–4). Many of the *uchelwyr* and their women-folk could now read for themselves. This probably explains the growing fifteenth-century demand for manuscripts and the increasing interest in lay education.

Most of the contemporary culture, however, was still an oral phenomenon; a delight for the ear rather than the eye. Poetry was declaimed or sung to the assembled company—and how vastly it gains in meaning and appeal when read aloud, even today. Romances and tales were told orally around the fire by the professional *cyfarwyddiaid*, or more amateur storytellers, and music and songs performed in the same way. What we are less sure of is how far down the social scale it all percolated; among all the freemen fairly certainly, and among many of the peasants, no doubt. Even if some of them never got into the *uchelwyr*'s halls, they could not have been kept out of the taverns where the same kind of entertainment, though more debased and less highly professional, certainly thrived. Delight in poetry and song seems unquestionably to have been widely diffused among all the population.

The whole populace may have lived in the remembrance of one festival and the anticipation of the next; the poor more than the rich since their enjoyments were so much more restricted. In the course of a single year, age-old folk-custom, some of it pre-Christian in origin, as well as the calendar of the Church, provided people with plenty of opportunities for celebration on whatever scale they could manage. The Christmas season and the days that followed into the New Year were a time for roistering when poets, musicians, and other entertainers looked to the halls, great and small, for a welcome. Lent was preceded by wild carnival delights, and Easter ushered in a season of mixed religious and secular pageantry. The onset of May, as abundant poetic references leave us in no doubt, was a time of outdoor jollification and sexual licence, of dancing and merrymaking around the maypoles. St John's Eve was an occasion to celebrate fittingly, as was the ending of the corn harvest. So, too, were the fairs of late summer and autumn, until the declining days of October brought shades of All Hallows Eve and the dark winter evenings once more. Much of the gaiety of the age seems to have a frenetic edge to it; an intense craving to make the most of what chance there was to forget life's perils and precariousness—plague, disease, drudgery, famine, and poverty—and squeeze whatever joy was to be got out of the moment. The censures of Siôn Cent, and other moralists like him, on the fierce and uninhibited indulgence in the pleasures of the world and the flesh that they saw on all sides may have been directed chiefly, but by no means exclusively, at the rich. For most men and women a warm fire, full belly, alcoholic drink, responsive company, tuneful verse or song, merry tale, and lively dance were delights to be keenly savoured whenever opportunity offered. In the solace, such as it was, of the taverns, where there was warmth and good fellowship, where home-made drink was plentiful and cheap, where morals were sometimes lax and girls of easy virtue not unknown, they drank, talked, sang, swore, grumbled, and made love with rare good humour but hardly less frequently quarrelled uproariously too.

CHAPTER 5

THE CHURCH AND RELIGION

FOR the Welsh Church the Glyndŵr Rebellion had been the culmination of a long period of difficulty and dislocation. During a century beforehand the Church had had to contend with the effects of increasing intervention by the State, especially following the outbreak of the Hundred Years War, the severe disruption caused by the Black Death and other visitations of disease, depopulation and economic set-backs, and the rise of anticlericalism and heresy.[1] By the beginning of the fifteenth century, therefore, it was already in poor state to face the onset of several years of brutal and exhausting conflict during the Rebellion of 1400–10. The effects on ecclesiastical and religious life were catastrophic, and their malign consequences were being experienced well into the fifteenth century. In 1421 the bishop of Bangor maintained that it would take at least ten years to start improving the fruits of his diocese. His brother of Llandaff in 1428 declared his church and diocese to be in danger of total desolation on account of the Rebellion and pestilences. In the 1430s and 1440s a number of Welsh monasteries, widely scattered in different parts of the country, Abergavenny, Beddgelert, Basingwerk, Carmarthen, Conwy, Strata Florida, and Cymer, were all reported to be in serious difficulties, mainly of a financial kind. As late as 1468 Richard Edenham recounted the extreme poverty of his diocese of Bangor as a result of wars and rebellions which had long prevailed in those parts.

Rehabilitation was a slow and uphill process. The very universality and depth of the damage to the economy as a whole made the recovery of the Church an arduous task. Many of the higher clergy were, in any case, royal nominees and strangers to their dioceses, who were loth to venture among the hostile population of unreconciled and disordered Wales in the aftermath of rebellion. Neither the monarchy nor the aristocracy was particularly well-disposed to extend a helping hand to the unfortunate clerics. The high-flying ambitions of the Lancastrians in France and their chronic financial predicaments, not to mention the inflammation of Anglo-Welsh antipathy, ruled out royal help on any scale. A few of the great aristocrats were rather more helpful and some of the religious houses benefited from their patronage and protection. But, in the main, Welsh

---

[1] G. Williams, *The Welsh Church from Conquest to Reformation* (Cardiff, 1976).

clerics, having no option but to learn that God helped those who helped themselves, ensured recovery largely as a result of their own efforts. Thomas Franklin, abbot of Neath and later of Margam, was an outstanding example. During a period of some forty years after 1422 he was acknowledged to have restored and repaired the abbeys of both Neath and Margam in respect of the number of their monks and ministers, their divine worship, and their possessions.

Thanks to the efforts of men like Thomas Franklin, and still more to the gradual healing process at work in the structures of economic and social life, the Church was slowly but undoubtedly recovering. The pleas of poverty, so common earlier in the century, died away, and some of the clergy, among the seculars and regulars, were living comfortable, not to say luxurious, lives again. Among them were men like Maredudd ap Rhys, one among many priest-poets of the period, vicar of Rhiwabon from about 1430, and sinecure rector of Meifod and Welshpool by 1450 at least. Like many of the more substantial of the parish priests, he was descended of gentle lineage and was a married man. Another of the same sort was Dafydd ap Thomas of Faenor in Cardiganshire. He was a patron to Dafydd Nanmor, a poet more than usually demanding in the standards of hospitality and comfort he looked for from his benefactors. But in Dafydd ap Thomas he found one who lived as well as any lay gentleman, and his well-spread table, and his comfortable beds particularly, fully matched up to the poet's exacting requirements. Siôn Mechain, parson of Llandrunio in Montgomeryshire, lived in a fine new hall, described with gusto by that discerning judge, Guto'r Glyn. Other clerics recovering their former status and material well-being were Cistercian abbots, also drawn from leading *uchelwyr* families. Abbot Rhys of Strata Florida (d. 1441) was ecstatically praised by Guto'r Glyn in the poet's early days. Rhys was a man of breeding as competitive and as insistent upon his rights as his lay brethren. His desire to assert what he considered to be Strata Florida's rightful position of leadership in Ceredigion emerged in his furious quarrels with the abbot of Vale Royal over Llanbadarn, his attempts to refurbish the abbey's buildings, his lavish hospitality, and his ultimate death in a debtor's prison at Carmarthen as a result of overtaxing his resources. His fellow-abbot, Siôn, at Valle Crucis was sprung 'from the heart of the Trefor clan' [*o ganol llwyth Trevawr*].[2] Patron of the master poet and genealogist, Gutun Owain, he is presented in the latter's poems as one of the *grands seigneurs* among Welsh Cistercians. A feature of Gutun's poems is the repeated suggestion that Siôn Trefor ought to be appointed bishop of St Asaph, something quite contrary to the normal royal practice for a century of insisting on intruding non-Welshmen into Welsh dioceses.

[2] *GO*, I, 125.

There are other signs of recovery in the Church from mid-century
onwards. One of the most notable is the wide-ranging programme of
churchbuilding, which parallels that remarkable wave of the building of
secular homes already commented upon. As with the houses, the best
churches are concentrated in the thriving north-east and south-east corners
of Wales. Nevertheless, in almost all parts of the country from about the
1460s, at least, down to the 1530s, all the indications are that parishioners
were eager to embark on ambitious schemes to enlarge and beautify their
churches. This activity has usually been attributed in the past to the
improved order and stability said to have been introduced by Henry Tudor
after 1485. But there is every reason to believe that it had begun a
generation before the battle of Bosworth was fought, though it also
proceeded in full swing for some fifty years after 1485. In a number of the
most impressive medieval churches surviving in Wales, rebuilding had
begun as early as the reigns of Henry VI and Edward IV. Gresford was
started c.1460, Wrexham c.1463, Tenby c.1461–75, and St John's, Cardiff,
c.1473. Other outstanding achievements are to be attributed to the early
Tudor period, when the enthusiasm for churchbuilding gained momentum.
Such were the works at the two northern cathedrals of Bangor and St
Asaph, the Perpendicular building at Clynnog, the tower of Wrexham, the
screen at Conwy, the roodloft at Newtown, and the 'Stanley' churches at
Gresford, Northop, and Mold. Many parish churches were enlarged
greatly by the building of an additional nave or aisle. The best-known are
the remarkable series to be found in Denbighshire and Flintshire, though
they also exist in other parts of Wales, including the south-western diocese
of St Davids. In the north-western diocese of Bangor, where the churches
tended to be smaller and poorer, the same purpose was attained more
simply and cheaply by adding a transept level with the east end of the
church. Such enlargements have occasionally been explained as resulting
from the need to house a larger population. That seems improbable,
however, in an age when population was lower than it had been in earlier
centuries and was either static or only increasing very slowly. It seems
more likely that the building programmes arose out of the growing
popularity of the cult of the BVM and the urge in many parishes to provide
a Lady Chapel. It is not inconceivable, of course, that the growth of the
cult itself may have attracted more people to attend church services.

Other parishes were set on adorning their churches with new towers or
windows. A number of handsome crocketed and pinnacled towers, which
were one of the special attractions of Perpendicular building, were
constructed in Wales late in the medieval period. Particularly handsome
specimens were erected in the south-east at Cardiff and Newport, and in
the north-east at Gresford and Wrexham, the latter of which was reputed
to be one of the 'seven wonders' of old Wales. Many churches also

proceeded to enlarge their windows in the Perpendicular style. The object of these windows was to give the chance to a worker in stained glass to display his art and, especially, to provide the illiterate worshippers with 'poor men's Bibles' illustrating stories from the Old and New Testaments, apocryphal literature, and the lives of the saints. Most of the stained glass has long since disappeared or survives only in shattered fragments.[3] But, at the little church of Llanrhaeadr Dyffryn Clwyd, the remarkable preservation of a 'Jesse window' depicting the royal lineage of Christ in the 'stem of Jesse'—an interesting comment on the contemporary passion for genealogy—gives an inkling of the beauty that once might have been common in parish churches. First erected in 1533, the window was taken down and hidden in Commonwealth times and re-erected at the Restoration.

Other outlets for the inspiration and craftsmanship of the contemporary masons were churchyard crosses and fonts. The Vale of Glamorgan must once have been rich in these crosses, judging by the three which still survive at Llangan, St Donat's, and St Mary Hill. Other fine examples also survive in north-east Wales, at Newmarket and Hanmer in Flintshire and Derwen in Denbighshire. The feature of them all is the exquisite care which the sculptor took to carve moving representations of the passion and death of Christ and images and symbols of the saints. The same was true of many of the fonts installed at this time, the best of which, the magnificent font at Wrexham, strikingly depicts the emblems of the passion. Some of the Welsh abbeys, too, embarked on ambitious and extensive building programmes in the fifteenth century. William Herbert, earl of Pembroke, who was buried at Tintern in 1469, left a hundred tons of stone for the works proceeding there when he made his will. At Valle Crucis a major reconstruction was undertaken in the fifteenth century to provide, among other things, a new hall and chamber for the abbot. Similar changes were also effected at Basingwerk, Conwy, and Neath. All these developments indicated a greatly improved financial condition within these abbeys and a desire not only to repair and refurbish buildings but also for greater comfort and a measure of ostentation on the part of the abbot.

The art of the mason, however, probably has less merit and individuality than that of the carpenter. Elaborate work in stone tends to be typical of rich low-lying country and prosperous towns. Not much of it could be expected in an upland country like Wales, where good timber was, in any case, in better supply than good building stone. The expertise of contemporary carpenters has already been commented on in the discussion of the number of fine houses built during this period (above, pp. 111–12). Much of the very best woodwork put up at this time may have been lost when monasteries and friaries disappeared during Henry VIII's reign and

---

[3] M. Lewis, *Stained Glass in North Wales up to 1850* (Altrincham, 1970).

again in the process of later 'restoration'; but a great deal survives even today. The roodscreens and roodlofts erected during the latter half of the fifteenth century and the first decades of the sixteenth remain the crowning glory of Welsh parish churches of the late medieval period.[4] They were found in all parts of Wales and traces of no fewer than 300 of them have been discovered, some in the south-western counties where not a single screen survives. Some of the best examples still left to us are to be found in churches off the beaten track, like Llananno in Radnorshire or Patrisio in the Black Mountains. The church at Llanfilo in Breconshire, where the loft has been sensitively restored with modern carvings of saints and a modern rood above, can today convey much of the overwhelming impact that the rood depicting Christ's sacrifice might have made on the medieval worshipper. Most of the roods in Wales appear to have been carved by native 'schools' of carpenters, whose work is characterized by vitality, exuberance, and a joyous inventiveness. The handful of wooden images and statues further indicate what we may well have lost by the disappearance of most of those which flourished in such profusion in medieval churches. One of the most striking remains of the masterly woodcarving that went into them is the 'Sleeping Jesse' at Abergavenny Priory. Massive, dignified, and assured in its detail as well as its conception, it must have been a figure of tremendous power and beauty when complete. Other vestiges, like the 'Bound Rood' of Mostyn at Bangor cathedral, the fragmentary roods from Mochdre and Kemys, now in the National Museum, and carvings at Betws Gerful Goch or Llanelian yn Rhos, give us more than a hint of the moving intensity with which they and many others like them once conveyed the anguish of the stricken Saviour to the medieval congregation.

Excellent woodwork by Welsh carpenters could also be seen in the many church roofs which were put up during this period, from the handsome St Davids roof of Irish bog-oak and the delightful carvings at Tenby and Haverfordwest to the excellent roofs at Cilcain and Llangollen at the opposite end of Wales. The roof at the little church of Gyffin, just outside Conwy, is one of almost unique interest, still preserving its canopy of honour, with its painted panels of saints, which may at one time have been a common feature in Welsh churches. Another means by which the woodcarver could remind parishioners of Christ's suffering was to chisel out the familiar emblems of the passion—the cross, ladder, crown of thorns, five wounds, cock, scourge, spear, sponge, nails, whip, pincers, and hammer—on the parish chest or any other wooden surface that lent itself to the purpose.

Though Welsh parishes were not as wealthy as many others, the art of

[4] F. H. Crossley, 'Screens, Lofts and Stalls stituated in Wales and Monmouthshire', *Arch. Camb.*, XCVII–CVII (1943–58).

the jeweller and craftsman in precious metals was nevertheless widely represented in church plate, ceremonial crosses, images, candelabra, and the like. Naturally the most lavish endowment was to be found in the cathedrals, religious houses, wealthier parish churches, and the most popular places of pilgrimage. Teilo's famous shrine at Llandaff, placed in the Lady Chapel there, was an elaborate treasure, containing the images of the three saints associated with the cathedral—Teilo, Dyfrig, and Oudoceus—and weighing many hundreds of ounces. There were, in addition, silver figures of the twelve apostles and a large quantity of silver plate. A particularly handsome golden chalice and paten, thought once to have belonged to the abbey of Cymer, were found in 1891 in rocky and inaccessible country near Dolgellau and are now preserved in the National Museum. However, the despoliation of so many of the Church's treasures during Edward VI's reign, and the wholesale remodelling of church plate during Elizabeth's, have meant that hardly any genuine pre-Reformation church goods have survived.

Only scattered fragments, too, remain of the costly and beautiful vestments which the inventories compiled in Mary's reign, or the bequests in contemporary wills, tell us were once so usual a sight in the parish churches. They not only brought warmth and colour into the services but were, again, designed to try to impress upon the illiterate the significance of what was being undertaken on their behalf. Each vestment had its own meaning: the long alb betokened the white cloth in which Christ was clothed; the chasuble the cloth of purple mockingly placed upon him as 'King of the Jews'. The colours, too, had their own symbolism: red for Holy Week and the Jesus Mass (celebrated on 7 August), blue for confessors, and white fustian for Lent.

Finally, many of the church walls were painted with frescoes which, perhaps, most unforgettably of all, reminded people of religious scenes and narratives. The setting most frequently depicted was that of the Last Judgement. It was normally painted above and on each side of the chancel arch, so that the whole congregation could not fail to be reminded of the final adjudication that awaited every earthly soul, with the divine judge rewarding the blessed and consigning the wicked to eternal punishment. Other popular subjects were the closing episodes of Christ's life on earth: the Last Supper, washing Peter's feet, the agony in Gethsemane, the arrest, the mockery, the mob clamouring for the Crucifixion, and the bearing of the cross on the *via dolorosa*. One such tableau, measuring 29 feet long by 6 feet high, once graced the walls of old Llanwddyn church before it was submerged under the waters of a new dam, and another of the same kind has come to light very recently in the shape of the remarkable series of frescoes discovered in the little church of Llandeilo Talybont, near Llanelli. Another favourite figure was St Christopher bearing the child

Jesus, which still livens the north wall of Llantwit Major church. But of all the surviving wall paintings in Wales probably the best-known is that of the 'Seven Works of Mercy' on the walls of Rhiwabon church.

It is not easy to tell who was responsible for providing the inspiration and the money for much of this churchbuilding. The bishops and clergy are known to have inspired and financed a good deal of it. Bishop Richard Redman of St Asaph (1471–93) took the initiative for restoring the transepts and perhaps the choir, building a new screen, and putting in the fine canopied stallwork at his cathedral. Bishop Thomas Skeffington (1509–33) built the tower, the nave arches, and the clerestory at Bangor. Prominent abbots like Dafydd ab Owain and Leyshon Thomas took the lead in building and extending at their own monasteries at Conwy and Neath, and almost certainly raised the finance to be able to do so. Many of their humbler colleagues were, within the limits of their capacity, just as active. A vicar of Brecon, Thomas ab Ieuan, as his fellow-townsmen testified, had contributed generously towards the building of churches, buying of vestments, giving of chalices, and other such charitable acts, 'together with the great reparations he had made in the priory [of Brecon] amounting about to the sum of one hundred pounds'.[5] Illustrious lay figures—Richard III, Henry VII, Jasper Tudor, Margaret Beaufort, William Herbert, Rhys ap Thomas, and Matthew Cradock among them—were all disposed to extend their patronage to churchbuilding. In some towns, guilds and fraternities made handsome contributions towards maintaining the fabric and services. At Brecon, chapels were kept up by guilds of craftsmen, while Presteigne's population of about 900 maintained four such fraternities. In most of the parishes, however, it was the well-disposed parishioners, whether formally grouped into guilds or not—and comparatively few of them seem to have been so organized in Wales—who were responsible for making a communal effort when extensions, adornments, repairs, or replacements were believed to be needed. A rare and revealing glimpse of what happened in Abergavenny and, *mutatis mutandis*, in many other towns no doubt, comes from a lawsuit of 1537. The parishioners there had had to find the money for placing a new peal of bells in the church tower. Elderly townsmen testified how they had each paid their share of the cost, and one recalled how his father had helped to set them up, as well as contributing his share of the expense. A number of others were named as having gone about 'into the country with games and plays' to raise funds. In the end, the town had had to launch a second round of subscriptions to raise all the money needed.[6] How reminiscent it is of many similar ventures in our own time. More information of the same

[5] *Records of the Court of Augmentations relating to Wales and Monmouthshire*, ed. E. A. Lewis and J. C. Davies (Cardiff, 1954), p. 23.

[6] Williams, *Welsh Church*, p. 459.

general kind comes from the wills of the period, where legacies in cash and in kind were regularly bequeathed to the testators' parish churches and other churches too. Sir Thomas Salusbury, for instance, left £20 in his will for the Carmelites' church at Denbigh and at the same time left them twelve mares and a horse called 'y glas benllyn'.[7]

One cannot but be impressed by the great fund of goodwill in the contemporary attitudes towards contributions to churchbuilding. All the evidence points to this as having been an age when local piety—and pride—were strong enough to have inspired the populace to contribute generously to the adornment of the churches. Many were deeply devoted towards their places of worship and anxious not only to enlarge and beautify them but also to do so in a way that should increase the effectiveness of the Church in conveying its message, especially to the large army of illiterates. It was not, of course, a simple uncomplicated matter of the devotion of lay folk to their churches and a widespread and deep-seated piety. Men's motives are rarely as unmixed or unworldly as that. If it would be invincibly cynical to doubt that sincere devotion was a primary and compelling force, it would be blissfully unsuspecting to conclude it was the only one. When testators left money for the churches in their wills they were moved by fear as well as fervour, by pride no less than piety. The clergy who drew up the wills for them were in a strong position, which they did not neglect, to influence such testamentary dispositions. Late medieval moralists were not without misgivings about the 'pomp and pride' of this world which impelled men to spend lavishly on churches.

One of the reasons for rebuilding, extending, and adorning churches was the upsurge of enthusiasm for pilgrimages. These building schemes were, to a surprisingly large extent, determined and financed by the worshippers who could be attracted to relics, images, and other sacred objects housed in churches. The urge to pay homage to holy places was, it need hardly be said, much older than the fifteenth century, and the best-known pilgrim attractions, abroad and at home, had been as familiar to people in Wales as those of other countries. Jerusalem, Rome, Santiago, Canterbury, Gloucester, St Davids, Bardsey, and Clynnog had long attracted the devout and the curious in their search for the health of body and soul. But in the second half of the fifteenth century and the beginning of the sixteenth, greater prosperity and more settled conditions gave a fresh impetus to pilgrimages. The Stradlings were but one of several families whose members ventured as far as the Holy Land to become Knights of the Holy Sepulchre. Additional pilgrims were attracted to Rome by the proclamation of a jubilee in 1450 by Pope Nicholas V, as poems by Robin Ddu and others testify. Santiago, too, attracted many, in spite of the

[7] Williams, *Welsh Church*, p. 460.

hazards of a long sea-journey across the terrifying rollers of the Bay of Biscay. The memory of Saint James and his pilgrimage is still perpetuated in a window at the church of Llanasa; and two pilgrims to Santiago, at least, lie buried in Wales beneath graves embellished with the saint's scallop shell, while a third, Siôn ap Rhys ap Siancyn of Glyn Neath, was buried at Neath in a now unidentifiable grave.

One of the most interesting features of the latter half of the fifteenth century was the sudden uprush in the popularity of many new local shrines, either in Wales or just over the border in places like Hayles or Chester. The two main focuses of this new devotion were the roods and the images of the BVM. Famous roods, which can hardly have been installed before the second half of the fifteenth century, like those at Llangynwyd, Brecon, Bangor, Rhuddlan (*yr Iesu gwyn*—'the blessed Jesus'), and Tremeirchion were regularly resorted to, as the many contemporary poems addressed to them testify. The aspect of Christ's death seized upon by all the poets is the agony of his sufferings. Like so much fifteenth-century art, it focused attention upon the pain and horror. Christ hung tortured on the cross, the crown of thorns biting into his head, and his wounded body dripping blood. The emphasis is on physical torment, which is portrayed in word, just as in wood, with that detailed and unsparing realism which seemed best able to release the deepest springs of medieval susceptibility. One senses the risk in all this that the individual rood was itself becoming a wonder-working icon and assuming the largest place in the worship of its devotees rather than the merits of the great sacrifice of which it was the symbol. It was this kind of attitude which was to give rise later to the comment of a sixteenth-century reformer that 'such was the habitual blindness' that 'images seemed better than the blessed God'.[8]

Along with her son, the BVM, who had throughout the Middle Ages been fervently venerated in Wales, was the subject of a new and more intense adoration in the fifteenth century. She seemed to her votaries to embody all that was tenderest and most compassionate in Christianity and to be the supreme expression of a mother's love and devotion. The cult of her Rosary acquired immediate and widespread popularity; and poets frequently make mention of carrying rosary beads in one hand, a taper in the other. Much of the contemporary churchbuilding was undertaken in honour of the Virgin and designed to accommodate her devotees. More chantries, guilds, fraternities, and bequests in wills honoured her name than that of any other saint, just as her shrines and wells outnumbered all others and drew greater numbers of pilgrims. She figured far more prominently than anyone except her son in miracle plays, poems, and prose texts, though most of this literary material is based not on biblical

---

[8] Williams, *Welsh Church*, pp. 506–7, 540–1.

narrative but on apocryphal literature or the *Legenda Aurea*. These authors were inclined heavily to stress her influence in the Last Judgement, almost at the expense of the merits of her son. Even when all allowance has been made for the inbuilt tendency of Welsh verse to exaggerate and overpraise, it is at times difficult to avoid the conclusion that there was a widespread and deeprooted belief that nothing mattered more in the final balance of souls than having Mary for one's advocate. Nowhere does this come out more pointedly than in those poems not specifically directed to her, as for instance in some of Tudur Aled's elegies, where Mary is frequently regarded as having it virtually within her power to grant admission to Heaven to the dead man.[9]

This kind of close association between the vogue for pilgrimages and poetry is a reminder that another symptom of the recovery of the Church is the renewed demand for religious literature during this period. There was a centuries-old tradition in Wales of such composition, in prose and verse, prolific in quantity and excellent in quality. Much of the prose consisted of translations into Welsh of a wide variety of biblical texts, manuals of instruction, prayers and hymns, works of piety and devotion, apocryphal literature, visions of Heaven and Hell, and lives of the saints. These vernacular texts, when they originated in the thirteenth century, had been designed to provide instruction in their own language for the more unlearned priests who had little knowledge of Latin. The translations still continued to fulfil that function; but they had come increasingly to meet the needs of the growing number of literate lay men and women who were deeply concerned about matters of faith and belief. Among the highly important collections of religious prose copied in the fifteenth century were texts such as Llanstephan MS 28, reputedly transcribed by Gutun Owain, and the now-lost White Book of Hergest. An important school of Glamorgan prose translators also flourished in the fifteenth and sixteenth centuries and was responsible for Welsh versions of texts like John Mirk's *Liber Ffestialis*, first published early in the fifteenth century, *Gesta Romanorum*, and Henry Parker's very popular *Dives et Pauper*. But the translators of this school continued their work into the sixteenth century, publishing post-Reformation works.[10] Lives of the saints were particularly in demand at the end of the Middle Ages, and Welsh manuscripts included the translation by Huw Pennant, antiquary and poet, of much of the most celebrated of all compilations of saints' lives, the *Legenda Aurea*.

The favourite themes of the prose literature were widely echoed in contemporary verse. Poems to Welsh and other saints, deriving their inspiration from the prose *vitae*, abounded. Many of these poems were closely linked with shrines particularly associated with an individual saint

[9] *TA*, pp. 284, 289, 324, 336, 349, 372, 375.
[10] Williams, *Tradd. Llen. Morg.*, pp. 176 ff.; Lewis, *GCH*, III, 550–4.

and seem likely to have been commissioned with the express intention of publicizing the power of the saint and his/her image or relic to convey favours to the devotees. Two of the most popular saints, and both the subject of a whole series of poems drawing freely on the prose literature, were the image of the BVM at Penrhys in the Rhondda, which attracted the addresses of three generations of Glamorgan poets, and the shrine of Gwenffrewi [Winifred] at Holywell, whose well was, and is, one of the most magnetic and sought-after sources of healing in England and Wales. Similarly, the frequent poems on the passion of Christ were inspired not only by the great roods which became so attractive to the pilgrims but also as a result of reading the much-favoured apocryphal 'Gospel of Nicodemus'. Another genre of contemporary religious poetry evoking a strong response was that given such extensive currency by Siôn Cent and his followers (see above, pp. 26–7). One of the most interesting of a number of poets profoundly influenced by Siôn Centian motifs was a gentleman-poet of Glamorgan, Llywelyn ap Hywel ab Ieuan ap Goronwy, whose surviving verses are almost wholly concerned with religion. Sombre in tone, gaunt and lapidary in expression, Llywelyn seemed preoccupied with man's awesome moral and religious responsibility. His poetry raises a number of considerations of more than ordinary interest. It gives us an exceptionally full and vivid impression of how the weighty issues of sin and repentance, judgement and grace, were balanced in the mind of an unusually thoughtful and articulate man of the period. The gloom is certainly illumined by hope; nevertheless, the prevailing tones are those of unease and apprehension. Moreover, much of the initiative for expressing this scrupulous concern for religious truth and meaning appears to have passed from clerics to devout laymen like Llywelyn. Finally, he was not alone in his preoccupations; they were shared by many others, judging by the relatively large number of manuscript copies of his poems and those of others like him which have come down to us.[11]

The southern parts of Wales—Glamorgan especially, Gwent to a lesser extent, and Carmarthenshire—were also the scene at this time of the emergence of what was to become a widely appealing form of poetic expression in the sixteenth and seventeenth centuries. This was the *cwndid* or religious poem in the 'free' metres, which certainly began to be composed in the fifteenth century, if not earlier, though hardly anything has survived from before the early sixteenth century. Such poems might be written by professional poets, literary-minded gentlemen, or clerics. Containing as they do the medieval sermon themes, they may well have been intended to counter-balance the shortcomings of the priests as preachers and the fewness of sermons preached in Welsh. Simpler and

[11] J. M. Williams, 'The Works of Some Fifteenth-Century Glamorgan Poets' (MA Thesis, Cardiff, 1923).

more debased in technique than the classical *cynghanedd* poetry, they made free use of colloquial and dialect forms. Poetry of this general kind was to become an extremely important medium later in the sixteenth and seventeenth centuries for conveying the truths of the Reformation in the work of men like Thomas Llywelyn of Rhigos, or still more significantly in the verse version of the Psalms by Edmwnd Prys or the poetry of Vicar Prichard (see below, pp. 444–5).

The most diverting of the new trends in literature was the appearance, for the first time in Welsh, of religious dramatic literature. Four Welsh plays have survived—two mysteries and two moralities. The linguistic evidence of the texts indicates that they were composed during the second half of the fifteenth century or early in the sixteenth. They were not mere translations and the most convincing explanation of their origin is that they drew heavily on the common stock of such literary material as was widely diffused throughout Europe. The plays were independently devised for, and perhaps by, Welsh players' guilds, at some time during the latter half of the fifteenth century. The strongly defined characteristics of the Powys dialect of the north-east and the less clearly marked traces of the Glamorgan dialect of the south-east to be discerned in the language of the plays give us an indication of the regions in which they may have been performed—once more the lead seems to be taken by the prosperous eastern communities. In the *cwndidau* and in the plays, we again have an expression of the steadily rising interest of some laymen in matters of religion and their willingness to take the initiative in trying to propagate religious ideas and bring them to the attention of others.

At the time, also, there are a few slight symptoms of the restoration of better ecclesiastical discipline. The absence of bishops' registers and of a reliable series of monastic records makes it difficult to be sure on this score. But in the registers of St Davids from 1486 onwards, the only ones to survive, discipline seems to be well maintained in such matters as putting checks on appropriations, inquiring into the illegitimate birth of certain priests, punishing criminous clerks and heretical talk, and regularizing grammar schools. The most influential of the religious orders, the Cistercians, were obviously going through a period of tightened discipline as compared with an earlier period. Houses were being more frequently visited and misdemeanours brought to light and punished. That formidable visitor and reformer of the 1490s, Marmaduke Huby, carried out a number of energetic reforms among Welsh houses, in spite of acrimonious rivalries between him and representatives of Clairvaux and his own ill-concealed animus against the Welsh. In the early Tudor period, under the leadership of such abbots as Dafydd ab Ieuan of Valle Crucis and Dafydd ab Owain of Conwy—both of them appointed bishops of St Asaph—and Leyshon Thomas of Neath, the Welsh Cistercians enjoyed a brief Indian summer.

For a short while, Cistercian abbots were again outstanding figures on the Welsh scene, six or seven of them, at least, being university graduates, some being in close contact with the General Chapter of the Order, and two or three employed on important disciplinary missions.

By the beginning of the sixteenth century, the Church had, to all appearances, come through its 'time of troubles' very well. It was a remarkable tribute to the essential stability of ecclesiastical life that the Church should have emerged with its possessions not seriously diminished. Only a few small alien priories had disappeared in the fifteenth century because of their connection with French mother houses. The prestige, privileges, and property of its clergy were still such as to attract some of the best-educated men of the age. Popular devotion appeared to be flourishing and heretical critics had been extirpated or driven underground. But there were inner weaknesses which belied this proud façade. The crises through which the Church had passed during the two preceding centuries had taken their toll. They had whittled away, from within, a good deal of the former strength and substance. Much of the life of the Church was controlled by laymen and many of its clergy were tainted by secularism. The life of the religious orders, once the spearhead of zeal and commitment, had become indolent and complacent. The higher clergy were most of them tied too closely to the State and too widely separated from the parish priests. The large majority of the latter were badly educated and, in many instances, incapable of giving the kind of lead and example looked for by an increasing minority of literate and earnest lay men and women. In much of the contemporary religious observance, an excessive emphasis tended to be placed on externals and too minute a concern displayed in the mechanical means of obtaining grace.

In the course of the fourteenth and fifteenth centuries the kings of England had greatly increased their control over the choice of bishops and other higher clergy in Wales. Bishops were often Civil Servants rewarded for their services to the Crown with their distant dioceses, which they rarely if ever visited and from which they were often fairly quickly translated to other more rewarding sees. Other bishops were abbots who derived their main income from their abbeys but craved the prestige and privileges of being a bishop—even in such small and unlucrative sees as those of north Wales. Some were friars, often confessors to the King or Queen, including the most extraordinary example of all, George de Athequa, Catherine of Aragon's confessor, made bishop of Llandaff in 1517. Most of the bishops were not Welsh and had little or nothing in common with most of their priests. True, Henry VII appointed two Welshmen to the diocese of St Asaph—Dafydd ab Ieuan and Dafydd ab Owain—and two to St Davids—John Morgan and Edward Vaughan—though less on account of their nationality than of their services to him. The large majority of the canons of cathedrals were men of the same sort: devoted servants of the Crown, rewarded for their services with a clutch of profitable, non-resident sinecure canonries at a number of cathedrals; big-scale pluralists and absentees to a man. The leadership in the Welsh dioceses was entrusted to men who, by training, experience, and inclination, were unlikely ever to put themselves in opposition to the Crown, whatever its line of policy.

Not all the higher clergy, naturally, could be absentees. Some of them had to be men drawn from local families and resident at the cathedrals. Many were of *uchelwyr* stock, not all that significantly different from their lay *confrères* in attitudes and values, sometimes married men with children, living in comfort, generous patrons of poets, and ambitious to make their way in the world for their own sake and that of their families. One of the most remarkable of them was Robert ap Rhys of the diocese of St Asaph. Son of Rhys Fawr, Henry VII's standard-bearer at Bosworth, Oxford graduate and protégé of Wolsey, he acquired a large number of benefices, leased monastic estates from Conwy, Strata Marcella, and the Hospitallers, bought up temporal lands, and was said to be able to lay his hands on £2,000 in plate and cash. He was married and had twelve sons and four daughters. Three of the sons became heads of the well-known gentry houses of Rhiwlas, Plas Iolyn, and Pantglas; two others became abbots of Strata Marcella and Conwy; and all the daughters married well. The career of Robert ap Rhys is a reminder that within the ranks of the Church was a potential fifth column of men largely secularized and not in the least averse from aligning themselves with royal policy to confirm and extend their gains.

There were others not unlike Robert ap Rhys among the parish clergy. Hywel ap Dai, sinecure rector of Whitford, one of the best livings in Flintshire, was also a married man. A descendant of the princes Rhodri Fawr and Rhirid Flaidd, he lived in comfort at his family home in Northop, cultivating his patrimony and keeping hospitality in traditional style. He welcomed poets as eminent as Guto'r Glyn and Dafydd ab Edmwnd, Lewys Môn and Gutun Owain. His son succeeded him there and, years later, in 1563, his grandson was still enjoying the rectory and was dislodged only as a result of a Star Chamber suit brought against him by the bishop of St Asaph. Clerics of this kind, though not uncommon among the clergy, were the exception rather than the rule. The evidence of the *Valor Ecclesiasticus* of 1535 concerning the monetary value of Welsh livings of the time makes it plain that most of the Welsh clergy were not particularly well-off and some were desperately poor. This analysis of the *Valor*'s evidence, set out in the table, serves to make the position clear. Of the 745 livings listed altogether in the *Valor*, 558 or seven out of ten were worth less than £10 a year, and 192 of them, at less than £5, were wretchedly

	Total	Over £20	£10–20	£5–£10	Under £5
St Davids	340	16 (4.5%)	62 (18%)	168 (50%)	94 (27.5%)
Llandaff	187	5 (3%)	34 (18%)	83 (45%)	65 (34%)
Bangor	112	17 (15%)	39 (35%)	43 (39%)	13 (11%)
St Asaph	156	15 (9%)	49 (32%)	72 (46%)	20 (13%)
Total	795	53 (6%)	184 (23.5%)	366 (46%)	192 (24%)

poor. Furthermore, these figures, depressing as they are, take no account of the equally numerous unbeneficed clergy who were even worse off. Closer examination of the evidence for typical deaneries, like that of Pembroke in Pembrokeshire or Subaeron in Cardiganshire, reveals the painful truth that the incumbents of a majority of the better benefices were non-resident and content to leave the cure of souls to miserably paid stipendiary curates and chaplains, who probably received no more than £3 or £4 a year for each cure they served. Nor could the latter hope to enhance their income very substantially by seeking additional remuneration as chantry priests, domestic chaplains, or mass priests, since openings of that kind seemed to be far fewer in Wales at this time than they were in England.

While it would be over-simplifying the position to postulate too facilely that there was an inevitable equation between poverty and ignorance, it nevertheless seems undoubtedly true that the fewer the substantial livings there were available for the clergy in the Welsh dioceses, the more difficult it was to attract men of talent and learning. Those who had proceeded through the long and rigorous training of the universities looked for something better at the end of it than to eke out a miserable existence in an impoverished backwoods parish. The result of the poverty of the parishes, the expense of a university education, the scarcity of schools, and the absence of seminaries for the formal training of clerics meant that a majority of the Welsh clergy must have been sadly ignorant, having little more than the bare rudiments of knowledge and training necessary to enable them to get through the services. Many of them could only have had an intellectual equipment inferior to that of the more able and literate of their parishioners. It is thus not to be wondered at that a gifted and highly educated Welsh humanist, Sir John Price of Brecon, should have been so censorious of the clergy in his introduction to the first Welsh printed book, which appeared in 1546. His sole purpose, he declared, was to compensate for the deficiencies of the clergy 'who either cannot or will not reveal to their parishioners those things which it is the duty of the one to teach and the other to learn'. It may be argued that Price was judging the clergy by the unduly severe criteria of contemporary humanists; but, in fact, he went to great pains to stress that his book was intended for the simple and unlearned and not the scholars. Because of the failure of the clergy in this respect, he saw a great number of his fellow-countrymen lying 'in the direst darkness, lacking a knowledge of God and his commandments and thereby falling into greater depth of sins and vices than other nations'.[12] It may be objected that, as a university-educated intellectual Price was setting too austere a standard for the average incumbent and his ill-instructed flock. But the contents of his book, consisting of translations of the creed, paternoster, and Ten Commandments, certainly did not raise the sights extravagantly high. These items constituted the very minimum which every medieval priest had for centuries been required to teach his flock. A few years later, in 1551, William Salesbury followed up John Price's criticism of the waywardness of the clergy with this onslaught: 'Woe unto the priests of the world who do not rebuke vice and do not preach. Woe unto him who does not guard his flock and he a shepherd.'[13] It would be difficult to accept that all the clergy were as remiss in fulfilling their duties as teachers and preachers as Price and Salesbury suggested, but it does seem incontestable that there were good grounds for sharp criticism of their shortcomings as instructors.

Nor were failures in the learning and effectiveness of the secular clergy being made good by greater zeal on the part of the regular orders. Monks and friars had suffered severely from the crises of the fourteenth and fifteenth centuries. They were no longer at the forefront of ecclesiastical dedication and reform as once they had been. One of their most serious weaknesses was that they were so reduced in numbers. Whereas in the heyday of great houses like Whitland or Margam a single convent might have had 100 or more monks, by the sixteenth century Cistercian monasteries had an average of about six monks, the Augustinian canons about five, and the Benedictines only three. From the fourteenth century right down to the dissolution of the monasteries, they seem to have been consistently under-manned. By 1536 only Tintern maintained the thirteen monks normally thought to be the minimum number who could maintain the proper round of services and devotions. The friars were hardly better off, having an average of about seven or eight inmates to each house, though the largest, Carmarthen, maintained fourteen. Not only had the numbers of the regulars fallen but the quality of life within the houses had also deteriorated. Occasional scandals defaced the good name of some; as when Robert Salusbury, abbot of Valle Crucis, was found guilty of highway robbery and a monk of Strata Florida was accused of forging coins. Furthermore, Dafydd, abbot of Margam, had no scruple about avowing his children and a former abbot of Conwy was charged with impoverishing his house to provide for his mistress and her child. Such

---

[12] *Yny Lhyvyr Hwnn*, introd.
[13] *Kynniver Llith a Ban*, ed. J. Fisher (Cardiff, 1931), title-page.

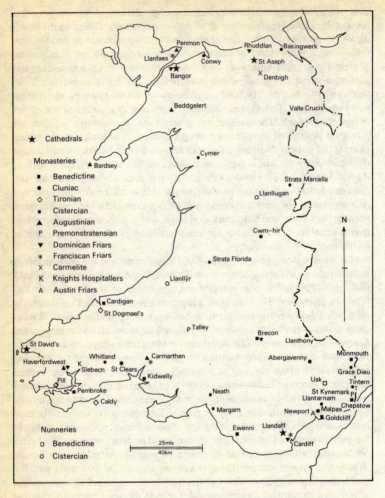

MAP 4 Cathedrals and Religious Houses

peccadilloes, harmful as they might be, were less detrimental in the long run than the tepid, laicized indolence which characterized most of the monastic inmates. Some of them may, indeed, have been afflicted with *accidia*, the spiritual sluggishness and melancholia to which men in the ascetic vocation were peculiarly prone, though there is little evidence of this in Welsh monasteries. More of them appeared to be quite content to drift complacently and agreeably along, unperturbed at maintaining a drastically reduced round of prayer and worship with their shrunken numbers. Even the life-style of the better-known abbots, like Siôn ap Rhisiart or Dafydd ab Owain, who are much more familiar to us from the poems addressed to them, seems often to be very similar to that of their lay counterparts in their addiction to the gentlemanly pursuits of hunting, feasting, and other delights of hall and hospitality. Admittedly, the monasteries still had a considerable role as patrons of poetry and they had resumed their work as copyists and conservators of manuscripts, including among them the famous Register of Neath and the White Book of Hergest. Abbot Wiliam ap Lleision of Margam was enthusiastically applauded by Lewys Glyn Cothi for his learning, and Leyshon Thomas, last abbot of Neath, seems to have kept a celebrated school at his abbey. Even so, it is obvious that the golden days, when Welsh monks and friars were undisputed leaders in the quest for scholarship and learning, were long past. A prelate of the calibre of Abbot Dafydd ab Ieuan ab Iorwerth, abbot of Valle Crucis and bishop of St Asaph, skilful politician, man of affairs, and generous host, and yet, withal, a man of genuinely scholarly interests coupled with an unmistakable strain of deep religious devotion, was now a distinct rarity among Welsh monks.

If monks were not the leaders in the intellectual and spiritual fields that once they had been, neither were they any longer affording the same pioneering example in the social or economic sphere. They had long since farmed out most of their lands and their other assets to laymen and become content to live the undemanding existence of *rentiers*. In the process they had found it necessary to hand over the management of most of their economic affairs to lay officers. Such a delegation of authority carried with it grave dangers to the life of the monasteries. It broke down still further the barrier which ought to have existed between the cloister and the outside world. The presence of a large number of lay officials and hangers-on led to excessive familiarity, even overweening arrogance, on their part. Richard, abbot of Tintern, was obliged to sue his 'servant', the earl of Worcester, on account of the latter's intolerable behaviour in 'borrowing' plate, refusing to honour various solemn promises, and interfering with the abbot's enjoyment of certain rights. Clement West, commander of the Knights of St John, had even more grievous cause for complaint against Rhys ap Thomas and his son, Gruffydd, for having unlawfully cut down timber, extorted large sums of money from the order's tenants, and having broken into West's house. More sinister still was the growing tendency for powerful local lay families to seek to control elections within the monasteries and, in so doing, to solicit the help of powerful ministers, like Thomas Cromwell, with no pretence at veiling the simony involved. When

Robert Salusbury, the bandit-abbot of Valle Crucis, was hauled off to gaol in 1535, the abbot of Cymer wrote to Cromwell offering him £20 for the privilege of becoming the new abbot of Valle Crucis with his assistance. But perhaps the worst danger of all was that, when Henry VIII dissolved the monasteries, the most powerful laymen would wholeheartedly approve of the King's decision to appropriate monastic wealth, hoping themselves to pocket at least a part of the proceeds.

The truth appears to be that among all classes of society the monastic ideal had largely exhausted its appeal. It had become altogether easier, for those among the laity who wanted to do so, to read and meditate for themselves and to seek to pursue a life of devotion and dedication outside the cloister. 'The world is wide enough and good enough to seek to win heaven in', said the English mystic, Richard Rolle,[14] thereby expressing the conviction of many that it was possible to find the means of regeneration within the world and not only behind cloister walls. By the beginning of the sixteenth century, Erasmus's criticisms of the abuses and hollowness of the monastic life found in Wales a few eager readers at least. William Salesbury described him as the 'most learned, eloquent and accomplished scholar in Christendom of our age and many ages before us'.[15] Through the agency of men like Salesbury and John Price, another enthusiastic admirer of the Dutch scholar, the criticisms of Erasmus, widely *de rigueur* among the educated, might well have percolated in vulgarized form among more home-keeping kinsmen and friends in Wales. Even some of the poets, who had earlier appeared to be good friends to their monastic patrons, changed their tune just after the dissolution. Lewis Morgannwg, once an ardent admirer of Neath Abbey, later denounced the 'false religious of the choir'.[16] Still more startling was Gruffydd ab Ieuan ap Llywelyn's change of front, since he, as a gentleman-poet, enjoyed a greater measure of personal independence in expressing his sentiments than Lewis Morgannwg. In his younger days he had been the friend of Dafydd ab Owain and an *habitué* of Conwy Abbey. Yet he turned sharply against his old allegiance and became a warm Protestant sympathizer.[17] It was the widespread conviction that the religious orders had long outlived their real usefulness that constituted the greatest danger to them. That they could have been reformed no one need doubt; but, in the atmosphere of late medieval Wales, there was no discernible source of inspiration that might have triggered off real improvement. As the late Professor David Knowles, himself a monk, reminded us,

---

[14] M. Aston, *The Fifteenth Century* (London, 1968), p. 149.
[15] *Oll Synnwyr Pen . . .* (1547), introd.
[16] Williams, *Welsh Church*, p. 548.
[17] Williams, *Welsh Church*, p. 498.

There is something fundamentally amiss, socially as well as spiritually, when a community of fifty or less men or women, vowed to the monastic life, administers vast estates and draws large revenues which are not used for any spiritual purpose, just as they have not been earned by any work of mental, material, or spiritual charity.[18]

When we come to consider the nature of religious beliefs and practices of the majority of the population, generalizing about such subjects is difficult and dangerous. Much of what we conclude about them must be vague and speculative, in view of the paucity of reliable evidence and, sometimes,of its contradictory nature. Piety and superstition, belief and credulity, often went hand in hand and were conjoined in the same individual. None the less, it is probably safe to begin with the assertion that there was virtually no sign of deep-seated opposition to the faith as taught by the Church, nor any serious criticism of it. Lollardy and other medieval heresies, though not unknown, had made little impact on Wales and, if they survived at all, showed little trace of active existence by the end of the Middle Ages. Anticlericalism there certainly was, as in most European countries, in the form of dislike of the clergy's pretensions and their financial exactions, and also in the shape of friction between laymen and monks over the latter's commercial interests. But all of this, such as it was, manifested itself only on a comparatively small scale and posed no alarming danger to the Church. The humanism associated with Erasmus and comparable scholars had made some progress by the beginning of the sixteenth century among the better-educated of the clergy, such as Richard Whitford, and laymen like John Price or Edward Carne. But though men with these sympathies deplored the superstitions and excesses that sullied contemporary religion, they were, for the most part, anxious for reform within the existing church rather than to challenge its authority. The mass of the population accepted without demur or hesitation the role of the Church in society and its teachings in so far as they understood them. They did not doubt the reality of the supernatural order or the painful presence in this world of the Devil and his minions, always alert, hostile and aggressive in seeking opportunities to lead men and women and their humble possessions into misfortunes and destruction. Life for most of them was hard and precarious; and its end could come suddenly and soon. It was only to be expected, therefore, that any thoughts they had about religion tended to concentrate on the four last things: death, judgement, heaven, and hell. It was unexpected death which continued to be the thing most dreaded; what Dafydd Nanmor so unforgettably described as *dwys ofn angau disyfyd* [the anguished fear of sudden death].[19] They believed that after death those who were damned went straight to hell; but even those who had confessed their sins and

[18] D. Knowles, *The Religious Orders in England: III. The Tudor Age* (Cambridge, 1959), p. 259.   [19] Williams, *Welsh Church*, p. 469.

received absolution still had to face the terrors of purgatory and the last judgement. Many poets consistently reiterated the need for human beings never to forget 'how brief was the life of man' and to 'study unceasingly' with seriousness and intensity 'what remained to come' in the last judgement.[20] In stone, wood, paint, and words, artists regularly depicted the everlasting horrors of the infernal cauldron [y pair du] with its extremes of unbearable heat and cold, its malevolent horned fiends, and its unspeakable torments.

Such were the appalling prospects held out for the wicked who ignored the warnings they so constantly received. Most men and women implicitly believed the teaching of the Church that it had been divinely instituted to save them from these eternal torments, though only on condition that they in turn obeyed its precepts and participated regularly in its sacraments. But the degrees of understanding and obedience varied widely. It is difficult to know, in the first place, just how often the Welsh people attended church. Many of the parishes in which they lived, especially in the upland areas, were of enormous extent, covering thousands of acres, served by poor trackways which were often impassable in winter. Their small, dark, and draughty parish churches were often inconveniently placed at one end of the parish and distant from much of the population. As late as the Religious Census of 1851, there were widespread complaints about how difficult it was for many of the populace to attend church at all.[21] Assuming, however, that many of them managed to get there, there is no certainty as to how much religious instruction they received. Many of their priests were under-educated and sadly deficient in the qualifications which would have enabled them to instruct their parishioners in their religious duties. Sermons, and other forms of teaching on the part of the clergy, seem to have been woefully lacking amid a population that was largely illiterate and much neglected. There existed a stultifying unawareness of the essential nature of religious truth and obligation, as Sir John Price and other critics observed. Most of the people appeared to regard religion as something that was performed on their behalf by the priesthood. Being present at mass and other services, with only a dim comprehension of what was going on, was enough for the majority. They performed these and other requirements of the Church in a largely mechanical if trusting way. The unflagging efforts of the small caring minority who tried to bring others to a suitably serious frame of mind seemed to show that many of the latter were largely immune to pious propaganda.

The Church proclaimed that divine mercy was infinite and that it offered the means of grace to every individual; only his own wilful acts could place

[20] Irene George, 'Syr Dafydd Trefor, Ei Oes a'i Waith' (MA Thesis, Bangor, 1928), pp. 226–32.
[21] I. G. Jones and D. Williams (eds.), The Religious Census of 1851 (Cardiff, 1976, 1981).

him beyond the reach of salvation. But the luxurious proliferation of cults, practices, customs, and assumptions being offered to would-be believers were of a very mixed kind. Many of those most frequently resorted to did not commend themselves to the official teaching of the Church or the approval of its most serious-minded sons; but they were not a whit less popular for that. Not a few of them were outward and unthinking observances, often riddled with superstition, from which reverence and understanding were largely absent. Others were astonishing exercises in credulity which bordered on idolatry and magic. A large number of them involved considerable expenditure, which could hardly fail to have aroused an uneasy suspicion that many of the poorer elements of the population might well fail to achieve salvation because they could not afford to pay for it. Not the least disturbing aspect of religion in the eyes of some of the most thoughtful of the age was that the tendency towards devotion was growingly divorced from morality. Yet, at the same time, it would be wrong to ignore the slowly spreading sense of earnestness and concern for religion among the more literate elements in the population, now found more often than previously. They were not infrequently painfully eager to find peace for their souls and to fulfil their obligations. As we saw earlier, many of them were pious enough to commission religious verse and manuscripts, to contribute generously to the improvement of their parish churches, and to seek ways of helping the Church to convey its teaching more effectively to the ignorant and the illiterate.

There were three main sources to which men and women looked for their salvation: the Godhead, the saints, and the Church and her sacraments. Fifteenth-century poetry to the Godhead revealed a new and mounting emphasis on the vision of Christ, the suffering redeemer. This is paralleled by the placing of so many new roods in the churches, all depicting the agony of Christ on the cross, and by the vogue for carving the emblems of the passion on lich-gates, parish chests, and the like. Stained glass and painted walls bore the same message. The very chasuble on the priest's back as he turned to celebrate mass might reveal to worshippers the crucifixion scene. When they emerged from church it greeted them again on the churchyard cross. In wealthier people's homes, too, though we know very little about their interiors, there were probably depictions of the passion. Everywhere there are signs of a widespread conscious attempt to bring home the profound love for humanity which led the son of God to suffer such anguish on its behalf. None the less, it is also true that one of the contemporary faults most commonly denounced was the prevalent custom of swearing by Christ's body, blood, and wounds. In this there was no conscious blasphemy; it was all to be attributed to thoughtless coarseness.

Veneration of the saints had been a feature of the Christian religion from earliest times and its dangers had always been apparent to theologians. The pitfalls were in danger of becoming even more noticeable in the late medieval era, with the increased appeal of pilgrimages and an intensified search for holy images and hallowed relics—the latter all too often the objects of a sordid and fraudulent trade. Visual representations of the saints became more realistic, while saints' lives and poems based on them became the most popular genres in religious literature. It has to be admitted that they were esteemed for their value as a source of entertainment as much as, if not more than, for their moral content. The Welsh, like other European peoples, were particularly attracted to their native saints, who, it was believed, naturally enough had a special regard for their own. David, Beuno, Teilo, Deiniol, Illtud, Derfel, Dwynwen, Ffraid, and Gwenffrewi, and many others, all had dedicated to them their shrines and holy places which drew devotees in large numbers. They came not only to pay their respects to the saint but also to purchase the indulgences which were normally offered for sale at the shrine. Invocation of the saints and the pilgrimages associated with them were, nevertheless, of all facets of contemporary devotion, among those most strenuously assailed by critics and moralists. Nor could it be denied that popular attitudes were badly tainted with credulity, abuse, and superstition. Yet it may be necessary to keep a sense of perspective about these matters. Normally the saints, with the exception of the BVM, were regarded as not much more than celestial mascots. In an age when life and property were desperately uncertain, it was hoped that the saints would ensure good fortune and good health. It was a benevolent vigilance which was usually sought from them: to keep livestock free from disease; to defend men on journeys by land or sea and in battle; to release them from prison, protect them from those who wished them ill, and expedite their love affairs; and, above all possibly, to restore them to health after injury or illness. It was as old and comforting friends who performed such favours that they survived for centuries after the Reformation. As late as 1721 Erasmus Saunders spoke of the Welsh as 'hardly yet having forgotten the use of praying to them. And there being not only Churches and Chapels, but Springs and Fountains dedicated to those Saints, they do at certain times go and bath themselves in them, and sometimes leave some small Oblations behind them.'[22]

The services and ritual of the Church were inextricably associated with the pageant of the seasons of the year and its sacraments intertwined with the great events of the individual's life from birth to death. A man's physical birth was quickly followed by his rebirth in baptism and, as he approached the threshold of death, he received forgiveness of all mortal

[22] *A View of the State of Religion* . . . (repr., Cardiff, 1949), pp. 35–6.

sins when extreme unction was administered. The central act of worship was the rite of mass, at which all were expected to be present on Sundays and holy days. The Church taught that mass was not only an act of thanksgiving and praise but also a sacrifice, availing the living and the dead, through which men and women might take hold of the merits of the death of Christ. The doctrine of transubstantiation was clearly understood by some of the poets, as far as we can judge. Morys ap Hywel, for example, explained how

in the sacrifice where He belongs, God, the guardian of man, is seen. From wheat of finest growth His flesh is made for the prospering of faith. The holy man with Latin words turns into blood the water and wine. Let our belief in this be flawless; for I know assuredly that God is there. Plainly in the chalice—let us all revere it—Christ is present in purity.[23]

Theologians were careful to lay down that, except by divine revelation, it was not possible to calculate how much benefit any particular mass or masses might confer on an individual soul. There was, all the same, a serious risk of popular misinterpretation. Contemporary documents, especially the wills of the period, show that in Wales as elsewhere, there existed a widespread assumption that the more elaborate masses were or the more they were multiplied in number, the greater was the benefit which accrued. Unfortunately, many priests depended upon the financial provisions made for increasing the number and frequency of masses for a large part of their income. The mechanical attitude adopted towards masses, and the increasing traffic in them, was a major factor in leading to the excessive growth in the number of mass priests and the debasement of the priestly calling.

Further grave perils were also associated with the sale of indulgences, a practice notoriously open to abuse. The root of the trouble, as with the mass, lay in the disparity between authoritative teaching and the way it was ordinarily construed. The Church continued to teach, in theory, that an indulgence must be obtained only by those who were truly contrite and had confessed; that it could only remit temporal penalties; and that it could not be automatically applied with a measurable and unfailing effect to every soul. But that was not the way it was usually looked upon nor even the way it was normally proclaimed by the more ignorant and unscrupulous emissaries of the Church. To many, it became the means of buying 'pardon from Purgatory' [*pardwn rhag y Purdan dig*], both for themselves and those who were dead. So eager were ordinary folk to avail themselves of this seemingly easy and far-reaching means of relief that they were ready prey to unprincipled vendors of feigned indulgences. Thus, in 1474, Hugh Huntley, chamberlain of South Wales, and the mayors of Carmarthen and

[23] NLW, Llanstephan MS 47, fos. 268–9.

Haverfordwest, had to take action against one Thomas Hochekyn for selling indulgences without authority to do so. 'For now of late days', they complained, 'divers persons have come into our coasts usurping upon them by feigned and coloured writings great power to assoil *a pena et a culpa* and afterwards found fickle and untrue.'[24] There are also extant poetic protests against the sellers of false indulgences and relics. The satirical poet, Phylip Emlyn, though himself a priest, hit off all too successfully the power of money and commercialization even in the sphere of obtaining the means of grace:

> And God's pervading grace within me dwell,
> Strength for my body, Heaven for my soul,
> With many a pope's indulgence furnished well.
> So am I sure to assuage each enemy:
> My purse, for this grammercy be to thee.[25]

[24] BL, Egerton MS 2410; cf. E. Owen, 'Strata Marcella Immediately before and After Its Dissolution', *Y Cymmr.*, xxix (1919), 17.
[25] Bell, *Trans. Cymmr.*, 1940, p. 241.

CHAPTER 6

LEARNING AND THE ARTS

THE demand for formal education, though it was growing perceptibly in the fifteenth century, remained relatively restricted in Wales. The mass of the population, made up of peasants, craftsmen, and labourers, often needed to undergo long learning periods of apprenticeship and training so as to acquire that skill and experience without which life would have been insupportable for them; but, for the most part, they could do well enough without formal education and the majority remained unable to read or write. Even among those who were better-off, there were serious obstacles to acquiring education and intellectual skills, all the more so in a thinly populated, relatively poor country like Wales, lacking concentrations of population and wealth in towns or villages of any size. Much of the education of the period was conducted in Latin, and reading materials, still consisting mostly of manuscripts, were scarce and expensive. Nevertheless, there were some callings and professions to enter for which men obviously required at least a modicum of education. Those who wished to become clerics, lawyers, physicians, administrators, and littérateurs, had to have passed through the schools and, in some instances, the universities or the Inns of Court.

The Church and her ministers still exercised an extensive measure of control over the means of education. Universities, schools, and the general processes of instruction continued to come under the dominance of clerics. Those who wished to receive the rudiments of education ordinarily went to an educated and well-disposed clergyman or came under the care of a household priest or domestic chaplain. Or else they attended the local chantry school, or song school if there was one; an institution like that chantry founded by James Walbeef at Llanhamlach in Breconshire, who stipulated that the chantry priest should also 'preach the word of God or teach children'.[1] At the cathedrals and in some of the larger towns and parishes, such as Oswestry or Haverfordwest, there were grammar schools to 'inform unlearned youths in grammar and other liberal sciences'.[2] There are indications, too, that monks occasionally acted as tutors and that some of the monasteries and friaries, like Neath or Conwy or Carmarthen, may have kept schools for the instruction of others besides their own novices.

---

[1] Williams, *Welsh Church*, p. 291.   [2] *St David's Regs.*, II, 524.

Pupils of all these kinds of teachers and establishments who were able and ambitious enough and who could find the means of support to maintain them for what might prove to be many years of study, then proceeded to the University of Oxford or Cambridge. It was only a select minority who went thus far, even among those with their eyes on the Church or the law or some other learned profession. When eminent clerics like John Blodwel or Robert ap Rhys, or leading abbots such as Dafydd ab Owain or Leyshon Thomas, had taken a university degree, it was sufficiently rare an achievement to be the subject of prolonged and enthusiastic comment on the part of the poets.

Among the laity, the demand for education was evidently growing in most European countries, and Wales was no exception. There had been signs in the fourteenth century of a marked interest and achievement on the part of some laymen. When the Glamorgan rebel leader, Llywelyn Bren, was executed in 1316, among his possessions were a number of manuscripts, including a French one of the *Romaunt de la Rose*. At the end of the fourteenth century, Hopcyn ap Thomas of Ynystawe was an exceptionally discerning and cultivated patron of learning, literature, and manuscripts; and at the same period, the heretic Walter Brut was a man who could hold his own in Latin debate with clerics sent to confound him. By the fifteenth century, all the indications are that literacy was spreading among lay men and women; landowners, lawyers, merchants, and traders were learning to read in increasing numbers. Early in that century that lively and successful Welsh burgess of Oswestry, David Holbeach, had perceived the need to found a grammar school in that town, and Sir John Wynn was to record how his great-grandfather was sent to Caernarvon to attend school there. In view of the common practice of intermarriage between Welsh and English families and the closer contacts of every kind between them, it may well be that there was a growing number of literates in both Welsh and English, and maybe in Latin as well in some instances. There was a keen interest in literature, and more desire to acquire manuscripts and even printed books. More and more professional scribes and copyists were appearing outside monastic walls among laymen to meet the demand. The greater availability of paper, so much cheaper than parchment, made it much easier to supply manuscripts. Among those who were quick to detect this new demand and to meet it were some of the leading poets like Gutun Owain and Lewys Glyn Cothi, both of whom were noted copyists. 'Vocational' literature of every kind—religious, legal, medicinal, and historical—as well as 'creative' writings were much in vogue, among women as well as men. There are frequent references in the work of the poets to the delight which they and their patrons took in reading and studying texts together (see below, pp. 160–1). Included among the twenty-four feats which everyone who aspired to be considered a gentleman must master was the ability to read and appreciate Welsh literature. Slowly there was a shift from an oral culture to a written one. But it should not be overemphasized; there were no printed books in Welsh before 1546; manuscripts were still rare and precious commodities; and most of the instruction continued to be by word of mouth, as did most of the diffusion of culture.

Among the better-educated of the laymen were lawyers. Lawyers had been a small but well-educated and highly influential element in the population. The use of Welsh for legal purposes at an early stage reflected not only the maturity and sophistication of the native language but also the expertise and training of the legal profession that expressed itself through it. Though it is true that Welsh law suffered serious set-backs as the result of the Edwardian settlement of 1284, it had nevertheless survived vigorously in post-conquest Wales. This suggests strongly that well-organized law schools of some kind continued to exist in Wales, together with teachers expert in Welsh law. It is confirmed by the existence of a body of manuscripts from the fourteenth and fifteenth centuries showing not only the continuance of native law but its capacity to go on developing. In many parts of north Wales, especially, there existed *ynaid* or professional judges, though in south Wales it was a body of men learned in the law and not a professional judge who gave the verdict. The growing influence of English law in Wales after the Edwardian conquest meant that an increasing number of individuals had also to be trained in that law. Sir Edward Hanmer had risen to become one of Edward III's leading judges; and his son-in-law, Owain Glyndŵr, probably received some of his education at the Inns of Court, as much if not more for the acquisition of the appropriate social graces as for a training in the law. Robert Trefor of Chirk, one of a number who became a lawyer and a collector of rents in the March, was in 1452 hailed by Guto'r Glyn as a receiver who had now gone to pay his dues to God as once he had done to Richard, duke of York.[3] Others, like Ieuan ap Rhydderch, went to university or Inns of Court to continue their legal studies. There must have been not a few like James Walbeef who were 'practised in the laws both of England and Wales'.[4] The increasing employment of individuals and families in financial and legal offices, by the Crown and the lords of the March, called for instruction and experience in the rudiments of law, finance, and administration; and that was ordinarily provided by some form of apprenticeship in the law.

Others who needed long and intensive instruction were the littérateurs. They had existed in Wales down the centuries as a powerful and well-organized group. They were drawn only from the free classes and some of them were well-established gentlemen of repute. In order to acquire the

---

[3] *GG*, p. 51.   [4] Pugh, *Marcher Lordships*, p. 249.

skills needed to become proficient in the craft of poet, prose-writer, story-teller, or declaimer [*datgeiniad*], a youth sought out an acknowledged master, who alone could take pupils for training, and stayed with him for some years. We know most about the training of poets, though doubtless that in the other literary crafts was broadly similar. The novice went to a *pencerdd* [master poet, chief of song], who was, strictly speaking, only supposed to have one pupil at a time, though this requirement was frequently ignored and the leading poets often had a number of young men in training. The instruction they received was essentially an oral one. By frequent repetition, intensive memorizing, and regular practice, they gradually mastered the literary art and the body of knowledge associated with it.

It would take the apprentice poet at least nine years, and possibly much longer, to pass through the successive grades of *disgybl ysbas heb radd* [temporary apprentice without a degree], *disgybl disgyblaidd* [apprentice appropriate for instruction], and *disgybl pencerddaidd* [apprentice of the master craft], before he became a *pencerdd* or master poet. Under rules minutely laid down and carefully observed, the pupil would normally attain his various grades of proficiency at recognized *neithiorau reiol* ('royal' wedding-feasts, i.e., the feast of a bridal pair claiming descent from the princes), when the acknowledged masters put him through his paces. But there were also at least three celebrated occasions during the fifteenth and sixteenth centuries—at Carmarthen *c.*1450, and at Caerwys in 1523 and 1567—when large-scale *eisteddfodau* or bardic gatherings were held. At these, poets graduated in larger numbers, though according to the same rules as were observed in the *neithiorau*. It was a long and demanding training, having much in common with other forms of medieval apprentice-ship. Its strength lay in the rigorous and exacting standards of classical achievement called for from the apprentice-poets, its weakness in the rigid and inflexible exclusivity of its conservatism. By 1523, and still more by 1567, there was an important political and administrative criterion, as well as a test of skill, underlying the *eisteddfod*. This was the determined effort being made to pluck out the 'weeds', i.e., to ensure that no unlicensed vagrant or idle person, describing himself as a poet or a minstrel, should be allowed to wander the countryside, pestering the gentry. Only skilled, bona fide poets who had graduated in the schools would now be allowed this privilege.

Closely associated with the art of poetry, *cerdd dafod* [song of the tongue] was the art of music, *cerdd dant* [song of the string]. For centuries, music and singing had been immensely popular in Wales. The ancient laws of Hywel Dda contained provisions relating to music and musicians; and Gerald of Wales's flattering references to the talents of the Welsh for singing in harmony are too well-known to need repeating. Musical science would seem to have been highly developed in medieval Wales, and the training and examinations to which medieval musicians were subjected were rigorous and demanding.[5] There were schools for musicians very similar to those of the bards, and both groups seem often to have been trained together. Both were certainly regulated by the same *eisteddfodau*, and the great Tudur Aled was hailed as 'Pencerdd y ddwygerdd'—master of both kinds of song, *cerdd dafod* and *cerdd dant*. Such status would have meant that Tudur was a master not only of performing music but also of composing it as well as verse. Unfortunately, we can no longer judge whether or not he attained the same mastery over music that he did over verse, because any music which he may have composed has long since been lost. If music never attained equal recognition with Welsh poetry, there were times when the poets, who themselves repeatedly show an intimate acquaintance with the sister art, felt their position of superiority to be in danger from the popularity of music.

The favourite musical instruments were the harp, regarded as the national instrument of Wales, the *crwth*—a kind of bowed lyre—and, to a lesser extent, the pipes, though many other instruments were well known too (see below, pp. 163–4). The Church played an important role in musical education. In a number of churches, organs are known to have existed, and where there was an organ there was, as a rule, a clerk who acted as organist and choirmaster. At St John's, Cardiff, for example, one Hugh Lamb received 26*s*. 8*d*. for his services every year; the same amount as his counterpart at Salisbury Cathedral was paid. The wealthy fraternity at Montgomery was able to maintain choirmaster, organist, and professional choristers. The townspeople of Brecon came to an agreement with their chaplain that he should 'keep Our Lady's mass daily, having sufficient company with him, with pricked song, also keep the organs and teach two children their pricked song and plain song'.[6] It is against this broad background of a naturally musical people providing many opportunities for musical discipline and training that we have to set the apparently sudden rise to prominence at court and chapel royal of so many Welsh musicians in the early Tudor period.

There also existed a wide range of craftsmen, all of whom had painstakingly to learn their trade from acknowledged masters. A unique list of thirteenth-century Merioneth occupations includes one or two exotic figures like a goldsmith and a painter—neither particularly highly assessed for tax purposes—but much the most common among them were the carpenters (16), blacksmiths (17), and weavers (29). The training they had received had made some of these men accomplished artists in their own right. Recent study of the making of a sword and buckler by a Welsh

---

[5] P. Crossley-Holland, *Music in Wales* (London, 1948).
[6] Williams, *Welsh Church*, p. 452.

medieval blacksmith has brought out the high quality of the craftsmanship that went into them and also the accuracy of a poet's description of them.[7] So we need not wonder that Tudur Aled should sadly bemoan the loss of one Ieuan ap Deicws—'prince of blacksmiths was he' [*pennaeth ar ofannaeth fu*].[8] But, of all the Merioneth craftsmen listed in the subsidy roll, the carpenters were assessed at a higher rate than anyone else, including even the beneficed clergy and the poets. Nor was that really surprising when we remember how expertly and artistically they had learned to handle wood. It is no coincidence that poets should have ranked the carpenters alongside themselves as artists and a striking tribute to the mastery of the woodcarvers over their medium that poets were fond of likening their own use of words to the carpenters' carving of wood. 'I am a full carpenter of the [poetic] measures' [*mi yw saer llawn mesurau*], Iorwerth Fynglwyd, one of the finest poets of south Wales, claimed with pride as he compared himself to the woodcarvers of his native Glamorgan.[9]

Nor, finally, should we overlook how much the ordinary farmer had to learn. He had to absorb the manifold arts and skills of growing crops and rearing livestock; the methods of simple butchery and salting meat; the techniques of spinning, weaving, and dyeing rough cloth; the making of simpler farm implements and bits and pieces of farm and household furniture and equipment; the methods of any by-employments in which he found himself engaged; and he had to know how to put up out-buildings and the ruder houses, together with how to thatch and waterproof them. There was much that he needed to pick up about the lore of the weather and how to observe its changes and portents, and to learn about the habits of fish, wildfowl, and wild animals. His wife was called upon to fulfil an even more demanding role. In addition to having absorb much of what her husband knew, she was also expected to learn the hard way about giving birth to children with minimal help, rearing them, looking after the family in face of the dangerous ailments and diseases that abounded, and preparing its food for it at all times, often having to store and eke out the meagre rations as best she might. The life of medieval peasants may have been that of superstitious, conservative, and illiterate creatures; yet there was a fund of skills, wisdom, lore, and folk-culture that they had to acquire as and how they could. It ill behoves twentieth-century folk to look down upon them pityingly and patronizingly. It might not be unreasonable to ask ourselves how well the products of our own schools, after years of formal education, compare with them in the range of their skills, discernment, and understanding.

Literature was the supreme cultural achievement of fifteenth- and early

---

[7] I. Edwards and C. Blair, 'Welsh Bucklers', *Antiquaries Journal*, LXII (1982), 74–115.
[8] *TA*, pp. 449–51.   [9] Williams, *Tradd. Llen. Morg.*, p. 52.

sixteenth-century Wales, as it had been for centuries. The country had never known the flourishing urban life, or the degree of wealth that went with it, to give rise to the high art that blossomed best in prosperous cities or thickly populated plains. Its artistic energies had been channelled into the sort of art that could flower readily outside major courts or wealthy towns. Welsh literature was, therefore, 'pre-eminently social in function, formal and conventional in both theme and treatment, archaic and polished in diction, impressively dignified in style and generally conservative in metrical patterns . . . such a high degree of artistic refinement and technical accomplishment was obviously the product of a long and rich tradition'.[10] It had maintained, presumably since Celtic times, but certainly for a thousand years, an unbroken continuity of literary tradition, preserved by a professional and trained class of littérateurs. They saw themselves and were seen by the *bonedd*, the free and gentle classes of Wales, as the guardians and transmitters not only of the language and literature of their country but of its cultural and historical heritage also. They were consciously conservative, fully aware of their inheritance from the past and equally determined to hand it on to future generations. Having survived the traumatic events of 1282–4 which had struck down those princes who had previously been their chief patrons, they had also come through the Glyndŵr Rebellion and the statutes passed against them, battered but unbowed. In spite of the many political divisions of Wales and its administrative fragmentation, its literary men had succeeded in maintaining a single literary language, intelligible in every part of Wales, whether used by bards from the north or the south, the east or the west. That language showed not a trace of the many dialectal or colloquial differences which characterized normal everyday speech then as now.[11] So when a north Walian like the poet Huw Cae Llwyd, from Llandderfel in Merioneth, found it necessary to move as a young man to Breconshire to live, he found no difficulty in being understood nor in acquiring many patrons in the south-east of Wales.

It was not only a single literary language that was preserved; a culture common to all parts of Wales was also kept flourishing. This has been brilliantly illuminated by the analysis made of the geographical distribution of the patrons of a single great poet of the fifteenth century, Lewys Glyn Cothi.[12] It shows that he visited all parts of Wales and the March and would seem to have been equally welcome wherever he went. On the basis of the present administrative divisions of Wales, his poems can be localized as follows: Dyfed (south-west) 75; Powys (mid and north-east) 74; West

[10] C. Lewis in *A Guide to Welsh Literature*, ed. A. O. H. Jarman and G. R. Hughes (2 vols. Swansea, 1979), I, 90–1.
[11] A. Thomas, *The Linguistic Geography of Wales* (Cardiff, 1973).
[12] E. D. Jones in Jarman and Hughes, *Guide*, pp. 245–6.

Glamorgan 10; Gwent 10; Gwynedd 9; South Glamorgan 3; and the English border 19. The high figure for Powys includes many poems directed to patrons living in those parts of Wales like Brecon and Radnorshire, which have long been anglicized. A number of his poems were addressed to patrons living over the border in what is generally considered to be England. What was true of Lewys Glyn Cothi would, *mutatis mutandis*, hold good for every major poet. Though rooted in his own native district [*gwlad*], where he would expect to find many of his patrons and from which he often took his poetic title—Lewys **Glyn Cothi**, Dafydd **Nanmor**, Tudur **Aled**, Ieuan **Deulwyn**, Lewis **Morgannwg**—he would nevertheless itinerate widely through many other parts of Wales. Studies of patronge which have been undertaken for a number of individual and widely dispersed districts of Wales—Flintshire, Merioneth, Cardiganshire, or Glamorgan—show that in all of them there were many devoted patrons and households.

Ancient though the tradition of Welsh verse was, it achieved the peak of its medieval development between *c.*1430–40 and *c.*1530–40. Its greatest individual poet, Dafydd ap Gwilym, may have belonged to the fourteenth century, but the outstanding feature of the poetry composed between 1430–40 and 1530–40 was the very large number of front-rank poets who then flourished. No fewer than eighteen of them were listed by Sir Thomas Parry in his classic *History of Welsh Literature*:[13] a larger number of poets of that quality than were ever known to have been active in any comparable period before or after. What is equally impressive is the enormous poetic output, most of it still preserved in unpublished manuscripts dating from this period or shortly after. It is quite extraordinary that a small population of about a quarter of a million should have been responsible for producing the poets and the patrons for so prolific an outpouring of poetry of remarkably high quality. It becomes all the more astonishing when we remember that a very large quantity of literature has been lost from medieval Wales as from many other countries in the medieval period. The work of some poets would hardly be known at all were it not for the survival of a single manuscript. Much may never have been committed to writing and so has disappeared without a trace. Such, for example, appears to have been the fate of much of the classical poetry and also of the very large corpus of poetry believed to have been composed in the 'free metres', which was not considered to have enjoyed sufficient status to warrant having been written down. A good deal of the poetry written by poets of the eastern side of Wales and the March was unfamiliar to the copyists of the north and west, who preserved most of what has come down to us and has therefore been lost. Many prose texts may also have

---

[13] *HWL*, pp. 162–3.

similarly been lost for various reasons. What has been preserved, however, constitutes one of the great literatures of medieval Europe.

That it has not been more widely appreciated is due to the special difficulties of translating it, for it is more than usually true of Welsh verse that what gets lost in translation is poetry. Its complicated and unique patterns of metrics and *cynghanedd* spring naturally and spontaneously from the genius of the Welsh language but are virtually untranslatable without crippling loss. Like many a good wine, *cynghanedd* simply does not travel. Briefly, there are four kinds of *cynghanedd*. The first two, *cynghanedd groes* and *cynghanedd draws*, depend upon corresponding patterns of alliteration and stress. This is an example of *cynghanedd groes*:

Y gwr marw | e gar morwyn
  g r m'r | g r m'r

Cynghanedd draws is similar but somewhat looser in that some consonants in the second half of the line are not included in the matching pattern:

Pwy sydd | mor gampus heddiw
 p s'dd| p s 'dd

Cynghanedd lusg is a pattern of internal rhyming where an earlier syllable rhymes with the accented penultimate syllable of the line, for example,

Asgell archangel melyn
     el mel

Cynghanedd sain is a combination of internal rhyme and consonance, for example,

Segurdod yw clod   y cledd
    rhyme rhyme
        cl'   cl'

Complex and demanding though the rules of *cynghanedd* and the fixed metres are, in the work of the great poets, far from being fetters which intolerably shackle the poet's ability to express himself freely, they become adornments which add to the power as well as the elegance of the verse. The rules governing *cynghanedd* were not finalized until the fourteenth century and only then was it obligatorily introduced into the three most popular forms of poetry of that age: the *awdl* [ode], containing more than one measure; the *cywydd* [rhyming couplet of seven syllables in each line]; and the *englyn* [a verse-form of four lines]. The *cywydd* became the measure particularly beloved of the poets of the age, and it was typical of the favour that it found with them that Tudur Aled should have left 125 *cywyddau* as compared with only 11 *awdlau*. Poets achieved astonishing mastery over the *cywydd* measure and, by the first decades of the sixteenth century, in the work of the supreme masters like Tudur Aled or Iorwerth

Fynglwyd, it had reached its pinnacle. Its capacity for further development was now severely limited.

The themes of the poetry were firmly laid down for the bards in their bardic 'Grammars' and other similar documents, the most celebrated and widely known of which was that associated with the name of Einion the Priest, a fourteenth-century compilation. Since their topics and the treatment of them were so rigidly stipulated, the key difficulty for the poets, as always in a conservative classical tradition, was to find ways of keeping to the established conventions and yet managing to introduce notes of originality and individuality, especially in the brilliance of their modes of expression. Central to the whole ethos of the poetic order was the theme of praise; praise rendered primarily in the form of eulogies to the living and elegies for the dead. There were, according to theory, two kinds of objects for praise: things spiritual and things corporeal. Among the former were God and the saints, for whom appropriate virtues were prescribed to be praised. God was to be extolled for those ineffable qualities of almighty strength, supreme wisdom, and overwhelming love to be associated with the Creator and Upholder of the universe; and the saints for their celestial virtue and holiness. Much of the religious poetry of the time was explicable in terms of those criteria. Among the corporeal objects of praise were the two categories of clerics and laymen; each being accorded the virtues which befitted them. The lay lord was to be applauded for his power, ability, military prowess, courage, strength, pride, meekness, wisdom, accomplishment, generosity, gentleness, amiability towards his friends and followers, beauty of countenance, dignified bearing, magnanimity of mind, nobleness of actions, and other honourable and kindly qualities. No mention was made here of his ancient and distinguished birth, although this was becoming increasingly prominent in contemporary poetry. Women also had an important place in Einion's scheme of things and they were figuring steadily larger in the fifteenth-century poetry. They, too, had the qualities suited to them carefully listed: wisdom, propriety, chastity, generosity, beauty of countenance, complexion and form, and guilelessness of speech and actions. Though not included here, a woman's nobility of birth was becoming increasingly significant as an object of praise and so, too, was her care for the sick and the poor.

Praise had been the function of poetry from time immemorial. In return for valuable but perishable gifts the poet had undertaken to render his patron's reputation imperishable. The weakness of the whole arrangement was that the poets tended to resort to flattery and exaggeration. The conventions of medieval rhetoric required authors to present things and people not as they really were but as ideally they ought to be. The disparity between reality and the image of perfection presented in literature could be very wide. Medieval men seemed more concerned to have an ideal than to live up to it. Thus Sir Thomas Malory projected for an admiring readership 'the noble acts of chivalry' used by the Knights of the Round Table by which they acquired honour and put vicious wrongdoers to shame.[14] Yet he himself had done much of his literary work from prison, where he had been immured for robbery, theft, and extensive raiding. The Welsh poets, for their part, were not unaware of the gap between truth and exaggeration, wart-faced reality and unblemished perfection, in their own work. Their self-constituted scourge, Siôn Cent, laid about him with righteous indignation in his condemnation of their servile and mendacious praise of earthly honours, good living, and high-handed behaviour. His censures of the obsequious hollowness of much of their praise were to be expected; but even Guto'r Glyn, widely acknowledged as the supreme exponent of the noblest genre of the poetic art, *moliant mab* [praise of men], had to confess that there were times when he yielded to the temptation of flattery:

> Ni cheisiaf, o chanaf chwaith
> Wedi gwin, wadu gweniaith.

[I will not deny that flattery comes if I sing after wine]

He extricated himself from his dilemma with supple finesse and a consummately deft poetic touch:

> Beth yw gweniaith ond iaith deg?
> O thraethir y gwir a'r gau,
> Y gair tecaf yw'r gorau.[15]

[What is flattery but fair language? If one must speak truth and falsehood, the fairest word is best.]

In the same way, another master of the art of *moliant mab*, Tudur Aled, well knew that patrons had few illusions about the excessive praise that was directed to them, but argued that the real justification for it was to deploy the words with an artistry which made the flattery unforgettable because of the sheer beauty with which it was expressed—*gweniaith brydferth* [artistic flattery]. Tudur knew of 'no worse venom in any language than poison expressed in flattery':

> Gwenwyn ni wn gan uniaith
> Mwy na gwenwyn mewn gweniaith.[16]

And Lewys Môn, in his most famous *cywydd*, the one in which he sought reconciliation with Siôn Puleston, urged that for the sake of his friendship with his patron he would come to sing his praise 'not for his gold or any desire' [*nid am eich aur na dim chwant*] but simply to be his minstrel and his man until the final hour' [*eich cerddawr hyd yr awr dranc a'ch gŵr wyf*].[17]

[14] E. F. Jacob, *The Fifteenth Century* (Oxford, 1961), p. 656.
[15] *GG*, p. 176.   [16] *TA*, p. lxx.   [17] *LM*, pp. 256–8.

The elegies [*marwnadau*] were more than usually prone to exaggeration and hyperbole, for death was the most solemn and final occasion on which to recount a patron's virtues. There would be no further opportunities for praise, and poets found it virtually impossible to refrain from over-pitching their encomiums. Elegies invariably referred to inconsolable grief at the irreparable loss. There were 'Noah's floods' of weeping and ear-shattering outbursts of grief. Lewys Môn, one of the supreme exponents of the elegy, in his poem to Angharad daughter of Dafydd recounted the three most awe-inspiring choruses of lamentation—when Adam was buried, Christ crucified, and Herod massacred the innocents. The fourth such piteous outburst greeted the obsequies of Angharad at the Dominican friary at Bangor. All the bells of Gwynedd would ever ring a knell for her, and the poor, needy, and ailing of the whole land would be for ever bereft of charity.[18] By modern standards it was all a little hard to swallow and even bordering on the farcical; yet medieval convention seemed to demand it and to accept that such extravagant expressions of loss were no more than fitting for the occasion. Nevertheless, some of the paroxysms of anguish, such as Dafydd Nanmor's grief at the death of a maiden, possibly Gwen o'r Ddôl, seem to express a heartfelt sense of loss that goes far beyond mere convention: 'Oh! God, if she be buried, would that I were a shroud wrapped about her!'

> Och Dduw Tad, o chuddiwyd hi,
> Nad oeddwn amdo iddi[19]

Two other kinds of poetry which were very usual at this time could be regarded as sub-categories of poems of praise. They were *cywyddau gofyn* [request poems] and *cerddi brud* [prophetic poems]. *Cywyddau gofyn* might be interpreted as double-barrelled attempts to please the patron to whom the request was directed and the one on whose behalf it was solicited, unless, as was very often the case, the poet was asking for the gift on his own account. A poem of this kind gave him the chance to flatter the owner of the object by finding all kinds of ingenious comparisons and conceits with which to praise it and also to blazon the virtues and the pedigrees of both patrons involved. Guto'r Glyn, seeking a hunting-horn from Geoffrey Kyffin, offered him delicate compliments on his legal skill and knowledge at the bench in London and reminded him of the close relationship of the would-be recipient, John Eyton, to him. He then proceeded to give a long, elaborate, and ingenious description of the hunting-horn, 'clarion of the hunting-dogs for a generous kinsman' [*clariwn helgwn i hael gar*].[20] Nearly all the *cywyddau gofyn* conform more or less to this general pattern.

---

[18] *LM*, pp. 157–9.   [19] *DN*, p. 85.   [20] *GG*, pp. 213–5.

The prophetic poems were intended to whip up enthusiasm for a leader of Welsh descent who could claim to be capable of fulfilling those ancient prophecies that forecast victory for a prince of 'British' blood who would regain rule over the island of Britain. If the contender were an established and well-known figure like Edward IV or William Herbert or Jasper Tudor or Rhys ap Thomas, it might not be necessary to conceal support for him. But on those occasions when the object of the poetry intended to set himself up in opposition to established authority and overthrow it, then a veil of obscurity had to be drawn over the plans and their authors. Animal symbolism, secret omens, and portentous prophecies, designed to give an air of greater mystery and significance to the venture, would be freely scattered about the verse. Some poets, like Dafydd Llwyd o Fathafarn, specialized almost exclusively in this kind of poetry. A Lancastrian for most of the time, he was not above changing his political allegiance on occasion and he has poems addressed to Yorkist leaders like William Herbert and Lord Ferrers. His zeal for the Lancastrian cause and the House of Tudor waned during the lean years between 1471 and 1483. The most impressive and unchanging features of his verse, however, are his intense partisanship on behalf of Welsh heroes, his confidence in ultimate Welsh victory, and his passionate Anglophobia. 'Those Saxons of false faith shall wade in their own blood up to their fetlocks', he prophesied in a typically hostile and embittered phrase.[21] At critical times in the civil wars, the verse of poets like Dafydd Llwyd was of more than ordinary importance. During the months leading up to the battle of Bosworth the active propaganda of such poets was of decisive value to Henry Tudor in arousing support for his venture.

Canu serch [love-poetry] was, in its own way, another variety of praise poetry and was widely enjoyed. It had been given tremendous appeal by Dafydd ap Gwilym's genius in the fourteenth century and appears to have developed side by side with the *cywyddau moliant* [praise poems] to such an extent that Dr Rachel Bromwich has suggested that it sprang from the work of a circle of poets rather than the inspiration of a single innovatory genius.[22] It was certainly in great demand during the fifteenth century. It gave endless scope for greater informality and flouting of convention; far more than the more sedate and sober *canu moliant*. The poets in their love poetry engaged in a lighter, more humorous, and satirical vein. They liked to poke irreverent fun at jealous husbands, old men, and coy and reluctant mistresses; above all, perhaps, they mocked themselves and their discomfitures in their *amours*. Their conventions were fairly well established: they loved to distraction but usually in vain; they sighed with unrequited longing for their loved one's figure, her hair, her eyes, her lips, and the

[21] *D. Ll. F.* p. 27.   [22] Jarman and Hughes, *Guide*, p. 167.

nectar of her kisses; they pined for love and became mere skeletons, miserably hanging about in despair. They hated the winter months and yearned for spring and Nature's rebirth to give them comfort and inspiration. They made wild promises and protestations of love and dispatched love-messengers [*llateion*] of every kind to convey them. Occasionally, their conceits were so daring as to border on the blasphemous; Ieuan Deulwyn said of one maiden that Jesus himself could not obtain her if he sought her. Even priests wrote love-poems, and one of them, Siôn Leia, claimed that Ovid's *Ars Amatoria* took precedence over the mass book in his thoughts.

Although some major poets regarded love-poetry as mere juvenilia on which an apprentice could try his hand before he graduated to the more serious matter of praise poetry, a number of leading poets—Dafydd ab Edmwnd, Gutun Owain, Bedo Brwynllys, and Ieuan Deulwyn—were known almost exclusively for their love-poems. Dafydd ab Edmwnd sang primarily for his own satisfaction and enjoyed the exercise in wit and satire which love-poetry afforded him. When his loved one was removed from his presence by her husband, Dafydd vowed to loose the 'hounds of his far-reaching muse' [*fytheiaid o faith awen*] and his 'greyhounds of the fair one's praise' [*mawlgwen oedd fy milgwn i*] to pursue her, slyly introducing into his verse his delight in hunting in more than one sense. He mocked his own discomfort, having waited vainly for his love on a winter's night: 'I got chilled waiting in the yard from time immemorial, with the dog barking.'[23] Another polished and amusing poet, if distinctly lacking in ardour in his quest for love, was that highly accomplished wordsmith, Gutun Owain. He likened himself to a pilgrim making the circuit of Rome's holy places as he tramped around his loved one's territory.

It is not easy to tell for whom this kind of poetry was intended. Love poetry of the kind expressed by the troubadours had long been popular among older men and women as well as young ones. A medieval winter was a time of cold and hardship, of lean, monotonous, vitaminless diet, made all the sparser by the long Lenten fast. One night of winter, complained Dafydd ab Edmwnd, lasted longer than a month in spring. When the vernal season came round again, the adrenalin flowed freely as the sap rose. People of both sexes and more than one generation heard with renewed delight the love-poetry, gladly indulged in song and dance around the maypole, and gave themselves to the joys of love in the fresh green countryside, free from the gaze of prying eyes and the comment of gossiping tongues. May was notoriously the season of the year when the constraints of the marriage bonds sat lightest upon them and when many heeded the siren voices that spoke of love and freedom and the delights of

[23] *D. ab E.*, pp. 31–5.

the senses. By contrast, for others who would never seriously have thought of such indulgence there was great pleasure to be derived around the blazing hearth on a winter night from a bard's merry tongue and his mischievous verbal shafts.

The other major category of verse was the religious poetry, about which a good deal has already been written. Much of it was yet another variety of poetry of praise, glorifying God, Jesus Christ, the Blessed Virgin, the saints, and holy places associated with them, for their virtues and powers. There also flourished a strong vein of didactic verse linked especially with the name of Siôn Cent. It deplored mankind's ineradicable hankering after ephemeral earthly delights and pleasures, emphasizing how short was its lease of earthly life, how perishable its apparent triumphs and riches, and how great the need for restraint, contribution, and obedience to the Church's teaching and for application to godliness and devotion.

There was also a considerable body of prose literature. Much of this consisted of tales and romances, some of which have survived in manuscript form, though many must have perished. These stories, handed down for generations, had been polished to a high degree of artistic effectiveness. They were learned, remembered, and transmitted by the professional *cyfarwyddiaid* [story-tellers] whose services, like those of the poets, were regularly called for and received with acclamation by the throngs assembled on feast nights in the halls of the *uchelwyr*. Most of the tales were aristocratic in their setting and provenance and were regaled to entertain an upper-class audience, which responded instinctively to them. Some were ancient Celtic legends of demigods and heroes, supreme among them the *Mabinogi*, which rank among the world's great stories.[24] Alongside them were preserved Arthurian tales, legends of the Grail, stories relating to Charlemagne and his men, and other old and similarly popular narratives. There existed, too, a wide range of 'vocational' prose literature—historical or quasi-historical texts like *Brut y Tywysogion* [Chronicle of the Princes] or Geoffrey of Monmouth's *Historia Regum Britanniae* in Welsh translation; bardic grammars; genealogies; triads; versions of the lawbooks; medical, scientific, and astronomical treatises; religious texts and saints' lives; and the like. Increasingly, these prose works were being recorded in writing at this period; an indication not only of the virility of the prose tradition but also of the growing interest among the literate members of society in acquiring available versions of such texts.

The culture embodied in the medieval Welsh poetry and prose constituted a choice and variegated inheritance. The littérateurs and their patrons had entered into a singularly rich, long-lived, and diverse cultural patrimony. Nor were they just rigid, inflexible heirs and guardians of an

[24] G. and T. Jones, *The Mabinogion* (London, 1948).

ancient native tradition. They were men who delighted to see the fashioning anew in every generation of an exquisite and sophisticated literature designed to gratify a truly cultivated taste and appetite for it. At its best, literature was created by an intelligentsia catering for an intelligentsia.[25] In their poetry, bards drew on a comprehensive range of references which displayed not only, as would have been expected, an intimate knowledge of the Welsh language, prose, verse, history, pseudo-history, genealogy, and heraldry, but also an equal familiarity with Celtic legends and traditions, scriptural and Christian knowledge, apocryphal literature and religious texts, and an awareness of the major figures of the classical, Arthurian, and medieval scenes. When they referred to the events and personages of this widely-ranging milieu, they appeared to take it for granted that these would reverberate instantly in the consciousness of those who listened to their poetry. They were working within a frame of reference which they could assume was nearly as familiar to their audience as to themselves.

The vigour and resilience of the literature owed as much to the patrons as to the poets. This spectacular flowering of Welsh poetry during the fifteenth century would have been impossible without the existence of a large number of enthusiastic, generous, and discerning patrons. There was unquestionably a rising wave of vitality and interest among the contemporary gentry. That growth in prosperity and self-awareness among the *uchelwyr*, to which attention has already been drawn, found a ready outlet in the patronage of the bards. Moreover, this was an age of unbounded ambition, resolute competition, and incessant striving among the upper classes. They sought fiercely to uphold, proclaim, and extend their own possessions and reputation and those of their family and descendants. They vied with one another to demonstrate publicly their wealth and position by building new halls, acquiring costly goods and chattels, and giving lavish feasts and celebrations on special occasions. There was a novel and particular emphasis on status as expressed in material possessions, lineage, kinship, and position. None could proclaim all this to the world of Wales with greater authority than the poets, accredited for centuries past with the role of publicists and propagandists. Something may still have prevailed of the 'mantic aura' of an earlier period when what a man received from a poet's plaudits was to be measured by the generosity of his own giving. The poet's goodwill could influence a patron's character, well-being, and prosperity. The bard spread his patron's reputation among all those invited to his hall: his friends and fellow *uchelwyr* and his *plaid* of kinsmen, dependants, and tenants. In a still largely oral culture these effusions must have been widely heard and appreciated among the class of freemen brought up to admire

[25] E. P. Roberts, 'Wiliam Cynwal', *TDHS*, XII (1963), 51–85.

and venerate the poetry. In all parts of Wales, the March, and the English border, wherever the Welsh tongue was spoken, there were patrons who welcomed poets. Some great houses, like Gwedir, Nannau, Corsygedol, Mostyn, Dinefwr, or Raglan, and some monastic establishments, such as Valle Crucis, Conwy, Strata Florida, or Neath, reinforced the tradition in generation after generation and became rightly renowned as outstanding centres of culture and hospitality. The more celebrated the hearth, the more the poets flocked there, like bees to honey in the hive of patronage.

We know comparatively little about the nature of the gifts actually received by the poets. But there are a few fragmentary indications. The 'Statute of Gruffydd ap Cynan' laid down that, from a gentleman having a living of £5 a year or more, a *pencerdd* could claim once in every three years eighty-one pence; and if he were a teacher he ought also to receive a jewel, weapon, or clothing. If he were to be made a butt for lesser bards at a wedding feast, his gift should be doubled and he should receive the bridegroom's second-best surcoat or doublet. On the three great feasts of the year, Christmas, Easter, and Whitsun, and at a wedding feast he ought to receive forty pence, and on lesser occasions a shilling. The poets of lower grades ought to receive proportionately less on such occasions.[26] But much, doubtless, depended on the poet's standing and on his own awareness of it. A good deal must also have been determined by the nature of the friendship existing between poet and patron.

Poets loved going on circuit of their patrons, of course. They often conveyed discreet and delicate hints to their patrons of their wish to travel the countryside on their poetic peregrinations by composing request poems for horses. Horses could be invaluable for warfare and hunting and the poets give magnificent descriptions of spirited steeds. But more often than not they wanted quieter nags for themselves so as to be able gently to perambulate the countryside on their visitations. Lewys Glyn Cothi has a number of amusing poems asking for tame horses, including one to the men of Elfael requesting one as lacking in spirit as a sheep and having a short bridle to prevent him from leaping wildly. Guto'r Glyn, by the end of his life old and blind, has a rather plaintive poem of gratitude to Dafydd ap Meurig Fychan of Nannau to thank him for the gift of a 'handsome hackney' [*hacnai hardd*], 'with careful trot bearing the blind man' [*da iawn ei duth yn dwyn dall*].[27]

There were particular times when the poets were expected to visit their patrons. The 'Statute of Gruffydd ap Cynan' tells us something about the seasons when they went: Christmas and a circuit following until the feast of the Purification of Mary (2 February); from Easter until Ascension Day; from Whitsun until Relic Sunday (the third after Midsummer); when a

---

[26] *TA*, p. xxii.   [27] *GG*, pp. 227–9.

nobleman built a new house; the patron saint's day [*gŵyl mabsant*]; and a wedding feast for a maiden bride. Lewys Glyn Cothi recalled how poets visited a patron, Llywelyn ap Gwilym ap Thomas Fychan, at Christmas, New Year, Lent, Easter, and Whitsun, and how, at the home of another, Dafydd Llwyd ap Dafydd, if they went on Mary's feast day (21 November) they stayed until Christmas, and having stayed at Easter they returned again at Whitsun.[28] Still more important were those occasions of special concern to the individual families—weddings and funerals. The wedding feasts brought together the representatives of two families to celebrate and to act as witnesses to the merging of two lines of gentle descent. It gave the poets a unique opportunity to glorify the lineage of both husband and wife and their respective families. Funerals were solemn occasions when the merits of the deceased had to be appropriately commemorated when 'the song was brought home' [*dwyn y cerdd adref*], as the saying went. Though subject to the conventional expressions of exaggerated grief and mourning, there were times when the loss of a real friend seems to have been keenly and genuinely felt. Tudur Aled, mourning the death of Tudur Llwyd of Bodidris, lamented thus: 'I called upon him, great was my grief; my cry went through the rock and oak and gravel. If he could but have heard me, even though his wall were locked, Tudur's grave would have been unsealed.'[29]

Such expressions are a reminder that friendship between patron and poet could be deep and real. Guto'r Glyn went so far as to describe the relationship between himself and Hywel ab Ifan Fychan as being akin to that between a married couple, between whom God Himself would allow no divorce. Oftentimes, the friendship between them was based on close ties of common aesthetic and intellectual interests. One of the most attractive vignettes presented to us in the literature of the age is that of Guto'r Glyn and Rhys of Glyn Neath in one another's company, avidly poring over the Brut, saints' lives, the triads, the romances, and the poems of Cynddelw.[30] Then again, Lewys Glyn Cothi tells us how he and his patron, Wiliam Siôn (also a poet), read and studied together history, chronicles, pedigrees, and the oldest poetry [*hengerdd*] and *rhieingerdd* [love-poetry].[31] Even the somewhat chilly Gutun Owain warmed when he recalled Robert Trefor's knowledge of poetry, story, song, grammar, and history; or Elisau ap Gruffydd ab Elisau's remarkable learning in law, scripture, heraldry, and the chronicles—'of the wise ones he is the choicest' [*o'r doethiaid ef yw'r dethol*].[32] From time to time, however, the most cordial friendship might come to grief—temporarily at least. At such a juncture the poet naturally wanted to achieve a reconciliation if that were at all possible; and it is often not hard to detect the note of pressing

[28] *LGC*[1], p. 76.   [29] *TA*, p. 318.   [30] *GG*, pp. 240–1.
[31] *LGC*[1], p. 315.   [32] *GO*, pp. 213–15.

urgency in his efforts to bring it about. Dafydd Nanmor enjoyed an unusual degree of intimacy with his leading patron, Rhys ap Thomas of Tywyn in Cardiganshire; but on one occasion a serious rift occurred between them. Seeking to regain Rhys's good graces, Dafydd expressed the fear that if he failed he might have to become an outlaw. In the end he was wise enough to resort to a device which many a poet had to adopt—he appealed to Rhys's wife, Margaret, to intercede with her husband on his behalf. The stratagem worked and the poet was restored to favour.[33] Guto'r Glyn could typically not keep his mischievous humour out of a poem urging reconciliation with Ifan Fychan ab Ifan. He likened himself, bearing the burden of Ifan's anger, to three other famous load-carriers—St Christopher, Hercules, and the man in the moon! He, too, sensibly besought the aid of Ifan's wife, Angharad, and his grandson, Hywel, to soften his patron's wrath.[34]

The social reason for the gentry's patronage of poetry—its main impetus probably—has already been discussed (see above, pp. 98–101). Yet it would be doing the *uchelwyr* a grievous injustice to overlook their genuine delight in literature for its own sake. They really did enjoy having poets in their homes and savoured their offerings with relish. Furthermore, when a number of bards assembled together—and we know of at least twelve in the company at a feast given by Rhisiart Cyffin, dean of Bangor, on one occasion—an inordinate amount of hilarity, leg-pulling, and rivalry ensued. It was not only the patrons who competed among themselves; the poets were also just as keen to excel. Beneath the lively chaffing and banter can be detected a sharp competitive edge to see who would come out on top and an eager desire to score points off rivals for a patron's gifts and favour. The poet Ieuan ap Hywel Swrdwal confessed that he had been sent to a Breconshire lady as a *llatai* [love-messenger] for another poet, Llawdden, only to find that when he approached her she would have none of Llawdden and much preferred his emissary. In mock indignation Llawdden retorted that Ieuan had been far too busy voicing two words on his own account for every one he uttered on Llawdden's.[35] More seriously, Ieuan Deulwyn accused his fellow poet, Bedo Brwynllys, of speaking with a forked tongue to Richard Herbert (a Yorkist) and Jasper Tudor (a Lancastrian) in order to deceive both; and on another occasion he complained that other poets were two-faced in their attitude to him, flattering him to his face and reviling him behind his back.[36] Guto'r Glyn figured in such altercations [*ymrysonau*] more than almost any other poet. He and Tudur Penllyn engaged in a fine-edged poetic debate, spiced with wit and not a little venom. In their poems to one another, each taxed the other for his shortcomings while droving sheep for the parson of Corwen.

[33] *DN*, p. 12.
[34] *GG*, pp. 73–4.
[35] *HS*, pp. 29–31, 37–8.
[36] *ID*, pp. 86, 89.

Guto further engaged in a highly entertaining verbal rough and tumble with the priest-poet, Sir Rhys of Carno, when he was confined to the house with illness but still got the better of the encounter. The most witty duel of all was that in which he crossed swords with Llywelyn ap Gutun who, in one of the most scintillating satirical poems of the fifteenth century, pretended to lament Guto's death in the Menai Straits by drowning—he was in Heaven because he could not swim. Guto tried hard to reply in kind but he clearly came off second-best in this encounter.[37] No less magisterial a figure than Tudur Aled was singled out as a butt for such bardic sallies; but his normal mode of reply was to remind the lesser fry with some hauteur of his aristocratic descent and his bardic accomplishments.

For all the point-scoring and sharp-tongued criticism that might have gone the rounds among the poets in their efforts to get the better of one another, there is also unmistakable evidence of the profound respect cherished by them for the unrivalled mastery over their art exercised by the acknowledged leaders of their profession. Even Llywelyn ap Gutun, when satirizing Guto'r Glyn unmercifully in his mock elegy on the latter's 'drowning', could nevertheless not forbear from conceding that he was the 'hawk of the *cywyddau* of praise' [*gwalch cywyddau gwŷr*], 'captain of the major poets' [*capten yr henfeirdd*], and 'a great oak towering above bards' [*caterwen uwchben beirdd*].[38] But it was in some of the elegies addressed to poets by their compeers that the sense of irreparable loss to the art of poetry after the passing of a great master can be most clearly detected. It was in these poems that the measure of their achievement can be best assessed. Exaggeration swells through them admittedly—nothing could prevent poets from indulging in that—but there echoes through them as well an undeniably sincere note of profound *hiraeth* [nostalgia] and admiration. When the *pencerdd* of the Carmarthen Eisteddfod, Dafydd ab Edmwnd, died, his nephew and most dazzling pupil, Tudur Aled, mourned his passing and that of two of his contemporaries, Dafydd Nanmor and Ieuan Deulwyn. 'God's hand has slain the muse, has killed the soul of the whole ancient art of poetry'. He went on to offer Dafydd ab Edmwnd as sincere and striking a tribute as any that could have been paid him: 'Never was there a poet of greater inspiration unless it was the bard of fair Glyn Teifi [i.e., Dafydd ap Gwilym], who will now not be without a companion, without a brother up aloft in Heaven'.[39] Tudur Aled's own death in 1526 occasioned even deeper and more widespread sorrow. The elegies of no fewer than nine poets have been preserved for us. Among them were some of the most accomplished masters of their craft then living—Lewys Môn from Gwynedd, Gruffydd ab Ieuan ap Llywelyn Fychan from Powys, and Lewis Morgannwg from the south. Gruffydd ab Ieuan, in a line of

---

[37] *GG*, pp. 98–103, 277–82.   [38] *GG*, p. 99.   [39] *TA*, pp. 282–4.

resounding onomatopaeic force, shuddered at the 'thunder-crash as the great beam of poetry fell' [*trwstan-gwymp trawst awen-gerdd*]. Lewis Morgannwg sighed for the loss of 'My carpenter of all the [*cynghanedd*] measures' [*fy saer i'r holl fesurau*]. Tudur Aled's own bardic pupil, Raff ap Robert, was inconsolable that 'my teacher has gone into earth; poetry has for ever passed from us; now that God of Heaven has taken our chosen one, what does it matter any longer what we sing?' But the most touching sadness of all was expressed by Tudur's bosom friend, Lewys Môn, who opened his elegy with an unforgettable couplet: 'I am an orphan without a father; my brother has been taken; I am a dead man'. Then he went on, 'Every ardent praise came from his lips; was his voice not splendid, chief Taliesin? He was livelier than a cauldron; who seethed with greater learning? He was chief of poets. . . . And now in St Mary's churchyard—it will ever be a vineyard—the muse dwells for ever.'[40]

'The muse dwells for ever.' [*Y trig awen tragywydd.*] It was a fitting epitaph on the excellence of Welsh medieval verse and the camaraderie of the poets as well as on Tudur. For he was the last of the really outstanding medieval poets. When he died in 1526 the whole of the Welsh bardic order of the Middle Ages was on the verge of fundamental change. There would be fine poets later in the sixteenth century; but none would have the same sense of unalloyed assurance nor the air of undisputed mastery over his medium that Tudur Aled, 'pen Taliesin', last of the giants of the golden age of Welsh medieval poetry, had enjoyed.

Tudur had been a double master—of *cerdd dant* [music] as well as *cerdd dafod* [poetry]. So, too, were other poets, including that Ifan ab Ifan Fychan before whose anger Guto'r Glyn's back had bowed so low. But Guto had all the same recognized that Ifan's silver tongue and harp had fully merited the praise heaped upon them.[41] It was usual for men of rank to maintain musicians as well as poets in their retinues. Music and song were as intensely enjoyed and appreciated in the halls of *uchelwyr* as poetry and story-telling. The poet Rhys Goch Eryri, in a poem praising the many facets of the excellent taste of his patron, Robert ap Maredudd, attached special importance to his delight in music. He commented on the many kinds of musicians and entertainers—crowthers, harpists, trumpeters, pipers, fiddlers, drummers, and sawtrie players—who, together with acrobats, jugglers, and conjurors, in addition to poets of course, were welcomed to his home.[42] Lewys Glyn Cothi similarly referred to the many musicians—pipers, crowthers, harpists, and organists—who played for Siencyn Hafard's delectation.[43] The harp was particularly favoured among the Welsh and was generally regarded as their national instrument. Poetry was often declaimed to the strains of the harp, and songs sung to its

[40] *TA*, pp. 725–52.
[41] *GG*, p. 74.
[42] *IGE*, pp. 302–3.
[43] *LGC*[1], p. 125.

accompaniment. An early manuscript of harp music, dating from 1613 and compiled by Robert ap Huw, was based on a sixteenth-century manuscript which may have incorporated a good deal of medieval harp music. Unfortunately, it does not seem possible, at present anyway, to decipher the musical notation satisfactorily.[44] A little more is known about church music which may have been more important at this time than any other form. It must have been in a fairly flourishing condition to have produced four early Tudor composers of such singular talents as John Lloyd (c.1480–1523), Robert Jones (c.1485–1535), Philip ap Rhys (*flor.* 1530) and John Gwynedd (*flor.* 1525–55). Robert Jones was the ablest amongst them. He had the distinction of being one of the composers whose work was included in Wynkin de Worde's unique book of *Twenty Songs*, published in 1530, and of being included in Morley's well-known list (1597) of famous composers who flourished before the Reformation. His Mass and Magnificat is held to have marked a distinct advance in musical technique and to show the first glimmering of the great polyphonic work later created by Tallis and Byrd.[45]

Traces of the other arts which flourished in medieval Wales were closely connected with religion and have already been referred to. The Church was the great matrix of architecture and the other visual arts which blossomed under its aegis. Pre-eminent among them were the woodcarvers. Close affinities of standards and inspiration can be discerned between woodcarving and poetry. In both, the artist was content to allow himself, both by the canons of his craft and the requirements of his patrons, to be confined to a limited number of highly stylized themes and patterns. In wood and word the flowing vitality and exuberance of the artist were enhanced not imprisoned by his strict adherence to the meticulous details and the exacting, strict classicism of his artistic conventions. The vines, the wyeverns, and the traceries so lovingly fashioned in a Welsh roodscreen could be as congenial an expression of Welsh medieval aesthetics as the poet's *cywydd* or *englyn*. The poetry and the roodscreens both reached their peak in the century or so before the Reformation.

---

[44] *The New Oxford Companion to Music*, ed. D. Arnold (2 vols. Oxford, 1983), II, 1958–9.
[45] Williams, *Welsh Church*, p. 451.

CHAPTER 7

WAR ABROAD AND TURMOIL AT HOME
1415–1461

HENRY V began his reign in a determinedly conciliatory frame of mind towards his own subjects. He seemed intent on tying up such loose ends as were left over from his father's reign, including the Glyndŵr Rebellion. He was concerned to bring peace and reconciliation to Wales, partly in order to forestall any attempts by the Lollards to take advantage of disturbed conditions there, but more importantly to be able once more to mobilize the resources of the country to help in prosecuting his wars in France. He therefore offered terms on which large numbers of Welshmen could come to his obedience—and pay for the privilege of doing so; peace with profit, an admirable outcome from Henry's point of view! In November 1413 he exacted a fine of no less than 1,600 marks from the war-torn shires of Caernarfon, Merioneth, and Anglesey. In the same year he tried to restore a measure of stability and recovery by promulgating a royal ordinance to the effect that the earls of March and Arundel, the lords of Powys, and the Chamberlain of South Wales should send back to their home areas those tenants who had decamped from the three north-western shires; and he also allowed £200 for the purchase of sheep and cattle to restock the devastated countryside. In 1413, too, he established a commission to examine the treasons and riots in which royal officials had themselves been involved; and, in consequence, he sacked the Chamberlain of North Wales, Thomas Barneby, whose behaviour had been self-interested and fraudulent. As further incentives to the Welsh, the native law of inheritance was guaranteed in royal lands, debts incurred before 1411 were cancelled, and many of the native population were restored to lands they had left before rebellion had broken out, though a number of new landholders were perforce introduced into some areas (above, pp. 29–30). In July 1415 Henry even empowered Gilbert Talbot to negotiate with Owain Glyndŵr himself and offer him and other rebels a chance of coming to the king's peace and obedience. Owain—if he were still alive—ignored the proposal, and his son, Maredudd, also held out for some years longer.

In general, though, Henry's initial policies worked well. No support was forthcoming in Wales for that plot devised in 1415 by Richard, earl of Cambridge, as elements of which the earl of March was to be taken to Wales and proclaimed king, and the former enemies, Owain Glyndŵr and

Sir John Oldcastle, were to be induced to collaborate with one another. Though Oldcastle came to the Marches of Wales and was able to maintain himself there for two years, he found little favour with the Welsh population. When he was eventually seized in 1417, his capture was effected by two Welshmen, Gruffydd Fychan and his brother, Ieuan. A reward of 1,000 marks had been offered for Oldcastle's capture and he was taken by the two brothers in a glade at Pant-mawr farm, Broniarth, and brought in triumph to Sir John Gray. His leading lieutenant, a man from Glamorgan called Thomas Payn, was captured some years later.

To wage his campaigns in France Henry could turn to Wales for men and money as confidently as his predecessors had done. Welsh freemen had always looked upon war as the most honourable and glorious activity in which they could indulge. Their bards, from sixth-century Taliesin and Aneirin onwards, had extolled valour in battle as the noblest characteristic of any man with pretensions to breeding and honour. They could praise these elemental virtues of an heroic society as enthusiastically as ever at the end of the fourteenth century and the beginning of the fifteenth, in tones bloodthirstily reminiscent of poets of an earlier age. Iolo Goch had described Owain Glyndŵr as

> Cannwyll brwydr, cân holl Brydyn,
> Mawr fu ei arswyd, crwyd crau,
> Blwyddyn yn porthi bleiddiau.[1]

[The candle of battle, the song of all Scotland; great was the fear of him, spiller of blood; for a year he fed the wolves [with corpses]]

and Guto'r Glyn, early in the fifteenth century, hailed Matthew Goch in France in similar vein as

> Enaid y capteiniaid da
> A blaenor y bobl yna.
> Broch â bar coch yn bwrw cant[2]

[The soul of good captains and the chief of all the people there. The badger with the blood-stained bar overthrowing a hundred.]

An upland country like Wales, where all the sons inherited equal shares in their fathers' lands, tended to produce a surplus population, many of whom could not be readily absorbed within the confines of their own pastoral economy and among whom existed widespread under-employment—a phenomenon common enough in other soldier-breeding mountain countries of Europe like Scotland, Switzerland, or parts of Castile. A soldier's life, therefore, had an irresistible appeal for many a Welshman. Since the thirteenth century English kings and Marcher lords had been recruiting them in large numbers for service in Scotland or France or even against

[1] *IGE*, pp. 34–5.   [2] *GG*, pp. 8–10.

their own countrymen. In Principality and Marches alike Henry could expect Wales to be a fruitful nursery of fighting men. An old tradition of soldierly prowess, an instinctive family or individual loyalty to king or lord, a desire to escape from depressing poverty, the prospect of good pay (an archer was paid twice as much a day as a labourer), ample booty, glory, adventure, wine-bibbing, wenching, a break from dull routine in exotic foreign lands, all combined to attract many recruits. The Welsh already had a name for being brave and dashing soldiers, eager for battle though somewhat boisterous and ill-disciplined, hard drinkers, enthusiastic womanizers, and much given to looting. It was a reputation that many of them would amply sustain in fifteenth-century France.

In his search for troops Henry V naturally sought to make use of the services of those who had hitherto been loyal to himself and his father in their campaigns against Glyndŵr. Men like David ap Llywelyn, better known as Davy Gam (the 'one-eyed' or 'squint-eyed'), whose family had long had a tradition of service to the lords of Brecon and who had himself stood resolutely on the side of the Crown against his compatriots in the course of the Rebellion from 1400 onwards, when as a king's esquire he first received his annuity of forty marks a year, were as willing to join the royal army for service in France as in Wales. Davy Gam himself and his son-in-law, Roger Vaughan of Bredwardine, fought and died at Agincourt, where the former was reputed to have been posthumously knighted. Rhys ap Thomas of Carmarthen was another who had been loyal to the Crown, and, for his steadfastness, had been rewarded with office and an annuity of £10 to compensate him for damage and destruction to his lands by the rebels. He was also granted denizen rights to free him from the taint, under existing statutes, of his Welsh origins.

But the King was by no means averse from availing himself of the services of those who, having opposed him during the Rebellion, had since come to terms with him and were now willing to fight under the royal flag. Owain Glyndŵr's own son-in-law, John Scudamore, in 1415 went to France with four men-at-arms and twelve archers and remained abroad for some years, being captain of Harfleur in 1416 and guardian of the port in 1422. The young Owain Tudor, Glyndŵr's kinsman and later to become Queen Catherine's second husband, in spite of the devastating sacrifices suffered by his family in the rebel cause, appears to have served in France with Sir Walter Hungerford. Maredudd ab Owain himself, Glyndŵr's son, eventually entered the royal service. Gruffydd Dwn, grandson to the indomitable rebel Henry Dwn, fought long and hard in France, from Agincourt down to 1445, when he was taken prisoner at Dieppe and ransomed by Walter Devereux. Three of Gruffydd's sons also won their spurs fighting against the French. David Howell of Pembrokeshire, implicated in the earl of Cambridge's plot of 1415, afterwards went to

France and had a distinguished career there, in the course of which he was knighted. Not all Welshmen abandoned their anti-English stance, however. One at least, Henry son of William Gwyn, a former Owainite, remained irreconcilably rooted in his hostility to kings of England. He was killed at Agincourt in the company of the King's French enemies. There could well have been others like him whose names have not come down to us.

For his French campaigns Henry raised troops by means of indentures with individual lords and captains, who engaged to bring a stipulated number of men-at-arms 'well-mounted, armed and arrayed as belonged to their estate' and a body of archers. They contracted for a specified term of service, ranging from forty days to a year or more, and in return the King paid them wages at an agreed rate. Recruitment in south Wales was particularly successful. No fewer than 500 men out of a total of 9,000 eventually mustered in England and Wales were raised in Carmarthenshire, Cardiganshire, and the lordship of Brecon alone, under the command of John Merbury, Chamberlain of South Wales. The mounted archers in their ranks were paid 6d. a day, the unmounted 4d., and the men-at-arms 1s. Richard Beauchamp, earl of Worcester and lord of Glamorgan, although he did not go overseas in 1415, performed valuable service at home by raising 5,000 men from his estates and concentrating them at Hanley castle, Worcs., in order to suppress any attempt at insurrection by the Lollards. In 1417 he was one of a large company of earls who accompanied Henry V on his second attempt to conquer Normandy. Many Welshmen accompanied these lords and their followers to France, though few details of their service have survived. Gruffydd Fychan went with Sir John Gray, who was killed at Baugé in 1421 and brought home to Welshpool to be buried. Edward Stradling of Glamorgan, John Perrot, and William Wogan joined Humphrey, duke of Gloucester; Henry Wogan, Gruffydd Dwn, and William ap Thomas were three of a number of prominent Welshmen gathered round the duke of York; John Griffith and John ap Thomas went with Sir William Bourchier; John Glyn and Nicholas Griffith with Lord Talbot; and John Edwards, who stayed in France at the end of the wars, accompanied Michael de la Pole, son of the earl of Suffolk. Richard Beauchamp, earl of Warwick and lord of Glamorgan, one of the greatest English generals in France, had many notable Welshmen, including Richard Gethin and Matthew Gough, under his command.

It was not only troops that were levied in Wales. Considerable sums of money, especially in view of how grievously impoverished the country had been by rebellion, were also raised to buttress the King's cause. War taxes were paid even in disaster-stricken north and west Wales. In 1417 Henry obtained payment of £1,000 from Cardiganshire and Carmarthenshire and squeezed £1,500 out of the Duchy of Lancaster's Welsh lordships in the same year, extracting loans of £53 from burgesses like Walter Brace and

Thomas ap David. There were further attempts, in 1420 and 1430 at least, to raise large sums of money again.

During the four decades from 1415 to 1453 a good many Welshmen, even if their numbers cannot be precisely quantified, went abroad to fight in the King's multinational forces in France. They often kept together in compact national groups; partly because of close local ties with one another and their captains, and partly because of the difficulty of giving orders to men who understood no language but their own. For example, the garrison at Falaise in 1429 under Thomas Gower contained a high proportion of men with Welsh names, while at Tancarville in 1438 Gruffydd Dwn had 77 men with Welsh names out of 137 under his command. From the midst of the Welsh emerged such notable captains as David Howell, Richard Gethin, Gruffydd Fychan, and Fulk Eyton. Most celebrated of all was the redoubtable Matthew Gough, who lived on as 'Matago' in the awed and often bitter French remembrance of him. He had terrified the hapless French civilians, who had suffered untold casualties and damage at his and his desperadoes' hands, as completely as he had thrilled his countrymen by his daring feats. He had fought with éclat at Cravant (1423) and Verneuil (1424), had subsequently commanded many French towns, was taken prisoner in 1432—an event which caused profound consternation among Welsh bards—but was soon released and fought finally at Formigny, where a stirring eve-of-battle address to the troops was attributed to him.

The kind of admiration which the exploits of such swashbuckling captains aroused in their fellow Welshmen, and no doubt fired many adventurous youths to follow them, is still vividly conveyed to us in the verses directed to them by that master-poet, Guto'r Glyn. Guto, himself a soldier renowned for his courage and his unexampled strength of arm, was a man who served in a number of campaigns during the 1440s and wore the badge and collar of the king's guard. He may have composed his *cywydd* to Matthew Gough about the year 1441. This and other poems like it vibrate with the excited, youthful hero-worship of a poet, then probably in his twenties, for these formidable warriors. In his eulogy of Gough, who originally hailed from Maelor in north-east Wales, Guto indulged freely in lavish plaudits of him as the admired adversary of the two most famous French captains, the 'Castor and Pollux' of the enemy armies, La Hire (Étienne Vignolles) and Poton de Xantrailles. La Hire, companion-in-arms of the immortal Maid of Orléans herself, had extended to Gough the hand of friendship during a truce, but that, vowed the poet, did not prevent Gough and his men from subsequently rousing the echoes among the French hills and woodlands with their cry of 'Ho-hw La Hire' as they hunted him like a stag. They had launched themselves on the French of Anjou and Maine with all the speed and frightfulness of cannon-balls, the most alarming of the new weapons of war (an unusually early example of the use of the term and metaphor in Welsh literature).[3]

Guto took back with him to Wales his memories of La Hire and Poton. Both figure centrally in his witty *cywydd*, written *c.*1444 perhaps, to Thomas ap Watcyn Fychan of Gwent, who intended to go to France with the duke of York. In this satirical poem about a 'skirmish' between poets and liquor, we sense the same uncontrollable excitement at the prospect of action on the battlefield coupled with a devil-may-care attitude of approval of deep drinking, regardless of any indiscipline that might follow. In this instance, the battle was won, for once, by the 'French forces' of the Dauphin represented by white wine, La Hire by metheglin, and Poton by heavy beer. They routed their 'enemies', the bards, who did battle with them. The poem ended, nevertheless, by assuring Thomas and his comrades of victory once the real-life fighting was joined in France.[4]

By the time Guto came to address his poems to Richard Gethin, probably about 1449, the days of victory and the spectacular gains that had enabled Gethin to lend as much as £1,000 to the duke of Bedford in 1434 were long since past. Many of the English and Welsh had left for home, the last towns in Normandy were falling inexorably to the French, and English armies had their backs to the wall. Guto was deeply grieved that Gethin, a native of Builth now captain of Mantes, was in danger of being captured. Tears flowed from the poet's eyes as he reflected that the 'flower of Welsh manhood' might already be a prisoner in enemy hands. Fortunately, the report proved to be untrue and Guto was able to exult in his idol's freedom. Trying to catch this hero, he boasted, was as futile as seeking to hold the wind in one's hands. In spite of heavy defeats, the old camaraderie, the courage in face of danger, the sheer joy in battle for its own sake, the heedlessness of civilian sufferings and misery—the contempt for them, even—and the total absence of any moral or humanitarian qualms are still unmistakably present in the poetry.[5] Guto'r Glyn shared Froissart's view, even if he had never heard of it, that 'gentle knights were born to fight and war ennobled all those who engaged in it without fear or cowardice'. The cries of those French men and women who at this time were wailing bitterly, 'Alas! I die of cold and hunger',[6] got scant hearing from Guto or the soldiery.

It is not at all easy to assess what these Welshmen who had fought in France gained or lost as a result of their experiences there. A few among them undoubtedly won lasting fame and remembrance as gallant, if often callous, soldiers—with Matthew Gough and Richard Gethin outstanding in their midst. Each of the leading captains had also done well in more material terms as a result of his exploits. Members of other rising

[3] *GG*, pp. 8–10.   [4] *GG*, pp. 11–3.   [5] *GG*, pp. 3–7.
[6] M. Bishop, *The Pelican Book of the Middle Ages* (Pelican, 1983), p. 376.

families—Games, Vaughans, Herberts, Dwns, Stradlings, Wogans, and Tudors, to name but a handful—had also gained a good deal; indirectly, in terms of increased and valuable contacts with the Crown or the aristocracy, rather than in terms of enhanced wealth or greater estates. Almost without exception the leading figures had been granted denizen rights and exempted from the interdictions of the penal statutes.[7] But not one family can be singled out as having made its fortunes solely on the basis of war profits. The lesser lights, the men of lower rank, no doubt acquired their share of booty from time to time; but their habitual addiction to drink, women, and gambling probably ensured that they lost their gains almost as quickly as they had won them. Yet Guto'r Glyn, at least, brought back with him to Wales as a present bestowed on him by Richard Gethin an elegant golden cloak which dazzled the eyes of many a beholder, especially of the fair sex, as Guto, dark, handsome, and resplendent in the cloak, swaggered among the halls and *plasau* and taverns back home. There may have been many other similar trophies which found no poet to record them.

Even though the wars did not make much difference to the process of acquiring gentry estates in Wales, a number of the captains had been granted lands in France. Matthew Gough had done especially well for himself, with estates at Rouen, Gisors, Caux, Evreux, and Harcourt between 1430 and 1432. Sir David Howell acquired the barony of Briars and the lordship of Aufreville in 1437, as well as other lordships later, while Gruffydd Dwn had got his hands on lands in Alençon in 1437 and later obtained the lordship of Aqueville and the fiefs of Orties and Fervaques. Men of lower rank, including one David, who was an assistant to the English tavern-keeper at Avranches, had managed to pick up lesser acquisitions. Two members of the Apowell family and John Gough had been students at the University of Caen; and the last-named became curate at Cherbourg. Most of the gains made by all ranks were lost, of course, when the tide turned so disastrously against the English in the last stages of the war. Only those who were prepared to accept the inevitable French victory and throw in their lot with the conquerors could hope to cling on to what they had won. One such was John Edwards, a Welshman, veteran of Agincourt and captain of La Roche-Guyon, who had risen high enough in the world to be able to marry a wealthy French lady, who had 'fine lands and revenues' [*belles terres et revenues*] and was related to the influential Count Denis de Chailly. Loth to lose his wife's possessions, Edwards surrendered his fortress and became a vassal of Charles VII, 'at the advice, prayer and entreaty of his wife, on condition that he should enjoy his wife's lands and become a subject of King Charles'.[8] Others of his fellow-

[7] *WWR*, pp. 63–4.

[8] C. T. Allmand, *Lancastrian Normandy, 1415–50* (Oxford, 1983), p. 80.

countrymen may have had few qualms about similarly switching their allegiance. Among them, just possibly, may have been Richard Gethin. He disappears from the records about 1450, and it is worth recalling Guto'r Glyn's comment that Gethin was extremely reluctant to 'leave the wealthy country' [*nis gad y wlad oludawg*].[9]

Those who did return to England and Wales brought back with them a wealth of campaigning knowledge and experience which they might not be averse from turning to their own and other people's advantage. Matthew Gough was killed as early as 1450 defending London Bridge against the rebel leader, Jack Cade. His death, profoundly lamented in Wales, evoked what must rank as one of the worst couplets of Latin doggerel ever perpetrated, when William of Worcester summed up the Welsh outburst of grief in these halting tones:

> Morte Matthie Goghe
> Cambria clamitavit Oghe[10]

[On the death of Matthew Goch, Wales in deepest gloom cried 'Och']

Another veteran of the French wars, Philip Vaughan of Hay, was described as the 'most noble squire of lances among all the rest' when he fought for the earl of March at the battle of Mortimer's Cross.[11] Dafydd ab Ieuan ab Einion, who was to conduct the famous long-running Lancastrian defence of Harlech castle between 1461 and 1468, had already had long and valorous service overseas. 'I held a castle in France until all the old women in Wales talked of it', he proudly boasted, and added, 'now I will hold a castle in Wales until all the old women of France talk of it.'[12] Ironically enough, the man who was ultimately to reduce Harlech castle, William Herbert, had served his military apprenticeship in France under the eagle eye of the most eminent of Welsh commanders there, Matthew Gough, in the last years of English rule. That early introduction to war would stand him in good stead during his meteoric rise in the 1440s and 1450s. On a more limited scale, Sir John Wynn told how Griffith ap John ap Grono, in a local feud with Hywel ap Rhys, employed tactics which he had seen in the French wars to burn the latter's barns and outhouses. The presence in England and Wales of all these men who had outfaced death in France would not, of itself, have sufficed to bring about the civil wars of the fifteenth century, but it certainly meant that when those conflicts broke out they would be fought with more professional expertise and greater ferocity than they might otherwise have been. Furthermore, it meant that in most areas of Wales there were many ex-soldiers who knew no trade as exciting or more profitable than war. They might not be loth to attach themselves to

[9] *GG*, p. 3.   [10] *WWR*, p. 62.
[11] A. Goodman, *The Wars of the Roses* (London, 1981), p. 166.
[12] *WWR*, p. 167.

ambitious leaders who, like themselves, had tasted war in France and were not unaware of what the resort to armed violence could achieve or afraid to employ it in order to attain their ends in disturbed or unstable circumstances.

The Wales to which these soldiers returned was, like the rest of the kingdom, in a restless and, not infrequently, lawless condition. In the 1430s and 1440s the state of affairs appeared to be getting worse. The unexpected death of Henry V in 1422 had been a serious blow to good government, leading as it did to acrimonious rivalries among the relatives of the child-king Henry VI, especially those between his uncle, the duke of Gloucester, and his great-uncle, Cardinal Beaufort. But from 1437, when Henry came of age, the situation deteriorated still more markedly. The young king proved to be a weak and ineffectual ruler, very much under the influence of favourites, to whom he was all too prone to make excessively generous grants of land and office, thereby creating an unhealthily large Household vested interest. Conversely, he kept other major figures, whom he ought to have admitted to his counsels, away from his person and the levers of power, thus making them dissatisfied and hostile. As a result, partisan rivalries and jockeyings for influence and position became all the more intense. That civil war did not break out before 1455 is a remarkable tribute to the stability of the fifteenth-century governmental system and the widespread respect felt for the Crown—even for such a woefully inept king as Henry VI and one so prone to become a prey to corrupt favourites.

From the border counties of Herefordshire, Shropshire, and Gloucestershire during these decades came repeated complaints to Parliament of the lawless state of Wales and of raids by Welshmen which left in their wake damaged buildings, spoiled crops, and stolen livestock. Merchants told of how by land or on the River Severn they felt themselves insecure, in danger of attack or kidnap. Redress or reparation was out of the question when the malefactors could escape to lordships where they were received and protected like very 'precious jewels'.[13] Nor were these misdeeds carried out by common criminals only. A soldier of such valour and breeding as John Talbot of Goodrich castle, later earl of Shrewsbury, considered it perfectly acceptable in 1424 that, before going to serve in France, he should compensate himself for arrears of wages as constable of Montgomery castle by embarking on a lucrative raid on wealthy farmers in Herefordshire. Among those who joined him in this nefarious enterprise were a number of retainers with unmistakably Welsh names. Similarly, in Shrewsbury a well-to-do widow called Alice Mutton hired a number of ne'er-do-wells from Powys to do her bidding by murdering some of her neighbours. Nor was the situation made any better by the considerable

[13] *HGF*, p. 41.

numbers of Welsh people who came to settle in these border areas, especially the towns, for short or extended visits, or even permanently.

The 1440s proved to be a still more troubled decade. Complaints to Parliament in 1442, 1445, and 1449 spoke of continuing thefts, disorders, and breaches of the peace. Welsh offenders were alleged to be passing from lordship to lordship with their ill-gotten gains in order to escape punishment. A number of Welsh abbeys, including Neath, Strata Florida, and Basingwerk also complained of grievous losses. The abbot of Vale Royal in Cheshire, who had valuable possessions at Llanbadarn and elsewhere in Wales, had a sorry tale to tell of Welshmen 'to whom the abbot has not given such rewards as they desired' falsely accusing him in court to compel him 'to give them rewards and fees' and of 'how he could not pass through certain lordships without being assaulted and beaten'.[14] Other Welshmen, accused of treason, were in 1445 alleged to have come into market towns and remained there for several days without being arrested, either because the sheriff did not know they were there, or 'for favour and amity' or 'for doubt of hurt'.[15] There were worrying reports of a monk who had been holding riotous assemblies in north and south Wales, stirring up the people to rebellion by recalling their history and their prophetic traditions. These were also the years when the fate of Sir Gruffydd Fychan highlighted many of the problems of Wales. Gruffydd had fought for many years in France and had been knighted there for his prowess, owing his promotion in large measure to the favour of Humphrey, duke of Gloucester. He had returned to Wales and on 10 August 1443 had pierced with a lance the heart of his master, Christopher Talbot, third son of the earl of Shrewsbury and a champion tilter. Because of a strong suspicion that Talbot's death was not accidental, Gruffydd was outlawed and a price of 500 marks put on his head. For four years he and his sons remained in outlawry until Sir Henry Gray enticed him to surrender with the promise of a safe-conduct and then promptly beheaded him on 9 July 1447. His death was greeted with a great outburst of grief and indignation, memorably expressed by the bards, Dafydd Llwyd and Lewys Glyn Cothi. Both spoke bitterly of this further instance of Saxon treachery, with Dafydd Llwyd lamenting particularly that his hero had not listened to his poet's warning but had overtrustingly placed his faith in a perjurous safe-conduct, only to have his head lopped off.

In that self-same year of 1447 many other Welshmen were both saddened and incensed by the fall of their great protector, Humphrey, duke of Gloucester. The duke had been interested in Wales since 1414, when he was made earl of Pembroke and acquired the lordships of Cilgerran, Tenby, and Llanstephan. In 1427 he had been appointed Justice

---

[14] *Rot. Parl.*, v, 43.   [15] *Rot. Parl.*, v, 106.

of North Wales and in 1440 Justice of South Wales. Over the years he had attracted many Welshmen to his service and, as pressures mounted against him by his enemies, he was accused of plotting rebellion in Wales to destroy his chief opponent, the duke of Suffolk. Following Gloucester's death at Bury St Edmunds on 23 February 1447, forty-two of his followers—most of them Welshmen—were arrested and imprisoned, among them such considerable figures as Gruffydd ap Nicholas, Henry Wogan, Owain Dwn, and Thomas Herbert. Some of them came within an inch of being executed before Suffolk would allow them to have the benefit of a royal pardon. There may well be a link between the anger caused by Duke Humphrey's downfall and the justification offered for the reinforcing of the garrison at Beaumaris in 1447, when it was claimed that the Welsh were more riotous than they had been and that Scots, Bretons, and other enemies were given to landing in Anglesey, whose only defence was Beaumaris castle.

Judging by the complaints presented to Parliament in 1449 the death of Gloucester and the dispersal of his retinue had not improved the state of Wales one whit. 'Misgoverned persons' were reported to be taking 'divers persons and cattle under colour of distress where they have no manner fee or cause to make such distress, but feign action and quarrels.' Further,

many times for taking of such distresses and in such resistance of them, great assemblies of people, riots, maims, and murders be made, and if it not be hastily remedied other inconveniences be like to follow, of which takings, bringings and carryings in their behalf no due punishment is made, whereof the people of the said parts daily abound and increase in evil government.[16]

To keep the lawlessness of Wales in perspective, however, we should remember what was said at this point about other parts of the kingdom. The Commons in 1449 complained to the King that 'murders, manslaughters, rapes, robberies, riots, affrays and other inconveniences greater than before now late have grown'.[17]

Attempts were made during these years to try to cope with at least the symptoms if not the underlying causes of the turbulence in Wales. Fearing that some of the more daring and violent of the offenders there might seize castles, efforts were made in 1436 to ensure that all constables of castles returned to their charge, and lords marcher were enjoined to maintain order within their lordships. A more far-reaching proposal of 1437 envisaged the setting up of a council to deal specifically with the affairs of the Principality and the March—an interesting anticipation of a device later to be adopted by Edward IV. Nothing came of the suggestion however; nor did much benefit ensue some years later when, in 1442, the lords of the March were instructed to confer together. In that same year the law of treason was extended to include abduction or theft carried out in the border counties by Welshmen, an innovation which lasted only six years. A more negative aspect of these efforts to restore stability was the reaffirmation of Henry IV's statutes against the Welsh in 1431, 1433, and again in 1447, following the upheavals caused in Wales by the death of Duke Humphrey. The statutes were then reaffirmed and 'all grants of franchises, markets, fairs, and other freedoms to buy or sell, or bake or brew or sell in the towns of north Wales made to any Welshman before this time' were to be 'void and of no value'. Furthermore, all bondmen of the King were 'compelled to such services and labours as they were accustomed to; and that the officers have power to compel them to do such labours and services'.[18] The constables of castles were once more required to fulfil their duties in Wales. But, as will have been seen from the reported state of Wales in 1449, little improvement was effected, even when the duke of Buckingham was sent there to deal with the difficulties.

The truth was that, as long as the King's administration at the centre and in the localities remained so feeble, there was small hope of improving matters. This paralysis of government was giving ambitious local men an unprecedented opportunity to gain the confidence of the leading figures in English politics—a Gloucester, Beaufort, York, or Suffolk—and thereby to seize power on the spot. The most striking examples of this in Wales were the rise of the families of Dynevor, Raglan, and Tudor. Gruffydd ap Nicholas of Dynevor and his sons, Thomas and Owen, had carved out a remarkable degree of authority for themselves under the patronage of the duke of Gloucester. When Gloucester came to grief, Gruffydd had no hesitation about making himself useful to his successor, Lord Beauchamp of Powick. That petition directed to Parliament in 1449 complaining of illegal *cymhorthau* or money levies may well have been aimed at men like Gruffydd and his agents. Gruffydd was neatly summarized in a seventeenth-century biographical account of his family as a 'man of hot, fiery and choleric spirit; one whose counsels were all *in turbido*'; a character 'naturally fitly composed and framed for the times; very wise he was, and infinitely subtle and crafty, ambitious beyond measure, of a busy stirring brain'.[19]

In south-east Wales William ap Thomas of Raglan, and his son, William Herbert, were likewise establishing themselves firmly as the result of the vacuum left by the non-residence of great magnates and their need for vigorous and reliable local adjutants. William ap Thomas married Elizabeth Berkeley, the 'lady of Raglan', in 1406 and bought the estate outright in 1430. He later married as his second wife the famous Gwladus Ddu, daughter of Davy Gam and ancestress of the energetic Vaughan and Herbert lines. For three decades, from the 1420s to the 1440s, William was

---

[18] *Statutes of the Realm*, II, 344.   [19] *Cambrian Register*, I (1795), 57.

busily building up his estates and his splendid castle at Raglan and simultaneously acquiring office and influence. He acted for both the Crown and leading magnates: as steward and receiver in the Duchy of Lancaster estates and others; and became deputy-justice of south Wales, and sheriff of Glamorgan, Cardiganshire, and Carmarthenshire. A prominent member of the duke of York's council, he served in France with him in the 1440s. Enterprising, vigorous, and astute, he had few scruples about using force to gain his ends where necessary, as was revealed in his rough-handed treatment of the prior of Goldcliff in 1437. He transmitted many of his own characteristics as well as much of his influence to his still more outstanding son, William Herbert. Herbert married Anne Devereux in 1449 and served as a young captain in France during the next two years. In the course of the troubled decades of the 1450s and 1460s he was to rise to become the most influential Welshman of his generation (see below, pp. 191–5).

Another family that was to rise even more rapidly but for different reasons was that of Owain Tudor. Owain ap Maredudd ap Tudur, born c.1400, was the son of that Maredudd ap Tudur who, like the rest of his family, fared so disastrously as the consequence of their participation on the rebel side in the Glyndŵr Rebellion. Appreciating how bleak were his prospects in Wales, Owain, a personable young fellow, made his way to court to seek his fortune and there succeeded probably beyond his dreams. He found a place in Dowager Queen Catherine's household and the susceptible young widow fell in love with her handsome servant, marrying him c.1430–1 in spite of a statute of 1427–8 which forbade such a union without official consent having been obtained beforehand. There is no suggestion, however, that the marriage in any way lacked the blessing of the Church or that children born of it were illegitimate. It was, nevertheless, kept secret until after Catherine's death in January 1437, when Owain was obliged to appear before the royal council and was imprisoned in Newgate gaol. Early in 1438 he escaped to Wales, where a sympathetic poet, Ieuan Gethin ab Ieuan ap Lleision, insisted that Owain's only fault had been to win the love of the daughter of the 'king of the wineland' (i.e., France). Of the four children born to Owain and Catherine, the two elder boys, Edmund and Jasper, were placed in the care of Catherine de la Pole, abbess of Barking, from 1437 to 1442. Both they and their father were generously treated by Henry VI. In 1449 he knighted both sons and in 1453 conferred earldoms upon them, making Edmund earl of Richmond and Jasper earl of Pembroke. Edmund's career proved to be brief, though his son's was to be momentous. Jasper, too, in his own way turned out to be one of the most remarkable figures in the politics and statesmanship of fifteenth-century England and Wales.

In the mean time, during the years between 1449 and 1453, disasters had been overtaking Henry VI and his realm. The King's own unwisdom and ineptitude in fulfilling his royal duties, combined with cupidity, corruption, and lack of ability among his favourites, had led to calamitous set-backs for the English armies in France and mounting criticism at home. Opposition came to a head in the Parliament of 1449 and outside it. It led to the impeachment and downfall of William de la Pole, duke of Suffolk, who held, among many other offices, the justiceship of North Wales. He was put to death in 1450 by an act of popular justice, though he was soon replaced in Henry's favour by Edmund Beaufort, duke of Somerset. The same year witnessed the dangerous rebellion of Jack Cade, suppressed only with considerable difficulty. During the next few years conditions at home and abroad continued to worsen. There were further defeats in France and dangerous quarrels broke out between rival magnates in more than one part of the kingdom. Because some of these great aristocrats who found themselves excluded from access to the Court and the power and profits associated with it had major interests in the Principality and the March—as, of course, did the Crown itself—Wales was bound to be drawn into these conflicts.

A crucial figure in English politics at the time, as well as being the greatest single Marcher lord, was Richard duke of York. From his mother, Anne, he had inherited in 1425 the vast and strategically placed Mortimer estates of the earldom of March. His territorial interests stretched from Caerleon and Usk northwards through the solid core of Mortimer lands in the middle March to Denbigh. This holding became the main centre of his power, though he held enormous possessions elsewhere in more than twenty shires of England. Even if, as the result of some not very efficient management, the income from his Welsh estates was diminishing, they still brought him £3,430 a year, as compared with £3,230 from his lands in England, and represented a vital source of men, money, and politico-military influence for him. The death of Duke Humphrey in 1447 had left York as the heir-apparent to the throne as long as Henry VI had no children. It also meant that he became the principal opponent of the Suffolk–Somerset clique. But his influence on politics was vastly reduced as a result of the dominance which the King's favourites exerted over the effete and incompetent Henry. York became particularly resentful and suspicious of Somerset's hold over the King. In 1449 York had been shipped off to Ireland as lieutenant in a transparent manœuvre to keep him out of the way. In August 1450, however, he returned from Ireland to Beaumaris, where he found representatives of the Household interest in north Wales, notably the Stanley family and their associates, trying to block his path. Symptomatic, too, of nervousness among the men surrounding the King was their attempt to put south Wales in a state of alert following York's landing.

Another leading lord in the Marches at this time was Richard Nevill, earl of Warwick, who had assumed the title of lord of Glamorgan since taking over possession of it as part of his wife's lands in 1449. He, as we shall see, would soon have his own reasons for making an alliance of convenience with the immensely powerful and deeply discontented York. A relative of Warwick—Edward Nevill—was lord of Abergavenny, while two influential client families to York and Warwick, the Herberts and Vaughans, were dominant at Raglan and the surrounding region. The other major figure in south-east Wales was Humphrey Stafford, duke of Buckingham and lord of Newport and Brecon, who was a loyal adherent of the Lancastrian dynasty. In the middle Marches were the Talbots of Goodrich, also Lancastrians, while further north were the Fitzalan earls of Arundel, substantial lords in Chirk, Oswestry, and Clun. In the coming years much would depend on the ability of the royal administration to retain these magnates in loyal and reasonably contented mood and on the relationships of the grandees with one another.

Any hopes of stability there might have been were soon dispelled between 1450 and 1455, which proved to be a disruptive period for more than one region. An unusually large number of magnates were divided amongst themselves by fierce local and personal dissensions, especially those in the west country between Lord Bonvile and the earl of Devon and in the north between the Percies and the Nevills. It has been estimated that not less than one-sixth of the peerage was put behind bars at this time for violent and lawless behaviour. Such indiscipline augured ominously for the peace and stability of the kingdom. It is difficult not to conclude that on the eve of the outbreak of the civil wars the country was in a more than ordinarily disturbed and disorderly condition. Contemporary writers clearly believed this to be true. John Hardyng in his *Chronicle*, completed in 1457, told how

> Misrule doth rise and maketh neighbours war;
> The weaker goeth beneath, as oft is seen,
> The mightiest his quarrel will prefer . . .
>
> Such sickness now hath take them and excess,
> They will not write of riot ne debate,
> So common is it now in each estate.[20]

In the Marches of Wales the duke of York began to drum up support for himself in 1451–2. There appeared to be considerable backing among the population there for putting him on the throne. Placing himself at the head of an army, he marched to London but found no more than minimal support for his plans. Too much loyalty to the King—for even a broken reed like Henry VI—survived, and York found himself humiliated and placed temporarily under arrest. He had done enough, however, to

---

[20] Scattergood, *Politics and Poetry*, pp. 174–6.

awaken alarm among the King's entourage and to rouse it into significant counter-action. In the summer of 1452 an ambitious royal progress was undertaken through the west country and the Marches with the aim of restoring the King's authority, punishing his enemies, and reassuring his friends. Judicial sessions were held at Ludlow, at which many of York's followers were brought to book for attempted rebellions. Even so, at the same time royal pardons were offered to some of the representatives of influential gentry families such as Walter Devereux, William Herbert, and Owen ap Gruffydd ap Nicholas, seemingly in an effort to win them over to the royal side. Further attempts to bolster the authority and prestige of the royal family, especially in Wales, came in January 1453, when the King's half-brothers, Edmund and Jasper Tudor, were created earls and given precedence over all the other earls within the kingdom. Jasper was not only made earl of Pembroke but was also entrusted with the important castles of Pembroke, Cilgerran, Tenby, and Llanstephan. Both brothers wasted no time in establishing contact with the bards and by means of lavish patronage seeking to create a favourable climate of support for themselves. Also in 1453, serious efforts were made to recover arrears of revenue and other debts and services due to the Crown from the Principality of North Wales as a result of negligence on the part of the officers.

The year 1453, nevertheless, in spite of the birth to the Queen in October of an heir, long awaited and almost despaired of, was anything but an *annus mirabilis* for the Lancastrian monarchy. In France the last English forces, except for the garrison at Calais, were driven out in July and in that same month Henry VI lapsed into madness. In spite of strenuous efforts by the Queen and her supporters to conceal the nature of her husband's malady the truth eventually came out and York had to be appointed Protector in March 1454. There followed a short burst of well-intentioned administrative reform by a government enjoying a wide basis of support. As far as Wales was concerned, York seems to have had the backing of those like Walter Devereux, his chief steward, and William Herbert, who had earlier given evidence of their support for him. In 1454 Devereux was at pains to assure the duke that Herbert 'saith he is no man's man but yours'.[21] That was to be expected; what was more surprising was that the two Tudor brothers also appeared to be backing him at this time. In addition, he could look for the still more powerful co-operation of Richard, earl of Warwick and lord of Glamorgan, who had been deeply alienated by the actions of the royal favourite, Somerset. In 1453 Warwick's claim to Glamorgan had been disputed by Somerset and the quarrel had led to serious disturbances at Cardiff and Cowbridge. The king's council was informed that the lordship was being kept by great

[21] T. B. Pugh in *Fifteenth-Century England, 1399–1509*, ed. S. B. Chrimes *et al.* (Manchester, 1972), p. 92.

numbers of men as if a state of war existed. Having failed to gain his ends by force, Somerset now played the card of royal authority to summon the sheriff of Glamorgan, William Herbert, and eight other men before the council to explain why they had been responsible for making 'great assemblies and routs of people'.[22] The custody of the lordship was entrusted to one of Somerset's cronies, Lord Dudley, much to the fury of Warwick, who now had his own compelling reasons for aligning himself with York's opposition to Somerset and King Henry.

York himself, though greatly preoccupied with disturbances in the north of England, came down to the Marches and dealt firmly with a boundary dispute between his own tenants of Chirbury and those of the lordship of Caus. He also took further steps to try to curb the unlicensed activities of the egregious Gruffydd ap Nicholas and his three sons in west Wales. Writing to them in May 1454, the Council expressed its 'great cause of displeasure' because all four were guilty of 'greatly grieving' the Crown's subjects and conveyed a broad hint that the penal statutes of Henry IV against Welshmen holding office might be invoked against them.[23] Not that such strictures had much practical effect, for even when Gruffydd ap Nicholas himself was arrested and charged in Hereford he was promptly rescued by his son-in-law, the influential local landowner, Sir John Scudamore. In fact, York's intensive and well-meant spate of law enforcement and good government proved to be a short-lived experiment. Late in 1454 Henry VI recovered his wits, York's protectorate came to an end, and Somerset was back in the saddle once more.

The subsequent summoning of a council at Leicester, ostensibly to 'provide for the safety of the King's person against his enemies',[24] was understandably viewed with the gravest suspicion by York and his allies, who feared for their own safety and armed themselves to resist any attempts made on them. There now opened the longest spell of intermittent civil war in British history—thirty confused years of struggle, or forty if we regard the battle of Blackheath (1497) as being the end of the 'Wars of the Roses'. In spite of the long period of unresolved, or partially resolved, conflict, the damage done to the economy and to society was to be much more limited than might have been supposed. The kingdom was geared for peace not war, and the battles, though often fierce and bloody, were fought out by relatively small contingents of men and directly affected only a minority. The actual fighting lasted for short periods only—some twelve or thirteen weeks in thirty-two years. The great magnates had for a long while been reluctant to take up arms against the King; but after the

[22] *GCH*, III, 196.
[23] R. A. Griffiths, 'Gruffydd ap Nicholas and the Fall of the House of Lancaster', *WHR*, II (1964–5), 218–19.
[24] *WWR*, p. 85.

first battle of St Albans (1455) the restraint shown up to that point was much weakened. Once the Crown and the influence that went with its possession were seen to be up for the taking, it became difficult to restore lasting peace again. Long after the battle of Bosworth was fought, even, it was by no means certain that the Tudor dynasty was irremovably established on the throne (below, pp. 229-30).

Wales and the Marches were to be heavily involved in the wars for a number of reasons. Wales was a country with a long military tradition where soldiers were readily recruited. Its population was inured to the prospect of warfare and rebellion, indoctrinated with the notion of fighting for Welsh or allegedly Welsh leaders, and very easily whipped up into anti-English sentiment. Any leader who could plausibly be represented as continuing the age-old national struggle would not have far to seek for a following among his compatriots. Among the politically conscious groups had emerged a class of aspiring gentry, many of them hardened by experience of warfare in France, greedy for power, influence, and land, only too eager to identify with the prevailing sentiments and prejudices of the people of Wales and exploit them for their own purposes. Intensely aware of their ancient lineage (real or assumed), they maintained close links with their kinsmen and renewed in each generation the bonds which held them together. The key figures in preserving an accurate record of such ties of blood, kinship, and alliance, as well as of the collective group memory of the Welsh, were the poets. The *uchelwyr* [gentry] readily associated themselves with the bards, who were in turn enthusiastically prepared to lend themselves and their muse in the battle for the allegiance of hearts and minds to the rival factions.

The aristocratic leaders of those factions, having a large stake in Wales in the shape of offices and/or possessions but not usually resident there, recognized the value to themselves of their gentry clients and the mutual ties of self-interest that knit lord and retainer together. Among the most valuable of their privileges as Marcher lords were those quasi-regal ones which allowed them to maintain their own autonomous administration, raise armies, and wage private warfare. In the process of upholding their rights, they exerted strenuous efforts to exalt their friends and abase their enemies. Furthermore, Wales was an upland country with a rugged landscape and indifferent communications, in which small bodies of troops could hold out defiantly when their faction had lost ground elsewhere. It was a land more thickly peppered than almost any other region in the kingdom with powerful stone castles, many of them masterpieces of Edwardian or concentric construction, which could provide sturdy bastions for defence or threatening springboards for attack, as the Glyndŵr Rebellion had tellingly illustrated. Finally, there was the long indented coastline of Wales, with its many favourable landing-places, relatively easy of access from Scotland, Ireland, or France. It offered possibilities for sea-borne incursions that were far more favourable to invaders than defenders. More than one such descent, including Henry Tudor's invasion, would take advantage of them.

It was from Wales that, in 1455, Duke Richard, accompanied by many Welsh followers, marched to St Albans. There ensued the opening skirmish of the Wars of the Roses rather than a battle between rival armies. It ended in victory for York and the death of his deadliest enemy, Somerset. The winner assumed power and summoned a meeting of Parliament. An important part of its business was declared to be to 'ordain and purvey for the restful and sad rule in Wales, and set apart such riots and disobedience as have been there before this time'.[25] The country was in all conscience restless enough, and the restoration of strong rule was urgently needed. But in the mean time Henry VI, who had fallen ill again in 1455, appeared to recover and York was deprived of his powers in February 1456. The direction of Lancastrian fortunes was now taken over by the formidable Queen Margaret, implacably opposed to York and fiercely protective of the interests of her feeble husband and those of her son. She withdrew to the Midlands, where she hoped to find more solid bases of strength. As far as Wales was concerned, a tense struggle for influence began.

Broadly speaking, the position appeared to be that Lancastrian support was strongest in west Wales, in the Principality shires—north and south—where the Crown had hitherto been able to manipulate official appointments in its own interest, and in the Duchy of Lancaster lordships of the south-west, where most of the local gentry also looked to it for patronage. The Yorkists, thanks to the vast Mortimer inheritance, largely dominated the eastern and central Marches. The situation was, however, more complicated than appeared at first sight, and each faction could hope to strengthen its position in the sphere of influence occupied by its rivals. In the Marches, for instance, in spite of the immense influence of York and the Nevills, there were to be found such steadfast Lancastrians among the aristocracy as the duke of Buckingham and the earl of Shrewsbury, as well as influential gentry families like the Scudamores or the Pulestons. Similarly, in the largely Lancastrian south-west the Dwn family was staunchly Yorkist. In almost all areas of Wales, moreover, there were opportunist families and individuals, less concerned with loyalty to either Lancaster or York than with the prosecution of their own interests, who might be induced to switch their allegiance when it suited their ends. Thus, the Stanleys, dominant in Cheshire and north Wales, where they had many gentry clients, although they owed most of their influence to Lancastrian favour, would reveal over the next thirty years an unrivalled propensity for changing sides and double-dealing when it suited them.

Endeavouring to strengthen the royal stake in Wales, Queen Margaret now sent the King's half-Welsh half-brother Edmund, earl of Richmond, there. The choice was a sensible one in view of his family's Welsh connections and their claim to be descended from Cadwaladr, his own recently conferred status (1453) as an earl, and his even more recently acquired bride (1455), the Lancastrian heiress, Margaret Beaufort, daughter of the first duke of Somerset. Edmund and Jasper Tudor had already discerned the propaganda value of the support of Welsh poets, thanks perhaps to the good offices of their father, Owain Tudor, who had long been a poetic patron like his predecessors before him. In an early poem of c.1453 addressed to both brothers, Dafydd Nanmor referred pointedly to Owain's role as the 'keeper of the hearth of Cadwaladr' [*i gadw aelwyd Gadwaladr*].[26] Edmund Tudor's arrival in west Wales had the immediate effect of infuriating Gruffydd ap Nicholas, that 'man of hot, fiery and choleric spirit', who had no wish to see a half-royal earl muscling in on his sphere of interest, even if he were a Lancastrian. Gruffydd may have hitherto liked to pose as the dutiful representative of Henry VI; but that had lasted only as long as the King's rule was nerveless and permissive of Gruffydd's increasing local autocracy. The arrival of Edmund Tudor on the scene quickly made the lord of Dinefwr bare his teeth and by June 1456 he and the Tudor were reported to be 'greatly at war'. Nor were the duke of York and his agents willing to see any change in the balance of power in west Wales go unchallenged. In August 1456 York, intent upon re-establishing his own authority in the region, dispatched a force of some 2,000 men, drawn mainly from Herefordshire and commanded by two of his most powerful and ambitious tenants, Sir Walter Devereux and the latter's son-in-law, Sir William Herbert. This pair proceeded to show that any friendship there may earlier have been between York and the Tudors had soon evaporated. They took Edmund Tudor prisoner, seized the key castles of Aberystwyth and Carmarthen, and held judicial sessions. The affair seems to have been sufficient to cause Henry VI to lose what last shreds of confidence he had in York and withdraw to the protection of his queen and her party at Kenilworth.

Queen Margaret, in the course of the year 1457, made a further determined bid to reinforce the Lancastrian position in Wales. In the spring and early summer Herbert and Devereux were summoned to appear before an inquisition taken at Hereford to answer for their misdeeds in terrifying the justices of that city during the previous year and forcing them summarily to hang a number of tradesmen as an act of vengeance for the

[26] *DN*, pp. 34–5.

murder of one of Herbert's kinsmen. But Herbert and at least twenty-one others, who included two of his brothers and a number of his relatives, were pardoned in an attempt to appease both sides. This act of clemency appears to have been instrumental, if not in winning Herbert over completely to the Lancastrian cause, at least in inducing him to maintain an attitude of guarded neutrality and outward loyalty to Henry VI. The poet Lewys Glyn Cothi went so far as to claim that Herbert had become an enthusiastic Lancastrian partisan, averring that he would be a mighty eagle in Jasper's ranks, willing to strike a blow for the Crown. But that may have been said more in hope than confidence, for with political circumstances being as fluid and as intensely competitive as they were, Herbert's own dynastic and local interests counselled caution. His long-standing family ties with York, not to mention the towering influence wielded by York and Warwick in the central and southern Marches, led him to play 'a watchful and waiting game between 1457 and 1460'.[27] Later in 1457 the Queen travelled through the border counties and granted a pardon to the now-ageing Gruffydd ap Nicholas and his sons.

More important than any other aspect of the Queen's policy was the faith she pinned on fortifying the authority of Jasper Tudor in Wales, in succession to his brother Edmund. The latter had died in November 1456 as a young man in his mid-twenties, to the acute dismay of the poets, one of whom, Lewys Glyn Cothi, saw his death as the end of hopes of 'freeing the captive land of Wales' [yn iach cwncweru gwlad Cymru gaeth].[28] Two months after Edmund's death his son, Henry Tudor, was born in Pembroke castle in January 1457. Lewys Glyn Cothi cannot have been aware of Margaret Beaufort's pregnancy since he made no mention of it; but other poets were quick to comment on the significance of the birth of her son. One of them, Robin Ddu, according to the chronicler, Ellis Gruffydd (temp. Henry VIII), had gone to the extent of prophesying that even if Edmund were dead, his body burned, and his ashes drowned, the son born to his wife would one day be king of England. Dafydd Nanmor, too, in a poem of 1458 hailed the infant as one who might hope to become duke of Somerset and even king. The long and successful connection between Jasper Tudor, his nephew, and the Welsh poets began early, for it can hardly be doubted that it was Jasper's patronage that inspired this early poetry to Henry Tudor. Yet we should be unwise to suppose that at this stage such bardic sentiments could be anything more than the extravagant wishful thinking that often accompanied poetic hyperbole. It must be regarded as extremely doubtful whether anyone took seriously Henry's 'claims' to the throne at this point. Another feature of the poetry of these

[27] D. H. Thomas, 'The House of Raglan as Supporters of the House of York' (MA Thesis, Cardiff, 1967), Chap. 2.
[28] LGC¹, p. 496.

years is the close link which it reveals as being forged between Jasper and Gruffydd ap Nicholas and his family:

> Y gŵr hwnnw a garwn
> A dry gwŷr gyda'r Goron

[That man whom we love will turn many men to the Crown]

and a host of them would wear his livery, with the historic three ravens of Dinefwr, as 'partisans of the lily' [*plaid i'r lili*]—a reference to Queen Margaret's royal arms of France.[29] Jasper was taking further practical steps to consolidate his hold on his earldom of Pembroke by strengthening the castles of Pembroke and Tenby and taking those of Aberystwyth, Carreg Cennen, and Carmarthen into his possession and thus displacing York, who had previously been their constable.

By 1458–9 the Queen had very largely assumed control of the direction of royal policy and, in the spring of 1459, was busily recruiting retainers in Cheshire, 'trusting through their strength to make her son king'.[30] Her activities could not fail to awaken alarm and suspicion on the part of York and the Nevills. York was at Ludlow, where he assembled about him a formidable force of men from the Marches. According to the chronicler Hall, the loyalty of the commons of Wales (presumably of those parts of the country loyal to him) and his 'affinity' there was such 'that they could suffer no wrong to be done nor evil word to be spoken of him or his friends'.[31] While the earl of Salisbury was marching towards Ludlow to join York he was attacked by royal troops at Blore Heath; but, in spite of Lord Stanley's holding aloof from the battle with typical equivocation, Salisbury beat off his assailants and succeeded in linking up with York and his eldest son, Edward, earl of March. Shortly afterwards, Salisbury's own son, the earl of Warwick, arrived with a contingent of veterans brought from Calais. The latter, however, had not anticipated being called upon to fight against the King's forces and defected when they realized that this was expected of them. Their action demoralized the Yorkist forces who, after the briefest of exchanges at Ludford Bridge, disintegrated and fled. York and his second son, Rutland, departed precipitately for Wales, breaking down the bridges as they went, *en route* for Ireland. In spite of what Hall had had to say about the loyalty of some parts of Wales to York, there were conspicuous absentees from the battle at Ludford Bridge, the most notable of them being William Herbert. He and a number of other Welshmen, including Owain Tudor and Henry Wogan, were well rewarded for their fidelity to Lancaster, or at least their refusal to take York's side.

---

[29] *LGC*[1], pp. 131–7.
[30] *An English Chronicle of the Reigns of Richard II . . . Henry VI*, ed. J. S. Davies (Camden Soc., 1856), pp. 79–80.
[31] Hall, *Chronicle*, p. 232.

The revenues of a number of formerly Yorkist families were raided to provide 500 marks for the prince of Wales so that he might retain knights and squires in order that those lordships where York had been strong might be 'brought back the more speedily to the King's obedience'.[32] The lordship offering the most stubborn resistance to the royalists was Denbigh; and here Jasper Tudor was made constable of the castle and steward of the lordship, being granted full powers to reduce it to obedience, to raise more troops in Wales, and to pardon or execute rebels. In February 1460 a powerful commission was set up to inquire into the granting of livery and the summoning of unlawful assemblies (the phrase normally used to describe gatherings of opponents of the regime in power) in the Principality of Wales, Flint, and Cheshire. Denbigh fell in March 1460 and Jasper made his way to south Wales. Here he was active in taking steps to ensure the defence of the area, particularly the large but very vulnerable landing-place at Milford Haven, which took a great deal of defending.

This Lancastrian triumph proved to be of short duration. In July 1460 Warwick, who a month earlier had landed at Sandwich with the earls of March and Salisbury, advanced rapidly and defeated the King's forces at Northampton, taking Henry prisoner in the process. Queen Margaret fled in haste and humiliation to Wales; first to Harlech castle and later to Pembroke, whence she eventually sailed to Scotland. Warwick, flushed with victory, took immediate steps to place Yorkist adherents in positions of strategic importance in Wales. Among them figured prominently Sir William Herbert who, despite his earlier wariness, had come out boldly for the Yorkist earls when they landed. On 17 August he, Sir Walter Devereux, and Roger Vaughan were given wide powers to prevent all unlawful assemblies—Lancastrian ones this time, in contrast to the Yorkists of a few months previously—to ensure the safe keeping of castles and stamp out the embers of opposition. The leader of the victorious faction, York himself, circumspectly made his way back to London via his strongholds in the Marches, where he spent some time reinforcing the bonds of loyalty to him. In the capital city he made his unsuccessful bid to become king, but was recognized once more as Protector and accorded the right to succeed Henry VI on his death. Alas for York! The only crown he ever won was a mocking paper one. His own death was to precede Henry's by eleven years or so and was to take place within a matter of weeks. On 30 December 1460 his armies were defeated at Wakefield, where he was killed and Salisbury executed. Their heads were placed on the gates of the city of York, and the duke's was scornfully adorned with a silver paper crown. Seven weeks later, on 17 February 1461, Queen Margaret, with an army

[32] C.Pat.R., 1460, p. 550.

composed of Scots, Welshmen, and men from the north of England, defeated Warwick at the second battle of St Albans and put him to flight.

Even now, the bewildering twists of this politico-military kaleidoscope were not done; there were yet two more quick turns to come before the first decisive phase of the civil wars was over. York's death had left his eighteen-year-old son, Edward, earl of March, as the hope of his house and leader of its cause. He promptly began the task of raising troops in the familiar recruiting-ground of his Marcher estates. He had the willing assistance of three experienced adjutants: Sir Walter Devereux, Sir William Herbert, and Sir Roger Vaughan. All had been blooded in campaigns in France; they were intimately familiar with the Levantine shifts and subtleties of Marcher politics; and Herbert and Vaughan, particularly, enjoyed close links with the native poets and and the national sentiments of Wales. The Yorkist contingents were, therefore, very largely recruited from the March and adjacent Herefordshire. The Lancastrians who turned out to oppose them were a decidedly motley band, made up of French, Breton, and Irish soldiers, raised in the main by James Butler, earl of Wiltshire, who landed at Milford Haven; and there was also a strong Welsh contingent, drawn mainly from Pembrokeshire and Carmarthenshire, and led by Jasper Tudor, Owain Tudor, the sons of Gruffydd ap Nicholas, and other gentlemen from the south-west. The original intention in recruiting them may have been to concert their actions with those of the Lancastrians who had fought at Wakefield. To effect a junction with the troops in the north, Wiltshire, Jasper, and their men marched up the valley of the Tywi and pressed on into Radnorshire.

Edward turned his army to confront them at Mortimer's Cross on the river Lugg, six miles from Leominster, so as to prevent them from linking with their allies further north. Taking heart from the strange portent of the appearance of three suns, which had sorely dismayed some of his men,[33] Edward roundly vanquished the heavily outnumbered Lancastrians on 2 February 1461. Jasper Tudor managed to make good his escape but his ageing father, who must he been about sixty years old, was captured. He was put to death in the market-place at Hereford, as an act of vengeance, possibly, for the deaths of York and Rutland at Wakefield. He had been brought to the place of his execution by Sir Roger Vaughan, an action which marked the beginning of a long and bitter feud between Tudors and Vaughans. The chronicler Gregory, referring to Owain's end, tells a macabre story of how a mad woman combed Owain's hair and washed the blood off his face. 'And she got candles and set them about him burning more than a hundred.' Owain himself, when he finally realized that his end was nigh and could not be avoided, murmured sadly, ' "That head shall lie

[33] So impressed was Edward that he was reputed to have taken the rising sun as his own particular symbol, 'the Golden Sun of York', ever afterwards.

on the stock that was wont to lie on Queen Catherine's lap"; and put his heart and mind wholly unto God and full meekly took his death.'[34] He was buried at the Friars Minor's chapel in Hereford. His son Jasper was deeply stung by this defeat and especially by his father's death. Some of the Welsh poets also took Owain's death far less meekly than he himself was reported to have done. Robin Ddu sadly lamented the 'severing of the sea-swallow's head' but rejoiced that the 'great eagle, the earl, [Jasper] had been left'

> Er torri pen y wennol,
> Mae'r iarll, eryr mawr, ar ôl.[35]

While Ieuan Gethin would have preferred to see him die, if he had to, on the field of battle, and could not forgive the English (overlooking Roger Vaughan's role!) for shortening the hero's life. He could console himself and his hearers only by remembering that in spite of Owain's death he could still look to his grandson, Henry, and his son, Jasper, to fulfil the old dreams of freedom and a better day for the Welsh. Yet, in general, the battle of Mortimer's Cross, significant though it was, aroused less interest among the Welsh poets than might have been expected.

Edward now proceeded triumphantly to London with his largely Welsh army and on 3 March was crowned king in the presence of a small group of notables, such 'chosen and faithful' of the aristocracy as he could muster. Among them were Sir Walter Devereux (now confirmed as Lord Ferrers of Chartley) and Sir William Herbert, who would soon be raised to the peerage. They and Edward's Welsh troops, among them perhaps Guto'r Glyn, engaged on his last campaign, also accompanied the new king on his journey to the north, where he sealed his triumph by once more defeating the Lancastrian army at Towton on 29 March 1461. This was a large-scale and bloody battle, in which something like 50,000 troops may have been involved, and it brought to an end the first phase of the civil wars. Edward IV had won the crown that had always eluded his ambitious father who had so eagerly coveted it. It remained to be seen just how worthy he was of it and whether or not he could retain it.

---

[34] *William Gregory's Chronicle of London*, ed. J. Gairdner (Camden Soc., 1876), p. 211.
[35] E. D. Jones, *Beirdd y Bymthegfed Ganrif* (Aberystwyth, 1984), p. 25.

CHAPTER 8

THE YORKIST ERA, 1461–1483

As ruler of the realm in 1461 Edward IV was faced by four overriding responsibilities with which he quickly had to come to grips. He had to pursue a successful foreign policy so as to reduce the risk of domestic rebellion or subversion being engineered from abroad; reinstitute confidence and more restrained behaviour among the mightiest of his subjects; restore a greater measure of public order; and nurture sound royal finances. All these obligations had their relevance for Wales. The country with its long stretch of indented coastline lay open to landings from abroad, especially while pockets of Lancastrian resisters held out in key bases. Some of the most powerful aristocrats in the realm guarded jealously the vital personal and clientage interests they had at stake in Wales and their freedom to act in defence of them. Public order and its maintenance had long given rise to intractable problems in the Principality and the March. Finally, the revenues of the Crown had, for a generation or more, been at the mercy of self-interested and loosely controlled officials. So pressing were the needs of Wales that it even looked at first as if Edward IV himself intended to take a hand in settling its affairs. When he returned from the north after his victory at Towton he gave orders on 8 July 1461 to William Herbert and Walter Devereux to raise men for him in the border counties and the Marches, and preparations were also made to assemble a fleet. Preliminary arrangements were drawn up for his army to muster at Hereford on 8 September and some of his equipment was sent there in advance of his own arrival. But although Edward progressed through the Marches and journeyed on via Hereford to Ludlow, he changed his mind about personally heading the campaign in Wales and soon showed himself content to leave the conduct of affairs to his two lieutenants, who 'with divers many other gentlemen' proceeded before him 'to cleanse the country'.[1]

Edward had already given clear indications of the trust he reposed in these servants, especially Herbert, and his intention to leave the government of Wales largely in the latter's control, even at the risk of irritating the dangerously powerful Warwick. At York on 8 May 1461, by an unprecedented concentration of power in south Wales in a single pair of hands, he had appointed Herbert as chief justice and chamberlain and

---

[1] H. Ellis, *Original Letters Illustrative of English History* (3 vols. London, 1825), i, 15–16.

steward and chief forester of Carmarthenshire and Cardiganshire, with his brother, Richard Herbert, as his deputy-justice. On the following day William Herbert and two of his brothers were granted a commission to take into the King's hands the county and lordship of Pembroke and other assets of Jasper Tudor, together with possessions belonging to the earl of Shrewsbury. He was similarly empowered on 11 May to take over for the King the lordships of Laugharne and Walwyn's Castle in south-west Wales, which had formerly belonged to James, earl of Wiltshire. When Edward was crowned in June, he elevated Herbert to the peerage as Lord Herbert—the first Welshman to enter the ranks of the English aristocracy if we exclude the Tudor brothers—formally recognized Devereux as Lord Ferrers, and created Sir William Hastings as Lord Hastings. The last-named was soon afterwards made chamberlain of North Wales; the earl of Worcester became chief justice there and, at the same time, the Yorkist stalwart, John Dwn, was appointed constable of Aberystwyth and Carmarthen and sheriff of Carmarthenshire and Cardiganshire.

Armed with this panoply of office and authority, Herbert and Ferrers could immediately turn their attention to the practical problems of Wales. Their Lancastrian enemies still looked to be firmly entrenched at Pembroke, Tenby, Carreg Cennen, Denbigh, and Harlech, all of them strong castles which, on the face of things at least, were capable of obdurate resistance. Yet, in south Wales, the Yorkist commanders encountered very little difficulty. Tenby offered no resistance, even though Jasper Tudor had bestowed much care and expense on its fortifications. Pembroke, 'victualled, manned and apparelled' for a long siege, was one of the most formidably sited and impregnable catles anywhere in Wales. But its commander, John Scudamore, trusting to the good offices of Herbert and Ferrers to save him from subsequent punishment, gave in without resistance on 30 September. The two Yorkists seemed genuinely to have intended to exert their best efforts on his behalf, but that did not save him from having to forfeit his livelihood as a result of a parliamentary statute.

The Lancastrians in north Wales were subjected to equally heavy pressure. Their two leaders, Jasper Tudor and the duke of Exeter, according to one of the Paston correspondents, had 'fled to the mountains' while 'the most part of gentlemen and worship' of all parts of north Wales were coming to the new king.[2] William Herbert assisted the process by turning his attention to north Wales once his victory at Pembroke had been completed and he defeated Jasper and Exeter at Tuthill just outside Caernarfon on 16 October 1461. The former once more contrived to elude his would-be captors and fled to Ireland, where he continued to stir up trouble, with one eye fixed on a possible return to the west coast of Wales.

---

[2] *Paston Letters*, II, 52.

The town of Denbigh succumbed in January 1462 and, on 23 February, was granted £1,000 by the King for the rebuilding of premises destroyed 'by occasion of burning of the same town violently done'.[3] Carreg Cennen in the south-west also yielded in May 1462, leaving Harlech alone to hold out for the Lancastrians. Indications of the widespread disorder and damage which the Lancastrian captains and garrison of Harlech could inflict come from a petition addressed to the first Parliament of Edward IV's reign by the 'Tenants and Commons of North Wales'. The petitioners alleged that many of them had 'been daily taken prisoners and put to fine and ransom as it were in land of war; and many and divers of them daily robbed and spoiled of their goods and cattle'. These captains and their men, moreover, 'reputed in all their doings the said late king for their sovereign lord and not the king our sovereign lord that now is' and took 'oxen, sheep, wheat and victuals of the said tenants for stuff of the castle with strong hand' and would not deliver to any 'such person as the late king has deputed to be his constable'.[4] In spite of all these outrages on the part of its defenders Harlech would be allowed to hold out for another six or seven years; a constant thorn in the flesh of Yorkist authorities and a possible landing-place for Lancastrians and other malcontents from Ireland and Scotland.

The effects of these initial Yorkist victories and of Edward's wholesale redistribution of land and authority in Wales soon became apparent. The King clearly intended to eradicate as completely as he could the last traces of Lancastrian opposition. In Wales, as elsewhere, he evidently proposed to depend as far as possible on the services of magnates who had been newly elevated by him. That meant entrusting power chiefly to William Herbert and his close associates as a reward for their past services and a guarantee of their future commitment. Edward may also have been sensitive to the need for harnessing the powerful appeal of Welsh patriotism as expressed in contemporary poetry and other sources of propaganda in support of his regime. Even if he were not himself inclined that way, his right-hand man in Wales and his allies were certainly well aware of those potentialities and bent on exploiting them. The situation in which Edward and his Welsh lieutenants found themselves in 1461–2 offered unprecedented scope to make a start on securing his aims. The attainder of the Prince of Wales and Jasper Tudor brought into Edward's possession all the lands of the Principality and those of Jasper in the earldom of Pembroke. Also in his hands were the lordships of the Duchy of Lancaster as well as his family inheritance of the former Mortimer estates. A final piece of good fortune for him was the uncovenanted bonus of there being minorities in the three major Marcher families of the Stafford dukes of Buckingham, the Mowbray dukes of Norfolk, and the Talbot earls of

[3] D. H. Owen in Griffiths (ed.), *Boroughs Wales*, p. 181.   [4] *WWR*, pp. 144–5.

Shrewsbury. The upshot of all this was that every important Marcher lordship in south Wales, with the exception of Warwick's lordships of Glamorgan and Abergavenny, was under the King's control.

William Herbert and his associates, therefore, stood to cash in handsomely from the cornucopia of rewards that Edward IV had at his disposal for deserving Yorkists. Herbert himself had already been appointed chief justice and chamberlain of South Wales; in 1461, custody of the lordship of Newport was committed to him during the minority of Buckingham; and he also received the lands of Jasper Tudor and the earl of Wiltshire, including the castles and lordships of Pembroke, Tenby, Emlyn, Cilgerran, Castlemartin, Llanstephan, and Walwyn's Castle (February 1462). To these were added, also in the same month, the custody and marriage of the five-year-old Henry, Edmund Tudor's son, whom he had captured at Pembroke in the previous year. Although Herbert had paid £1,000 for this privilege, which he badly wanted, the move may have owed even more to the King, who was keen to reconcile the two families by a marriage alliance. That there was every intention of marrying Henry to Herbert's daughter, Maud, in due course is clearly expressed in a contemporary poem by Dafydd Llwyd and later in Herbert's own will of 1469. In the mean time, the boy Henry was being reared in Herbert's household by his wife, Anne, along with their own children 'well and honourably educated and in all kinds of civility brought up'.[5] Herbert was further given custody of the Mowbray lordships of Gower and Cil-fai during the minority of the heir, and also the town and castle of Haverfordwest, paying 100 marks a year for it for twenty years. He was given titular recognition by the King, admitted to the House of Lords, and created a Knight of the Garter. Well might Lewys Glyn Cothi hail him as the Roland to Edward's Charlemagne, the Gawain to his Arthur.

His rise during the next few years was meteoric. Not even Warwick enjoyed so complete a delegation of power in any one region. Herbert's own unswerving loyalty, his burning ambition and indispensability in Wales, the persistence of Lancastrian opposition, the growing friction between Edward and Warwick, and the rise of a new court party around the family of Edward's queen, all helped Herbert to obtain more and greater rewards and power. In 1463 his influence was extended into north Wales when he was appointed chamberlain and chief justice in the county of Merioneth, jurisdiction over which was now withdrawn from the principality of North Wales. He was at the same time made constable of Harlech castle. These appointments were intended to endow him with ample authority to tackle the outstanding problem of Harlech, but without any immediate success. In October 1464 these powers were extended by

[5] Thomas, 'Herberts of Raglan', p. 72.

the issue of a commission to him and others to receive all rebels in Harlech and the county of Merioneth, except a few, into the King's obedience. A grant of 1463 had already conferred upon him Crickhowell and Tretower, and the manor of Dunster in Somerset and other lands in that county and Devon. Following Edward's marriage to Elizabeth Wydevill in 1464, he sought to build up alliances between the Queen's relations and some of his other peers; prominent among them Lord Herbert, whose son, also William, was married to the Queen's sister, Mary, in 1466 and created Lord Dunster. Just previously to this, Edward had created the lordship of Raglan for Herbert senior—the last Marcher lordship to be established in Wales. He had done so, in his own words, to acknowledge the valour of William Herbert, 'whom . . . we have raised to the estate of baron and magnate of our realm'. The lordship had been created by adding to the Raglan estate part of the royal lordships of Usk and Monmouth and all were now to 'form one united royal lordship called the lordship of Raglan . . . and the said William and his heirs shall have within the said limits all royal rights'.[6] He also acquired the grant of the lordship of Haverfordwest as part of the marriage deal between his son and Mary Wydevill. In August 1467 came further influential offices in north Wales: chief justice there, and steward of Denbigh, Montgomery, Ceri, and Cedewain, together with wardship of the lands of Richard Gray, Lord Powys, and Sir Thomas Talbot. Further evidence of the domination exercised in Wales by him and his faction was seen in the way in which Herbert and his associates made up most of the commissioners appointed in 1467 to deal with clippings and falsifications of money. In September 1468 the duke of Norfolk conveyed to him the lordships of Gower and Chepstow. In the same month the coping-stone of his advancement was set in position when he was created earl of Pembroke, even though Henry VI's creation, Jasper Tudor, was still very much alive. By this time Herbert is estimated to have enjoyed the enormous income, by the standards of Welsh gentry, of £2,000 per annum. His loyalty and his usefulness to his royal master had made his fortune—literally and metaphorically.

Others in Herbert's circle had also profited extensively from Edward's favour and his own elevation. His father-in-law, Walter Devereux, Lord Ferrers of Chartley, acquired Richard's Castle, though he obtained most of his lands in the Midlands. He served on a number of commissions in Wales and was also constable of Aberystwyth. William's brother, Richard, a tall and mighty man—'an Anakim in stature'—proved to be a devoted lieutenant to William and to the King. He profited from the confiscated lands of the Lancastrians Thomas Fitzhenry and Sir John Scudamore and built himself a greatly admired house at Coldbrook. Herbert's kinsmen,

---

[6] C.Pat.R., 1461–67, pp. 425–6.

the Vaughans, got their share of the rewards, too. Roger Vaughan of Tretower secured extensive lands in the west country, and his son, Thomas, was appointed receiver of the lordships of Brecon, Hay, and Huntingdon during the minority of the Stafford heir. Another Vaughan— Thomas, son of Roger Vaughan of Monmouth—who was to have a particularly distinguished career as a diplomat and administrator in Edward IV's service, was also well rewarded at this time. John Dwn, like the Herberts and the Vaughans, had steadfastly adhered to Edward's cause and received Laugharne, part of the confiscated property of the earl of Wiltshire, and other lands.

The Yorkists were, in addition, unmistakably keen to create a favourable climate of public support for themselves in Wales by encouraging the composition of Welsh poetry. Their faction had earlier tended to have a livelier appreciation than the Lancastrians of the value of propaganda in the kingdom generally and in the 1450s could be said to have come off decidedly the better in the battle for publicity. This may have been less true of Wales, where English-language propaganda would have cut little ice with the majority of the population and where, in any case, a number of the main agents of publicity, the leading poets, had evinced strongly Lancastrian sympathies. Nevertheless, it was crystal clear that William Herbert and his circle perceived the value to themselves and their party of poetic endorsement. They may even have convinced Edward IV of its importance. It would not be difficult to credit the King, alert as he always was to the value of all kinds of propaganda, with having grasped how attractive this poetry would be to his Welsh subjects when the point was put to him by Herbert or some one else among his followers in Wales. Whatever may have been their King's reactions, the Herbert faction certainly enlisted the services of a number of poets during the 1460s. Some were obvious choices; keen supporters of the house of York like Guto'r Glyn, who had been closely associated with the duke of York and William ap Thomas, or Huw Cae Llwyd, or Hywel Swrdwal. Huw Cae Llwyd, for instance, recalled how Sir William ap Thomas had once been 'the lock and key of the whole country, loosing and binding' [*yn glo ac allwedd, yn gollwng neu'n rhwymo*], and proceeded to praise his sons, William and Richard Herbert, and a whole galaxy of lesser lights among related Herberts, Vaughans, Harvards, and Gameses.[7]

Other more unexpected poets were employed by them, too; especially the two Lancastrian stalwarts, Lewys Glyn Cothi and Dafydd Llwyd, both of whom were already closely associated with Jasper Tudor. Lewys Glyn Cothi, like Guto'r Glyn, not unnaturally sought to emphasize Edward IV's descent from Gwladus Ddu and impress upon his hearers how closely he

[7] *H.C.Ll.*, p. 35.

and Herbert worked hand in hand with one another. Herbert was the 'great ear of Wales in London' [*unclust holl Gymru'n y Gwindy gwyn*] and Edward's 'master-lock in Wales' [*unclo'r King Edward yw'r Herbard hwn*]; the Roland to his Charlemagne, the Gawain to his Arthur.[8] Similarly, Lewys in his poem to Richard Herbert hailed Edward as 'royal [or privileged] Welshman' [*Cymro breiniol*] and made extravagant forecasts of his future conquests. Dafydd Llwyd, too, could be induced to tune his harp to William Herbert's praise as a Briton 'of our own language' but warned him

> Gochel gwnsel a gwensaeth
> a gwin Sais, gwenwyn sy waeth

[Beware the counsel, fawning smile and wine of the Englishman—it is worse than poison]

and urged him to ensure that his daughter married the young Henry Tudor, 'offspring of the swallow, a man of Gwynedd' [*gyw'r wennol, gŵr o Wynedd*].[9]

The Yorkists did not have it all their own way with the poets, though. Jasper Tudor particularly, and other Lancastrians as well, were equally alive to the crucial significance of bardic support and just as determined to try to obtain it. In some ways they may have been even hungrier for it, since they were fighting desperately to preserve the remnants of the Lancastrian cause. They knew well how vital the poetry was to maintain the bonds between lord and client and kinsman and kinsman, to keep up morale, and to give news and hope to their adherents. The poet Tudur Penllyn gives us a penetrating insight into the way in which Jasper Tudor, now flitting restlessly hither and thither in exile, was able to remain in close contact with Gruffydd Fychan of Corsygedol and, through him, with his other friends in north Wales. Gruffydd had built a house in Barmouth, 'a house built half in the waves' [*tŷ â'i hanner mewn tonnau*] as a perfect rendezvous on the coast of Gwynedd for Jasper's comings and goings overseas. Gruffydd, swore the poet, knew just when to expect the arrival of Jasper, that 'black eagle' flying in from Anglesey or the Isle of Man.[10] These poets, Lewys Glyn Cothi, Dafydd Llwyd, Tudur Penllyn, and others like them, in spite of their contacts with the Yorkists, continued to maintain their intimate links with Jasper and other Lancastrians.

This apparent inconsistency in their attitude is sometimes cited as testimony to how unreliable the poets were and what pliant lackeys at the mercy of their patrons, obliged to play the tune for which their paymasters called. They would praise anyone who commissioned them to do so, it is argued, and in the process would raise ill-founded hopes and exaggerated expectations among their more naïve and unsuspecting countrymen. Such

[8] *GG*, p. 63.   [9] *D.Ll.F.*, p. 75.   [10] *TP*, pp. 5–6.

arguments have some force but may themselves be too simplistic. They ignore the essential consideration that the poets were felt to be needed by both sides and their services keenly competed for. It has also to be borne in mind that, given the nature of the contemporary patronage system, it would hardly be reasonable to expect poets to refuse commissions offered by powerful men, especially when the Yorkists largely dominated Wales in the 1460s. The really surprising feature is that many poets remained independent enough to be able to render their services to both sides and to do so seemingly with impunity. There is the further and more important point that, though the poets might serve both factions, they showed over and over again where their sympathies primarily lay, i.e., with their fellow-countrymen. No one who has any familiarity with this verse can doubt that its authors' loyalty to the Welsh heavily outweighed that to any political faction. Even in an otherwise light-hearted love poem, Ieuan Deulwyn cannot refrain from getting his dig in at the hated English—his loved one cares no more for him than she would for a surly and destestable Englishman.[11] Poets could only give life and meaning to their verse when they were backing Welshmen against Englishmen. None but those who wanted to see authority in Wales wielded by the Welsh at the expense of subordinating the English, if not of expelling them, were worthy of their plaudits. It may well be that this was the tacit and instinctive understanding between poet and patron; the only way in which both could be got to operate the system.

It could be argued, of course, that this was no more than a convention which papered over the dangerous inherent contradictions in the arrangement or threw an elegant poetic mantle over the unbridled personal ambitions of the gentry. The poets did indeed exaggerate their patrons' virtues, idealize their intentions, and ignore their shortcomings. Yet it is impossible to ignore the underlying substratum of sincere belief. The poets' pride in their Welsh past, their desire to see the rights and aspirations of their countrymen validated, and their intense resentment against the English who denied them justice, formed too integral a part of the literary and cultural patrimony on which they drew for their education and training to be ignored. These traits had, on the contrary, become so instinctive that again and again they could not refrain from giving expression to them in their poetry. Guto'r Glyn, for example, though a Yorkist poet greatly devoted to Edward IV and his faction, nevertheless protested furiously against the 'injustice' meted out to another Yorkist, John Davy, from Cemaes in Powys. John had fought valiantly for the King of Towton and 'shaved the north' [*eillio'r nordd*] but had had his hand cut off for striking a man before the judges at Westminster Hall in 1462. Guto was incensed by

[11] *ID*, pp. 23–4.

the Yorkist Englishmen's treatment of John Davy and contrasted it furiously with what would have happened in Powys in those circumstances:

> Ni rôi Powys y bys bach
> Er naw-Sais a'u harneisiach[12]

[In Powys they would not have allowed his little finger to be cut off for nine Englishmen and all their equipment]

Nor was it only Welsh poets on their side who saw their patrons in this light. An interesting glimpse of the reverse image of the Welsh as seen by the English through the opposite side of the fifteenth-century looking-glass comes in 1469. At that point a Gloucester annalist presents the attitude towards William Herbert and his men of the English citizens of Gloucester, who were presumably familiar enough with the characteristics of Welshmen as they perceived them. At a critical point in the dissensions between Edward IV and his antagonists, although Herbert was one of the King's most trusted lieutenants, the chronicler saw him and his entourage as a terrible threat to the English. Herbert he described as 'a cruel man' and stigmatized him and his followers as being 'prepared for any crime and, it was said, they plotted to subdue the realm of England and totally plunder it'.[13] The Welsh, in his eyes, seemed even more of a threat than the detested Northerners, who ranked with English Southerners much as the barbaric Highlanders did with eighteenth-century Lowland Scots. Similarly, in 1470, Thomas Talbot, challenging William, Lord Berkeley, to single combat, hotly rebutted the latter's taunt that he intended to bring in the detested and fearsome Welshmen to 'destroy and hunt my own nation and country. I let thee wit I was never so disposed nor never will be.'[14] Here, then, from an English standpoint were the expressions of an anti-Welsh prejudice as biased, racist, and alarmist as those of the Welsh poets on the other side.

If we could date much of the Welsh poetry with greater precision that would be likely to give us a clearer idea of how to interpret it more accurately. If, for example, we knew how to link the poetic outbursts with attempts being made by both factions to concert military actions against one another in the 1460s, the objects of the poetry would become much more intelligible. Undoubtedly, much of the poetry that now survives was intended to kindle enthusiasm for the Lancastrian efforts to stir up trouble for Edward's regime in Wales in 1463–4, or conversely for the Yorkist campaign to smoke out the wasps' nest at Harlech in 1468; but there remains a good deal that cannot be connected with military activities in that way. Furthermore, one of the largest and most significant bodies of

---

[12] *GG*, pp. 104–5; cf. S. Lewis, 'Gyrfa Filwrol Guto'r Glyn', *YB*, IX (1976), 80–99.
[13] Scattergood, *Politics and Poetry*, pp. 318–19.
[14] J. Blow, 'Nibley Green, 1470 . . .', *History Today*, II (1962), 598–610.

politically oriented verse of this period—the prophetic poetry [*canu brud*]—remains largely in manuscript form, unedited and unexplored. Yet that poetry embodies some of the profoundest hopes and instincts of the people of Wales: their desire to see the vindication of those ancient and time-honoured prophecies indissolubly associated with their history, real and mythical, and with their awareness of themselves as a people. The myths embodied in it were central motifs of the mentality and emotions of the Welsh. Though most of the poems cannot as yet be reliably attributed to the authorship of a particular poet and few of them can be precisely dated, the very existence of large numbers of them surviving from the fifteenth century shows that they were greatly in demand. There were obviously many patrons who believed it important that they should be composed and a body of poets willing and able to supply them. Contemporary chroniclers provide striking evidence of the force of these prophecies as practical inspiration in battle, as for example in the fateful battle of Edgecote in 1469 (below, pp. 204–7).

Additionally, there is every reason to suppose that much of the poetry composed in the 'fixed' or *cynghanedd* metres of the kind referred to in preceding paragraphs has been lost over the centuries. Moreover, a whole corpus of verse in the 'free' metres has disappeared virtually completely. Knowing from those which have survived from the sixteenth and seventeenth centuries how immensely popular such verses and songs were at that time and how prominently political and social themes figured in them, we may reasonably assume that a great mass of material of this kind has been lost to us for ever. This kind of poetry would have been particularly well-suited to appeal to the wide audience among the minor gentry, clergy, freeholders, and more substantial farmers. Its motive—and emotive—power would surely have been harnessed to the politico-military chariots of the contemporary factions, and its disappearance is an especially serious loss to us in trying to understand the nature of popular political allegiance and how it was appealed to and reinforced at this period.

In spite of the immense authority wielded by Herbert and the Yorkist faction in Wales during the 1460s, the country, like the north of England, remained far from being completely subdued; and, not surprisingly, close contacts between these two insubordinate areas were kept up. As long as the Lancastrian garrison continued to hold out in Harlech, it offered hope and encouragement to other dissidents in Wales and elsewhere. Thus, towards the end of 1463, the duke of Somerset, although treated favourably by Edward IV—over-sympathetically in all probability—renewed his intrigues against the King. From his refuge in north Wales he communicated with Henry VI at Bamborough and assured that weak and wavering ex-ruler that many of the chief men in Wales were ready to rise on his behalf. Jasper Tudor, too, was no less active in the Lancastrian interest. In December 1463, Somerset departed for the north of England to concert plans for rebellion, leaving Roger Puleston and John Hanmer to lead the risings in north Wales. It may have been at this time that one of the defenders of Harlech, Rheinallt ap Gruffydd, seized Robert Bryne, a former mayor of Chester, as his prisoner and hanged him. Down in the south Jasper Tudor had succeeded in persuading Philip Mansel of Gower and Hopcyn ap Rhys of Llangyfelach to head a revolt. It was to counter these plans that John, duke of Norfolk, was dispatched to Denbigh, while John Dwn and Roger Vaughan were deputed to deal with disaffection in the south. By March both risings had been effectively crushed. On 1 March 1464, according to a letter from John Paston the younger, Norfolk was still in Denbigh, busily engaged with the rebels. Paston thought it would take the duke another fortnight to complete his task, that most of the trouble-makers would be pardoned, 'and as far as I can understand, they shall have grace'.[15] Down in south Wales, on 4 March, Dwn and Vaughan had shattered the Lancastrian forces at the battle of Dryslwyn, and both were well rewarded for their victory. A month or two later, the duke of Somerset and the Welsh troops accompanying him were among those heavily defeated at Hedgeley Moor (April) and Hexham (May), where Somerset was killed. In 1464 Parliament called unavailingly on Harlech to submit, deploring the fact that it was a refuge for malefactors, a centre of intrigue and disturbance, and an easy port of entry into the kingdom for Lancastrian dissidents. In October 1464 William Herbert was empowered to deal with all rebels in Harlech and Merioneth.

The most troublesome of Herbert's enemies was Jasper Tudor. In spite of the many set-backs and disappointments he had had to endure, he remained immovable in his loyalty to the Lancastrian dynasty and unresting in his machinations on its behalf. Finding it impossible to remain unharassed in any place for long, 'he moved from country to country in Wales', recorded Hall, 'not always at his heart's ease, nor in security of life or surety of living. Such an unstable and blind goods is fortune.'[16] The Welsh chronicler, Ellis Gruffydd, provided an even more detailed snapshot of the straits to which Jasper was reduced. Gruffydd told how Jasper, after the pacification of the north in 1464, took ship at a place called Pwll Picton near Mostyn. He was there 'constrained to carry a load of pease-straw on his back as he went to the ship lest he should be recognized because there were not wanting those who searched for him' and managed to sail to Brittany, thanks more to his own navigational skills than those of the mariners.[17]

[15] *Paston Letters*, II, 151–2.   [16] Hall, *Chronicle*, p. 261.
[17] Mostyn MS 158, fos. 323v–4.

Two years later, in 1466, the garrison of Harlech embarked on a raid which took them as far as Wrexham, seventy miles distant. This venture served to arouse even more acutely the apprehensions of the agitated captains of Beaumaris, Caernarfon, Conwy, and Montgomery, some of whose town and castle garrisons had already had to be strengthened during these years. They were reassured once more that adequate reinforcements would be sent 'for the safeguarding of our strongholds, considering our rebels be daily in the said country'.[18] But an expedition under the command of the earl of Worcester sent to reduce Harlech castle completely failed in its purpose. Large parts of the revenue due from Caernarfonshire and Anglesey still remained unpaid, and this intransigence was in no small measure to be explained by the resistance of Harlech.

In 1468 Edward IV was eventually brought to see the necessity for reducing this stubborn outpost of Lancastrian resistance. By the summer of that year it appeared as if relations between England and France were deteriorating to the point of open warfare between the two countries. That wily operator, Louis XI of France, invested a tentative speculation to the extent of three ships and fifty men in Jasper Tudor's capacity to create diversions. With these he was encouraged to descend on the coast of Wales to cause trouble for his own and Louis's adversary, the king of England. Having landed, probably at Barmouth, about the end of June, Jasper found himself gaining a good deal of support and was able to gather 2,000 men about him. He was emboldened to advance to Denbigh, where he caused a good deal of damage in the suburbs of the town and in the lordship as an act of vengeance against the Yorkist population but failed to take the castle. Stung by Jasper's latest act of daring, and seeing its importance in a wider context, Edward on 3 July empowered William Herbert to raise a formidable contingent of some 7–10,000 men from the Marches and the border counties. Herbert and his brother Richard divided their army into three sections, according to Guto'r Glyn, and marched northwards. Jasper was defeated and, in retaliation for the damage wrought by him at Denbigh and for that done by the Harlech garrison over the years, the Yorkist army waged a savagely punitive campaign and 'wasted with fire and sword all Nanconway and all the country lying between Conway and Dovey'. 'The whole borough of Llanrwst and all the vale of Conway besides carried yet the colour of the fire', testified John Wynn over a hundred years later.[19] Herbert was a hard man even by the standards of this unpitying age; iron-willed, ruthless, determined, and convinced that his opponents had to be taught a dire lesson—no wonder the Gloucester chronicler shuddered at his approach! Chilling stories have been preserved of his granite-faced inexorability. William of Worcester

[18] C. D. Ross, *Edward IV* (London, 1974), p. 120.
[19] *HGF*, pp. 29, 34.

recorded how he had hanged seven brothers in Anglesey despite their mother's piteous pleas that one, at least, should be spared. Failing to move the remorseless Herbert, the distraught woman eventually fell on her knees and cursed him; 'which curse fell upon him at Banbury', added William of Worcester portentously.[20]

The siege of Harlech itself was graphically described by the poet, Hywel Dafi, who told of men being 'shattered by the sound of guns' [*a tharfu gwŷr â thwrf gwns*], with 'seven thousand men shooting in every port, their bows made from every yew tree':

> Saethu 'mhob porth seithmil pen,
> A'u bwa o bob ywen.[21]

The garrison may have been disheartened by the size of Herbert's army, its ruthless treatment of the countryside, and the defeat of Jasper; at all events, the final siege lasted no more than a month. The castle surrendered on 14 August and fifty prisoners were taken. Included among them was the indomitable Dafydd ab Ieuan ab Einion, who had kept 'little Harlech for so long, alone faithful to the weak crown':

> Ni bu ond Harddlech fechan
> Gywir neb i'r goron wan.[22]

Thanks to Herbert influence, however, neither he nor Gruffydd Fychan suffered for their part in defending it. One of those not captured by the victorious Yorkists was that Houdini of the civil wars, the great escapist Jasper Tudor. True to form, he once more eluded his pursuers: 'men ween that he was not out of Wales when that Lord Herbert came with his host; but favour at some time doth great ease, as it is proved by the hiding of that lord, sometime earl of Pembroke'.[23] The *ci-devant* earl might have escaped; but his title was appropriated and now passed to the Lord Herbert as his reward. The costs of the expedition had been large: in November 1468 King Edward recognized his debt of £5,521 for services in Wales; but Herbert was at the pinnacle of his power. Guto'r Glyn felt it necessary to warn him against the temptation to overstretch his authority in retaliation against his countrymen who had stood by Lancaster: 'Tax not Anglesey beyond what it can bear. Let not the Saxon rule in Gwynedd and Flint. Confer no office upon the descendants of Horsa.'[24]

These warnings to Herbert against alienating his compatriots and counselling him to beware of devious stratagems and sinister deceits on the part of the English may well have been prompted by the increasing friction not only between Richard, earl of Warwick, and the King, but also

[20] Ross, *Edward IV*, pp. 114, 120.
[21] E. D. Jones, *Beirdd y Bymthegfed Ganrif a'u Cefndir* (Aberystwyth, 1984), p. 31.
[22] *D.Ll.F.*, p. 92.   [23] *Gregory's Chronicle*, p. 237.   [24] *GG*, pp. 130–1.

between the former and Herbert himself. By 1468–9 it was not the opposition of outright Lancastrians like Margaret of Anjou and Jasper Tudor that Edward had to fear so much as the pride and hostility of the so-called 'kingmaker'. The rift between Warwick and Herbert had begun as early as 1461. Handsomely as Earl Richard and his family had been rewarded, their greed was insatiable. In Wales, Warwick had especially coveted control of the Buckingham lordships which ran alongside his own possessions in Glamorgan and Abergavenny. He had actually been given custody of them at first, only to see it transferred to Herbert four days later. Edward's decision had signalled unmistakably that if it came to a choice between Herbert and Warwick in Wales, the Welshman was the more likely to win his favour.

The action sparked off eight years of rivalry between the two men. Warwick became further exacerbated in 1464 when the King's unbargained-for marriage to Elizabeth Wydevill wrecked the earl's plans that Edward should contract a foreign marriage alliance. Not only that, but the promotion of the interests of the Queen's relatives, particularly the marriages arranged for them, severely restricted Warwick's freedom of manœuvre in planning alliances for his own daughters. One of those who benefited at the expense of Warwick's discomfiture was Herbert, whose son was married to the Queen's sister in 1466. The following year, fuel was added to the flames when Herbert was one of a small, select company who went with Edward to demand the Great Seal from the Lord Chancellor, Warwick's brother, George, archbishop of York. To compound this set-back, Warwick's hopes of an alliance with France were blasted by Edward's negotiations with the Burgundians in 1468. In Wales Herbert's agents seized a messenger carrying letters from Queen Margaret to Harlech and he accused Warwick of Lancastrian sympathies, as a result of which Warwick was taxed with being guilty of being in secret communication with Lancastrians. Sorely vexed, he now moved closer to the King's discontented brother, Clarence, so as to detach him from the court party, and sealed their alliance by marrying his daughter to the Yorkist prince. The two newly found friends and allies were responsible for a joint letter of 12 July 1469 in which they brooded darkly on Edward's propensity for making confidants of ambitious and newly created lords. 'The king', they wrote, 'estranges great lords from his council and takes about him others not of their blood inclining only to their counsel.'[25] Even if Herbert had not been specifically named in the letter, there was no mistaking him as one of the two or three most obvious targets for these shafts.

The threat to Edward from Warwick and Clarence was all the more perilous because one Robin of Redesdale or Robin Mend-all (probably Sir

[25] *WWR*, p. 173.

John Conyers, a kinsman to Warwick) had already raised rebellion in the north. Inspired partly, at least, by the intrigues of the Nevill family, the rising was gaining ground to such an extent that Edward felt obliged to march north to suppress it. Finding less support than he had hoped for, he turned back to Nottingham to await the arrival of reinforcements being brought up from Wales and the west by William Herbert and Humphrey Stafford, earl of Devon. Herbert had raised a formidable army of several thousand men, variously estimated as being from 6,700 to 18,000 strong. Drawn mainly from south-east Wales and Pembroke, they included in their midst a large number of gentry of the best blood in south Wales, with the prolific Herbert, Vaughan, Morgan, Havard, and Games clans prominent among them. Their ranks were also liberally laced with hardened veterans who had experience of warfare in France. Herbert came 'with the extremity of all his power', Hall assures us, 'joyous of the King's summons, partly to deserve the King's liberality which of a mean gentleman had promoted him to the estate of an earl.'[26] Before the expedition had set off, Herbert had entertained all the leaders to a sumptuous feast at Raglan, described by Guto'r Glyn in terms reminiscent of all those well-remembered eve-of-battle repasts prepared for warriors from time immemorial since the legendary banquets of Caswallon and Arthur. Yet again the loyal poet aired his deep misgivings about the bribery and treachery to be feared from the English:

> A'i bribwyr oll yn bwrw brad . . .
>
> Gwenwyn gantun' ugeinwaith,
> Gael yn iarll ŵr glew o'n iaith.[27]

[Their venomous envy is aroused a score of times to see a fine man of our nation made an earl]

From Raglan, Herbert and his troops made their way to Gloucester, much to the trepidation of its annalist, and thence to the Cotswolds to link up with the earl of Devon.

By Sunday 23 July 1469 they must have reached the neighbourhood of Banbury, for on the following day there was a short but fierce skirmish. One of those killed in the course of it was Thomas ap Roger Vaughan of Hergest, whose marble monument set up by his grieving widow, Ellen Gethin, can still be seen at Kington. It is not certain whether it was on the Monday night or the previous evening that a flaming altercation broke out between Herbert and the earl of Devon. Ostensibly the quarrel concerned a dispute between them over billets and a pretty girl to whom the libidinous Herbert had taken a fancy. In reality the rift might have gone much deeper and may well have been an irreconcilable argument about who should take

---

[26] Hall, *Chronicle*, pp. 273–4.   [27] *GG*, p. 135.

precedence in commanding the army. Herbert may have been the offending party, but, whatever the provocation, Devon's conduct in storming off in high dudgeon and taking his troops away some ten miles distant on the eve of battle can hardly be excused. The poets were later to reproach him for it scathingly and, with considerable justification, to blame his defection for the defeat. His precipitate departure left Herbert in a dangerously vulnerable situation because most of the archers of the combined force were to be found in Devon's contingent.

The Welsh now took up a strong position at Edgecote Lodge, some five miles from Banbury. Though they had been left in the lurch by Devon that, curiously enough, may have made them more not less eager for battle. They were reported to have been in euphoric mood, buoyed up by that immortal prophecy, reportedly delivered to King Cadwaladr and recorded by Geoffrey of Monmouth, of future victory for the Welsh descendants of the ancient Britons. 'They imagined that now the long-wished-for hour had arrived and used every possible exertion to promote its fulfilment.'[28] They fought with great determination and seemed to have won the day, but were finally overcome when confronted with reinforcements led by John Clapham, fighting under Warwick's banner. Ellis Gruffydd preserved for us the brief conversation which reputedly passed between the brothers William and Richard Herbert. Richard urged his brother to flee, but William's disdainful reply was that his brother had better take flight if he feared their enemies. Richard countered with equal hauteur that he feared none but God and the old woman of Anglesey's curse. On the day after their defeat both brothers were executed at Northampton in spite of an urgent plea by William that his brother be spared because he was 'young, lusty and hardy, meet and apt to serve the greatest prince in Christendom'.[29] The execution of the Herbert brothers, for which there was no legal justification because they were not up in arms against the king, was a typically malevolent act of spite and vengeance carried out on the orders of the earl of Warwick, who had for years been eyeing Herbert's rise to power with consuming envy and waiting for an opportunity to settle old scores with him. The list of those killed in battle or put to death afterwards reads like a roll-call of the most honourable and distinguished names of the gentry of south Wales. Estimates of losses range from 2,000 to 5,000, among them 168 members of the gentry. In the whole annals of the civil wars of the fifteenth century the battle of Edgecote (or Banbury) exacted a much more fearful price in Welsh blood than any other. The bards were right to see it as a calamity of unparalleled proportions.

This battle made an extraordinarily deep impression on those Welsh poets. Its impact appeared to have been branded more searingly on their

[28] *Croyland Continuator*, pp. 446–7.   [29] Hall, *Chronicle*, p. 275.

recollections than that of any other of the clashes of the civil wars, with the possible exception of Bosworth. It is from their verses that we derive our sharpest impressions of its agonizing repercussions amongst the Welsh. Naturally the poets recorded the exceptional courage of many of the participants—was not valour in battle at the very heart of the heroic tradition of praise, even when defeat resulted? One of those who fought on the Welsh side, identified by his great-great-grandson, Lord Herbert of Chirbury, English chroniclers, and the poet Bedo Brwynllys as Richard Herbert, though Dr John David Rhys and Lewys Glyn Cothi claimed him as Thomas ap Roger Vaughan, had fought his way through the enemy ranks twice, cutting them down like a reaper lays a swathe, 'which is more than is famed of Amadis de Gaul or the Knight of the Sun'.[30] Inevitably, however, it was grief at the carnage among so many brave men, the flower of their country's manhood, which tended to overwhelm them. The death toll was so frightful that Guto'r Glyn likened it to the horrifying *danse macabre* fresco at St Paul's, with implacable Death's grinning skeleton gloatingly leading his myriad victims away. Ieuan Deulwyn saw his world turned upside down and the end of all things close at hand. All the poets viewed with utter dejection the loss of so many courageous heroes, so many generous patrons; hardly one was left to sustain them, mourned Huw Cae Llwyd.

No aspect of the battle kindled their vehemence more explosively than the earl of Devon's dereliction of duty in failing to support Herbert and his desertion of his Welsh comrades in the face of the enemy. Hywel Swrdwal contemptuously branded all Englishmen as 'Lollards' (a rare example of any reference to these heretics in Welsh poetry) and traitors. Tudur Penllyn thought that they compared with the Turk for barbarous cruelty and denounced those responsible for executing the Herberts as 'whoresons of Hengist and Horsa' [*hwr-swns o Hors a Hengist*]. Ieuan Deulwyn believed that, with their natural instinct for treachery and betrayal, the English had repeated at Banbury what they had earlier been guilty of at Builth in 1282 when they had killed Llywelyn the Last. Guto'r Glyn had a certain savage satisfaction in reminding his fellow-countrymen that at least the treacherous earl of Devon had had no long life since he had been executed in August 1469.

Worst of all, the bards sensed what a catastrophe for their country was implied in the loss of a man who, from relatively modest beginnings, had hoisted himself into so exalted a place in the counsels of the King and so influential a role as Edward's viceroy in Wales. 'The defeat at Banbury cut down this mighty wide-branching oak into a mass of shapeless chips', grieved Huw Cae Llwyd:

[30] Lord Herbert, *Autobiography*, ed. S. Lee (London, 1906), p. 6.

Maes Banbri'n torri caterwen—osglawg
yn asglod anghymen.[31]

Hywel Swrdwal implored Edward 'to come to Wales to rekindle the nation':

Edward hyn, dyred unwaith
I Gymru enynnu'r iaith.[32]

If there is any truth in the tradition about the effect of the old prophecy on Welsh hopes before the battle of Banbury—and there seems every reason to conclude that there was—then how much more shattering was the consequence of defeat? William Herbert may have been a proud, ambitious, and domineering figure, as Dafydd Llwyd confessed in a rare moment of unvarnished and uncomfortable truth, yet the poet must have believed that it was better that a ruthless Welshman of that type should exercise authority in Wales than an Englishman like Warwick, who would certainly be no more gentle or scrupulous in his methods but infinitely less *simpatico* to the Welsh. And so the poet wished Heaven to Herbert and all the host who died in his cause at Banbury.

Nef ir iarll a'i nifer wŷr
A fu farw yn rhaid f'eryr.[33]

With William Herbert safely disposed of, Warwick lost no time in taking over the offices in Wales his rival had previously occupied. He became chief justice and chamberlain of South Wales, constable of Carmarthen and Cardigan and assumed other lesser posts once held by Herbert. For some months, Edward's own position in the shadow of his 'super-noble' was uneasy and incongruous. By November 1469, however, he felt strong enough to install his brother, Richard of Gloucester, as chief justice of North Wales and chief steward and surveyor of the Principality of Wales and the earldom of March. At this stage Richard was intended by Edward to fill Herbert's vacant shoes in Wales, and this became even plainer in February 1470 when he replaced Warwick as chief justice and chamberlain of South Wales during the minority of the young Herbert earl of Pembroke. Edward also entrusted authority in Wales to other men upon whom he clearly thought he could depend, notably Lord Ferrers, Sir Roger Vaughan, Sir William Stanley, and in west Wales John Dwn. Dwn's elevation took place greatly to the annoyance of the grandsons of Gruffydd ap Nicholas, who seized Carmarthen and Cardigan castles, from which they had to be evicted by Richard of Gloucester. In the spring of 1470 Warwick and Clarence fled to France, where Louis XI managed to cobble together an alliance between them and Margaret of Anjou and Jasper

---

[31] *H.C.Ll.*, pp. 41–3.   [32] Jones, *Beirdd y 15fed Ganrif*, p. 37.
[33] *D.Ll.F.*, pp. 123–5.

Tudor. On the strength of it they landed at Dartmouth in September and put the washed-out Henry VI back on the throne. Warwick and Jasper once again took over the government of Wales for a short period before Edward returned to Ravenspur in north-eastern England in March 1471.

Though many were wary of revealing their sympathies too soon, there were Welshmen who were glad to welcome Edward on his return. Such was Roger Kynaston, one of the first to greet him after his landing, and the subject of a poem by Guto'r Glyn. In the ensuing battle at Barnet, Warwick was defeated and killed. Yorkist propagandists hailed Edward's triumph as a twofold victory—for legitimate descent, and for the will of God as revealed on the field of battle. Guto'r Glyn greeted the news with delight, interpreting the victory as vengeance for the defeat at Banbury, while John David Rhys was later to record the tradition that the man who had killed Warwick was none other than the Welshman, William Fychan, who had thereby avenged his uncles killed at Banbury. Following the Lancastrian set-back at Barnet, Margaret of Anjou, who had landed in England that very day, retreated to the west country but was soon defeated at Tewkesbury by Edward IV's armies, in which John Dwn and Roger Kynaston fought well and were knighted. Tewkesbury was a particularly black day for the Lancastrian cause; after the battle the Prince of Wales was executed. Within a very short time Henry VI died in mysterious circumstances in the Tower of London—so conveniently for Edward that everything points to his having been responsible for Henry's death; 'crushing the seed', as one Welsh poet put it. Rumours were soon widespread that the deed had been committed in the presence of, if not by, Richard of Gloucester.[34]

Jasper Tudor, fortunately for him perhaps, had not been present at the battle of Tewkesbury, and he now withdrew to the castle of Chepstow. Here he was confronted by Sir Roger Vaughan of Tretower, dispatched by Edward IV to seize him. Jasper, however, 'got his retaliation in first', took the initiative and quickly put Vaughan to death. The dead man had been a munificent patron to the bards, some of whom were not slow to condemn Jasper for what he had done and especially for behaving treacherously. Llywelyn Goch y Dant hoped that since he had shown no pity to Vaughan neither would he himself receive any when he died. Huw Cae Llwyd went further and maintained that Jasper had broken the oath he had given on the sacrament that no harm would come to Roger. Two sixteenth-century commentators, Hall and John David Rhys, on the other hand sought to defend Jasper; Hall by maintaining that Vaughan had been sent by Edward IV to capture Jasper by a ruse but that he had got wind of it first; while John David Rhys recorded an old tradition that Jasper had put Vaughan to

---

[34] Jones, *Beirdd y 15fed Ganrif*, p. 56.

death because it was he who had led his father Owain Tudor to the scaffold. We need not expend too much sympathy on either of the two; in that lawless world it was indeed a case of the 'devil take the hindmost'.

Jasper Tudor was himself in sore straits at this time. Although a Milanese emissary reported that Louis XI had ordered financial help to be given to him because he was holding a number of towns in Wales and it was even rumoured that he intended to make himself king, he found himself under increasingly heavy pressure, even after he had withdrawn from Chepstow to Pembroke. At Pembroke he had his fourteen-year-old nephew, Henry, in his custody. The subtle and worldly wise Jasper realized the increased importance of the youth as a possible Lancastrian claimant to the throne now that Henry VI and his heir were dead, though any claims he had to the throne were not canvassed by anyone at this time. Jasper therefore decided to flee abroad for safety, taking his nephew with him. They sailed from Tenby in 1471 with the help of a local merchant, John White. Their original intention was to make for France in the hope of gaining the help of Edward IV's enemy, Louis XI. Fortunately, they never reached that country or they might have been handed over to Edward when Louis later came to terms with him. Instead, they found themselves blown off course to Le Conquet in Brittany and in that duchy they were to spend the next twelve or thirteen years.

From 1471 onwards, with his Lancastrian opponents crushed and scattered, Edward IV remained securely seated on his throne until his death in 1483. He was now in a position to take steps not only to rule firmly the more settled parts of his kingdom but also to restore a measure of order to some of the more notoriously turbulent areas like the north of England and Wales. In Wales the death of the all-powerful William Herbert in 1469, followed by the upheavals of the next two years, had created a power vacuum, especially when, in 1471, Richard duke of Gloucester was obliged to turn his attention to the north of England. Edward's immediate solution was to fall back once more on the Herbert family and allow the youthful William Herbert, junior, second earl of Pembroke, to inherit the offices of justice and chamberlain of South Wales, which had been granted to his father in tail male. The earl of Shrewsbury was at the same time installed as chief justice of North Wales. Meantime, in the Marches Edward found himself occupying a more powerful role *vis-à-vis* other lords of the March than any previous king had done. Having inherited his own family's extensive lordships, acquired the Lancastrian ones, and taken over those formerly belonging to the earl of Warwick, he had become lord of almost the whole of the March. The only major figure on the horizon there besides himself was the duke of Buckingham. Though the situation was unprecedently favourable to him, he could not be said to have had a preconceived and carefully worked out plan for dealing with it. But he did improvise and extend new arrangements over the next few years with some measure of success. In 1471 he created his son Prince of Wales and set up a council for him. When the prince took up residence in the Marches in 1473 an inner council, of which Lord Rivers, Bishop Alcock, and Sir Thomas Vaughan were the most active members, was established. The Prince and his officers now began to reside at the old Mortimer 'capital' of Ludlow and were given additional supervisory powers (see above, pp. 52–3). In 1479 the earl of Pembroke, who had inherited his father's title and offices but not his ability or his ruthlessness and had proved a disappointment, was forced to surrender his earldom in return for the title of earl of Huntingdon and somewhat inadequate territorial compensation and was pushed increasingly into the background as the Herbert position of influence was dismantled.

In general, during the years of Edward's second reign, from 1471 to 1483, Wales accepted his rule without demur. But, in spite of the eclipse of the Lancastrians and the establishment of the Council of the Prince, Wales remained far from being peaceful and subdued. In 1473 the Council at Ludlow was obliged to try to suppress the turbulence caused in the Marches by robberies and disorders committed by the men of the counties of Shropshire and Hereford as well as by those of the Marches. It found itself confronted with an old and familiar dilemma on the part of witnesses who wanted good government but were loth to 'tell the truth for dread of murder and to be mischieved in their own houses considering the great number of misdoers and the bearers up of the same'.[35] In the following year, Thomas ap Gruffydd ap Nicholas, widely renowned as a swordsman and victor in many notable fights with Henry ap Gwilym, met his end. He was an unruly and aggressive son not unworthy of his masterful and ambitious father and was killed following a skirmish at Pennal, in the course of which he had himself earlier slain Dafydd Goch. Disorders ensued and provided the opportunity for Thomas's son, Rhys, to make his entrance on the stage of Welsh politics, where he was to play so long, dominating, and illustrious a part. But he was now charged with having taken up his inheritance without licence to do so. Members of the Herbert family were involved that winter in 'divers offences committed by them in Wales and the Marches', whereupon they 'withdrew to Wales and stirred up rebellion'.[36] Additionally, in 1475 there were 'heinous complaints of robberies, murders, manslaughters, ravishing of women, and burning of houses' committed by 'errant thieves and rebellions of Oswestry hundred and Chirkland', whom the marquis of Dorset and Sir Richard Gray were commissioned to punish.[37] It was symptomatic of the continuing turbulence of the Marches that all the Marcher lords were summoned to be at Ludlow on

---

[35] *Rot. Parl.*, v, 159–60.
[36] *Paston Letters*, III, 107.
[37] H. Owen and J. B. Blakeway, *A History of Shrewsbury* (2 vols. London, 1825), I, 252.

24 March 1476 to discuss among themselves the best means of restoring order.

It may possibly have been these upheavals and disorders which led some of the poets to appeal urgently to Edward IV to take action in Wales to restore stability and eliminate injustice there. Even a former sympathizer with the Tudors' cause, like Dafydd Llwyd, had lost faith in their future as the men who might fulfil the venerable prophecies of Welsh victory. The Welsh would now be better engaged in looking to Edward IV, himself sprung 'from the trunk of the old stocks'—a reference to the King's descent from Gwladus Ddu, daughter of Llywelyn the Great. Dafydd was confident that, whatever Welsh faults had been in the past, they could make amends and turn to serve the King's present needs.[38] Less surprisingly, the old Yorkist stalwart, Guto'r Glyn, addressed a memorable poem to Edward when he was engaged in preparing for a campaign in France in 1474–5. True to type, Guto appealed to him to look to his grandmother's Welsh kin for support in Wales, reminding him of the Mortimers' descent from the ruling house of Gwynedd. More especially he appealed to him to free the Welsh from all the 'deceit and oppression' [*dwyll ac amraint holl Gymry*] under which they laboured.[39] How much effect these poems had on Edward, and who was responsible for the patronage which evoked them, it is impossible to say. But they do serve to show that the Yorkist king was popular in Wales and that Welsh hopes for better government after the death of William Herbert were largely pinned on Edward's personal influence.

Whatever the reason for it, Wales during the last years of Edward's reign seems to have been much quieter, with far fewer references to disorder than there had been earlier. Had Edward lived to a ripe old age, as there seemed every prospect of his doing, the fortunes of the Yorkist dynasty might long have been secure. But on 9 April 1483, he died suddenly, just short of the age of forty-one, without having taken adequate precautions for the safe succession of his son. His heedlessness in this matter, the limited base of the aristocratic support on which he relied, the unpopularity of the Queen's family, and the ambitions of his brother, Richard, were rapidly to transform the political situation.

[38] *D.Ll.F.*, pp. 73–4.   [39] *GG*, pp. 157–9.

CHAPTER 9

TO BOSWORTH AND BEYOND, 1483–1497

EDWARD IV had been a popular and experienced ruler, whose son, Edward V, might ordinarily have been expected to succeed to the throne without serious difficulties, just as the youthful Richard II and the even younger Henry VI had done in earlier generations. Had the late king's brother, Richard duke of Gloucester, named as Protector in his brother's will, been content to fulfil his appointed role, the continuance of the Yorkist dynasty might have been assured. Admittedly, in the struggle for power during the minority of the young king, there was almost bound to be cut-throat political in-fighting, given the grasping, place-hunting instincts of Edward V's mother and her relations. What was not foreseeable was that Richard would unlawfully have seized the throne for himself. This was an acquisitive and unrelentingly competitive age, however, in which men of the blood royal and others of distinguished aristocratic lineage had brutally been put to death over the previous quarter of a century or more. Richard was morbidly suspicious—not without good cause—that the aggressive intentions of the Wydevilles and the influence they were certain to exert over the youthful and immature Edward might tempt them to go for his jugular, literally as well as metaphorically. To forestall any danger to himself, therefore, he immediately took steps to seize the person of the boy ruler.

Edward V and his entourage were making their way from Ludlow to London when, at Northampton, they encountered Humphrey Stafford, duke of Buckingham. A vain and self-seeking individual, convinced that he had been excluded from the role to which he believed his birth and ability entitled him, Buckingham had already been in close touch with Richard of Gloucester. If he had not sowed the first seeds of disloyalty in the royal uncle's mind, he had actively promoted their germination. At Stony Stratford the party was joined by Richard who took charge of young Edward and proceeded to London. The first council he attended confirmed his title as Lord Protector; but he discharged his responsibility by having the King and, later, his younger brother, detained in the Tower—hardly the kind of 'protection' or even 'protective custody' originally envisaged for them. On 26 June, less than three months after his brother's death, Richard was proclaimed king. Both Lord Stanley and his wife, Margaret Beaufort, Henry Tudor's mother, played a conspicuous part in Richard's coronation ceremony on 9 July 1483. But, in general, his usurpation of the throne proved to be a singularly unpopular action, even in an age hardened to violent politics and abrupt fluctuations of fate. It mortally offended not only the Wydevilles and their friends but other loyal supporters of Edward IV and his sons as well. Naturally, it was completely unacceptable to what remained of the Lancastrian faction; but it was also repellent to many people of all parties—and none—because it appeared to be so blatant a violation of what was widely regarded as one of the most sacred principles on which society depended: the immutable right of lawful heirs to succeed to their inheritance. In addition, socio-economic circumstances were particularly unpropitious in this summer and autumn, which proved to be a time of acute scarcity and soaring prices, the result of a bad harvest in 1481, followed by the atrocious one of 1482. By the autumn of 1483, in the midst of all this disturbance, simmering discontent with Richard's regime was rife.

Richard's usurpation dramatically transformed the prospects for the Lancastrians. The altered situation was almost tailor-made for a rival claimant, even one as remote and obscure as the exile in Brittany, twenty-six-year-old Henry Tudor. Penurious though he was and shaky as his Lancastrian claim may have been, events had now had the effect of changing him into a genuine contender for power. The way looked to be open for his irrepressible uncle, Jasper Tudor, to make yet another come-back, in a bid this time on his nephew's behalf. Among the first to discern the new possibilities open to Henry was his mother, Margaret Beaufort, who had at one stage during Edward's reign worked hard for his peaceful return. In spite of her religious and unworldly disposition and the fact that she had seemed to countenance Richard's coronation, she was ambitious for her son and a shrewd judge of politics and the realities of power. She promptly began to intrigue with Edward IV's widow in the hope of arranging a marriage between the latter's daughter, Elizabeth, heiress of the house of York, and her son Henry, so that the claims of York and Lancaster to the throne might jointly be pressed. She used as her messenger her doctor, Lewis Caerleon, because he was also Queen Elizabeth's physician and had ready access to her. She opened secret negotiations with the duke of Buckingham, too. He, for his earlier help to Richard, had been amply rewarded by being made constable of England and virtual viceroy of Wales; but he quickly became disillusioned by Richard's conduct of affairs or disappointed that he had not gained more for himself. He was now prepared to conspire against the King and may indeed have had claims of his own on the throne.[1] The plotters were also in touch with other opponents of Richard, mainly disenchanted Yorkists in

[1] He had royal blood in his veins, being descended on his father's side from the daughter of Thomas Woodstock, son of Edward III, and on his mother's side was connected to John of Gaunt.

the south and east of England. By October rumours were freely circulating that Edward IV's sons had been done to death at their uncle's command, and the moment seemed ripe for rebellion.

Margaret Beaufort sent her emissary, Hugh Conway, to Brittany to urge Henry to make for Wales, where he would find help awaiting him. When this news reached him, Henry sought out the aid of Duke Francis of Brittany to launch his campaign. The duke promised Henry help in the form of ships and money. Success would depend to a large extent on careful timing and co-operation on the part of various groups of Richard's enemies in raising rebellion. But details of the conspiracy were leaked to Richard and co-ordination between the rebels was almost non-existent. When they rose in revolt, therefore, in October 1483 they failed disastrously. In Wales torrential rainstorms and severe flooding prevented the duke of Buckingham from crossing the Severn. His army, alleged to have been 'recruited against their wills and without any lust to fight', deserted him and left him to his fate. Buckingham was a harsh and unsympathetic character, 'a sore and hard-dealing man', unpopular with his tenants who could make no appeal to national sentiment in Wales. Around him he had a number of enemies, among them the Vaughan family and their associates. Besides their hatred of Buckingham, these opponents had other old scores to settle with Lancastrians too. Their feud with the Tudors still rankled unforgivingly as they recalled how Jasper Tudor had savagely executed Sir Roger Vaughan, head of the Tretower family, at Chepstow. Taking advantage of their enmity, Richard had encouraged them to rise against Buckingham and seize Brecon castle in his absence. The duke was soon captured at Shrewsbury and put to death. Not only had his rebellion in Wales collapsed ignominiously but he had also failed to rally support there. There were no Welshmen among the ninety-seven supporters of Buckingham later attainted, while twenty-two men of south Wales who remained loyal were given annuities by Richard.

Henry Tudor's expedition from Brittany fared little better. He had hopefully set off on 10 October with fifteen ships, 5,000 men reputedly—though that figure seems exaggerated—and a gift of 10,000 golden crowns from Duke Francis. The expedition ran into severe gales in the Channel, the same storms which had battered Buckingham's troops and caused the Severn to flood. Thirteen of Henry's ships were scattered and driven helplessly back, though his own craft and one other managed to arrive just off the English coastline. Henry sent a boatload of his men to discover what had happened ashore. Waiting for them they found some of Richard's victorious troops who, by pretending that they were Buckingham's men, tried to entrap their enemies. But the members of the landing-party were too wary to be deceived, refused to go ashore, and returned to their mother ship. Having heard their report, Henry returned to Brittany via

France, to be greeted with the news that the rebellion had been snuffed out and Buckingham executed.

Buckingham's failure was not by any means the complete disaster for Henry's cause that might have been supposed. It was almost certainly an advantage to the Tudor that he did not owe his throne to the help of a man as self-interested and unscrupulous as Buckingham, who might have turned out to be as undependable an ally for Henry as for Richard. Furthermore, Henry was joined in Brittany by a number of disaffected Yorkists as well as leading Lancastrians, and something like a 'government in exile' was taking shape around him. On Christmas Day 1483, with snow lying deep on the ground, Henry took an oath at Rennes cathedral in the presence of his supporters that he would marry the Yorkist heiress. They in turn swore homage to him as though he were already king. No previous claimant to the English throne had gone as far as to call himself king before winning his victory; but Henry clearly felt confident enough to be able to claim the throne on behalf of the families of Lancaster and York.

These events emboldened him to appeal once more to the duke of Brittany for help. There could be no question henceforward that he was established as a valid pretender to the throne; the hope of all those who opposed Richard III, for whatever reason. The King himself was becoming seriously worried about the threat that loomed from his rival. Early in 1484 he induced Parliament to attaint Henry and his followers and seized Margaret Beaufort's lands and possessions, transferring them to the care of her husband, Lord Stanley. These actions availed him little or nothing. Within a year or two, his plight became perceptibly more wretched. In April 1484 his only son and heir died, leaving the whole question of the succession, the central issue of politics, more open than before. A year later, when his wife Anne died, it was symptomatic of the deep-seated and widespread suspicion of Richard among his subjects that wild rumours should circulate to the effect that he intended to marry his own niece, Elizabeth of York. There was almost certainly not a shred of truth in them; but their very existence showed how low Richard's reputation had sunk.

Richard's capacity to resist his enemies should not be underestimated, however. He was a vigorous and experienced soldier who instituted active measures to defend his realm. In Wales, which he had good reason to suspect might be Henry's landing-place, he took a number of precautions against possible attack. He organized a system of signalling news quickly by means of a number of well-sited lamps on hills adjoining Milford Haven, the likeliest invasion-point. He entrusted many strategically placed castles to the command of a reliable follower, Richard Williams; and also placed his old allies, the Herberts and Vaughans, in positions of vantage. William Herbert, earl of Huntingdon, though not a very effectual personality, was made justiciar of South Wales and entrusted with castles and the stewardships of a number of lordships. Another of the King's men, Sir James Tyrrel, was appointed to take charge of the upper Tywi Valley and the lordship of Glamorgan. In 1484, too, Richard initiated two policies which, if they had succeeded, might have eliminated the threat from Henry altogether. First, he encouraged Edward IV's widow, Elizabeth, and her daughters to come out of sanctuary at Westminster. The effect of this could very well have been that her eldest daughter, whom Henry had agreed to take as his wife, would have been married to some one else before ever he had returned from exile. Indeed, when news reached Henry of Richard's alleged intention to marry Elizabeth, improbable as that suggestion must have seemed, it was reported to have 'pinched him at the very stomach' with disappointment. Second, and even more dangerous for the pretender had the plan succeeded, was Richard's scheme to have Henry brought back from Brittany with the agreement of the authorities there. In the summer of 1484, when Duke Francis was ill, Richard arrived at an understanding with his minister, Pierre Landois, that Henry should be returned to England. Luckily for him, Henry got wind of the plan from John Morton and was able to devise a stratagem to escape to France in the nick of time. There he became a useful pawn in French hands in the international crisis that was now brewing. The main objective of French policy at this time was to ensure that when the elderly and ailing Duke Francis died, Brittany would fall into French possession. Such an outcome would certainly be resisted by Richard III and it was to foil his anticipated opposition that the French offered to help Henry. They did not expect his role to be very significant and the help they extended to him was distinctly modest. Indeed, on 9 August 1485, two days after Henry had landed in Wales, the French came to terms with Brittany. Had they done so sooner, they might never have aided him at all and Henry might have remained a poverty-stricken exile, incapable of taking any initiative.

Henry had realized for some time that the later he left his invasion, the weaker his position was likely to become. It was essential for him to take advantage of such help as he could get and not to delay any longer than he had to. He had already received messages of support from England and Wales. Morgan Kidwelly had conveyed promises from his step-father Lord Stanley, Sir William Stanley, and Gilbert Talbot; and John Morgan had brought similar news from Rhys ap Thomas and John Savage. Henry, in turn, would send confident letters to his supporters, proclaiming his rights to the throne and giving them promise of ample rewards if they supported him. Letters to his Welsh friends were particularly interesting. Such a letter—no doubt one of many—was later written to his kinsman, John ap Maredudd, and preserved for posterity by the latter's descendant, John Wynn of Gwydir. Henry again wrote as though he were already king, dismissing Richard as an 'odious tyrant' and 'usurper'. He went on to promise to restore his 'realm of England into its ancient estate, honour and prosperity' and the 'principality of Wales and the people of the same to their dear erst liberties, delivering them of such miserable servitude as they have piteously long stood in'. If the people supported him, he promised in the terminology characteristic of the age, to become their 'good lord' and to reward them handsomely.[2]

In the mean time, in spite of the apparent loss of confidence in the Tudors during the 1470s and the further disappointments of 1483, there had been a renewed outburst of poetic effort on Henry's behalf. Poets energetically whipped up expectations that the coming of the 'Bull of Anglesey' was imminent and that he would land without delay. Throughout the spring and summer of 1485 expectant eyes were watching for the arrival of the Tudors from Brittany. In a poem to Jasper Tudor, Lewys Glyn Cothi anxiously asked him what his intentions were:

> Siasbar, pa ddarpar yr wyd?
> Pa fôr y mae d'angorau?
> Pa bryd (pa hyd y'n hoedir?)
> Y tarw du, y trôi i dir?[3]

[Jasper, what preparations do you make? In what seas are your anchors? When, O black bull, will you turn to land? (How long shall we have to wait?)]

By the end of July 1485 Henry's preparations were complete. In the port of Harfleur at the mouth of the River Seine he had assembled a force of about 4,000 troops, many of them mercenaries paid for by the king of France, Charles VIII, who had also given him the sum of 40,000 livres. The chronicler, Philippe de Commines, acidly described these troops as 'the worst rabble one could find'; but his comments may well have been unduly brusque. Mercenaries of this period often fought well and reliably, and there is no suggestion that Henry's men did not acquit themselves bravely at Bosworth. Henry also had with him some Breton adventurers, Scots archers, and about 500 English exiles. The expedition was small in size, but its numbers compared favourably with those of any invasion force mounted from abroad to attack the kingdom since 1460. As the expedition was on the point of setting sail, Henry was reputed by one of his biographers, Bernard André, to have offered a prayer for its success. In that prayer he was said to have disclaimed any suggestion that he was embarking on the venture from human vanity or ambition but wanted only to free the population. He commended his troops to God and trusted to Him for victory. On 1 August the force sailed from Harfleur for Wales and nearly a week later, on 7 August, just before sunset they landed in Milford Haven, the anchorage where a French expeditionary force had landed in August

[2] *HGF*, p. 28.
[3] W. G. Jones, 'Welsh Nationalism and Henry Tudor', *Trans. Cymmr.*, 1917–18, p. 18.

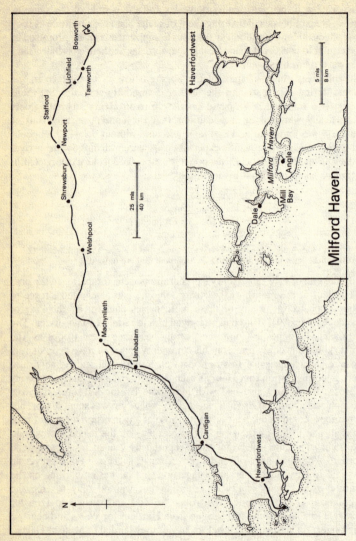

Bosworth
Lichfield
Tamworth
Stafford
Newport
Shrewsbury
Welshpool
Machynlleth
Llanbadarn
Cardigan
Haverfordwest

25 mls
40 km

N

Haverfordwest

Dale
Milford Haven
Mill
Bay
Angle

5 mls
8 km

Milford Haven

MAP 5 Henry Tudor's March to Bosworth

1405 to help Glyndŵr and in 1461 the earl of Wiltshire had come ashore from Ireland to aid the Lancastrian cause. The spot where Henry landed was probably Mill Bay, near St Ann's Head on the north-western side of the Haven.[4] It may have been carefully chosen so that the invaders should remain out of sight of the garrison at Dale castle, two miles further north, though the force must have been clearly visible from Angle, a short distance away on the eastern side of the Haven. In any event, the disembarkation could not be kept secret for long, and Richard's followers in the area were quick to carry news of it to the King at Nottingham. Within a very short space of time, by 11 August, he had been appraised of his rival's home-coming to the shores of Pembroke.

Henry's choice of a landing-place in Wales could hardly have been unexpected. The area was about as far distant from Richard's main centres of power as it could be. West Wales had always been a Lancastrians' stronghold and they had planned landings there before in the 1460s and 1470s. Jasper Tudor, still titular earl of Pembroke, had throughout these years kept up his connections with Wales; and it was there that Margaret Beaufort had suggested Henry should land in 1483. Henry knew beforehand that he had influential supporters in Wales on whom he hoped he could count, like Rhys ap Thomas, no less formidable than his fearsome grandfather, Gruffydd ap Nicholas, and his numerous kinsmen and allies. The poets—no fewer than thirty-five of them have been traced—had been active in stirring up public opinion to accept Henry as the promised *mab darogan* [son of prophecy] and could be expected to exert themselves even more strenuously on his behalf once he had landed.[5] Their help in reinforcing Welsh adherence to nationality and kinsman might be critically important. From a military point of view it was essential that Henry should be able to disembark in a land where his army could hope to come ashore and deploy quickly without meeting opposition in the first days, when it was likely to be at its most nervous and vulnerable. Equally important was that it should find itself in a sympathetic countryside when it was obliged to forage for supplies—there may be hint of this in the chronicle of Ellis Gruffydd, who tells how a large party of men from Gwynedd brought with them 'a great gift of fat animals, oxen and cows' when they joined Henry.[6] Most necessary of all, perhaps, was that he should be able to attract support so as to be able to build up his numbers without undue delay. And if, after all this, his campaign went awry, he might be glad of the mountains of Wales as a refuge, just as Owain Glyndŵr and Jasper Tudor before him had been.

In spite of all the build-up beforehand, Henry may have been a little

---

[4] S. B. Chrimes, 'The Landing Place of Henry of Richmond, 1485', *WHR*, II (1964–5), 173–80.

[5] Jones, *Trans. Cymmr.*, 1917–18, pp. 1–59.   [6] NLW, Mostyn MS 158, fo. 344.

disappointed that there was not more support for him from Wales after he had landed, and must certainly have noted with dismay how little enthusiasm there appeared to be for his cause in England. Some individuals and families in Wales remained loyal to Richard. Richard Williams and James Tyrrel, to whom many strongpoints had been entrusted, were two; and many of the Herberts and Vaughans, old Yorkist stalwarts in south-east Wales, were others. It may well have been these men or others like them who ensured that news of Henry's landing reached the King within four days, a remarkably short time considering that he was two hundred miles away at Nottingham. They, too, were strategically placed to deter the most direct thrust by Henry into England, and it could well have been their presence that partly accounted for his decision to march north-eastwards in the first instance. Many may have been sympathetic to Henry's cause but were too cautious to come out openly in his favour at once. Some, no doubt, remembered Buckingham's débâcle in 1483; others may have been unwilling to show their hand too soon—just as the men of northern England had been when Edward IV landed at Ravenspur in 1471. Warily calculating the chances before openly declaring one's loyalty had almost become a way of life during the civil wars of the fifteenth century. Not a few, therefore, waited to see how much support Henry attracted before joining him. The attitude of even of those who appeared to have been committed to his cause beforehand, like Rhys ap Thomas and Walter Herbert,[7] gave rise to some initial anxiety. As for the Stanley family, which exercised so decisive an influence on many of the gentry of north Wales, they were a considerable distance away in the north-eastern Marches and Lancashire, and it might be some time before Henry learned how they were going to react. On the other hand, if there was no rush to join Henry's army, there seemed to be a greater reluctance to come to Richard's defence.

During the fortnight after he had landed, Henry and his men pushed on at an average rate of about fourteen miles a day (see Map 5). In the course of his march he took care to send out parties of scouts, or 'scourers', to carry out reconnaissance and he depended heavily on the news they brought back of the lie of the land and of potential support. From Mill Bay, his troops avoided the direct route eastwards, fearing perhaps to run into opposition too soon, and also, more importantly, by pressing northwards, intending to link up with allies from north and mid Wales. Twelve miles north-east, over the hummocky route from Mill Bay, the invaders arrived at their first town of any consequence, Haverfordwest, where they were well received. Thence they proceeded over the Prescelly Hills to Cardigan, and from there they continued their northerly push along the coast of

---

[7] He was the second son of William, first earl of Pembroke, and a much more vigorous man than his elder brother. Despite his family's strong Yorkist tradition, he joined Henry Tudor.

Cardigan Bay to the neighbourhood of Aberystwyth. Then they turned inland along the valley of the Dyfi to Machynlleth. Nearby, in the vicinity of Cemaes, they stopped at Mathafarn, home of the celebrated poet, Dafydd Llwyd, a committed supporter of their cause. A well-known anecdote preserves the memory of Henry's consultation with the poet about his prospects. Dafydd's wife advised him to forecast victory, since if Henry won, the poet might be rewarded; but if he lost they would hear no more of him! From Cemaes they made their way eastwards to Welshpool and Mynydd Digoll [Long Mountain], which they reached after just a week on the march.

If Henry before this had been at all perturbed about the reactions of the Welsh to his campaign it was here that he got his assurance of the reality of their support. Substantial contingents from almost all parts of Wales joined him at this strategic central point. Here, on 13 August, only the seventh day of his march, reinforcements had arrived with such speed and in such good order that, considering how notoriously rough and difficult were the trackways in Wales, they must have reached this rendezvous almost certainly in accordance with a pre-arranged plan. The convergence of Henry's adherents from Wales may account for Ellis Gruffydd's somewhat over-enthusiastic account of his reception that, as soon as the gentry heard of his arrival, they rose in every commote and shire and came to him.

The largest and most impressive of the contingents to arrive was that of Rhys ap Thomas, who brought with him a great company of soldiers from south-west Wales. There had been some initial confusion about Rhys's attitude, though the picturesque story that he had salved his conscience over his loyalty to Richard by allowing Henry to cross over his body while he crouched under Mullock Bridge near Dale must be rejected as legendary.[8] His initial hesitation had doubtless been caused by his desire to negotiate suitable terms for his own reward by Henry in the event of victory. He had then quickly rallied his men and led them enthusiastically under his family's banner, blazoned with the historic three ravens of the deathless northern hero, Urien. They had proceeded by a different route from the main band and had come via Carmarthen, Llandovery, Brecon, and Newtown, swelling their numbers as they came. This alternative path may have been taken deliberately to keep the two contingents separate in case they should quarrel and also to mislead Richard III concerning Rhys's intentions. One old English ballad credits Rhys with having brought 'eight thousand spears', though two thousand would be a more likely figure; while another narrated how

> . . . Rhys ap Thomas draws Wales with him,
> A worthy sight it was to see

[8] *Cambrian Register*, I, 99–100.

> How the Welshmen rose wholly with him
> And shogged them to Shrewsbury.[9]

Later, a Welsh poet, Guto'r Glyn, was to claim that Henry won the day at Bosworth because of the strength of Rhys ap Thomas's men. But another hardly less encouraging sight for Henry was the arrival of companies of hardy warriors from north Wales: the men of Môn and Arfon under William Gruffydd ap Robin of Cwchwillan, those of Hiraethog led by Rhys ap Maredudd, and the men of Richard ap Hywel and Hugh Conway from the north-east.[10] Thanks to the response of his fellow-countrymen Henry had come close to doubling the size of his army.

Henry had now reached the borders of England. The critical question still hanging over his campaign was, in spite of earlier promises, how much help could he expect from men as prominent—and shifty!—as the Stanley brothers, who exerted an unrivalled influence in north-west England and north-east Wales? His venture still seemed nearly as great a gamble as he approached Shrewsbury at the crossing of the Severn as it had been at Mill Bay. He was first of all refused permission to enter the town; but the following day was allowed to enter without being challenged. It meant that there was now no longer any chance of confining the rebellion to Wales. Henry had crossed the most important river barrier into England and captured his first English town of consequence. Arriving at Newport (Salop) he was met and joined by Gilbert Talbot with 500 men. On the next day he reached Stafford and had his first conversation with the younger Stanley brother, Sir William. The result was probably inconclusive; but Stanley must have said enough to encourage Henry to continue with his march. The Stanleys were a family undeniably notorious for changing sides as it suited their advantage; but they were placed in an unenviable position at this time. Although Lord Stanley was the husband of Henry's mother, Margaret Beaufort, his eldest son by an earlier marriage, Lord Strange, was being held as a hostage by Richard III and with him was one of the most prominent gentlemen of north Wales, William Gruffydd of Penrhyn. Both were virtually certain of being put to death if the young Strange's relatives moved against the King. Lord Stanley's younger brother, Sir William, had raised some three thousand men from his lordships in Wales, and an English ballad declared that 'all the Welshmen love him well'.[11] One such was John Edwards of Chirk, whom Guto'r Glyn welcomed on his return from Bosworth, having believed, ironically enough, that he had gone to fight for Richard! On 20 August Henry had a further meeting with the Stanley family at Atherstone. It is not certain whether he met both

---

[9] A. F. Pollard, *The Reign of Henry VII from Contemporary Sources* (3 vols. London, 1913), I, 14.

[10] *WWR*, p. 223 lists the men from north Wales rewarded by Henry.

[11] *WWR*, p. 224 n.

brothers or only Sir William; but it seems evident that even at this stage he was unable to extract a cast-iron promise of their support.

By the time Henry reached the vicinity of Bosworth on 21 August his enterprise, on any objective assessment, still seemed distinctly hazardous. Even now, he had no more than a comparatively small force of about 5–7,000 men, confronting a royal army nearly twice as large. His troops had had a fortnight's hard marching, whereas Richard's for the most part had come a much shorter distance. Henry's artillery, too, may well have been inferior to that at his enemy's disposal. Worst of all, on the very eve of battle, he could not be sure what those forces commanded by the Stanleys would do. All he knew was that they were there in suficient strength—6–7,000 of them in all, perhaps—to carry the day one way or another.

Richard, meanwhile, had not been inactive. For some weeks before Henry landed, the King had established his headquarters at Nottingham. On 11 August he had received news of the invasion and had begun his preparations to counter-attack. He issued a proclamation denouncing Henry and his followers as traitors and began the calling-up of additional troops to come to his aid. All things considered, he seemed to be in a much stronger position than his challenger. He had vastly more experience of warfare and military command than Henry and had had ample time to prepare his defences. He commanded a larger and better-equipped army and was able to occupy the more favourable tactical position on the battlefield. But his position, too, had its weaknesses. He had grave doubts about the morale of some of his troops, and was far from certain of the dependability of one of his most important commanders, the earl of Northumberland. As for the Stanleys, Richard had probably more cause than Henry to doubt on which side they would commit their men. A day or two earlier, his hostage, Lord Strange, had confessed that his uncle, Sir William Stanley, had conspired to join Henry, though he maintained that his father was still loyal. But Richard must have been acutely worried by the thought that neither of the Stanley brothers had hitherto made any move to fulfil their duty to resist Henry in the course of his march; that hardly augured well for their loyalty to their sovereign. Whatever advantages Richard may have enjoyed, he still had many reasons on the eve of battle to feel doubt and uncertainty. On paper, the odds favoured him beforehand. Bosworth was a battle that he should perhaps have won; but the result was no foregone conclusion. Most men of the fifteenth century held the unshakable belief that the outcome of every battle lay in the hands of God. Finite men might submit themselves to the ordeal by battle; but only the Almighty in His infinite wisdom, they were convinced, would decide which of them had the better right to victory. He would grant it to the man whose cause had deserved His goodwill.

Important as the battle between Richard and Henry turned out to be, there is still a great deal we do not know about it and can now never hope to know. The main reason for the gaps in the record is that no contemporary account of it has survived. The fullest description was that given by the Italian, Polydore Vergil, who did not compose his history until about twenty years later. A careful and critical scholar, he had the opportunity of questioning many of those who had fought in the encounter, and we remain deeply indebted to him for his account of it. From what he wrote, it is clear that although the battle lasted only a few hours, it was not a shapeless slogging match, but one that was fought with skill and intelligence by the commanders on both sides. Among other things we cannot be sure of was where it was fought. The site at Ambien Hill, traditionally accepted for so long, has been challenged recently by scholars who have argued for the nearby village of Dadlington,[12] though without commanding universal acceptance. And although elaborate plans of the disposition of troops and their movements during the course of the battle have often been constructed, much of the detail is uncertain and remains open to conjecture.

On the morning of 22 August 1485 Richard's armies appear to have occupied a strong tactical position on the crest of a hill. In the van were a force consisting mainly of archers under the command of the duke of Norfolk. Behind him, in the centre, Richard was stationed with a picked body of men, and to the rear were the troops of the earl of Northumberland, whose constancy and morale were rated doubtful. Confronting them at the foot of the hill were Henry's men. His vanguard, like Richard's, included many archers and was commanded by John de Vere, earl of Oxford. On Oxford's right was a force commanded by Gilbert Talbot and on his left were troops under Sir John Savage. Also on that wing, at some distance from Oxford, was Henry Tudor, accompanied possibly by his uncle, Jasper.[13] The separation between Henry and Oxford was almost certainly deliberate and intended to give the former a chance to escape if the battle turned against him.

Somewhere on the flanks, between the armies of Henry and Richard, were the contingents led by the Stanleys. It is not certain where they were positioned, but Lord Stanley was probably to the south, with Sir William to the north, nearer to the battlefield. Neither of the main protagonists knew for certain on which side they would intervene, but Henry had the better hope of their help and Richard the greater uncertainty.

Before the battle began, Henry is described by the sixteenth-century chronicler, Hall, as having issued a stirring manifesto to his followers. In one of those unconvincingly appropriate and carefully worded eve-of-

[12] C. Richmond, 'The Battle of Bosworth, August 1485', *History Today*, 35 (1985), 17–22.
[13] There is no certainty that Jasper was at Bosworth. No contemporary source makes any mention of his being present at—or absent from—the battle.

battle speeches, full of that emotion remembered in tranquillity so beloved of chroniclers, he is reported to have said:

We have without resistance penetrated the ample region and large country of Wales . . . If we had come to conquer Wales and achieved it, our praise had been great and our gain more; but if we win this battle, the whole rich realm of England . . . shall be ours, the profit shall be ours and the honour ours.[14]

Even if Henry never in fact spoke those eloquent words before the battle, they give an interesting impression of what a later Tudor observer thought he ought to have said about his and his men's intentions in launching their venture.

The battle itself began with an attack by Oxford's men on those commanded by the duke of Norfolk. Oxford, a wary and battle-hardened general, gave orders to his men not to advance too far from their standards so that they should not be in danger of being overwhelmed. The fighting, therefore, was inconclusive and there was something of a lull.

There then occurred an unpredictable twist which changed the whole course of events. Henry, it has been suggested, had hoped that, when the battle began, the Stanley contingent would have been forming the left wing of his army. That had not happened and Henry, seeing his troops outnumbered and in danger of defeat, had ridden towards Stanley to appeal to him for his immediate intervention. At that stage, Richard took a fateful decision. Having spotted Henry making his move in the midst of a relatively small company of his followers, Richard, accompanied perhaps by no more than a hundred men, had launched a furious assault on him. This sudden impulse was out of keeping with his normally cautious self, but may have been inspired by his other most typical characteristic—calculation. He knew well enough that, in most fifteenth-century engagements, the death of the main leader on either side usually ended the contest between the armies. He may well have felt, therefore, that he could turn the ordeal by battle into a trial by single combat between himself and the pretender. Having always hitherto shown an undisguised contempt for Henry and his men, he was probably confident that he could strike him down at an early stage and thereby gain a quick and brilliant victory. Moreover, he had other pressing reasons for wanting to get the encounter over speedily. He himself had had a troubled night and been beset by bad dreams which had unsettled him. Many of his men, he feared, had no great enthusiasm for battle and he was afraid that the earl of Northumberland might play him false. Most serious of all, possibly, was his fear that the Stanleys intended to intervene on Henry's side.

Whatever his motives, he and his cavalry plunged forward fiercely into the attack. Richard had never lacked courage and he fought with vigour

[14] Hall, *Chronicle*, pp. 416–18.

and spirit. Henry's standard-bearer, Sir William Brandon, was struck down early on, only for the Welshman, Rhys ap Maredudd, 'Rhys Fawr' [Rhys the Mighty], immediately to pick up Henry's Red Dragon banner and bear it high and proud, thus making a lasting name for himself. Henry himself, in spite of his lack of military experience, fought surprisingly stoutly: 'He bore the brunt longer than his own soldiers would have weened, who were now almost out of hope of victory.'[15] All the same, he was in desperate straits and it looked as if Richard's gamble was about to pay off.

But in launching that cavalry charge, Richard had taken the grave risk of riding across the van of Sir William Stanley's men and exposing himself to attack. At that very time, Stanley may have been preparing his own move to come to Henry's aid. He now swept forward at this critical juncture in the engagement and came to Henry's rescue. His onslaught turned the tide decisively. For all Richard's prowess he was overpowered by the sheer weight of numbers. He had the opportunity to escape but refused it. Surrounded and outnumbered he was struck down dead—by the hand of the Welshman, Rhys ap Maredudd, said the sixteenth-century poet, Tudur Penllyn; by Rhys ap Thomas, according to his seventeenth-century biographer. Seeing their commander killed, the rest of Richard's men either fled or surrendered. The God of battles had disclosed His purpose. Richard had not only been defeated, he had also been slain; the first English king since Richard I to be killed on the field of battle. To make Henry's victory still more complete, Richard had left no heir to fight another day with Henry for his crown. The new king was crowned on the battlefield and acclaimed by his troops with joyous shouts of 'God save King Henry'. This was a ritual act of crucial significance: the recognition that Henry had won his crown by right of conquest, echoing the plaudits that had greeted Edward IV after the battle of Barnet. As Henry would later tell Parliament, placing the crown on his head was 'the true judgement of God in granting him victory over his enemies in the field'. Soon, the poets would be rejoicing over Richard's downfall and Henry's triumph. Lewys Glyn Cothi, in a terse line of chilly finality, greeted the former's death:

A'r baedd oer i'r bedd a aeth

[And the cold boar to the grave has gone]

and Dafydd Llwyd exulted even more delightedly:

Llyna feirdd yn llawenach
Llwyddo'r byd a lladd R. bach . . .
Harri fu, Harri a fo,
Harri sydd, hir oes iddo.[16]

---

[15] Polydore Vergil, p. 244.   [16] *LGC*[1] p. 481; *D.Ll.F.*, pp. 69–70.

[Here are bards much happier, the world is all the better for killing little R. . . .
Harry was, will be and now is—long life to him!]

Henry wasted no time in issuing from the battlefield a proclamation
forbidding robbery and violence. Its opening words boldly asserted his
royal title: 'Henry, by the grace of God, King of England and of France,
Prince of Wales and Lord of Ireland.' He had thus already confirmed his
royal position by right of conquest. Within a few days, on 3 September, he
proceeded to St Paul's cathedral in London to offer to God the banners he
and his troops had borne in battle as a token of the debt he owed the one
who had given him victory. Three banners, each highly symbolic, were
presented. The one was of the arms of St George, typifying his right to the
crown by conquest. Another was the Red Dragon of Cadwaladr,
representing his claim by his Welsh or 'British' ancestry. The third was the
Tarteron and Duncow, which stood for the Lancastrian and Beaufort
connection. At Henry's coronation on 30 October the arms of Cadwaladr
were again given a prominent role, when the king's champion, Sir Robert
Dymock, had his horse's trapper emblazoned with them.

Nor, in the early months of his reign, did Henry forget to reward those
who had loyally stood by him before and during the battle of Bosworth.
His mother and his step-father were, of course, suitably honoured. But
many of his Welsh followers were also appropriately remembered. Chief
among them was the most steadfast and longest-serving of all, Jasper
Tudor, now created duke of Bedford and loaded with offices and lands,
many of them in Wales, including the office of Chief Justice of South
Wales. Another with strong Welsh connections, Sir William Stanley, was
made Chamberlain of the Household and later Chief Justice of North
Wales. Rhys ap Thomas was knighted three days after Bosworth, and
created Chamberlain of South Wales and given other offices there. Many
other Welshmen who had rallied to his ranks were given lesser rewards,
like the pension given to one Hugh ap Howel, 'for his services at Bosworth,
where it happened him to be sore hurt and maimed'.[17]

A further stage in recognizing Henry as king came when Parliament met
early in November and passed an act which acknowledged, in the simplest
and bluntest terms, that Henry was king and said nothing at all about any
right by which he claimed the throne. All that now remained was for him to
seal his position by fulfilling his promise to marry Elizabeth of York. On 18
January 1486 this was done, and the claims of York and Lancaster, so long
and fiercely contested, were united at least in the title of the royal couple.
Just as important in most Welshmen's eyes was that the scion of
Cadwaladr's line had married a lady who could claim to be sprung from the
stock of Llywelyn the Great. So were merged the two most significant royal

[17] G. Roberts in Roderick (ed.), *Wales through the Ages* (Llandybïe, 1959), 1, 198; cf.
C.Pat.R., 1485–94, p. 158.

lines in the history of Wales. Just over a century later, the greatest of
English dramatists proclaimed that peace had come again to the realm:

> Now civil wounds are stopt, peace lives again,
> That she may long live here, God say Amen.

(Richard III, v. v. 140–1)

Shakespeare was a little too optimistic in his comment, however. There
were still some Yorkists who refused to accept Henry as the rightful king.
The Wars of the Roses were not over; there were battles yet to be fought.

Many dissidents were by no means reconciled to the idea that victory in
one battle and marriage to Edward IV's heiress had given Henry an
incontrovertible title to the throne. Throughout the first half of his reign he
was to be plagued by a number of risings on the part of rebels and
pretenders. As early as April 1486, even in Wales, where he might have
been supposed to have been especially popular, there was disaffection on
the part of a group of dissatisfied Yorkists drawn from among the
Vaughans and Herberts. There had long been bad blood between these
families and the Tudors, and the poison still curdled in their veins. Led by
Sir Thomas Vaughan of Tretower, the malcontents raised rebellion against
the King at Brecon, Hay, and Tretower, all old Yorkist strongholds. They
conspired to kill Henry and seized Brecon castle. Fortunately for the
Tudor, he could call upon Sir Rhys ap Thomas to put down the rebellion
with a firm hand.

A year later, in 1487, the first of the two best-known rebels against
Henry appeared in Ireland. He was Lambert Simnel, who posed as the earl
of Warwick, son to Edward IV's brother, Clarence. Having drummed up a
good deal of support in discontented Ireland, he crossed over to Britain,
but was defeated at Stoke near Newark. Strong contingents from Wales
were recruited for Henry's forces on this occasion. There were 500 cavalry
under the command of Rhys ap Thomas alone. A vivid memory of their
exploits is preserved in Lewys Glyn Cothi's poem to Rhys's brother, Siôn.
It was the steel-tipped talons of this family's ravens which had once more
saved the monarchy and ripped its enemies asunder, contended the poet.[18]

The second impostor, Perkin Warbeck, trying to pass himself off as
Edward IV's younger son, Richard, duke of York, appeared in 1491. One
of those who became implicated in his schemes was a man high in Henry's
esteem, Sir William Stanley. Henry owed him an almost irredeemable
debt, of course, since it was his intervention at the decisive moment in the
battle of Bosworth which ensured victory for him. For these services
Stanley had been well rewarded. He had grown extremely wealthy as a
result of Henry's favour, reputedly having some 40,000 marks (£27,000) in

<hr>

[18] LGC[3], pp. 67–8.

cash, plate, and jewels at Holt castle and an income of £3,000 a year from land, though it may be indicative of some slight mistrust that he had never been raised to the peerage. He had become involved in Warbeck's plottings as early as 1493, and, in 1495, according to Polydore Vergil, had declared that if Warbeck was Edward IV's son he would not fight against him. Much of the wind was taken out of the plotters' sails as a result of Henry's planting spies in their midst. The value of such agents had been borne in on him during his years in exile and, thanks to their information, the plot largely collapsed in 1495. For his part in it Stanley was executed. At first sight this seems an untypically savage reaction on the part of a normally cool and level-headed king, who treated Perkin Warbeck himself leniently. But his spies may have furnished him with damaging information about the nature of Stanley's ambitions and the reasons for his disaffection. In any case, the knowledge that the loyalty of someone in his immediate circle of associates had become suspect may have pushed him into this harsh decision. A century or so later, Francis Bacon, in his life of Henry, was to declare that God had punished him for this act of cruelty and ingratitude by the failure of his family to produce heirs—Elizabeth being the last of the direct line. However, Bacon's anxiety to please James I by hinting that it was God's hand which had brought the Stuarts to the throne cannot be ignored in the consideration of this assertion.

Two years after this episode Henry was faced with the last serious rising of his reign, this time on the part of Cornish rebels. Once again, Henry depended heavily on Welsh loyalty in crushing the rebellion. Troops under the command of Sir Rhys ap Thomas, created a banneret for his services, Sir Robert Salusbury, and others, played a notable part in defeating the Cornishmen at Blackheath. The poet Tudur Aled hailed Sir Rhys as a mighty warrior who had shattered his foes:

> Ni ddaliodd, gan eiddilwyr,
> Y Blac Heth, blwc, ith wŷr.[19]

[Blackheath did not hold, with its feeble men, for one moment against thy warriors.]

and Lewys Môn, with that harsh realism in which the poets delighted to indulge themselves when describing battles, told how the gauntlets of Owain ap Meurug of Anglesey were liberally bestrewn with fragments of human flesh, so fiercely had he mown down his enemies:

> Ni chymynodd eich menig
> Y Blac Heth heb ôl y cig.[20]

[Your gloves did not cut at Blackheath without having on them the remains of flesh.]

With the crushing of the rebellion in 1497 the civil wars and dissensions of the fifteenth century were at last at an end. Yet, even now, there was

[19] *TA*, p. 40.   [20] *LM*, p. 28.

still doubt whether or not Henry's son would be able to follow him on the throne. As late as 1503 or 1504, after the death of Prince Arthur, prominent personages were discussing, in the light of the King's own precarious health—he being 'but a weak man and sickly, not likely to be no long lives man'—who might succeed him on the throne in the event of his death. Various names were mentioned, including those of the duke of Buckingham and Edmund de la Pole, 'but none of them . . . spake of my lord prince' (i.e., the future Henry VIII).[21] This episode is a further reminder of how precarious Henry's position was, in some respects, for almost the whole of his reign and how limited his freedom of manœuvre. None the less, in due course Henry VIII was to succeed to his father's throne without difficulty or dispute.

[21] *L. and P.* I, 231–40; cf. S. B. Chrimes, *Henry VII* (London, 1972), p. 308.

CHAPTER 10

THE TUDOR DYNASTY INSTALLED
1485–1536

HENRY TUDOR came to power as a largely unknown and untried adventurer and parvenu. Apart from a short visit to see Henry VI in his Uncle Jasper's company in 1470,[1] he had never even set foot in his capital until he made his bid for the throne in 1485. Twenty-eight years old when he won the battle of Bosworth and became Henry VII, he had hitherto spent the first quarter of his life as a boy in Wales (1457–71) and the second as an impecunious exile in Brittany and France (1471–85). Though he was Welsh by birth, having been born in Pembroke castle in January 1457, only one of his four grandparents, Owain Tudor, his paternal grandfather, was Welsh. His paternal grandmother, Catherine of Valois, was the descendant of French kings and the rulers of Bavaria, while his mother, Margaret Beaufort, from whom he inherited such Lancastrian claims as he had to the throne, was of characteristically mixed though distinguished aristocratic and royal blood. There had originally been dispute and discussion concerning his name, so Ellis Gruffydd reported. Some maintained that he had first been christened Owain, 'which name the prophecy showed that he would do much good to the men of Wales'.[2] But whether or not he had been christened with that name so replete with meaning in Welsh history and prophecy, it was as Henry, the name insisted on by his mother, he became known to subsequent history.

As a young child he had a Welsh nurse, Joan, wife of Philip ap Hywel, whom he was as king to reward with a pension; but no means exist of knowing how much Welsh she or anyone else may have taught him. While he lived in the English-speaking town of Pembroke from 1457 to 1462 he would presumably have heard little of the language. But when, in 1462, he was taken to Raglan to be brought up in William Herbert's household, it may have been a very different story. Raglan in the 1460s was the foremost household in Wales; the main focus of its literary patronage as well as its

---

[1] This episode was recalled by Shakespeare, when he put the following words into Henry VI's mouth: 'This pretty lad will prove our country's bliss . . . Make much of him my lords, for this is he/Must help you more than you are hurt by me' (*Henry VI, Part III*, IV. vi. 67, 72–3). See also R. A. Griffiths and R. S. Thomas, *The Making of the Tudor Dynasty* (Gloucester, 1985), pp. 70–1.

[2] NLW, Mostyn MS 158, fo. 346v.

leading political centre. While he lived in such an atmosphere a bright and observant boy like Henry may well have been given a remarkable introduction to Welsh political activity and, through the processes of osmosis and observation, have absorbed a keen awareness of what gave it life and meaning: ambition, rivalry, faction, intrigue, and opportunism; the importance of blood, lineage, kinship, and connection; the ineluctable role of king, magnates, office-holders, gentry, and retainers; the place of lordship and dependence, patronage and clientship; and all the other bonds that held politics and society together.

One of the other features of Henry's life at Raglan which has not hitherto been sufficiently emphasized was its significance for him as the leading forum of poetic patronage, literary culture, political propaganda, and their subtle inter-connections with one another. More poets were attracted to Herbert's court at this time than to any other household in Wales and their value as publicists was keenly appreciated. But being propagandists and entertainers was not their only office; they also had an important part to play as the preceptors of Welsh boys of good birth. Their function was to instruct them in genealogy, heraldry, and the cultural and political history of their country. It is difficult to believe that as an adopted member of the Herbert family and the Raglan household, Henry Tudor would not have come under the aegis of schoolmaster-bards during these years. It is equally hard not to suppose that they would have highlighted for their young pupil his claim to be descended from Cadwaladr, the place of his Welsh kinsmen in the tradition, and the high hopes of his countrymen that one day the ancient prophecies of a future Welsh victory would be fulfilled—especially in the expectant atmosphere of the 1460s. Nor is there any reason to believe that William Herbert would have discouraged the poets from such proceedings. He had, after all, been quick enough to discern the usefulness of the boy as a possible ally and a husband for his daughter; and no one employed the services of Welsh poets for his own ends more effectively than Herbert. Until late in Henry's life Welsh poetry continued to hold its appeal for him. He was reported to have called in 'Welsh rhymers' from time to time to dispel the brooding melancholy with which the cares of government sometimes engulfed his spirit.

But before William Herbert's plans for a marriage between his daughter and Henry Tudor could be consummated he had been executed on the morrow of the battle of Edgecote; and very soon afterwards Jasper Tudor recovered control of his nephew. Whatever Yorkist influences had previously been brought to bear on Henry he was now swung sharply back into the Lancastrian orbit—permanently, as it turned out. Jasper was an irrefragably steadfast supporter of the Lancastrian cause and had always been devoted to the interests of his half-brother, Henry VI, and the latter's son, Edward, prince of Wales. A contemporary English poet had aptly singled him out as the 'sail-yard' of his party;[3] durable, trustworthy, and impervious to set-back, defeat, or exile. In 1471, however, following the death of Henry VI and his son, he perceived the much-increased importance of his own brother's son as a Lancastrian claimant to the throne and would continue as dedicatedly and tenaciously loyal to him as he had been to Henry VI. The immediate prospects for the young Henry Tudor were so bleak, however, that Jasper felt obliged to remove him into exile. For Henry it was the influence of this near kinsman, so conscious of the Tudor descent, of his links with powerful kinsmen and allies, of the inspiration of Welsh ideals and how they could be exploited by the poets, which now came to reaffirm the earlier connection with the poets in the Herbert household. Nor did this influence necessarily end when uncle and nephew took refuge in Brittany; for Brittany was a land in which Geoffrey of Monmouth, himself probably sprung from Breton stock, and his 'matter of Britain' were extremely popular, though during the chilling tedium of those years of exile, Jasper and Henry must have been hard put to keep aflame the flickering embers of the old inspiration. Not until after 1483 did events conspire to enable the Tudor phoenix to soar upwards in a renewed and more scintillating existence.

When Henry came to power in 1485 his paramount responsibility for the rest of his reign was to keep himself securely seated on the throne and hand on an unchallenged succession to his descendants. For this task he had had very little training or experience. He had never succeeded to the oversight of a great patrimonial estate nor held a major office. Before 1484 he was largely unfamiliar with the art of managing men of great gifts and maturity or keeping a team of advisers and collaborators working in harmony. Bosworth was the first battle in which he had ever fought and it was won for him rather than by him. Not many of his subjects were convinced that the internal vendettas and civil wars from which the country had suffered for a generation or more were over, or that Henry would necessarily remain as king for very long. The obligations which now confronted him were extremely formidable. He had to achieve his own security against pretenders, rivals, and rebels, and enhance the supremacy of royal power. To maintain his monarchy in an unassailable position, its finances needed to be nourished and augmented and the trade and prosperity of his realm vigilantly fostered; for years he had himself been poverty-stricken and so, as Ellis Gruffydd commented, he knew 'only too well what wise princes could do with worldly wealth'.[4] Furthermore, the perennial tasks of maintaining effective government and establishing law and order, especially among the more powerful of his subjects, called for his immediate and unremitting attention. Finally, in his relations with European countries he

[3] 'Political Poems', *Archaeologia*, 1842.   [4] NLW, Mostyn MS 158, fo. 349v.

must ensure peace if he could, partly in order to secure his own and his dynasty's position against intrigue inspired from abroad and partly to win recognition by foreign states. By any reckoning, all this was an awesomely demanding agenda, especially for a new, insecure, and inexperienced ruler, still to serve out his political apprenticeship. Yet, on balance, Henry achieved considerable success in all his commitments, though during his later years his character and the quality of his regime deteriorated. As deaths in his family and old age and illness took their toll, he became more suspicious and greedy. He had never possessed those extrovert gifts that might have made him a popular king with his subjects, but in his last phase he was deeply feared and even hated by some of his subjects, especially the wealthier and more powerful among them, on whom he pressed relentlessly. He nevertheless founded what turned out to be one of the most famous, if not the most celebrated, of all British ruling families; and at his death in 1509 his son, Henry VIII, was able to enter into his inheritance confidently and unhesitatingly, in spite of the defeatist remarks about the Tudor succession voiced as recently as 1503 (see above, pp. 229–30).

The credit for Henry VII's achievements must go in the main to his own qualities of mind and temperament. Paradoxically enough, his own lack of experience may have contributed much to his later success. Never having previously wielded authority himself, once he had obtained it, he would share it with no one: he was his own master and no minister was ever allowed to overshadow him. Excluded from the citadels of power before coming to the throne, having once arrived there he applied himself to his *métier* with unexampled meticulousness and single-mindedness. Polydore Vergil's percipient and closely observed character-sketch portrays him convincingly as a prudent, astute, resolute, and dedicated monarch. As a ruler he may have been much more of an innovator and far less committed to following Yorkist precedents than has often been supposed. Though cautious, he breathed new life and imparted greater resolution into customary institutions and practices. He was firm, determined, and cool in face of danger; excellent in his choice of servants and staunchly loyal to those who had served him well, particularly those who had stood by him during the bleak and barren years in Brittany and the hectic few weeks of the Bosworth campaign. His record as a person shows him to have been a devoted son, affectionate husband, and wise father; genuinely pious and deeply, if conventionally, religious; cheerful in company; fond of sports and amusements but also a lover of music and poetry and a patron of scholars and books.

Henry's application to the tasks of government in his realm as a whole was bound to benefit Wales to some extent. The restoration of a relatively strong and secure monarchy and the slow reimposition of more stable law and order brought a measure of better government to Wales as well. A curb was put on some of his more turbulent subjects there, although a powerful individual like Rhys ap Thomas was reputed to have done virtually as he pleased with all the freeholders for twenty miles around his main residence. The statutes against Livery and Maintenance, i.e., against keeping unlawful retainers as opposed to bona fide household servants, were made applicable to Wales as well as England, even though their enforcement was everywhere less successful than Henry might have wished. Welsh suitors were encouraged to take their cases to the great courts at Westminster like Chancery and Star Chamber, though they evinced little interest in doing so as yet. As part of the wider attempt to control the activities of great magnates by frightening them with recognizances for good behaviour, heavy pressure was put on a number of Marcher lords and stewards of lordships, who were required to sign indentures from at least as early as 1490 which gave guarantees for better order and less lawlessness in their jurisdictions. These were the first signs of a royal policy which would go on seeking more effectual means of overseeing the divided and troubled lordships of the March, until eventually Henry VIII would decree their abolition and reconstitute them into shires. Trade between England and Wales, notably that in cattle and woollen cloth, also gained from restoring good order and encouraging economic links between the two countries. Welsh ports and shipping, though still small, were included within the provisions of the Navigation Acts and may have benefited to some extent from them.

Henry's preoccupation with his wider problems necessarily absorbed almost the whole of his time and energy and left him with little to spare to devote to the particular concerns of Wales. For this he has not always escaped the censure of some Welsh writers—on two counts. First, and the more venial of the two criticisms, he is blamed for having been an opportunist, and not an inspired one at that. Second, and a much more fundamental impeachment, is that he was an adventurer, cynically angling beforehand for the support of his countrymen by means of a confidence trick, making his appeal to them as the 'son of prophecy' and holding out extravagant hopes and promises. Then, having duped them into being mainly responsible for enabling him to win his crown, once in power he callously forgot all about his earlier promises and left them in the lurch. If we take the poetic evidence at face value, it could certainly appear that Henry had aroused euphoric expectations in Wales of what could be expected if he won the crown. Many might have yearned with Dafydd Llwyd for the 'coming of the long golden summer' [*pan ddêl yr haf hirfelyn*] and with it the 'long foretold triumph of the red dragon over the white' [*A'r un haf hefyd yr awn am ben y ddraig wen i gyd*].[5] Henry had thus been

5 *D. Ll. F.*, p. 49.

eulogized as the man of destiny who would give substance to the cherished
hopes that had, over the centuries, buoyed up his people's confidence in a
brighter dawn, in spite of earlier defeat and disaster. In the mystic light of
that long-heralded sunrise three of its promised rays seemed to glow with
dazzling refulgence. First, the belief that he would rehabilitate the 'true'
ruling house of ancient Britain in its rightful place of supremacy and might
even give his countrymen dominance over the English. Second, he would
free Wales from Saxon oppression and, in his capacity as a 'good lord',
would reward his Welsh followers with office and authority in their own
country. Third, he would restore dignity and confidence to the Welsh and
emancipate them from the inferior position of serfdom—their 'miserable
servitudes' in Henry's own words—to which they had been reduced.
Intoxicating prospects of a brave new world indeed!

Before considering how far Henry, or any mortal man, could implement
such aspirations, we should remind ourselves that it was part of the
accepted poetic convention of the age that the bards should pitch their
praise and their desires at the very summit of expectation. The ideal which
they sought to present, whether they were eulogizing achievement (present
or future), courage, beauty, hospitality, magnanimity, or any other
excellence, always far outstripped flawed and insufficient reality. The bards
knew that perfectly well and so did their patrons. So, if Henry fell short in
important respects of that idealized image of him as the fulfiller of
vaticinations and the saviour of his people, the poets and their patrons and
hearers might have been far less surprised or disappointed than a literal
interpretation of their verse might lead us to suppose. Just as few modern
voters would be disenchanted if the lofty principles proclaimed in the much
more prosaic and matter-of-fact political manifestos of our own age were
far from wholly realized! Nor should we forget that Henry was not a
political revolutionary. He had no intention of changing medieval life and
institutions out of all recognition; he wanted only to make the existing
systems work much more effectively. Moreover, in the few scraps of
evidence of his attitude before Bosworth that we have available to us, his
was not the language of a hero who had come to redeem his people; it
carries much more conviction as the 'appeal of a leader . . . to the bonds of
kindred and the self-interest of individuals'.[6] It expresses the aspirations of
a Lancastrian claimant with Yorkist support who was well aware of how
much he needed to bolster up his somewhat tenuous claims to the throne
by the powerful emotive appeal to the Welsh of his 'British' descent. But,
in practice, all that that committed him and his supporters to was mutual
loyalty in the coming campaign. It was not interpreted by either side as a
blueprint for a Welsh Utopia.

    [6] J. D. H. Thomas, *A History of Wales, 1485–1660* (Cardiff, 1972), p. 23.

As far as restoring the true ruling house of Britain was in question, there was no doubt in the minds of poets and others that the ancient ruling house of 'Troy' and the veritable line of British royal descent had once more been accorded its rightful place in the polity of the realm. Henry was 'the long bulwark from Brutus'[7] [*efo yw'r ateg hir o Frutus*], sang Lewys Glyn Cothi:

> O Droia fawr draw i Fôn,
> Dewr a phert yw'r ffortun.[8]

[From great Troy over to Anglesey, brave and fair is the fortune]

Even though the rhetoric of the descent from Brutus and Cadwaladr, so enthusiastically recalled by Henry's most ecstatic admirers, may have meant less to him than it did to them, it would be a mistake to assume that it conveyed nothing to him. On the contrary, it was not only Welsh poets who stressed its significance; the French poet and friar, Bernard André, also saw the necessity for laying great emphasis on Henry's descent from Cadwaladr and the duty it imposed on him to tame the 'ferocity of the English' [*Anglorum saevitia*].[9] Two Italian poets, Pietro Carmeliano and Giovanni d' Giglis, and the Scotsman, Walter Ogilvie, also extolled Henry as Cadwaladr's heir; and a Venetian emissary reported to his government that 'the Welsh may be said to have recovered their former independence, the most wise and fortunate Henry VII is a Welshman'.[10] The writer of the Worcester pageant early in Henry's reign greeted him as the descendant of Cadwaladr come to fulfil the ancient vaticinations:

> Cadwaladr's blood lineally descending,
> Long hath been told of such a prince coming.
> Wherefore friends, if that I shall not lie,
> The same is the fulfiller of the Prophecy.[11]

The fact that all these very different commentators were unanimous on the point seems strongly to suggest that his lineage meant a good deal to Henry himself. He seems to have had a genuine pride in what he believed to be his royal British descent and was at pains to show it. Beneath the hard shell of wary realism, which the frustrating years of boyhood and exile had taught him to grow, there was an inner man, pious, sensitive, and responsive to medieval ideals of honour and religion. To such a man, who can hardly have been unaware that his Lancastrian claims to the throne were not unimpeachable, the distinction of his ancient Welsh descent, vindicated by

---

[7] In the *Historia Regum Britanniae* Geoffrey had depicted Brutus as the Trojan leader who had pressed on from Rome to settle in Britain and found the monarchy.

[8] *LGC*[1], p. 500.

[9] James Gairdner, *Historia Regis Henrici Septimi* (RS, 1858), pp. 9–10.

[10] *A Relation . . . of the Island of England . . . about the Year 1500*, trans. C. A. Sneyd (Camden Soc., 1847), p. 19.

[11] Scattergood, *Politics and Poetry*, p. 214.

God's evident token of approval in the fight at Bosworth field, gave the deepest satisfaction.

Throughout his reign Henry made a number of gestures designed to show where his sympathies lay. Each was small in itself but the cumulative impact of them all was substantial. The Red Dragon of Cadwaladr and Wales was clearly very significant for him. He bore it on his green-and-white banner at Bosworth and then presented it at St Paul's. He adopted it as one of the supporters of the royal arms and displayed it prominently on his coinage. In the later ceremonies of his reign it was always well to the fore. High on that wonderful eastern window of King's College Chapel, Cambridge, itself a shrine of the early Tudor myth, the Red Dragon occupies a place of supreme honour over the head of Christ crucified.

Neither Henry nor his Welsh supporters were unaware that his wife, Elizabeth of York, could also claim, through the Mortimers, descent from the greatest of Welsh princes, Llywelyn the Great, via his daughter, Gwladus Ddu. When Henry and Elizabeth's eldest son was born in 1486, the King, knowing how much importance attached to the name to be given to the boy who was the symbol of the union of York and Lancaster and the hope of his dynasty, called him Arthur, 'in honour of the British race, of which [he] himself was',[12] in Francis Bacon's words. This was a name charged with significance for the Welsh; the name of the mightiest of all the early British heroes and the central figure in the *Historia Regum Britanniae*. Though not unknown among the personal names of the English royal family, Arthur was certainly unprecedented as a name for the heir to the throne on whom so much depended. The Welsh poets naturally responded to its magnetic symbolism, prophesying all kinds of wonderful future feats for the young prince, comparable to those of the hero after whom he had been named. Dafydd Llwyd rapturously greeted the two Arthurs: the famous one of history, and the new one to come:

> Arthur benadur ydoedd
> Mawr draw, ac ymherodr oedd . . .
>
> Bid Arthur, mae'r byd wrthaw—
> Ym mrwydr drom, ymherawdr draw.
> Gwylied am fuddugoliaeth
> Ydd wyf, wrth yr enw ydd aeth.[13]

[Arthur was a great leader of yore, and an emperor . . . May Arthur—the world lies open to him—be a great force in battle and an emperor. I watch for the victories that go with his name.]

When he died prematurely, the bards were understandably cast into the

---

[12] Francis Bacon, *The History of the Reign of King Henry VII*, ed. F. J. Levy (New York, 1972), p. 81.
[13] *D.Ll.F.* p. 28.

deepest gloom. Rhys Brydydd, one of many who mourned the tragic loss, was distraught at the death of one from the line of Llywelyn the Great—'casting down the kin of Aberconway' [*bwrw cenedl Aberconwy*];[14] a reference to Aberconway abbey, the 'Westminster Abbey' of north Wales, where Llywelyn the Great and other princes of Gwynedd were buried.

Henry also proclaimed his pride in his Welshness in other ways. He patronized a number of poets in Wales and welcomed them and Welsh musicians to his court. He directed a commission to the abbot of Valle Crucis, Dr Owen Poole a canon of Hereford, and John King, herald, to inquire into his pedigree. They consulted distinguished bard-genealogists like Gutun Owain, Siôn Leiaf, and others, 'in the search of the British or Welsh books of pedigrees, out of which they drew his perfect genealogy from the ancient kings of Britain and princes of Wales'. The Tudor historian, David Powel, said that it could be seen in his time and, indeed, a manuscript copy of it, Cardiff MS 50, still survives. Like many other genealogies of the period, it is accurate enough for the more recent generations, but the further back it goes, the more fanciful it becomes, especially in its attempts to trace Henry's lineage all the way back to Brutus.

Henry also encouraged Welshness at his court. He gave £2 so that the feast of St David, Wales's patron saint, might be fittingly celebrated. He kept a number of Welshmen near him in his personal service: Lewis Caerleon as his doctor and David Owen as his carver; and included a number of Welsh archers among his bodyguard. John Puleston of Hafod-y-wern, who had fought at Bosworth and received an annuity of twenty marks for life, became a gentleman-usher of the King's Chamber. Henry encouraged many others among his compatriots to come to court and to London; and gave them minor patronage: making Piers Lloyd, one of his yeomen, Customer at Calais 'for true and faithful service', or giving another, Edward ap Ryse, a beerhouse in Fleet Street appropriately named 'The Welshman'. One of the most notable of the Welsh *emigrés* was David Seisyllt of Alltyrynys, reported as having 'fled out of England with Henry of Richmond'.[15] He became a sergeant of the guard, a landowner in Northamptonshire, and founder of the Cecils, the most brilliant administrative dynasty of Tudor England. This kind of migration had often happened before—Henry's own grandfather, Owain Tudor, was a noteworthy example of it. What was new about the process in Henry's reign was the much greater scale on which Welshmen were encouraged to go. So many Welshmen appeared at court and in London and were so eager in their pursuit of honour and profit that the poet Skelton, reflecting the prejudice they aroused, suggested that St Peter's precedent of shouting 'caws pôb'

[14] *RBRR*, pp. 24–5.
[15] A. L. Rowse, 'Alltyrynys and the Cecils', *EHR*, LXXV (1960), 54–76.

[toasted cheese]—of which Welshmen were inordinately fond—and locking the gates of heaven as soon as all the Welshmen ran out, should be followed in London![16]

However, if there were those who cherished notions that the enthroning of a king of British descent would also mean that the Welsh would be in a position to pay off old scores against the English and lord it over them, then they must have been sadly disappointed. Some notes of disillusionment were in fact detectable in the contemporary poetry. Lewys Glyn Cothi, for example, bemourned:

> Mae bywyd trist, mae byd llwm,
> Meibion a gweision oedd gaeth,
> Mynd weithian maent waethwaeth.

[Life is still sad, the world is still hard; men and servants who were captive, find themselves getting worse and worse.]

A gentleman-poet of Glamorgan, Llywelyn ap Hywel, believed that Henry and Jasper preferred the odious men of the North (i.e., Englishmen north of the Trent) to their own countrymen [*Gwell gan Siaspar a Harri y gwŷr o'r Nordd na'n gwŷr ni*].[17] Yet for every one of these notes of disapproval a score or more strongly in favour of Henry and his regime could be quoted. It must be considered very doubtful whether the bards had ever expected Henry literally to lead some sort of campaign of Welsh vengeance against the English. Certainly, their leading patrons, men like Jasper Tudor, Rhys ap Thomas, or William Gruffydd, would never have had any illusions on this score. They knew perfectly well that Henry had other prior claims on his time and attention. His position in England was so insecure and his problems there so demanding that he must devote his energies almost exclusively to maintaining his control over the larger and wealthier part of his kingdom; to have done otherwise would have been a recipe for disaster. Hard-bitten politicians would have known better than to expect a wise and cautious realist like Henry to give a clear priority to Wales and would not have been surprised when he did not do so. They may not have known the saying that 'politics is the art of the possible' but they understood well enough the truth that underlay it. Jasper Tudor, for instance, the most lavish patron of all the political and prophetic poetry before 1485, was content to live in England at court and on the broad estates given him by his nephew after 1485 and hardly ever visited Wales in spite of the valuable lordships he possessed there. He and men like him realized that they and Henry had to come to terms with the world as it was. It was enough for them that they had succeeded in installing a representative of the British

---

[16] D. Williams, *Modern Wales* (London, 1950), p. 23.
[17] C. Thomas, *Historical Foundations of Welsh Nationalism*, ed. D. M. Lloyd (Cardiff, 1950), pp. 76–7.

line on the 'throne of the whole island', that he was well-disposed towards his fellow-countrymen and had handsomely rewarded his supporters. There seems no reason to doubt that Henry's greatest gift to the Welsh was himself and that his triumph implied that the emotional and psychological union of England and Wales had been achieved as a result of his victory. But it is also worth emphasizing that Henry's son and grandchildren on the English throne showed none of his partiality for the 'British' descent and made little or no boast of their own share in it.

As for the second hope, that Henry might free Wales from its English rulers and reward his Welsh followers with office and authority, that was, again, in part fulfilled. Many of his most loyal supporters were given rewards, great and small. Here, too, there were precedents for what was done. William Herbert had been made virtual ruler of Wales in the 1460s by Edward IV, Jasper Tudor by Henry VI in 1470–1, and Buckingham by Richard III in 1483. What was different in Henry VII's reign was the greater scale of the grants given. Not only were the bigger fish rewarded but a large number of lesser men were given office as well—as sheriffs, constables, receivers, coroners, escheators, woodwards, bailiffs, and the like. Jasper Tudor was made duke of Bedford and justice of South Wales; Rhys ap Thomas chamberlain of South Wales and William Gruffydd chamberlain of North Wales. Huw Lewys of Prysaeddfed and William Gruffydd ap Robin of Cwchwillan, having each led a contingent to Bosworth, became sheriff of Anglesey and of Caernarfon, respectively, in 1485. John Morgan and Edward Vaughan were appointed bishops of St Davids, and Dafydd ab Ieuan and Dafydd ab Owain bishops of St Asaph, after a long period in which almost no Welshmen had been appointed bishops at all. Many Welsh families were again able to benefit from the absence of great magnates and dignitaries by acting as their deputies and exercising authority on the spot, to an even greater extent than they had done in the fifteenth century. In the great lordships of Glamorgan and Gower, for example, in the absence of Sir Charles Somerset, their nominal lord under the King, the effective ruler of both lordships was his deputy, Sir Matthew Cradock of Swansea.

Nevertheless, it would be quite wrong to suppose that all was changed and that those *bêtes noires* of the bards, the detested 'plant Alis' [children of Alice] or the descendants of Rowena [the English], no longer ruled in Wales. There was much that remained as before. In those parts of the Marches of Wales where great English families, like the Staffords in south-east Wales or Sir William Stanley in the north-east, were the Marcher lords, the King could not and did not try to interfere with their lordship. Even in those areas where he had the power to intervene, Henry did not by any means always favour the Welsh. Although William Gruffydd had first of all been made chamberlain of North Wales, he was unceremoniously removed from office in 1490, when the King's men in the Principality proposed to embark on a new and harsher policy, which actually led to an outbreak of rebellion in 1498. Men like Sir Richard Pole and other English servants of Henry VII were now in charge. Similarly, when from about 1489–90 onwards Henry had established a council in the Marches, later to become the council of the Prince of Wales, it was staffed almost entirely by Englishmen. Its object was to set up overriding authority in the Marches and to install a stronger, even more dictatorial, regime. Henry had needed to reward his faithful Welsh followers and had done so; but in the course of his reign it was efficiency and profit, not patriotism or sentiment, which governed his choice of servants in Wales. It may well be this aspect of his policy which accounted for the bardic notes of chagrin referred to earlier.

As for the third expectation, that Henry might restore the confidence and dignity of the Welsh and raise them from the status of a conquered and mistrusted people, his freedom to act in this sphere was distinctly limited. He did nothing official to repeal the statutes most hated by the Welsh—those passed in Henry IV's reign. They remained on the statute book unchanged until as late as 1624. It was still illegal, in theory at least, for Welshmen to buy land in England or in English boroughs in Wales, to hold office there, or for an Englishman to marry a Welsh woman without losing his privileged status. Welshmen had chafed against these restrictions from the time that they were imposed, and the more ambitious and enterprising among them had eagerly sought their emancipation by acquiring denizen rights. Many were accorded such privileges by Henry VII. Commenting on his reign, George Owen went so far as to claim that the Welsh 'willingly submitted themselves in heart to his highness, being paternally of their ancient princes of the British line . . . they who in former times were termed so disobedient to the Crown of England . . . might be governed by laws as the subjects of England, and not by the thraldom and cruelty used by the Lords Marcher'.[18] The main evidence attesting such a glowing testimonial comes from late in Henry's reign. Between the years 1504 and 1508 Henry was induced to issue charters of privilege to his Principality of North Wales (1504 and 1507) and to the north-eastern lordships of Bromfield and Yale (1505), Chirk and Denbigh (1506), Ceri and Cedewain (1507), and Ruthin (1508). By the terms of these charters, four considerable privileges, in the main, were granted to the inhabitants of these regions. They were given the right to buy and hold land and to hold office in England and the English boroughs in Wales; they were freed from many burdensome and outmoded financial payments originally imposed in the Middle Ages; and they were also allowed to inherit land according to English law by the custom of inheritance by the eldest son

---

[18] Owen, III, 171–2.

(primogeniture) and not according to the Welsh custom of *cyfran* (equal rights of inheritance by all the sons). Many individual Welshmen had been keen to secure such rights previously by obtaining grants of denizen privileges. This, however, was the first time that inhabitants of the whole Principality or entire lordships had been accorded such benefits which, in important respects, anticipated the provisions of the Acts of 1536 and 1542–3 (the 'Act of Union'). These charters, therefore, marked a notable concession. At first sight they could be construed as a more constructive act of statesmanship on the part of Henry VII, designed to elevate the status of a large body of his Welsh subjects, thereby fulfilling some of his most expansive earlier promises.

Closer examination reveals, however, that his subjects in north Wales had been clamouring for these concessions long before Henry became king. When he did belatedly grant them, he did so in return for large sums of money; the Principality, for instance, paid no less than £2,300 for its grants. Moreover, it seems as if in going contrary to the terms of existing statutes Henry may have made grants which he was not empowered to concede. At all events, the burgesses of North Wales, traditionally the most obdurate upholders of English privileges, reacted strongly and protested in vigorous terms against the new rights now being claimed by the Welsh. Henry himself died before the controversy could be resolved. Even so, whatever may have been the limitations on his motives or his actions, Henry had, in this matter, moved nearer the future in meeting the wishes of his subjects for improved status than in any other act of policy.

Henry's reign can perhaps best be described as the 'happy ending' of what had been a century of acute unrest and instability for Wales since the Glyndŵr Rebellion. He had left many issues unresolved; had indeed made no attempt to settle them. He had only partially been able to fulfil the most grandiose of those expectations proclaimed by his bardic partisans when he came to the throne. Nevertheless, his reign had marked a watershed between the Wales of medieval times and the decidedly different Wales which was to emerge in the sixteenth century. Without knowing it, he had prepared the ground for the far-reaching changes introduced in his son's reign. A strangely symbolic foreshadowing of those changes took place at Carew castle in 1507, just two years before Henry VII's death. Sir Rhys ap Thomas, most influential of the native and resident Welsh magnates and pre-eminent patron of Welsh poets, held a resplendent tournament at the castle. It reached its climax at that point when two figures representing the supreme champions of Welsh and English patriotism, St David and St George, embraced one another as if to show that no shadow of hatred or enmity came between them. It seemed to prefigure the uniting of Wales within itself and the closer relationship with England which was brought about by the legislation of 1536–43. The way for that development had been paved by Henry's ascension to the throne in 1485, which had made much easier the achievement of union half a century later.

In Henry's own lifetime the poets of Wales had applauded him as a prince of their own race, claiming descent from Cadwaladr through his grandfather Owain Tudor. He appeared to the bards and the majority of his politically conscious Welsh followers as the rightful heir of prophecy, come to set them free after centuries of oppression and restore their dignity as a people, even though his practical achievements in that respect were, as we have seen, distinctly limited. His right to that place of honour which his contemporaries conferred upon him was enthusiastically confirmed by later poets of the sixteenth and seventeenth centuries. They, too, viewed him as a hero-deliverer in the same mould. They looked back at him not only through the normal spectacles of Tudor propaganda, as the man who had ended the civil wars which had plagued England and Wales in the second half of the fifteenth century, but also through a rosy-tinted Welsh eyepiece, which revealed him as a king who had initiated a new era of greater freedom and opportunity for his own particular people, the Welsh. In their eyes he was the founder of a Welsh dynasty which had put the earlier oppression of Wales behind it and begun a regime of benevolence and goodwill. Cadwaladr's prophecy was at last fulfilled; Owain had indeed returned; Arthur had emerged from his cave and seized his throne. However exaggerated and over-romanticized that view may now seem to us to be, the stereotype became firmly installed as an irremovable part of the Welsh mental furniture for centuries.

Typical of many poets who gave voice to it in the later sixteenth century was Siôn Tudur (1530?–1602) who, in a poem to Queen Elizabeth, Henry's granddaughter, likened her great forebear to one of the divinely sent liberators who had freed the chosen people of the Old Testament from captivity in Babylon; thus, too, had Henry emancipated the Welsh:

> Harri lân, hir lawenydd,
> Yn un a'n rhoes ninnau'n rhydd.
> I Gymru da fu hyd fedd
> Goroni gŵr o Wynedd.[19]

[Fair Harry, our long-lasting joy, in the same way set us free. Good for Wales was it all his life that the man from Gwynedd was crowned.]

Well into the seventeenth century a leading poet, Edward Morris (1607–89), harped on the same theme:

> Nes cael brenin, gwreiddin gras,
> Archdeyrn ar ucha'i deyrnas

[19] *ST*, I, 379.

O Frutanwaed, fryd doniau,
Dan ei rwysg i dynnu'r iau.[20]

[Until we had a king, rooted in grace, chief ruler of all his kingdom, a man of British blood, of splendid gifts, under his power to free us from the yoke.]

Nor was it only the higher-ranking poets of the classical *cynghanedd* metres who reacted thus; some of the free-metre bards were equally laudatory. One of them, in a poem to Elizabeth, referred admiringly to her grandfather:

Sidanen ŵyr Harri seithfed;
A hwnnw oedd ben y brytanied
Ac a 'nillodd i gyfiownder
Wrth i gleddef ai wrolder.[21]

[Sidanen [Elizabeth], grand-daughter of Henry VII; he was head of the Britons and he won his just deserts by his sword and bravery.]

Joining the bards in their paeans of praise came the newer kind of antiquarian and historian emerging into view during the Tudor period, who was just as fervent in his estimate of the worth of the founder of the Tudor line. Ellis Gruffydd wrote of Henry: 'indeed, our ancestors said that he was one of the wisest and most intelligent kings and the one with the largest aims and intentions in the whole world among those who were ruling at his time'.[22] A short time afterwards, Arthur Kelton, a Welshman from Shrewsbury and a rather indifferent English poet, published his 'Commendation of Welshmen' in 1546. He referred with immense pride to Henry VII 'being of Cadwalader's line, rightful King of Britain called England' and assured his readers that the meaning of Henry's triumph was that

Thus God above
of very love
His Kingdom hath assured[23]

and that was why his 'princely name was had in such memory'.

Four of the best-known antiquaries of sixteenth-century Wales—William Salesbury (1520?–1584?), Humphrey Llwyd (1527–68), David Powel (1552?–1598), and George Owen (1552?–1613)—all contributed lavishly their meed of praise to Henry's memory. Salesbury was convinced that after centuries of 'apostasy', 'long wars', and 'rigorous laws', it 'pleased God . . . to look down again upon them, sending them a most godly and noble David [Henry VII] and a wise Solomon [Henry VIII] . . . who graciously released their pains'.[24] Humphrey Llwyd believed Henry Tudor to be a most prudent prince, 'who lineally descending from his grandfather,

[20] G. Williams, *Harri Tudur a Chymru: Henry Tudor and Wales* (Cardiff, 1985), pp. 94–5.
[21] Williams, *Tafodau Tân*, p. 142.   [22] Mostyn MS 158, fo. 349*v*.
[23] A. H. Dodd, 'A Commendacion of Welshmen', *BBCS*, XIX (1960–2), 235–49.
[24] *A Dictionary in Englyshe and Welshe* (1547; rep., London, 1877), dedication.

Owen Tudor, a Welshman born in the Isle of Anglesey, quite delivered all the Welshmen from such laws of bondage as in other kings' days they were subject unto'.[25] George Owen saw him as a 'Moses' and a 'second Solomon' sent by God to free his people:

this noble prince, achieving the crown of England and being lineally descended from the ancient British Kings of this land, so drew the hearts of Welshmen to him as the lodestone doth the iron . . . that there hath not been found in England any country or province more obedient in heart than this country of Wales hath been and is to the progeny of the said King Henry VII.[26]

Even the Roman Catholic exile of Queen Elizabeth's reign, Morys Clynnog (c.1525–81), commented warmly on the 'prophetic oracles' which had ensured that all the inhabitants of Wales joined Henry when he landed and marched into England to win the battle of Bosworth.

However much Henry may have been pilloried by some authors of our own century for having cynically led the Welsh by the nose and exploited them to his own advantage, those views were not shared by sixteenth- and early seventeenth-century Welshmen. On the contrary, all those who recorded their impressions regarded him as a heaven-sent, historic deliverer of his people of epic, scriptural proportions. Naïve, fulsome and hyperbolic as their opinions may now seem to be, they are not to be dismissed on that score as having had no reality for the men and women of the Tudor era. Whether we like it or not, there can be no mistaking their belief that a transformation of the state of Wales and of the relationship between Wales and England, greatly for the better, had occurred during Henry's reign, for which he himself was almost wholly responsible. When he had landed in Milford Haven in 1485, nowhere had his coming been more warmly welcomed than in Wales; conversely, nowhere had his death been more sincerely mourned in 1509. When Henry was on his death-bed he was reported by George Owen to have given a 'special charge' to his son and heir that he should have a particular care for the welfare of his Welsh subjects.[27] Owen, a well-informed antiquary of outstanding ability, may have had good grounds for attributing this request to the dying king. But it seems not to have made any memorable impact on his son. Henry VIII was the most selfish of men, wrapped up in his own pleasures and pursuits. For some twenty years he was too preoccupied with his own personal concerns to pay any special attention to Wales, and his father's last wish—assuming it to be accurately reported—seems not to have weighed at all heavily on his conscience.

When Henry VIII, young, confident and assertive, succeeded his father on the throne, the reception given him in Wales was at least as enthusiastic

[25] *Commentarioli . . . Fragmentum*, p. 49.
[26] Owen, III, 37.   [27] Owen, III, 39.

as that accorded to him elsewhere in his realm. Bards and chroniclers welcomed him warmly as heir to his father. Ellis Gruffydd, who was accustomed to seeing him at close quarters, described him as 'a fair, gentle man, of good appearance and handsome body, with a great ability and desire to perform all those manly feats on foot and on horseback, and full of playfulness as his years expected of him'.[28] An Anglesey priest-poet, Dafydd Trefor, mourned the loss of a great and good king by the death of Henry VII, and, greeting his successor warmly, urged him not to undo any of his father's work nor take away any of the benefits he had 'given the Welsh', but to leave all things as they were.

There is little reason to believe that the new monarch ever actually heard the good wishes or the earnest supplication directed to him by Dafydd Trefor, but the poet's plea that nothing should be changed from what it had been in Henry VII's time was in practice accepted. All the leading Welsh servants of the Crown, men like Rhys ap Thomas, William Gruffydd, Matthew Cradock, Edward Stradling, Robert Salusbury, or Roger Puleston, were confirmed in office. The Council in the Marches, though decidedly moribund, was at least kept in being, even though there was no prince of Wales for it to serve, nor would there be one for nearly thirty years. But the King's own preoccupation was to cut a masterly figure on the European stage of war and international diplomacy. In raising troops for his ventures in France and Scotland he relied as heavily on Wales as a number of his predecessors had done. When he mustered his armies for service in France in 1512–13 nearly all his leading servants and vassals in Wales rallied conspicuously to his banner. Charles Brandon, later duke of Suffolk, although not himself Welsh, depended heavily on his interests in Wales to raise large bodies of men. In the campaign of 1513, all but 222 out of the 1,800 common soldiers raised by him came from Wales or the Marches, and again in 1514 and 1523 many of his men were Welsh. Sir Charles Somerset, KG, illegitimate son of Henry Beaufort, third duke of Somerset, not himself a Welshman, had married the heiress of William Herbert, earl of Huntingdon. Ever since being knighted by Henry Tudor when he landed at Milford, Somerset had acquired increasing stature as a result of royal favour, and he fought so stoutly at Thérouanne that in 1514 he was rewarded with the earldom of Worcester, thereby founding one of the most influential aristocratic lines of Tudor and Stuart Wales. Outstanding among the resident native Welsh gentry, it need hardly be said, was Sir Rhys ap Thomas, described by one of his many bards as 'pinagl holl Gymru' [pinnacle of all Wales]. Now turned sixty years of age, he nevertheless played a leading part in the campaigns of 1512–13, whence he returned to be saluted by his admiring poet:

[28] NLW, Mostyn MS 158, fo. 375v.

> Trecha un draw yn trychu'r drin
> Tair Brân ond Duw a'r brenin.[29]

which was rendered into an English couplet by his equally impressed seventeenth-century biographer:

> Next after God and the King that day
> Rees and his Ravens did bear the sway.

His courtier son, Gruffydd, accompanied Sir Rhys to Guienne in 1512, but after making rather a hash of it there, was noticeably not on campaign in the following year. Two younger men, later to be dominating figures in the history of Tudor Wales—William Herbert and Rice Mansel—served the earliest phases of long and distinguished military careers in France at this time. Most prominent among the men of north Wales was Sir William Gruffydd, whose control there during the next few years was to be virtually complete. Lewys Môn, the Anglesey poet, wishing Gruffydd Godspeed, success, and a safe return, gives us a striking snapshot of the various dread misfortunes that might befall a soldier going to fight in France. He prayed that Christ and His mother would preserve his patron from piracy, shipwreck, wild waves, the effects of French wine, poison, prison, injury from a portcullis, quarrels, gunfire, crossbows, and all other causes of death and wounding; and finally, he hoped that Gruffydd, like Jason, would return with his golden fleece![30]

With Henry wrapped up in the delights of war, hunting, and courtly pastimes, much of the overall responsibility for the government of his realm devolved into the capable hands of his great minister, Thomas Wolsey. Naturally enough, the cardinal had his own agents in Wales, to whom he entrusted great authority. Among those on whom he placed a good deal of dependence was Sir Rhys ap Thomas, affectionately known to Henry VIII as 'Father Rhys', who remained as virtual viceroy of Wales until his death in 1525. Even after the old knight's death, Wolsey appeared to have exercised his good offices to protect the young heir, Rhys ap Gruffydd, for a time at least, against the effects of his own rash behaviour (below, pp. 255–6). In the Principality of North Wales, the justice, Charles duke of Suffolk, was an absentee, and so control of the government and patronage of the northern Principality was concentrated in the hands of the resident chamberlain and deputy-justice, William Gruffydd, who exercised his authority in a singularly high-handed style. When challenged on account of his dictatorial methods in 1519 Gruffydd justified them on the grounds that north Wales was so desperately difficult to govern that a very firm hand was essential there. Wolsey must have agreed with him, for Gruffydd remained in office. One of the cardinal's best-known agents in the north-east was a man remarkably like himself, only on a more limited scale. This was Robert ap Rhys, third son of Rhys Fawr, who had borne Henry Tudor's standard at Bosworth. Intended for the Church, he had studied ecclesiastical law at Oxford and acquired an extensive range of ecclesiastical benefices and a wife into the bargain. Becoming Wolsey's chaplain and cross-bearer, he carved out a notable career for himself in north-eastern Wales, thanks to his powerful master's favour. In the process he became one of the principal founders of gentry families in the area, in spite of his clerical vows.

A potentate of much higher social status than Robert ap Rhys, who failed to maintain the good relations he had once enjoyed with Wolsey and Henry VIII, was Edward Stafford, third duke of Buckingham. A grandee with royal blood in his veins and the greatest of the surviving Marcher lords, he lived in almost princely state at his newly built castle in Thornbury, where he once entertained 500 people to dinner and 400 to supper at his Epiphany Feast of 1508. This kind of ostentatious and luxurious life-style gave credence to rumours that, as a student of astrology, the duke believed it was his destiny to wear the crown of England. In the Marches of Wales he ruled over a number of lordships, including those of Brecon, Hay, Huntingdon, and Newport. He was regarded by his Welsh tenants as an overbearing and oppressive lord, and their opposition to his financial exactions was so intense that in 1518 the King's Council had to intervene to decree a final settlement between him and them. In the early years of Henry's reign he had been on terms of close friendship with the King and high in his favour. But his pride in his own exalted station, his persistence in seeking to retrieve his title to the constableship of England and to recover the royal moiety of the Bohun inheritance, his undisguised dislike of Wolsey, and his readiness to criticize the latter's domestic and foreign policy, brought him under the grave suspicion of King and Cardinal. Henry may not have forgotten the conversation of 1503, when Buckingham's name had been preferred to his own as possible heir to the throne, and it is significant that as late as 1519 the Venetian ambassador had told his masters that he felt sure that Buckingham would easily obtain the throne if Henry were to die without an heir.

In 1520 Buckingham withdrew from court and in November of that year asked for permission, as he had done on several occasions since 1517, to raise a bodyguard of 300 to 400 men, which he considered necessary to accompany him on a visit to his estates in Wales. He requested this on the grounds 'that we cannot be there for our surety without three or four hundred men'—a telling indication of the unpopularity in which he stood with his tenants there. The request raised disturbing echoes of his father's rebellion against Richard III in 1483 and he had plenty of enemies all too willing to carry malicious tales about him to Henry and Wolsey. The latter had the prickly sensitivity of a middle-class minister easily offended by aristocratic hauteur, while Henry's malevolence against aspiring over-mighty subjects with royal blood in their veins lay very near the surface. Buckingham's bad relations with his Welsh tenants and his general unpopularity made it easy for Henry to destroy him, even if the Emperor Maximilian and others attributed his downfall to the malice of what they contemptuously described as the 'butcher's dog'. Buckingham was brought before a court of dubious legality, presided over by the duke of Norfolk, condemned and executed. He may have done nothing to merit so savage an end, but it was an object lesson to the great aristocrats, who accepted it with surprising docility, that the heads of even the tallest poppies might be lopped off by their masterful and easily offended sovereign. It also meant that the last of the great Marcher lords had disappeared and another large and lucrative inheritance had come into the King's possession. His position *vis-à-vis* the lords of the March was now quite unchallengable.

A few years after Buckingham's fall, significant changes took place in the administration of Wales, when the Council in the Marches was reorganized, partly to coincide with changes in royal policy and partly to meet the needs of the Princess Mary. It was one of a series of changes instituted by Henry and Wolsey at this time. In the north of England a council was set up, with the King's illegitimate son, the duke of Richmond, nominally in charge. In Wales another council, like the northern one remarkably similar to the council of any great nobleman of the period, was also established. Richmond was at this point being considered as a possible husband for the ten-year-old princess, after a number of other suggestions for a marriage between her and Charles V, or James IV of Scotland, or one of the French princes had, for one reason or another, fallen by the wayside. A large part of the reorganization of Mary's household, which involved some 300 people, was concerned with providing appropriate conditions for her upbringing and education. But much of the change was intended to ensure that the Council carried out its function of administering the law in one of the remoter and less well-controlled areas of the kingdom (see above, pp. 52–3). In north Wales, the duke of Suffolk, who had failed to produce adequate revenue and was too frequently absent on courtly and other duties, was dismissed from his office as justice and replaced by John Salter. William Gruffydd's control as chamberlain was left intact, but the Council of the Princess was given powers to oversee his activities. Down in south Wales, the last of the great Welshmen of the truly medieval era, Sir Rhys ap Thomas, died at the age of 76, full of years and honour. He had held a dominating place in the government of Wales since 1485. His son, Gruffydd, had predeceased him, and his grandson, Rhys ap Gruffydd, was regarded as unsuitable to fill his grandfather's shoes. A new era was soon to open, not simply for the house of Dynevor but for the whole of Wales.

PART II

WALES REORIENTED AND REFORMED 1536–1642

CHAPTER II

THE ASSIMILATION OF
ENGLAND AND WALES

THE first phase of Henry VIII's reign came to an end in 1525 as far as Wales was concerned. Up until that point the King and Cardinal Wolsey had been to content to rely on the methods and, to a large extent, the personnel employed by Henry VII to govern the country. Much the most influential figure there had been Sir Rhys ap Thomas, KG, who had concentrated into his own hands a formidable array of dignities and offices. When, in 1525, 'Father Rhys' had died, his young heir, Rhys ap Gruffydd, was not appointed to any of the offices in Principality or March previously held by his grandfather. This may have been because he was deemed too young and lacking in experience and, possibly, unfitted by his bookish ways to hold office. The King may also have been reluctant to appear to be countenancing hereditary succession to office and authority by the representative of a house which could raise larger bodies of troops than any other Welsh family. Instead, on 22 August 1525, Henry conferred for life the key office of justice of South Wales on Walter Devereux, Lord Ferrers, and on 25 May 1526 appointed him chamberlain of South Wales, also for life. Head of an influential Marcher family, Ferrers was steward of Princess Mary's household and a notably active member of her council. The decision to appoint him and not Rhys ap Gruffydd, whatever the reasons for it, was unquestionably interpreted as a snub to the most powerful family in south-west Wales—more, perhaps, by the young man's wife, the imperious Catherine Howard, and by some of his kinsmen than by Rhys himself. It was an affront calculated to cause much heartburning and upheaval in the coming years.

The year 1525 also witnessed a move by Wolsey to instil new life into the Council in the Marches. The previous two years had seen obstinate resistance to his plans for taxation and had highlighted how necessary it was to attain firmer control over outlying areas. Furthermore, there was a need to delegate some of the responsibilities of Star Chamber to regional bodies. The result was the setting up in 1526 of a Council in the Marches consisting of some 340 people to attend upon the Princess Mary. Issued with a set of instructions for the upbringing of the princess and the administration of justice, they were charged with inquiring into the decline of 'good order, quiet and tranquillity', 'by reason of the long absence of

any prince making residence either in the Principality or in the Marches'.[1]
They were also to impose upon all holders of Marcher lordships fresh
indentures after the pattern of Henry VII and to examine closely claims to
sanctuaries and liberties. The council's newly appointed president was
John Veysey, bishop of Exeter, a protégé of Wolsey whose legal training
and administrative experience ought to have made him a good choice,
though in practice he proved to be sluggish and ineffectual. Nor were other
leading personalities in the area of his jurisdiction of any great help to him.
In the south-east, Henry, second earl of Worcester (1526–49), inherited his
father's comprehensive range of offices as steward of a number of lordships
as well as being lord of Gower, Chepstow, and Raglan in his own right; but
he was no more capable or energetic than Veysey and some of the worst
abuses existed in those parts where he had authority. Lord Ferrers and
William Brereton both acquired considerable powers in the south-west and
north-east respectively. Each was vigorous and enterprising; but both were
also self-seeking, brash, and prone to give offence. Too many of the
officials in the Marches, great and small, were so guilty of unchecked self-
interest and venality that honest administration and impartial justice were
hardly even an afterthought for them.

Such conditions became more disquieting as the realm moved towards
the crisis of the Henrician Reformation. From 1527 onwards matrimonial
discords between Henry and his queen raised the increasingly complex and
intractable issue of the annulment of their marriage. By 1529 it had led to
the summoning of the Reformation Parliament, the downfall of Wolsey,
and worrying international tensions. With the rise to power of Thomas
Cromwell, the completion of the breach between king and pope, and the
consummation of the royal supremacy over the Church in 1533–4, the
foreign situation became even more fraught and the peril of conflict
between England and one or more of the great Catholic powers more
acute. The risks inevitably threw into sharper focus any disorders—of
which there were ordinarily more than enough—in an area as loosely
governed and vulnerable to invasion as Wales and made the king's
government all the more sensitive to the inadequacies of its officers there
and more dissatisfied with their performance.

An unusual invasion was reported from Pembroke in the mid-1520s,
when the region was inundated with a great wave of Irish refugees fleeing
from Desmond's rebellion. With that statistical inflation characteristic of
the period they were calculated to number about 20,000, which, if true,
would have been virtually equal to the whole of the estimated population
of the later shire. The correspondent who transmitted news of this alarming
influx urged stern measures against these unauthorized immigrants and

---

[1] P. R. Roberts, 'The Union with England and the Identity of "Anglican" Wales', *TRHS*,
v, xxII (1972), 49–70, on p. 59.

those who encouraged them.[2] In view of the earlier precedents for successful invasions launched against Milford Haven, the government was understandably nervous about any potential insecurity or disturbance there. More tidings of trouble in the south-west came when Lord Ferrers wrote on 9 January 1526 to say that, in spite of Wolsey's instructions that no subpoenas were to be served in Wales, they were then being directed to Carmarthen and Cardigan. Their inhabitants declared 'plainly that they would not pay one groat . . . if any man do appear otherwise than they have been accustomed, but they had liever run into the woods'.[3] Ferrers judged this to be the most serious crisis he had known in Wales, but no further news about it was forthcoming. In 1528 a complaint was received by the Council at Ludlow from the tenants of the town and lordship of Brecon that justice was not maintained, the king's tenants impoverished, and his income diminished (above, pp. 47–8). About the same time John Puleston deplored the outrages committed in the lordships of Powys and Cyfeiliog and the maintenance of thieves and murderers by the gentlemen of Merioneth and expressed his alarm at how far removed from good order much of north Wales was. There were also reports of a perennial source of friction—the continuing animosity between the burgesses of the garrison boroughs of north Wales and the surrounding Welsh population.

A much more serious outbreak of violence occurred in the royal 'capital' of south Wales, Carmarthen, in 1529 between Lord Ferrers and Rhys ap Gruffydd. The latter, still nursing his grievance at not being recognized as his grandfather's successor, was popular with the Welsh and when he returned from London to south Wales was warmly received by the populace. This led to more ill-will on the part of Ferrers who, irritated by this display of favour, according to Rhys ap Gruffydd put severe pressure on some of the latter's tenants and servants. These smouldering tensions flared up into open conflict when Ferrers came to Carmarthen to hold a sessions in June 1529, as a result of which some of Rhys's men were imprisoned. When on 15 June their lord, accompanied by forty armed followers, arrived at Carmarthen castle to release the prisoners, he and Ferrers were soon literally at daggers drawn. Rhys was imprisoned and on the following day his wife, Lady Catherine, roused his men to rescue him. Ferrers wrote in profound agitation to Wolsey to describe these episodes as the worst insurrection anyone could remember in Wales. His panic had led him to overstate his case. What had happened has been more accurately described by a modern writer as no more than an 'unpremeditated riot'.[4]

Both parties were summoned before Star Chamber, where each was severely censured by Wolsey and both dismissed with an exhortation to make peace with one another. The cardinal's attempts at conciliation met

[2] L. and P., III, appx. 44; IV, 4485.   [3] L. and P., IV, 1872.
[4] W. Ll. Williams, 'A Welsh Insurrection', Y Cymmr., XVI (1903), 18.

with little success. As soon as Ferrers arrived back in Wales, the intrepid Lady Catherine assembled a large company of followers and laid siege to Carmarthen castle. Rhys himself, living quietly in Islington, had nothing to do with this clash; but on 7 October 1530 his uncle, James ap Gruffydd ap Hywel of Castell Maelgwn, was arrested for allegedly conspiring with his nephew to take vengeance on Ferrers. Both were imprisoned in the Tower, though, in June 1531, Rhys was released on bail on grounds of ill-health. In November he was brought before King's Bench on charges of treason and conspiracy, found guilty, and executed on 4 December 1531.

The evidence offered against him of plotting Henry VIII's death and conspiring with James V of Scotland to help the latter conquer England and in the process procure Wales for Rhys was meagre in the extreme. Even Ellis Gruffydd, prejudiced though he was against the house of Dynevor, thought it most unlikely that Rhys had ever been fool enough to believe that James would make him prince of Wales; and Chapuys, ambassador to the Emperor Charles V, also maintained that Rhys had refused to enter into a conspiracy proposed to him. His execution was brought about less by anything he had done than by the suspicions of the government about what he might have it in mind to do. There had certainly been bad blood between him and the Crown's principal agent in strategic and vulnerable south-west Wales, where Rhys could muster a powerful military following and where memories of the decisive role of his grandfather in helping Henry VII to his throne had not yet faded. Rhys may, in addition, have allowed himself to become seduced by prophecies, which had often loomed so large in his family's past history. One William Neville deposed that the 'late Duke of Buckingham, young Ryse and others had cast themselves away by too much trust in prophecies'.[5] Dabbling in ominous vaticinations was a hazardous predilection in the reign of the suspicious and unforgiving Henry VIII. No less dangerous was it to make disparaging remarks about the King's mistress and his religious changes; and Chapuys was convinced that if Rhys had but held his tongue on those matters he might have escaped his unfortunate end.

The execution of this flower of the Welsh aristocracy sent ripples of alarm fluttering along many nerve-ends in Wales, even as far north as the household of Sir Richard Bulkeley, who was hard put to rebut accusations of complicity. But it provoked hostility as well as fear. In 1534 Charles V received a report that, on account of the people's attachment to Princess Mary and to Rhys, the whole of Wales was alienated from the King. In the same year, Chapuys, always inclined to make the most of any rumours of opposition to Henry, claimed that it was freely being said of Wales that its people only waited for a chief to take the field.[6] An accusation brought

[5] *L. and P.*, v, 1106.   [6] *L. and P.*, vii, 1368.

against John Hale, vicar of Isleworth, taxed him with saying, 'And what think ye of Wales? Their noble and gentle Ap Ryce so cruelly put to death and he innocent.'[7] Rhys's uncle, James ap Gruffydd, escaped to Ireland, then Scotland, and thence to Flanders and Germany, there to engage with Pole and others in active plotting against Henry and finding frequent mention in Cromwell's memoranda and in reports to Henry and his ministers.

Meantime, other causes for profound misgiving and anxiety had arisen, especially in the Marches of Wales. The now-familiar indentures for good behaviour had had to be reimposed in 1531, and evidence from Glamorgan indicates that they were not without some effect. However, under Veysey's slack and indolent presidency, the Council's authority was manifestly not being enforced, corrupt or negligent officials were undisciplined, and lawbreakers unpunished. A memorandum presented to Cromwell in 1532 told of serious frauds being perpetrated in Glamorgan by responsible officials, including the king's attorney. Similar embezzlements, committed by the deputy-steward to the earl of Worcester, were uncovered in Elfael in 1533, and George Herbert's shameful behaviour in Gower has already been described (above, p. 46). Other members of the Herbert family, notorious for its unprincipled pursuit of power and profit, had turned the lordship of Magor into a veritable sanctuary for criminals. No fewer than twenty-three murderers and twenty-five notorious thieves and outlaws lurked there under the protection of the deputy-steward, Walter Herbert, and some of this lawless crew were involved in serious riots in Newport in 1533. All the same, it would be wrong to conclude that conditions in Magor were typical of the Marches as a whole, or that within a short time the state of law and order had everywhere deteriorated appallingly, with officials far more contemptuous of their responsibilities than before and lawbreakers greatly increased in numbers and daring. The basic problems remained what they had always been: the fractionization of jurisdiction, the ease with which criminals took advantage of it, and the readiness of officials to connive at, and even encourage, their misdeeds for their own profit. What *had* changed, though, was the emergence of a keener awareness of misrule in the Marches and the dangers to be apprehended from it at a time of growing crisis for the realm as a whole. The consequence was a stream of correspondence directed to the King's government during the early 1530s with the intention of bringing the problems to its notice and suggesting possible remedies.

One of the first and most radical plans for reform had been outlined as early as 1531, when Dr James Denton, chancellor to the Council in the Marches, had proposed that the Marches be shired. To press his point he

---

[7] *L. and P.*, VIII, 609.

went to court, where both Henry VIII and Norfolk approved of the idea;
Henry expressing the view that 'it were a gracious deed to reform Wales'.[8]
But, with his matrimonial impasse unresolved, the King was loth to arouse
possible opposition in the Marches and nothing was done. In May 1532
Thomas Phillips deprecated the Council's failure to suppress cattle-stealing
or control officials and urged the establishment of a body which would
make every official shake with fear. In the same year, probably, worried
communications commenting acidly on the prevalence of perjury, maintenance, and unlawful assemblies were sent to the Council in the Marches by
the earl of Worcester, John Salusbury, steward of Denbigh, and John
Salter, justice of North Wales. Another correspondent, John Parker,
advocated stricter constraints on officers, urged that they be forbidden to
pardon murder or felony in return for a fine, and called for *commortha* to
be prohibited. In 1533 Thomas Holte, the king's attorney, submitted a long
and detailed memorandum. He contended that murder and cattle-stealing
were going unpunished and *commortha* was too prevalent. In the same
year, another influential figure, Sir Edward Croft, vice-chamberlain of
South Wales, claimed that Veysey was too frequently absent and that, as a
cleric, he could anyway not impose the death penalty, with the result that
many murderers were not hanged. Croft pressed for a president who would
'use the sword of justice . . . throughout the Principality. Otherwise the
Welsh will wax so wild it will not be easy to bring them to order again'[9]—a
suggestion which might well have rung an urgent bell in Cromwell's mind!
Croft's son, Thomas, a few months later estimated that a hundred men had
been killed in Veysey's time without retribution falling on one of the
murderers. These representations had the effect of making Cromwell note
in 1533 the 'necessity of looking to the state of Wales'.[10] In December,
among the measures for the defence of the realm he wished the King's
Council to consider was one for reforming the administration of Wales 'so
that peace should be preserved and justice done'.[11] The Council never in
fact considered this issue, but disorder in Wales was evidently coming to be
seen less as a problem in itself than as part of a wider panorama involving
the need to secure the whole kingdom in face of possible religious
opposition, insurrection, and invasion.

The situation during 1534 was particularly worrying. Though Henry had
annulled his first marriage, married Anne Boleyn, and completed his
supremacy over the Church, he remained deeply unsure how Charles V
and Francis I might react. In spite of their incorrigible mutual mistrust
there could be no guarantee that they might not combine—temporarily at
least—against England. If they did, then Scotland could be expected to
abandon its flimsy truce with Henry. There had already been disturbing

[8] Pugh, *GCH*, III, 567.   [9] *L. and P.*, VI, 210.
[10] *L. and P.*, VI, 286.   [11] *L. and P.*, VII, 293.

rumours that the Scots and the Welsh would assist Andrea Doria in an attack he was preparing on Calais, and Chapuys feared that, as a result, Catherine of Aragon would be accused of stirring up insurrection in Wales. Rebellion in Ireland, too, encouraged Chapuys to hope that Welsh sympathies could be turned to the advantage of the Irish and Charles V. He played up suggestions of Welsh concern for Catherine and the Irish rebels and the likelihood of their rising against Henry. Over-sanguine his dispatches may have been but they were not entirely groundless. Difficulties in recruiting men for service in Ireland were reliably reported and John Barlow in 1536 alleged earlier sympathy on the part of papist gentry in Wales for the Irish rebels. Meantime, in Wales as in other parts of the realm, there were a number of widely scattered protests—mostly from disgruntled priests—against the King's religious changes (below, pp. 280–1).

In face of these mounting anxieties Cromwell acted with his customary decisiveness. Early in 1534 he ordered the officers in Wales to apprehend any papist preaching in support of the pope's authority. In May he changed King Log for King Stork by appointing the dynamic, coarse-grained, and unclerical cleric, Rowland Lee, bishop of Coventry and Lichfield, to replace the lethargic Veysey, with positive instructions to restore order in the Marches and maintain it with an iron fist. A few weeks later, in response to complaints made in Parliament about outrages in the border counties, Cromwell arranged for the King to meet the Marcher lords at Shrewsbury. There they agreed on a series of ordinances, designed to recruit more reliable officers, prevent the harbouring of known offenders, and ensure the regular holding of courts. A year later, Henry was back in the Marches, exerting his personal influence by 'traversing the country to gain the people'.[12]

To strengthen the hands of the new President of the Council a number of statutes was pushed through Parliament in 1534. Their provisions were modelled largely on the recommendations adumbrated in the memoranda and correspondence of preceding years. Cromwell and his draftsmen may further have been helped by Rowland Lee and Welshmen at court and in governmental circles like William Herbert, later earl of Pembroke, Sir Richard Herbert, Sir John Price, and Sir Edward Carne. The first of the statutes, 'An Act for Punishment of Perjury of Jurors in the Lordships Marcher' (26 Henry VIII, c. 4) was intended to safeguard jurors against illegal pressure to which they were regularly subjected but at the same time to punish them for any manifestly false verdict they might return. The next, 'Act for Keepers of Ferries on the Water of Severn' (26 Henry VIII, c. 5), aimed to establish a tighter grip on ferries and ferrymen providing thieves with such convenient escape routes, particularly after nightfall. The third,

[12] *L. and P.*, IX, 58.

'Bill concerning Councils in Wales' (26 Henry VIII, c. 6), was the longest and most important of the Acts. Its preamble delineated, in the admonitory phrases beloved of Tudor draftsmen, what it saw as the wilful inclination of the inhabitants of Wales and the Marches to commit crimes and the pressing need for 'sharp correction'. It outlined a number of remedies: enforcement of suit of court; compensation for wrongful imprisonment at the rate of 6s. 8d. a day and punishment of the officers responsible for it; prohibition of the carrying of weapons to courts and other places of assembly; and abolition of the old Welsh practices of *commortha* and *arddel*, which had long been grievously abused and distorted. It authorized justices of the peace from neighbouring English shires to extradite known offenders from the Marches and bring them back to their own shires for trial and conviction. Any fines imposed on those who found sureties for their future good behaviour were to be paid to the king's use. In spite of a saving clause purporting to protect the privileges of the Marcher lords, the Act represented a serious incursion into the autonomy they had hitherto enjoyed. Two further Acts (26 Henry VIII, cc. 11 and 12) sought to discourage men from laying ambushes to waylay officers from the border counties who pursued them to implement legal process and also limited benefit of clergy in cases of murder, petty treason, and felony.[13]

Taken altogether, these statutes of 1534–5 laid down a number of important principles. First, they recognized that the whole area of Principality, March, and border English counties should be regarded as a unit where law enforcement had been woefully lax and was in sore need of being tightened. Second, they conferred upon the Council enhanced powers of dealing both with offenders and those officials by whose connivance they prospered. Third, they curtailed the privileges of each lordship and suppressed widely prevalent abuses. Finally, by empowering English justices of the peace to intervene in the Marches, they introduced shire administration there for the first time—indirectly, at least. It may well have been the difficulty of implementing this provision effectively which was to contribute most to the speedy shiring of the whole of Wales. Shortly after these Acts had been passed, Chapuys commented that they had taken away the native laws and customs of the Welsh, 'the last thing in the world they can endure patiently'.[14] How easy it was even for an intelligent and well-informed observer to misinterpret what was happening!

Fortified by these statutes and backed up by royal authority, Lee embarked upon the duty he found so congenial of suppressing criminals and enforcing law and order with that boundless vigour and irrepressible gusto which characterized all his doings. For the next eight years he

[13] The text of all the above statutes may be seen in Bowen, *Statutes*, pp. 51–6.
[14] *L. and P.*, VII, 1554.

terrorized the lawbreakers of the Marches into an unprecedented state of quaking alarm and galvanized his council into an unparalleled spate of hectic activity. He had come to the fore as a royal agent in the divorce and may even have officiated at the marriage of Henry and Anne; but though he remained utterly devoted to the King and Cromwell, he had little sympathy for the Reformation, being castigated by Stephen Vaughan as 'a papist, an idolater and a fleshly priest'.[15] Yet in spite of being a cleric of the old school he had no qualms about shedding blood and obtained an indulgence to allow him to carry out the death penalty on convicted criminals. He was aptly summed up by the Elizabethan lawyer, William Gerard, as 'stout of nature, ready-witted, rough in speech, not affable to any of the Welshry, an extreme severe punisher of offenders, desirous to gain (as he did indeed) credit with the King and commendation for his service'.[16] Equally memorable was Froude's vivid pen-picture of him as the 'last survivor of the old martial prelates, fitter for harness than a bishop's robes, for a court of justice than a court of theology, more at home at the head of his troopers in the gorges of Llangollen than hunting heretics to the stake'.[17]

Together with his willing henchmen, Sir Thomas Englefield and Sir Richard Herbert, Lee wasted no time in launching his campaign against the miscreants of the March. During 1534 he was at Hereford in July, Shrewsbury in August, Ludlow in November, and Presteigne in December. The following year saw him rampaging widely through the Marches, claiming exultantly that the 'Welshmen of Shrewsbury' had been brought to a 'reasonable stay touching such robberies and other malefacts as were there used' and boasting he had 'hanged four of the best blood in Shropshire'.[18] In 1536 he extended his activities as far as Brecon and Monmouth, gleefully defying the offenders he stalked to do their worst: 'Although the thieves have hanged me by imagination, yet I trust to be even with them shortly in very deed.'[19] During the next year, 1537, however, Lee was cast down by Englefield's death and obliged to admit, in some trepidation, that 'there was never more rioting in Wales than there is now'.[20] His perturbation may have been caused in large part by the acrimonious dispute which broke out between Lord Ferrers and the earl of Worcester over the stewardship of Arwystli, though Lee was quick to intervene and keep the conflict within bounds. By September 1538 his ebullience had resurfaced and he was able confidently to assert that 'in the

[15] *L. and P.*, vi, 1385.
[16] PRO SP12/107/10; cf. *Y Cymm.*, xiii (1899), pp. 134–63.
[17] *History of England* (Everyman edn., 1909), iii, 35.
[18] *L. and P.*, vii, 1393.
[19] *L. and P.*, vii, 1393.
[20] W. Rees, 'The Union of England and Wales', *Trans. Cymm.*, 1937, p. 50.

Marches and in Wales, in the wild parts where I have been, there is order and quiet such as is now in England'.[21]

During Lee's term as president between May 1534 and January 1543 he carried out his function as the rough-riding executant of Tudor rule in Wales with undeviating conviction, inexhaustible *élan*, and ruthless efficiency. Murderers and cattle-thieves were the most common offenders with whom he had to contend and he concentrated on them with forbidding resolution. He delighted in hanging them publicly 'for a sign' to deter others; and took special pleasure in executing a gentleman on the grounds that that would do more good than dispatching a hundred 'petty wretches'.[22] The two aspects of his presidency which left an indelible mark on the minds of his contemporaries were its rigour and ubiquity. An indication of Lee's ferocity in prosecuting criminals was that Ellis Gruffydd should have credited him with hanging no fewer than 5,000 in the space of six years. That estimate was doubtless an example of the incautious partiality of Tudor commentators for an inflated and reverberating round number; but even if we need not believe that Lee's behaviour was as savage as that figure would imply, the fact that an astute and seasoned observer should make such a calculation at all provides thought-provoking evidence of the impression which Lee's policy of 'thorough' and his reputation for unsparing prosecution made on his contemporaries. A generation later, William Gerard reinforced Gruffydd's testimony with his declaration that 'this stout bishop's dealing . . . generally so terrified them as the very fear of punishment . . . wrought first in them the obedience they now be grown into'.[23] Lee's other characteristic, his ubiquity, was brought out in his own letters as well as in Gerard's comments. He and his colleagues made their presence felt and their name feared by their incessant journeyings: 'They spent their whole time in travelling yearly . . . and by that travel knew the people and found their disposition',[24] favouring those willing to preserve law and order and discountenancing others who were not. Lee's legendary reputation lasted long. A state paper of the early seventeenth century advocated the adoption of a similar policy in Ireland, and a Shrewsbury chronicle of the same period attested that he 'had brought Wales into civility before he died and said that he would make the white sheep keep the black'.[25]

His aims throughout these years had been simple and uncomplicated; his political vision circumscribed and unimaginative. Asked in 1536 for his opinions concerning further 'articles for the helping of Wales' all he could recommend was an Act for compelling corrupt officers to compensate wronged parties and another to prohibit the discharge of felons except in

[21] *L. and P.*, XIII, i, 222; ii, 276.   [22] *L. and P.*, XIV, ii, 384.
[23] PRO SP12/107/21.   [24] PRO SP12/107/21.
[25] C. A. J. Skeel, *The Council in the Marches of Wales* (London, 1903).

open court.[26] His attitude towards the Welsh or even the English of the border counties was as blinkered as that of an old-fashioned colonial administrator in the north-western frontier districts of India: convinced that the natives had regularly to be taught their lesson by the representative of a higher civilization whose method was that of imposing forceful but impartial justice and order. Such uncompromising law enforcement none the less remained indispensable throughout his term of office, even after a new approach had been embarked upon.

Long before 1543, Lee's limited concept of his task had been overtaken by a more expansive and adventurous line of policy for which Henry and Cromwell had opted. It was one which Lee from the outset openly and hotly opposed and to which he never became reconciled. The first portents of a different line being adopted in Wales became apparent in an Act of the Parliament of 1536 for the making of justices of the peace in Wales (27 Henry VIII, c. 5), which provided for their appointment by the Lord Chancellor in the six existing shires and the two counties palatine of Glamorgan and Pembroke. The Act implied that shire administration, as it operated in England where local authority was entrusted to the county gentry, was being envisaged for Wales. Within a matter of weeks this measure was to be superseded by an Act which divided the whole of Wales into shires, suggesting that some confusion and uncertainty existed in the minds of those responsible for policy, possibly because of the sheer volume of business that had to be pushed through Parliament. As soon as Lee heard of the alarming notion of entrusting authority to the disorderly natives, he at once pronounced his opposition: 'There are very few Welsh in Wales above Brecknock who have £10 in land', he informed Cromwell and added tartly, 'and their discretion is less than their land.' He pointed out that Cardigan and Merioneth, though shire ground, were as disorderly as the worst parts of the Marches. Sure that he could convince Cromwell of the extreme unwisdom of the proposal he exclaimed despairingly, 'Would God I were with you one hour to declare my mind therein at full'.[27] Nor was his the only dissenting voice. There exists a set of articles purporting to prove that it would be 'hurtful to the commonwealth of north Wales' to have justices because its inhabitants were poor and quarrelsome and most of its gentry 'bearers of thieves and misruled persons'.[28] Sir Richard Bulkeley was another who added his pennyworth of opposition; not least because he feared that his mortal rivals, the Gruffydds and the Glyns, might benefit from being made justices, 'for which Dr. Glyn will give large sums'.[29] John Salusbury, fearful of losing some of his fees, claimed that the country had already been well ruled with fewer officers and less expense than under the proposed new arrangements.

[26] L. and P., x, 330.
[27] L. and P., x, 453.
[28] L. and P., xi, 525.
[29] L. and P., x, p. 176.

The hostility of Lee and others to the proposals cut little ice, however. In the offing were larger plans, of which those being prepared for Wales were only a part. An Act of 1536 for the 'recontinuing of Certain Liberties and Franchises heretofore Taken From the Crown' was one of the most significant Acts passed by this Parliament. Under its terms, from 1 July 1536 onwards, only the King would have the right to pardon a murder or other felony and to appoint judges in any part of the realm; and all writs were to be issued and indictments made in his name. The end was at hand for all those traditional rights, privileges, and diversities still vested in individual subjects of the Crown; the whole structure of authority in the localities throughout England and Wales was to be uniform, coherent, and royal. Such a concept left no future for outmoded anomalies like the Marcher lordships and necessitated new arrangements to replace them. The lumber left from earlier centuries was to be unceremoniously removed to clear the ground for the creation of a new order within Wales as a whole so as to facilitate its integration into the realm of England. Heralding these changes, the first of the Acts making up what has usually been known as the Act of Union—'An Act for Laws and Justice to be ministered in Wales in Like Form as it is in this Realm' (27 Henry VIII, c. 26)[30]—was now to be steered through Parliament.

In some respects the time could be said to have long been ripe for the assimilation of the two countries. The policies being promoted in 1536 were in one sense no more than the culmination of a centuries-old drive to extend the authority of the king of England over Wales. It has rightly been argued that the union of England and Wales had been achieved in the Statute of Rhuddlan in 1284. Even in the Marches, left largely unchanged in 1284, the King had, during the intervening centuries, become incomparably the most powerful landowner. While there were still important lords left there in 1536, Henry VIII held the large majority of the lordships in his own possession. By inheritance, purchase, attainder, escheat, or as duke of Lancaster, he enjoyed a supremacy which no combination of lords, still less any individual lord, could dream of challenging. The potential threat to royal power from a Marcher coalition, which had more than once been real enough in earlier centuries, was now virtually inconceivable. Furthermore, the changes in the social and economic life of Wales already noted (above, pp. 78–89) had brought it far more closely in line with that of England. The increasing disintegration not only of the manors of the south and east but also of such institutions peculiar to Wales as the *gwely*, *gafael*, and *cenedl*, had placed an enhanced premium on thrusting individualism in economic activity and social relationships. This was fostering the emergence of patterns of landownership, consolidated estates, enlarged farms,

---

[30] Bowen, *Statutes*, pp. 75–93.

landlord–tenant–labourer structures, the supremacy of a landowning gentry and commercial values, and the expansion of trade and industry not fundamentally unlike those which prevailed in England. It was intuitive realization on the part of Henry and his advisers that these developments had prepared Wales to receive the kind of changes embodied in the legislation which in no small measure accounted for the nature of its provisions.

The King and his ministers had had their awareness further quickened by representations made to them by some of their Welsh subjects. Many of the Welsh gentry were conscious of their changed position and eager to avail themselves of a more secure legal status and improved political and economic opportunities. Ever since Henry VII's reign a number of them had jumped at the chance of going to London and others had infiltrated into towns and offices from which Henry IV's statutes theoretically debarred them. A reliable indication of their ambitions had been their readiness to pay for letters of denizenship and charters of privilege. Other symptoms of the same eagerness were the petitions compiled in Wales at this time. One emanating from the inhabitants of Montgomery, in 1536, complained that they had 'ever lived under the oppression of their lords and their officers' under customs 'always applied and interpreted after the pleasure . . . of the lord and his officers to their best profit' without respect to 'any good equity or conscience'.[31] The most celebrated of these documents was that published by Lord Herbert in his *History of the Reign of Henry VIII*, the authorship of which has been variously attributed to Sir Richard Herbert or Sir John Price. In it the petitioners craved to be 'received and adopted into the same laws and privileges' enjoyed by the King's other subjects and expressed their earnest wish to 'unite ourselves to the greater and better parts of the island'.[32] They were pushing at an open door in so far as the Tudor monarchy, like others of its kind in France, Spain, and elsewhere in Europe, was showing itself anxious to bring about greater unity and uniformity in law, administration, institutions, and language within its domains. As early as 1520 Henry VIII had expressed the hope that Ireland could be brought into closer conformity with England 'by sober ways, politic drifts and amiable persuasions founded in law and reason'.[33] Nor was it entirely a coincidence that Brittany, another land speaking a Celtic language, had been absorbed into the French monarchy in 1532, or that England should at this time embark on a 'forward policy' within the British Isles for greater control in Ireland and in its relations with the kingdom of Scotland.

[31] W. Ll. Williams, 'The Union of England and Wales', *Trans. Cymm.*, 1907–8, pp. 54–6; Pugh, *GCH*, III, 579.   [32] Rees, *Trans. Cymm.*, 1937, p. 54.
[33] *State Papers published under the Authority of H.M. Commission, Henry VIII* (London, 1830–52), II, 52.

Yet, however much Wales had been brought into a state of greater readiness for assimilation as a result of these evolutionary changes, it was not they which determined the timing of the Acts. Even as late as 1531, the King had declined to shire Wales while the 'great matter' of his divorce was still undetermined. By 1534, however, the breach with Rome was complete, his annulment secured, his second marriage achieved, and the royal supremacy consummated. Furthermore, that supreme architect of governmental revolution by statute, Thomas Cromwell, now had the King's ear. The implementation of the epoch-making changes in relations between Church and State gave a new and urgent relevance to the related issues of order and security in Wales and the possibility of an invasion along its coastline. Wales and the Marches were one of the badly governed and disorderly areas of the kingdom whose problems gave rise to more pressing anxiety at a time when the military response of Spain and France to the English Reformation was unpredictable and full of risk for Henry. In addition, the Welsh were, religiously, a conservative people among whom there was widespread sympathy for Queen Catherine and her daughter and for the Irish rebels. Reports of disaffection of this kind loomed larger in the official mind because of the possibility of foreign landings in a thinly populated country like Wales, far from the main centres of strength, and offering many tempting landfalls, well-known to foreign enemies.

In the light of this William Rees argued that the Act of 1536 was 'a necessary expedient to meet the new political situation which had suddenly arisen as a result of the breach with Rome';[34] necessary for two reasons: in order to enforce the new religious settlement in Wales since the legislative enactments of Parliament did not apply there; and because of the grave fear that the Welsh might assist an invasion from Ireland directed by the Spaniards. Though Rees's view held the field for a long time, neither of his explanations can readily be accepted. No constitutional hindrance existed to the introduction of the Reformation. Ever since 1284 Parliament had assumed the right to legislate for Wales, and all the key Reformation statutes of the 1530s had already been applied there. Again, it would seem an act of doubtful political wisdom to meet a military crisis two years after it had passed its peak by a far-reaching constitutional change, especially one that was opposed by the Crown's chief official on the spot. It might surely be preferable to infer that the dispatch of the dictatorial Lee, the statutes of 1534, and the rearming and fortifying of the coastline constituted a more practical prescription for coping with the dangers of possible invasion. Nevertheless, Rees's general point that it was the crisis caused by the Reformation changes which largely served to draw attention to the condition of Wales remains valid.

[34] Rees, *Trans. Cymm.*, 1937, p. 44.

The explanation does not end there, however. The achievement of royal supremacy over the Church was but one part of the fundamental reorganization being undertaken in the 1530s, largely at Cromwell's instigation. With the King recognized as ruler of Church and State, the next stage was to extend his authority over the outlying parts of his domain so as to create a single unified and effective sovereign entity. In the north of England, the power of the great quasi-feudal families of Dacre, Clifford, and Percy was broken and the Council of the North set up to exert firmer governmental control. In the county palatine of Chester, justices of the peace were now introduced for the first time. The administration of Calais was reorganized and the town given the right to return members to Parliament. In 1541 Henry proclaimed himself king of Ireland, which hitherto he had ruled as lord of a papal fief. Scotland, too, was to be brought within his orbit, though his campaigns for military conquest compromised his more diplomatic approach to cement closer relations by a marriage alliance and a possible union of crowns. Tudor policy for Wales may best be understood when viewed as a part of this wider strategy, rather than as a solution dictated first and foremost by Welsh needs and problems, even if the preambles to the Acts of 1536 and 1543 concentrated exclusively on the King's alleged reactions to circumstances prevailing in Wales.

Closely associated with this reorganization were the financial needs of the Crown. Thomas Cromwell, main architect of all these changes of the 1530s, had promised to make his master the richest ruler in all Christendom and part of the revenues needed towards achieving that goal must come from Wales. Hitherto it had made little contribution to the royal coffers by way of taxation and for over a century the income accruing to the King from the Principality and his lordships in the March had been slumping drastically. Even Rowland Lee, in his efforts to bring the Marches to a more law-abiding state, had found himself chronically short of money, while his royal master could never obtain enough to meet all his needs. All parts of Wales and the Marches were therefore to be subject to taxation after 1 November 1536. The Subsidy Act of 1543 was the first of its kind to be extended to Wales, and £4,291 out of the total of £74,070 was raised there.

The Act of 1536 proceeded quickly through Parliament and received the royal assent on 14 April 1536. It betrayed signs of haste, muddle, and incompleteness in its drafting, but in view of the huge programme of legislation having to be pushed through during the session that was hardly surprising. The preamble referred to Wales as 'ever' having been 'subject to . . . the Imperial Crown' of the realm. If 'ever' was to be taken literally, its use could only be justified by reference to the ancient empire alleged to have existed in early Britain and appealed to in the Statute in Restraint of

Appeals to justify Henry's pretensions to jurisdiction over the Church. This may have been a hint of the kind of status claimed by Geoffrey of Monmouth on behalf of the early rulers of Britain, from whom Henry VII had traced his descent. Otherwise, the claim to authority over Wales could go back no further than 1284. The preamble also drew attention to the differences in rights, laws, and customs and in speech between England and Wales, on account of which 'rude and ignorant people' had drawn 'distinction and diversity' between the Welsh and the King's other subjects. This would appear to have had in mind the legal disadvantages under which the Welsh had laboured, though it would hardly have been politic to draw attention to Parliament's own part in imposing those burdens. Therefore, the King, out of his 'singular zeal, love and favour' for his Welsh subjects— to which he had never previously found it necessary to give expression in twenty-seven years on the throne!—and, minding to bring them under the laws of his realm and 'utterly to extirp all and singular the sinister usages and customs differing from the same', with the agreement of Parliament had ordained that Wales should be 'incorporated, united and annexed' to his realm of England. Constitutionally, there was nothing innovatory in that; what was new was that all his Welsh subjects should henceforth enjoy the same freedoms and laws as his subjects in England. Critics of the Act have often drawn attention to that part of the preamble purporting to extirp 'sinister usages and customs' and have claimed that the Welsh language was included among them. A more reasonable interpretation, especially in view of the reactions to the Act of such ardent upholders of the Welsh language as William Salesbury and John Price (below, pp. 275–6), would be to read this as a reference only to outmoded legal customs, like *commortha* and *arddel*, which had contributed greatly to lawlessness in the past.

The Act went on to lay down that laws relating to inheriting land should be changed from the Welsh practice of equal partition among all the sons to the English system of 'tenure without division' and inheritance by the eldest son. In practice, such a change had already been adopted by many Welsh families. The Act swept away the Marcher lordships on the grounds of the high incidence of crime committed within them and because a majority of them was in the King's possession. Marcher lords were no longer to try pleas of the Crown, though they could continue to hold minor courts and retain rights to treasure trove and wreck. In place of the lordships the new shires of Monmouth, Brecknock, Radnor, Montgomery, and Denbigh were created, and a Chancery and Exchequer established at Brecon and Denbigh. Other lordships were attached to the counties of Shropshire, Hereford, and Gloucester, thereby removing Welsh-speaking areas like Oswestry and Ewyas Lacy to English counties. The counties of Carmarthen, Cardigan, Pembroke, and Glamorgan were enlarged by attaching a number of lordships to each and the lordship of Mawddwy was added to Merioneth. In what was subsequently to prove its most controversial clause, the Act laid down that all administrative and judicial proceedings were to be conducted in English and that no one using 'the Welsh speech or language shall have or enjoy any manner office . . . unless he or they use the English speech or language'. Each of the Welsh shires was granted regular parliamentary representation on the basis of two members for Monmouthshire and one for every other shire, together with one member for all the ancient boroughs within each shire, except those of Merioneth. The members were to be paid wages, those of the boroughs being met by the burgesses of all other ancient boroughs within the shire, thus bringing into existence a system of contributory boroughs peculiar to Wales. The county franchise was conferred upon all forty-shilling freeholders, while in the boroughs only freemen had the vote. Immediately after the prorogation of the Parliament of 1536 the Lord Chancellor was to appoint a commission to arrange for the division of all the new or extended shires into hundreds. Finally, the Act reserved to the King the power of repealing the whole or any part of its provisions within three years after the end of the existing Parliament.

During the years which intervened between this Act of 1536, which laid down the main principles on the basis of which the two countries were to be integrated, and that of 1543, which filled in the details, there ensued considerable delay, confusion, and uncertainty. This may have been caused partly by continuing threats from European powers and disturbing fears of a joint invasion by them in 1539; a year which saw Lee actively fortifying castles and coastal defences in Wales. Relations with Scotland and France deteriorated to the point of open war between 1542 and 1546, the possibility of invasion loomed more menacingly than ever in 1545, and Welsh coasts were again under serious threat. But quite apart from these dangers from foreign powers there were domestic difficulties too. The Boundaries Commission, which was to have presented its report on 1 November 1536, had its powers extended for three years in 1536 and for another three years in 1539 because the King had 'such great affairs and urgent causes' that he had 'no convenient time nor leisure to accomplish and execute' the divisions.[35] Lee mentioned that great uncertainty prevailed over the trial of felons because of doubts over the jurisdiction of Marcher lordships, which had been abolished but without new shires being brought into existence. To help with the shiring Justice Sulyard was sent to the Marches. In 1538 Lee reminded Cromwell that he had asked several times for guidance 'but you are too busy'.[36] In 1539 he and Sulyard both

[35] P. R. Roberts, 'The "Act of Union" in Welsh History', *Trans. Cymm.*, 1972–3, pp. 49–72.
[36] Rees, *Trans. Cymm.*, 1937, p. 54.

wrote again and the Act of 1539 to extend the Boundaries Commission may have been passed in response to these representations. As late as 1540 Lee was still busy converting 'Denbighland into shire ground'. Appointing sheriffs and justices of the peace was also a slow and piecemeal process. Glamorgan, for instance, had a clerk of the peace by July 1539 and some of its justices of the peace began to operate about the end of 1541. An Act of 1540 cleared the way for the appointment, in November of that year, of new sheriffs for one year only. On 28 June 1541 four justices were appointed for the four new assize circuits being envisaged. The first of the new sheriffs for Glamorgan, Sir George Herbert, was appointed in 1542. His had long been a familiar but hardly well-loved face in local administration; while up north, in the long-standing shire of Caernarfon, Sir Richard Bulkeley, who took office as sheriff in 1542, had held the post from 1527 to 1540.

Yet another reason for the delay involved the King himself. A ruler obsessed with the problems of the succession, Henry was turning over in his mind proposals which, if they had come to fruition, would have assigned a special position to the Prince of Wales. It may have been the birth of his heir, Edward, which prompted Henry to issue a proclamation of 1537 invoking the powers of veto reserved to him in the Act of 1536. Well aware of the particular importance to the King's eldest son of the Principality of Wales, he did not wish lightly to abandon it. He appears to have explored the possibilities of enlarging that inheritance and making use of the experience of governing that it could confer upon his son. A plan along these lines devised in 1540–1 found expression in an early draft entitled 'a breviat of the effects devised for Wales'.[37] This envisaged placing all Wales under the authority of the Prince and supervising its judicial hierarchy not by the Council of Wales but by a Welsh Court of Chancery. Nothing actually came of these initiatives, however,—presumably because Edward was too young and Henry becoming too old and too much concerned with his heir's succession to the whole of his inheritance.

In the parliamentary elections of 1542 the Welsh elected their first representatives to a Tudor Parliament. They could, therefore, be said to have been consulted and heard on the subject of the 'Act for Certain Ordinances in the King's Dominion and Principality of Wales (34 and 35 Henry VIII, c. 26)[38]—for all the difference which that may have made. Passed in 1543, this Act was a long one of 130 clauses, spelling out *in extenso* the arrangements for future administration and justice in Wales. Its preamble again adopted a conciliatory and persuasive tone towards the Welsh, whose 'greater wealth and prosperity' were alleged to be Henry's

[37] P. R. Roberts, 'A Breviat of the Effectes Devised for Wales', *Camden Miscellany*, (RHS, 1975).
[38] Bowen, *Statutes*, pp. 101–33.

chief reason for passing the Act. Its terms were claimed to have been framed in response to the 'humble suit and petition' of the populace, which may be an allusion to the petitions already mentioned, or others like them. It confirmed the creation of the shires and the delimitation of hundreds within them, though it made some adjustments. The lordships of Hope, St Asaph, and Hawarden had already been transferred from Denbigh to Flint by a statute of 1541. In 1543 the town of Haverfordwest was recognized as a county in its own right, Abertanad was transferred to Shropshire, and the lordships of Llansteffan, Laugharne, and Ystlwyf from Pembrokeshire to Carmarthenshire.

The Act put the Council in the Marches, previously a prerogative court of the Crown, on a statutory footing and made provision for it to hear and determine such causes as should afterwards be referred to it by the King. Another institution peculiar to Wales set up by the Act was the Court of Great Sessions. This extended the arrangement already in being in the three counties of the north-west to three other new circuits of three counties apiece: in the south-west (Pembrokeshire, Carmarthenshire, and Cardiganshire), south-east (Glamorgan, Brecknock, and Radnorshire), and north-east (Flint, Denbighshire, and Montgomeryshire). In each of them the Justice was to hold his sessions for a week, twice annually at fifteen days' notice, and the court was given powers to act in 'as large and ample a manner' as King's Bench, Common Pleas, and Assize Courts. Monmouthshire was excluded from these dispositions and attached to the Oxford Assize Circuit—perhaps to maintain the symmetry of four circuits rather than for any other reason. The Act specified in detail the jurisdiction and procedure of the Council and Great Sessions. It also empowered the Lord Chancellor to appoint in each county eight justices of the peace and *custos rotulorum*, waiving the normal stipulation that every justice must have an income of £20 a year from land. They were regularly to hold their Quarter Sessions, which effectively became the ruling administrative and judicial body within each shire. A sheriff was to be appointed in each county; serving for a year only, he was to be nominated by the Council in the Marches and chosen by the Privy Council. Arrangements were also made for the appointment of escheators, coroners, and high and petty constables in every county. An interesting feature was that the Act granted the King powers to legislate independently; Henry never invoked the authority but there are indications that had he lived he might have done so.

The legislation of 1536–43, especially the two major Acts of 1536 and 1543, has usually been referred to in this century as the 'Act of Union'. The name was prompted by the use of the word 'united' in the Act of 1536 to describe what it was intended to achieve and was first employed by O. M. Edwards in 1901 and given wider currency by A. F. Pollard.[39] More

[39] O. M. Edwards, *Wales* (London, 1901).

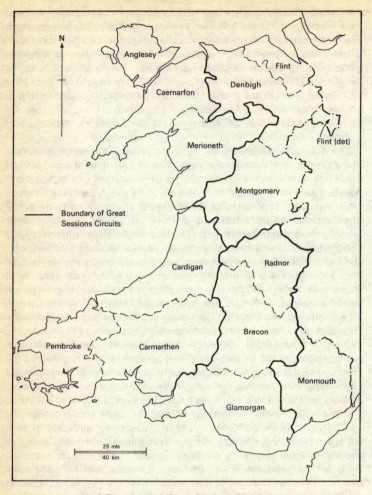

MAP 6 Counties and Great Sessions Circuits, 1543

recently its use has been criticized by Goronwy Edwards on the grounds that the 'real' union was effected in 1284 and what happened in Henry VIII's reign was not that Wales was united with England but rather that Wales was unified politically and judicially within itself.[40] Valuable as it

[40] J. Goronwy Edwards, *The Principality of Wales, 1267–1967* (Caernarfon, 1969), pp. 35–9.

was to indicate the inadequacies and even inaccuracies of the label 'Act of Union', the point may have been taken too far. Not only was Goronwy Edwards obliged to admit that in three important respects the Act united Wales to England: it gave both countries a single, uniform law; it conferred on Wales representation in Parliament; and it created justices of the peace in Wales. But he also tended to ignore how much closer Wales became tied within the English state by the operation of forces which had little or nothing to do with the provisions of the Act: the vastly increased power of the Crown to control the life of Wales through the Privy Council, prerogative courts, common taxation and defence, royal supremacy over the Church, and the closer social and economic as well as political and legal contacts between the two countries. His criticism of the term 'Act of Union' nevertheless remains largely valid. A more appropriate label might be the 'Act of Assimilation' since that would cover the changes which took place within Wales itself to make easier the process of integrating it within the English monarchy. But, given the convenience of the term 'Act of Union' and the regularity with which historians have used it, there may be little to be lost in continuing to employ it, as long as its inadequacies, like those of nomenclatures such as 'Renaissance monarchy' or 'Industrial Revolution', are duly recognized.

Whatever label is attached to the Henrician legislation, there can be no doubt that over the next four hundred years it was to be immensely formative in the life of Wales. For the first time it defined the territorial boundaries of the country. The process by which this was achieved was not entirely logical or satisfactory, when the new eastern limits did not conform with existing ethnic, linguistic, or ecclesiastical boundaries. Considerable areas with a Welsh-speaking population and several parishes belonging to Welsh dioceses were now included in England. The worst anomaly was that Monmouthshire was so included for judicial and administrative purposes, in spite of its thoroughly Welsh background and traditions. Since, however, in the eyes of those who drafted the statutes, the main purpose was to assimilate Wales into England, disputation over details of demarcation and division would have appeared pointless and irrelevant.

Secondly, within those newly defined boundaries, the Act created unity of jurisdiction and administration for the first time. Whatever may have been the merits of Edward I's settlement of 1284 he had not tackled the main problem of medieval Wales—the parcelling-out of authority. That remained as marked as ever, in the shape of the division between Principality and March, and still more obviously and detrimentally in the fragmentation within the March itself. From these long-standing divisions had arisen all kinds of pernicious consequences about which enough has already been said. Even Rowland Lee had been grappling with the symptoms of disorder rather than its causes. In the long term, the only solution was the abolition of the lordships and their replacement with a single uniform regime in jurisdiction, law, justice, and administration. It is difficult to suggest or envisage any workable arrangement at this time other than one based on the creation of shires throughout Wales with a machinery of local government and justice comparable to that already existing in England. The shires now established proved their value and durability by remaining in existence until 1974. Interestingly enough, the bodies entrusted with supervising the working of shire institutions and officials, the Council in the Marches and the Court of Great Sessions, were peculiar to Wales and thereby the Act acknowledged in some measure constitutional autonomy for Wales, though it is difficult to believe that this was done for any motive other than administrative convenience.

Thirdly, by making the Welsh citizens of the realm it gave them equality under the law with English subjects. Admittedly, the penal statutes passed in 1401–2 remained on the statute book even though they had been superseded. It is also true that those earlier legal restrictions had rarely been strictly implemented and that there were ways of getting round them; but as long as they might be enforced they were a source of resentment and frustration. The upper classes of Wales had long chafed against them and tried to find ways of evading their consequences. At last they had had their wish and been granted by statute the full 'freedoms, liberties, rights, privileges and laws' of the realm. By conferring upon them legal authorization to become members of parliament, sheriffs, justices of the peace, and the like, the Act had done little more than give statutory confirmation of rights they had already acquired *de facto*. Yet, in formally handing power to members of the gentry, the Crown had conferred self-government upon Wales in the sixteenth-century sense of that term, even though in practice authority continued to be exercised by much the same people after the Act was passed as before.

Fourthly, it introduced into Wales coherent governance in law, justice, and administration. Though it was a grievous loss to the cultural patrimony of Wales as well as to the practice of law to see the Laws of Hywel abolished, it has to be admitted that they had suffered very serious erosion even in their former strongholds. Had the legislation of 1536–43 never been passed, it is hardly conceivable that the remnants of native Welsh law could have lasted indefinitely. Interestingly enough, however, the custom most intimately associated with it—that of *cyfran*, or equal partition among heirs—survived vigorously in some parts of Wales like Builth, Cyfeiliog, Gower, Dinmael, and Abergavenny long after it had been statutorily abolished. On balance, there was much to be said for the introduction of English law. The Marcher lords were thereby deprived of any legal basis for continuing their obsolete privileges. Moreover, English law had penetrated deeply into the theory and practice of law in Principality and March, where ambitious Welshmen in their representations to the Crown had already asked to be brought under its aegis. The courts of justice introduced under the Act to minister that law were a marked improvement on what had gone before them, especially in the Marches. One of the most welcomed changes was that the Act had made it impossible for sessions to be bought off. The delight of those who had previously suffered was expressed in 1559 in the evidence of Glamorgan plaintiffs who testified that Henry VIII, 'of his godly and charitable mind', 'had clearly annulled and put away for ever all such sessions and the redemptions of the same'.[41]

In the light of the significance of these changes it may be a little surprising that their introduction did not evoke more reaction among contemporaries. The most immediate and outspoken observations were those of a negative kind uttered by Lee and other critics of what they saw as 'setting a thief to catch a thief'. Oddly enough, Ellis Gruffydd, who offered many illuminating reflections on other events, dismissed the legislation summarily in a single sentence as an Act 'to turn the whole of Wales into shires'. Nor had the classical bards anything much to say by way of praise or censure, except for Lewis Morgannwg's warm praise of Henry as a masterful ruler who dealt effectively with enemies and traitors. Some of the free-metre poets passed sharp judgements on the social ills of the age; but these related to inflation, bad harvests, the greed of the rich, and sufferings of the poor rather than the impact of the legislation. In two of the earliest Welsh printed books, published within three or four years of the Act of 1543, there are brief but complimentary references. In the first Welsh book, Sir John Price, the man usually regarded as a key adviser on Welsh affairs to Henry and Cromwell, referred to the King as a prince 'as godly as he is powerful. And since he has already bestowed on the Welsh nation so many temporal blessings he will be no less willing to allow them spiritual gifts'.[42] Similarly, William Salesbury in his introduction to his *Dictionary in Englishe and Welshe* (1547) drew attention to the King's 'excellent wisdom' in ensuring 'that there shall hereafter be no difference in laws and language betwixt your subjects of your Principality of Wales and your other subjects of your Realm of England'.[43] They were the first of a whole series of Tudor and Stuart authors to pass favourable judgement on the legislation. Both were well-educated gentlemen, humanists, widely familiar with law and politics, and each was an ardent enthusiast for the language, literature, and antiquities of Wales. Those who followed were men of the same kidney—Humphrey Llwyd, Rice Merrick, Sir Henry Sidney, George Owen, and Sir John Wynn. So the paeans of praise continued all the way down to the twentieth century, through commentators

---

[41] *Cardiff Recs*, III, 75–7.   [42] *Yny Lhyvyr Hwnn* . . . (1546), introd.
[43] *Dictionary* (1547), dedication.

as diverse as James I, Charles Edwards, Edmund Burke, and W. Llewelyn Williams.

Llewelyn Williams was the last scholarly historian to write in terms of almost unqualified praise of what he described as Henry's 'grant of a constitution'.[44] As long as the political connection with England went unchallenged as a source of pride and esteem, the Reformation as a giant step forward in the direction of enlightenment and progress, and Henry VIII as a masterful but benevolent monarch, his legislation was accepted as a beneficial and praiseworthy achievement. But in this century, with mounting criticism in some quarters of the 'English connection', a sharper attitude towards the Tudor gentry and their successors, a more tolerant understanding of and even admiration for medieval values and beliefs, and a correspondingly hostile view of Henry's character and intentions, the Act has come in for much more derogation. Authors deeply sympathetic to nationalist ideals have argued that its real object was to destroy the distinctiveness of Wales by launching a calculated attack on its language and the culture based upon it. The Welsh could enjoy the privileges of English citizenship, argued A. O. H. Jarman, on condition that they forgot their own particular past and personality, denied their Welshness, and merged with England.[45] Other historians, while considerably more sceptical of Henry's allegedly liberal and benign motives, have nevertheless sought in effect to maintain that Tudor rulers and statesmen were, above all, practical men, who must be judged by the standards of their own age, that the past is not answerable to present-day ideals, and that sixteenth-century men viewed the issues of language and the image of nationality very differently from those of the twentieth century.

Whether applauding or denouncing the Henrician legislation, its supporters and critics have tended to attribute too much to the effects of royal policy for good and ill; to assign to it greater consequences than either a powerful monarch or Acts of Parliament could of themselves achieve. The measures enacted in the name of King and Parliament were a success not because they initiated anything very much but because they took cognizance of and gave the seal of official approval to major administrative, legal, social, and economic changes that had long taken place or were already far advanced. Most of the major provisions of the legislation had either come about in practice, if not in theory, or had long been urged upon the government by interested parties. 'Legislation alone will not change the habits of a people and the history of the past is littered with the debris of ineffective legislation; ineffective because it departed too far from the social habits and practices of the people',[46] observed William

[44] *Making Modern Wales*, Chap. 2.
[45] Jarman, *Historical Foundations Nationalism*, pp. 79–98.
[46] Rees, *Trans. Cymm.*, 1937, p. 27.

Rees. Curiously enough, however, he viewed the Acts as being hastily conceived and *ad hoc* in nature, failing to emphasize sufficiently that though this verdict may have been true of some of the details it was not applicable to the underlying principles. Moreover, the statutes have often been, and still are, viewed not in the context of the wider developments of which they were a part but from the distinctly narrower and potentially misleading standpoint of conditions in Wales itself, as though these had very largely if not entirely determined the nature of the legislation. Lastly, it is important not to attribute to the sixteenth century conceptions of government, language, culture, and nationality, which formed no part of its mental furniture but have been very much the product of the last century and the present one.

In essence, the controversies over the effects of Henrician policy centre on the issue of whether or not the price paid by the Welsh in terms of cultural losses has been too crippling in return for any material or political benefits conferred. 'The sacrifice of a nationality', wrote Lecky, 'is a measure which naturally produces such intense and enduring discontent that it should never be executed unless it can be accompanied by some political or material advantages that are so great and at the same time so evident as to prove a corrective.' For a long period it was assumed that those benefits in the case of Wales were substantial and self-evident. A coherent and uniform regime in law, justice, and administration had been introduced, sweeping into the limbo of history old inequalities and anomalies. Power had been vested in native hands and parliamentary representation conferred. The outcome had been a greater measure of law-enforcement and stability, bringing in its train economic advance and prosperity. But such arguments have heavily overestimated the direct benefits of the Act. English law and methods had pervasively infiltrated before 1536. There was no abrupt transfer of power; most of the former (and often corrupt) officers continued to exercise authority in their localities under different titles. There was certainly no 'instant' peace or respect for law and order; and Elizabethan Wales, as will be seen, had its share of altercations and disorders. Stronger and stabler government there may, indeed, have been; but it owed far less to these Acts than to the augmented power of the Crown and its central instruments of government, without which the statutory provisions relating to Wales might have been so many useless pieces of paper. Neither did greater economic prosperity derive directly from the effects of the legislation; it stemmed chiefly from the impact of the increase in population, the inflation of prices, and the growth of demand.

Conversely, critics of the Acts have contended that they had a disastrous effect on the Welsh language, literature, and identity. Until the 1530s, it is argued, the gentry took a pride in their language, were enthusiastic patrons of literature, and the guardians of national awareness. The terms of Henry's legislation were deliberately calculated to offer them the lure of status and power in return for their willingness to sacrifice their language and their sense of nationality, of which it was the chief ingredient. Having eagerly swallowed the deadly bait, they rapidly became anglicized in speech and cultural affiliations. They ceased to patronize bards and writers, and Welsh literature slithered into steep decline. The gentry became Wales's lost leaders, separated from the mass of the people by a yawning chasm of class, wealth, status, language, and culture. The hypothesis is neat and, at first sight, persuasive. Closer scrutiny of the historical reality raises doubts; life was, as usual, more complex and loose-ended than theory. For a long while before the 1530s, many of the Welsh gentry had already acquired a knowledge of English and saw great value in doing so. But, on the other hand, long after the Acts were passed, many of them saw no incompatibility whatever between accepting with open and willing hands any benefits that Tudor policy had to confer on them while at the same time maintaining much of their traditional Welshness. One of the most prominent themes of later Welsh poetry is the eager eulogy of any office such as that of sheriff or justice of the peace which their patrons may have held. Nor did those patrons desert the Welsh language and literature until well into the seventeenth century. That a sad decline in Welsh literature set in during the sixteenth century is undeniable; but to attribute it solely to the 'language clauses' of the Acts is an example of the fallacy of arguing *post hoc ergo propter hoc*. It takes too little account of some major social and economic forces which are likely to have contributed much more to the nature of the changes than did Tudor legislation. And if poetry declined, prose flourished in the same era as it had seldom, if ever, done before (see below pp. 449–50).

CHAPTER 12

THE REFORMATION: CHANGE AND CHANGE-ABOUT, 1527–1558

THE ROYAL SUPREMACY

ALONG with those major changes of Henry VIII's reign in government and law came the first phase of an equally profound transformation of medieval religion. From about 1527 to 1533 the Tudor kingdom was plunged into one of the most momentous crises in its history as a result of Henry's determination to have his first marriage annulled so as to enable him to marry Anne Boleyn and perhaps ensure the birth of a male heir and successor. His 'great matter' led to a series of laws being passed which, by 1534, shattered papal authority over the Church in England and Wales and replaced it with a royal supremacy based on parliamentary statute. Yet even without Henry's matrimonial complications, the Reformation might well have come anyway, though more gradually. The Church as it had existed in the Middle Ages was one of those outmoded franchises which a reformer of Cromwell's temper would have wanted drastically to modify. Moreover, revolutionary Reformation doctrines were percolating from the Continent and taking possession of groups and individuals among university graduates, clerics, and literate and pious lay people—landowners, lawyers, merchants, and artisans. It would have been virtually impossible to keep the lid pressed down indefinitely on this pressure cooker.

Wales at the beginning of the sixteenth century was far removed from the epicentres of religious upheaval and controversy. The faith was unquestioningly accepted by almost all its population but was dimly apprehended. Habit rather than conviction was its mainspring; and the Welsh were nearly as ill-prepared to defend the existing order as they were to welcome the appearance of challenges to accepted beliefs. Many circumstances had conspired to restrict severely the circulation of late medieval concepts of religious enlightenment, such as mysticism, the *devotio moderna*, or the reformed religious orders. Among them were the geography of the country with its large areas of inaccessible hill and moorland; the conservative, isolated, and thinly dispersed pastoral communities; the absence of a capital, royal court, and university; the fewness of wealthy and cultivated households; the poverty of Welsh sees and monasteries; the smallness of the urban population and trading classes;

and the lack of a printing-press, together with the poor circulation of books and manuscripts. Nor, in these conditions, had the more militant and heterodox critiques propagated by heretics made much impact either. The native heresy of Lollardy had been apparent in some border districts but never made much progress among the population at large. Towards the end of the fifteenth century and beginning of the sixteenth, humanist ideas of improvement began to impinge upon the growing number of university graduates from Wales. Clerics like Richard Whitford or Edward Powell, or laymen like John Price or Edward Carne, came under the Erasmian spell. But the more extreme propositions of Luther and other advanced reformers like Tyndale gained hardly any ground. Isolated individuals—a Richard Davies or William Salesbury—might be converted at university, but seem to have made little impression in Wales. There appeared to be few signs of any agonizing crises of the soul or much evidence of an unslaked spiritual thirst observable in other parts of Europe.[1]

Therefore, the deeper potential religious implications of the royal annulment proceedings took the Welsh largely unawares. Nevertheless, from 1527 onwards, their sovereign's desire for a second marriage and his longing for an heir moved him and them steadily nearer a decisive break with tradition. As relations between Henry and Pope Clement VII became frayed to breaking-point, all those major anti-papal statutes enacted by the Reformation Parliament between 1529 and 1534 were as applicable to Wales as to England, even if Wales was not as yet represented in Parliament. To many of the King's ordinary subjects in Wales, the whole affair may have seemed remote and unreal, having little bearing on their obscure routine. Chapuys, the imperial ambassador, however, informed his master more than once of warm feelings on the part of the Welsh for Queen Catherine, their antagonism towards Anne Boleyn, and how they might make common cause with Irish and Scots in opposition to Henry. Rhys ap Gruffydd and his uncle seem to have voiced such sympathies and there were a number of isolated instances of seditious protests uttered by individual critics. Typical of the latter was the outburst of one William ap Llywelyn, who was reported to have said on 4 July 1533 that he would like to have Henry upon Snowdon where he would 'souse the King about the ears till he had made his head soft enough'.[2] Another cleric of Dyffryn Clwyd, Robert ap Roger Heuston, gave it as his opinion that Henry had left the Holy Church and people ought to die for the faith rather than let the King despoil them. A prominent poet, Lewis Morgannwg, castigated Anne Boleyn as the reincarnation of Alice and Rowena, classic symbols of English treachery; but though his censure may have been typical of the sentiments of many, he would hardly have dared publicize it until after her

[1] Williams, *Welsh Church*, Chap. 14.   [2] PRO SP 1/99/79–81.

fall. Both Bishop Barlow of St Davids and Sir Richard Bulkeley in the north-west gave broad hints of sympathies between the Welsh and the rebels of northern England; yet this may have been not much more than an excuse to blacken their enemies.

Whatever qualms or misgivings there may have been in Wales about the King's actions, there was little sign of their being translated into serious or concerted opposition to the government. When, for example, Observant Friars, whose order was more unyieldingly opposed to Henry than almost any section of the clergy, arrived in Cardiff, they were immediately packed off to London as prisoners. Furthermore, virtually all the Welsh clergy obliged by law to take the oath under the Act of Supremacy did so without demur. Even the inmates of monasteries, suspected of being the most tenacious upholders of the pope's authority and required to take a more comprehensive oath than the parish clergy, including a categorical rejection of any acknowledgement of papal jurisdiction, complied unhesitatingly. Only a tiny handful of clergy associated with Wales refused the oath. One was George de Athequa, bishop of Llandaff since 1517, a Spanish friar and confessor to Catherine of Aragon. True to his Iberian upbringing and his loyalty to his mistress, he refused the oath and, after hair-raising adventures, was allowed to return to Spain. Another who resisted and was later executed was Richard Fetherston, archdeacon of Brecon and physician to Princess Mary. Henry's most recalcitrant opponents among Welsh-born priests were all domiciled in England and influenced by opposition there. Richard Whitford, monk of Sion, would not take the oath at first but later gave in. John Davies, a Carthusian, died in prison; John Griffith, chaplain to the marquis of Exeter, and John Eynon of Reading Abbey were put to death in 1539; and Edward Powell, a secular priest, was executed in 1540. Robert Morreby, a monk from a dissolved Welsh abbey, testified to the abbot of Fountains in 1538 that some in Wales had been 'in readiness to have taken your part if ye had been so happy to have come forward' (i.e., rebelled).[3] Yet the overwhelming majority of the clergy, high and low, regular and secular, accepted the royal supremacy without any obvious hesitation. It may have been this lack of any leadership on the part of the clergy which partly induced prominent laymen also to accept the royal policies. None of the leading figures, remembering the fate of Buckingham and Rhys ap Gruffydd, were willing to put themselves at risk. Sir Richard Bulkeley doubtless spoke for many besides himself when he confessed tremblingly to Cromwell, 'I know right well it lieth in your hands to undo me with a word of your mouth'.[4] Even someone like Sir Rice Mansel who, with his wife, stood loyally by Princess

---

[3] *L. and P.*, XIII, i, 346.
[4] *L. and P.*, XI, 1329.

Mary, nevertheless served in the royal forces on land and sea and participated prominently in the dissolution of the monasteries.

In addition to ensuring acceptance of the oath under the Supremacy Act, vigorous efforts were set on foot in all the Welsh dioceses to disseminate from the pulpit propaganda against the pope and in favour of royal supremacy. Rowland Lee admitted that he had never been in the pulpit in his life but was willing to give it a try if Cromwell believed it necessary. At Bangor, the bishop, Thomas Skeffington (1509–33), also abbot of Beaulieu, was in 1529 reported not to have visited his diocese for fourteen years but nevertheless found himself embroiled in furious rivalries between the families of Bulkeley and Glyn, in which rows over the royal supremacy became an integral part of the disputes. His successor, Bishop John Salcot, was in 1535 obliged to confess to being sorely handicapped in 'the diligent setting forth and sincere preaching' of government policy because he knew no Welsh.[5] Though he alone admitted to this grievous disability, it was one shared by a majority of the higher clergy in Wales. For most of Salcot's diocesan clergy, paradoxically enough, one of the first effects of the breach with the pope was the tightening-up of erstwhile Roman discipline in relation to clerical marriage. In January 1536 the Bangor clerics sent a plaintive petition to Thomas Cromwell asking for permission to be allowed to keep their women so as to be able to maintain such hospitality as they had customarily done and pleading that laymen, knowing their frailty in relation to the fair sex, would not allow them in their houses. Another complication in Bangor, not unknown elsewhere in Wales, was that the royal supremacy was seized upon as an issue in faction struggles which really had little to do with religion. The old quarrel between Bulkeley and Glyn was infused with new animus by the latter's adoption of a strongly reforming pose in contrast to the conservative stance of Bulkeley's protégé, Robert Oking, with both parties trying to curry favour with Cromwell. Violent clashes ensued between them in Bangor cathedral and Bulkeley heatedly accused his adversaries of disloyalty to the King, warning that if decisive action were not taken against them 'the King shall have as much to do with his subjects here in north Wales as ever he had in Ireland'.[6] Much of the heat went out of the struggle with Glyn's death in 1537 and the seal was set on Bulkeley influence in 1541 when Dr Arthur Bulkeley became bishop of Bangor.

The King's visitors were active in St Asaph diocese as well during the late summer and autumn of 1535. As in Bangor, John Vaughan and Adam Becansaw had taken prompt steps to put an end to the concubinage practised by priests and laymen alike, though their efforts had been undermined by the shameless conduct of their fellow-visitor, Ellis Price,

[5] *L. and P.*, VIII, 832–3.   [6] PRO SP 1/116/117–8; 117/10–11.

who caused scandal by riding about openly with his mistress. They had also commissioned preachers to denounce the pope and his errors, with the result, they claimed, that the people were convinced of how they had previously been deceived by the priests. While the visitors were in the diocese, elaborate manœuvrings were going on to secure the succession to the vacant see. The rival parties competed to gain the ear of the all-powerful Cromwell, with Foulk Salusbury offering to place his deanery at the disposal of the vice-gerent. In the end, however, it was William Barlow, a fiery reformer and client of Anne Boleyn and Cromwell, who was elected on 16 January 1536, only to be translated within months to St Davids.

Before becoming bishop of St Davids, while he was still prior of Haverfordwest, Barlow had already stirred up the waters in south-west Wales in 1534. He had denounced in unmeasured terms the hostility of the clergy and the 'enormous vices, fraudulent exactions and heathen idolatry' of the diocese.[7] Shortly after his appointment as bishop, he had violently locked horns with his clergy over their resistance not merely to his reformed teachings but also to his attempts to enforce what his canons regarded as an unconstitutional extension of his authority over the chapter by seeking to make himself head of it. In the other southern diocese of Llandaff, Athequa's conservative inclinations had led to delays in eliminating 'the corrupt and unsavoury teaching of the bishop of Rome and his disciples'.[8] When Vaughan and Becansaw arrived in November 1535 they deputed preachers to mount the attack on Roman survivals; but, in March 1536, Vaughan wrote despondently that the people 'were never so far out of frame concerning the spiritual jurisdiction by reason of naughty bishops and worse officers'.[9] Hugh Latimer, too, had reason to complain to Thomas Cromwell about what he had heard of the extreme backwardness of the diocese of Llandaff.

THE DISSOLUTION OF THE MONASTERIES

Once the assertion and enforcement of the royal supremacy had been more or less successfully accomplished, exploitation of its financial possibilities could be followed up. An Act of 1534 decreed that annates (i.e., the first year's revenue from an ecclesiastical benefice) were not to be rendered to the papal curia as hitherto, and another statute of the same year stipulated that they were to be paid to the Crown. Some of Cromwell's memoranda compiled about the same time suggest that he was turning over in his mind much more far-reaching plans for making his master one of the richest rulers in Christendom. Whatever enterprises were ultimately embarked

[7] T. Wright, *The Suppression of the Monasteries* (Camden Soc., 1846), p. 79.
[8] *L. and P.*, x, 45–6, 481.   [9] *L. and P.*, xii, ii, 1266.

upon, the Crown would need without delay as comprehensive and accurate a report on the property of the Church as could be compiled. To that end, on 30 January 1535, Cromwell appointed commissioners to conduct the inquiry in the Welsh dioceses. Headed by the bishops and a representative range of leading figures from the local gentry, they were to list all dignities, prebends, benefices, monasteries, and other ecclesiastical institutions and provide a full and accurate return of their possessions and revenues. Theirs was not an easy commission. Sir Richard Bulkeley in north Wales reported how he and his fellows had done their best to get reliable persons to give them true estimates of the value of ecclesiastical preferment but had sometimes found others coming forward with higher figures. Sir William Morgan, who executed the return for Llandaff largely on his own because he found it difficult to get anyone to help him, sent in details for his own area of Monmouthshire which are much the best and fullest for any part of Wales. On the whole, the information provided in the report, known as *Valor Ecclesiasticus*, is reasonably accurate and reliable, even though the monastic assets of which the commissioners took no account meant that their estimates of income were about 20 per cent lower than they should have been.

Meantime, Cromwell was also preparing to make use of the powers conferred upon him as the King's vice-gerent in matters spiritual to appoint his own deputies to visit cathedrals and monastic houses, even those normally exempted from episcopal control. It is usually supposed that the thinly veiled object of the visitation was to provide evidence to justify the dissolution; but the eighty-six questions to be put to the monks, drafted by Richard Layton, were not unreasonable. The visitors for Wales were Dr John Vaughan, probably a Carmarthenshire man, who begged Cromwell to let him have one of the abbeys so that he could do him more service, Dr Adam Becansaw, a canon of St Asaph, and Dr Ellis Price, the notorious 'Doctor Coch' [Red Doctor]. Their visitation took nine months to complete, from August 1535 to April 1536, though they may have spent part of that time in London. In their dozen or so letters from Wales which still survive, the visitors do not appear to have gone out of their way to uncover scandal and, in one instance at least, that relating to Carmarthen Priory, made a point of commending the state of the priory and the behaviour of its head.

During August 1535 they dealt with the unworthy abbot of Valle Crucis, Robert Salusbury (above, pp. 133–4), and reported that the abbey was in great decay and up to its eyes in debt. At Conwy they received the abbot's resignation and replaced him with Ellis Price's brother, the youthful Richard ap Rhys. This they did in the teeth of opposition from Sir Richard Bulkeley, who viewed the visitors, and Ellis Price in particular, with unconcealed distaste, and on 21 November wrote to Cromwell on behalf of the prior of Penmon in Anglesey, 'shut up in his house by Dr. Ellis Price and William Glyn, the King's commissioners and yours'.[10]

By November Vaughan and Becansaw had reached Llandaff but only two letters concerning south Wales monasteries survive from them. In the one Vaughan was severely critical of Monmouth Priory, which had been in deplorable state when the bishop of Hereford deposed the prior in 1534. Vaughan intended to suppress it, 'for it is the voice of the country that whilst you have monks there you shall have neither good rule nor good order'. He added that people reported that other houses, including Tintern, were 'greatly abused'.[11] On the other hand, the comments on Carmarthen were very favourable. It was well built and in good repair; its monks were of good report; they maintained charity and hospitality; and the king of Portugal, no less, had gone out of his way to convey his thanks for the excellent treatment of his merchants.[12] Though fuller visitors' reports of this kind would have been welcome, their scantiness makes very little difference in the sense that the fate of the monasteries did not ultimately depend on the condition of discipline within them. They were to be dissolved not on moral grounds but primarily for financial and political reasons.

What we know of Welsh monasteries from all sources at this time suggests that they had little capacity to withstand the impending dissolution themselves or to inspire others to resist on their behalf. None of the reformed orders—Carthusians, Brigittines, or Observant Friars—from whom came the King's most intransigeant opponents, had taken root in Wales. Some of the houses were deep in debt to influential local notabilities. Valle Crucis was virtually in William Brereton's pocket, and Strata Marcella, largely in ruins in 1529, had actually been sold to Lord Powis before the dissolution, while the steward of Pill, Sir John Wogan, who forbade the monks to lease their estates without his permission, took possession of them after the dissolution. Several of the gentry families who controlled much of monastic life were chiefly concerned to ingratiate themselves with Cromwell so as to be in a favourable position to take advantage of changes in the offing. Included among them were the Bulkeleys, Pennants, Gruffydds of Penrhyn, and the family of Robert ap Rhys, in the north; and the earl of Worcester, Herberts, Devereux, Wogans, Barlows, Mansels, and Sir John Price, in the south. Even Richard ap Rhys, after a difficult year as abbot of Conwy, when he had found it very costly to maintain charity and hospitality in a season of acute scarcity, was primarily concerned to ensure that one of his brothers should be farmer of his house if it were dissolved. In general the attitude of landowners and merchants during these critical months seems to have been

[10] L. and P., IX, 1291.   [11] L. and P., X, 160.   [12] L. and P., X, 1246.

to brace themselves to protect their own interests as officials, lessees, and tenants and to seize any benefits that might accrue to them from the ending of monastic life rather than to take up the cudgels, literally or metaphorically, on behalf of the abbeys over which the sword of Damocles hung.

In March 1536 an Act was passed whereby all monasteries with possessions worth less than a clear yearly value of £200 were to be given up to the King's Highness on the grounds that 'manifest sin, vicious, carnal and abominable living' was rife in those small houses where 'the congregation of religious persons is under the number of twelve'. Although two of the Welsh houses, Tintern and Carmarthen, were actually worth more than £200 and Tintern also maintained the minimum number of thirteen monks, they had all been valued at less than £200 in the *Valor*. Under the Act they should all have been dissolved; but it was necessary to make provision for those monks who wished to continue in the monastic life to be transferred elsewhere, so three houses in Wales, all belonging to the Cistercian Order, were spared. Strata Florida paid £66 for the privilege, Neath £150, and Whitland the huge sum of £400. All three had to exert strenuous efforts to raise the necessary sums by means of leasing land and other devices. All of Whitland's leases were dated later than 1536 and Sir John Price wrote of Leyshon Thomas, abbot of Neath, when his house was on the point of being surrendered, that 'he hath of late dangered himself and his friends very far with the redemption of his house'.[13] Not that it availed them very much, for within two or three years they, too, were extinguished. A few of the smaller Welsh houses, like Brecon, Ewenni, Malpas, or Cardigan, which were daughter houses of the major English monasteries of Battle, Gloucester, Montacute, and Chertsey, managed to eke out an attenuated existence until their mother houses were surrendered.

By the time that the greater monasteries were dissolved the friaries, now in a deplorably reduced condition, had also disappeared. Some of the friars, anticipating the extinction of their houses, had already departed. Behind them they left depleted communities deeply in debt and hopelessly diminished in morale. When, therefore, Richard Ingworth, bishop of Dover and himself a former friar, was appointed to visit the friaries in February 1538, he found them to be a soft target. His tactic was, in the presence of the mayor and aldermen of the town in which the friary stood, to give the inmates an apparent freedom of choice. He disclaimed any authority to suppress them but nevertheless offered to accept their voluntary surrender. It was an approach which rarely failed to produce the desired result, for by 1538 the friars were almost universally in a state of indigence and despair, brought about by the 'failure of their world to

[13] *L. and P.*, x, p. 434.

support them any longer and the failure on their part to hold or recapture the favour of their world'.[14]

In Wales it took Ingworth only three weeks to proceed from his starting-point at Rhuddlan on 17 August, via Denbigh, Bangor, Llanfaes, Ludlow, Brecon, Carmarthen, Haverfordwest, and Cardiff to Newport, where he completed his operations by 8 September. Although he had discovered some sympathy for the friars in Wales, where many pleaded on their behalf for a reprieve—a sympathy borne out by the bequests to friaries being made in wills as late as May 1538—Ingworth had no difficulty in persuading all the Welsh friars to surrender their impoverished houses and attenuated possessions to him. The only friary he found to be in fairly healthy condition was Carmarthen, the largest one in Wales, boasting a double cloister and having fourteen inmates even in 1538. It also possessed a considerable quantity of vestments and furniture, though the fact that some of its possessions were 'abroad' in the town suggests that here, too, attempts had been made by the friars to alienate their goods before the suppression. Most of the other houses had as little left as the Dominican Friary at Cardiff, where vestments worth £7 were missing and 'there is gone many other things of the which we can have no knowledge'.[15] The visitation completed, and inventories compiled of whatever goods and possessions could be sold or leased to the King's advantage, it only remained for the friars to sign the deed of surrender. Finally, in 1540, the houses and possessions of the Order of St John were dissolved. The Commandery of the Knights at Slebech in south-west Wales was wound up, and its possessions and those of the Order in north Wales confiscated.

Once the religious houses had been dissolved, measures had to be devised for dealing with their former inmates, buildings, and possessions. In Wales there were, in all, about 250 monks, nuns, and friars to be resettled. All the former heads of monasteries, in spite of their supposedly 'deplorable lives' to which the Act of 1536 referred, were awarded pensions ranging from the £40 paid to the abbots of the three houses spared in 1536 down to the £4 doled out to the abbot of Grace Dieu and the £3. 6s. 8d. to the abbess of Llanllugan. On the whole they were adequately compensated, especially when, as frequently happened, they acquired ecclesiastical preferment as well, like Leyshon Thomas of Neath's nearby rectory of Cadoxton, valued at £21 a year, or Richard Price of Aberconway's rectorial tithes of Maenan and Llanbadrig in the area where he settled. All those monks still left in the monasteries in 1538–9, as well as some of those whose monasteries had disappeared in 1536, were assigned pensions of the order of £3. 10s. to £4. Such payments were not lavish, amounting to no more than their recipients would have received as

<hr />

[14] Knowles, *Religious Orders*, III, 261.
[15] G. T. Clark, *Cartae et Alia Munimenta* . . . (6 vols. Cardiff, 1910), v, 1873.

stipendiary priests; but still, they provided a minimal subsistence for men who were often too old to make a living in any other way. Furthermore, the pensions were regularly paid. In 1553, nearly twenty years after the dissolution, Welsh monks still figured on Cardinal Pole's list of pensioners, while Richard ap Rhys, so worried about the future in 1536, lived to enjoy his pension until 1589 at least. Those who came off worst were the friars who, having little or no landed possessions for which to be compensated, received no pensions at all. When monastic life came to an end, many of the former religious were given ecclesiastical dispensations allowing them to wear secular dress.[16] Some of them now picked up handsome preferments, including a number of English monks who became bishops in Wales—Holgate at Llandaff, Wharton at St Asaph, and Barlow at St Davids. Welsh monks like Lewis ap Thomas, last abbot of Cymer, who became suffragan bishop of Shrewsbury, and John ap Rhys, last abbot of Strata Marcella, who became dean of Pontesbury, did well enough. Others may have become incumbents of parishes, chantry priests, stipendiary curates, or household chaplains, though in the absence of diocesan registers it is difficult to be quite sure. Some may even have returned to lay life. A handful of the most dedicated and determined in their midst, it has been claimed, withdrew to the wilder, more wooded, and inaccessible regions such as the hills of north Glamorgan around Penrhys, or the more desolate country east of Strata Florida, and there surreptitiously carried on their monastic existence.[17] The evidence on which this suggestion was based, however, is thin and speculative, and it is noticeable that none of these monks ever emerged into the open in Mary's reign when it was safe for them to do so and when their presence would surely have been welcomed as the Queen sought to reinstate monastic life.

As for the considerable body of servants and labourers maintained by each monastery, no evidence exists concerning their fate. What little we know of their numbers suggests that Welsh monasteries had not been 'over-staffed' with menials and it is distinctly possible that most, if not all, of them would be needed by the new owners and lessees of former possessions and would continue to be employed in much the same way as before. It seems unlikely, therefore, that any serious material hardship was caused to monks and their servants. Some of the religious who had no very strong vocation may possibly have welcomed the opportunity of turning their backs on the cloister. What we have no way of measuring or even discovering is the mental or emotional distress which may have been created by turning out into a very different, if not unsympathetic, world men and women who had taken a vow to live the whole of their lives according to the rule of religion, though older and more sentimental

[16] D. S. Chambers, *Faculty Office Registers, 1534–39* (Oxford, 1966).
[17] D. Mathew, *The Celtic Peoples and Renaissance Europe* (London, 1933), pp. 490–4.

accounts of the painful hardships suffered by monks and nuns turned adrift without provision can almost certainly be discounted.

Once a monastery had been dissolved, such of its contents as were moveable or saleable were quickly disposed of. Jewels, plate, cash, and valuable manuscripts were dispatched to the royal treasury. All other assets like glass, vestments, missals, candlesticks, organs, timber, and other furnishings were auctioned on the spot. Many of the monastic churches, especially those belonging to the Benedictines and Augustinians and often located in towns such as Brecon, Abergavenny, Chepstow, or Haverfordwest, had for centuries been used for parish as well as monastic worship. They and a number of outlying Cistercian chapels built for the convenience of worshippers were either sold or given to parishioners to meet their continuing needs. So, too, was Margam abbey church, though most of the Cistercian churches, where they were not plundered down to their foundations, have, like Valle Crucis or Strata Florida, survived only as romantic ruins preserving nostalgic recollections for poets and other sensitive souls of an age of devotion long dead. A small number were turned into schools. Strata Marcella's Capel Dolwen, and three friaries—Carmarthen, Brecon, and Bangor—became grammar schools. Iron and lead belonging to the monasteries were greatly prized. Bells were cut down and sold to local men or even distant merchants; like the two from Llanllŷr and four from Carmarthen acquired by Sir William Thomas, or Margam's six, Neath's four, and Grace Dieu's two, all sold to a London merchant and shipped to Bristol for him. Lead from the roofs was stripped and melted down for the King's use or sold. Basingwerk's lead went to repair Holt Castle and Margam's, valued at £372, was sold to three Glamorgan merchants. Official instructions to royal agents in charge of the dissolved houses ordered them to pull down to the ground the walls of churches and buildings there; but demolition cost money and these men contented themselves with making places uninhabitable by removing roofs and stairs. Many of the surviving structures were exceptionally convenient sources of timber, stone, and glass, and were consequently the objects of extensive plundering. Some of it was authorized and undertaken on behalf of the Crown. Stones and timber were taken from Maenan at a cost of £150 to repair Caernarfon Castle, and others were taken for use by purchasers of sites and buildings, like John Bradshaw at St Dogmael's. Much was unauthorized, like Nicholas Purcell's depredations at Strata Marcella, where he made a handsome profit out of sales of stone, glass, and timber, or those of local men at Cardiff who carried away stones, timber, windows, and tiles from the Grey Friary. A number of religious houses were snapped up by prominent gentry families to be adapted or transformed into dwelling-houses; thus, John Price acquired Brecon, Rice Mansel Margam, Edward Carne Ewenni, and Roger Barlow Slebech.

More important than the fate of their buildings was that of the monasteries' temporal and spiritual possessions. Had they all remained in royal possession the revenues from them would have more than doubled the King's income. The original intention was probably for the Crown to retain a large part of the gains from the biggest measure of land nationalization in British history, though from the outset Henry and Cromwell were evidently prepared to acquiesce in gifts and sales to some of their favourites. From 1535 onwards they had found themselves inundated with requests for concessions in the form of gifts, leases, or purchases of monastic land. As early as March 1537, the site and much of the possessions of Tintern had been bestowed on the royal favourite, the earl of Worcester, to compensate him for losses sustained in the abolition of the Marcher lordships. Immediately after the dissolution, leases for twenty-one years of vacant sites, demesnes, and rectories not farmed out were concluded at rents based on the assessments made in 1535. The majority of these early leases were entered into by members of the royal household or men in close touch with it. Three of those connected with monastic visitations who took advantage of their inside information and connections to obtain leases of Welsh houses were John Price (Brecon Priory), Edward Carne (Ewenni), and John Vaughan (Grace Dieu, Pembroke, and Whitland). From 1539 onwards the Crown found itself obliged to begin selling former monastic lands on an appreciable scale, ordinarily at the rate of twenty years' purchase. The first sales in Wales were recorded on 26 February 1539 when Cardigan Priory and three of its rectories were sold to William Cavendish, auditor of the Court of Augmentations. There was something of a lull in 1541–2, but after 1543 lavish expenditure on wars with Scotland and France, and an urgent need for money, led to further sales. They continued during the reigns of Edward VI, Mary, and Elizabeth, by which time a large proportion of the former monastic possessions had been disposed of.

Only a very small amount of this property came back to the Church or to educational foundations. The newly created dioceses of Gloucester, Bristol, and Chester were allowed to take over some of the former interests in Wales of the abbeys of Tewkesbury, Gloucester, St Augustine's Bristol, and St Werburgh's Chester; and four grammar schools were founded out of part of the buildings or endowments of Abergavenny, Bangor, Brecon, and Carmarthen. Nor, apart from Tintern, was any significant part of monastic land given away or disposed of on favourable terms. Most of it was bought in hard cash; for rarely less than the market rate of twenty years' purchase, and sometimes for considerably more, as when Sir Edward Carne paid no less than twenty-seven years' purchase for the Austin Friary at Newport. Neither were any Welsh properties bought by large-scale speculators, other than for quick resale to local men. Sooner or later, nearly all the gains accrued to the native landowners. The biggest buyers of Welsh monastic land were local gentry who made direct application to the Court of Augmentations for the properties they wished to purchase. Often they were lessees of sites and demesnes who now wished to acquire larger estates—Sir John Williams at Cwm-hir, John Scudamore at Dore, John Price at Brecon, Rice Mansel at Margam, John Bradshaw at St Dogmael's, Edward Carne at Ewenni, and Nicholas Arnold at Llanthony were among the most notable examples. The only individuals who could thus benefit were those who had the ready cash or the credit to raise it quickly. In a number of instances they were men who had done well out of service in war or diplomacy to the Crown, in trade, at the law, or by all or a number of these means. To acquire their new estates they were often able to raise impressive sums of money. Rice Mansel, for example, put up no less than £2,482 for the estates of Margam, which he bought in four instalments between 1540 and 1557. James Gunter, who bought the site and lands of Abergavenny, was only a minor royal servant but was evidently regarded as worthy of favour and was allowed to pay by instalments the large sums needed for his purchases.

Gunter was one of those speculators who usually made substantial profits out of his deals; for example, in 1545 he bought the manor of Priorsmead for £40 and in 1554 sold it to David Lewis for £300. But many of the purchasers, though not without an eye to business, were men more concerned with prestige than immediate profit. There is little evidence that they were unduly oppressive or inequitable in their treatment of tenants. At all events, there are very few of the protracted lawsuits that might have been expected to result in so litigious an age if they had been. Often, indeed, the boot was on the other foot, with new monastic proprietors complaining of being unable to get former monastic tenants to fulfil their obligations. The Crown had gone to great lengths to secure existing tenant interests and had, thereby, probably ensured that the dissolution could be achieved without upheaval or protest.

Nor can the purchasers of monastic land be said to have constituted a 'new' gentry. Certainly, a new family might be established in a county, such as the Barlows at Slebech, the Bradshaws at St Dogmael's, or the Steadmans at Strata Florida in 1571. But, in general, the families that profited most were well-established and rising clans. In Glamorgan and Monmouthshire, the two counties with much the highest concentration of monastic land in Wales, those who benefited most handsomely—the Somerset earls of Worcester, the Herberts, the Morgans of Llantarnam, Arnolds of Llanthony, Williamses of Llangybi, Gunters of Abergavenny, Mansels of Margam, Carnes of Ewenni, Stradlings of St Donat's, and Lewises of Y Fan—were not new families but their stake in monastic property undoubtedly served to emphasize the difference between them and the less successful ones. It has often been suggested that their acquisitions from this source, especially when paid for at the market price, helped to create a vested interest that ensured the permanence of the Reformation. That did not necessarily follow by any means. A number of the Welsh families which gained most out of monastic properties were stubborn recusants: the Edwardses of Chirk, the Wynns of Melai, the Mostyns of Talacre, and the Owens of Plas-du, in the north; the earls of Worcester, Morgans of Llantarnam, Barlows of Slebech and Turbervilles of Pen-llin, in the south.

The dissolution was unquestionably a landmark in the history of religion in this country and yet it is not easy to assess the gain and loss which resulted when the monasteries disappeared after four hundred years of existence. Without doubt, the loss to art and architecture was considerable and with the religious houses disappeared many of the finest treasures in sculpture, woodcarving, glass, plate, and vestments from a country not overendowed with them. Scholarship and learning were despoiled when monastic libraries were often dispersed and lost, though some of the new owners like John Price and Thomas Stradling were careful to preserve what they could. Welsh poetry was also deprived of a number of its most lavish patrons when the Cistercian abbeys disappeared. Economically and socially, the monks were no longer the pioneers they had been of yore; formerly leaders in wool production, advanced agriculture, and industrial initiative, they had long been content to surrender to laymen much of the responsibility for the direction of their economic fortunes. Nor is there much evidence to suggest that the change-over from monastic to secular landlords led to any significant differences in the management of estates, partly because laymen had been running them previously and also because the Crown had leaned over backwards to protect tenants' interests. Neither had the monks been conspicuously good rectors of their appropriated churches, though admittedly the laymen into whose hands they now passed were certainly no better. The real criticism in this respect should be applied to the government for failing to see that tithes were returned to parishes whence they came to be applied to worthwhile purposes. Though the monasteries were still maintaining charity and hospitality, much of the inspiration and momentum had ebbed from these functions. Their charitable donations tended to be perfunctory, haphazard, and not very closely related to need; their hospitality had too often become flawed by ostentation and luxury which bore too little relation to the Rule of St Benedict. Even so, in a poor upland country like Wales these activities were missed all the more than they might have been in south-eastern England.

In the last resort, however, it is as centres of religious and spiritual life that the monasteries must be judged. Reduced in numbers, zeal, and morale, the monks were but a shadow of what they had once been and now seemed incapable of giving a lead or inspiring devotion. It could be argued, nevertheless, that the life of the whole community was much the poorer when the acts of worship and prayer offered on its behalf by the monks were extirpated. All that can be said on that score is that some of the most devoted lay Catholic families and individuals did not appear to wish to defend the monasteries nor, indeed, did they refuse to participate in and benefit from the dissolution. In four hundred years of existence the monasteries had made an immense contribution to the secular and spiritual life of Wales; but for a long while before their extinction they had been a sadly dwindling asset. That is not to say that they could not, even in 1536, have been reformed had the will to do so existed on the part of the monks themselves, the lay population, or, above all, the Crown.

THE LAST YEARS OF HENRY VIII'S REIGN, 1536–47

During the last ten years of his reign the King's overriding objective was to maintain the unity of his realm, if necessary at the price of burning those heretics, such as Thomas Capper of Cardiff (1542), who denied transubstantiation, while at the same time executing any 'traitors' like Edward Powell (1540), who still acknowledged the authority of Rome. Some willingness to countenance cautious reform was shown from time to time in the choice of bishops. Among those elevated to the Welsh sees was one of the keenest Protestants of all, the pushing and impetuous William Barlow, who also took the opportunity of introducing ardent young reformers like Thomas Young, Rowland Meyrick, and George Constantine into his diocese. Other milder and more reticent reformers were Wharton, bishop of St Asaph, 1535–54, Bulkeley at Bangor, 1541–51, Holgate of Llandaff, 1537–45, and his successor, Kitchen, 1545–63. Holgate, particularly, was an able man of scholarly bent who, unfortunately for his see, was whisked away to serve on the Council of the North in 1538. Meanwhile, Barlow was all too present and active at St Davids to suit the taste of the more conservative of the brethren—clerics and laymen.

Another step away from long-cherished observances was the campaign which followed on from the Injunctions of 1538 against offering money and other gifts at centres of pilgrimage, especially those associated with cathedrals or religious houses. Officially, the move was one directed against idolatry but another compelling motive was the confiscation for the King's use of the rich treasures at the shrines. One of the pilgrim attractions most resorted to in north Wales was that of Derfel Gadarn (Derfel the Mighty) at Llandderfel, connected with neither cathedral nor monastery. Its downfall was attributed by Ellis Gruffydd to friction between the parson of Llandderfel and Ellis Price, who reported very adversely on it to Cromwell. Relics seized by Ingworth when visiting the friaries were 'Malchus' ear'[18] and another described by him as the 'holiest relic in all north Wales',[19] worth twenty marks a year to Bangor's Dominicans. Two of the most celebrated shrines now attacked were Winifred's Well, associated with Basingwerk Abbey, and the shrine of the BVM at Penrhys in the Rhondda Valley, part of the possessions of Llantarnam Abbey. Fearing that public opinion at Penrhys, seemingly unmoved by the fall of the monasteries, might be very much more hostile at the removal of the Virgin's image, the Privy Council ordered William Herbert to take it down as secretly as possible. It and Derfel's image were carried off to Smithfield to be burnt. In south-west Wales, at the priories of Cardigan and Haverfordwest, Barlow suppressed the images of the Virgin and their associated miraculous tapers, reputed to burn without ever wasting. He was even more delighted to be able to set upon the shrine of St David at his cathedral church, despite incurring the wrath of his canons by doing so. The other cathedral shrine known to have suffered was the richly endowed one dedicated to Sts Teilo, Dyfrig, and Eudogwy at Llandaff, where the canons tried to forestall expropriation by dividing the treasures amongst themselves, only to be detected and punished by Cromwell's agents.

More positive steps towards reform were outlined in proposals put forward by Bishops Wharton and Barlow. The former wanted to move his cathedral from St Asaph to either Wrexham or Denbigh and found a grammar school for the instruction of his clergy. Barlow likewise wanted to transfer his see from St Davids to Carmarthen, in order to wipe out the 'memorial monuments' of Rome's 'puppetry'. The move would also have brought the cathedral clergy more firmly under his control. He, too, wanted to set up a grammar school, because his clergy were 'unlearned, the people ignorant and the English tongue nothing preferred'; and finally, he proposed to endow regular preaching in English.[20] There was much to be said for both bishops' schemes. Wrexham and Carmarthen were two of the biggest and liveliest market towns in Wales; and in both dioceses preaching and grammar schools were badly needed. Nothing came of these plans, however; though in 1541 Barlow was able to set up a grammar school, not in Carmarthen but in Brecon. Barlow was too hot a gospeller, too arrogant and tactless in his approach, too selfish in pursuing his own and his family's interests, and too out of sympathy with the needs of the large Welsh-speaking majority of his flock, to succeed.

What Barlow and others had done, nevertheless, was to give a marked

---

[18] Reputedly the ear of the high priest's servant, struck off by Peter when Christ was being arrested.

[19] Wright, *Suppression*, p. 212.

[20] G. Williams, *Welsh Reformation Essays* (Cardiff, 1967), pp. 110–24.

stimulus to the use of the vernacular languages in worship and devotion. As early as 1535 one of Barlow's servants living in Tenby had a copy of the English New Testament, to the scandal of many conservatives; and in 1538 the bishop had ordered the prior of Cardigan to preach and declare the epistle and the gospel in the 'mother tongue'—presumably in English. In the English-speaking towns and along the borders some may well have become familiar with these vernacular devotions. The Marian heretic and martyr, Rawlins White of Cardiff, at the time of his trial gave the firm impression that he and his associates had been reading the English Bible for many years, possibly since Henry VIII's reign. In 1546 Richard Devereux, son of Lord Ferrers, and his chaplain were brought before the Privy Council on charges of Protestant heresy. An occasional Welsh will, too, like that of Sir Thomas Gamage of Coety (1543), is redolent of Protestant influence in its phraseology and makes no provision for prayers or masses after death.

A hesitant start was also being made in catering for the needs of the mainly monoglot Welsh-speaking population. In 1542 Bishop Bulkeley of Bangor required his clergy, schoolmasters, and heads of households to give religious instruction to their charges in Welsh, though the vernacular literature available to help them to do so was scarce and confined to manuscript sources. Before 1543, however, Tyndale's English New Testament had become popular enough in Wales for parts of it, along with extracts from Cranmer's litany and order of communion, to be translated into Welsh, presumably in support of budding Protestant sympathies in the dioceses of Llandaff and St Davids. In the last year of Henry's reign there occurred a pioneer development of the utmost importance, when Sir John Price of Brecon, inspired by a variety of motives—religious, humanist, and political—published at his own expense the first Welsh printed book, *Yny Lhyvyr Hwnn* . . . . It was a relatively straightforward religious primer, containing the Creed, Lord's Prayer, and Ten Commandments among other things. In the preface he deplored the widespread ignorance of religious teaching and urged his countrymen to take advantage of the printing-press to lighten their darkness.

All Henry's policies had been received in Wales with virtually no overt opposition; not on account of any profound or general desire for change or reform, but because of the combined impact of royal authority and the willingness of the gentry to co-operate with it or, at least, not to oppose it. The increasing hold of the Crown on the Welsh in terms of its psychological appeal, the inducements it could offer, and still more in its greater ability to enforce its will effectively, has already been traced. So, too, has the rise to authority of the native gentry. The latter's power depended largely on being *en rapport* with the Crown; for even the most influential offfice-holders—Somersets, Devereux, Bulkeleys, and the like—were virtually

Tudor creations. There was, moreover, no really profound attachment to a Church which had such grave institutional weaknesses as an alien, largely absentee higher clergy, an unlearned priesthood, monastic houses in decline, and an ineffective administration; and one which was widely regarded as being overendowed with material possessions and excessive jurisdictional privileges. Laymen had already installed themselves in key positions as officials, lessees, and almost *de facto* possessors of Church property. They stood to gain much from royal policy and a great deal would depend on the manner in which innovations in the relationship between Church and State were presented to them. If the Reformation were portrayed as an act of stronger and more effectual government, in which a masterful king deposed a distant foreign pontiff, and clipped the endowments and pretensions of ecclesiastics to redistribute them in favour of the laity, then far from being resented, it might be welcomed. All the more so if his Welsh subjects regarded Henry, as he did himself, as an orthodox believer, whose changes made little or no difference to the worship, appearance, or language of the churches as they had always known them. Their customary beliefs, assumptions, and practices could be maintained with little modification under such a regime. Under his son's rule circumstances would be very different.

THE REIGN OF EDWARD VI, 1547–53

Whereas under Henry VIII the Reformation had in the main been a political revolution, during the six-year reign of his son, the boy-king Edward VI, it assumed the dimensions of a religious transformation: first under the direction of the duke of Somerset from 1547 to 1549 and later, from 1549 to 1553, under the still more radical and dominating duke of Northumberland. The repercussions of change radiated to the remotest parishes and could hardly be ignored by even the humblest of Edward's subjects. Broadly speaking, two aspects of policy were enforced: first, the elimination of practices and beliefs associated with the Roman Church and the implementation of reformed doctrine and worship by means of the English Books of Common Prayer of 1549 and 1552; and second, the further confiscation of ecclesiastical property, for which the changes in doctrine were offered as a justification, though more truly they were little better than an excuse for lay expropriation.

Almost immediately after seizing power Somerset prepared the ground for reform by repealing the conservative Six Articles Act of Henry's reign, measures against heresy, and restrictions on reading and circulating the English Bible. Early in 1548, sweeping changes in popular religious practice were introduced when traditional medieval observances, such as pilgrimages, keeping of holy days, creeping to the cross on Good Friday (when the clergy and people kissed a crucifix on the sanctuary steps), or burning candles at Candlemas, were abrogated. The mayor and corporation of the biggest Welsh town, Carmarthen, to conform to these instructions, were obliged to take a priest, Nicholas Byford, to the Court of Chancery for persisting in observing holy days as before. The appearance of parish churches was also drastically modified when images, pictures, and frescoes were ordered to be removed or defaced, and roods and roodlofts were to be mutilated. In the same year, an English Order of Communion was published. In 1549 the Latin services were abolished and replaced by those of the English Book of Common Prayer, the use of which in all churches, including those of Wales, was legally enforced from Whit Sunday (9 June) onwards by an Act of Uniformity. This created grave dilemmas for those parts of the realm like Wales where English was not the language of everyday use. A French version was prepared for Calais and the Channel Islands; but although John Oswen, a Worcester printer, was given the right to print prayer books for Wales, this almost certainly meant producing copies of the English version for use in Wales. To a minority of the population, the new order of worship, though a startling novelty, was at least intelligible and some may have welcomed it. But to most of the Welsh-speaking population it must have been almost completely incomprehensible and unacceptable. We do not know how they, or a number of their priests whose knowledge of English was sketchy, made shift with this new prayer book. Possibly some of the officiants resorted to subterfuges known to be common enough elsewhere of mumbling the words indistinctly so that no one knew quite what was being said, and continuing to intone and chant in the former fashion, while many of their congregation carried rosaries, burnt candles, crossed themselves, beat their breasts, and generally comported themselves as before. That, at least, was what happened in a town as important as Carmarthen, where Protestant influences had made considerable headway.

In 1549, also, priests were given the legal right to take wives. Though many of them had been 'married' previously, Bishop Ferrar of St Davids deemed it necessary to defend the practice over and over again in his sermons until his hearers complained that they 'wearied with hearing one tale'. In 1550 it was ordered that altars, hitherto the centre-piece of worship, should be taken down and replaced with communion tables: an outward reflection of a profound shift away from the concept of the mass as a sacrifice in the direction of a commemorative communion of all believers. One of the first places anywhere in the kingdom to carry out this instruction was Carmarthen, where a group of ardent reformers were so insistent on change that they provoked fierce altercations, in the course of which the communion table was moved a number of times within a short space. A leading figure who favoured the destruction of the altars was

William Salesbury, author of an English pamphlet which assailed them as the pope's buttresses.

It was Salesbury, too, who in 1551 published his *Kynniver Llith a Ban*, a translation of the epistles and gospels of the Prayer Book and the first printed version of substantial portions of the Scriptures in Welsh. Since 1547 he had urged upon his countrymen the indispensable need for a Welsh translation of the Bible. In his introduction to his new book he recalled how he had been touched to the quick by the thought of how the Welsh were 'ignorant of sacred knowledge yet burning more than most men with a fervent zeal for God'. His appeal to the Welsh bishops to give official authorization to his translation went unheeded, but it was used and copies of it survived into Elizabeth's reign. In spite of its many excellent qualities, it suffered from Salesbury's idiosyncratic views about language and was less useful than it might otherwise have been.[21] In the same year, 1551, Bishop Bulkeley of Bangor issued articles of inquiry to discover whether or not the clergy of his diocese—of all the Welsh dioceses the one in which English was likely to be least understood—had acquired English Bibles and Prayer Books, whether any prayed on beads or said masses, and whether there were any images, tabernacles, shrines, or feigned miracles in churches. His inquiries give us a broad hint of how little change there had been in many places. A year later, the Second Prayer Book, more unmistakably reformist and far less of a compromise than the first, was published and its use enforced everywhere by a Second Act of Uniformity.

These transformations of doctrine and worship were accompanied by further raids on chantries and other church property. Occasioned partly by changing spiritual attitudes towards the efficacy of prayers and masses for the dead, they were even more obviously the outcome of thinly disguised material cupidity. Following an Act of 1545 against chantries, which was never implemented, a fresh Act was passed in 1547. A report was drawn up in time for the Act to operate from Easter 1548. It not only gave details about the larger institutions in some of the more important towns but also included valuable information about a number of more modest endowments sufficient only to maintain a light, add to a priest's income, or contribute to the repair of a church. It also gave useful estimates of the number of communicants in some places and details about plate, vestments, and other possessions. All were now dissolved and treated much as the monasteries had been. Priests were allocated pensions of £4–5; and readily realizable assets like plate, vestments, or jewels were sold locally or sent to London. Houses or lands were leased or sold, with no shortage of willing buyers for compact blocks of property. Sir William Herbert bought a good deal of chantry property at Cowbridge, Llantwit, Caerleon, Newport, and Usk,

<hr>

[21] *Kynniver Llith a Ban*, introd.

and his brother, Sir George Herbert, picked up the former large hospital at Swansea. Not a little of the property was 'lost' or confused, accidentally or deliberately, as is revealed by commissions of concealment appointed well into the seventeenth century. Pious hopes expressed in the preamble to the Act that the proceeds of the dissolution would be used to found schools or be devoted to charity went unrealized. No new schools or hospitals took the place of those which disappeared. In addition, some towns like Cardiff or Tenby felt the loss of chantry income which had previously been used to subsidize municipal amenities, such as quays and bridges. Chantries had impinged much more directly than monasteries upon the religious and social life of ordinary people, especially in urban communities, and their disappearance must surely have fuelled dislike.

If attacks on chantries were unpopular, the confiscation of the treasures of parish churches was probably even more hotly resented. First mooted as early as 1551, the scheme was not put into execution until April 1553 and was still incomplete when Edward VI died in July. The returns for this act of spoliation are complete only for one Welsh county, Glamorgan; but if the consequences there were typical, then most Welsh churches were deprived of treasured possessions. The Glamorgan commissioners summoned representatives from each parish to present an inventory of parish plate, ornaments, vestments, and other valuables. Most of these had been rendered superfluous by the liturgical changes of the Second Prayer Book and were confiscated in the King's name. Many never reached the royal treasury, however, but were appropriated by Sir George Herbert and Sir Rice Mansel, the local commissioners appointed to act for the King. Others, like the 292 oz. of Llandaff's cathedral plate, sold for £73, half its real value, only benefited the archdeacon who had purloined it.

Serious losses were caused by the pressures exerted on episcopal and cathedral property by powerful laymen. Already, in 1546, Barlow of St Davids had alienated the valuable manor of Lamphey in favour of the Devereux family, in return for inadequate compensation in the form of tithe. Not a little of the troubles of his successor were caused by his efforts to recover property squeezed from Barlow by powerful laymen. In 1553 the manor of Llandaff, responsible for one-third of the bishop's income, was acquired by George Mathew, who had married into the family of the earl of Pembroke. Godwin, a later bishop of Llandaff, described Bishop Kitchen, who agreed to the transaction, as the 'calamity of the see', who had 'sold in parcels all the episcopal farms with the exception of a very few, and let out the rest on very long leases, receiving extremely small payments'.[22] Well might Bishop Babington aver with rueful humour that he was bishop of Aff, because all the land had gone! In the northern

---

[22] E. J. Newell, *Llandaff* (London, 1902), p. 143.

diocese of St Asaph, Sir John Salusbury had obtained illegal possession of the chapter seal and was using it for forged leases with the connivance of his kinsman, the dean. The attitude of such men was admitted by Sir William Petre who, in a rare moment of honesty, confessed, 'We, which talk much of Christ', have left 'fishing for men and fish again in the tempestuous seas of this world for gain and wicked mammon'.[23]

Of Welsh people's reactions to this spate of revolutionary changes we have conflicting evidence. On the one hand, there was a small minority which received them favourably. Apart from those who gained from the plunder, there was a handful of intellectuals, of whom Salesbury was the most prominent, who welcomed them effusively, though they were convinced that the Reformation could make little headway among their compatriots until it was presented in Welsh. The gentleman-poet, Gruffudd ab Ieuan ap Llywelyn Fychan, voiced Protestant convictions and condemned the relics of 'superstition'. In some of the larger towns, notably Cardiff and Carmarthen, and conceivably others for which no evidence has survived, there was a reforming minority which read English Bibles, listened eagerly to sermons, and called for wholesale modifications, even censuring a bishop like Ferrar for being too slow-moving.

Our knowledge of the majority comes mainly from the poets, though Bishop Ferrar admitted that in Carmarthen a multitude of medieval practices survived and had to be tolerated. The pace of reforming change there was deeply unpopular and provoked what Ferrar described as 'the grudge of the people' to such an extent that he seriously feared rebellion in support of the West Country Rising of 1549. The criticisms of the poets were so indignant that it could hardly have been safe for them to make such denunciations public until Mary was on the throne. Siôn Brwynog, though he had spoken of Henry VIII with admiration, made a furious onslaught on Edwardian changes. Contrasting the two faiths, old and new, he proceeded to attack in anger and outrage the married clergy, the absence of masses and confession, and the 'icy coldness' of the churches without altars, candles, incense, or holy oil. He accused the priests of not understanding the Prayer Book when they read it.[24] In south Wales Thomas ab Ieuan ap Rhys was no less condemnatory, denouncing Protestant teaching as an alien English faith [ffydd Sayson] imposed on the Welsh against their will. He flayed the alterations in religion and the appearance of the churches— now bare and empty as barns; and contemptuously dismissed the new-style married clergy as 'conceited goats'.[25] That the poets spoke for the majority we need hardly doubt. The Reformation, presented in a foreign tongue and accompanied by the abrupt destruction of many features of parish church and popular worship and practice that had been interwoven with

---

[23] W. G. Hoskins, *The Age of Plunder* (London, 1976), p. 131.
[24] Williams, *Welsh Ref. Essays*, p. 49. [25] *GCH*, IV, 218–19.

the fabric of the people's lives since childhood, might almost have been calculated to give the maximum offence. During these years there may have been a real danger of rebellion in Wales, and anxiety was expressed about the possibility of serious trouble in 1549, 1551, and 1552–3. That it never came cannot be attributed to any absence of strong dislike of the new regime; rather is it to be explained by the continuing loyalty of aristocrats as powerful as the earl of Pembroke, the Herbert clan, the earls of Worcester, and the Devereux, in the south, and of notable gentry figures like the Salusburys, Bulkeleys, and Prices, in the north. All had lined their own pockets handsomely and consolidated their positions of influence during Edward's reign.

THE MARIAN REACTION, 1553–8

The fidelity of these notabilities was to be acutely tested at the beginning of Mary's reign. Some of them had been drawn into Northumberland's conspiracies to divert the succession, including Walter Devereux, Viscount Hereford, Sir Richard Bulkeley, Ellis Price, and much the most significant of them all, William Herbert, earl of Pembroke. Lady Jane Grey was actually proclaimed queen at two places at least, Beaumaris and Denbigh; and Pembroke's task was to have been to hold Wales securely for Northumberland. He was, however, at best a very tepid participant in these plans and he quickly deserted to Mary's cause. The new queen was received by the Welsh with unmistakable enthusiasm; but as the rightful heir to her father far more than as a Catholic claimant to the throne. A few men, Welsh by birth or association, such as William Thomas, former clerk to the Privy Council, Sir James Crofts, and Sir Nicholas Arnold, were implicated in plots to raise rebellion in Wales in conjunction with the Wyatt Rising. Nothing came of them and the loyalty of Wales was strongly reaffirmed.

In the autumn of 1553, without any Act of Parliament or proclamation, Catholic worship was increasingly reintroduced in piecemeal and haphazard fashion, and was welcomed by the poets with open arms. Siôn Brwynog acclaimed the return of the 'old masses' and the 'privilege of the saints' as 'God's right hand come to make us whole'. This may have been the voice of the majority, though one cannot help wondering what were the reactions of those once-vocal minorities of reformers in Carmarthen and Cardiff, or Protestant clerics like Thomas Young or Rowland Meyrick. By 1554, following Mary's marriage to Philip of Spain and the return of Cardinal Pole, the Queen embarked on a more stringent policy designed to eradicate Protestantism and restore Catholicism in full. Between the spring of 1554 and that of 1555 active steps were taken against the married clergy, anti-papal legislation repealed, the schism with Rome ended, heresy laws revived, and the burning of notorious heretics begun. In some places, unyielding opposition was offered by a hard core of Protestant bishops, clergy, middle-class men, and artisans. They had but few representatives in Wales. The only Protestant bishop was Robert Ferrar, who was already in prison. A number of other clergy were proceeded against for marriage rather than heresy; in the diocese of St Davids something like one in six of them, and in Bangor about one in eight, were deprived for this reason. Many, if they consented to part from their wives, were shuffled round to other benefices—at least ten of them in Bangor alone. The number of deprivations for marriage was unexpectedly large in Wales and occasioned more upheaval among the clergy than any other change during the century. Only a small number lost their livings for heresy, however; and some of them, like Thomas Young and Richard Davies, both to be Elizabethan bishops, went into exile. Most of the others stayed in this country, not a few of them resorting to such dubious practices as entering into fraudulent leases of their benefices with relatives or friends so as to safeguard an income for the support of themselves and their families. What was much more typical was that a large number of the clergy, including three out of four bishops, were able to comply with Mary's requirement with the same obliging pliability they had shown in respect of earlier changes. One with a particularly supple conscience was Ellis Price. Agent of Thomas Cromwell and later of Northumberland, he remained as chancellor of St Asaph and lay rector of Llanuwchllyn, Llandrillo, and Llangwm; yet in 1553 he was MP for Merioneth and sheriff in 1555, but was still in a position to be recommended warmly as bishop of Bangor in 1565. If leading figures like Price could thus trim their sails so readily it was hardly to be wondered at that hundreds of parish priests, beneficed and unbeneficed, should accept the government's dictates and keep their own counsel about the rights and wrongs of the matter.

For the laity, the restoration of Catholic belief and worship caused less disturbance than for the clergy. In the eyes of many the Edwardian revolution had slighted the fabric of the faith with almost intolerable abruptness and lack of preparation. Its English liturgy was neither as familiar nor as reassuring as the Latin rite, nor even more intelligible. In addition, much revulsion had been aroused when the Church had been robbed of its possessions and stripped of its beauty by greedy pillaging hands acting under the pretext of reform. None the less, the general picture among laity and clergy alike was one of caution, apathy, confusion, or even demoralization as a result of a bewildering succession of changes. Most of the politically conscious gentry were willing to conform to the Church 'by law established' rather than to the pope's revived authority, but on the tacit understanding that their obedience did not require of them anything more than outward acquiescence. The mass of the population, in so far as it had views at all, seemed content to follow the gentry's lead. None of those who had acquired former Church possessions showed the slightest inclination to part with them; not even Edward Carne of Ewenni or William Morgan of Llantarnam, both staunch Catholics, the former Mary's ambassador at Rome and the latter encouraging renewed pilgrimages to Penrhys. But the gentry were not unwilling to connive at the revival of medieval statutes against heresy. Under the authority of such legislation three were burnt in Wales—Robert Ferrar and Rawlins White in 1555, and William Nichol in 1558. The first two were among the earliest Marian martyrs and their fate was intended to frighten other Protestants in the south-west and south-east into submission. The tactic may well have succeeded, since neither district figures thereafter in the annals of heresy. The fewness of these martyrdoms has often been cited as proof of the lack of Protestant sympathizers in Wales. But too much can be made of the point; the intensity of persecution varied widely and depended not only on the number of heretics but also on the zeal of individual bishops. Much depended, too, on the degree of social influence enjoyed by Protestants. Upper-class reformers were usually able to depend on the protection of family to escape punishment. Neither Sir John Perrot nor William Salesbury, in spite of strong Protestant sympathies, suffered serious inconvenience at this time. Other heretics—mostly clerics and less than a dozen from Wales in all—found safety from persecution by going into exile.

To dwell only on these repressive aspects of Mary's regime is to do it less than justice. Cardinal Pole's overriding concern was not to suppress heresy but to encourage genuine Catholic reform. To this end he secured the appointment in Wales of ardent reformers of the calibre of William Glyn, bishop of Bangor, Thomas Goldwell, bishop of St Asaph, Gruffudd Robert, and Morys Clynnog. He also encouraged Bishop Henry Morgan of St Davids, Kitchen of Llandaff, and Goldwell of St Asaph in their strenuous efforts to recover possessions pillaged from their dioceses by laymen. At St Asaph, where the cathedral was in 'great ruin and decay', 'destitute of decent and convenient ornaments' needed for services,[26] the resolute Goldwell was undeterred by the influence wielded locally by the Salusburys and Conways in his campaign to recover lost possessions. He also summoned a synod in 1556 and issued injunctions to his clergy designed to improve their morals and behaviour. There are indications that the reforming efforts of these clerics were beginning to bear fruit when Mary's short and unhappy reign came to an end in 1558.

Though the events of the decade from 1547 to 1558 had served to draw the lines of demarcation more sharply and irreconcilably between

---

[26] G. Williams, 'Wales and the Reign of Mary I', *WHR*, x (1981), 355.

Catholics and Protestants, by 1558 the large majority of the people were not pledged to either group. Most of the Welsh were admittedly conservative by inclination and addicted to customary practices, from habit rather than conviction. In all ranks of society prevailed a mass of uncertainty, time-serving, incomprehension, and inertia. The upper classes wanted primarily to see the whole structure of authority, central and local, securely maintained and were more concerned to preserve their own interests than to uphold any religious dogma. A legitimate government, whatever its complexion, which guaranteed them these, would get their support. If Mary's reign had lasted, say, another ten to fifteen years it might all have been very different. With the advantages of a Catholic sovereign and establishment, bishops of the calibre of Goldwell and Clynnog, and exposure to the full inspiration of the Council of Trent and revived Catholicism, enough impression might have been made on clergy and laity to have created a powerful and instructed Catholic opposition. As it was, Mary's reign had lasted only five unsuccessful years, being bedevilled by military defeat, disastrous harvests, and decimating outbreaks of disease, as well as envenomed religious animosities. Even so, it had not been a complete failure. The foundations of Welsh Counter-Reformation opposition to Elizabeth had been laid during her half-sister's reign; its leaders would be men brought forward by Pole—Goldwell, Clynnog, Robert, and Morgan Phillips—and its main supporters some of the families which traced the origins of their militant Catholicism back to these years. But what the period from 1527 to 1558 had shown, and the Elizabethan experience would confirm, was that the support of the monarch and his government was extremely significant, if not decisive, in religion. Without a Catholic ruler the Catholic opposition had scant hope of victory. That is why the Marian interlude provided the Catholic Church with a last chance of success, which it was unable to consolidate. The long era of the erastian and cautiously reforming Elizabeth would seize the opportunity to secure the foundations of an Anglican establishment.

CHAPTER 13

THE REFORMATION SECURED, 1558–1603

THE ELIZABETHAN SETTLEMENT, 1558–70

AT her accession Elizabeth faced a situation calling for the utmost circumspection on her part. A disastrous foreign war, an exhausted treasury, an insecure title, and a realm badly divided in religion and politics all forced her to move warily. From the outset her principal concerns in things ecclesiastical were to establish a church that would ensure the widest possible measure of unity among her subjects and one that would remain securely under her control; basic objectives that continued unchanged throughout her reign. In the spring of 1559 she assumed the title of Supreme Governor as one less likely to cause opposition than Supreme Head, and promulgated her church settlement in the Book of Common Prayer, published and enforced by the now-familiar device of an Act of Uniformity. Based on the Second and more distinctively Protestant Book of 1552, her Prayer Book judiciously offered a number of substantial concessions of a conservative hue designed to secure its wider acceptance. It was imposed by a royal visitation, for the purpose of which the four Welsh dioceses were joined with those of Worcester and Hereford in a single western circuit. Between August 1559 and January 1560 they were traversed by visitors who administered the oath of loyalty to the clergy under the Act of Supremacy, issued the royal injunctions, and enforced the use of the Prayer Book. In the course of the visitors' itinerary three of them, Richard Davies, Thomas Young, and Rowland Meyrick, were elected bishops of the dioceses of St Asaph, St Davids, and Bangor, respectively.

There was less opposition to the settlement than had been expected initially, and by November 1559 John Jewel could jubilantly proclaim that 'the ranks of the papists had fallen almost of their own accord'.[1] In Wales, Kitchen of Llandaff proved to be the only bishop prepared to take the oath. The others were men of more resistant fibre. Goldwell of St Asaph, most formidable of Mary's Welsh prelates, had been allowed to deliver the funeral oration of his master, Cardinal Pole, but in the summer of 1559 fled into exile in Europe. The bishop-elect of Bangor, Morys Clynnog, another of Pole's protégés, also went abroad in 1559. The fourth Welsh bishop,

---

[1] *Zurich Letters* (2 vols. Parker Soc., 1842–5), I, 27, 45; II, 19.

Henry Morgan of St Davids, refused the oath, was deprived of his see, and retired to Wolvercote, where he died in December 1559. About a dozen or so of the other Welsh clergy would not subscribe to the settlement either and were deprived of their preferments. They included Gruffudd Robert, archdeacon of Anglesey, Morgan Phillips, precentor of St Davids, and Owen Lewis, fellow of New College Oxford, all of whom were to be leading Catholic exiles, and John Lloyd, dean of St Asaph. Some of the laity were also opposed to the new arrangements. Sir Edward Carne, Mary's ambassador to the Holy See, did not return from Rome and died there in 1561. Sir Thomas Stradling of St Donat's was another soon to be in bad odour with the government for fostering belief among fellow-Catholics in the so-called 'miracle of St. Donat's, in which the image of a supernatural cross was alleged to have been left on an oak-tree when it blew down in a gale. For his activities he was clapped in the Tower in 1561 and remained there until 1563. Another who may have had serious mental reservations was Sir Richard Bulkeley, who was reported to have abstained from Anglican communion services for sixteen years; and other leading landowners may have shared his hesitations.

The overwhelming majority of the clergy and the laity, however, was content to accept the Queen's instructions, though doubtless with a wide variety of inward misgivings. David Augustine Baker was later to give a graphic sketch of how unmoved by the change the townsfolk were in his native Abergavenny and, quite likely, in a number of other places as well:

. . . after the said change made by Queen Elizabeth the greatest part even of those who in their judgements and affections had before been Catholics, did not well discern any great fault, novelty or difference from the former religion . . . save only the change of language . . . in the which difference they conceived nothing of substance or essence to be. And so easily digested the new religion and accommodated themselves hereto; especially in Wales and other like places remotest from London.[2]

Typical of them was Thomas Bulkeley, rector of Llanddeusant in Anglesey, who had been there since 1543 and would go on serving the parish until 1579, adapting himself without apparent discomfort or embarrassment to all the abrupt switches in direction ordered by four very different monarchs. Other men similarly absorbed the effects of these upheavals for a variety of reasons: some out of respect for a church 'by law established'; others because they were uncertain what the future might hold in the event of Elizabeth's marriage or death; many out of bewilderment induced by a series of contradictory changes; not a few from an understandable caution about revealing their position too boldly or

[2] A. H. Dodd, 'The Church in Wales in the Age of the Reformation', *Welsh Church Congress Handbook*, 1953 p. 31.

precipitately; yet others because their commitment to religion was not so intense as to impel them to put themselves at risk; and the mass of ordinary men and women from sheer ignorance of what was involved, or indifference to it. Thus, arising from some or most of these perplexities, the result was that not only during the first years of the reign but for almost the whole of it there continued to be great clouds of uncertainty, ambivalence, mind-changing, uneasy compromise, and downright apathy or unawareness. There were to be some 'church papists', other luke-warm conformers, and a great many stolid and indifferent 'neuters' who had no very discernible opinions at all. The initial reception of her settlement may not have been at all unacceptable to the Queen, whose principal concern was for political loyalty not religious zeal; but it did not bode well for a church whose adherents were required—in theory at least—to have an intelligent understanding of its tenets and worship.

Responsibility for instilling these new doctrines into the population rested largely with the bishops. Out of sixteen bishops appointed to Welsh sees during Elizabeth's reign, thirteen were Welshmen; a proportion unheard-of in the later Middle Ages or indeed at any time during the sixteenth and seventeenth centuries, apart from the brief reign of Mary. Most of them were graduates, resident in their dioceses, men of good character, and genuine reformers. They numbered among them one or two undesirables like Middleton of St Davids or Hughes of St Asaph, but, on the whole, they were above average in quality and included such outstanding churchmen as Richard Davies, William Morgan, and Richard Vaughan. Whatever the failings of the Elizabethan Church in Wales, unworthy bishops were not among them.

The reports returned by some of these prelates during the first decade of the reign bring out clearly the major difficulties with which they had to grapple. They may, to some extent, have exaggerated the weaknesses since they were setting a distinctly higher standard for their clergy and laity than had previously been expected. Much of what they said, however, was corroborated by other sources. Some of the blemishes they reported were to continue throughout the reign. The poverty of the Church, for instance, was centuries-old and would defy eradication until the eighteenth or nineteenth centuries. Other shortcomings, like poor clerical education, the absence of vernacular services and literature, and a widespread illiteracy, would be tackled during the Elizabethan era, with varying degrees of success.

One of the most serious problems facing the bishops was the poverty of the Church, by which it had been perennially bedevilled. Before the Reformation, its income at all levels had been low and inadequate. Reformation changes themselves had extinguished some earlier sources of income, like pilgrims' offerings, the sale of candles, or payments for masses and prayers for the dead. When the monasteries were dissolved those parishes previously appropriated to them had passed into the hands of the Crown, which in turn had sold or leased them to lay impropriators. Such changes had further encouraged an inveterate tendency on the part of the State and powerful laymen to pillage the property of the Church. Lay subjects were not loth to follow Elizabeth's own rapacious example in relation to Church possessions and from all four Welsh bishoprics there were to be protests by bishops against unprincipled pressures on them by the laity. Furthermore, allowing the clergy to marry had the effect of increasing their domestic and family liabilities. Finally, the inflation of prices during the century imposed a heavy additional burden on those stipendiary priests whose slender remuneration certainly did not keep pace with inflation and, at worst, remained obstinately static. Beneficed priests, admittedly, coped much better since the value of the products of glebe and tithe increased along with that of agricultural commodities generally; and in 1583 Bishop Middleton of St Davids claimed that the incomes of his beneficed clergy had trebled since 1535. Certainly, the surviving wills of beneficed clergy show them to have lived on the level of prosperous minor gentry or yeomen. Nor, indeed, could the Church have recruited into its ranks the younger sons of gentry and substantial freeholders if its benefices had offered only a bleak and unremunerative return. Nevertheless, the overall picture was one of poverty and a poverty which was getting relatively worse. One of the most outspoken of the bishops, Richard Davies, pilloried those 'insatiable cormorants', 'greedy for Church spoils' and contemptuously intolerant of the clergy. He himself had suffered at the hands of marauding courtiers like the earls of Leicester and Pembroke, Sir John Perrot, or George Cary, who reduced the income of the diocese of St Davids diocese from £457 per annum to £263 by his acquisition of Llanddewibrefi and its dependent churches. Davies's outburst on the rapacity of the age was understandable:

There is so much covetousness of the world today for land and possessions, gold and silver and wealth, that only infrequently wilt thou find one who trusts in God and his promises. Violence and theft, perjury, deceit, hypocrisy, and arrogance; and with these, as if with rakes, every condition of men gather and drag to themselves.[3]

The impoverishment of the Church was a taproot from which sprang many other malign growths. It accounted for some of the gravest abuses of the Elizabethan Church, though deficiencies like the lack of clerical education, pluralism, non-residence, and simony had been common enough in the Middle Ages too. Poor remuneration meant that many of the

---

[3] 'Letter to the Welsh Nation' (1567), trans. A. O. Evans, *A Memorandum on the Legality of the Welsh Bible* (Cardiff, 1925), p. 107.

parish clergy with cure of souls were often men of meagre education and indifferent moral quality, whose level of training and moral character were, and would continue to be, too low to enable them to shoulder the major new responsibilities of instruction and example that the Reformation laid to their charge. Bishop Robinson of Bangor wrote in 1567 of the 'blindness' of his clergy; most of them 'too old (they say) to be put to school'.[4] Moreover, because of the poverty of the livings, the twin evils of pluralism and non-residence were rife among the clergy, from the highest to the humblest. As a result of pluralism, some churches fell into a state of disrepair, clerical hospitality and charity were badly maintained, some of the beneficed clergy were strangers to their parishioners, and their curates were paid miserable stipends. All the Welsh bishops were obliged to hold other benefices *in commendam*, and even the best of them were accused of being inordinately desirous of acquiring worldly wealth. Edmwnd Prys, though himself a distinguished churchman, commented acidly on the excessive greed of the clergy in 'bagging' money and complained that the parson sheared to the quick and then wanted more.[5] The medieval practice of handsomely providing the higher clergy with a number of preferments still continued. Sons, nephews, friends, and clients had a range of benefices duly conferred upon them, often to the detriment of parish and locality. A great deal of non-residence ineluctably ensued. The registrarship of St Davids was held by a Breconshire gentleman, while the archdeaconry of St Asaph was leased to a member of the Salusbury family by an archdeacon who lived in London. 'Non-residencies', thundered John Penry with characteristic vehemence, 'have cut the throat of our Church. Some that never preached have three church livings.'[6]

While the greater luminaries collected benefices to keep themselves in comfort, the lesser lights among the clergy did so to keep themselves alive. Richard Davies in 1570 referred in distressed tones to the sore straits in which some of the poorer parsons found themselves and to those churches which did not have 'whole service once a year; but upon Sundays and holy days the epistle and the gospel only'. This came about because the farmers of livings refused to give competent wages but made shift with a priest 'that shall come thither galloping from another parish, which for such parishes shall have 40s. a year, four marks, or £4 at the best'.[7] Sixteen years later that was still the situation in Breconshire, where an anonymous observer told of 'ignorant and unlearned stipendiary priests' serving a number of cures and scampering through part of the service 'in such posting manner that the hearers are little or nothing the better for it'.[8] Other bishops testified to the wretchedly small stipends allowed to curates, who

---

[4] D. Mathew, 'Some Elizabethan Documents', *BBCS*, VI (1931–3), 77–8.
[5] Williams, *Tafodau Tân*, p. 159.   [6] *Treatises*, p. 40.
[7] PRO SP12/66/26, 26(i).   [8] PRO SP12/191/17.

continued to be badly paid down to the Stuart era and beyond. To make up their income some of the poorest clerics sometimes took up unsuitable by-employments or indulged in dubious pursuits, such as exercising a menial craft, keeping a tavern, counterfeiting documents, or gambling. Yet it had not escaped a bishop like Richard Davies that part of the blame lay with the clergy, who took on 'four or five cures . . . but never one aright' in collusion with the gentry and the sheriffs. Among the places which suffered as a result were some of the most important centres of population like Cardiff, Cowbridge, Neath, Swansea, Carmarthen, and Llansteffan. Evidence also exists that, almost inevitably, the less scrupulous entered into agreements which savoured strongly of simony. Andrew Vayn, a Llandaff cleric, referred to 'diverse simonaical offers' known to him, and another Glamorgan parson, William Fleming, wrote of the 'silver or golden key' which alone could unlock the 'door which leads men to any preferment, be it never so mean'.[9]

The greatest cause of distress resulting from the poverty of the Church for the bishops was the lack of preachers. Throughout the realm there was a 'great and alarming scarcity' of preachers;[10] but in Wales they were even thinner on the ground because of the greater poverty of the livings and the added handicap that no Bible, Prayer Book, or apologetic literature existed in Welsh. The first bishops' reports of 1561 revealed how desperately short of preachers Wales was; with only five in St Asaph, five in Llandaff, and no more than two in Bangor. Even allowing that much more stringent criteria were applied before a man could be licensed to preach then than now, this was a truly desperate situation. In 1570 Bishop Davies made an impassioned plea to the Privy Council to help ensure that 'the small patrimony of the Church which is yet remaining . . . may still continue to the sustentation . . . of preachers and teachers after that the incumbents now being no preachers shall happen to depart'.[11] Eighteen years later, however, Penry's onslaughts were more devastating than ever: 'My brethren for the most part know not what preaching meaneth . . . they think it sufficient to hear one sermon once perhaps in all their life'.[12]

All these circumstances considered, it was not surprising that the quality of the Welsh clergy was mediocre, to say the least. At the beginning of Elizabeth's reign there was a marked shortage of clerics of any kind, seemingly on account of the upheavals and confusions of the two previous reigns. In Bangor, the sole Welsh diocese for which reasonably full registers survive, only eleven priests were recorded as having been ordained between 1544 and 1552—not enough to make good normal wastage. So acute was the shortage that some bishops were driven to ordain manual workers and other unfit persons, for which they were

[9] *The Stradling Correspondence*, ed. J. M. Traherne (London, 1840), pp. 83–91, 331.
[10] *Zurich Letters*, I, 98.   [11] PRO SP12/66/26(i).   [12] *Treatises*, p. 7.

sharply rapped over the knuckles by the Queen. During the 1560s, however, there was a marked improvement in Bangor, where Meyrick ordained 47 candidates in his first two years, and 114 were ordained between 1570 and 1580. At St Davids, too, Davies between 1561 and 1566, when his registers stop, ordained about 90 candidates, though this was a much larger diocese. Few of these ordinands, however, were graduates or well-educated men. Contemporary Welsh poets condemned the clergy for being unable to read the Scriptures on Sunday, though they could swear and get drunk freely enough, and if any of them could read English they were up and away to England to 'spout the new gospel'.[13]

Bishops had therefore to make do as best they might with an undistinguished body of priests largely inherited from their predecessors. Their clergy's ready complaisance in accepting the Elizabethan settlement, though they had no deep conviction in favour of it, was itself a mixed blessing. Some of them, in spite of taking the oath of loyalty and ostensibly accepting the Prayer Book, were unduly sympathetic to the Catholic religion and continued to minister mass in secret. William Luson, archdeacon of Carmarthen, was described in 1564 as one of the 'chief and principal receivers and maintainers' of a band of Marian priests. Another was Walter Powell, dubbed the 'bishop of Llandaff' and a 'priest ordered in Queen Mary's days', who continued to be 'a recusant and a common mass-monger' until 1604.[14] Other priests, 'too old to go to school', carried on in much the same way as before, adapting as well as they could to new demands made on them but maintaining as many of their customary ways as they dared. Even in the cathedral chapters considerable slackness prevailed. The vicars-choral of St Davids, like their fellows in other dioceses, were poorly educated and some were found 'insufficient in reading'. Others of them were insubordinate, badly behaved, and too fond of drinking, gaming, and madcap pranks to devote much time to study. When the Thirty-nine Articles were being read at St Davids 'the people thronged out of the church, it being towards dinner time' and the clerk himself 'tarried not to hear anything read' for the same reason.[15]

Such clerics could be replaced only very slowly. When Hugh Puleston died in 1566 he had been vicar of Wrexham since 1520, undisturbed by all the intervening changes. Thomas Bulkeley remained in Llanddeusant from 1543 to 1579, Humphrey ap Richard in Llanbeulan from 1544 to 1587, and Robert ap Huw at Newborough from Mary's reign until the end of the century. Even when the 'old guard' disappeared, their replacements might not necessarily be very different. The low stipends paid to curates offered no inducements for recruiting men of better calibre. Graduates and men of

[13] W. A. Bebb, *Cyfnod y Tuduriaid* (Wrexham, 1939), pp. 140–1.
[14] *HMC, Wells Cathedral MSS. 10th Report*, III, 249.
[15] NLW, St. David's Chapter Acts, I, 52, 89, 113–14, 239, 241.

ability were attracted to England in considerable numbers, so the beneficed clergy might not be all that better than their predecessors. Geoffrey Kyffin, vicar of Llanrwst in 1581, was a sad example. He and his family were accused in Star Chamber of violence, affrays, counterfeitings, kidnappings, and forced marriages. This was one of the worst instances of deplorable allegations being brought against a clergyman; but it was not at all unusual for members of the clergy to be among those accused in the courts of various unbecoming misdeeds, sometimes committed in churches or their surroundings.

Many of these shortcomings were connived at, even encouraged, by the laity, almost all of whom strongly disliked any suggestion of maintaining, still less extending, the authority of the clerical hierarchy. Some of the laymen were 'church papists', i.e., they acknowledged the Queen's jurisdiction by attending services but made no pretence of accepting her doctrine as set out in the Prayer Book. While present in church they showed their dislike of the new ways by coughing, talking loudly, walking about, praying on beads, or even reading Catholic books. Though as Catholics they had been forbidden by the Council of Trent in 1562 to attend the state church, as late as 1598 Robert Parsons was obliged to admit that some Catholics were still attending. Conservative inclinations on the part of the laity as well as the clergy had prevented the appearance of many churches from being changed. True, in a town like Swansea, churchwardens' accounts record altars and roods being taken down early in the new reign but in many of the more off-beat country churches nothing was done to remove medieval furnishings, vestments, and books. At St David's cathedral itself, the sexton, Ellis ap Howell, had hidden under the noses of the bishop and chapter 'ungodly papish books, as mass books, hymnals, grails and such like (as it were looking for a day)'. The bishop also had to give orders to convert 'massing garments, viz., chasubles and tunics to carpets for the Lord's table'.[16] In 1583 his successor found it necessary to order that images, pictures, windows, altars, and roodlofts be destroyed throughout his diocese. Many of the traditional practices associated with medieval worship also survived. Llandaff in 1565 was denounced as a place of 'extreme darkness' where no reformation or redress had taken place. Robinson at Bangor in 1567 deplored the 'dregs of superstition'; 'images and altars standing in the churches undefaced, lewd and indecent vigils and watches observed, much pilgrimage-going, many candles set up to the honour of the saints, some relics yet carried about, and all the country full of beads and knots'.[17] Other commentators confirmed the persistence of poverty, ignorance, superstition, or apathy.

Some men and women may indeed have 'wished the Romish religion

[16] NLW, St. David's Chapter Acts, I, 236, 239.   [17] BBCS, VI, 77–8.

again'—that 'crew of obstinate idolaters', stigmatized by Penry, that would 'be fain in execrable Rome again'—yet for most people, 'slow and cold in the true service of God' or 'even careless for any religion',[18] the relation of these vestiges to Catholic dogma was very tenuous or even non-existent. Such habits were far removed from the Council of Trent and the Counter-Reformation; they had nothing to do with papal authority or doctrinal certitude; they arose from no struggles of conscience or a painful search for salvation. What they did represent was the carry-over by an unchanging country population of a fixed round of custom and observance into a period of rapid, officially enforced religious change. This routine was as age-old, familiar, and reassuring as their farming tasks. It was linked with the seasons of the year and the great milestones of human existence—birth, marriage, and death. Maintaining such practices could be, and usually was, far removed from open recusancy. These habits might, with minimal stress or contradiction, be combined with outward conformity to the Queen's Church. So, too, could the regular resort by hard-pressed peasants to soothsayers, wise men, magicians, charmers, and witches, who could offer their clients what the latter conceived of as much-needed help against theft, evil spirits, malign spells, sickness in humans and beasts, and other misfortunes.

These perennial religious and other practices were maintained because of the laxity of ecclesiastical and secular administration. Churchwardens, on whom rested the duty of implementing the church settlement in the parishes, were notoriously under the thumb of local notabilities among the gentry and negligent in fulfilling their role. Bishop Davies denounced sheriffs and their officers for having blunted the 'ecclesiastical sword' of excommunication and made it impossible to punish incorrigible priests, blatant moral offenders, or 'supporters and bearers of superstition and idolatry'. Many magistrates, he contended, defended papistry and its survivals in the shape of pilgrimages to wells and chapels. They gagged churchwardens or obliged them to commit perjury at times of visitations and forced them to wink at all manner of offences. He also deplored that hundreds of those excommunicated for vicious living—mostly adultery and bigamy—remained in that state for more than four years, in some instances, with no further punishment imposed.[19] Penry later confirmed this contempt for ecclesiastical jurisdiction. 'A conscience must be wrought in our people', he fulminated, 'else they will never leave their idolatry, swearing, adultery and thieving.'[20] Not that such immorality was peculiar to the Welsh; in many parts of England, too, the populace was subjected to comparable puritannical denunciation.

[18] *Treatises*, p. 32.
[19] *Funeral Sermon Preached . . . on the Death of the Earl of Essex* (London, 1577), no pagination.   [20] *Treatises*, p. 36.

Yet of all the obligations laid upon the reforming bishops the most pressing was that of ensuring that the new doctrines were intelligibly presented to their people in a language they could understand. This could not effectively be undertaken as long as the Bible and the service book were 'closed up from them in an unknown tongue', to quote Bishop Robinson. A Welsh translation of both was at once the paramount need and the supreme achievement of the Elizabethan Church in Wales. Early in Elizabeth's reign those who most passionately wanted to bring this about were two men in the diocese of St Asaph: its newly elected bishop, Richard Davies, and William Salesbury, who ever since 1547 had been advocating the need for a translation with single-minded fervour. The friendship between the two ripened quickly and it was very probably they who were responsible for a succession of measures designed to secure a speedy translation. Among them was an anonymous petition for Scripture to be had 'in the vulgar Welsh tongue that the prince of darkness might not altogether possess the principality of Wales'.[21] Then there were articles pleading that Welsh and Cornish children should be taught the Catechism in their native tongue. Salesbury's earlier translation, *Kynniver Llith a Ban* (1551), may now have been brought back into circulation, since Thomas Davies, bishop of St Asaph, in November 1561 required his clergy to read the epistle and gospel in Welsh and to declare the Catechism in Welsh every Sunday. Most important of all was the effort mounted by Davies and Salesbury, with some help from Humphrey Llwyd, to bring about the privately sponsored measure of 1563 for the translation of Prayer Book and Bible into Welsh. It may well be that a statute was not needed at all for a Welsh Bible but since the Act also called for a Welsh service book and was intended to authorize its use in Welsh-speaking parishes, its promoters were probably justified in supposing that such a modification of the practice laid down in the Act of Uniformity in 1559 needed parliamentary authorization to ensure that the change had legal force everywhere in Wales. The Act made no financial provision to meet the costs of publication and the time it allowed for completion of the work was very short. It was, none the less, a major milestone. For the first time it provided official sanction and a specific mandate for these translations and their use in parish worship. It may very well have met with stiff opposition in the Lords, which resulted in a proviso being added to ensure that copies of the Welsh and English Bible were placed side by side in the churches so as to enable parishioners to learn English—an early indication, it seems, of that resistance sustained throughout Elizabeth's reign to the idea of there being any need for a Welsh version at all.

Once the Act was passed, Davies and Salesbury collaborated closely for

---

[21] D. R. Thomas, *The Life of Davies and Salesbury* (Oswestry, 1902), p. 4.

a year or two at the bishop's palace in Abergwili, though Salesbury may very well have executed much of the work before this time. It was he who translated the Prayer Book and most of the New Testament, with Davies undertaking a number of epistles and Thomas Huet the Book of Revelation. None of Davies's fellow-bishops gave any help or even undertook to authorize the translation as the Act required them to do; but Edmund Grindal did give his approval to the Prayer Book. Both the New Testament and Prayer Book were printed at the costs of Humphrey Toy and published in 1567. An edition of some 1,000 copies must have been run off if enough were printed to allow one to be placed in each of the churches of Welsh-speaking parishes. The translations have often been subjected to criticism on account of Salesbury's linguistic idiosyncrasies—in the sixteenth century and since. Penry described the Welsh service as 'most pitfully evil read . . . and not understood of one among ten of the hearers'[22] and Maurice Kyffin was equally dismissive. They may well have been over-harsh and other contemporaries thought differently. Robinson testified in 1576 to his pleasure at knowing that 'all things are done in Welsh', and when Morgan came to dedicate his Bible in 1588 he paid a remarkable tribute to Salesbury 'who, above all men, deserved well of our Church'.[23] Davies and Salesbury had undoubtedly intended to translate the whole Bible, but never again published anything in collaboration. Possibly they disagreed fundamentally over their respective approaches to the task; Davies having the needs of priests and people more in mind, as opposed to Salesbury's emphasis on the appeal to scholars and savants. Or they may perhaps have encountered financial difficulties, or there may have been other reasons of which we know nothing. They left much still to be accomplished; but what they had achieved was of the utmost importance for the future. They had contrived to secure official recognition of the need to establish Welsh as the language of public worship in Wales. They had also provided the means, though as yet incomplete, to begin to make Protestant services meaningful for the majority of their countrymen. Yet the labour of implanting reformed doctrines in Welsh minds and hearts had been no more than begun.

During the first ten or twelve years of Elizabeth's reign, therefore, the reformed church had made singularly slow progress among the Welsh. For Catholics and those who sympathized with older modes of belief and practice, those years formed a generally peaceful and untroubled period. Little pressure was put upon them; outward conformity was all that was asked of them and that was willingly enough rendered. Nevertheless, this temporizing was perceived by some ardent Catholics as a mortal peril to their faith. They feared that Catholicism would die a lingering death of

---

[22] *Treatises*, p. 56.   [23] Evans, *Memorandum*, p. 130.

spiritual malnutrition as the people were increasingly deprived of the sustenance of the sacraments with the dying out of older Marian priests. To counter the threat, William Allen, greatly assisted by his Welsh friends, Owen Lewis and Morgan Phillips, founded a seminary at Douai in 1568 with the intention of preparing young men for the Catholic priesthood to reconvert England and Wales. These recruits were to be educated, indoctrinated, and disciplined with a thoroughness hitherto unparalleled among the priesthood. A second instrument of reconversion was literature. In the same year of 1568, another of the exiles, Morys Clynnog, followed a pattern set some years earlier by English exiles and published the first Catholic book to be printed in Welsh, *Athravaeth Gristnogawl* [Christian Doctrine]. It was intended to provide a simple and intelligible foundation for the faith of all good Catholics.

Already, too, the third prong of Catholic counter-activity, that of politico-military intrigue, had for some time been taking shape. As early as 1561 Clynnog had written to urge that Elizabeth be overthrown by military invasion; better for his countrymen, he declared, 'to attain eternal blessedness under a foreign lord than to be cast into the nethermost hell'.[24] But not until Mary Stuart's arrival in England in 1568 did the conspiracies really warm up. A report of 1569 by the Spanish ambassador, Guerau de Spes, claimed that a majority of the Welsh was Catholic and supported Mary; and the Irish rebel, Fitzgerald, was equally confident that most of them longed 'for nothing more than to see the sacraments of Christ restored again to their country'.[25] No sign of disloyalty emerged in Wales, however, during the dangerous year of 1569. But, in the proceedings of that year leading up to the excommunication of Elizabeth, among the witnesses examined by Pope Pius were Thomas Goldwell and Clynnog. The Papal Bull of Excommunication of 1570 drew the line much more sharply between supporters and opponents of the Queen. The former closed ranks behind her, including among them many who still cherished Catholic sympathies. Her enemies were now obliged to make their opposition clearer and more pronounced. The three means by which they would mount resistance were already manifest: seminary priests, literature, and conspiracies. In support of one or more of these methods a tiny but resolute minority showed themselves prepared to come out in open opposition to the government.

THE MIDDLE YEARS, 1570–88

During the two decades of the 1570s and 1580s resistance to Elizabeth's settlement polarized at both ends of the religious spectrum. It was

---

[24] Williams, *Modern Wales*, p. 68.   [25] *Carew MSS*, I, 398.

Catholicism, not surprisingly, which had the more decisive impact on Wales; Puritanism was unmistakably slighter and more peripheral in its influence. Among the first consequences of the Bull of Excommunication was the passing of a statute of 1571, the first of a series to be directed by Parliament against Catholics. Another outcome was the Ridolfi Plot of 1570–1, intended to secure the marriage of Mary Stuart to Norfolk and put the Queen under severe pressure. It failed, but among those deeply implicated were the Welshmen, Hugh Owen of Plas Du in Caernarfonshire, and Thomas Morgan of Monmouthshire. Both fled to Europe and were to become for many years the leading Welsh conspirators against Elizabeth; Owen as the 'intelligencer-in-chief' of Philip II, and Morgan as Mary's chief agent in Paris. In 1575 Clynnog outlined a proposal to the pope that he should raise 6,000 men for an invasion of Wales, on account of its separate language and history, its fidelity to the Catholic faith, and its potential for resistance. The scheme was too wild and impractical to be taken seriously and nothing came of it.

Disturbing reports in 1576–7 of the ambitions of Philip II's half-brother, Don John of Austria, on the English throne occasioned all the more apprehension because the first effects were now being experienced of the missionary activities of the seminary priests who had been entering the country since 1574. They represented a vastly more dangerous challenge to the Elizabethan Church than anything posed by the ageing remnants of the Marian priesthood. Whereas Robert Parsons criticized the latter for being content with a 'stage-play where men do change their persons and parts, without changing their minds or affections', the newcomers by contrast were less concerned with doctrine and more preoccupied with 'interior conversion and godly discipline'.[26] Typical of the new generation was the Welsh priest, Robert Gwyn, who was decidedly sharper in his comments on the deficiencies of his countrymen and of the *naïveté* he detected in the attitude of older men like Clynnog. Seminary priests like Gwyn, thoroughly imbued with the inspiration of the Catholic Reformation and Douai's intense training, burning with zeal to convert their countrymen, were emissaries willing to face any danger, even death itself. They returned aflame with a courage and a commitment hitherto unparalleled and by 1577 were actively proselytizing in some areas; secretly saying mass, baptizing children, burying the dead, and instructing the faithful.

In 1578 a new seminary opened in Rome, with Clynnog as its warden. From the outset acrimony was kindled there by his alleged favouritism towards the Welsh students and also by Welsh suspicions of the Jesuit teachers. Underlying these racial animosities there may also have been a deeper schism over what it was that the College was intended to achieve.

[26] J. Bossy, *The English Catholic Community, 1570–1800* (London, 1975), p. 17.

Owen Lewis, Clynnog, and the Roman establishment envisaged it as a house of studies to secure employment abroad for the exiles while they awaited their return home. Parsons and the Jesuits, however, wanted it to be a missionary college and won Gregory XIII over to their view. Rancour came to a head in 1579 when Clynnog was removed. Ill-will continued to fester and created profound mistrust on both sides. Lewis left Rome and, like Gruffudd Robert, came deeply under the influence of Cardinal Borromeo and his concept of a church in which the hierarchy and the rights of bishops had a prominent role, and was markedly hostile to some aspects of Jesuit activity. One of the unhappy consequences of these disputes and enmities for the Catholic campaign of reconversion was that they conspired to reduce sharply the number of priests who returned to Wales and also limited the production of Welsh Catholic literature. Something like 218 students from Wales and the March have been traced between 1568 and 1642 at various Catholic seminaries. About 100 of them went in Elizabeth's reign, of whom some 70 were ordained and 64 sent on mission; but of these only a small minority were active in Wales or chose to write in Welsh. The English exiles who chiefly directed Counter-Reformation enterprises did not properly understand or take into account Welsh national sympathies or the necessity of appealing to the people through the Welsh language. Moreover, as time went on, the numbers of priests being recruited from Wales fell steadily. Eleven went from Bangor during Elizabeth's reign, only two between 1603 and 1642. St Asaph numbers declined during the same period from twenty to six; and Llandaff's from sixteen to four.

The first appearance of these missionaries caused enough discomfiture in the Privy Council for it to set afoot in 1577 inquiries by the bishops to find out how many objectors refused to come to church. Replies were reassuring enough on the surface: no objectors were reported from St Asaph, and one apiece from St Davids and Bangor. Only in Llandaff, where there were thirteen, including at least one justice of the peace, Thomas Carne of Ewenni, were recusants numerous. Considerably less than pleased with the state of Wales, none the less, was that stern disciplinarian, John Whitgift, who complained with some asperity of clandestine Catholic activity. His representations led to a follow-up at Bangor and Llandaff. At Bangor, Bishop Robinson and Ellis Price were thwarted by a tip-off given to the offenders. But when Thomas Owen returned to Plas Du in the summer of 1578 he was brought before Star Chamber by an energetic justice, Robert Vaughan. The subsequent hearing blew the lid off widespread recusant activities in Llŷn, where missionary priests had been enthusiastically received and mass said in secret. These disclosures sent tremors of acute apprehension rippling along many nerve-ends in Llŷn and elsewhere in north Wales between 1579 and

1581, shrivelling up the Catholic loyalties of a number of squires. For their efforts at this time, Robinson and Vaughan gained a reputation for being unrelenting recusant-hunters. Bishop Bleddyn of Llandaff was equally active in 1579 but found that his efforts, too, were being undermined by fellow-commissioners who warned priests in advance. He suspected that leading families like the Lewises of Y Fan and the Kemeyses of Cefnmabli were themselves harbouring priests and recusants. A year later, when the President of the Council in the Marches himself, Henry Sidney, unsuccessfully searched out recusants in Monmouthshire, he was warned by Walsingham that 'great hold is taken by your enemies for neglecting the execution of this commission'.[27] The advent of the Jesuit mission of Campion and Parsons in the same year gave rise to still sharper anxiety and led to a further anti-Catholic statute of 1581, making it an act of treason to attempt to withdraw any persons from their 'natural obedience' to the Queen to accept the 'pretended authority' of Rome.

During these years the government was made aware of the widespread persistence of medieval and quasi-papist practices in Wales. A traveller of 1578 had deplored the prevailing 'ignorance of God's word' and the 'deep darkness' he found. Again, in 1583, Bishop Middleton of St Davids, whose diocese covered the greater part of south Wales, issued visitation articles which constituted one of the severest indictments of medieval survivals ever uttered by any Elizabethan bishop. They disclosed that some 'blind, ignorant priests and ministers' continued to elevate the host and engaged in other customs retaining a memory of the 'idolatrous mass'. They were ordered to desist from these and other popish rites still observed at baptisms, burials, and churching of women, and were commanded to remove images, pictures, and other 'monuments of feigned miracles' and to stop observing holy days.[28] Such practices were thought by many reformers to offer an all-too-fertile breeding ground for the activities of seminary priests. Conversely, though, the unknown author of *Drych Cristnogawl* [Christian Mirror], c.1585, the ablest Catholic apologist to write in Welsh, saw Wales in a very different light. It grieved him to the heart to see the population of whole shires, as he thought, 'living like animals' without a single Christian among them; the poor blithely following the debased example of the gentry 'without thinking of any faith'.[29] He was convinced that the majority of the wealthy and influential were too afraid of the dire social and economic consequences for themselves and their families to stand four-square as recusants. The sad truth was that sincere men on both sides of the religious divide saw only too

[27] W. W. E. W(ynne), 'Herbertiana Supplement', *Mont. Colls.*, IX (1876), 382-3.

[28] W. P. M. Kennedy, *Elizabethan Episcopal Administration* (3 vols. Alcuin Club, 1925), I, 145-52.

[29] G. H. Hughes, *Rhagymadroddion, 1547-1648* (Cardiff, 1951), pp. 52-3.

clearly from their respective standpoints what a daunting assignment lay before them in having to convert the ignorant and the heedless.

In spite of this and the mounting persecution being launched against them, Catholic priests and laymen redoubled their exertions. They even established a secret printing-press in a cave on the Little Orme and there printed part of *Drych Cristnogawl* before being detected. Two more short-lived secret presses were to follow; one at Brecon, the other in Flintshire. At least five priests have been traced as having been particularly active in north Wales during these years. One of the earliest Douai men in Flintshire was John Bennett; caught in 1582, he was banished in 1585, only to return later, travelling all over Wales, mostly on foot, for thirty-five years. One of the bravest and most admirable of the recusants was the lay schoolmaster-poet, Richard Gwyn, the first Catholic martyr of Elizabeth's reign, who was executed at Wrexham in 1584, with the deliberate intention of providing a terrible example to all gentlemen and heads of families nearby.[30] Increased Catholic effort brought intensified persecution in its wake. The numbers of recusants brought before the courts were stepped up, especially in the border counties of the south-east and north-east, where their numbers were greatest. The increase was due not only to the success of the priests but also to more rigorous prosecution, inspired in north Wales very largely by Sir George Bromley, Chief Justice of Chester and an ardent Protestant. In Glamorgan, for example, the number of recusants presented at Great Sessions rose steeply from four in 1584 to seventy-seven in 1587, a year when the nerves of all Elizabeth's subjects were badly stretched by preparations for the Armada.

Mention of the Armada is a reminder that during the years before 1587 the intrigues against Elizabeth had been thickening fast. Thomas Morgan had been implicated in the Throckmorton Plot of 1583 and with the double-agent William Parry. The assassination of William the Silent in 1584 aroused almost hysterical apprehension among Elizabeth's subjects for her safety. Echoes of this can be heard in the repeated questioning of Richard Gwyn at his trial as to his loyalty to the pope as opposed to his allegiance to his sovereign. The Bond of Association of 1584, designed to protect the Queen and her realm, was signed by all the leading gentlemen of Wales, among whom William Parry's conspiracy against her aroused deep revulsion in 1585. But of all the intrigues the most serious, and the one which had the most dangerous implications for Wales, was the Babington Plot of 1586. Two leading Welsh gentlemen, Thomas Salusbury and Edward Jones of Plas Cadwgan, were heavily involved and, having fled to Wales, were caught and executed for their part in it in September 1586. Salusbury was described as a 'comely personage, valiant and extreme lover

[30] D. A. Thomas, *The Welsh Elizabethan Catholic Martyrs* (Cardiff, 1971).

of his nation' who had always protested that he was unwilling to offer any violence to Elizabeth.[31] The role of Salusbury and Jones was abhorred by most of their countrymen, with whom Elizabeth was not only genuinely popular but was also regarded as the principal bulwark against chaos and invasion. Most of John Penry's compatriots, who agreed with him in little else, would have joined in his denunciation of 'these insatiable blood-suckers Babington and his adherents' and the Spaniard and the 'forces of Romish Cain', who put in peril the political stability as well as the religious settlement of the country.[32]

In contrast to the Catholic resistance, the more radical Puritan voices found few echoes in Wales, even though in England during the 1570s and 1580s such opposition to Elizabeth's Church was on more than one occasion forcefully pressed. In view of the faltering progress which even the cautious brand of Anglican reform had been making, the brasher Puritan version not surprisingly made infinitely less headway. A trace of earnest episcopal Puritanism was discernible in a man like Richard Davies or Richard Vaughan, bishop of Bangor and later of Chester. Davies was a close friend of Grindal, Spenser, and others of their circle; but all his surviving expressions of opinion are those of a fervid reforming bishop and well within the limits of the accepted Elizabethan positions. One or two of the gentry may also have espoused Puritan convictions. Edward Downlee, an English immigrant to Carmarthenshire and MP for the county, joined Job Throckmorton in sponsoring Penry's *Aequity* (1587) in the Commons. Another betraying sympathies with the Puritan standpoint was the poet Thomas Llywelyn, though accounts of his having founded advanced Puritan congregations in the hills of Glamorgan are no more than legends. Symptoms of Puritan leanings are also apparent in one or two Welsh towns. At Wrexham in the 1580s sabbath-breakers and maypole dancers were hounded by 'hot Puritans, full of the gospel', who are also known to have infuriated Richard Gwyn.[33] In Cardiff, home of early Protestant martyrs Thomas Capper and Rawlins White, townspeople insisted on burying punctiliously according to Protestant rites at the expense of causing affrays in the churchyard, while others sternly prosecuted those who played games or worked on Sundays.

Only one contemporary Welshman, however, is known to have proceeded to a hard-core Presbyterian standpoint and finally all the way to Separatism. John Penry published three pamphlets in 1587–8 giving an unrelievedly sombre picture of Wales as it appeared to an out-and-out Puritan. He was unsparing in his excoriation of its ignorance, backwardness, negligent hierarchy, and absence of Welsh Scriptures. No one could doubt the sincerity of his passion for reform, though it may be argued that his

[31] Mathew, *Celtic Peoples*, p. 70.   [32] *Treatises*, p. 27.
[33] Thomas, *Welsh Martyrs*, p. 93.

Puritanism took priority over his patriotism and not vice versa as has usually been supposed. Penry exercised virtually no direct influence on Wales, however.

His indirect influence on the greatest event in the religious history of Elizabethan Wales may, paradoxically enough, have been of considerable significance. When in 1587 he had let fly his barbed shafts at the hierarchy for being responsible for the failure to produce a Welsh Bible, those criticisms may well have had the effect of stinging Archbishop Whitgift into realizing that the most effective response to this Puritan gadfly would be to speed up the publication of a Welsh translation of the Bible that was already in hand. One of the exquisite ironies of sixteenth-century history is that Penry, often likened to a voice crying in the wilderness, may decisively have spurred his worst and most relentless enemy to hasten the consummation of a project so dear to Penry's heart and that of the translator, William Morgan. Morgan, a Cambridge graduate and vicar of Llanrhaeadr ym Mochnant, prefaced his Bible of 1588 with a dedication to the Queen in which he confessed that he would have despaired of publishing anything more than the Pentateuch had it not been for Whitgift's moral and financial encouragement. To expedite publication Whitgift put pressure on Morgan to come to London, where he lived for months with another Welshman, Gabriel Goodman, dean of Westminster. By September 1588 the new Bible was ready and the Privy Council issued instructions to the Welsh bishops to ensure that copies were bought and used by their clergy. The year in which English independence was preserved by the defeat of the Armada was also the one in which the linguistic and cultural integrity of Wales was saved by Morgan's Bible.

A lively awareness of the need for a Welsh Bible had long existed. From Salesbury's first plea of 1547 there had been urgent requests for it, down to those of Penry or Dafydd Johns of Llanfair Dyffryn Clwyd, who in 1586 launched his impassioned appeal for it in the aftermath of the hideously devastating famine of 1585–6, attributed by him as God's punishment on men's sins and ignorance. When, two years later, Morgan had published his translation, it was to be justly acclaimed with rapture by his contemporaries as a peerless gift to the Welsh. Bards like Siôn Tudur and Ieuan Tew, or prose-authors such as Maurice Kyffin, Huw Lewys, or Siôn Dafydd Rhys (and he a papist!) had nothing but lavish praise for it. One of the earliest and most intriguing reactions was that of the poet-parson, Thomas Jones of Llandeilo Bertholau in Monmouthshire. At Christmas 1588 he urged his hearers, a generation or more before Vicar Prichard did the same, to sell their shirts in order to buy a Bible. He was wildly over-optimistic in supposing that laymen would be able to buy copies at this time—there were only enough to go round the churches—but it was symptomatic of his enthusiasm for Morgan's translation that he could exhort them to try.

What he and other eulogists instinctively recognized was that Morgan had produced an incomparable masterpiece. Clearing away all Salesbury's earlier archaisms, obscurities, and quirks, he had given an appropriately majestic and dignified rendering that was nevertheless beautifully lucid and intelligible. It combined all the strength and purity of the ancient literary language with a flexibility and modernity that enabled Welsh to measure up to the new demands being placed upon it. In addition, it had made the Reformation message come alive in their own language for the first time for many Welshmen who knew no tongue but their own. 'The greatest gift the Welsh people ever had',[34] was how Sir Ifor Williams, most eminent Celtic scholar born in Wales in our time, described it. It would be hard to dissent from that judgement.

THE LAST YEARS, 1588–1603

Morgan's Bible triggered off other publications in Welsh during the last ten or fifteen years of Elizabeth's reign. In 1595, the layman Maurice Kyffin published his *Deffynniad Ffydd Eglwys Loegr*, an admirable translation of John Jewel's classic apologia for the Anglican faith written a generation earlier. In the same year, from the pen of a Caernarfonshire cleric, Huw Lewys, appeared *Perl Mewn Adfyd*, a Welsh version of Coverdale's *A Spiritual and Most Precious Pearl*. In 1599 was published a new Welsh edition of the Prayer Book based on the text of Morgan's Bible and having all the appearance of having been prepared for the press under his direction. Morgan himself was immersed in revising his New Testament but the completed manuscript was unfortunately lost in a fire and never saw the light of day. Welsh versions of the Catechism, desperately needed if the parish priests were adequately to carry out their functions as preceptors of their people, were published, along with another work of considerable benefit to the average incumbent, *Llyfr Plygain* [Book of Matins].

The pace was accelerating in the production of poetry as well as prose. The *cynghanedd* poets did not find their classical genre easy to adapt to the function of religious instruction. They achieved their ends more congenially by means of their customary praise poems, in which the virtues not only of the individuals addressed could be applauded but also those of the reformed faith. Edward ap Raff neatly inserted into a poem extolling the Queen some highly complimentary observations on the superiority of her church settlement over the 'superstition' of papists and referred to her as 'opening the faith of the saints to the Welsh in place of former dishonour'.[35] This kind of encomium occurred more usually in poems to

---

[34] 'Ar Gymraeg William Salesbury', *Y Traethodydd*, 1946, p. 32.
[35] E. D. Jones, 'The Brogyntyn Welsh Manuscripts', *NLWJ*, VI (1950), 223–48.

prominent clerics. A whole series of bishops of St Asaph, for instance, extended their patronage to poets, while some of the more notable prelates maintained their own scholarly and literary households to which Welsh bards and men-of-letters flocked. None of these poets, however, seemed at all enthusiastic about responding to pleas from scholars that they should become new-style poets of Christian learning and the printed book (below, pp. 446–9).

Much better suited to the purpose of religious teaching were the free-metre poems, which were more easily composed and remembered than the *cynghanedd* verse with its minute and intricate regulations. They were far more popular among the mass of the population, were often sung to catchy airs and circulated freely. Most of their content was non-controversial and consisted of strict moralizing and trenchant social criticism. They denounced with intense puritannical flavour the unbridled sensual passion, rapacity, and oppression, the frenetic pursuit of ephemeral worldly wealth, pleasure, and satisfaction, and the heedless trampling underfoot of the weak and poor. Some of the most effective were the *cwndidau*, not inappropriately categorized as 'sermons in song', even though most of them were written by laymen and not cleric-poets. One of the most celebrated of the *cwndidwyr*, Thomas Llywelyn, in his best-known poem, 'The Tavern and the Church', linked the drink, sloth, and loose-living of the tavern to medieval religion and insisted that the deceitful, money-spinning practices associated with the mass and the images had been justifiably replaced by the purer ideals of reformed religion.

These poems reveal as plainly as any source the slowly growing awareness of their religious responsibilities being evolved among a minority of the more thoughtful and literate. Much of the credit for it should be attributed to the lead being given by a number of late Elizabethan bishops—Bellot, Vaughan, and Rowlands at Bangor, Bleddyn and Babington at Llandaff, Rudd at St Davids, and Morgan at Llandaff and St Asaph. What Bleddyn, one of the most dynamic among them, said of himself, might with equal truth have been applied to the others: 'More than all others I have laboured and toiled for years, travelling about at need that I may preach the Gospel'.[36] Supporting the bishops were clerics of outstanding ability among the higher clergy: men of the calibre of Edmwnd Prys, Henry Perry, Huw Lewys, Richard Parry, David Powel, Edward James, or John Davies; all of them distinguished graduates, accomplished authors, and conscientious reformers. The number of graduates ordained in Bangor rose from four in the decade 1560–9 to forty-one between 1600–9, though not all served in the diocese itself and many were still being enticed away to English sees. Among the parish clergy of

---

[36] L. Thomas, *The Reformation in the Old Diocese of Llandaff* (Cardiff, 1930), p. 133.

all the dioceses in Wales there was a sharp increase in the number of graduates coming from the now almost wholly Protestant climate of the universities and in the number of preachers. Their interest in religion and literature was reflected in the many poems directed to clerical patrons by poets like Wiliam Llŷn or Wiliam Cynwal. Not a few of the clergy also showed their enthusiasm for learning by making provision for it in the form of gifts or bequests. Their wills, too, showed them leaving an increasing number of books behind them. Many were drawn from among the younger sons of gentry families, like the Glynns of Glynllifon or the Wynns of Gwydir in north Wales, while in the southern county of Pembrokeshire, out of 131 landed families recognized by Lewys Dwn 31 were those of beneficed clergymen. Between men of this kind and their kinsmen among the gentry there existed a close liaison and a common interest, like the bonds which tied George Owen Harry, rector of Whitchurch, to George Owen of Henllys for nearly thirty years. There had come into being among the clergy in every diocese the nucleus of an articulate, well-trained Protestant intelligentsia. In any dialectical contest with them, it must have been increasingly difficult for laymen with Catholic susceptibilities to hold their own, unless they were aided by systematic and regular instruction by priests of their own persuasion.

No less significant had been the gradual change in the attitude of the laity towards the Church. The Welsh gentry may have been criticized by recusant, Anglican, and Puritan sources of the sixteenth century for being greedy, lax, and devoid of religious principle; and doubtless much of that censure was justified. But there is another side to the case which ought also to be put. The rhetoric of pulpit critics, of whatever religious complexion, was partisan and highly coloured and ought not to be taken completely literally. For all that has been said of the laity's deficiencies, if a share in stimulating religious literature be any index of their interests, then they had been nearly as active as the clergy. Take away men like William Salesbury, Maurice Kyffin, John Penry, or Thomas Llywelyn from among the authors, or Humphrey Toy, Edward Stradling, or Thomas Salusbury from among the patrons, and the history of Welsh religious literature would have been sorely impoverished. The extent and seriousness of their commitment were eloquent testimony to the value of the Reformation's shift of emphasis to the role of the layman in religious life. We should not underestimate the force of a cultural change that was making the more well-to-do sections of gentry and yeomen better educated and more articulate as education at a grammar school, or possibly even a university or Inn of Court, became more common among them. In all these institutions they were likely to encounter Renaissance learning strongly tinged with Protestant values and loyalties. It was at individuals such as these, at heads of households down to the level of yeomen and substantial farmers, that much of the reformed teaching of the age was directed. The outcome was that the list of distinguished clerics and laymen produced 'especially in north Wales cannot be equalled in a similar period [the Elizabethan and early Stuart age] either before or since'.[37]

The Church and its clergy and laymen were, however, far from being free from imperfections. Improvement, where it existed at all, could be detected mainly among the more literate and dutiful elements in the upper reaches of society. Lower down the scale, many of the ingrained characteristics noted earlier appeared to be as unchangeable as ever. Poverty, especially among the lower clergy, was hardly less in evidence than before. At Llandaff the cathedral itself was in 'ruins and decayed state', 'more like a desolate and profane place than a house of prayer' in 1594, and in 1603 Bishop Godwin spoke of it as 'fallen into such decay . . . that it must needs in short time fall to the ground without some relief'.[38] A return of the same year concerning impropriations in the diocese revealed how very little vicars and stipendiaries continued to receive: Cardiff livings were worth £100 to the appropriator, the vicar received £20; Margam yielded £100 and the curate was paid £10. Was it to be wondered that the bishop found many unlicensed curates plying their trade? George Owen, farther west, deplored the 'scared consciences' that allowed men to 'search any part of the church livings, yea the church itself, if we see it but hang loose'.[39] In north Wales conditions were hardly any better. A number of Bangor incumbents were kept at university for most of the year on the proceeds of their benefices, but the effects on their parishioners, left to the ministrations of badly paid curates or neglected altogether, can only have been sadly detrimental. At Churchstoke in Montgomeryshire parishioners complained late in Elizabeth's reign that their curates were paid such miserable sums that they were always 'unlearned, poor, bare and needy fellows', 'forced to leave their wives and children to the mercy of the parish'.[40] They added that this kind of 'mischief and inconvenience' happened very often in Wales. Sir William Meredith of Stansty could not remember a 'learned or godly minister' at any time within Bromfield and Yale. Penry, predictably, dismissed them all as 'rogues and vagabonds', 'spendthrifts and serving-men', 'known adulterers, drunkards, thieves, roisterers, most abominable swearers';[41] but we may heavily discount his evidence as that of an excessively biased witness. Yet even the godly and orthodox Anglican, Huw Lewys, castigated his fellow-clergy for still performing only a sacerdotal rather than an instructing role; 'like bells without clappers or a candle under a bushel', with the result that old people

[37] A. I. Pryce, *The Diocese of Bangor in the Sixteenth Century* (Bangor, 1923), p. xl.
[38] *GCH*, IV, 226–7.   [39] Owen, III, 85.
[40] PRO E112/62/40 Monts.
[41] *Treatises*, p. 63.

of sixty and upwards could give no more account of their faith than new-born children.[42]

The task of transforming the 'collective Christians' of the Middle Ages into individual believers with a strong sense of personal responsibility had hardly begun. Huw Lewys's standards may have been high, but his evidence of religious backwardness was heavily reinforced by other observers' critical reports. A visitor to Clynnog, Caernarfonshire, in 1589 was scandalized by the 'abominable idolatries' he saw: the sacrifice of bullocks to Beuno; pilgrimage-going; open carrying of beads to church by many who claimed to read upon them 'as well as others can upon their books'; calling on saints to help in all extremities; and crossing themselves persistently, when closing windows, leaving cattle in fields, and burying the dead.[43] Ten years later, another commentator told of the constant resort to wells and other places and gave it as his opinion—much exaggerated, it must be supposed—that the people knew nothing of God and that those under thirty years of age had no religion at all. Conditions in Wales were very similar to those described in Lancashire and elsewhere in the north of England in the 1590s. Old conformities died hard. A letter of c.1590 complained that the Welsh went 'in heaps' to the 'wonted wells and places of superstition'.[44] The Council in the Marches reported in 1592 that people in Carmarthenshire still repaired to places where in the past there had been pilgrimages, images, and offerings. In north Wales the appointed times for pilgrimages were announced by 'pencars' [*pencerdd*—a bard]. Wells such as those of Trillo at Llandrillo or St Winifred's famous well—recommended by the Catholic physician and author, Siôn Dafydd Rhys, on religious as well as medical grounds presumably—were favourite resorts.

It was on those occasions when such medieval survivalism provided cover for the much more subversive activities of Catholic priests that the Elizabethan authorities became particularly outraged. Their main agents for the suppression of recusancy were justices of assize like Sir George Bromley, whose 'affection towards religion' was closely noted by the populace, who 'drew forward or backward' according to how they saw 'the temporal magistrate to be affected'.[45] In 1591 assize judges at Carmarthen tried David ab Ieuan of Margam for having allowed 160 people to participate in Catholic worship at a former chapel of Margam Abbey near his home. The years following 1592–3 were critical ones, when the Privy Council launched a major campaign against recusancy. In 1592 it warned the Council in the Marches of the flight of English recusants into Wales and of seminary priests linked with them. Commissions to inquire into the recusancy were ordered for a number of single shires, and the president of

[42] *Perl Mewn Adfyd*, ed. W. J. Gruffydd (Cardiff, 1929), p. xxi.
[43] PRO SP12/224/74.
[44] F. Jones, *The Holy Wells of Wales* (Cardiff, 1954), p. 62.   [45] PRO SP12/66/26.

the Council in the Marches instructed to choose reliable men for the task of arresting Catholics. In 1593 the Council was required to prevent the Welsh from worshipping at former shrines. Its president had already written that the inhabitants of the shires near the vulnerable Milford Haven were 'in religion generally disaffected, as may appear by their use of popish pilgrimages, their harbouring of masspriests, their retaining of superstitious ceremonies and the increase of recusants'.[46] A tell-tale symptom of the Privy Council's marked concern over the state of Wales at this time was the show trial of the Anglesey martyr-poet, William Davies, in 1592–3. Whereas, eight years earlier, John Bennett had only been banished, Davies was obliged to suffer death after a long trial intended to make a lasting impression in such a sensitive area as Anglesey and probably in the whole of north Wales. When invasion was greatly feared in 1596, the screw was again sharply turned. The home of the Turbervilles, Glamorgan's most notorious recusant family, was searched for two seminary priests, Morgan Clynnog and Fisher, who brought seditious literature there in 'considerable quantity'. A leading Breconshire justice of the peace, John Games, was charged in Star Chamber with reading Catholic literature. As late as 1601 the Council in the Marches reported 'great backsliding', especially in 'the skirts of the shires' between England and Wales, with 'many runners abroad and carriers of mass books . . . and all other things used at or in the singing of mass'.[47] A Catholic poem sent to Whitgift by William Morgan in 1601 was believed to be associated with the Essex Rising and openly incited Catholics to rebel against 'the Ammonite destroyer'.[48]

To the very end of the reign recusancy was alive and vigorous in parts of Wales. Sir Richard Lewkenor, an experienced judge, in March 1603 gave it as his view that many of the Welsh were given to 'superstition and papistry, and for the most part irreligious for lack of understanding and good preaching', even though he allowed that the bishops were doing their best to remedy this.[49] In the same year, a return for all the Welsh dioceses gave a total of 808 avowed recusants as opposed to a churchgoing population estimated at 212,450. That figure for objectors probably needs to be multiplied by four or five in order to give something like an accurate impression of the real number of recusants. There were likely to be a comparable number of Catholics who did not communicate or were 'church papists'. Further, it would not be unreasonable to allow another 50 per cent for inefficiency and negligence on the part of those responsible for the return and 40 per cent for children.[50] That would give in all about 3,500 for Wales. Such a figure may seem only a small proportion of open

[46] *HMC Salisbury MSS*, XIII, 478.   [47] *HMC Salisbury MSS*, XI, 460.

[48] R. G. Gruffydd, 'Awdl Wrthryfelgar gan Edward Dafydd', *Llên Cymru*, V (1958–9), 155–63; VIII (1964–5), 65–9.

[49] *HMC Salisbury MSS*, XII, 680–1.   [50] Bossy, *Cath. Community*, pp. 191–2.

Catholic objectors in relation to the total population. But it is important to notice that, as compared with all the dioceses in the kingdom, the two Welsh ones of Llandaff and St Asaph were third and fourth behind Chester and Durham in relation to the number of recusants per parish, while the diocese of Llandaff had a higher proportion of recusants to Anglican churchgoers than any other diocese in England or Wales.

The largest concentrations of Welsh recusants were to be found in the old centres in the north-east and south-east. The high figures for Flintshire owed much to the remarkable esteem in which St Winifred's Well was held and to the proximity of Flintshire and Denbighshire to the strongly recusant centres nearby, in the diocese of Chester, with which they formed a single area of activity. The very high figures for Monmouthshire similarly owed much to adjacent recusant strongholds on the Herefordshire border and to the protection of the Somerset family at Raglan and the Morgans at Llantarnam. Recusants everywhere, if they were to flourish, looked to the patronage of powerful families; and tenants who did not avow recusant beliefs were usually put under strong pressure by such landlords to do so. Only the aristocracy and the bigger gentry had the resources of wealth and influence to shelter Catholic priests and give patronage to Catholic authors. Most of the bigger landowning families in Wales had been unwilling to risk their necks in such ventures; but some of the lesser figures, like the Turbervilles of Pen-llin, the Pughs of Creuddyn, or the Edwardses of Chirk, were notably staunch in their resistance. It was to such influential upper-class sponsors that yeomen and tenants looked for leadership and protection. One of the most striking features of the statistics relating to recusants was the high proportion of women found among them. Women found the Catholic religion attractive for a number of reasons: because of the disappearance of monastic orders; and on account of the unacceptable Protestant emphasis on literacy and the priesthood of all believers. Women often remained defiant in their recusancy when their husbands had conformed and they exerted considerable pressure on their children, servants, and others about them to follow their example. One young Welsh woman, born at Overton Madog in Flintshire, made a name for herself by experiencing visions, accounts of which were written up and circulated among the people to such effect that she herself was sent for by the Privy Council to be examined.

Yet, courageous and upright as was the resistance of many Catholics, the success of the Counter-Reformation in Elizabethan Wales was distinctly limited. The reasons for this were not far to seek. The English Catholic leaders had concentrated too much on England; had neglected Wales even to the extent of diverting many Welsh-speaking priests to labour in England. Robert Parsons himself confessed that priests had not ventured into many parts of Wales and the north which, in spite of or perhaps because of their 'spissa ignorantia', were most likely to respond. This was borne out by the extraordinarily low figures for recusancy in the two westernmost Welsh dioceses. The Catholic leaders may have been induced to miscalculate their real strength in Wales as the result of the persistent survival there of medieval practices. As late as 1602 a report from Douai suggested that recusancy was so strong in Wales that no official dare apprehend a recusant. This misplaced confidence in their numbers may have led Catholic leaders to concentrate their efforts where they deemed missionary activity to have been most urgently needed and to provide less well for Wales in the belief that it could safely be left. Even without such neglect, recusancy would have found the going very hard. It could be propagated only in secret and outside the law; and it was smeared with accusations of disloyalty, subversion, and conspiracy. It debarred men from positions of power and brought them in danger of heavy fines, long imprisonment, and social ostracism, even if the favour of some justices of the peace, the inadequacies of the fining system, and the evasions of recusants themselves managed to soften much of the rigour of the penal statutes of 1581, 1585, 1587, and 1593. The seminary priests found it difficult to get into the country and even more difficult to work undetected in face of constant harrying by magistrates, spies, and informers, though a few like Walter Powell or John Bennett somehow contrived to spend many years actively ministering to the faithful. Some determined men also continued assiduously to copy and circulate Catholic literature like Robert Gwyn or Llywelyn Siôn; but they were often hauled before the Courts of Great Sessions to answer for their recusancy. In addition to all the pressures exerted upon them by persecution, Catholic priests and writers encountered the same difficulties as the Protestants amid a population apathetic and largely illiterate. Catholic labourers and servants, like their Protestant counterparts, in the midst of their 'continual slavery', found it difficult to manage even a short prayer at the beginning and end of the day, and God alone knew how often, through hurry and drowsiness, they omitted these as well. All these difficulties considered, the wonder was less that there should have been so small a number of recusants than that there should have been any who had had the spirit and resilience to resist and go on resisting Elizabeth, her government, and her church.

That church, whatever its continuing weaknesses may have been, enjoyed overwhelming advantages. By 1603 it had been in existence for over forty years and its services were the only form of public worship that the population under about fifty years of age—the vast majority—could remember. During that time it had had a virtual monopoly of not only the means of open worship but also of instruction and education through pulpit, schools, and press. It was synonymous with legality, order, and patriotism, and, in return for outward conformity, could offer security and prospects for advancement. Therein lay an essential key to the role of the ruling class of landowning gentry. Like the laity elsewhere in Europe, they could not separate the question of authority in the Church from that of authority in State and society. What decisively counted with most of them was the security and stability of the political and social order in face of threats internal and external. An essential pillar of that order was the Queen's Church. It gained in strength because it was backed by the full authority of law and government and was not being agitated for in tumult and upheaval by dissident groups of nobles, merchants, or artisans. The settlement was the more attractive for being erastian, comprehensive, and undemanding. It offered the further incentive of a church over which the landowners could exercise a large measure of influence in terms of patronage and livings, choice and control of incumbents, and enforcement of statutes regulating attendance at church. The Church had become increasingly associated in their minds with two kinds of loyalty; the one Tudor, the other Welsh. Fidelity to the Tudors sprang from the gentry's participation in politics and local government, which led to a growing attachment to a whole complex of institutions, including the Crown and the dynasty, common law and parliament, and the Established Church and the Protestant settlement. Devotion to things Welsh was further fostered by the use of the vernacular language in church services and the concept of reformed religion as a return to that great fountain-head of Welsh religious life, the Celtic Church. The Roman religion, on the other hand, was becoming inseparable from sedition and disloyalty, the menace of internal disorder and foreign invasion and domination. 'I protest I would sooner spend my living and my life also than that the enemy should possess any part of Her Majesty's dominions', said Sir John Wogan, a Pembrokeshire gentleman in 1602.[51] He spoke for most of his fellow-gentry. No matter what shortcomings may have defaced the Elizabethan Church, however much ignorance and superstition might survive in its midst, it was, in the eyes of the social groups that mattered, a central and irreplaceable bulwark of continuing order and prosperity. That mattered more than anything else to the dominant élite.

[51] *CSP Dom., 1598–1601*, p. 269.

CHAPTER 14

ELIZABETHAN GOVERNMENT
AND POLITICS

WALES AND GOVERNMENT AT THE CENTRE

ELIZABETH'S reign saw Wales being brought much more completely within the orbit of the English monarchy and the full effects of the assimilation achieved in 1536–43 become increasingly apparent. Elizabeth herself enjoyed an invaluable advantage in dealing with Wales: from the outset she was, like her father and grandfather before her, greatly esteemed as a representative of what the Welsh chose to regard as their own native dynasty. Their loyal sentiments were voiced by Lodowicke Lloyd among others. A servant of Sir Christopher Hatton, he was a poet of modest talents who expressed himself thus:

> From Brutus' brood, from Dardan line,
> Sidanen [the silken one, i.e., Elizabeth] is that Phoenix fine,
> From Cambria's soil, from Hector's seed,
> Sidanen princely doth proceed.[1]

Sidanen's monarchy retained in the public mind most of those attributes associated with the kingship of the Middle Ages. The authority of the sovereign had ultimately been delegated to her by God as His representative on earth. As such, she was the fount of justice; maintaining what contemporaries regarded as an acceptable level of law and order, punishing wrongdoers and lawbreakers, and providing redress for those who had suffered from crime, misdemeanour, or injustice. Her subjects also looked to her to uphold the interests of her realm against the machinations of external powers (especially the pope!) and to defend it against attacks by foreign enemies, rebellious subjects, pirates, and other marauders. Hers, too, was the duty of maintaining true religion and the lawful Church, an issue of mounting relevance which, in the ideologically riven second half of the sixteenth century, raised the gravest questions of war and peace, external menace, and internal subversion. She was expected, in addition, to do all she could to protect, encourage, and foster agriculture, industry, and trade, promote economic and social harmony, safeguard employment, and succour the deserving poor.

[1] Jones, *NLWJ*, VI, 283–309.

On the whole, Elizabeth's monarchy was strong, stable, and popular. There were, none the less, serious and insurmountable limitations to its power to influence events. Without a standing army, police force, or salaried bureaucracy, or any means of levying taxation at a level that might have brought such desirable instruments of coercion, persuasion, and control within its grasp, the ability of government to direct the life of the Queen's subjects was narrowly restricted. It had perforce to rely on the goodwill and co-operation of the 'political nation', i.e., that minority of subjects sufficiently propertied, educated, informed, and interested to participate in the tasks of government, either at the centre or, more particularly, in the localities. These subjects comprised about a quarter or a fifth of the adult male population (women were largely, though not wholly, excluded). They consisted in the main of landowners, ranging from yeomen up to the nobility, and of the more substantial burgesses of towns and cities. Between them and the government there existed an unwritten but well-understood arrangement that, in executing the authority entrusted to them, public policy might frequently have to take second place to the private interests of powerful individuals. Without such a tacit understanding, government could not have functioned at all.

The particular problems facing the Elizabethan administration in Wales were much the same as those existing throughout the realm. The country was still prone to outbursts of turbulence and lawlessness, which would continue into the seventeenth century. Earlier ideas that the Act of Union had brought instant solutions to disorder like a day-star dispelling darkness were not well-founded. Landowning families, great and small, maintained their retainers and followers and were prepared to threaten antagonists, browbeat officials and juries, and, if they saw fit, resort to force. In an atmosphere of unceasing competition for office, land, possessions, and influence, there was almost unlimited scope for illegal pressure, bullying, sharp practice, intrigue, and excessive or malicious litigation. Another sphere fraught with hazards was that of religion. The government constantly faced refusals to accept its dictates, outbursts of controversy, dissension, and the possibility of meddling by foreign powers tempted to take advantage of internal divisions and resentment. Wales, was, moreover, economically backward, with its population outstripping resources; feeding it gave rise to severe problems of food supply in times of poor harvests and acute shortage like those of 1585–7 and 1593–7. On such occasions the government intervened to mitigate as best it could the hardships being suffered. Meeting all these responsibilities cost money and Wales was now required to contribute its share to royal taxation. It was also brought within the scope of arrangements for levying indirect taxation by means of customs collection.

One major difficulty about this whole extension of royal authority was that all official proceedings had to be conducted in the English language, of which the majority of the Welsh had little or no command. Much had therefore to be translated into Welsh for their benefit, but even so some litigants felt themselves at a painful disadvantage. William Gerard suggested in 1576 that one of the judges of Great Sessions should understand Welsh, because 'many times the evidence is told according to the mind of the interpreter, whereby the evidence is expounded contrary to that which is said by the examinate, so the judge giveth a wrong charge'.[2] But whereas in Ireland English administrators were convinced that they had to annihilate native customs to reduce it to order, in Wales, though they wanted to abolish what was left of Welsh law and establish English as the official language, they did not intend to destroy Welsh culture but to shape society after the English fashion. They were not unwilling to sanction the informal use of Welsh in the courts and elsewhere to enable the people to understand the proceedings.

The competence of royal government in Wales no less than England depended largely on the effective working of its major institutions at the centre—Privy Council, departments of state, courts at Westminster, and Parliament. The impact of all these bodies on Wales was steadily increasing and, had it not been that by the standards of the age they worked tolerably well and consistently, the arrangements for the government of Wales, created by the legislation of 1536–43 would hardly have been worth the paper they were written on. What ultimately accounted for the increased effectiveness of government in Wales in contrast with that of an earlier period was the cutting edge of the central instruments of authority, and the stability they ensured as compared with the vicissitudes of the fifteenth century.

At the centre of government the dynamo generating power which radiated to all corners of the realm was the Privy Council, the compact group of Elizabeth's most influential and authoritative advisers, hand-picked by the Queen herself for their talent and dependability. Its daughter body in Wales, the Council in the Marches, came under its close and watchful scrutiny, as did all the courts of justice, together with the activities of their officers from the Lord President down to the humblest parish constables. Nothing was too great or too small for the Privy Council to concern itself with—from instructions for the defence of Wales in 1588 down to a begging licence for one David ap Richard of Caernarfon. Its principal concerns, however, were with military security, religious conformity, and restraining those quarrels which seriously threatened the general peace. More often than not it operated through the Council in the Marches and stood foursquare behind it; but it also appointed its own commissioners

2 PRO SP12/107/21.

when it saw fit and might order them to act or report back without reference to anyone else. The scope of all Privy Council interventions in Wales widened and their frequency increased during Elizabeth's reign. By its very existence the Council contributed enormously to order and good government in Wales.

Reinforcing the jurisdiction of the Privy Council was that of conciliar courts at Westminster. Litigiousness increased prodigiously in Wales no less than England, and a rising tide of Welsh suits flowed into the courts of Chancery, Exchequer, Requests, and Star Chamber, in spite of the facilities offered by the Council in the Marches and Great Sessions for hearing actions similar to those taken to Westminster. This litigation increased the prestige of the Westminster courts, augmented royal revenues, and accustomed the Welsh to the notion of looking more regularly to London as the main seat of authority and justice. Most influential of the courts was Star Chamber, in essence the Privy Council sitting as a court of law. It became immensely respected as a body which could administer punishment to even the most powerful subjects. The number of suits taken there from Wales rose from 9 during the first five years of the reign to 243 between the thirty-fifth and fortieth years, dropping to 127 for the last five years.[3] By going to Star Chamber the Welsh had not necessarily lost confidence in the Council in the Marches. Nor were all their suits taken seriously when they reached there. Out of 67 Star Chamber cases relating to Breconshire, for example, only 31 can be shown to have been proceeded with in earnest by hearing them in full in London or taking depositions of witnesses locally in Wales.[4]

The High Court of Parliament was another central institution where the Welsh voice was heard—however rarely and mutedly. Welsh members' participation in the parliamentary proceedings was slight and under-active; they rarely spoke in debates, regularly applied for leave of absence, and attended poorly at the House. Out of 770 bills passing through Parliament between 1559 and 1581 only 16 related to Wales.[5] Evidently the main reason for their becoming members was to put up a marker indicating their status in their own county and to make known their family name in the hope of extending their influence and estates and enhancing their chances of arranging favourable marriages for their children.

REGIONAL INSTITUTIONS

Before turning to the regional and local institutions of government we

[3] H. A. Lloyd, 'Wales and the Star Chamber', *WHR*, v (1971), 257–60.
[4] P. Williams, 'The Star Chamber and the Council in the Marches of Wales, 1558–1603', *BBCS*, xvi (1956), 287–97.
[5] G. R. Elton in Davies (ed.), *Welsh Society and Nationhood*, pp. 108–21.

should remember that appointments continued to be made to many of the Crown and Marcher offices which had existed before 1536. Some of those appointed might be tempted, from time to time, to try to revive the ancient privileges associated with those posts in order to repair their fortunes. A native of Montgomeryshire, one William Herle, hoped to recoup his earlier losses by pressing the claims of his office of *rhaglaw* in Cardiganshire, only to find to his chagrin that sixteenth-century 'Cardis' were no more prepared to part with their money than their twentieth-century counterparts. Herle ran head-on into unyielding opposition led by John Pryse of Gogerddan, who, by virtue of his extensive estates, his office as *custos rotulorum*, legal training, and domineering personality, placed himself in the van of resistance.[6] Magnates like the earl of Pembroke or George Owen of Henllys were also bent on seeking to revive the potentially profitable perquisites of Marcher lords, lapsed or overlooked to the profit of quick-fingered tenants. Owen's attempts to resuscitate his rights as lord of Cemaes made him, in the words of his biographer, an 'unpopular reactionary'[7] retarding the movement for change and greater freedom.

These older offices and customs had been deprived of much of their importance by the legislation of 1536–43, which had conferred a new or enhanced role upon the two regional bodies, the Council in the Marches and the Great Sessions. The Council, placed on a statutory footing for the first time in 1543, had its scope and competence more precisely defined later by instructions sent down to it by the Privy Council from time to time—in 1553, 1574, and 1586, for example. Its authority and jurisdiction became so wide that George Owen had to admit in 1594 that they were 'not certainly known'. It held sway over an extensive area of Wales and the Marches, including all the Welsh counties and four English border ones, though Bristol escaped its control in 1562, Cheshire in 1569, and Worcester tried unsuccessfully to free itself in 1576. Early on, the Council had met in various places; but during Elizabeth's reign, it came to be located permanently in that 'town of noble fame', 'for Wales most apt, most fit and best' (Thomas Churchyard) and natural centre of the Marches, Ludlow.

Its two most eminent Elizabethan presidents, covering nearly the whole reign between them, were Sir Henry Sidney (1559–86) and Henry, second earl of Pembroke (1586–1601). Sidney, a man of tolerant and generous nature, liked his Welsh charges, took a genuine delight in their history and culture, and treated them with trust and liberality. 'Europe hath not a better country to govern' was his verdict on Wales. But his regime was much weakened by three long spells he was obliged to spend in Ireland and by opposition from the more rigid and authoritarian Whitgift, his vice-president for some years. The earl of Pembroke, scion of the most famous

---

[6] D. L. Jones, 'William Herle and the Office of Rhaglaw . . . ', *NLWJ* XVII (1971), 161–82.
[7] B. G. Charles, *George Owen of Henllys* (Aberystwyth, 1974), p. 98.

of Welsh aristocratic families, also took his duties seriously and was anxious to carry out reforms. Much debilitated by illness and absence, however, he found himself unable to cope adequately with the difficulties of the 1590s, arising, on the one hand, from Essex's meteoric rise to power, and the steadily rising tide of opposition from common lawyers, on the other. These presidents were supported by a council consisting of a handful of noblemen, bishops, and assize judges, and a larger number of gentry and lawyers. Out of ninety-six members appointed between 1560 and 1603, seven were nobles, forty-seven lawyers, forty gentry, and two were indeterminate. Lawyers were the most active and useful members, though by 1602 numerical precedence had passed to the county gentry. Very few Welshmen were included, and, apart from the bishops, they were recruited from major landowners like Sir John Perrot or Sir William Herbert of Cardiff. In addition, the Council had a small army of its own officials, major and minor, and a large retinue—too large was the common complaint—of barristers, attorneys, and clerks.

The Council, like many other Tudor bodies, functioned both as a court of justice and an administrative organ, though contemporaries would not have deemed it necessary or desirable to distinguish too finely between its responsibilities. As a court it exercised a jurisdiction over misdemeanours and breaches of the peace very similar to that of Star Chamber. In addition it held a commission of oyer et terminer which allowed it to inquire into cases of murder, treason, and felony that were excluded from Star Chamber and also to use torture to extract evidence. It could, additionally, try those offences against penal statutes, so called because of the penalties they carried against those who infringed them. These laws, enacted by the government in its attempts to regulate social and economic life by means of legislation, covered matters such as defence, commerce, industry, food supplies and prices, and relations between employers and workmen. They were enforced by the Council in the Marches in common with a number of other courts. It also came to be regarded as a court for implementing all statutes relating to ecclesiastical and religious issues. Finally, on the civil side, it enjoyed an ample equity jurisdiction, i.e., it could try those issues for which no remedy existed at common or statute law. By the early seventeenth century, equity cases dominated the work of the Council and made it known as the 'Chancery Court of Wales', in spite of the many suits from Wales taken to the Chancery Court in London. In its capacity as a court of justice the Council was widely embracing in scope, relatively quick and cheap in procedure, convenient of access, and so frequently resorted-to that it was described as the 'very place of refuge for all the poor oppressed of Wales to fly unto'.[8]

---

[8] Owen, III, 23.

Contemporary observers of the Council evidently regarded it as being primarily a court of justice, to the extent of virtually ignoring its function as an administrative body in their comments. In this latter capacity, none the less, it had major duties to fulfil. Dominating all others in the Council's surviving administrative record for the years from 1569 to 1591[9] were its military functions. From 1586 onwards the President of the Council was ex officio Lord Lieutenant of all the counties in his charge except Gloucestershire. To assist him, he appointed deputy-lieutenants in each county and sought to secure the co-operation of sheriffs, justices of the peace, and other local functionaries. In this respect and a host of others he needed reliable officials, and so it was essential that the Council should have a say in choosing them. In recommending who should be chosen for the three key offices of deputy-lieutenant, sheriff, and justice of the peace, the Council did have an important voice. But not the only one; for magnates at court and locally were importunate in pressing for the selection of their own friends and clients. Not that choice by the Council was necessarily any guarantee of a good appointment. One of the worst of the deputy-lieutenants was Cadwaladr Price of Merioneth, who had to be turned out of office in 1601 for gross corruption. Yet, even after his dismissal, he was strongly supported by the Council's president, Pembroke, in an-all-too clear example of the pressure of patronage on behalf of an unsuitable officer. The Council was also supposed to keep a vigilant eye on the activities of local officials in order to anticipate, restrain, or punish disorder. Thus it intervened in 1573 and 1576 to control the licensing of alehouses, notorious as potential hotbeds of crime, disorder, and illegal games. In 1571 it moved to take action against possible violence at a Merioneth election, and thieving and disorder at Ludlow Fair in 1576. Again, in 1585 it roundly tongue-lashed all the officials of local government for their scandalous failure to prevent or report 'outrageous offences and misdemeanours'. Other typical administrative activities on its part were its attempts to ensure fair distribution of food in times of famine in 1585–7, or its efforts to check the still prevalent cattle stealing and also to prevent the over-stocking of the commons of mid Wales (see below pp. 387–8).

During Elizabeth's later years the Council encountered critics who complained that the President and judges were neither as vigorous nor as respected as Lee and Englefield had been; certainly not in relation to powerful and self-interested members of the Council itself, like Sir John Perrot or Sir Richard Trevor. Others contended that the attendance of judges and officials was poor and that there were far too many cases—'great heaps of unfit trifling suits'—many trivial, others malicious.[10]

[9] R. Flenley, *The Register of the Council in the Marches of Wales, 1569–91* (London, 1916).
[10] David Lewis, 'The Court of the President and Council of Wales and the Marches, 1478–1575', *Y Cymmr.*, XII (1897).

Such litigation was encouraged by the low costs awarded and by the presence of too many attorneys and officials, who, paid out of fees, found it very greatly to their own advantage to encourage unjustified actions. In justice to the Council, it could be argued that many of these shortcomings were common to other courts as well. It was an excessively litigious age and the Queen wanted her courts, like every other aspect of her government, run on the cheap, so she made over-heavy demands on the Presidents of the Council and others. But, whatever the deficiencies of the Council, it had performed, and was performing, an extremely valuable service in slowly bringing Wales to a more peaceful condition and more general acknowledgement of the rule of law. An observer as perceptive as George Owen in 1594 warned those who believed they could do without it altogether that it was still indispensable for good government and that those who called for its abolition might be among the first to experience the ill effects if their wish were granted.

Another major instrument for enforcing law and order and encouraging respect for the judicial process was the Court of Great Sessions. Extended to all the counties of Wales in 1543, these courts were a vast improvement on the unsatisfactory conditions which had previously obtained in the Marches. They met regularly, could not be bought off, and brought fairly efficient justice within easy reach of the populace. Sessions met in each county twice a year for a period of six days. In addition to its assize judge, each circuit of three shires had its own complement of officials, of whom the protonotary (recorder), attorney-general, chamberlain, and chancellor were the most important. Great Sessions was endowed with extensive powers. It was charged with holding all manner of pleas of the Crown in 'as large and ample a manner' as King's Bench, 'pleas of Assizes and all other pleas and actions, real, personal and mixed' comparable to Common Pleas, and generally 'to minister common justice to all and singular the King's subjects'.[11] It also acquired an equity jurisdiction at an early, if not precisely determinable, stage in its history. It attracted so 'many great and weighty causes' that by 1576 an additional justice had to be appointed to each circuit. The judges evoked this glowing tribute from George Owen: 'the guilty condemned with pity and the innocent delivered by justice', with rich and poor being treated impartially.[12] The detailed operations of Great Sessions are still shrouded in veils of darkness; but it appears that the court rarely dealt with cases of equity or serious disorder, which were almost always sent to the Council. The cases most frequently heard seem to have been those relating to debt (rarely less than 50 per cent of the actions), trespass, minor disputes over land, and many thefts of livestock (especially cattle and sheep), wool, clothing, and household goods. Punishment was

---

[11] Williams, *Making Mod. Wales*, p. 129. [12] Owen, III, 143.

harsh; those convicted of minor offences were flogged or pilloried, and those found guilty of grand larceny or more serious crimes were hanged.[13] In spite of George Owen's eulogies, Great Sessions was not without its deficiencies. Some of its judges were of inferior quality and guilty of corruption. The courts were held at inconvenient times when people were busy on the land with sowing or harvest. There was much evidence of pressure on jurors. It was difficult to ensure attendance at court and the implementation of verdicts. Finally, it was alleged that there were far too many shady out-of-court settlements and compositions and too many under-valuations of stolen objects so as to reduce the crime from grand larceny (theft of an object worth more than a shilling), for which an offender might be hanged, to petty larceny; though one can hardly blame juries for wanting to spare life in this way.

LOCAL INSTITUTIONS

As far as local government and justice were concerned, the basic unit was the shire. Many of the Welsh shires had only come into existence in 1536; even so, by Elizabeth's reign all had become fully absorbed into the popular consciousness as the natural units for government, administration, justice, and politics. Denbighshire might have been one of the newly created shires in 1536 but its poets were nevertheless wont to praise their patrons for participating freely in shire activities.[14] In each county, administration and justice were carried out by virtue of the authority entrusted to its officials by various commissions, chief among them the commission of the peace issued to justices of the peace. The core of their activities lay in Quarter Sessions, the records of which have unfortunately been lost for every Welsh county except Caernarfonshire. If, however, Caernarfonshire is typical—and, as one of the ancient Edwardian shires, it may not be—its gentry took in their stride the arrangements instituted by the establishment of Quarter Sessions. In practice, the new machinery made surprisingly little difference to the pattern of authority previously wielded. As justices of the peace, those of Caernarfonshire were as keen as the gentry everywhere to turn their office to their own advantage and rarely scrupled about neglecting their duty or distorting it whenever it seemed beneficial to them to do so. The editor of the Caernarfonshire records has argued vigorously, though perhaps a shade too indulgently, that they carried out their tasks in the searchlight of an active public opinion, conscious of being watched from above by the gimlet eyes of Privy

---

[13] K. O. Fox, 'An Edited Calendar of the First Pembrokeshire Plea Roll', *NLWJ*, xiv (1965–6), 469–84; E. J. Sherrington, 'The Plea Rolls of the Courts of Great Sessions', *NLWJ*, xiii (1964), 363–73.

[14] J. G. Jones 'Patrymau Bonheddig Uchelwrol Sir Ddinbych', *TDHS*, 29 (1980).

Council, Council in the Marches, and judges of assize, and from below by those of lesser gentry, yeomen, and burgesses.[15] Such scrutiny might not be able to make good the deficiencies caused by self-interest or the non-existence of a regular, disciplined police force; but, as a system, rule by justices of the peace was probably preferable to the kind of regime which had existed in the Middle Ages, and it worked reasonably well.

Quarter Sessions met four times a year, with varying numbers of justices present. In its capacity as a judicial court it dealt only with petty lawsuits and misdemeanours, the more serious matters being referred to superior tribunals. The Caernarfonshire records disclose the existence of a good deal of minor violence, in which women were involved hardly less than men and which often occurred in churches or churchyards, and much petty theft, some illegal games, and other minor offences. In its administrative role, Quarter Sessions was required to implement a vast and growing body of statutes. Among its most important responsibilities was the working of the Poor Law, which involved determining the paternity of bastards, arranging apprenticeships, controlling vagrants, and relieving the deserving poor. The justices also licensed and controlled alehouses, determined wage-levels, checked abuses of common rights, and carried out a miscellany of comparable functions.

A number of minor courts continued to operate at a lower level. Within each county the sheriff held the monthly freeholders' court, and his deputies conducted the hundred courts every two or three weeks. Both were concerned chiefly with the innumerable cases of petty debt and trespass arising in a pastoral society chronically destitute of ready cash, living much of its time on credit, and pasturing its animals in open unenclosed fields and commons. Manorial courts leet and courts baron also continued to be summoned in former Marcher areas. They dealt with minor affrays and disputes springing from the ownership and administration of landed property. Trivial as their concerns may now appear to have been, in the eyes of ordinary inhabitants their proceedings probably assumed much more significance than those of more prestigious courts. Another unit of local administration increasing in importance was the parish. It was charged not merely with its customary functions of maintaining the church and its fabric but also with registering births, marriages, and deaths, the upkeep of parish boundaries, roads, and bridges, and, above all, with discharging in detail the provisions of the Poor Law.

Towns corporate stood apart to some extent from the shire administration outlined above. They were governed by the terms of the charter granted to them by the Crown or Marcher lord, allowing them a considerable measure of self-government, which they jealously upheld. Their privileges may have

---

[15] Williams, *Caerns. Q.S. Records*, p. lxxxiii.

varied widely in detail, but most towns were governed by a mayor (sometimes known as portreeve or bailiff), aldermen, and common council of burgesses, who usually comprised a minority of about 8–10 per cent of the population. The mayor, elected annually, exercised within his own town many of the functions of the deputy-lieutenant, sheriff, justice of the peace, coroner, and escheator. Each town also had its company of officers, including recorder, common attorneys, and such picturesquely named individuals as ale-taster, steward of the mountain, and guardian of the market. Every borough was empowered to make its own by-laws for such matters as the regulation of trade and manufacture, conduct of markets and fairs, measures for rudimentary public health and cleanliness, punishment of offenders, and, most important of all by the end of the century, relief of the poor and control of vagrants. Borough finance was raised by means of rents, tolls, impositions, and fines. Though these towns were no longer the *capita* of Marcher lordships, their lords were still anxious to exercise some degree of control over them, partly for financial reasons and partly because the boroughs had the right to return members of parliament. This residual oversight was normally exercised through the lord's steward, usually drawn from among the local gentry.

OFFICE-HOLDERS

In each of the counties there were, broadly speaking, three levels of office-holders. It would be misleading to try to define them too sharply or precisely, or to imagine that all levels remained set hard and fast in position without any individual or family slipping down or others climbing up. At the topmost level there was a small group of perhaps two, three, or four families who held the most important and prestigious office of deputy-lieutenant. Very near to this group and hardly distinguishable from it came the remaining top county families—some half-dozen perhaps—from whose midst were drawn the next most important officials: sheriffs, members of parliament, and justices of the peace, who held the dignity almost as 'of right'. Then came the other esquires and substantial gentry, numbering by the early seventeenth century as many as 30–40 households, who could expect to provide a justice of the peace from time to time. Below them were a large number of families of 'parish' gentry, freeholders, and yeomen, not easily distinguishable from one another. From them were drawn coroners, escheators, high and petty constables, jurors, and the like. All these groups, together with substantial lawyers, clerics, merchants, and burgesses, were the people who had 'voice and authority' in the commonwealth (though a few enjoyed a great deal more of both than others). In short, they constituted the 'political nation'. Speaking of those mainly engaged in local government, Bishop Richard Davies, who had considerable experience of north and south Wales and who sat in the Lords, Council in the Marches, and on the justices' bench, expressed a distinctly unfavourable view of them. He charged them with 'partial dealing to pleasure rich men' and justifying the wicked; they 'pill and poll the country, beggar their poor neighbours' and dress their houses 'with the goods of the poor'.[16] A senior Welsh judge, David Lewis, was equally condemnatory of those 'men of no substance nor of credit made sheriffs and justices of the peace, which most live by polling and pilling'.[17] Both these critics may have been too one-sidedly severe; but that there was a good deal of truth in their censures will become more apparent as we come to examine in detail the way these officials bore themselves in office.

The ranking office of local government was the deputy-lieutenancy, appointment to which was usually a sure sign that the man chosen was pre-eminent in his county. Not unexpectedly, there was often intense lobbying to obtain the dignity. Typical of the reactions of a candidate for the office in a county where faction was rife was Sir John Salusbury's emotional plea of 1602 to Sir Robert Cecil to remember his father's precedents and 'have him [Salusbury] in mind upon the setting down of deputies' at a time when Salusbury's enemies were exerting powerful leverage in high places.[18] After 1586 deputy-lieutenants were regularly appointed; most Welsh counties having two, though Glamorgan in 1590 had five. It was an office which could burden the holder with heavy expenses. Sir John Wogan claimed that he had spent £1,000, which he believed to be too 'great for a man of so small a living'.[19] It was onerous in other ways. It entailed the regular mustering of troops and might also mean raising loans for military purposes and controlling the illegal export of food to enemy countries. Such activities often aroused resentment and unpleasantness among neighbours. Even a conscientious deputy-lieutenant like George Owen was not above taking bribes, while such prize rogues as Cadwaladr Price and John Lewis Owen of Merioneth were found guilty of embezzling £1,000 worth of armour, levying illegal taxes, and making illicit profits out of the musters.

Sheriffs were most frequently drawn from major landowning families, though from a wider group than deputy-lieutenants. Though they now carried less weight than in the fifteenth century and served for a year only, within their counties they were still the chief executive officers of central and local government. They were appointed annually by the Crown from a list of names supplied by the Council in the Marches. They impanelled juries, kept prisoners in custody and produced them for trial, levied fines,

[16] *Funeral Sermon*, no pagination.   [17] *Y Cymmr.*, XIII, 131.
[18] W. J. Smith (ed.), *Calendar of Salusbury Correspondence, 1553–c.1700* (Cardiff, 1954), pp. 43–4.
[19] *HMC Salisbury MSS*, XI, 164.

and carried out sentences. They served writs, promulgated proclamations, delivered royal letters, and collected taxes. They conducted those county and hundred courts so much resorted to because justices of the peace had no jurisdiction over debts. As returning officers in parliamentary elections they were able to determine the outcome with scant regard to the actual voting figures. In spite of the heavy expenses that might be incurred when serving as sheriff, of which George Barlow complained bitterly, avowing that some had been 'utterly undone and others greatly weakened . . . and impoverished',[20] there is no indication that men were loth to compete for the office or offer inducements to obtain it. Thomas Martyn told John Wynn in 1592 that a *douceur* of £10 would greatly have helped to make his son, Robert Wynn, sheriff; but if men relied only on words and used no more effective means they must take what befell.[21] So eager was Ellis Price for the office that he served no fewer than fourteen times—seven in his own Merioneth and seven in neighbouring Denbighshire (4), Anglesey (2), and Caernarfonshire (1). Men who thus served outside their own counties prompted the barbed criticism of 1572 that, having 'neither lands nor goods in the county', they 'lay in alehouses and lived of the spoil of the county'. Such accusations were confirmed by the sharp reprimand administered by the Council in the Marches in 1572 to those sheriffs who had 'used their office to their own private gain' by selling posts within their gift, a practice which led to extortion, bribery, and *commortha*.[22] Neither this nor any similar censure seems to have made much difference in practice, for some of the most flagrant examples of corruption occurred during Edward Kemys's four terms as sheriff of Glamorgan between 1576 and 1595. He was as bad an example of a dishonest sheriff as Elizabethan Wales could offer: packing and intimidating juries, selling offices, practising blackmail, and accepting bribes. 'If the consistency and scope of his abuses are unique, the fact of corruption is not.'[23] Not even heavy pressure from the Council in the Marches would necessarily abash a sheriff well entrenched in his own locality. Thomas Lewis of Y Fan, at the time of the notorious disagreement over the appointment of coroners in Glamorgan in 1572, defied the injunctions of the Council, maintaining contemptuously that if it came to the worst it was but a matter of paying the fine. Nor did much better result always arise from the remonstrances of assize judges. Walter Vaughan of Golden Grove, found guilty of serious offences, was mainly concerned with not having to eat humble pie before Justice Atkins at Great Sessions. Some of the sheriffs' underlings—under-sheriff, gaoler, and hundred bailiffs—were just as rapacious and unprincipled as their superiors. George Owen commented that as a hundred bailiff was obliged

---

[20] H. A. Lloyd, *The Gentry of South-west Wales* (Cardiff, 1968), pp. 146–7.
[21] *CWP*, p. 25.   [22] PRO SP12/235/18; Flenley, *Register*, pp. 98–9.
[23] G. E. Jones, *The Gentry and the Elizabethan State* (Swansea, 1977), pp. 65–9.

to pay £10 or £20 for his office, which he held only for a year, he did not shrink from 'pilling and polling the poor people' to recover his outlay.[24]

The backbone of local justice, policing, and administration, and the most important and typical local officials of England and Wales, were the justices of the peace. Presiding over them in each county was the *custos rotulorum*, normally the most consequential landowner in the shire. He was assisted by the clerk of the peace, usually a gentleman who had gone through the Inns of Court or else a county lawyer connected with the *custos*. The justices were, in theory, to be selected from the 'best sort of gentlemen in the shire' by the Lord Chancellor or Lord Keeper on the advice of the Privy Council, Council in the Marches, and the judges. All these nominating bodies, it need hardly be added, were deluged with copious streams of advice, solicitation, pleading, and pressure from interested parties, chief among them the would-be justices and their patrons. Those ultimately chosen were supposed to be 'good men, lawful men, no maintainers of evil, best of reputation', learned in the laws, and most worthy in the counties wherein they were appointed.[25] Welsh poets had no doubts about the virtues which should distinguish them either: noble lineage, intelligence, graciousness, wisdom, fairness, justice, godliness, and public service. In practice few of the justices would have dared peer too closely at themselves in these mirrors of perfection. Contemporary judicial records were all too often littered with evidence of their cupidity, misuse of power, and persistent quarrels; their proneness to taking bribes, protecting murderers and felons, resorting to threats and violence, obstructing the processes of the law, supporting friends, and thwarting enemies. Even so, the system worked about as well as anyone might have expected from a group of ambitious, self-seeking, unsalaried administrators.

Originally, the statute of 1536 had limited their number to eight in each county. Because of the additional responsibilities placed upon them, and still more on account of the increasing numbers coveting the honour of being a justice, their ranks had expanded rapidly. By 1575 there were ninety-nine justices in seven counties; and in Glamorgan they rose from eleven in 1542 to about twenty by the 1590s and thirty-three in 1642. Increased numbers precipitated complaints that 'divers men of mean living had climbed up on to the bench' to its discredit; and urgent appeals were made that the property qualification of £20 a year in landed income, waived for Welsh justices in 1536, should be strictly applied. Although their numbers had just about doubled, justices were not evenly distributed over the countryside. They were very thin on the ground in Cardiganshire, where as late as 1594 brigands still flourished on the old road between Rhayader and Aberystwyth. There were no justices resident in the

[24] Owen, III, 71–4.   [25] Owen, II, 53.

hundreds of Dewsland or Cemaes in 1575, nor any in the hills of Glamorgan. As late as 1617 Sir John Wynn was oppressed by the burden of having only one justice living between Gwydir and the towns of Ruthin and Denbigh and for the hilly and waste part of the shire extending for over twenty miles from the confines of Merioneth to the sea.[26]

POLITICS AND RIVALRIES

The Elizabethan era was as intensely acquisitive and fiercely competitive an age, at all levels in society, as the fifteenth century. Men were acutely conscious that they had not only to be engaged in a constant struggle to maintain their own position and possessions in face of ambitious competitors but that they had also to be perpetually on the alert to secure additional advantages for themselves and their friends. The choice of all the officers of local government from the highest to the lowest depended very largely on the outcome of the interplay of those ties of patronage which permeated the whole of society from the Queen through her courtiers and great aristocrats down to the county gentry and their clients and dependants. George Owen, authentic voice of the politically conscious orders, described the earls of Pembroke, Worcester, and Essex as the 'chief patrons and careful conservators and protectors of this poor country of Wales'.[27] The society in which they lived was an ordered hierarchy, with its norms and conventions of precedence; but it was also a torridly and incessantly competitive one, in which those who possessed 'clout' had no compunction about using it. The leading figures at court vied fiercely with one another in their efforts to secure office and advantage for their protégés, in order to satisfy both their own and the latter's ambitions and to place them in strategic positions. Men aspired to office at all levels appropriate to them because it conferred prestige, satisfied their pride, helped them make money, and afforded them added control over their own and others' clients or prevented their rivals from acquiring such influence. The greatest magnates needed to maintain their links with county society and secure a power base in the localities as well as at the centre. Apparently small local rivalries, like the keenly fought contest in Glamorgan for Barbara Gamage's hand in marriage (1574), could bring intervention on opposing sides from such luminaries of the court as Francis Walsingham, Howard of Effingham, Walter Ralegh, Henry Sidney, and James Croft; even the Queen herself knew what was going on.

All men of substance exhibited an oriental awareness of the importance of 'face' and status, and were almost unbearably sensitive to any insult to their honour, actual or imaginary. Ordinarily, they could look for a

[26] *CWP*, p. 131.   [27] Owen, III, 44–5.

compliant deference from lesser men; but if it was not forthcoming they showed no hesitation in brusquely reminding subordinates of what was expected. The classic case-study of the urge to power at its most insistent, and of a perilously short fuse when it was thwarted, is that of the second earl of Essex. Young, hot-blooded, and overweeningly ambitious, he dominated the politics of Wales from the mid-1580s to 1601. As early as 1585 he pronounced, 'I am desirous to countenance my friends and servants in this country as far forth as I am able'. The following year, writing of his friend, Walter Vaughan of Golden Grove, fined by Star Chamber, he declared, 'If I and all the friends I have can help it, he shall have no wrong'. The 1590s witnessed the rapid rise of the Essex faction, engineered in Wales by the earl's able but unscrupulous steward, Sir Gelly Meyrick. No fewer than eleven justices of the peace in south-west Wales could be described as 'serving men in livery . . . belonging to the earl of Essex' and four out of the seven members of parliament there in 1593 were his clients. When in 1595 the government issued an order threatening to remove such retainers from the commission of the peace, Essex replied with hauteur that he would free them from his service rather than that they should lose 'any jot of their former reputations', confident that he was sure of their love anyway.[28] The earl of Pembroke, now in ill-health and isolated from court, saw the need to thwart Essex as far as he could. He hotly resented Meyrick as Essex's 'household servant, not residing in Radnorshire . . . and only brought thither by marriage to his wife'. When, however, Pembroke failed to get John Bradshaw nominated as deputy-lieutenant for Radnorshire, where Meyrick was particularly influential, he felt 'very sensible of the unkindness lately offered unto me' and nothing incensed him more than the 'scoffing laughter' of Essex, who succeeded in getting Meyrick appointed.[29] Another who had cause to be offended was Susan Morgan of Whitland, who wrote of Essex's men that they were insatiable for office: 'everything is fish that comes to their net' . . . 'so with their offices and brags they oppress all her Highness' poor subjects'.[30] Nemesis eventually caught up with Essex; and when his revolt had failed, Sir Richard Lewkenor could complacently inform Robert Cecil that the 'fall of the earl in those parts where he was greatest is not grieved at . . . Sir Gelly Meyrick himself lived by such oppression and overruling over them that they do not only rejoice at his fall but curse him bitterly'.[31] That, doubtless, may be no more than the tendency to join in rejoicing after the fall of a once-great figure.

Competition stemmed not only from the rivalries of the greatest magnates but was also reciprocally stimulated by the factions which existed

---

[28] BL Harleian MS, 6993, fo. 116; cf. Williams, *Council Marches*, pp. 282–8.
[29] Williams, *Council Marches*, p. 288.
[30] *HMC Salisbury MSS.*, VIII, 423.   [31] *HMC Salisbury MSS*, XI, 81.

among the leading landowners in Wales itself. Among the gentry there were comparable tussles and manœuvrings for position and influence on a smaller scale, though leading courtiers were often drawn in. All the counties were plagued by contests in which the gentry displayed an avid appetite for power and possessions. In some shires one family was cock of the walk. Sir John Perrot in Pembrokeshire had the 'most part of the gentlemen and freeholders of the county at his commandment'.[32] Edward Herbert dominated Montgomeryshire, Richard Bulkeley Anglesey, and John Wynn Caernarfonshire; though, in each of these counties, lesser bantams were game enough to challenge the most powerful birds' right to crow uncontested. Perrot, 'somewhat friended but more feared of the gentlemen and freeholders' of his county because of the heat of his own 'private malice and displeasure', stirred up enemies. They complained in 1570 that he avenged himself on their servants because they 'had not served his turn in juries or inquests or had displeased him in any other matter or they depended upon any gentleman with whom he was offended'.[33] Yet no single house was so strong as not to have its wings clipped by the Privy Council or go unresisted by its opponents. Perrot died in prison in 1590 and Richard Bulkeley was severely censured for his conduct in 1589. The Herberts had to fight a very closely run election against the Prices of Newtown in Montgomeryshire in 1588, which they won only because of the sharp practice of the sheriff. Nor could there be any guarantee that a family would be able to retain its position intact from one generation to another. Powerful though the Salusburies may have been in Denbighshire before 1586, the execution of Thomas Salusbury for his part in the Babington Plot eclipsed his family's influence for many years; and after Sir John Perrot's death, his descendants never enjoyed the same position of domination in Pembrokeshire.

In other counties there was no single paramount family and a number of influential houses battled for leadership. In Monmouthshire it was Morgan versus Herbert, in Breconshire Games versus Aubrey, in Denbighshire Salusbury versus Trevor, in Cardiganshire Lloyd versus Pryse, and in Merioneth Owen versus Nanney. Merioneth was a particularly interesting county. Remote and isolated, having little commerce and no mining, with Harlech its county town so decayed that it had no borough member, it might have been thought to be just a stagnant backwater. For many years the Prices of Plas Iolyn and the Owens of Llwyn shared the position of being the biggest frogs in the Merioneth pond. But before the end of Elizabeth's reign they were being successfully challenged by the Nanneys, especially, and the Lloyds of Rhiwgoch and the Vaughans of Corsygedol,

[32] Owen, II, 511; cf. B. E. Howells, 'The Elizabethan Squirearchy in Pembrokeshire', *Pembs. Hist.*, I (1959), 17–40.
[33] P. C. C. Evans, 'Sir John Perrot' (MA Thesis, Cardiff, 1940), p. 80.

to such effect that the county became hopelessly split asunder and its public life sadly impaired by relentless competition.[34] These influential families were rarely confined to a single household. In many districts they had cadet and allied branches powerfully installed alongside the main line to press the family interest. None had proliferated more successfully than the Herberts, who could almost be said to be like Woolworth's—'having branches everywhere'! Not that those branches always worked in the closest harmony. The Herbert earl of Pembroke was hopelessly at loggerheads with the chief resident representative of the family in Glamorgan, Sir William Herbert, over the disputes at Cardiff in the 1590s. The Salusbury branch at Rug, again, were sworn enemies of the senior branch at Lleweni.

The power of each great house still depended to a large extent on the number of men it had at its call as well as the depth of its purse. It was a matter of honour for every gentleman to gather around him in medieval fashion a following as large as his purse could be stretched to maintain—or possibly rather larger—and to preen himself on the body of kinsmen, retainers, freeholders, tenants, and servants he could muster to uphold his pretensions when any show of strength seemed necessary. Many of these followers were uncomplimentarily designated by Judge David Lewis as 'idle loiterers', who would 'pick and steal and kill or hurt any man' and 'yet would wash their hands thereof when the ill fact was done'.[35] It was probably no coincidence that a county like Glamorgan was as notorious for its frequent quarrels and outrages as for its large number of retainers. Many of the latter were certainly as touchy and disputatious as their master, possibly even more so, in upholding his 'honour' and were prompt to exacerbate an old quarrel or pick a new one on his behalf. Their lord must then, according to David Lewis, 'after the manner of the country, bear [them] in all actions be they never so bad'. Sir Richard Lewkenor, after trying to reconcile the Salusburies with the Trevors, warned Robert Cecil in 1601 that the people were 'factious and ready to follow those they do affect in all actions without respect to the lawfulness or unlawfulness thereof'.[36] A family as well known as the Salusburies could be accused by their Myddelton rivals of protecting retainers alleged to have committed no fewer than sixteen murders within eight years in the 1590s and compounding in cash for their offences.

Violence and bloodshed were always prone to break out in a society where people were thin-skinned and easily offended, and where most men

[34] H. G. Owen, 'Family Politics in Elizabethan Merionethshire', *BBCS*, XVIII (1959), 185–91.

[35] Lewis, *Y Cymmr.*, XIII, 130.

[36] A. H. Dodd, 'North Wales in the Essex Rising of 1601', *EHR*, LIX (1944), 348–70; W. J. Smith, 'The Salusburies as Maintainers of Murderers . . .', *NLWJ*, VI (1952), 235–8.

carried weapons as a matter of course. High words and threatening talk
were likely to degenerate quickly into open conflict and deadly blows. On
those occasions and in those places where men ordinarily congregated
together in any numbers the possibility existed that hot-tempered
individuals or rival factions might swap insults or more lethal exchanges. In
county towns at election times, when a show of 'party' strength had to be
assembled; in sessions, when clients needed to be protected and juries
might have to be pressurized; or at fairs and markets, when force of
numbers might be necessary to overawe opposing groups, trouble lay never
very far below the surface. Taverns, too, where passions were apt to be
inflamed by drink and reckless talk, not to mention their being haunts of
idlers, blackguards, thieves, and other shady characters, were liable to add
fuel to quarrels and disorders. Even churches, where men also gathered in
numbers, were not immune from outbreaks of emotion and disturbance
notably unchristian in nature.

It was, however, a positive sign of the slowly growing ascendancy of the
lawcourts and increased deference to the rule of law that such conflicts and
breaches of the peace were usually followed by court action. Much of our
information concerning them is culled from the records of suits subsequently
fought by the contending parties in the courts, especially Star Chamber.
But litigation not only followed breaches of the peace; it could itself be a
weapon with which to belabour an opponent. Excessive litigiousness tends
to be one of the features of a society moving from a violent phase in its
history to a more law-abiding one; feuds which were wont to be settled by
physical encounter become transferred to the lawcourt. When men went to
law so often and for so long, it was a golden age for lawyers. Some of those
suits involved issues of life and death and justified the fees and energy
spent on them. Others seemed hardly worth the effort, except that it was
presumably a matter of prime importance for any man of property not to
acquire the reputation of being a 'soft option' for the lynx-eyed,
determined, and malicious suitors in which the age abounded. The mental
attitudes of Elizabethans towards legal proceedings are nowhere brought
more vividly to life than in Sir John Stradling's animated and colourful
chronicle of the lawsuit fought over the sand-blown burrows of Merthyr
Mawr.[37] True to the propensities of the age for ex-parte legal pronouncements, his narrative indicts his antagonists alone as being prepared to use
violence, skulduggery, corruption, purloining of documents, abuse of
office, and any and every other device that came to hand. But from his own
story, in fact, it becomes plain that both parties were tenacious, ingenious,
and about equally unscrupulous. The ethics of litigation were far removed
from those of the twentieth century, and almost anything was fair in legal

[37] 'The Storie of the Lower Borowes of Merthyr Mawr', *SWMRS*, I (1932).

war as in love. Lawsuits were a convenient device to use in seeking to damage, even ruin, an opponent of more slender means. A great master of employing costly and vexatious lawsuits no less than a show of force to browbeat his enemies was John Perrot. Those who suffered heavily in legal battles against him have their names recorded in a list of 1581: John Barlow of Slebech lost 2,000 marks; Richard Barlow of St Davids £700; Rice ap Morgan £500; Edward Banester £500; Alban Stepney £400; William Philipps £300; George Owen £200; and Griffith White £300. Some smaller men, including Thomas Folland, a burgess of Haverfordwest, were said to be utterly ruined and reduced to beggary.[38] While suits continued to be referred to all lawcourts in growing numbers, a comment by William Harrison suggested that the Welsh were more addicted than almost anyone else in going to law. That may be so, but it is as well to remember that many actions were not seriously proceeded with, and others were cross-actions relating to the same dispute, which tended to give a misleading impression of the number of disagreements actually at issue.

The intensity of these antagonisms, outside and inside the court, may be gauged on a number of different occasions and a variety of issues which indicate where the epicentres of disruption lay. Some of the most dramatic and irreconcilable clashes occurred at contested elections. Then the prestige and honour of predominant houses were 'laid on the line' and almost the whole county pulled in behind one or other of the rivals in a way seldom otherwise equalled. The Member of Parliament for the shire was normally the head or the favourite son of the pre-eminent family, or the accepted representative of the ruling faction. Borough representation was far less honorific and offered scope for local burgesses, lesser gentry, or carpet-bagging lawyers seeking their place in the parliamentary sun. Ordinarily, the likely outcome in county constituencies was so predictable and widely accepted that elections were not fought. Contests were unpopular; they could fracture the peace of the whole county with disturbances which had an unpleasant habit of smouldering on threateningly for a long while afterwards. If they could be avoided so much the better in all men's eyes. As a result, there were signal instances of the long domination of a seat by the same family or families. In Breconshire, between 1542 and 1610, two families, Games of Newton and Vaughan of Porthaml, virtually monopolized the seat; in Carmarthenshire the Vaughans of Golden Grove sat seventeen times between 1563 and 1640; and the Pryses of Gogerddan thirteen times in Cardiganshire between 1553 and 1621. There were those rare and untoward occasions, nevertheless, when the nicest calculations went awry so that contests could not be avoided. They were all the more likely in Wales, where the single-member constituency made it impossible to accommodate the aspirations of two opposed factions—though even in two-member Monmouthshire in 1572 the Morgans and Herberts decided to slug it out.

If an election was contested, the candidates were obliged to drum up every last freeholder who had the vote, having 'scant left a boy at home to drive the plough', as they said of Denbighshire in 1588.[39] There might be an electorate of as many as 1,500–2,000 all pouring into the cramped and narrow streets of the county town, most of them bearing weapons of some sort. The key to the result lay less in the number of voters mustered than in the person of the sheriff. That worthy made no pretence of being impartial but was openly and unblushingly committed to one of the candidates. As returning officer he could and did practise many stratagems to favour his own side: canvassing support before and during the election; holding back the parliamentary writ or serving it early as it suited his party best; conducting the election at an unusual time or in an unfamiliar place; and polling the electors in an order favourable to his man. If all else failed, he was prepared to declare his candidate elected irrespective of the number of votes cast, confident in his expectation that if need be his allies would 'save him harmless' (i.e., pay his fine). Such chicanery was in evidence at a number of Elizabethan elections in Wales: Merioneth 1571, Haverfordwest 1571, Radnorshire 1572 and 1597, Montgomeryshire 1588, Denbighshire 1588 and 1601, and Cardiganshire 1601. Details of all of them have been elegantly recounted by Sir John Neale.[40]

Other issues which provoked tension and conflicts were defence and the mustering of troops (below, pp. 368–72), religion, and divisions between town and country. From the 1570s onwards the government, greatly perturbed by the relationship between recusants and disloyalty to the regime, regularly chivvied its agents in the localities into inquiring minutely concerning the allegiance of their neighbours who were recusants or suspected papists. Early in 1588 the Privy Council informed Lord Pembroke of its profound suspicions of Catholic sympathizers in Wales, avowed and secret, expressing its conviction that those planning invasion would 'never attempt the same' were it not for the 'hope which the fugitives and rebels abroad do give . . . of those bad members that already are known to be recusants'.[41] Further inquiries were set afoot in the 1590s (above, pp. 327–8), including one of 1593 concerning those 'beyond the seas, sent over . . . under colour of learning languages', and their 'parents and patrons at home'.[42] Few even of the Catholic gentry were seduced from their loyalty. Those who did allow themselves to waver, usually found that retribution was swift and severe. Others discovered that dangerous

---

[39] J. E. Neale, *The Elizabethan House of Commons* (London, 1949), p. 115.
[40] Neale, *Elizabethan Commons*, Chaps. 1–4.
[41] *CWP*, p. 20.   [42] *CLP*, pp. 19–20.

accusations of papist disloyalty might freely be bandied about in efforts to blacken reputations and weaken legal positions. Morgan Jones, justice of the peace at Llandeilo, was accused in Star Chamber by the servants of the Vaughans of Golden Grove and in turn brought counter-actions against them, in relation to an affray involving a killing, in which he appeared to be as much on trial for his religious beliefs as for any other misdemeanours. The county where, more than in any other, the struggle between Anglicans and Catholics dominated the feuds of the gentry, was Monmouthshire, where the recusants had uncommonly influential patrons and were to be found in larger numbers than anywhere else in Wales.[43]

Relations between town and country frequently became strained. Corporate towns, jealous of their burghal privileges, resented any attempts by the surrounding gentry to control them. Some of the burgesses were themselves descended of gentry stock but, like their fellow-townsmen, had no wish to be brought under over-zealous gentry surveillance. The bigger and more prosperous the town, the more it tended to cherish a robust spirit of independence. The earl of Worcester, lord of Gower and the borough of Swansea, was moved to protest indignantly against the behaviour of his burgesses there: 'for that they will bear their money against me in any suit I think they might as well come to cut my throat . . . I am loth to deal with them in any kind of way.'[44] Those members of the gentry living close to towns, appreciating their importance as venues of elections, sessions, fairs, markets, and other activities, dearly loved to try to get their hands on the levers of power when they could. They built town houses and installed their servants or clients in the boroughs. With men of pride and spirit on both sides, it was to be expected that teeth were often bared, and threats or blows exchanged. Some of the clashes were heated but short-lived; others rumbled on for years, flaring up at intervals like partly dormant volcanoes irrupting into life. There was a bloody clash between the retainers of John Perrot and those of Francis Laugharne in Haverfordwest in 1569. When, in 1587, Sir John Wogan was required to recover pirated cargo and apprehend the thieves in Haverfordwest and Carmarthen, the towns' officials point-blank refused him entry. Kidwelly had a less happy outcome to its resistance and was overwhelmed by local gentry, who sacked it and put much of it to the torch. In north Wales, John Wynn found the towns very obstinate about co-operating with the country in military matters. He deplored the persistent envy and ill-will between towns and the rural areas, 'each seeking to lay the burden on the other for its own case'.[45] There was a riot in Caernarfon between townsmen and the sheriff of the county in 1575 and again in 1595 over the choice of bailiffs. The vendetta between

[43] F. H. Pugh, 'Monmouthshire Recusants in the Reigns of Elizabeth and James I', *SWMRS*, IV (1957).
[44] NLW, Penrice and Margam MSS, L3.   [45] *CLP*, p. 9.

the town of Brecon and the Games family lasted throughout the 1590s and spawned a series of hotly disputed Star Chamber suits. Denbigh's bailiffs, early in the seventeenth century, strongly rebuffed efforts by the Salusburys to regain control of a borough that had once been in their pockets.

The most serious fracas, however, occurred in Cardiff during the 1590s. Hitherto the town had been very much in the hands of its overlord, the earl of Pembroke, who had supported it against most of the county gentry in a long-running feud of the 1570s and 1580s over the repair of the town bridge. In the 1590s, when Pembroke's health had badly deteriorated, leading him to withdraw from active control, the growing hostility of bailiffs and townsfolk towards the local gentry, especially Sir William Herbert and the Lewises of Y Fan, erupted into the open. Between 1593 and 1595 repeated demonstrations of strength were mounted in the streets and some of them degenerated into violent affrays and bloodshed. No fewer than ten Star Chamber suits and counter-suits resulted, and Sir William Herbert ended up having to pay a fine of 1,000 marks and £100 damages. Some of the smaller towns, lacking the muscle to assert their independence, found themselves becoming theatres in which spectacles of hostility between local gentry factions were played out. The Vaughans of Llwydiarth in Montgomeryshire battled out their long-running feud with Richard Herbert and the Prices in the streets of Llanfyllin; but it spilled over into Shrewsbury in 1588 with 'such abundance of people that the like hath not been seen'.[46] Thelwalls and Salusburys clashed in Ruthin, and the Lloyds of Abermâd and Pryses of Gogerddan affrighted the streets and townspeople of Aberystwyth with their noisy and violent exchanges.

Yet, even when the towns were not subjected to pressures from the gentry neighbours, their burgesses found plenty of reason or excuse for quarrelling over place, precedence, or profit among themselves. At Blaenllyfni and New Radnor there were furious rows about the rights of 'strangers' vis-à-vis those of burgesses. In 1573 Carmarthen was convulsed by the feud between David Rees and Richard Phillips. At Denbigh, in 1599, a self-appointed leader of a minority faction, Jenkin Atkinson, declared his intention of organizing a 'mutiny' against the majority—a term of more than ordinarily sinister overtones at the best of times and especially frightening in view of the partiality of some men in the vicinity for the Catholic religion and the Queen's enemies.

CONCLUSION

In the course of Elizabeth's reign the government of her realm had certainly become more complex. By 1603 a whole military command

[46] A. H. Dodd, *Life in Elizabethan England* (London, 1961), p. 24.

structure had long been in place. The duties of sheriffs, justices, and others had also increased in range and weight, and as the work of justices had become more intricate, they had evolved their own more intimate organization of petty sessions to cope with it. Yet, from what has been said, it will be obvious that officials, from highest to lowest, were all the while apt either to neglect their official responsibilities or else to exercise them in pursuit of their own advantage. They continued to react instinctively, in the first instance, as interested individuals and only secondly, if at all, as representatives of a distant government. Physically they were at a long and awkward distance from London or even Ludlow and were, mentally, even farther away from the Privy Council's hawkish eye. Thus, Milford Haven could be recommended to the Spaniards as a safe place where they 'could not be offended with the Queen's power'.[47] Down to the end of the reign, reports were regularly received of laxity and partial dealings, especially by sheriffs, who were at times literally getting away with murder! The 1590s were an extremely difficult and unsatisfactory decade. Adversity caused greater pressure to be imposed by central and local government; this, in turn, sharpened the drive for power, place, and profit. Envy and competition kindled dispute; dispute bred conflict and corruption. The years from 1593 to 1597 witnessed an unprecedented number of suits in Star Chamber and Council in the Marches, and frequent convictions in Great Sessions for thefts of food by men and women driven to desperation. Complaints against dishonest and oppressive deputy-lieutenants and other officials reached their peak during these years. The new decade began with the rising of the earl of Essex, who for some twelve of fifteen years had been building round him a large faction of ambitious and ruthless followers, even if most of them lay low when the moment of decision arrived. Gloriana's sun seemed to be setting in a lurid and overcast sky, with a number of Welsh counties disastrously torn asunder by faction and corruption.

Whatever the shortcomings of government in the 1590s—which provide a salutary reminder that the era was far from witnessing an automatic, unbroken, upward progression in order and prosperity—Elizabeth's rule had, on balance, conferred distinct and positive gains on Wales. Not just because contemporary commentators like Rice Merrick, George Owen, John Wynn, or Lord Herbert of Chirbury said so, though while such men were favourable to the Tudors, they were not fools. When a highly intelligent and discerning observer like Owen declared (1594), 'comparing the present government of Wales with the government of this realm, I find ourselves now in far better estate than any other part thereof, governed with more care and less charge',[48] it does not do curtly to dismiss

---

[47] *HMC Salisbury MSS*, XI, 459–60.   [48] Owen, III, 3.

his evidence as merely the fawning gratitude of one who had done very well out of the Tudor regime. The structure of post-1536 administration had, indeed, furnished the whole of Wales with lawcourts which met regularly and where impartial justice was at least occasionally possible. The increasing number of suits taken to them and to the London courts is symptomatic of the slowly germinating respect for the processes of law. The fact that Star Chamber could, when needed, impose stringent penalties on such commanding local shoguns as Sir William Herbert or Sir John Wynn was itself the most eloquent testimonial to the power and authority of the courts. This was further attested by the development of the civil jurisdiction of the Council in the Marches to such a degree that by the early seventeenth century it had become overwhelmingly an equity court, no longer greatly concerned with its former principal role of punishing crime and lawlessness.

The truth was that the instinctive recourse to violence was abating slowly among aristocracy and gentry alike; they were gradually becoming more peaceable and less disposed towards taking the law into their own hands. A notable barometer of the drop in the prevailing level of violence was the county of Glamorgan, the government and society of which have been more intensively studied for Elizabeth's reign than those of any other Welsh county. Hitherto one of the counties most prone to retaining, faction, brawling, disturbance, and, at times, severe breakdowns of order, Glamorgan was, by the early seventeenth century, a county where even the mightiest members of its gentry had had to learn that contempt on their part for the law could and would be punished. During early Stuart times it was as orderly as any Welsh county. Still more impressive was the belief of contemporaries that Wales had been largely pacified in the course of the sixteenth century and their eagerness warmly to advocate that methods successfully applied to Wales should be extended to other less tranquil areas. In 1574 Lord Huntingdon was urged to follow, in the north of England, precedents from Wales, where 'good quiet' had already been ensured by these means. In dealing with troublesome Ireland Sir Henry Sidney was to have authority there 'for hearing and determining of causes as the President and Council had' in the Marches of Wales. Most striking of all was Sir William Gerard's advice to the Privy Council from Ireland: 'A better precedent, I told their Honours, could not be found than to initiate the course that reformed Wales.'[49] There were limitations, naturally, to what Tudor rule could achieve in Wales. It did not lie within the bounds of possibility for any sixteenth-century government to create a wholly law-abiding community. The most it could do was to induce men to turn more readily to the lawcourts than the sword to find outlets for their aggressive instincts. Nor did its influence over the gentry necessarily make much difference to the lives of the mass of ordinary men and women, whose experience of the higher courts was very limited. 'Probably the lives of husbandmen, artisans and labourers continued to be as violent as before; and the substitution of gentry rule for the authority of Marcher lords may not have seemed too great a change.'[50]

[50] Williams, *GCH*, IV, 200.

CHAPTER 15

DEFENCE, RECRUITMENT, AND PIRACY
1558–1635

THAT reputation which Wales had won for itself in the Middle Ages as a fertile recruiting-ground for fighting men was maintained in the sixteenth and seventeenth centuries. Troops continued to be raised there in large numbers for Henry VIII's early campaigns in France, his actions in Ireland in the 1530s, and again for his wars against Scotland and France in the 1540s. In the summer of 1545, when a possible French invasion hovered sombrely at the forefront of most men's fears and imaginings and the government maintained throughout the realm an army estimated at no less than 120,000, a leading Welsh commander, Sir Rice Mansel, could raise 2,000 men and a large quantity of armour and equipment in his own county of Glamorgan alone. Though from 1546 onwards musters were organized by muster commissioners not by local landowners on their own initiative, the Crown still depended heavily on the willingness and ability of influential nobles and landed gentlemen to recruit troops in the customary manner in their own vicinity. Thus, in 1549, substantial contingents were raised in south-east Wales by Sir William Herbert to help in suppressing the Western Rising of that year, as a reward for which he was created earl of Pembroke; and the same commander, again with many Welsh followers, was even more instrumental in putting down the Wyatt Rebellion of 1554. Queen Mary yet again had cause to be grateful to him in 1557, now as President of the Council in the Marches, for levying large bodies of men and vast sums of money in south Wales to be employed in her wars in France. On this occasion, his agent, relative, and namesake, William Herbert of Cogan Pill, and his underlings were less than scrupulous in the methods they employed and ended up in Star Chamber as the result of an action successfully brought by a number of Glamorgan gentry. The same fate befell Sir John Salusbury on account of opposition to his recruiting activities in the north-east.[1]

During these years the threat of invasion had served once again to expose the vulnerability of the Welsh coast at two points in particular: Milford Haven and Anglesey. In 1539 Thomas Cromwell drew attention to the need for surveying and fortifying Milford Haven. Two blockhouses

---

[1] PRO STAC 4/4/29 (Herbert); *APC*, VI, 153; PRO STAC 4/3/19 (Salusbury).

may have been begun on opposing sides of the Haven and, four years later, the President of the Council in the Marches was ordered to provide ordnance for the bulwarks 'lately made at Milford', though these towers seem never to have been properly completed.[2] In the spring of 1539, too, Sir Richard Bulkeley aired his fears that Anglesey lay open to all countries: it was but a day's sail from Scotland, the Bretons knew it well, and so did the Spaniards, who were familiar with every creek and haven. Similar anxieties were expressed in 1545; and in February 1558 Queen Mary voiced her deep unease that her ancient enemies, the French and Scots, might have sinister designs on Anglesey in its weakened state.[3]

In that last year of her life, Mary gave her assent to two bills dealing with military recruitment and the defence of her realm: 'An Act for the Taking of Musters' and another 'for the Having of Horse Armour and Weapon'. Both symbolized a major change whereby the government was coming to assume a primary role in the recruitment and training of soldiers and in raising finance to meet the costs of doing so. The county militia, of course, had been in existence in England for centuries, though it was only some fifteen years' old in Wales; but the system badly needed to be brought up to date. Under the terms of the second Act the adult population was divided into ten income groups, from £5–10 a year upwards, and stipulations were laid down for the contributions towards arms and equipment expected from each group. The object of both pieces of legislation was to infuse into the militia a more professional attitude and a higher standard of training and equipment.

By Elizabeth's reign it had become painfully apparent that her armies were falling far behind the standard of Continental forces, in whose midst a military revolution was fast taking place. The Spanish armies, especially, were the foremost in Europe; compared by the celebrated Welsh captain, Roger Williams, to a military university always in session. The quality of Spanish recruitment, weapons, training, tactics, and, above all, discipline, was vastly superior to anything English armies could present. Within a short space, during the perilous years from 1567 to 1572, the widening gap between English and Continental forces yawned more frighteningly. It was highlighted by a number of dangerous developments: the arrival of Alva's army in the Netherlands in 1567; the flight of Mary Queen of Scots to England, where she provided all too convenient a focus for Catholic dissentients at home and abroad; the Rising of the Northern Earls in 1569; the imminent danger of war with Spain, 1568–9; Roberto Ridolfi's machinations, 1571–2; and the Massacre of St Bartholomew, 1572. Already in 1569 William Cecil had been acutely pessimistic and with good reason. He surveyed with inspissated gloom the military and diplomatic

[2] APC, i, 385.   [3] Flenley, Register, p. 49.

weaknesses of England's isolated position and the threats impending from
a possible coalition of great Catholic powers spearheaded by the papacy.
He concluded that the realm had become so feeble 'by long peace, as it
were a fearful thing to imagine if the enemies were at hand to assail the
realm, or what force the resistance would be'.[4] Peace was precariously
preserved until 1585; but the threat of war hung oppressively over the
minds of Elizabethan statesmen from 1568 onwards, and after 1585 they
were to be constantly embroiled in open warfare until 1604. Small wonder
that Sir Walter Ralegh should believe that the 'ordinary theme and
argument of history is war',[5] or that war and preparations for it should
figure so prominently in the public archives of the time and also in such
collections of family papers as have survived.

Ancient and renowned though the military tradition of Wales was, and
early though Welsh captains and volunteers were found serving in
Elizabethan armies— the first mercenary company in the Netherlands in
1572 was commanded by Sir Thomas Morgan of Monmouthshire, and Roger
Williams and other Welshmen went with him—the defence of Wales itself
constituted a heavy liability for the Elizabethan government. The country
was relatively poor and thinly populated, and its mountainous terrain,
uncertain weather, and wretched roads made communications within
Wales itself and between it and England very arduous. It had a long,
serrated coastline with many favourable landing-places; yet its ports and
shipping were small and undeveloped. John Wynn outlined his difficulties
as deputy-lieutenant in Caernarfonshire: the county 'near 60 miles long
and the most rugged, unpassable country in all Wales, with wild roads and
many harbours and landing-places upon its long promontory';[6] but his
recital of his problems might have been echoed in many other Welsh
counties. The people of Wales were conservative in religion and
Protestantism had made little headway. On the eve of the Armada's
sailing, Mendoza could confidently report to Philip II that the population
was much attached to the Catholic religion and Mary Stuart. Though
Wales could boast of having an unusually large number of once-formidable
castles and a few walled towns, many of these were now badly decayed
and unfurnished with ordnance. Back in 1539, Edward I's mightiest
fortresses, Conwy, Caernarfon, and Harlech, were said to be so short of
weaponry and defences that they could not resist for an hour, yet if they
were lost 'it would cost his majesty one hundred thousand pounds and the
loss of many men before they should be gotten again'.[7] In Elizabeth's reign
those castles were reported to be in still poorer shape.

Panic concerning Anglesey and Milford Haven resurfaced regularly at

[4] C. Read, *Mr Secretary Cecil and Queen Elizabeth* (London, 1955), p. 438.
[5] *Works*, ed. Oldys and Birch (Oxford, 1829), VIII, 253.
[6] *CWP*, p. 30.   [7] *CLNW*, p. 37.

times of crisis. In 1569 the inhabitants of Anglesey agitatedly petitioned the Privy Council, urging decisive measures to ensure that no men were withdrawn from the island and that neighbouring castles be strengthened and properly manned. The government was again reminded in 1574 that the island, environed on all sides by the sea, was always 'in danger of sudden invasion of enemies' and in 1577 of the 'weak state of this poor island, destitute of power, armour, weapons and strength'.[8] The other weak spot, Milford Haven, offered the prospect of secure and convenient anchorage for the largest enemy ships; there was plenty of room to manœuvre against hostile vessels; and the haven was well-known as having been a landing-point for previous invasions. George Owen had counted 'sixteen creeks, five bays and thirteen roads' there; and Camden believed there was no port in Europe 'more spacious or secure; so many creeks and harbours had it on all sides, which cut the banks like so many fibres'.[9] Like Cornwall, another notoriously sensitive area, Pembroke was slenderly manned, weakly fortified, and easily invaded, having the sea on all sides but one.

The first serious military crisis of the reign came in 1569, when the Rising of the Northern Earls irrupted. Not only was there the risk that a host of Catholics and other sympathizers might rally to Mary Stuart but also that if the insurgents were successful the Spaniards would invade from the Netherlands in their support. The need for the speedy call-up of troops and resolute measures for the defence of the coastline was obvious. Positive action was taken against JPs thought to be sympathetic to Mary, though this occasioned little difficulty in Wales in spite of confident Catholic pronouncements beforehand. Instructions were swiftly dispatched by the Council in the Marches to reliable men in all Welsh counties to take charge of the armour already stored and to equip men as necessary. In this respect, Wales was, for once, ahead of England; a number of Welsh counties, including Radnorshire, Caernarfonshire, Montgomeryshire, Denbighshire, and Anglesey, having already established armouries and spent money on equipping and maintaining them. Musters were also taken, horsemen and horses made ready, and considerable sums of money raised. It looked as if all the necessary steps had been taken promptly; but, in practice, the outcome was far less than satisfactory. The muster certificates first returned were so 'uncertain' that fresh instructions had to be issued and the commissioners required to send one of their number to the Council in the Marches to report in person. Only five out of twelve did so; six others failed to appear and one was excused.[10]

From 1569 onwards, more systematic attempts were made to build up

---

[8] PRO SP12/98/19; 123/29.
[9] Owen, II, 63; *Camden's Wales* (Carmarthen, 1984), p. 52.
[10] Flenley, *Register*, pp. 72–3.

the country's military muscle. Musters were taken more or less regularly at four-yearly intervals. Normally held in the summer months at some time other than harvest, the musters required all able-bodied men between the ages of sixteen and sixty within the shire to present themselves and their equipment for inspection so that a comprehensive inventory of the county's resources could be compiled. In 1573 an important innovation was introduced when a select number of men were chosen from those who had been mustered and singled out for special military training every year during three periods amounting to ten days in all. The cost was to be borne by the population of the county, and levies, usually known in Wales as 'mises', were exacted for this purpose. Though those responsible for raising the money were expected by the government to take care 'not to burden the poorer householders, especially the cottagers', there were endless complaints of malpractice and oppression. The captains of the trained bands were ordinarily recruited from the local gentry, 'the best affected in religion, which we could wish to be some of the principal gentlemen in those counties or their eldest sons', whose influence enabled them to command the loyalty of their men. The rank and file were, in theory, to be drawn from the more well-to-do farmers and their sons: men who had a stake in the county and who would be more likely to defend it stoutly, since members of the trained bands were exempt from service outside its borders. There was, however, a good deal of 'fiddling' in this and other respects; and substitutes, if they could be paid for, were often allowed. The cavalry was to be provided by the squires at their own expense in accordance with their wealth and possessions; and we have at least one complete list for Wales which survives.[11] But the gentry, who controlled the musters, were notoriously given to evading their responsibilities wherever they could and transferring the burden to the shoulders of others less able to bear it. The horse soldiers were proverbially less well prepared than the foot and remained so well into the seventeenth century. Justices of the peace and their retainers were expected to be present at the musters to help with the training and to keep the peace, for in an age much given at all times to faction-fighting, violence was even more likely to break out when large numbers of men came together officially bearing arms. Justices of the peace as some of the main instigators of factional squabbles, were hardly the people best qualified to restrain them. Even a well-known ecclesiastic like William Morgan could be accused of using musters as an excuse to overawe his opponents with armed force!

There were musters again in 1577, when Don John's ambitions to win a crown at Elizabeth's expense caused a rare fluttering in the dovecotes, and once more in 1581. Perceiving the pressing need for greater expertise in the

---

[11] Flenley, *Register*, pp. 165, 219, 73–5, 160–7, 200–8.

training than most of the county gentry were able to provide, the government in 1584 appointed a number of muster-masters, professional soldiers with experience of war in the Netherlands, to help the local captains. Richard Gwynne was thus made muster-master for the three north-western counties but ran into no little trouble with some of the gentry who resented his efforts, especially Sir Richard Bulkeley, whom Gwynne was later to accuse of trying to blow him up![12] These muster-masters should have had the opportunity of exercising their talents in 1585; but the appalling weather of that summer and the resultant famine, nowhere worse than in Wales, obliged the Queen to call off the musters. That was the year, nevertheless, when her government embarked on an openly anti-Spanish policy and dispatched a military expedition to the Netherlands, for which the earl of Leicester recruited 200 men in south Wales out of a total force of 7,000. By this time, fears of possible invasion were mounting fast and in 1586 the President of the Council in the Marches was appointed lord lieutenant of all the counties of Wales. He in turn appointed deputy-lieutenants in each county to be responsible for its military security, training its men, and organizing its defences; and from now on these officers existed permanently in all the counties. The papers of the Gwydir and Clenennau families afford illuminating insights into how onerous the duties of the deputy-lieutenants were and how active they were required to be.

These officers had not been appointed a moment too soon, for the years 1586–8 proved to be a time of feverish crisis. The perils of Spanish invasion loomed over the country like a thunder-cloud growing more menacing with every month that passed. The Welsh faction among the Catholic conspirators was reported to be willing to encourage the Spaniards as conquerors and to be prepared to live under their rule. It seemed that they might have their way, since from several different parts of Wales came direful accounts of weakness and lack of preparedness to resist invaders. Anglesey in 1586 petitioned the Privy Council that it was weak and exposed. In neighbouring Caernarfonshire Sir John Wynn complained to William Maurice in August 1587 that there was no match, powder, or bullet to be had in the county for any money and urged him to keep a careful watch on the coastal beacons so that any invasion might be signalled without delay. Down in south Wales, where Roger Williams was sent in a short and belated effort to inject some expert stiffening into the defensive preparations, Spanish informants reported to their Council of War in November 1587 that captains and soldiers had been appointed at Milford Haven but no ammunition had been sent because the government hesitated to arm a large body of troops for fear of revolt. A more likely

[12] PRO STAC 5/G38/5.

explanation might be that it had neither the money nor the organization to do so. In 1588 the experienced and energetic John Perrot was appointed lieutenant-general for the three south-western counties and, sinking for the nonce his normal hostility to his old adversary, George Owen, summoned him to help beat off a possible attack by their common enemy. In an amusing comment made later, Owen told how the Pembrokeshire men that summer were unconcernedly playing their traditional game of *cnapan* so vigorously that if the Spaniards had seen them thus buffeting their opponents at play they would have been mightily scared at the blows they were likely to inflict in war![13] But, even a month before the Armada sailed, the deputy-lieutenants of Carmarthenshire agitatedly informed the Privy Council that only with the utmost difficulty could they induce the inhabitants to provide arms and munitions. By this stage a plan for the defence of Wales had been agreed upon. The two decisive points were held to be Anglesey and Milford Haven. To defend the former the trained bands of Flintshire, Caernarfonshire, and Denbighshire would converge; while all the troops of south Wales were held in readiness to go to the aid of the latter. When the Privy Council received news that the Armada had set sail, it sent immediate warning to the President of the Council in the Marches, ordering him to have his officers and men ready at an hour's notice, his beacon watches alerted, and all rumour-mongers sternly punished. Fortunately, perhaps, the fighting mettle of these defenders was never put to the acid test of combat with Spanish veterans; and a Welsh ballad-singer could add his mite to the general chorus of relief:

> Yno Duw mewn eirad hynt
> Ddanfones wynt ystormus,
> Ag i soddwyd llongau llon
> Ym min Iwerddon ynys.[14]

[Then God in a fortunate moment sent a stormy wind, and those merry ships were sunk near to the island of Ireland]

The failure of the 'invincible Armada' was not seen by either the Spaniards or Elizabeth's subjects as a conclusive defeat. It signalled the beginning not the end of the struggle for supremacy at sea. For the remainder of Elizabeth's reign warfare would continue by sea and on land; along the sea-lanes, on the Continent, and in Ireland, taking a devastating toll of manpower, equipment, and money, to which Wales was obliged to make a heavy contribution. On top of these oppressive demands occasioned by warfare there were other circumstances which made the 1590s an exceptionally comfortless decade: harvests, especially those between 1594 and 1597, were poor; food shortages, high prices, and

---

[13] Owen, I, 281.
[14] E. R. Williams, *Elizabethan Wales* (Newton, 1924), p. 100.

unemployment were rife; and outbreaks of infection, disease, and high mortality were frequent. As if that were not enough, these sombre years were also overshadowed by constant threats of possible Spanish onslaughts on the vulnerable shores of Wales among other places.

The first dark hints of invasion were bruited in the spring of 1590, when rumours spread of the sinister intentions of William Stanley, the renegade with Welsh captains in his ranks who had yielded Deventer to the Spaniards, to enter by way of Anglesey and north Wales in order to carry out his plan for putting Fernando, earl of Derby, on the throne. In response to this Sir Richard Bulkeley declared himself ready to burn the corn on Anglesey and drive its cattle into Caernarfonshire. In the summer of 1591 the Privy Council feared an attempt on the Welsh coast and thought the situation critical enough to warrant releasing Sir Richard Bulkeley from gaol to defend Anglesey. Later that year the earl of Pembroke as President of the Council in the Marches was deeply vexed by the persistent quarrels among some of the Welsh gentry. 'For how can your minds be united in public defence when they are divided by private quarrels?', he asked them reprovingly. 'And what hope of succour in the field may any man have from him who is his professed enemy at home?'[15] In 1593 he was profoundly anxious about the state of the fortifications at Milford Haven and even more worried about the possible susceptibilities of many inhabitants of south-west Wales, 'ill-affected in religion', to the pope's 'wicked persuasions' and the 'Spanish King's corruption'.[16] This was the very year when George Owen was actively engaged in compiling the information at Milford that would enable him to draw up his superb chart of the Haven, so badly wanted by the earl of Pembroke.

He needed that map still more urgently in 1595. A large-scale rising led by Tyrone had set Ireland ablaze, and there seemed every likelihood that the Spaniards would launch a heavy attack against Milford in an effort to assist the Irish by disrupting English defences and communications. In response to a desperate appeal by Pembroke, Owen sent him his map of the Haven and his plans for fortifying it. They included an ingenious stratagem for demolishing the customary mariners' landmark, St Anne's Chapel, and building a decoy which would lead sailors steering by it to 'a very perilous place full of cliffs and rocks' with 'no way out but death for them'.[17] Owen's plans were not carried out; but the reality of the possible threat to Milford emerges from a letter of July 1597, from Pedro Lopez de Soto to the Spanish Council of War, in which he impressed upon them the need to strike at the 'trunk' (the mainland), for 'all the rest is simply climbing in branches'. He earnestly advocated sending the fleet to Milford,

[15] *CLP*, p. 15.
[16] *HMC Salisbury MSS*, XIII, 478.
[17] Owen, II, 552.

'only 40 leagues further from Ferrol than Plymouth'. Within two days the invaders could powerfully establish themselves at the entrance to the Haven and be ready to repel all attacks by sea. The English, at such short notice, would have no hope of landing a force to batter the land side and, he concluded, 'the only thing to be feared is our delay in deciding to take this course'.[18]

A formidable armada, in fact, left Spanish shores that year but, luckily, its ships were again dispersed by gales. Three of the scattered vessels eventually found their way to the Welsh coast. One fetched up off Aberdyfi and in November 1597 the deputy-lieutenants of Merioneth reported to the Privy Council that they had ambushed Spaniards who landed, killed two and captured four. Having no ships or ordnance of their own capable of subduing the Spanish vessel, they had sent to the vice-admiral, William Maurice, for his assistance but to no avail. The Cardiganshire militia on the south bank of the Dyfi were equally helpless, though their muster-master, Robert Jones, had wanted them to attack the enemy craft in boats. Eventually, the Merioneth men tried to burn the Spanish vessel, but the wind changed and they were all obliged to watch 'the sailing of the ship but could not resist it'.[19] Two Spanish ships were also driven ashore on the Pembrokeshire coast where, ironically enough, the only warlike action arose out of the rivalry of the local gentlemen, Hugh Butler and John Wogan, reminiscent in miniature of the furious competition among English captains at Cadiz. Wogan fired on Butler and wounded him before rifling the ship of all her goods, money, and things of value. The other ship, coming ashore near Caldey, was carrying treasure for Dunkirk and was allowed to escape unscathed because of the disorderly behaviour of some of the locals.

Philip II's death in 1598 led to no slackening in Spanish hostility, and in July 1599 Robert Cecil received reports that a huge armada of 70 galleys and 100 ships carrying 15–16,000 Spanish troops was in readiness to invade. There followed national mobilization in England and Wales on a scale not seen since 1588. Richard Bulkeley vowed to John Wynn that he would defend the island of Anglesey or make it his grave. Still greater apprehensions centred on Milford Haven, regarded by Sir Francis Godolphin, an experienced defender of Cornwall, as the 'chiefest place for the enemy to covet', having no population or fortifications to speak of, and which, if seized and fortified, could prove extremely dangerous.[20] In July 1599 a merchant of Le Conquet testified that the Spaniards were eager to find mariners conversant with the Welsh coast, especially the area around Milford Haven, and would pay well for their services.[21] Throughout that summer close and apprehensive inquiries were made of captives newly returned from Spain concerning enemy intentions in relation to Pembrokeshire. Once more, however, the worst fears were not realized, though alarms continued to be raised. A report of 1602 from Genoa told of great Spanish preparations for war, with strong suggestions of projected attacks on London, the Isle of Wight, Plymouth, Scilly, and Milford Haven. As late as 1603, after the accession of James I, Guy Fawkes made a last despairing and unsuccessful attempt to persuade Philip III to send a fleet to Milford Haven.

Throughout all these years, large contingents of Welsh troops had volunteered for, or more usually been pressed into, service in all the main theatres of war. As the pressures mounted, the earlier understanding that members of the trained bands would not have to serve outside their own county was more often honoured in the breach than the observance. In the Netherlands, many had volunteered to serve since 1572 and the army lists are peppered with such Welsh names as Morgan, Price, Owen, Gwynn, and Vaughan. One of these captains, Walter Morgan, left a delightful sketch-book, now in All Souls College, recording his impressions;[22] and another, the most famous of them all, Roger Williams, published two books on warfare based on twenty years' experience of soldiering in the Low Countries.[23] Contingents were also raised between 1589 and 1594 in the eastern counties of Denbigh, Flint, Montgomery, and Radnor for service in France. In 1596, 800 men were recruited in north Wales and 800 in the south to serve in the Cadiz campaign; and the magnetism of the second earl of Essex attracted many ardent young Welsh captains about him.

All this paled into insignificance as compared with the enormous demands made by Ireland on Welsh manpower. Many went there in the 1570s with Sir John Perrot and the first earl of Essex in the hope of finding fortune and adventure. But it was the outbreak of rebellion in the 1590s and the campaigns which followed that led to the most cripplingly heavy impressment. Many captains are to be found in the Irish muster lists with Welsh names like Lloyd, Trevor, Vaughan, Mostyn, and Morgan. There were very heavy Welsh casualties at the battle of Yellow Ford in 1598, where one Welsh captain, Edmund Owen, was cut to pieces 'for he would not part with his colours until he was slain'.[24] The commander, Henry Bagnall, was also killed and the event awakened intense regret in Wales, commemorated in a popular 'carol':

[22] C. Oman, 'Walter Morgan's Illustrated Chronicle . . .', *Arch. Journ.*, 1930.
[23] *The Actions of the Low Countries*, ed. D. W. Davies (Ithaca, NY, 1964); *The Works of Sir Roger Williams*, ed. J. X. Evans (Oxford, 1972).
[24] J. J. N. McGurk, 'A Survey of the Demands made on Welsh Shires . . . for the Irish War, 1594–1602', *Trans. Cymmr.*, 1983, pp. 56–68.

Y siwrnai oedd atgas, gwanhawyd y deyrnas,
Marwolaeth a gafas llawer gŵr tal.
Sawdwyr Cymru llwyr gwae ni
O ladd Syr Harri Bagnal.[25]

[The expedition was hateful, the kingdom was weakened, many a fine man met with
his death. Soldiers of Wales, woe unto us that Sir Harry Bagnall was killed.]

Between 1594 and 1602, 6,611 men or 2.9 per cent of the estimated
population of Wales were called up for service in Ireland, as compared
with 0.76 per cent for England. None of the Welsh counties was
exempted—not even Anglesey or Pembrokeshire—and some, notably
Caernarfon (4.1 per cent), Flintshire (3.9 per cent), and Merioneth (3.5
per cent) were exceptionally hard pressed. Because the Welsh counties
were so conveniently near the main ports of embarkation—Chester,
Bristol, and Milford—men were raised in particularly large numbers in
them. In a county like Caernarfonshire, with an estimated population of
15,000, if we take the adult male population to have been 3,500–4,000,
something of the order of 15 per cent (600 men) were obliged to serve in
Ireland. Remembering how labour-intensive contemporary agriculture
was, this must have represented an appallingly severe drain on able-bodied
adult manpower and, as the war went on, there were sour complaints at the
lack of labourers. Nor, in view of how grim were conditions of service in
Ireland, can we fail to understand the widespread evasions, the many
desertions, en route and in Ireland, and the almost permanently near-
mutinous state of the troops there. Was it to be wondered at that, when
Tyrone passed through Wales after his defeat, the women, recalling the
wretched fate of many of their menfolk in Ireland, should have pelted him
mercilessly?

The military dangers faced by the Elizabethan regime and the scale of
the war-effort mounted to meet them in Wales have tended to go largely
unrecognized. Yet any reading of the contemporary sources brings out the
herculean exertions demanded of the men in charge and their constant
and, at times, almost overwhelming fears of the scope and nature of the
military threat. It was an uphill battle all the way to try to convey to
ordinary people in England and Wales, many of them already poor and
hopelessly overburdened, how great was the possible danger from an
enemy, who must have seemed to many of them remote and unreal. The
men of Caernarfonshire sullenly asked in 1598 why they should have to
raise money when they were unconvinced of any immediate threat to their
own safety. Their reluctance was all the more pardonable when they saw
justices of the peace and gentry quarrelling among themselves for
precedence, turning the musters to their own advantage, taking bribes,

25 Jones, NLWJ, vi, 160.

exercising blatant favouritism, and transferring a large part of the burden from their own backs to those of poor men. Yet, in spite of how inequitable, cumbersome, dilatory, and inefficient arrangements might seem to be, the military machine had greatly improved in the course of Elizabeth's reign. It had gradually developed an organization for taking the musters at regular intervals, training select companies, building armouries, storing weapons, and raising the money to pay for training, feeding, clothing, equipping, and transporting county levies. The deputy-lieutenants, justices of the peace, and captains had learnt a great deal; not least from the professional muster-masters appointed to assist the 'unskilful' captains.

The records provide telling glimpses of the actions and anxieties of those on whom the burden of responsibility chiefly fell. There is the earl of Pembroke nervously requesting George Owen in 1595 'forget not to note in how many places you shall conceive fortifications to be needful' at Milford Haven;[26] in 1596 indignantly chiding his deputy-lieutenants for all the faults and 'fiddles' still too prevalent in the musters; and in 1600 being himself on the receiving end of a reprimand from the Privy Council because the choice of men in Wales 'was so bad as to appear that they were picked out to disburden the counties of so many vagrant, idle and lewd persons rather than for their ability and aptness to do service'. Or John Wynn, 'hammering at his certificate' as the Armada crisis rolled inexorably to its climax, painfully conscious that the Privy Council wanted 'a greater garment than our cloth will reach to make'; or urging William Maurice in 1595, 'Do all you can that under officers bribe not the country, for what they do will be laid to our charge'.[27]

Truth to tell, all the same, the military machine was riddled with the defects that characterized other aspects of Tudor local government, carried out by an unpaid bureaucracy of county bigwigs. The key deficiencies were lack of tight control by the government, its inability to subject officials' declarations to independent verification, and its dependence on administrators with vested interests. All its 'servants' saw a position of influence as a personal perquisite to be turned to the advantage of self, family, and friends, and were unable to resist putting private gain ahead of public good. The result, inevitably, was the familiar scene of intriguing for selfish ends, jockeying to outmanœuvre rivals by fair means or foul, and indulging personal pique and factional enmity. Exasperated beyond endurance by personal rivalries in Caernarfonshire—no worse than any other county and typical of them all—Pembroke burst out in 1591: 'How shall her Majesty's service go foward . . . in this time of danger if one of you cross the same because the dealing therein is committed to another? All men cannot be deputy-lieutenants; some must govern, some must obey.'[28] Not that his

[26] Charles, *Owen*, p. 154.   [27] *CLP*, pp. 33–4, 47, 5, 24.   [28] *CLP*, p. 15.

deputy-lieutenants were beyond reproach. In the late 1590s, when the campaigns in Ireland were at their peak and the President of the Council in the Marches sick and largely absent, there were at least four counties whose deputy-lieutenants figured in serious Star Chamber cases. Sir Thomas Jones of Carmarthen was alleged to have made £2,000 by selling old armour for new, and the Prices of Gogerddan, Cardiganshire, were accused of collecting £3,300 by fraud and illegal *commorthas*. In two other counties, deputy-lieutenants were found guilty of comparably grave offences and dismissed from their offices: Cadwaladr Price and John Lewis Owen in Merioneth, and Richard Trevor in Denbigh.

Corruption was rampant throughout the Elizabethan forces at home and abroad. Sir John Neale was convinced that 'only the common soldier' 'shared the honour of being a victim with the Queen'.[29] Deputy-lieutenants, justices of the peace, captains, muster-masters, and constables were all in on the game; determined to milk the system to the utmost for their own gain. When it came to food, weapons, equipment, uniform, pay, and health, captains were hell-bent on squeezing the last penny of profit out of their men. The Welsh soldier and author, Maurice Kyffin, given responsibility in Chester and Ireland, told Burghley that corruption and falsehood among officials and captains were so inveterate and brazen-faced that they had 'irrecuperably damnified the state'.[30] A popular Welsh poet, Richard Fychan, presented a comparably lurid picture of the innumerable petty tyrannies, briberies, and victimizations being committed, as they were seen through the eyes of the common man, on whom they fell ever more burdensomely as the wars went on. In those circumstances, men resorted to all kinds of devices to avoid serving in the army: taking advantage of links of kinship or friendship; offering *douceurs*; finding substitutes; pleading that they were retainers of great men; and hiding or withdrawing from their counties while the press was on. Nor was it surprising that counties like Breconshire or Radnorshire should be accused of emptying their gaols and pressing their vagabonds into service to make up their numbers. There were endless complaints of desertions, which ran at a very high level: the men seized every opportunity to escape on the way to embarkation, again at the ports, and after getting abroad. Sickness, especially dysentery—known to Elizabeth's troops in Ireland as 'Irish ague'—was prevalent to such an extent that, after six months, as a result of desertion and disease, an army was down to half its normal complement. Of the 3,500 sent to Ireland in 1596, of whom 580 were Welsh, only 1,000 were left after six months. Pestilence had every right to mock War in Dekker's *Dialogue* of 1604, 'War, I suppress the fury of thy stroke'.[31]

[29] 'Elizabeth and the Netherlands, 1586–7', *EHR*, XLV (1930), 373–96.
[30] *CSP Ireland, 1596–7*, p. 231.
[31] *The Plague Pamphlets*, ed. F. P. Wilson (Oxford, 1925), p. 109.

Service in Ireland, falling so heavily on Welsh soldiers, was utterly detested. The boggy and trackless terrain, wet and inhospitable climate, appalling food and quarters, virulent diseases, and savage hostility of the inhabitants led men to 'venture any imprisonment rather than go for the Irish service where they hear of so bad usage of soldiers that they hold it better to be in prison here than at liberty there without meat, provision, pay or regard'. More than a dozen years later, William Maurice was to recall that people 'hid in rocks and caves, some flying into foreign countries, so that they were fain to hunt them by the pole like outlying deer and, having caught them, to commit them to the gaol until they had found sureties to appear at the next muster'.[32] In spite of everything, thousands of Welshmen went, or were forced to go, into the army. They fought doggedly and died bravely 'in the bogs of Ireland, the sand dunes of the Low Countries, under the walls of French and Breton towns, and in the harbours of Spain and Portugal'. Rarely did they leave any trace behind them, except for an occasional one like that Ambrose Pryce who made his will in Brittany in July 1591, 'being shot through my body at the entering of the breach'.[33] Those who managed to escape the perils of battle and the ravages of sickness and return home generally found civilian life hard and ungrateful. Few were able to roister uproariously like lions, letting pandemonium loose in the taverns of Llanrwst with a retired adventurer of Thomas Prys's ilk. For many a poor soldier the end of war meant the beginning of beggary and calamity. Robert Cecil himself admitted that the soldier came from the wars 'poor, friendless and unhappy . . . never relieved with such contribution as his misery requireth and his service hath deserved'.[34]

Nevertheless, the achievement of the Elizabethan government in raising, equipping, and organizing its armies should not be underestimated. It sustained, on a variety of fronts and theatres, much the longest continuous uninterrupted spell of warfare of the whole period between 1453 and 1642, facing the possibility of total disaster on more than one occasion. Despite the all-too-apparent weaknesses already noted, it had evolved a system which recruited large numbers of men and levied huge sums of money— £1,800,000 for Ireland alone between 1595 and 1603. It had met the vastly increased expense of equipping the troops with firearms in place of the bow and arrow and had given them much better training. Between 1585 and 1603 it had mounted an enormous war-effort against the most formidable power in Europe. So intense had been the strain that by the end of the period exhaustion and war-weariness had become heartfelt and nation-wide. If by 1603 it had become almost impossible to exact men and money in London or from a wealthy English county like Gloucestershire or

<hr />

[32] *CWP*, pp. 174, 112.   [33] Owen, *Elizabethan Wales*, p. 73.
[34] BL Add. MSS 48,041, fo. 365B.

Shropshire, we may well ask what price the bleak and poverty-stricken counties of Wales? William Maurice had good cause to complain to Robert Cecil c.1601–2 that Caernarfonshire was 'hilly, mountainous and bare . . . rather spacious than populous . . . there went out of that poor county three score and one [in October 1601], out of Shropshire but three score, which might better have spared 300'.[35] Yet even as late as 1600, though the effort had taxed them nearly to the limit, the Welsh had been reported as 'very forward to answer all commissions that come for H.M.'s service'.[36] The quality of the men mobilized was inevitably very mixed; but, even in 1601, fifty men from Anglesey were singled out for special commendation by the mayor of Chester as well-equipped, and well turned-out with excellent clothing. Many of those recruited had no desire at all to serve in the army and little stomach for a fight; yet it is worth remembering that Parma, greatest soldier of the age, expected that if he had landed in 1588 he would have had to fight many encounters and win only Pyrrhic victories. The Elizabethan wars had without doubt bled the Welsh white; but they had also had the effect of binding them into the kingdom more firmly, exulting in its victories and sharing its defeats, hating its Catholic enemies, and identifying its interests as their own.

With the peaceable accession of James I, his subjects, reduced by warfare and its incessant exactions to the point of near-exhaustion, welcomed their monarch's pacific intentions and gratefully allowed the musters to fall largely into abeyance for some years. Instructions issued in 1606 to equip horse and foot to guard against invasion seem to have been virtually ignored. Not until 1613 were serious attempts made to bring the county forces once more up to scratch. Considerable emphasis was laid on the need to modernize weapons and ensure they were in a good state of combat-readiness. As soon as the pressure was thus turned on again, the old well-worn excuses of poverty, natural disasters, and other difficulties were plausibly trotted out and were doubtless not without genuine foundation. William Maurice, faced by demands for troops to strengthen the garrisons in Ireland in 1615, found his nerves twitching painfully as he recalled all the earlier resistance to recruitment. He was seconded by his colleague, William Thomas, who suggested that local recalcitrance was still just as strong.[37] When the Thirty Years War broke out in 1618 it underlined the necessity for improving the quality of weapons and, for the first time, the term 'exact training', soon to become a catchword in military circles, was given currency. Among those considered particularly eager for improvements was the earl of Northampton, President of the Council in the Marches, whose enthusiasm soon became apparent. He was quick to draw the attention of his deputy-lieutenants to large sums of money,

[35] CLP, p. 127.   [36] CSP Ireland, 1600, p. 340.   [37] CWP, p. 112.

collected for the militia, which had got no further than the hands of the officials. A year later, he reminded them that the situation had hardly changed.

'Exact militia' was a term on every military spokesman's lips in the first year or two of Charles I's reign. The King called on his troops to learn the most recent drill with the most up-to-date weapons. He probably did not share the fear of invasion which in 1625-6 ran like fire through the stubble in his domain, especially in those parts like Wales with a long unguarded coastline already much plagued by pirates; but he sensed the value of making the utmost use of it in an effort to modernize his forces. He organized a pool of eighty-four experienced professionals to act as sergeants in training and drilling the men, and at least two Welsh counties, Pembrokeshire and Glamorgan,—there may well have been others—made use of their services. Oaths of allegiance and supremacy were exacted in a number of counties, Anglesey and Glamorgan included. One of the best of the lords lieutenant was the earl of Northampton, a knowledgeable and active man who tried hard to insist on better training in the Welsh counties, for most of which he was responsible. In Glamorgan and Monmouthshire, at least, his efforts bore fruit. Glamorgan claimed to have held a series of 'exact views' and to have trained its foot every week. Monmouthshire's deputy-lieutenants, for their part, described how they had worked to eliminate 'pristine errors' and believed that no one would be able to accuse them of neglect. The infantry were, as usual, in considerably better shape than the cavalry. To bring the latter up to standard, two great regional musters were arranged—at Denbigh for the north and at Cardiff for the south—but both had to be cancelled. Attempts were also made to standardize weapons in 1626, 1628, and 1635 but with scant success. Glamorgan, for all its boasted forwardness in training, went to the extraordinary length of acclaiming the hopelessly retrograde proposal to reintroduce bows and arrows with this amazing declaration of misplaced confidence: 'We are bold . . . to express how greatly it rejoiced us to see that most noble weapon begin again to come into esteem, which hath often heretofore made our kings and their armies victorious'.[38] The greater cheapness of bows and arrows as compared with firearms was doubtless what prompted this nostalgically rhetorical excursion into military history.

Welsh enthusiasm for the war, such as it may have been, was speedily diminished by the events of 1625 to 1627. Distressing memories of earlier hardships and disasters were brought to mind when 800 men from Wales were drafted to Ireland in the winter of 1624-5. Caernarfonshire, Merioneth, and Denbighshire resisted the payment of subsidies. Anglesey pleaded financial strain, the defencelessness of the island, and the

---

[38] PRO SP16/81/46.

interruption of its trade with Ireland by pirates. Pembrokeshire felt the financial as well as the emotional burden of relieving the famished tatterdemalions who had managed to survive the Cadiz expedition. Glamorgan complained of trade lost to pirates, tenants impoverished, rents in arrears, and money tight; and Breconshire could produce only seven subscribers out of nineteen to demands for a royal loan. From Wales and the Border generally, the President of the Council in the Marches told of 'backwardness' and lack of co-operation. The King's appeal for a 'free gift' to help prop up his woefully insecure finances fell flat on its face in Wales. Monmouthshire bluntly refused to pay subsidies unless granted by Act of Parliament, and other Welsh counties were just as uncooperative, if less forthright in their opposition. Nor were they any more forthcoming in the provision of thirty-ton barques for the Navy, which they were required to find singly or in groups; most of the Welsh counties pleading that they simply did not have such vessels available. When in the following year, 1627, France joined Spain in the war against England, old nightmares of a joint invasion by the two great Catholic powers came back to haunt the population, and the customary paranoia concerning links between internal recusants and external enemies was freely aired. To meet the threat of enemy action, 700 men were raised in Wales—fifty from each county, except Anglesey, and a hundred each from Glamorgan and Monmouthshire—and the King resorted to a forced loan. But, by this time, Parliament had to be called, and the whole issue of reluctance to give military and financial assistance had become linked to the constitutional opposition to Charles I and is perhaps better postponed to a later chapter (below, pp. 479–86).

PIRACY

Piracy was a problem much older than the sixteenth century. The line between orthodox trade and unlawful adventure had always been indistinct, and it had never proved easy to distinguish between privateering and piracy. But, from the 1540s onwards, Tudor governments had had to grapple more seriously than ever before with the difficulties of insecurity, lawlessness, and financial loss caused by the activities of pirates along the coastline of England and Wales. As sea-borne trade multiplied in volume and value, so did the swarm of predators who lurked around western coasts to batten on shipping. Prime targets of their assaults were French and Spanish ships carrying fish, grain, iron, and salt and wine especially, though more exotic cargoes such as spices, tropical fruits, ivory, and other luxuries were not unknown. Piracy was one of the most profitable 'trades' of the age, and the pirate captains and crews engaged in the carefully controlled and organized racket were in the business for gain not adventure. Their ships were small but speedy and well-armed, usually able to overcome whatever resistance was offered. The nature of the Welsh coastline, which made it so difficult to defend against possible invasion, also favoured the operations of pirates. It lay close to the main sea-routes of the English Channel, Bristol Channel, and Irish Sea, and it offered long and sparsely populated shores, studded with small ports, creeks, landing-places, and convenient off-shore islands like Caldey or Bardsey. It enjoyed the further inestimable advantage, from the pirates' point of view, of being anything from 150 to 300 miles distant from the prying eyes of the Privy Council and the High Court of Admiralty. The only possibility of these authorities being able to deal successfully with the pirates was to cut them off from their land bases. That was easier said than done and called for a stronger navy at sea and more honest officials ashore. As things stood, all the local representatives of the Privy Council and the Admiralty—deputy-lieutenants, vice-admirals, justices of the peace, mayors of towns, customs officials, even John Kift, one of the sergeants of the Admiralty, and other officers—were, almost to a man, acting in connivance with the marauders. Links in the pirates' shore-based network, they were anxious to avail themselves of any benefits on offer in the way of bribes, presents, or other shares in the illicit profits. Nor were the local inhabitants, by and large, at all undisposed to buy pirated goods brought ashore and offered for sale at cut prices. It was all a cosy 'closed shop', which the Privy Council could hope to break up only on those occasions when the rivalry between local magnates proved greater than their normal desire for gain.

During the later half of the sixteenth century, the three main areas of Wales involved in piracy were the south-west, centring on Milford Haven; the south-east, around Cardiff and Newport; and the north-west, in Beaumaris and Caernarfonshire. The worst place for piracy, and one of the most notorious in the whole kingdom, was Pembrokeshire. The county lay close to the sea-borne trade passing up to Bristol, main port of the west, and not far from the English Channel trade routes. It was admirably placed for conducting illicit operations, with the harbours and creeks of Milford Haven, especially Haverfordwest and Pembroke, not to mention the little port at Tenby, offering pirates excellent facilities for disposing of their booty ashore. The dominant figure in the county's politics and local government was the masterful John Perrot who, providing his supremacy was fittingly recognized, did little to discourage the pirates. Appointed vice-admiral in 1562, he was within two years in difficulties with the Privy Council for his partiality towards a local pirate, Philip ap Rice. In 1564 he was again sharply taken to task for the 'marvellous insufficiency' of one of his deputies, John Parrot of Tenby, who had bungled matters, deliberately or accidentally, when trying to arrest pirates; a blunder that led the Privy Council to censure Perrot for not appointing 'some more skilful and discreet man' to be his deputy.[39] There were so many complaints from various parts of the English and Welsh coast at this time about attacks against Spanish shipping that, in the following year, a permanent Piracy Commission was appointed for each of the maritime counties of the kingdom. In theory, the Commissioners were to deal not only with the pirates but with their confederates on land as well; excellent in principle but unlikely to work in practice, when a number of the Commissioners themselves dipped indiscriminate fingers into the illegal pies they were meant to abolish!

From 1570 to 1573 Perrot was busily engaged on Crown business in Munster. Once returned, however, he renewed his connections with pirates, and between 1574 and 1578 a number of them, including such well-known operators as John Callice, Luke Ward, Robert Hicks, John Johnson, and Edward Herbert, came and went freely in Pembrokeshire on their nefarious errands. It has been suggested that John Perrot was the mainspring of an effective organization for trading with pirates. That seems less likely than that, knowing very well what was going on, he let it be understood that he expected a 'rake-off' for turning a blind eye to the trade. In 1577 the Privy Council, incensed at the jiggery-pokery in Pembrokeshire, addressed a heated letter to Perrot, dressing him down severely for allowing the 'notable pirate', John Callice, to be 'lodged and housed at Haverfordwest' and, 'being there known, was suffered to escape'. They marvelled at the 'negligence of such as are justices in those parts'—Sir John Perrot was *custos rotulorum* there—for allowing so notorious an offender thus to depart. Not until 1578 did most of the details come to light, when a neighbouring Carmarthenshire gentleman, Richard Vaughan, acting deputy to Sir William Morgan, vice-admiral for the three south-western counties, intervened in an attempt to queer Perrot's pitch. It was not that Vaughan was a pillar of rectitude in these matters; he had himself been the recipient of bribes and presents from pirates. Rather was it the old story of local rivalry and a determination on Vaughan's part to thrust himself into a seat of regional authority at Perrot's expense. He presented a long, detailed, and damaging bill of complaints against Perrot for his complicity with piracy, which was referred to Drs Dale and Lewis of the Admiralty.[40] Vaughan was no match for Perrot, however, and the latter and his witnesses were easily able to rebut Vaughan's evidence against them. Nor did an independent inquiry come up with any further evidence against Perrot; indeed, in so far as it mentioned him, it tended to refer to him as a suppressor of pirates. Certainly it did not sustain Vaughan's depiction of him as a kind of sixteenth-century super-'fence' and receiver. After the inquiries of 1578 much less was heard of piracy in

[39] *APC*, VII, 148.   [40] PRO SP12/124/12, 28, 31, 66, 67.

Pembrokeshire. Later in the century it was the Wogan family, two of whom—John Wogan of Wiston and John Wogan of Boulston—were Commissioners of Piracy, and more tender in their treatment of local pirates than was warranted by their official responsibility for its suppression.

In the meantime, the 1570s and 1580s had seen a similar burst of activity in efforts to suppress piracy in Glamorgan and Monmouthshire. Among the ports most favoured by pirates was Cardiff, described by a Pembrokeshire justice as the 'general resort of pirates and there they are sheltered and protected'. Cardiff's own citizenry was forced to admit that the town had such a bad reputation for associating with pirates that its merchants, when travelling elsewhere, dared not 'avow the place of their dwelling at Cardiff'.[41] Its ill reputation arose for two reasons: partly because of the partiality shown for it by that scandalous malefactor, John Callice (originally of Tintern in Monmouthshire); and partly because of the collusion between him and the leading men of the town and neighbourhood, and members of the unchallengeable Herbert family most of all. Ordinary townsmen found themselves torn between dislike of the pirates' arrogant ways and evil repute and their desire to buy stolen goods cheaply, not to mention their fear of the pirates' powerful protectors. Between 1574 and 1576, Callice sold in Cardiff and the vicinity the cargoes of at least three ships which he had seized. He did so with such brazenness that one whole meeting of the Privy Council had to be devoted to the discussion of his misdeeds. During 1576–7 four lots of inquiries into piracy were set to work by the Privy Council: one by John Croft, the next by David Lewis, another by Fabian Phillips and Thomas Lewis of Y Fan, and finally the three-man inquiry by Sir Edward Stradling, Sir Edward Mansel, and William Mathew. A number of prisoners, mostly small fry, were taken and confessions extracted. A bizarre story unfolded of the relationship between local gentry and pirates, including their merry parties in taverns and tippling houses. Not surprisingly, perhaps, one of those appointed to make the inquiries, Thomas Lewis of Y Fan, turned out to be deeply implicated.

Gradually, some improvement was effected. Early in 1578, the sheriff of Glamorgan, Nicholas Herbert, and others were heavily bound over and warned not repeat their offences. When another well-known pirate, Tom Clarke, next put into Cardiff in 1578, he had to exercise compulsion to get people to revictual his ships. In 1581 a special commission of Great Sessions tried six pirates and hanged one. Eleven more were brought to trial in 1584. But even in 1586–7, pirates were able to escape with the connivance of Cardiff's bailiffs. When, as a result, the Privy Council put pressure on their patron, the earl of Pembroke, his reaction was to write a testy letter to Stradling, Mansel, and Mathew, reproaching them for having

[41] *Cardiff Recs*, I, 349–57.

acted rather 'from malice to me or contempt of me than from an upright meaning to redress offences or punish offenders'. The commissioners refused to be browbeaten and retorted boldly: 'we never learned of any pirate arrived in this road wherein they [the Cardiff bailiffs] have not showed their inclination'.[42] Their dogged line may have brought the desired results; at least there are no further references in the records to piracy at Cardiff. The only other incidents of piracy in Glamorgan were recorded at Swansea. The *Primrose* arrived there in 1581, carrying a cargo of tropical luxuries—brazil wood, cotton, pepper, monkeys, and parrots. The ship's captain claimed to have bought these from a well-known pirate whom he had encountered by chance in Torbay. His improbable story was accepted by piracy commisioners rendered less disposed to censure, perhaps, by the judicious donation of a monkey apiece to two of their number and two parrots to the Swansea customs official.

The other centre of interest was north-west Wales, where the trade of the region was dominated by shipping proceeding in and out of Chester. Two places became associated with pirates: Beaumaris in Anglesey and Pwllheli, with the neighbouring islands of Bardsey and St Tudwal's. Undisputed cock of the walk at Beaumaris was the third Sir Richard Bulkeley (1533–1621), whose family had been vice-admirals of the three north-western shires from 1539 to 1585. He swaggered over the Menai Strait as autocratically as Sir John Perrot over Milford Haven. Not until 1589 were his enemies, the Wood family of Rhosmor, confident enough to launch a major suit against him in Star Chamber, where he was accused of many misdeeds, including the encouragement of pirates.[43] There is little doubt that he was guilty of complicity; but as this was not the main point of the charges made it is not easy to tell how much weight to attach to it. At least, though, Sir Richard was severely censured by Star Chamber for his misdeeds; but was nevertheless regarded by the Privy Council as too indispensable a man not to be released from gaol to defend Anglesey (above, pp. 365–6).

The other scene of piratical activity was the coast of Llŷn in the vicinity of Pwllheli and Bardsey. Bardsey's hallowed association with the 20,000 saints of Welsh hagiographic legend did not deter pirates from making use of it as an eminently suitable base for their own unsanctified transactions. It had been granted in 1551 to John Wyn ap Huw by the duke of Northumberland as a reward for his prominent role in helping put down Ket's rebellion. In 1563, a Lancashire pirate named Thomas Woolfall had landed there with corn and rye and had disposed of them to Caernarfonshire men, in spite of an abortive attempt by John Gruffydd of Cefnamlwch to capture him. Similar proceedings seem to have continued there during the

[42] *Stradling Correspce.*, pp. 78–83, 294–5.   [43] PRO STAC 5/J18/1.

1560s, being revealed in an action of 1568 brought against John Wyn ap Huw by a local yeoman, Morgan ap John. In this he was accused of using Bardsey as a pirate headquarters for storing and revictualling pirate ships and carrying their booty to Chester, where it was sold in fairs and markets. It seems a plausible enough accusation; but as only the bill of complaint survives, it is difficult to tell how much credence should be placed upon it.

The most exciting and colourful episodes associated with this area occurred in the 1590s.[44] A local gentleman, Hugh Gruffydd, third son of Gruffydd ap John of Cefnamlwch, who had an active and adventurous career in command, first, of the *Pendragon* and later of the *Phoenix*, arrived with his illicit cargoes off St Tudwal's Island. He got in touch with Sir Richard Bulkeley at Beaumaris and, in order to avoid the possibility of his ship's being seized by Admiralty officers, contrived to sell it to Bulkeley. After another two or three years of adventure, Gruffydd subsequently met his end in north Africa. There, too, died Edward Bulkeley, who had taken over Gruffydd's former ship, abruptly ending a short but successful career in Algiers.

By the reigns of James I and Charles I, the nature of piracy in the waters around Wales had dramatically changed. It was pirates from the Barbary Coast who were now terrifying the inhabitants of western Britain with their devastating raids on merchant shipping, carried out from long, light, formidably armed ships, expertly designed to give chase and hunt down their prey. They were feared all the more on account of the extensive use they made of bases along the south coast of Ireland, which had become their nursery and storehouse. The inhabitants of south Wales, formerly willing accomplices of pirates, were now loud in their cries of distress at the serious losses they incurred as a result of the depredations being made on their shipping and vociferous in their demands to be adequately protected. Deputy-lieutenants in Glamorgan told of farmers being unable to pay their rent and the whole county impoverished because shipping carrying Glamorgan butter to France and Ireland had been preyed upon by pirates to such an extent in 1625-6. A year later, justices of the peace for the same county bewailed that 'within the space of little more than a year . . . five several good barques within the port of Cardiff have been taken by the Turkish pirates of "Sallie" to the utter undoing of many poor merchants here and discouragement of all others'.[45] Comparable lamentations emanated from the men of Pembrokeshire in the 1630s. They wanted to see prompt action taken against all the pirates haunting their coast, the 'Moors' worst of all. They pressed for the fortification of Milford Haven because it had become 'a receptacle for all rovers and robbers', 'a place too

[44] Owen, *Elizabethan Wales*, pp. 137-44.
[45] *CSP Dom., 1625-6*, p. 213.

well-known unto pirates and not unknown unto Barbary'.[46] The answer, they were convinced, was for a powerful royal vessel to be sent to guard the Haven. Piracy was also rife in north Wales at this time. Here, however, although the officials wanted firmer action taken against the pirates, the common people seem still to have hankered after their earlier practices of participating in illicit trade with them.

Steps were slowly taken to try to cope with the problem. A royal ship was dispatched to Milford Haven in response to the Pembrokeshire men's pleas; but its commander concentrated his efforts mainly against Lundy and other small islands which he found infested with pirates, though with little success. Having small faith in these tactics, the Pembrokeshire population now advocated that the Admiralty appoint local men of proven experience and ability to take resolute action. Predictably, perhaps, the first two names they suggested for the task were Perrot and Wogan. Further east, the most successful commander was Sir Thomas Button, a notable Glamorgan sailor with a distinguished track record. He was praised by Bristol merchants for being pre-eminent in trying to wipe out 'those common enemies of human society, the Turkish pirates', and this although his ship, *Phoenix*, had incurred 'imminent danger . . . for want of men, the coast of Ireland and Channel of Severn being very dangerous in winter time'.[47]

[46] C. M. Thomas, 'The First Civil War in Glamorgan' (MA Thesis, Swansea, 1963), pp. 30–9.

[47] P. McGrath, *Merchants . . . in Seventeenth-Century Bristol* (Bristol Rec. Soc., 1955), pp. 181–2, 187–8.

CHAPTER 16

ECONOMIC ACTIVITY AND CHANGE
1536–1642

MOST of the essential features of the economic life of Wales of an earlier period remained largely unchanged between 1536 and 1642. The growing number of travellers who commented on the nature of the Welsh economy mostly remarked on its poverty and backwardness. A Venetian noted in 1551 that though the land was rich in meadows and pasture, it was badly cultivated and its inhabitants much given to theft. Robert Lindsay, a Scot writing in the 1570s, commented that Wales was for the most part barren and unfruitful, its farmers living sparsely on oaten cakes and drinking milk mixed with water. Such testimony was confirmed by native observers of the early Stuart era. William Vaughan of Llangyndeyrn wrote critically of its lands 'not half stocked' and its 'cornfields . . . so bare of corn that a stranger would think that the earth produced such grain naturally wild'; while another writer dismissed disdainfully the poverty of some of the remoter farmers in Anglesey living upon 'oat and barley, bread and buttermilk and whey, *glastwr* [skim milk] and such like trash'.[1] Camden was a little more optimistic. Forced to concede that Wales was not very prosperous, he nevertheless maintained that the 'diligence and industry of the husbandman hath long since begun to conquer the barrenness of the land'. Thomas Churchyard was even more sanguine:

> Wales is this day (behold throughout the shires)
> In better state than 'twas these hundred years.[2]

The overwhelming majority continued to win its hard-earned livelihood from the none-too-generous land and its resources; and climate, contour, and soil still set the same close limits to its economic potential. If anything, climatic conditions may have worsened and become less favourable to corn production, causing a larger proportion of indifferent and really bad harvests than before. There was a succession of poor seasons in the 1580s leading up to the appalling harvest and famine of 1585–6 and another very bad run between 1594 and 1597. But probably the grimmest years of all were those between 1620 and 1623 and much of the 1630s, which may well

---

[1] W. Vaughan, *The Golden Fleece* (London, 1626), II, 29–36; Dodd, *Seventeenth Century*, p. 16.
[2] *Camden's Britannia*, ed. E. Gibson (London, 1695), p. 679; Churchyard, *Worthiness*, p. 52.

have been among the most desperate eras of dearth in the whole history of England and Wales.[3] They pressed all the more mercilessly on a populace much increased in numbers because, although there had been some improvement in farming methods, there was no startling breakthrough in agricultural production.

If, however, there was no dramatic alteration in the means of production, there were highly significant changes in land ownership and tenure. These were occasioned in part by the intensification of those trends towards individual accumulation and enterprise already so conspicuous in the fifteenth century. Some of the more successful families like the Bulkeleys and Herberts continued to forge ahead and were joined by new ones, like the Maurices of Clenennau, the Barlows of Slebech, and many others. More important still was the impact of the two crucial influences in contemporary European economic life—the increase in population and the inflation in prices. Population in Wales rose from an estimated 278,000 in 1536 to an estimated 405,000 in 1630 (below, pp. 406–08). From about 1580 onwards Wales, like the rest of Europe, was feeling the effects of the pressure of an increasing population with no growth in employment prospects. The consequent increase in demand, especially for food, and the upward movement in land values, may well have been the principal causes of the parallel inflation of prices, the most rapid and painful in the history of England and Wales before the twentieth century. Other contributory factors to the price-rise were the effects of the debasement of the coinage in 1540, the heavy expenditure on warfare in the 1540s and 1590s, the influx of Spanish silver from the New World, and the expansion of credit facilities. Prices rose dramatically beween 1540 and 1640, when, according to the most accurate calculations that economic historians are able to make, the price index of a 'basket of consumables', following a long period of stable prices, increased from an estimated 103 in 1510 to 158 in 1540 and to 607 in 1639. During that latter interval of a hundred years there had been two phases of convulsive upward leaps—one during the 1540s and 1550s, the other during the 1590s. In both instances a combination of heavy expenditure on warfare and a spell of bad harvests had drastically pushed up prices. The rise had been uneven as between one commodity and another: grain had gone up from 154 to 569 between 1540 and 1639 (375 per cent); cattle from 152 to 622 (410 per cent); but wool had moved up much less sharply, from 190 to 370 (190 per cent).[4]

Inflation unmistakably loaded the dice heavily in favour of the bigger men: gentlemen, who had the power to change tenants' conditions of tenure, exploit the resources of demesne and estate fully, and capitalize on office and influence; freeholders, yeomen, and bigger tenants, who could

---

[3] *Agrarian Hist.*, IV, 815–70.
[4] *Agrarian Hist.*, IV, appendices I and II, cf. Chap. 4.

manage to keep overheads down and work on a sufficiently large scale to gear production to the needs of profitable markets; and merchants, lawyers, and others with an elastic income from a profession or trade who had the capital and wit to invest in acquiring land and improving techniques. It was the small men who suffered most: paupers and labourers who grew no food were hardest hit; while cottagers and smaller peasants and craftsmen were not much better off. In these circumstances, powerful men were accused of adopting harder and more grasping attitudes; land hunger among all classes became almost inappeasable; a greater acreage was brought under cultivation; its use was made more efficient; subsistence farming lost out increasingly to commercialized production; old estates were enlarged and new ones rose and flourished; all available resources, including non-agrarian ones, were exploited. These forces affected the whole of Wales, but the pressures of change were uneven and somewhat haphazard. They were at their most pronounced in the lowlands in the east and south and along the main highways to Ireland in the north-west but were making inroads all the while in the more conservative upland areas as well.

The most telling insights into the spirit of the age are derived from the work of the poets. Major *cynghanedd* poets like Simwnt Fychan and Siôn Tudur criticized sharply the unscrupulous litigation, dishonest land transactions, pride and avarice, corruption in office, and oppression of tenants. This line of condemnation is even more prevalent in the popular free-metre verses of the age, especially the religious poetry and verses on the 'state of the world'. Over and over again, their authors depict a harsh, greedy, acquisitive society, insatiable in its cupidity for land, wealth, and material possessions. Poets were convinced that gain had become the mainspring of human existence and that, at all social levels, avarice and self-seeking were enthroned in place of true charity. In their eyes, such incorrigible selfishness brought down condign divine punishment in the form of frequent harvest failures and food shortages. That there was throughout England and Wales a compulsive craving for land and incessant competition for it among all classes can hardly be denied. 'Do not all strive to enjoy the land?', asked Gerrard Winstanley, in tones reminiscent of the Welsh poets. 'The gentry strive for land, the clergy strive for land, the common people strive for land; and buying and selling is an art whereby people endeavour to cheat one another of the land.'[5] Sir John Wynn's own brother, Ellis, reproached him for his 'unquenchable thirst of purchasing more land (God having blessed you with sufficiency already far above any of your neighbours)'.[6] This restless and unremitting search for land left its

[5] C. Hill, *Puritanism and Revolution* (London, 1968), p. 154.
[6] J. G. Jones, 'The Wynn Family and the Estate of Gwydir' (Ph.D. Thesis, Cardiff, 1974), p. 99.

traces in the thousands of deeds recording innumerable small transactions for the purchase, lease, mortgage, and exchange of land. One particularly interesting indicator is the increasing care with which families recorded the terms of marriage settlements entered into by all classes having land or money for which to make provision.

In the absence of striking innovations to improve the quality of farming, the easiest way of raising production was to bring more land into use for cultivation or grazing. Wherever doubt existed over the ownership of land, or where it was weakly or inefficiently enforced, men of all social grades were quick to make encroachments favourable to themselves. In the upland commote of Cyfeiliog, where hill pastures and wastes were extensive and population increased by 50 per cent from c.2,400 to c.3,500 between 1545 and 1600, all the farmers had surreptitiously sidled their way into these pastures, though typically it was the bigger freeholders who had been most active. Many of the former *hafotai* [summer dwellings] here and in other upland districts had been converted into permanent farms. It had been the same story in four commotes where the Crown had been very slack in its administration of them until they were granted to the earl of Leicester by the Queen in 1574. His agents recorded no fewer than 631 encroachments on hill commons. Of these, 322 were less than ten acres in extent; only 36 (5.7 per cent) exceeded 100 acres but these nevertheless covered 5,000 acres in all, or 40.2 per cent of the 12,279 acres surveyed. The tenants had increasingly treated the lord's *ffriddoedd* [hill grazings] as their own, often claiming that the land enclosed was in fact *cytir* [land held in common]. What had happened in the Crown lordship of Kidwelly, where 'great enclosures and encroachments'[7] had been secretly effected by a large number of tenants without paying extra rent, had taken place in many parts of Wales where the Crown enjoyed extensive possessions. Similarly, the earl of Worcester, whose agent, Edward Mansel, had been deplorably remiss, claimed to have lost 3,000 acres to 1,000 of his tenants, ranging from Sir William Herbert, one of the most powerful men in Glamorgan, down to some very poor husbandmen. In other cases, it was the extensive felling of woodland for industrial fuel which cleared the ground for farming for the first time, as at Talyfan in Glamorgan, turned into a large sheep leaze in 1596 after timber had been cut down for iron-smelting. Many such timber fellings were greatly resented by small farmers who had previously enjoyed extensive rights of using them as a source of timber for firewood, building, and implement-making, and gained nothing when they were cleared.

As well as taking in new or neglected land, it was even more essential to use existing farmland more intensively and effectively. If the growing

[7] PRO DL Misc. Books, 120/27B.

needs of townsfolk were to be met and extra mouths in every rural parish
fed as population increased, then crops had to be more fruitfully cultivated
and more livestock raised. A number of printed books existed to help
farmers, though we have no means of gauging how widely they were read.
More enlightened landlords, like George Owen, the Mansels, the Wynns,
or the Nanneys, made careful observations and kept strict accounts. The
Nanneys' account book of 1599–1608 gives evidence of 'extremely careful
purse management'.[8] George Owen's own land at Henllys may have been
something of a model farm, and we know that he could be sharply critical
of the unchanging and primitive methods of small farmers around him. But
it is as well to remember that the accumulated wisdom of many generations
had given farmers a working knowledge of what was likely to be best for
their lands and livestock and within the reach of their pockets. Thomas
Churchyard, at all events, had kind words for their efforts to improve their
methods:

> They have begun of late to lime their land
> And plough the ground where sturdy oaks did stand,
> Convert the meres and marish everywhere . . .
> They tear up trees and take the roots away,
> Make stony fields smooth fertile fallow ground,
> Bring pasture bare to bear good grass for hay.[9]

There is certainly evidence for the increased use of fertilizers such as lime,
marl, seaweed, and dung by those who could afford to do so. Evidence of
selective breeding is more difficult to come by, though it may be supposed
that the more enterprising landowners went in for it. When Sir John
Perrot, for instance, wanted to improve his stock, he earnestly solicited Sir
Edward Stradling's help in buying dairy cattle in Glamorgan.

To obtain maximum profits in return for their efforts, producers had to
become increasingly commercial in their outlook and specialize in those
commodities they were best fitted to produce, in order to meet the
demands of a wider market as well as local needs. The period between 1500
and 1750, lying between feudal and industrial Europe, has aptly been
labelled the 'age of commercial Europe'. To meet the needs of such an
epoch much depended on ease of access to the market and, in an age of
continuingly difficult land transport, having the sea within easy reach was
invaluable. The producers of the low-lying and more productive districts in
the plain of Gwent, vale of Glamorgan, lower Tywi valley, and south
Pembrokeshire benefited enormously from being conveniently placed near
a number of small but flourishing ports. Thence they could export to an

---

[8] B. R. Parry, 'Huw Nanney Hen (c.1546–1623), Squire of Nanney', *JMHRS*, v (1965–8),
197.
[9] *Worthiness*, p. 82.

expanding market in Bristol and the west of England; even to Ireland, France, and the Iberian Peninsula. Demand was principally for meat, dairy produce, hides, wool, and corn, in which all these areas could specialize. Glamorgan thus became one of the three biggest butter and cheese producing regions in the kingdom. On a smaller scale, the same was true for those areas of north-east Wales which had easy access to Chester, and even for parts of the north-west in Anglesey and Caernarfonshire near enough to the sea. Most of upland Wales, however, almost entirely cut off from convenient water communication, was forced to depend almost exclusively on the production of cattle, which could transport themselves to market, and wool and woollen cloth moved by pack-horse.

Commercialized farming put a premium on larger holdings. Those inequalities in the size of farms already visible in the fifteenth century became more pronounced as the pace of engrossing (bringing holdings together) speeded up dramatically in the sixteenth century. In Monmouthshire, by 1610, the break-up of the former manors had enabled some copyholds to be increased to as much as 150 acres, and mixed freehold and copyhold farms up to 250 acres. In Glamorgan, both in the vale and upland areas, the size of farms increased as the number of tenants and freeholders dropped. In Pentyrch, Thomas Mathew whittled down the freeholders of the manor by half, acquired much of the copyhold land, and rented the whole of the demesne. The growth of the Owen estate at Henllys Isa in north Pembrokeshire furnishes another characteristic illustration of the way in which large farms took the place of small ones, as minor or impoverished freeholders were ousted by more powerful ones, and scattered holdings consolidated or enlarged by purchase or exchange. In all parts of Wales, at greater or lesser speeds, the squires and well-to-do farmers were emerging more and more into view.

Engrossment and consolidation became most effective if accompanied by enclosure by means of hedges, ditches, fences, or walls. All contemporary experts were agreed that enclosures improved the value of land and increased the chances of its being more efficiently managed. Only after enclosing could the cultivator be sure of being able to manage crops and livestock in his own interest, free from hindrance by lazier or less competent neighbours. Leland commented on the spread of enclosures in Anglesey, and Rice Merrick noted approvingly how enclosures had changed the face of Glamorgan in the sixteenth century. A Crown surveyor in Pembrokeshire in 1625 warmly advocated purchase and exchange so that 'tenants may enclose and thereby make their best profit'.[10] Some landlords even hedged a whole area including other men's lands beside their own and then opened negotiations with a view to purchasing the land they did not

[10] B. E. Howells, 'Pembrokeshire Farming, c.1550–1620', NLWJ, IX (1956), 315.

already possess, doubtless exerting a good deal of pressure in the process when necessary. Demesne lands were everywhere enclosed by ambitious proprietors and intensively farmed. Freehold land, like demesne, was also susceptible to enclosure because of the greater security of tenure and the absence of restrictions on methods of cultivating it. Enclosure of freehold land in some of the old Welsh areas like Ceredigion or Cyfeiliog was slower, being retarded by the effects of the old Welsh practice of *cyfran* and also by the conservatism of the inhabitants. Customary land on the former open fields of manors was, by its very nature, somewhat resistant to enclosure. Vestiges of the old open fields continued to survive well into the seventeenth century, with intermingled small plots of land still open and unenclosed belonging to a variety of owners, though the system was clearly in state of rapid decay. The same held good for some of the much smaller 'open fields' which had once formed part of the arable lands of the native Welsh townships in Nannau, Cemaes, or Cyfeiliog, for example. They, too were being increasingly brought into the newer patterns of ownership and tenure.

Up to about 90 per cent of even the commons had been enclosed in many of the lowland manors in south Wales by 1640. This kind of enclosure engendered a number of intense and protracted disputes. The ones centred on Llewelli Green in Denbighshire were not settled until the eighteenth century. Those at Ystrad Marchell in Montgomeryshire involved yeomen attired in women's clothing and seemed to have anticipated the Rebecca Rioters by 250 years. There were furious rows between Henry, second earl of Pembroke, and his tenants of the manors of Usk, Caerleon, and Trelech, which ended up in fiercely contested suits in Star Chamber.[11] Yet, by and large, enclosure of the commons, or encroachment upon tenants' rights on them, did not create anything like the furore in Wales which they evoked in England. This was because enclosure in Wales was frequently intended for arable cultivation not pasture and so did not give rise to eviction and depopulation, and also because the hundreds of thousands of acres of unenclosed hill and mountain wastes continued to provide the pasture on which many Welsh farmers were desperately dependent. Indeed, what gave rise to protest was not the enclosure of these pastures so much as the danger that tenants were being deprived of their common rights for another reason. Petitions to the Council in the Marches objected bitterly to the depasturing of such large numbers of 'strangers'' cattle on the commons of counties like Montgomery or Radnor for commercial gain as to weaken the grazing to such an extent that beasts of smaller freeholders and tenants could not be sustained. To restrict such abuses it became necessary to introduce the practice of 'stinting', i.e., to control the

[11] Owen, *Eliz. Wales*, pp. 89–90.

number of beasts which residents could turn out on the commons to graze.

Central to all these activities was the increasingly active build-up of gentry estates, great and small, the nuclei of some of which had been brought into existence as early as the fourteenth century. It was, however, the century between the Act of Union and the Civil War which was the most creative phase; when incentives were at their most compelling and opportunities for accumulation most numerous. In the free-for-all in land it was the gentry and yeomen who participated from positions of strength. They had the secure economic base, knowledge, influence, and money; and they made the most striking gains. Such well-tried expedients for accumulating lands as purchase, mortgage, lease, exchange, and marriage were still much in evidence and intensively pursued. Tudor policies were newer factors in the process. The Act of Union formally introduced English land law, legalized mortgage, free buying and selling, and entail, though many of the gentry had long before availed themselves of these provisions in practice. Even more important was that the Act introduced what a contemporary termed a 'wonderful uncertainty' in relation to traditional tenures and, in the confusion which resulted for the best part of a century, powerful proprietors took full advantage to press their own interests at the expense of those of weaker men. Union also entrusted offices of local justice and administration to the native gentry and put them in a situation of further advantage. Reformation changes released an enormous amount of former ecclesiastical possessions onto the market for lease or sale, and sooner or later most of them came into local gentry's possession; though it was only the most successful who had the cash, credit, or connection to be able to invest in such property. The same was true of other Crown lands. Those vast estates in Glamorgan and Monmouthshire once in Jasper Tudor's possession were largely acquired by the first earl of Pembroke. On a smaller scale, in Caernarfonshire John Wynn was able to buy up in effect all the king's lands in Gwydir, Trefriw, and Dolwyddelan. In south Wales, John Vaughan of Golden Grove acquired many Crown leases, including a number of former Dynevor lands. Royal favour was almost indispensable in building up the biggest estates. Nearly every one of the front-rank families in Wales numbered at least one among their members who had served the state with distinction and been rewarded for doing so. Service to a leading aristocratic family might also be potentially a very valuable asset. Ellis Prys did very well out of his services to the earl of Leicester, and Gelly Meyrick even more lavishly out of the earl of Essex. Another ladder to the ranks of the privileged might be remarkable success in a profession, most often the law, followed by investment of the profits in land. William Jones of Castellmarch was a notable representative of the successful lawyer in Anglesey, David Williams in Breconshire, and John Vaughan in Cardiganshire. Hugh Owen of Bodeon in Anglesey neatly combined a highly profitable legal practice in the Carmarthen circuit with marriage to Elizabeth Wirriot, heiress of Orielton, and thus founded one of the most prominent families in Pembrokeshire. John, son of Sir Richard Bulkeley II, a physician 'taken to be a man of great repute and esteem and learning in his profession',[12] was able to buy the estate of Cleifiog out of the proceeds. No one in Wales made money more successfully out of commerce than Thomas Myddelton of Chirk, late of London, or Richard Clough of Bachygraig, formerly of Antwerp, though Evan yr Halen [Evan the Salt], patriarch of the Evanses of Gnoll, in spite of never having left Neath, profited sufficiently by the salt trade to set his family up in an influential way. Churchmen, too, might be just as eager as their lay brethren to set themselves up as gentlemen, even though the incomes of clerics were relatively much less than they had been. Richard Davies and his precentor, Thomas Huet, were accused—not without some justification —of using the patrimony of the Church to enrich themselves and their families. John Davies of Mallwyd was another who built up a small estate and constructed a handsome new rectory.

Just as vital as the acquisition of new estates was the effective management of what had already been won. Accumulation and management were inextricably linked in the successful landowner's mind. It was successful management which gave him the profits for further acquisition, and the latter was barren without the former. A large part of the recipe for efficient management lay in the landowner's being able to reside on his estates so that he could apply himself to overseeing, either in person or through his agents, all activities on his own and his tenants' lands. Even temporary absence could be damaging, as Lady Jane Mansel reminded her son, Bussy, when urging him to 'come and live in the country and not go abroad to consume and waste your estate and discomfort your poor friends and tenants'. To be more or less permanently absent was to run the risk of 'sustaining many damages', as Lord St John complained had happened to him.[13]

Direct farming of his demesnes was crucial for every landowner. It provided his household with basic foodstuffs, supplemented and diversified by vegetables and herbs from his garden, fruit from his orchard, venison from his deer-park if he had one, conies from his warren, fish from his pond or neighbouring rivers and estuaries, and wildfowl and other game from the teeming woods and marshes. John Perrot lavished much money and attention on his fine demesne at Carew, and Richard Bulkeley was furnished with 'excellent beef, mutton, lamb, butter and cheese' from his

[12] W. O. Williams, 'The Anglesey Gentry as Businessmen in Tudor and Stuart Times', *AAST*, 1948, pp. 100–14.

[13] D. R. Phillips, *A History of the Vale of Neath* (Swansea, 1925), p. 386; *Stradling Correspce.*, p. 101.

Anglesey demesnes. These home farms, properly managed, could be very profitable. In 1572 the Mansels of Margam were drawing an income of £375 from their demesnes; by 1638–9 this had risen to £976.

The major source of revenue as a rule was derived from rents and entry fines. The general tendency everywhere was for landlords, wherever they could, to push up rents as a hedge against inflation. This was not always easily achieved, as the rents of freeholders and customary tenants by inheritance were protected by law. So landlords were obliged to recoup on other rents as best they could and to bring pressure to bear on tenants to change the nature of their tenures. Leasehold was being increasingly substituted for copyhold, tenancy-at-will, and other customary tenures. The change to leasehold was not without benefits for tenants, especially tenants-at-will. It represented enfranchisement and stipulated more precisely the obligations of the landlord. But it carried greater advantages for the landlord since it enabled him to raise the rent and impose a stiff entry fine. George Owen, himself by no means an easy landlord, testified to the change whereby 'the poor tenant . . . is taught to sing unto his lord a new song . . . and now the world is so altered . . . that two or three years ere his lease end he must bow to his lord for a new lease and must pinch it many years before to keep money together'.[14] The beauty of entry fines from the landlord's viewpoint was that they could be bid up by competition whenever a holding fell vacant. Landlords like George Barlow of Slebech went to the extent of enthusiastically pursuing antiquarian trends so as to be able to discover what forgotten or neglected rights they could revive to increase their income. Others were restrained by a strong sense of family pride which dictated that those of their tenants drawn from families of long standing on their estates merited protection and consideration. The message delivered to a young heir by the poet Rhisiart Cynwal embodied the traditional advice and wisdom that much of an *uchelwr*'s strength and good name depended on the *plaid* of contented tenants and dependants around him:

> Dygwch drwy degwch draw
> Ych deiliaid yn eich dwylaw;
> A nâd byth yr un di-ball
> O'th wŷr at bennaeth arall.[15]

[By just dealings keep your tenants in your hands; and never let the blameless one among your men go to another lord]

Nor were there, in fact, all that number of lawsuits in which tenants accused their landlords of harsh treatment. Doubtless the squires were helped in this respect not only by restraint on their own part but also by the

14 Owen, I, 190.
15 Dodd, *Seventeenth Century*, p. 19; cf. *Llên Cymru*, IX, 89.

hectic competition for holdings and by the reluctance of tenants to go to court against them except when *in extremis*.

From about the 1570s onwards, nevertheless, there is evidence of a sharp upward movement in rents. In England and Wales generally from then on there was a wholesale revision of rents, with rising land values, when 'rent-rolls on estate after estate doubled, trebled and quadrupled in a matter of decades'.[16] Quantitative evidence for Wales is scarce; but on the Herbert estates in Glamorgan rents rose from £449. 19s. 3¾d. in 1570 to £1,169. 9s. 9d. in 1631, some of the biggest increases being recorded in the upland districts of the north of the county. Rents on the Mansel estates, where the landowners were resident, show even bigger proportionate increases. On the Gower estates they rose from £106 in 1559 to £400 in 1632; and on the Margam estate from £109. 2s. 7d. in mid-century to £1,098. 9s. 8½d. in 1632. Myddelton rents on their Chirk estates also increased tenfold between 1595 and 1631, the Mostyns' from £194. 1s. 7d. in 1576 to £537. 17s. 5d. in 1619, and George Owen's from £161 in 1583 to £252 by 1594. This rise in rents was accompanied by a vigorous drive to increase the incidence of leasehold tenure and a tendency, seen widely elsewhere in Wales, to reimpose labour services and renders in kind on a limited scale. Entry fines were also much increased, though evidence of the scale on which this took place is difficult to unearth. An estimate for the Gower estates of the Mansels between 1600 and 1632 suggests the annual rent as yielding £360. 10s. 4d. and fines £1,672. 3s. 4d., while a similar estimate for their Margam estates in 1633 gives £801. 2s. 5½d. for rents and £2,270. 13s. 0d. for fines.[17]

Nothing like a full picture of the degree or nature of the letting that went on emerges from the rent-rolls and surveys, since they rarely shed light on the incalculable number of transactions concluded between tenants and their under-tenants to whom they sublet. An unusually apt illustration of the process is afforded by the doings of Edward Lewis of Y Fan within some of the lordships and manors of the earl of Pembroke in Glamorgan. By 1570 Lewis dominated the lordships of Senghennydd Supra and Subtus, holding thirty-two tenements in the former and fifty-two in the latter, all of which he had sublet. By 1625 his grandson had acquired tenancies of two-fifths of the tenements in Senghennydd Supra and nearly half in Senghennydd Subtus, being tenant of 300 miscellaneous holdings when he died. The Lewises had mainly acquired freeholds; but it was not only freeholds which could be sublet in this way. Subletting by leaseholders presented no difficulties either, and enterprising gentry were quick to avail themselves of opportunities to make money which the process provided.

[16] *Agrarian Hist.*, IV, 690.
[17] D. M. Cole, 'The Mansells of Oxwich and Margam' (MA Thesis, Birmingham, 1966), pp. 150–67.

Richard Seys, for instance, demanded of his under-tenant that he discharge all the chief rents and other obligations in respect of the property being sublet and also render a cash rent, capons, and labour services. It was these smaller under-tenants and cottagers, with little or no protection against their landlords, often having to borrow from richer neighbours, who got deeply into debt, and tended to be pushed out into the swelling ranks of labourers and paupers.

Another valuable source of income for some landlords was tithe. At a time of rising prices for agrarian products, control of tithes could be nearly as profitable as demesne farming, especially tithes from parishes close enough to the gentry's houses to be collected easily and inexpensively. Following the dissolution of the monasteries, a number of landlords became lay impropriators of tithe on a big scale, and some of the most favoured and productive parishes passed into their hands. Others leased tithes on advantageous terms from the Crown and the diocesan authorities. The potentially large increment accruing to them from such tithes is illustrated by the long and tense struggle waged by the chapter of Llandaff to keep its tithe lessees under control. In the diocese of St Davids, where the Queen's farmer was allowed to rent for £40 a year possessions of the collegiate church of Llanddewibrefi, of which the see was deprived, he was reputed to be making £400 on the bargain. It is noticeable, however, that from the 1590s onwards, in a time of agricultural depression, the Crown found it decidedly more difficult to lease out its tithe possessions.[18]

On a number of estates there were non-agrarian sources of income to be exploited. Mills, fisheries, and timber were all the subjects of profitable leases. Timber was in great demand for domestic fuel, building, ship-construction, industrial smelting, and other uses. A good deal of the woodland in Wales was too poor and too far from centres of population for anything other than charcoal-burning. The earl of Pembroke made about £50–100 a year on his felling in Glamorgan and Monmouthshire, though his operations were hotly contested by his tenants. Sir Richard Bulkeley also stocked up his estates with timber to the value of £1,000, worked quarries at Penmon, and traded fish from Greenland for sherry and other wines in Malaga. There were a few favoured estates on which metal or mineral deposits were found. These could either be leased to individual entrepreneurs or worked by the landlords themselves. A number of north Welsh families profited handsomely out of the coal trade, including the Mostyns in Flintshire to the tune of £700 in 1619 and the Myddeltons in Denbighshire; and in the south the Mansels, Evans of the Gnoll, and Prices of Briton Ferry were profitably engaged likewise. The Vaughans of Llanelli, cadet branch of Golden Grove, not content with acquiring many

---

[18] *Agrarian Hist.*, IV, 386–90.

landed properties from neighbouring freeholders described as yeomen and gentlemen, were also busily engaged in mining coal and trading in it. John Wynn of Gwydir had extensive industrial interests in coal, lead, copper, alum, and other commodities, as well as enticing Irish manufacturers to set up linen weaving in Llanrwst and encouraging sea and river fisheries at Conwy and elsewhere. In Ganllwyd Valley in remote Merioneth Huw Nanney, anxious to develop the resources of his estate, encouraged English speculators and skilled labourers to develop an embryonic iron industry, though the neighbouring farmers frequently cursed the Nanneys for their ruthless felling of the timber of Penrhos Common.

Manorial lords enjoyed a number of miscellaneous minor sources of income. They included proceeds of lesser courts, heriots, mises, avowry fees, and survivals of medieval payments like *commortha*. None of these amounted to a particularly substantial sum, though there were attempts to enforce them more strictly and to increase the amounts accruing from them. Furthermore, most of the gentry of any consequence aspired to hold office, paid or unpaid, under the Crown. Ordinarily, the aspirants for royal patronage far exceeded the number of jobs available. One well-informed estimate puts the ratio among the aristocracy at 2:1; among the leading county families at 5:1; and among the minor gentry at 30:1.[19] Only a fraction of the gentry could, therefore, expect to add to their income from the proceeds of office and it was unknown for any but the greatest figures, secure at court and befriended by the sovereign, like the earls of Pembroke or Essex, Sir Robert Mansel, or Sir John Herbert, to make vast sums. They might even lose very large amounts, as did the first earl of Carbery, who claimed to have been £20,000 out of pocket as a result of his service over nine years to the Prince of Wales, later Charles I. For most office-holders it could well have been that the income derived from office was less important than the opportunities which it gave them to pick up land or augment other revenue. For the lesser men, service to some of the great aristocrats could be a comparably valuable source of influence on a more limited scale. Sir Thomas Morgan of Ruperra, who became an exceedingly rich and influential man in south-east Wales, was the seventh son of a not very wealthy Monmouthshire family. The foundations of his later position were laid when he was steward of the Pembroke estates, which enabled him to marry a rich heiress and become Surveyor of the King's Woods to James I. He was an outstandingly successful example of the go-ahead type in the self-centredly thrustful era in which he lived. A number of others pushed their luck too hard, for which Nemesis caught up disastrously with them. Essex and Gelly Meyrick were executed and John Perrot might well have been, had he not died in the Tower. Other over-eager contemporaries

---

[19] L. Stone, *The Crisis of the Aristocracy, 1558–1641* (Oxford, 1965), p. 467.

severely censured by the courts were Richard Bulkeley and Huw Nanney (both imprisoned for a term), John Wynn (heavily fined and turned off the Council in the Marches), William Herbert (heavily fined), and a number of deputy-lieutenants (above, pp. 369–70). Even so, their punishments rarely proved more than a temporary set-back.

The century under discussion unquestionably witnessed vast changes in the balance of land distribution, accompanied by a huge reallocation of wealth and income in favour of the upper classes. True, the situation became less favourable from 1620 onwards. Between 1621 and 1624 Wales encountered a crippling depression, with a sharp decline in all those commodities which gave the country a modest cash income—cattle, sheep, wool, hides, butter, cheese, and cloth. But, by that time, most of the landlords and yeomen were in a position to weather the storm. By contrast, the smaller men had found it fearfully difficult to hang on to their existing position and many had slipped into the ranks of cottars, wage-earners, and even paupers. This polarization had undeniably made their living conditions much grimmer. It is difficult to estimate the decline in their standard of living because we do not know what proportion of their wages may have been paid in kind or how much of their own food they were able to produce. But one salient fact is abundantly clear: the labourer of 1326 who was receiving 1½d. a day could buy much more with his wages than his counterpart of 1615 who was in receipt of 6d. a day. Whereas in 1326 it would have taken him two days' wages to buy a bushel of oats and six to buy a bushel of wheat, in 1615 he would have had to lay out eight and twenty days' wages, respectively, to buy the same amount. It has been estimated that an artisan of 1615, earning 9d. a day, would have taken 43 weeks to earn his yearly stock of provisions, and an agricultural labourer, earning 7d. a day in summer and 6d. in winter, would not earn a similar stock in a whole year.[20] Before the days of the worst inflationary pressures Sir Thomas More had written in a mood of sad reflection, 'God help me, I can perceive nothing but a certain conspiracy of rich men procuring their own commodities under the name and title of a commonwealth.' Later in the same century a Welsh poet put the same point much more tersely:

> Ag ymhob gwlad yn gyfan
> Mae y mawr yn lladd y bychan.[21]

[And in every country the great kill the small completely.]

INDUSTRIES

Industrial activities, or 'trades', as contemporaries preferred to describe all occupations other than agriculture or domestic service, as in the Middle

---

[20] Davies, *Econ. Hist. S. Wales*, p. 78.
[21] Hoskins, *Age of Plunder*, p. 121; Williams, *Tafodau Tân*, pp. 156–8.

Ages, were concerned mainly with the small-scale processing of native raw materials—corn, wool, hides, timber, malt, limestone, metals, and the like. They did not create a new class of capitalists or an industrial proletariat. As late as 1700 most of the industrial activities were far more like what they had been in 1400 than what they would be in 1850. Many of them continued along the same lines as before, though virtually all showed increased output as the result of growing demand from a rising population, even if large sections of the population did not have the wherewithal to purchase much in the way of industrial products. Growth was also stimulated by various forms of encouragement on the part of authority—State, landowners, entrepreneurs, town, or guild. Attempts were made to bring in highly skilled foreign specialists and technicians, who were accorded special privileges to encourage them to settle. To raise the capital necessary for the more expensive ventures embarked upon, monopoly joint-stock companies were set up, especially in relation to mining and smelting. Such enterprises arose partly from the State's wish to foster native industry and render the country less dependent on foreign imports, though it was also in large part a device to raise additional revenue for the monarchy and profits for individual initiative. Many of the gentry, merchants, and yeomen were also alert to the possibility of developing their resources and augmenting their income in this fashion.

Some industries felt the pull of increased demand more than others. The widespread reconstruction between 1550 and 1640 of the dwellings of the more prosperous social groups in many parts of Wales, town and country alike, benefited the building industry greatly. Though much of the work was seasonal in its nature, it absorbed large quantities of raw materials and employed many people in allied trades. Lime was also being used in decidedly greater amounts for fertilizer on the land, but had to be burned in kilns before it could be used. Brewing, too, seems 'to have thrived enormously in Elizabethan Wales' and increased significantly in importance.[22] Yet although we get tantalizing glimpses of greater activity in all these trades—many Tudor and Stuart buildings still standing, frequent references to lime-burners in contemporary records, and evidence from the port books of much greater imports of malt by local brewers—we know very little in detail about their operations. Many were located in or near towns; but the sixteenth-century history of these towns is still a largely unworked field. Some features of urban development are clear enough, however: many towns grew in size, population, and prosperity from c.1560 onwards. Like the towns generally, they attracted a larger-than-average share of the growing population. Some of the immigrants were gentlemen and yeomen or their sons, who set up profitably in trade and industry; but many

---

[22] E. A. Lewis, *The Welsh Port Books, 1558–1603* (London, 1927), p. xli.

were poor men and women attracted by the possibility of contriving a less uncomfortable living by work or charity than they could hope for in an overcrowded countryside. One of the features of the influx was the large number of Welsh speakers who came in, making the urban centres far more strongly Welsh in speech and culture than they had ever been.

Among the industries still conducted in towns was cloth-making. Weavers' guilds were incorporated in Carmarthen, Haverfordwest, Brecon, and elsewhere, and an Exchequer suit of 1600–1 shows that considerable quantities of cloth were still being woven in the towns of Glamorgan and Monmouthshire.[23] But it was an industry which found the restrictions imposed by town guilds more than ordinarily irksome and was rapidly escaping into the countryside. An Act of 1542 which first defined Welsh cloths by statute gave as the reason for doing so the regrettable out-movement of cloth-making from the towns of south Wales. Rural industry might have its disadvantages: wide dispersal in scattered locations at some distance from its markets, difficulties of control, and frequent disruption by the demands of agricultural work. But these were more than offset by compensations like lower taxation, freedom from guild restrictions, and lower costs and wages. The most important aspect of this shift for Wales was the move of the main centre of cloth-making from south to north. This was explained, in part, by the growing tendency for the farmers of south-west Wales to export their wool 'unworked' to the cloth industry of the west of England. What counted for even more was the suitability of the industry to the needs of the rapidly growing population of the upland counties of the north, where there were ample supplies of grazing, wool, water, and labour, in an area whose leaner agriculture could not alone sustain the expanding population. Cloth-making, there, necessarily remained a truly dispersed and domestic trade, mopping up the surplus labour of women and children as well as men. Rarely did the weavers employ any but family labour, except possibly for one or two assistants. Since the Welsh wools used, and those bought in considerable quantities in markets like Oswestry, were generally coarse, the cloth made from them was inferior in quality and relatively expensive. It nevertheless commanded a growing market down to about 1620. By its very nature it produced neither capitalists nor proletariat; its producers remained poor and dependent on a speedy return for their cloth. Obliged in many instances to look to wool broggers and 'putters out' for their wool, they were never in a position to introduce significant improvements in technique. The result was a 'scattered, vaguely-organized industry, incapable of cutting costs or even maintaining high standards' and forced to hand over the marketing of its

---

[23] PRO E112/61/Glam. 23; cf. *GCH*, IV, 46–8.

products to the wealthy and strategically placed Shrewsbury Drapers.[24]

The pulse of activity in mining and metals also beat perceptibly more robustly as the result of larger output from a number of different enterprises. However, earlier notions that there occurred an industrial revolution, based on much wider use of coal in industry and the introduction of superior technology, which anticipated the Industrial Revolution of the eighteenth century, have been sharply modified.[25] The development which took place is now seen as more modest, sporadic, and haphazard; more dependent on the initiative of entrepreneurs and less continuously maintained or successful than used to be supposed; barely able, indeed, to keep pace with the current growth in population. There were, even so, important changes, particularly in coal, iron, lead, and copper.

Demand for coal increased greatly; partly as a result of a pressing shortage of timber, resulting from its extensive felling for a variety of purposes. Coal was consequently much more widely used, not only for domestic heating in places where wood was scarce, but also in industries like malting, lime-burning, salt-refining, soap-making, brick and tile manufacture, glass-making, dyeing, and the preparation of saltpetre, copperas, and alum. Most of this demand came from outside Wales and a flourishing export trade sprang up to meet it (below, pp. 403–5). Coal continued to be mined in much the same sort of places as in the Middle Ages, though on a markedly bigger scale. In Flintshire it was mined at Ewloe, Holywell, and other sites in the neighbourhood; and in Denbighshire at Coedpoeth, Brymbo, Rhosllannerchrugog, and other places near Wrexham, and also in and around Chirk. The workings in south Wales, especially in the vicinity of Swansea and Neath, Llanelli and Kidwelly, and various points in south Pembrokeshire were even more important. Technology remained primitive, however, and the problems of ventilation and drainage acute, so that pits were comparatively small and shallow. The best contemporary description of methods of winning coal comes from George Owen's pen.[26] He describes a shaft some six or seven feet square, lined with timber, sunk to a depth of from 70 to 120 feet. In an average pit there would have been three hewers, seven bearers, one filler, four winders, and two riddlers; a team capable of producing 80 to 100 barrels a day. When men toiled from 6.0 a.m. to 6.0 p.m., with an hour off at noon, their work was exhausting. It was also very dangerous, with the possibility of death or crippling injury never far away. In spite of these risks, men and boys seemed to be easily recruited, and in the Swansea and Neath area

[24] T. C. Mendenhall, *The Shrewsbury Drapers and the Welsh Wool Trade in the XVI and XVII Centuries* (Oxford, 1953), p. 214.
[25] S. M. Jack, *Trade and Industry in Tudor and Stuart England* (London, 1977).
[26] Owen, I, 90–1.

mining became a full-time occupation. Coalmining, when undertaken on a commercial scale, could be a costly operation, involving a sizeable outlay of capital. It was some of the wealthier landowners, like the Myddeltons and Mostyns in the north, or the Mansels, Evanses, and Vaughans in the south, who put money into the industry from Elizabeth's reign onwards.

The same years witnessed major developments in metal-mining and smelting enterprises. In iron-making there was a primary technological advance with the introduction of the blast-furnace. It transformed the industry from the stage of pygmy bloomeries blown by hand-bellows to that of big furnaces in which blast was produced by large water-driven bellows. Expensive construction of these furnaces at carefully selected locations on the banks of streams required heavy capital outlay, led to much higher consumption of fuel, and called for the employment of highly skilled foreign workers. But, when successful, they resulted in highly commercialized concerns producing for an external market. The scarcity of timber in older iron-producing areas may not have been as severe as used to be thought and could have been met by skilful coppicing; but some districts in south-east Wales, none the less, held real attractions for the established ironmasters of the Weald. In Monmouthshire and Glamorgan they found an enticing abundance of resources: plentiful woodlands, iron ore deposits, limestone, and water-power, and all within fairly easy reach of ports. Richard Hanbury, a London goldsmith, set up works at Pontypool, Aber-carn, and elsewhere, employing 160–200 men daily, most of them unskilled local labourers. Sussex ironmasters, including Henry Sidney, were attracted to Glamorgan and established works at a number of points in the Taff Valley, with variable degrees of success. Around Chirk Sir Thomas Myddelton was very active in the years preceding the Civil Wars. Though cargoes of iron were being exported from Newport, Cardiff, and Swansea, early in the seventeenth century, serious difficulties remained to be overcome. The ironmasters had still to learn the techniques of realistic costing and financing, more frugal husbanding of fuel resources, and successfully managing the export and marketing of their product.

During the Elizabethan age the Crown firmly insisted upon its exclusive rights to 'mines royal', i.e., the ores of metals needed for coinage: gold, silver, quicksilver, copper, and tin. Such policies were strongly disliked by local landowners, who objected to the blocking of their own desire to exploit resources and enlarge income. But the royal ambition was to encourage discovery and exploitation of metals in the wider interests of national wealth, employment, and economic self-sufficiency. To achieve those ends, the technologically more advanced German experts were encouraged to settle in the country, with their technical operations being financed mainly by native capital. To raise the money needed, it was necessary to encourage joint-stock partnerships on the German model, with even some German capital. In 1568 two joint-stock chartered companies, the Mines Royal and the Mineral and Battery Works, were given monopoly rights to discover and work 'mines royal' throughout England and Wales. It was originally intended that the operations of the two companies should supplement each other, but they soon went their own separate ways.

The only Welsh county in which the Mineral and Battery Works had rights was Monmouthshire, where it established a wire-works at Tintern. The principal use for wire was in the manufacture of cards for carding wool and the company was given statutory protection against foreign competition. In spite of initial difficulties, by 1603 some 600 men were employed at Tintern, though the brass-making enterprise there never got beyond the experimental stage.

The Mines Royal, with its monopoly rights in all other Welsh counties, was chiefly concerned with lead and copper mining and smelting. It leased its lead mines in Cardiganshire to Thomas ('Customer') Smyth of London, whose devoted agent, Charles Evans, found them in badly neglected condition in 1586. Drainage and ventilation, as in coalmines, proved to be intractable problems. Prices for lead were poor because of competition from Polish mines, and the chief incentive for lead-prospecting was the hope of discovering silver-bearing strata. Luckily, silver was found at the Cwmsymlog mine and, until Smyth's death in 1591, operations went fairly well. Thereafter there was little progress until 1617, when Hugh Myddelton obtained a lease for fourteen years at a yearly rent of £400. Strongly backed by James I, he was given extensive powers to deal with 'ill-affected' landowners preferring their 'private ends and profit before the common good' and to control workmen who might 'prove mutinous and disordered'.[27] Myddelton was an able entrepreneur who made a success of his venture, though the oft-quoted figure of his profit of £2,000 a month needs to be received with marked scepticism. He died in 1631 and was succeeded by Thomas Bushell in 1637. Bushell solved some of his problems by driving adits to drain the mines and introducing a German ventilation device. He further managed to secure the setting up of a royal mint at Aberystwyth in 1638 and by 1642 had succeeded in minting £13,069 of silver coin. To keep his operations going he was obliged to bring in peat as fuel and to import quantities of coal from Pembrokeshire via Aberystwyth.[28] Lead was also mined in other parts of Wales in small quantities: in Flintshire, where the interests of lessees clashed with those of the Mostyns; in Denbighshire, where John Wynn was active; and in Pembrokeshire on a small scale by Sir Thomas Canon.

[27] W. Rees, *Industry before the Industrial Revolution* (2 vols. Cardiff, 1968), II, 445.
[28] Bushell left two books recounting his activities: *A Just and True Remonstrance of H.M.'s Mines Royal . . .* (1640); and *The Case of Thomas Bushell* (1649).

Modest amounts of copper as well as lead were mined in Cardiganshire and were taken for processing to a Mines Royal smelting-house near Neath. This choice of site at Aberdulais had much to recommend it. Copper smelting demanded large supplies of coal and timber, neither of which was readily available in either Cornwall or Cardiganshire, the two main sources of copper ore. There was a strong fall of water in the Dulais cascade; the site had easy access to the sea; and the chief local landlord was the earl of Pembroke, himself closely associated with the Mines Royal as an investor. A skilled German technician, Ulrich Frosse, was brought to supervise the working of two furnaces reputedly capable of dealing with 560 tons of ore in 40 weeks. Intractable difficulties arose, however: deliveries of ore from Cornwall were erratic and very difficult to smelt; and timber supplies and finance gave rise to serious concern. Although smelting continued until 1605, the significance of the venture lay in what it portended for the future not what it actually achieved. It was, all the same, an interesting episode, neatly illustrating three distinctive characteristics of the period: the exploitation of new or neglected resources; the employment of foreign technical expertise; and the creation of inter-regional economic interdependence. A further interesting pointer to the future was Ulrich Frosse's reputed experiments with coal as fuel for smelting.

About many other 'trades' we know surprisingly little. In spite of the importance of leather-making in virtually every town, the considerable capital outlay required for constructing tanneries and buying hides, and the long time-scale involved in the tanning process, little is known in detail of the leather industry and its associated crafts. The quarrying and export of slates, again, were obviously increasing in scale, with 100,000 slates being sent to Ireland alone in 1587; but apart from such indications in the port books little can be traced of the industry. Ship and boat building was another occupation growing in importance as sea-borne trade and fishing increased in volume. Of at least thirty-seven local vessels known to have plied in and out of Swansea between 1558 and 1640 many, if not all, must have been built locally, and the town's records present a busy scene of boat building along the Swansea strand, paralleled in many other places doubtless.[29] Fishing for herring in Cardigan Bay and cod in Newfoundland expanded considerably after 1560 and must surely have stimulated the building of many boats at various points along the coast.

A number of other industries had one thing in common, i.e., each was making greater use of coal in its manufacturing processes. They included brewing, lime-burning, potteries, glass-making, and salt-refining. Robert Mansel started a glass-works at Milford Haven in 1615, using Pembrokeshire coal in the process; and later set up at Swansea but without much success.

[29] Univ. Coll. of Swansea, Swansea Common Attorneys' Accounts, 1623, 1633, 1635.

A 'salt works' at Barry supplied salt to Gloucester and a particularly interesting experiment was the attempt to set up a salt refinery near Aberdyfi in the 1560s. The German expert, Christopher Schutz, was brought in to advise on the venture; but his many commitments elsewhere, the inclement Merioneth winter weather, and the slump in prices caused by the Huguenot seizure of the Biscayan salt-producing provinces in the end posed too many problems.[30] Apart from such attempts calling for large-scale investment and the employment of foreign experts, there must have been a number of 'trades' organized on a widely dispersed, small-scale local or domestic level, requiring little more than simple craft tools or just plain hard work and muscle-power, e.g., the widespread collecting of seaweed for burning so that its ashes could be used to nourish the soil or in the making of soft soap and for other cleaning purposes.

TRADING PATTERNS

Successive Tudor and Stuart governments were greatly preoccupied with the need to foster trade; and, economically, Wales gained much as the result of their policies. It was brought more closely within the political and economic orbit of the realm; statutes were enacted to promote law and order and to regulate and encourage trade; vice-admirals were appointed to protect the coast and suppress piracy; customs were reorganized and other measures promulgated to stimulate commerce. Such royal solicitude would have availed little had there not been new economic energies independently coursing through the country's arteries. Agriculture and industry were responding in lively fashion to the attractions of the wider market as well as local demand, and resultant increases in production were mirrored in contemporary trading patterns. The commodities exported were the fruits of Wales's mixed and pastoral farming: livestock, dairy produce, hides, wool, cloth, and corn. A quantity of fish and timber, and a mounting volume of its industrial production—coal, especially; iron, copper, lead, and slates, to a lesser extent—were also sent out. Though most of this output was directed to destinations within England and Wales a significant proportion went to foreign markets. The return traffic made good some of Wales's own deficiencies: imports of corn and fruit, and also wine, salt, tar, pitch, tobacco, and exotic tropical fruits and commodities, for instance. They came either directly or by re-exports from Bristol and Chester.

Difficult though land transport continued to be, two of the most important items in Welsh trade—livestock and cloth—were still delivered largely by overland routes. A reminder of how vital both had been and still

[30] W. J. Lewis, 'A Welsh Salt-making Venture', *NLWJ*, VIII (1953–4), 419–25. Cf. also, Vaughan, *Golden Fleece*, III, 65 for another venture.

were to the Welsh economy came in a petition from north Wales to the King in 1643. Its authors, sorely pressed by wartime exigencies, reminded Charles that 'cattle and cottons' were their 'principal and most considerable commodities . . . the only support of your petitioners' being and livelihood';[31] a declaration reinforced by Archbishop John Williams's oft-quoted remark about the cattle-trade being the 'Spanish treasure galleons' of Wales. Demand for meat had expanded greatly, and to feed the insatiable maw of the vast and growing population of London and other towns, large numbers of cattle and sheep were driven every year from Wales into England. Court records and the toll-books of Shrewsbury and Leominster tend to show that fewer found their way to the south-east than is often thought; most were sold to farmers and traders in the borders and Midlands to meet local needs. Nor should we overlook the fact that many animals from the south Wales coastal plains were sent by sea to satisfy the needs of Bristol and the west. The livestock were mostly bought at fairs, a chain of which existed across Wales and the border. The surviving toll-books of fairs at Eglwyswrw and Machynlleth reveal the existence of a substantial internal trade between the poorer counties of north Wales and those of the south for local fattening and consumption.[32]

Welsh cloth was also sent partly by sea but mainly by land. Cloth from south Wales continued to be sent coastwise to Bristol, but with the steady growth of the industry in north Wales, most of the cloth made there was transported by pack-horse to the towns of the border, especially Oswestry. There it was bought by the Drapers of Shrewsbury, who enjoyed a virtually complete monopoly of the trade, which they were tenaciously to defend for a century and more against their potential rivals from London, Chester, and even from within Shrewsbury itself. They in turn dispatched the cloth to Blackwell Hall in London and smaller quantities down the Severn to Bristol to be exported overseas. The chief markets abroad were France, and later Portugal, Spain, Leghorn, Barbary, and the islands. The trade had its ups and downs, and between 1615 and 1620 ran into a particularly severe depression which lasted until 1622 but from which it recovered sooner than might have been expected.

It was on sea and river communications that Wales depended for conducting a great deal of its commerce. Many parts of south Wales prospered because of its easy outlets to the sea, not only through the main ports but through many lesser creeks and harbours also. The resources of this coast the Tudor governments were determined to exploit more effectively, in their own rather than their subjects' interests. Early in Elizabeth's reign, a serious effort was mounted to rationalize the customs

[31] Mendenhall, *Wool Trade*, p. 11.
[32] E. Evans, 'Two Machynlleth Toll-books', *NLWJ*, vi (1949–50); E. A. Lewis, The Toll-books of Some North Pembrokeshire Fairs (1599–1603)', *BBCS*, vi (1933–5), 284–318.

organization, when all the Welsh harbours were grouped under the three head ports of Cardiff, Milford, and Chester. The intention was unmistakably to place in the appropriate ports the main customs officers—controller, customer, searcher, and surveyor. They were first appointed in Milford in 1565, Cardiff in 1573, and Beaumaris in 1577. But, for many years afterwards, there was strong local resistance to customs duties, widespread corruption and misdemeanours among officials, and a great deal of evasion, smuggling, and other malpractices.

In view of the many shortcomings of the customs organization, its records—the port books[33]—are an imprecise instrument for measuring the nature and volume of trade. Quite apart from the officers' own misdeeds there are other difficulties too. Their purpose was to keep a financial not a trading record; they give little information about smaller creeks and havens; they do not record the movement of livestock; and there are long periods for which no port books have survived. But whatever their imperfections, when supplemented by other sources, they succeed in giving an invaluable broad survey of Wales's sea-borne trade and the ships and merchants taking part in it.

They shed light on both the foreign and coastal trade. The most valuable aspect of foreign trade in the Middle Ages had been interchanges with France, whereby wine and salt came in, and wool, cloth, and hides were exported in return. This pattern continued for much of the sixteenth century, though exports of coal increasingly displaced those of wool and cloth. Figures for the export of coal from Neath and Swansea, the ports mainly involved, increased sharply from an average of 2,400 tons to 12,000 tons in the 1630s; but of the 12,000 tons only about 2,000 tons may have been intended for foreign ports, the fall being due to the taxes imposed on coal exports in 1620 and 1634. The former trade links with Spain and Portugal, whereby wines, salt, sugar, and iron were imported in return for Welsh cloth continued down until about 1580. Thereafter, largely as a result of the deterioration in relations between Elizabeth and Philip II, trade dwindled badly. Trade with Ireland concentrated mainly on Milford Haven, north Pembrokeshire, Cardigan Bay, and Beaumaris, with coal and culm going out in considerable quantities from the south, and slates from the north. The later years of Elizabeth's reign saw a big jump in corn exports, as the result of the increasing amount being grown in south Pembrokeshire. The years after 1593 similarly witnessed a sizeable increase in imports of salt, herrings, wool, flax, cloth, livestock, and timber from Ireland.

Coastal trade during this period was briskly stimulated by a number of

[33] Lewis, *Port Books*; E. A. Lewis, 'The Port Books of Cardigan in Elizabethan and Stuart Times', *Trans. Cards. Antiq. Soc.*, VII and IX (1930–3); W. Rees, 'The Port of Cardiff and its Member Ports, 1606–1610', *SWMRS*, III (1954).

developments: the increasing exploitation of mineral and metal resources; the growth of native iron, salt, and cloth industries in England; the influence of national economic policy aiming at making the kingdom self-sufficient in food supplies, by moving grain to Wales, in times of need, from regions in England with a surplus; importing exotic commodities into centres of regional trade such as Bristol; and, finally, the investment of large sums of capital in the metal industries of Wales. All these phenomena were reflected in the pattern of coastal trading. Coal became the most important item in the coastal trade of south Wales and the 'sea-sale' traffic was responsible for exporting it to many parts of western and southern England. Iron, lead, and copper figured more largely, and cloth exports continued to be a significant item, though they fell away sharply towards the end of the sixteenth century. Corn appeared prominently in exports from Pembrokeshire and Glamorgan, especially to Bristol, which, 'being very populous', explained to the Privy Council its urgent need to import food from south Wales,[34] though considerable cargoes of malt and barley came back in return. Livestock and wool also went across the Bristol Channel from Wales in large quantities. Butter and cheese were made in large enough amounts for members of the Bristol Society of Merchant Venturers to establish a monopoly in the export of them. In return, Bristol re-exported many luxury and exotic goods. In north Wales, Beaumaris enjoyed valuable outgoing trade with Chester, Liverpool, and other ports of north-western England. The commodities dispatched were dairy produce, hides, leather, and slate; but Beaumaris imported much larger quantities of pitch, tar, brass, pewter, wines, salt, and iron.

One of the features of the sea-borne trade was how small and numerous the ships engaged in it were. Vessels plying coastwise were usually between ten and twenty tons; some were as small as five or six. They tended to get bigger in the seventeenth century; but the coasters leaving Swansea in 1629–30 had an average burden of only twenty-nine tons and those from Neath twenty-seven tons. Yet, when considering vessels of this size, it should be remembered that they could carry as much as 100 horses. Larger vessels were used for foreign trade. By the seventeenth century, ships as big as *Long Thomas* of 200 tons or *Great Thomas* of 100 tons plied from Aberthaw to the Continent and even across the Atlantic. Many of the vessels engaged on the run to and from France were, none the less, much smaller than this, like the forty-ton *Jonas* of Swansea, which made at least half a dozen round trips to La Rochelle in 1587–8. Because the ships were so small, the trade of even a little port was shared by many. For example, in 1602 Cardiff's twenty-eight outward shipments were shared among fifteen boats and its seventeen inward shipments among ten. Provisioning,

---

[34] *APC, 1630–1*, p. 125.

supplying, repairing, and loading and unloading foreign and local vessels must have been a useful source of income and employment for merchants, shopkeepers, shipwrights, and labourers. A rare glimpse of the logistics involved comes from 1637, when *Long Thomas* required thirty-two men and women to unload her over a period of nine days, the men being paid 6*d*. a day and the women 4*d*.

Those engaged in the trade were drawn from a wide mixture of social backgrounds—merchants, traders, gentlemen, yeomen, farmers, and craftsmen. Men as mighty in their own localities as Sir John Perrot or Sir Richard Bulkeley took a hand in various ventures; and so did gentleman-industrialists like Sir Henry Sidney or Edmund Mathew. Nor did the commercial relationships of the Bristol Channel recognize any boundaries between England and Wales. Many south Wales men entered partnerships with associates on the English side of the Channel and a number of Bristol men were active in south Wales. Overall, in spite of sharp fluctuations of fortune from time to time, we derive the impression of buoyant and expanding trade at least until the 1620s.

CHAPTER 17

SOCIAL HISTORY, 1540–1642
RICH AND POOR MOVE FURTHER APART

POPULATION TRENDS

FORMING some estimate of the population of Wales in the sixteenth and seventeenth centuries is a little less difficult, though not much, than it was for the Middle Ages. In the first place, Wales has benefited indirectly from the excellent research undertaken on the population of England. Although the conclusions cannot be automatically applied west of Offa's Dyke, at least they give us as reliable an account as we are likely to be able to derive of what was happening in neighbouring counties within the same kingdom.[1] Furthermore, there exist for Wales a few sources of a kind which might be used to compile a tentative sketch of the size of its population and the changes which took place within it. Five sources in particular have been employed for this purpose: the subsidy assessment of 1545; the hearth-tax returns of 1670; the bishops' estimates of households within their dioceses of 1563 and 1603; a few of the handful of surviving parish registers; and the use of Gregory King's figures of 1689 and the first census of 1801 to work backwards proportionately from them. All these sources are in one way or another incomplete and unsatisfactory, some being much more deficient than others; but at least the evidence of them all points in the same general direction—to a considerable increase in population between 1540 and 1642. Much more analysis and local study are urgently needed in a field of Welsh history whose surface has barely been scratched as yet. But it has to be admitted, such is the nature of the surviving evidence, that it appears very doubtful whether we can ever hope to arrive at anything better than a very rough approximation, open to a wide degree of error, of the size of the population or the kinds of variation which overtook it.

What does seem well-established, nevertheless, is that the population of Wales, like that of the rest of Europe, grew substantially during this century, though even by as late as 1600 it may not have done much more than catch up with what it had been in 1300. The timing of all these

[1] E. A. Wrigley and R. S. Schofield, *Population History of England, 1541 to 1871* (London, 1981); B. E. Howells, 'The historial demography of Wales: some notes on sources', *The Local Historian*, x (1973).

increases may also have varied markedly from locality to locality within the country. Following the long medieval decline and near-stagnation, Thomas Starkey in 1536 maintained that there still existed 'a great lack and penury of people and inhabitants'.[2] Not until the second or third decade of the sixteenth century does a really significant recovery seem to have got under way. This growth was sharply checked by the outbreak in 1557 of a disease called 'the sweat' by contemporaries—it may well have been a virulent form of influenza—which 'commenced in Wales and then traversed the whole kingdom, the mortality being immense amongst persons of every condition'.[3] Population afterwards continued to rise fairly steadily, though doubtless with many regional disparities, until the late 1580s and 1590s, when famines, war casualties, and outbreaks of plague certainly slowed it down. The early 1620s were also a very bad period, when severe food shortages may have led to crises of subsistence in some parts of Wales (below, p. 428). The overall estimates of population in Wales for this period, which, it should be emphasized, are not much more than informed guesses, are listed in the table below.[4]

These estimates are too liable to error for us to generalize at all confidently on the basis of them. We need to be careful not to assume too readily that trends discernible in England are equally applicable to Wales, even though the growth of population in Wales appears to have been broadly similar to that of north-west England, an area very comparable in geography, climate, and social structure. Nevertheless, bearing these caveats in mind, there appear to be three features which stand out. First, the increases for the counties of north Wales between 1545 and 1670 are greater than those for the south. Second, there also seems to be a proportionately greater increase in a number of upland hundreds, which may well have been abandoned or neglected in the withdrawal from poorer land in the late medieval period. Finally, some though not all Welsh towns appear to have benefited from a considerable influx of population.

All the counties of north Wales show an estimated increase of 66 per cent and upwards, and two of them, Merioneth (85 per cent) and Montgomery (84 per cent) show the biggest gains of any of the Welsh counties. It should be noted, however, that three of the southern counties, Cardigan, Carmarthen, and Brecon, look so unconvincingly low as to give rise to the suspicion that the sources from which these statistics were derived were seriously defective. The northern counties might have been expected to benefit more than the southern ones from the movement back to pastoral upland areas and especially to those districts where a rural

[2] J. Youings, *Sixteenth-century England* (Penguin, 1984), p. 130.
[3] *CSP Ven.*, v, 541.
[4] Williams, *BBCS*, VII, 359–63; Owen, *Trans. Cymmr.*, 1959, pp. 99–113; Wrigley and Schofield, *Population History*, pp. 528, 566.

WRIGLEY and SCHOFIELD[a]

1541	194,000 (214,000)	1576	239,000 (263,000)	1611	309,000 (340,000)
1546	200,000 (220,000)	1581	252,000 (277,000)	1616	316,000 (348,000)
1551	211,000 (232,000)	1586	266,000 (292,000)	1621	329,000 (361,000)
1556	221,000 (243,000)	1591	273,000 (300,000)	1626	330,000 (363,000)
1561	209,000 (230,000)	1596	281,000 (309,000)	1631	343,000 (377,000)
1566	219,000 (241,000)	1601	288,000 (317,000)	1636	354,000 (389,000)
1571	229,000 (252,000)	1606	298,000 (330,000)	1641	356,000 (393,000)

DAVID WILLIAMS

1536	278,000	1600	379,000	1670	408,000
1570	325,000	1630	405,000		

LEONARD OWEN

county	1545–63	1670
Anglesey	9,770	16,175
Brecknock	21,190	27,185
Cardiganshire	17,320	20,015
Caernarfonshire	14,920	26,225
Carmarthenshire	34,375	37,225
Denbighshire	22,482	40,820
Flintshire	12,570	22,899
Glamorgan	29,493	49,928
Merionethshire	10,470	19,435
Montgomeryshire	18,972	34,907
Pembrokeshire	20,079	31,535
Radnorshire	14,185	16,295
Plus an estimated 10% for Monmouthshire	22,582	34,167
TOTAL	248,408	375,841

[a] The second figure in brackets represents 10% extra for Monmouthshire.

cloth-making industry flourished. Yet there is plenty of evidence of encroachments on upland wastes and the carving-out of new farms and holdings in upland areas of the south such as the hill districts of the lordships of Kidwelly or Gower or Blaenau Morgannwg. It is worth noting that in two particularly fertile and well-populated 'fielden' districts in Glamorgan and Pembroke, Dinas Powys and Castlemartin, neither of which had much in the way of spare or marginal land in 1545, the estimated increase in each instance was very small—Dinas Powys 19 per cent and Castlemartin 27 per cent—whereas in two upland hundreds within the same counties, Caerphilly or Cemaes, it was estimated at 88 per cent and 114 per cent respectively.

A number of Welsh towns seem to have benefited disproportionately, some even spectacularly, from the growth in population, in line with most of the urban populations of Europe. Whereas in the 1530s Leland commented pessimistically on the dilapidated state of towns like Mold, Cricieth, Hay, or Llandovery, which had suffered severely as a result of the decay of their castles or the loss of their former privileged position within Marcher lordships, strenuous attempts to renew urban growth had later been made by Parliament from time to time. Some towns clearly gained from such statutory encouragement and also from contemporary economic development. Those towns which were centres of trade or industry proved to be powerful magnets in attracting to themselves young unmarried people looking for employment. Some of those in north Wales grew especially fast. Caernarfon's population rose by an estimated 120 per cent from 800 to 1,755 between 1536 and 1670, and Wrexham's by 112 per cent from 1,515 to 3,225, making it perhaps the most populous town in Wales by 1670. Towns associated with the rise of a surrounding cloth industry also flourished. Montgomery appears to have increased from 308 to 678 (137 per cent) and Llanidloes still more, from 324 to 814 (150 per cent). In south Wales the coalmining in and around Swansea led to an estimated increase of 80 per cent in its population, from 960 to 1,733, and the inflow of migrants from a wide range of surrounding parishes, including places as far away as Llangadog, Defynnog, Cardiff, and even Bristol, has been traced within the town. Pembroke and Cardiff were two other prosperous southern towns whose population increased notably. Two of the largest and richest towns in Tudor Wales, Carmarthen and Brecon, experienced such modest increases of 26 per cent and 2 per cent, however, as to suggest some inherent deficiency in the sources used to arrive at those estimates. Another feature of the urban immigration worthy of comment was the big influx of Welsh-speaking people. Such an in-movement of Welsh settlers had been characteristic of late medieval towns; but, since the Act of Union had emancipated Welsh people from all previous legal restraints on their entry, they took advantage to flock in in much larger numbers. At Swansea they were present in sufficient force to demand Welsh-language church services as of right in 1592, while in Denbigh it was thought desirable to proclaim James I king in Welsh and English.

It is not altogether easy to explain this general increase in numbers. One reason may be the relative freedom from plague and other epidemic diseases during much of the second half of the sixteenth century, though individual towns and districts might be sorely stricken. Another factor may be the good harvests of the 1570s and 1580s. Yet another may be the tendency to marry younger and so to increase the child-bearing span of the wife and the number of children born. Better housing, for those comfortably enough off to have afforded it, certainly made a notable contribution to increasing the size of the population.

SOCIAL DEGREES AND MOBILITY

Surviving from the Middle Ages, in many important respects largely unaltered, were the structure of the social order, the assumptions traditionally cherished about differences of degree and status, the respect to which they entitled a person, and belief in the need to keep up a stable and unchanging chain of authority and dependence. Rural society still consisted of aristocrats, knights, esquires, gentlemen, yeomen, husbandmen, craftsmen, cottagers, labourers, and the poor, as before; and the town populations were made up, all the while, of urban gentry, merchants, shopkeepers, artisans, labourers, and paupers. The professional groups of clergy, lawyers, physicians, and others also knew their places and fitted into their respective niches as they had previously done. What was unmistakably different, however, and men were under increasingly fewer illusions about the reality of it, was that, within the existing structure, the economic changes earlier described (see pp. 381–401) were leading to a social polarization more pronounced than that already seen developing in the fifteenth and early sixteenth centuries between the upper social groups and the lower ones, between those who prospered and waxed fat and those who lost ground and grew poorer. Those who could benefit from this widening chasm had no hesitation about doing so. They could in consequence—at more than one social level—look forward with lively expectation to living standards of hitherto undreamed of comfort. Those who could not were, together with their children, pushed further and further down the slope to a depth of poverty and hardship hardly conceivable in the previous century. The pace of upward and downward social mobility was being dramatically accelerated.

Inflation threatened all ranks of society with the ominous prospect of seeing their income savagely eroded. Simultaneously, it also opened up avenues of fresh advancement for those whose control over land or other resources was such as to enable them to exploit their assets advantageously. Those best placed to do so, as already seen, were the gentry, great and small. In 1536 Rowland Lee had contemptuously dismissed most of them as having less than £10 a year in land and even more limited discretion, while as late as 1655 Major-general Berry commented disparagingly that it was easier to find fifty Welsh gentlemen of £50 a year than five of £100. It was certainly true that Wales was a land full of small estates; to such an extent that Professor R. T. Jenkins once remarked with characteristically mischievous insight that, seeing how thick on the ground were the one-time gentry houses, it was difficult to know where the tenantry had ever found room to bestow themselves in between the *plasau*! Yet many of these gentry families had been Argus-eyed in their vigilance to seize the possibilities of acquiring more land and adding to their estates during this century. By 1594, George Owen, from the Elizabethan comfort of a typically compact and well-managed estate built up at Henllys by his father and himself, looked back two generations to the world of 1536. He confessed that then there might have been 'scarce two gentlemen' to be found worth £20 a year in any shire, but claimed that by his day there were to be found 'some that doth receive yearly £500, some £300 and many £100 good lands'.[5] Even making allowance for the devaluing effects of inflation on money incomes, this was progress indeed. Owen's point was in 1645 reinforced by Richard Symonds. In a poor county like Anglesey, he could record three landowners worth more than £1,000, five between £500 and £1,000 and twenty worth over £100, while in Glamorgan he found thirty-five heads of families worth £300 a year or more (twelve of them worth £1,000) and upwards of 100 families worth £40–200 a year.[6] Throughout Wales, in every county, there were several dozen families regarding themselves as gentry and being accepted as such by their neighbours. Many of them might have applied other criteria besides strictly economic ones in determining their status.

Naturally, within so comparatively large a social group as the gentry there were wide variations of wealth and degree. At the topmost levels of county society came those superior families who would be worth at least £500 a year and upwards, with some of them enjoying an income which put them on a par with lesser members of the aristocracy like Lord Herbert of Chirbury. Men of this kind could normally expect to be knighted in each generation and some were to be found, like Sir John Stradling or Sir Thomas Mansel, among the first baronets created by James I in 1611. Just below them came the esquires, the title customarily bestowed on younger sons of peers, deputy-lieutenants, sheriffs, and justices of the peace. By Charles I's reign there would be two or three dozen families of this standing in every shire, monopolizing shire justice and administration. Some indication of the growing numbers of upper gentry families may be derived from the increasing number of justices of the peace in the early seventeenth century; but, equally, this increase may be as much an indication of the wider range of duties expected of them. What is even more impressive is the effort made by leading families to establish important cadet and collateral branches on the part of their younger sons within their own county or a neighbouring one. Among the thirty-five leading families noted in Glamorgan in 1645 were six belonging to various branches of the Lewis family of Y Fan; four of them were brothers, all sons of Sir Edward Lewis, who had been careful to provide for them by buying lands in his own lifetime. Even illegitimate sons might set up new families

[5] Owen, III, 57–8.
[6] *Diary of the Marches of the Royal Army during the Great Civil War*, ed. C. E. Long (Camden Soc., 1859), pp. 216–17.

in this way. The immediate ancestor of as high-flying and influential a stock as the Herberts of Swansea and Cardiff and the Herbert earls of Pembroke was the bastard Sir Richard Herbert of Ewias.

Others who had similarly seized the chances of establishing themselves as founders of new gentry families were successful lawyers, clergymen, physicians, and others who had purchased landed estates by deploying those steady profits, unaffected by agrarian vicissitudes, made out of their professions. They were themselves usually the younger sons of gentry who had been given an education appropriate to set them on the road to carving out their own future. The comment made by Sir Thomas Smith on those who had studied in the universities, professed the liberal sciences, and thereby established themselves as gentlemen has long become a cliché among historians, but it is no less true for being so. The complaint often heard about such men—doubtless not without its strong undertones of envy and exaggeration—was that in pursuit of their own interests they did not hesitate to trample over others. Lawyers, it was said, 'by the ruin of their neighbours' contentions are grown so rich and so proud that no other sort dare meddle with them' and 'they undo the country people and buy up all the lands to be sold'.[7] The legal profession was 'loth to be troubled with anything except making money, wherein they have a great facility', Sir John Stradling believed, and he described them as preying on young men as 'the eagles do on a carrion'.[8] However they came by their fortunes, a multitude of lawyers planted themselves and their descendants as leading gentry in every county in Wales. Nor were lawyers the only ones on the make. Those who should have been men's spiritual shepherds were all too often alleged to be most concerned with 'fleecing' them in other ways. Edmwnd Prys, himself an archdeacon, had tart comments to offer on men of his own calling who sought to make profits as avidly as the rest of the world and financially would have 'sheared the sheep' even more closely if they could.[9] Even Bishop William Morgan was accused of being too covetous for worldly goods; and his obsession with commendams, declared Sir Roger Mostyn irascibly, would 'commend them all to the devil'.[10] If the popular poets were to be believed, the clergy, along with gentry, lawyers, physicians, merchants, and the rest of the rich, were obsessed with gain and fatally tainted with greed for lands and possessions.

It was not only the gentry and their social equivalents, however, who stood to benefit by the opportunities of the age. Yeomen and prosperous farmers, by hard work, application, and enterprise, could also expect to

---

[7] Thomas Wilson, 'The State of England, 1600', ed. F. J. Fisher (Camden Soc., 1936), p. 24.
[8] *SWMRS*, I, 80.   [9] Williams, *Tafodau Tân*, p. 159.
[10] J. G. Jones, 'Bishop William Morgan's Dispute with John Wynn of Gwydir', *JHSCW*, XXII (1972), 70.

flourish. Yeomen could not easily be distinguished from those towards the lower reaches of the gentry scale, especially when large numbers of the latter were not ashamed to get their hands dirty when working alongside their servants in the fields or with livestock. Technically, of course, a yeoman was a freeholder worth 40s. a year, and in Rice Merrick's survey of the parishes of east Glamorgan he ranked nearly all those freeholders who were not gentlemen as yeomen. Over many other upland areas of Wales there were large numbers of such freeholders, many of them proud of their ancient gentle pedigrees and their distinctive life-style. But by the early seventeenth century William Vaughan, more in keeping with the trends of the time, had extended his definition of a yeoman to include all those who tilled the soil, derived their living from selling corn in the markets, and were worth 40s. a year. Such a classification embraced the many substantial copyholders and leaseholders who were to be found in lowland areas. They numbered men like John Hillen of Penally (d. 1613), who left behind him goods worth £86. 8s. 4d., including an unusually luxurious array of textiles, down even to table napkins; or Richard Love of Penmark (d. 1639), who farmed 120 acres, lived in a fine eight-roomed house, and possessed household stuff worth £38. 10s. The significant feature of the way of living of yeomen such as this, as Vaughan suggested, was that they were not working just for their own subsistence but on a scale big enough to have the wider markets in view. While they were eager to add to their holdings where they could, it was often true of yeomen that they preferred to enter trade rather than acquire more land, and engaged in a variety of other profitable commercial activities. They might keep alehouses, bakehouses, or smithies, engage in crafts and services, take part-shares in boats and trading ventures, and rent out livestock or crops. They often lent money on an ambitious scale to many neighbours in a countryside always starved for ready cash. When a man like Ievan Thomas of Robeston Wathen died in 1601, no fewer than thirty-one men, including two prominent Pembrokeshire squires, owed him sums of money amounting in all to nearly £40. In parishes where there were no gentlemen resident, it was yeomen who normally led their neighbours as churchwardens, overseers of the poor, and petty constables. In the average county there may well have been 100 or more families of yeomen. For the most successful and aspiring in their midst it was but a short step upwards into the ranks of the acknowledged gentry.

The most prosperous husbandmen or tenant farmers overlapped with the smaller yeomen. Comparing the inventories of their possessions which men of both groups left behind them, there is little if any difference between them, and the designation of one as 'yeoman' and another as 'husbandman' seems to have virtually no economic significance. Indeed, a 'husbandman' like John Beynon of Llanddewi, perhaps because he had none of the pretensions or expenses of a 'gentlemanly' life-style, died leaving possessions worth £76, which put him well ahead of a 'yeoman' of Llangyfelach, worth only £10. 6s. 6d., and even of 'gentlemen' like Morgan Bennett of Loughor (£18. 1s. 8d.) or Thomas Rees of Llandeilo Talybont (£57. 7s. 8d.). This could be seriously misleading unless we remember that analyses of the recorded possessions of husbandmen reveal that three-quarters of them left property worth less than £50, usually considerably less, which shows that most of them were middling to small farmers. Furthermore, many husbandmen—the majority of them, possibly—left no inventories because they had no possessions worth recording. Even farmers who held by a favourable tenure did not necessarily prosper; witness Henry Adams, a copyholder by inheritance, who died in 1603 worth no more than £6. 1s. 8d., while a censory tenant of Pembrokeshire in the same period died worth £26. 7s. 2d. in 1613.

In every one of the larger Welsh towns, too, there were successful gentry, merchants, craftsmen, and traders, no less well placed to take advantage of the more favourable economic circumstances. Leading town gentry like Sir George Herbert were able to symbolize their enhanced status by building fine new houses like his New Place, which stood proudly in the heart of Swansea until 1840, or his son William's Greyfriars, which only vanished from Cardiff in the second half of this century. Robert Wynn's even more sumptuous and ornate Plas Mawr still stands in Conwy and, next to the Edwardian castle, is that town's most-prized architectural gem. A prominent merchant and tanner of Carmarthen, Humphrey Toy, could afford to publish the first Welsh New Testament at his own expense, and a Brecon merchant made a fortune sufficient to leave behind him £2,500 to be invested in land to turn his family into gentlemen. The wealthiest man in early Stuart Swansea was a tanner, Thomas Hopkin, who died leaving possessions worth £753. 6s. 0d. in a rather mean house, described as having only one very large store-room and one other room. Not all were as 'tight' in their expenditure as Hopkin. Other merchants were as prepared to spend lavishly on their creature comforts as a Cardiff cordwainer, Edward Collins, who had indulged himself in a well-furnished house with several rooms, including a shop, parlour, four bedrooms, two other rooms, and a cockloft.

Most of the population, however, fell within the less fortunate, even disadvantaged, groups who, from the second half of the sixteenth century onwards, found it a steadily grimmer battle to contend with increasing population pressures and surging inflation. They belonged to the lesser husbandmen, small urban and rural craftsmen, cottars, labourers in town and country, and the poor. Among the husbandmen or tenant farmers, the largest group in the population, there were many gradations. The arable acreages they held might vary from five to fifty or sixty, with an average of about twenty perhaps, though size mattered far less than the quality and situation of the land. Their possessions, as valued in their inventories at death, might also range from £10 to £100, but inventories of husbandmen are not truly representative, since numbers of the smallest among them were to poor to have left one. The individual small farmer's nuclear family was not only the unit of habitation but also of production. He rarely employed hired labour, relying almost exclusively on members of his own family, including wife and quite young children. He also depended a good deal on his neighbours for co-operation and mutual help in agricultural operations, and 'good neighbourliness' was still accounted a cardinal social virtue. Even so, small farmers who could produce only a meagre surplus were finding it hard to hold their own in face of rising rents, entry fines, and prices. It was still more difficult for them to provide adequately for their children in terms of farms for their sons, or dowries—in cash or kind—for their daughters. It was becoming more and more of a struggle for their sons to find holdings of a viable size in the teeth of fierce competition from bigger men or even tenants of their own status. Many had to take over poorer upland crofts, former *hafotai*, or newly carved intakes from the wastes. Other family holdings, already barely viable, might have to be divided among brothers. It was this frantic search for appropriate tenancies and sub-tenancies that doubtless accounted for the large degree of movement, much of it short-distance migration to nearby parishes, that took place in rural areas. In the desperate scramble for tenancies many younger sons must undoubtedly have had to sink into the ranks of cottars and landless labourers, or drift into the towns and join the growing army of the urban poor.

Between the smallest farmers and the labourers there was no clear-cut social or economic division either, and the one group merged imperceptibly into the other. Many husbandmen and small craftsmen held such tiny acreages and so few beasts that they might be obliged to seek occasional by-employment. They were not easily distinguishable from those cottagers with perhaps two to four acres, common rights, and a few livestock, who were mainly dependent on employment as labourers by the day, when they could get it. More and more labourers had no land or stock to speak of and were therefore without any hedge against inflation or adversity. This kind of labourer was much more commonly found in those lowland areas where arable farming was more important. In Boverton and Llantwit in 1614, cottage holdings of four acres and less accounted for 43 per cent of all tenancies. In more upland Hafod-y-porth and Margam, not all that far away, they came to only 18 per cent, and in many truly hill districts might have formed a lower percentage still. The lot of the labourers in town and country was hard. Hours were long, usually from dawn to dusk with two-hour breaks for meals. Looking at the small farmers and labourers, George

Owen was struck by their weather-beaten aspect and the adverse effect on their physique of their 'continual labour in tilling the land, burning of lime, digging of coals, and other slaveries and extreme toils'.[11] Wages did not keep pace with inflation; and though many were paid partly in kind, this failed wholly to offset the remorseless effects of rising prices. Work was not easily obtained and many were without gainful employment for long periods. The grinding pressures on the poorer classes are revealed to some extent by the high incidence of petty theft in their midst. In years of dearth like 1586–7, 1594–8, and 1602–3, the cases of petty theft, often of food, showed a steep increase, though it should be emphasized that it was by no means only the poor who were convicted of theft.

An increasing problem was that of poverty. Contemporaries recognized various classes of poor people. Two categories covered the 'deserving poor' and efforts were made to provide for their relief: the 'poor by impotency' and the 'poor by casualty'. The former were the aged, widowed, orphaned, those permanently sick, infirm, or disabled; and the latter were made up of wounded soldiers, decayed householders, and those visited with grievous or painful disease. A third category, growing rapidly from the later sixteenth century onwards, was that of the able-bodied or 'thriftless' poor, treated as if they comprised only work-shy beggars, vagabonds, and rogues, though they included a growing number of married people with families as well as young single people, all involuntarily reduced to poverty because they were unemployed or severely under-employed. In the country parishes, where paupers were more dispersed and manageable in numbers, they depended for relief far more on charity dispensed by their neighbours than on the working of the poor law. But in the towns, where the problem was appearing on a bigger and more concentrated scale from the 1580s onwards, they were increasingly dependent on the poor law legislation of the years between 1597 and 1601.

The clearest picture which has so far emerged for Wales of the essentially urban nature of the problem and the steps taken to cope with it comes from the remarkably fine run of Swansea municipal records.[12] There, prompt measures were taken from the 1560s, including the regular collection of a poor rate, the establishment of a house of correction, the distribution of food and clothing, the keeping down of the price of corn, the administration of bequests for the relief of the poor, and the placing of children in apprenticeship. Nevertheless, by 1603 grave concern was voiced at the large numbers of paupers drifting into the town, their lawless and disorderly behaviour, and the potential cost to the burgesses of having to keep so many poor people. The municipal authorities were frequently

[11] Owen, I, 42–3.
[12] Univ. Coll. of Swansea, Swansea Book of Orders, Churchwardens' Accounts, Common Hall Book.

harsh in their treatment of paupers, flogging them unmercifully and driving out old, disabled, or pregnant wanderers. Popular poets uttered the appeals of Christian conscience against the savage and inhuman punishment meted out to these paupers: to their plight men went unmoved and the 'penniless, needy and starving pauper got no welcome but was sent packing brutally beaten, bare-backed and bleeding'.[13] Nevertheless, there was still a great deal of philanthropy and goodwill shown towards these unfortunates. The attitude of Sir Lewis Mansel was spoken of by an anonymous biographer as being but 'the glimmering of the moon' in his secular generosity as compared with the sun of 'his silent liberality towards the poor';[14] and in Swansea, where the corporation seemed so hard-faced, one Hopkin David (d. 1626) had his merits commemorated in flowery doggerel:

> The reliques of a saint here lie
> Who spent his days in Piety;
> The poor here come and raise their cry
> To feel their alms deeds with him die.[15]

Issues relating to the social order and the degrees that comprised it preoccupied Tudor and Stuart commentators, who were profoundly concerned to see stability and cohesion maintained at all levels. Yet, however much desired, an unchanging structure of society and its deferential acceptance by all ranks were bound to be no more than an ideal; in some respects, even, an illusion. For there were many on the 'right' side of the social divide who spared no exertion to pursue their own advancement and that of their families, usually at the expense of others. Families of gentry, professional men, traders, yeomen, and successful husbandmen throve prodigiously. Yet even among the favoured groups there were serious obstacles which could not always be overcome. There were, inevitably, differences of individual ability, temperament, and fortune; some were better blessed with intelligence, perseverance, or good luck than others; some were abler, worked harder, enjoyed better health, and lived longer. Quite apart from these differences in individual circumstances, there were other intractable difficulties inherent in the family and social structure of the time. Gentry families were generally large and tending to get bigger. Fathers tried to do the best they could for their children, but however far-seeing, prudent, or affectionate they might be, there were often younger children who could not be adequately provided for. The more of them there were, the greater was the likelihood

---

[13] *HG*, pp. 105–6.
[14] GRO, MS History of the Mansels, D/DC F48.
[15] T. Dinely, *An Account of the Progress of the First Duke of Beaufort through Wales, 1684*, ed. R. W. Banks (London, 1888), p. 172.

that some might have to find a niche in society lower than that into which they had been born.

Younger sons might have to enter the professions or trade or become working farmers. Being thus thrown in at the deep end like so many kittens did not necessarily mean that they all sank. Given a good education or an apprenticeship to a rich merchant and the right breaks, many of them achieved notable careers for themselves. Thomas, Hugh, and Robert Myddelton were all younger sons of the same family who abundantly proved the point. Not all could make their mark as the Myddeltons did, however, and a number became frustrated retainers to gentlemen or resentful unmarried hangers-on at home. Younger branches of a family were not usually able to give their children much of a start beyond the first or second generation. To make matters worse, by the second and third decades of the seventeenth century, opportunities for younger sons in trade, the Church, the law, or in soldiering were noticeably less plentiful than they had been. Even among the favoured elements of the population there must have been considerable numbers who sank in the social scale. One thinks particularly of the depletion that took place in the one-time large numbers of Welsh freeholders, whose sons and grandsons must have found it especially hard to maintain their predecessors' footing in society, even if *cyfran* or something akin to it prevailed in their midst. Such failure or near-failure leaves far less mark in the records than success and becomes much more difficult to spot.

Something like three-quarters of the population belonged to those social orders on the unprivileged side of the social divide who never had much if any chance of success. Most of them made up so large, amorphous, and unrecorded a mass that it is risky to make too many generalizations about them. Yet is is surely safe to conclude that for most there could be little prospect of moving up in the world. Only a fortunate minority, capable of hard work and shrewd judgement, and blessed with good luck in health and harvest, could ever have hoped to add sufficiently to their small stock of capital and land for them or their descendants to rise to the status of yeoman or burgess. Those who could just manage to hold their own probably counted themselves lucky, when most of their fellows at the lower end of the scale lay under the ever-present threat of drifting downwards. Not to mention any personal misfortune or accident, they were under constant social and economic pressure from the growth in their own numbers, the inflation of prices and rents, the relative stagnation of wages, the increasing scale of unemployment and under-employment, the engrossment and consolidation of farms, the erosion of common rights, and the existence of many holdings already so small that any further subdivision made them economically unviable. The combined effect of all these circumstances can hardly have failed substantially to enlarge the number of landless or near-landless labourers and paupers. Add to this that their lives were short, that they were weakened by precarious health, back-breaking labour, insufficient wages, insanitary housing, a diet at best inadequate and at worst at famine level, that they were easily the most vulnerable section of the population when natural or man-made disaster struck, and it becomes difficult not to believe that such mobility as existed among them must have been almost exclusively in a downward direction.

SOCIAL RELATIONSHIPS

Within their own localities the major gentry exercised an almost unquestioned mastery. A contemporary description of an Elizabethan squire, Piers Holland of Abergele, vividly conveys how arrogant and domineering they could be at their most masterful:

He is all in all and ruleth and commandeth all men as him listeth, using his will for law and his affection for reason, so as by his wilful and extortionate dealing . . . he purchaseth to himself great riches, for within three parishes next adjoining there is neither marriage agreed upon nor wedding concluded between rich nor poor, gentlemen nor yeomen, servants nor labourers, whereof the said Piers hath not some reward . . . there is no jury sworn nor inquest impanelled between party and party . . . but the same is led by the brief of the same Piers and where he willeth there it goeth, be it right or wrong.[16]

Similarly, one of Sir John Wynn's yeoman neighbours thought he 'could prove anything against him, though the same was never so untrue' and that he was 'able to make these stones to be green cheese if he list'.[17] Not all were quite so overbearing, perhaps; yet, fortified by wealth, influence, and public office, they took their supremacy over lesser orders as their birthright and spared no pains in manifesting, underlining, and upholding it among those around them. Their lineage, real and fictitious, was inscribed in book and manuscript, acclaimed by bard and herald. Their family arms and motto were emblazoned in hall and church, on fireplace and ceiling, window and panel, hatchment and tomb, in portrait and effigy, wood and stone, glass and paint. Sir Edward Stradling even left a silver ring with his arms and crest as a family heirloom. The lone voice of Henry Vaughan the Silurist echoes down to us reproaching the gentry for their insatiable pride:

> O why so vainly do some boast
> Their birth and blood, and a great host
> Of ancestors, whose coats and crests
> Are some ravenous birds or beasts?[18]

[16] NLW, Great Sessions Gaol Files, Denbigh 5/1.
[17] PRO E134, James I, Mich. 3.
[18] G. T. Clark, *Limbus Patrum Morganiae* (London, 1886), p. 233.

Only a few of the material remains of their departed greatness have not long since disappeared. On that unique and graceful italianate porch of Beaupré (1600) the Bassetts have left their proud motto, 'gwell angau na chywilydd' [better death than shame], and their arms for all to admire. The Mostyns' arms grace their overmantel at Mostyn and Sir Edward Herbert's decorate the fireplace of his long gallery at Powis Castle. Perhaps the most impressive memorials of their family pride still to be seen are their tombs and portraits. Among the most striking is the tomb of Humphrey Llwyd at Llanfarchell near Denbigh, with its Corinthian aedicule, ornamented frieze, and other details, having 'all the purity of Elizabethan High Renaissance architecture'[19]—a fitting memorial to so noble an ornament of Renaissance scholarship. Not too far away, at Gresford, two generations later, a quintessentially Jacobean monument was raised for Sir Richard Trevor and his wife, complete with Corinthian columns and kneeling effigies below the arches, during his own lifetime in 1638. More distantly, at Margam abbey in the southern county of Glamorgan, at about the same time, the sorrowing widow of Sir Lewis Mansel (d. 1638) erected as beautiful and striking a group of tombs as can be seen anywhere in Wales. It consists of four separate monuments commemorating four generations of her late husband's family: Sir Rice, Sir Edward, Sir Thomas, and Sir Lewis Mansel. All were made to the same general pattern with their elegantly carved effigies and little troupes of supporting 'weepers', all worked in the same white marble, now weathered to a darker cream.

Of the many portraits that were probably painted at this time, only a handful survive. From the hall of Penrice Towers Sir Thomas Mansel looks down on the observer with the calm unruffled confidence of one who might be saying, 'Look hard, fellow, you will not see my like again for many a year'. Or Colonel Thomas Davies, gentleman-in-attendance to Prince Henry of Wales, resplendent in his brown and gold doublet and breeches, with helmet and cuirass close by, still stands bold and haughty in his portrait on the walls of Gwysaney. Rarely are these pictures great works of art, and from a form critic's angle might justifiably be dismissed as stiff, stereotyped, and aloof. But they were created primarily for limited and clearly envisaged purposes of domestic assertion and dynastic needs and, as social documents, they reveal much about the attitudes of those who posed for them. Telling us little, perhaps, about the subjects as individual personalities, they tell plenty about how they wished to be seen as strong, dignified, and confident people; men who had no shadow of doubt about their place in society or their fitness to occupy and enjoy it.

Each squire and squireen kept as large a household of servants and followers as he believed his status warranted and his purse could be made

[19] E. Hubbard, *Clwyd: Buildings of Wales* (Penguin, 1986), p. 43.

to stretch to. On his surrounding lands and estates lived a further body of freeholders, burgesses, and tenants, dependent upon him, ranging perhaps from a dozen or two to several hundreds. Over all of them he exercised the authority of lord and master, and from all he expected obedience and support. As late as 1647, after all the upheaval, dislocation, and disaster of the Civil War, the ordinary people of Wales publicly and stubbornly insisted that they 'would not offend their landlords come what may'.[20] In the highly competitive and acquisitive society of Tudor and early Stuart times, with its myriad gentle families, proud and acutely sensitive to points of honour, tenacious of their economic interests and social position, and horrified at the prospect of any loss of face in the eyes of peers or underlings, quarrels were bound to break out from time to time between individuals and factions. Old habits of violence died hard among men and women who were fiery, mettlesome, and quick to take offence and slow to relinquish a grudge.

Many offences arose out of endless quarrels over precedence, land, and disputes over rights and boundaries. Nor was violence the prerogative of one social class; it was common among all ranks. The records of Great Sessions, Quarter Sessions, and manorial courts reveal a great deal of violent crime committed by men and women from all classes. Four kinds of offence were most common. First, there were homicides, most of which were not coldly premeditated crimes but usually arose from acts committed in the heat of the moment. Then there were assaults and affrays, or threats of violence. Theft was the commonest of all, and included stealing livestock, highway robbery, burglary, and housebreaking. Lastly, there was a wide range of penal offences, e.g., failure to attend church, vagrancy, and breaches of the licensing laws. Punishments were primitive and violent, and intended to be ferociously deterrent. Even trivial thefts, by culprits of either sex, might be punishable by flogging or pillorying, while conviction for more serious offences carried the death penalty, which was carried out at nearly every Great Sessions and often on a number of offenders. Amid a people so conditioned and inured to violence and with such a low emotional flashpoint, there was always the risk that bad feeling might explode into open conflict on those occasions when folk congregated in numbers, and rival groups or hostile individuals were likely to meet—in markets, fairs, taverns, elections, judicial sessions, and even in church.

Yet, in spite of the widening social cleavage, there was very little sign of a war between rich and poor. Nearly all the clashes that took place were those between town and country, or yeoman and yeoman, or, most frequently of all, between individual gentlemen or factions of gentlemen. True, there were riots and active physical protests from time to time. But

[20] T. Richards, *Religious Developments in Wales, 1654–1662* (London, 1923), p. 134.

they were usually orderly and ritualistic; intended to proclaim what men took to be the legal rights of a community *vis-à-vis* aggressors against the general good, like enclosers of the commons, or forestallers of the market. In the Brecknock lordship of Dinas a band of yeomen threatened to tie the workmen enclosing a common to horses' tails if they did not desist. On a common formerly belonging to Neath Abbey, another group of yeomen destroyed hedges with 'great rejoicing and triumphing', saying that 'they would not desist from that said riotous . . . enterprise so long as one hedge or mound were there standing'.[21] In James I's reign inhabitants of large parts of north Carmarthenshire furiously opposed attempts to levy rates and taxes at a higher rate and appeared in leet courts proclaiming 'trech gwlad nac arglwydd' [a community is greater than its lord]. The earl of Worcester's reference of 1570 to the possibility of a head-on clash between rich and poor, 'partly through the wilful disobedience of the meaner sort towards their superiors, and partly also by the wealthier sort meaning to oppress their inferiors by ravine' never amounted to anything and appears to be an isolated one-off expression of alarm.[22] In spite of widespread fears of the many-headed hydra of revolt by the poor, the risks of violent uprisings by the paupers and the property-less were not really as great as they sometimes appeared in the fevered and frightened imaginations of the upper class. The poor and downtrodden, conditioned to accept the superiority of their rulers, dependent on charity, ill-fed and ill-armed, poor in health and spirit, lacked the will, numbers, organization, or force to put themselves in armed opposition to those who ruled them.

HOUSING, DRESS, AND DIET

The gap in the standard of living between privileged and unprivileged was steadily widening, and polarization between them in terms of comfort and luxury becoming unmistakably more pronounced. The increase in production, trade, and wealth was accompanied by a steep and evident rise in the living standards of many individuals and social groups. The fortunate members of society attained hitherto unimagined levels of creature comfort in the shape of better houses, more luxurious furnishings and household goods, finer and more sumptuous clothing, and a richer and more varied diet. There was, of course, nothing new in lavish expenditure on items of this kind; such spending had been a notable characteristic of the medieval ruling classes. But it was now intensified not merely as a result of higher incomes but also of the diffusion of new and more expansive concepts, derived from Renaissance Europe, of the *mise-en-scène* and life-style appropriate to a nobleman. The resultant craze for splendour and

---

[21] PRO STAC 8/41/13.   [22] NLW, Penrice and Margam Correspondence, L5.

ostentation was seen at its most feverish among the scintillating leaders of fashion of court and capital; but its modes and manners, in reduced and more modest guise, also spread into Wales. In the main, it was the higher gentry who followed these styles, but even among more sober and cautious squireens, merchants, and yeomen the ways of their social superiors to some extent rubbed off.

Nowhere can the improvement in standards be more plainly seen than in the sphere of housing. When the Act of Union was passed, virtually all the dwellings in Wales were medieval in character. A hundred years later, at the outbreak of the Civil War, in many areas of the country, notably in the north-east, along the eastern border, in the south-east, the Vale of Glamorgan, and south Pembrokeshire, most of the accommodation occupied by the well-to-do had undergone a revolution. The rich in Wales, too, had seen their share of the 'great rebuilding' which had prevailed in so much of the kingdom between 1550 and 1640. The new or reconstructed homes then put up had been designed to secure greater privacy, convenience, comfort, warmth, and light. Medieval houses, with halls previously open to the roof, had ceilings inserted, upper floors created, and stairways installed. New houses were built with two or more storeys to provide more private rooms, bedrooms, and storage space. Windows were enlarged, mullioned, and glazed; and stone fireplaces and chimneys installed. The spate of new and remodelled houses flowed from a society becoming—for some of its members at least—more populous, prosperous, and secure; and the better housing conditions may in themselves have contributed significantly to a larger and healthier population. Such building was expensive and could be afforded only by those who had benefited most from the economic advances of the age. One of its striking features was the large number of houses belonging to the smaller gentry, 'clearly the centres of working farms', 'whose strongly regional style suggests owners embedded in their locality'.[23] One thing all the successful men, gentry or commoners, tended to share was the desire to modernize an old house or build a new one as soon as they could afford to do so.

Some of the wealthiest landowners transformed castles or abbeys, the grandest buildings known to the Middle Ages, into mansions where the emphasis was on ease and luxury not security or austerity. The families of Perrot and Somerset spent a fortune to bring Carew and Raglan up to date by contemporary standards. Both castles are today no more than magnificent ruins; but the home of the Myddeltons at Chirk, the two Herbert families at Powis and Cardiff, the Philippses at Picton, and the Stradlings at St Donat's still rank among the stateliest homes for families or institutions in Wales. Abbeys at Margam, Neath, Llantarnam, Brecon, and

[23] Smith, *Houses*, p. 141.

elsewhere, after their dissolution, housed families of gentry. The nature of the kind of transformation they undertook may best be judged by the remarkable inventory surviving from the Carnes' home at Ewenni which lists the rooms and their contents as they existed in 1650.[24] Refashioned abbey granges, such as those at Maenan, Mynachty, or Sker, also indicate what could be achieved by vigorous and imaginative new gentry builders. Eminent courtiers like Sir John Trevor, secretary to Lord Howard of Effingham, or Sir Thomas Morgan, built themselves large and ostentatious new houses at Plas Teg and Ruperra, deeply influenced by Renaissance concepts and yet preserving resonant echoes of older castellated styles of medieval origin. Around many of the great houses their owners constructed deer-parks, in which they and their friends could indulge in the delights of the chase, still the favourite upper-class pastime. They also added eyries, coney-warrens, dovecotes, fishponds, flower and herb gardens, possibly even a vineyard. The Latin poet, Thomas Leyshon, in a moment of exaltation, vowed that the Stradling rose-gardens at St Donat's were so fragrant that they enticed Neptune and Thetis from their salt-water depths to savour their perfume!

More impressive in numbers, if not in size, were the hundreds of smaller houses interspersed among those built by the greater gentry. In the single county of Glamorgan, in spite of its extremely heavy industrialization in subsequent centuries, about a thousand surviving houses of this kind have been found by the RCAHM (Wales). All were substantial, craftsman-built dwellings, the homes of minor gentry, merchants, yeomen, and successful farmers, scattered all over the Vale of Glamorgan, with many others, now nearly all disappeared, in the towns. There are hundreds of others, elsewhere in Wales, some built of stone, others timber-framed. They fall into three main types: one has the chimney built on an outside wall; another has it internally with its back to the cross-passage; and a third has two chimneys in the middle of the cross-passage. The houses might vary a good deal in size and lay-out, some having only one unit (the hall), others having two or even three units. Included among them were the particularly elegant black-and-white houses of Montgomeryshire, one of the most striking of which is Berriew Rectory built in 1616; a reminder that some clergymen were among those who flourished at this time.

Not for the majority of the population this vastly improved housing, however. They continued to live, as they had previously done, in miserable, windowless, one-roomed hovels with earthen floors and open hearths, built by their own efforts. In early seventeenth-century Caernarfonshire, one of Sir John Wynn's tenants, John ab Ifan Goch, was required to build his own house, 24 feet long, 15 feet wide, and 6 feet high.

---

[24] J. P. Turbervill, *Ewenny Priory: Monastery and Fortress* (London, 1901), pp. 93–101.

Presumably he and his family not only lived, cooked, ate, and slept in a house no bigger than a single good-sized room in a modern dwelling, but also housed some of their livestock and found storage space as well. Many lived in dwellings which can hardly have been better than those in Scotland described in 1679 as

Such miserable huts as never eye beheld; men, women and children pig together in a poor mousehole of mud, heath and some such like matter; in some parts where turf is plentiful they build up little cabins thereof with arched roofs of turf without a stick of timber in it; when their house is dry enough to burn, it serves them for fuel and they remove to another.[25]

As late as the nineteenth century, an observer noted the large numbers of tumbledown hovels, wretchedly cobbled together of clay, turf, and twigs in the Golden Valley on the borders of Wales; and rural cottages elsewhere were stigmatized as 'deplorable . . . old thatched buildings, very low, with one living-room, a portion of which is generally portioned off for a pantry and a general garret or sleeping-room for the whole family'.[26] Squalid as these may have been, for them to have been inhabited at all in Victorian Wales they must have been of better standard than most of the hovels of the sixteenth century.

The interiors of the bigger households were richly embellished. The more important rooms—hall, dining-room, gallery, and best chamber— were often panelled and wainscoted, their ceilings might be plaster-moulded, and their windows brightened with coats of arms in coloured glass. Their walls would frequently have been enlivened with frescoes or hung with tapestries and pictures. Furnishings, too, were becoming richer and more abundant. Edward Carne's inventory at Ewenni (1650) included a large quantity of miscellaneous furniture, furnishings, cloths, linens, utensils, tools, and implements. They were worth, in all, £245. 3s. 4d., £150 worth of which was accounted for by the contents of the gallery with its silk carpets, cushions, 'arrases', and pictures. John Moris (d. 1608), a gentleman of Swansea, left a long list of expensive furniture and furnishings, including a Spanish bed, Turkish carpet, rugs, carved and embroidered chairs, cushions of gilted leather, taffeta curtaining, a mass of clothing, much silver plate, and a number of silver spoons. Sir John Perrot's library contained many French, Spanish, Greek, Latin, and English books, and his music room boasted sackbuts, cornets, flutes, two recorders, violin, Irish harp, and a pair of virginals, together with books of music and a set of psalm-books.

Yeomen and merchants, on the other hand, spent far less on furnishings

---

[25] T. C. Smout, *A History of the Scottish People, 1560–1830* (London, 1972), pp. 140–1.
[26] R. Mathias, *Whitsun Riot* (London, 1963), p. 4; I. C. Peate, *The Welsh House* (Liverpool, 1944), p. 106.

than did the gentry and usually left a far smaller proportion of their possessions in household goods than in livestock, crops, materials, or tools of their trade. A backwoods gentleman like Edmund Harries of Freystrop was not very different in this respect and lived very close to the soil among his animals, crops, and an extraordinary hugger-mugger of utensils and implements in widely varying states of repair, from nearly new to almost totally derelict.[27] But men of humbler station could nevertheless follow from afar the lead given by the gentry in seeking improved comfort. Feather beds—once a rare and coveted luxury—were becoming widespread, and with them came coverlets, flannel blankets, and sheets. Tables, cupboards, benches, forms, chairs, stools, chests, and coffers, all made by skilled carpenters, were increasingly common. Status-conscious owners could frequently rise to silverware, especially spoons, as well as table-cloths, napkins, curtains, and rugs. Pewter platters and mugs, brass or pewter candlesticks, brass or copper pans, iron cauldrons, pots, skillets, gridirons, spits, dripping-pans, bakestones, and other utensils, along with earthenware crockery and dishes, are all freely in evidence in surviving inventories of yeomen and richer husbandmen. There had been a revolution in furnishing as well as housing, in their midst, between 1550 and 1640.

For the poorest sections of the community these possessions were far too costly to hope for. They could boast of little or nothing in the way of furnishings and household goods. They ate and drank from wooden vessels and platters, lay on straw, and owned only the barest minimum of belongings. Because the poor almost never left wills and inventories, we get scarcely any inkling of the number and nature of their possessions. One such rare insight comes from the inventory of Owen Griffith, a mason of Pentyrch (d. 1632). Apart from two kine, a calf, three sheep, and 6s. 0d. worth of corn, the only things he appears to have had worth leaving were an iron crock, a coffer, and a rake for his son, and a coffer, skillet, bakestone, pail, and candlestick for his daughter. Yet there must have been in Wales thousands of others as poor as or still poorer than Owen Griffith, pathetically scanty though his worldly goods were.

The same wide divergences are observable in the realm of costume and jewellery. For the rich this was an age when high fashion, dictated by the arbiters of style in Italy, France, and Spain, was introduced into England and Wales. A wide spectrum of sumptuous clothing materials in furs, velvet, camlet, sarcanet, silk, satin, taffeta, cloth of gold, cloth of silver, and fine lace and linen became available at luxury prices. The poet, Siôn Hywel Siôn, reflecting embitteredly on the contemporary love of fine clothing, deplored men's greed for 'garments of gold and satin that would never be sated, were they to obtain the worth of a hundred islands', and

[27] Howells, *Pembs. Hist.*, I, 37–40.

another, Thomas Siencyn ab Ieuan, drew a pointed contrast between the 'poor flannel' in which the infant Christ was wrapped and the 'dainty holland, lawn and cambric' now to be found in rich men's homes.[28] Surviving portraits show the leading gentry dressed in elegant and fashionable clothing, resplendent with jewellery.

Some of the richer yeomen had likewise taken to aping their betters with fine shirts edged with gold, attractive doublets lined with orange sarcenet, purple Venetian hose, and white woollen stockings. Their wives were just as colourfully turned out in frieze gown, red petticoat, and blue mantle. Farmers wore 'solid leather shoes, knitted woollen stockings, and a doublet or jerkin of fustian, canvas, or frieze, the whole attire being set off by a felt hat or cap'.[29] But here, again, the gulf between social groups was painfully wide and evident. The poorer elements in the population at best wore shapeless garments of rough home-made cloth and at worst were clad in pitiful rags and worn-out cast-offs. The rare comments we have on the clothing of the poor always refer to its meagreness and inadequacy to keep out the cold.[30] In Wales, William Vaughan referred to lack of clothing as contributing, together with lack of food, to the extremely high mortality rates (see p. 428).

The medieval virtues of *perchentyaeth*, that art of maintaining a bountiful hospitality to all and sundry, were still extolled as vociferously and eloquently as ever by Tudor and Stuart poets as the distinguishing marks of the true gentleman. Wiliam Llŷn hailed John Conway of Bodrhyddan as the proverbially munificent provider of feasts, the Ifor Hael [Ifor the Generous] of his age, one of innumerable bardic plaudits in the same vein.[31] Gentry correspondence, too, reverberates with gratitude for the hospitable welcome received by visiting guests, as when Humphrey Gilbert conveyed to Sir Edward and Lady Stradling 'a million of commendations'[32] for receiving him so generously at St Donat's. But Elizabethan observers also told how the middle classes in town and country ate heartily and well. According to George Owen, even the poorest farmers in Pembrokeshire enjoyed a remarkably good diet: 'the poorest husbandman liveth upon his own travail, having corn, butter, cheese, beef, mutton, poultry and the like of his own sufficient to maintain his house . . . Their diet is as the English people use, as the common food is: beef, mutton, pig, goose, lamb, veal, and kid, which usually the poorest husbandman doth daily feed upon.'[33] That glowing description of the smallest farmer's bill of fare might be thought to owe more to Owen's staunch local patriotism than to strict accuracy. Certainly when it came to

[28] *HG*, pp. 107, 137.   [29] Owen, *Eliz. Wales*, pp. 42–4.

[30] R. H. Tawney and E. Power, *Tudor Economic Documents* (3 vols. London, 1924), II, 317.

[31] *W.Ll.*, p. 91.   [32] *Stradling Correspce.*, p. 158.   [33] Owen, III, 33, 83.

estimating what food the ordinary labourer ate, Owen's calculation was decidedly more modest and restricted. He reckoned that the annual consumption was six and a half bushels of oats, one bushel of oat malt, three-quarters of a Cardigan stone of cheese, one and a half gallons of butter, and half a quarter of meat. This would have been supplemented by whatever he could grow, buy, or beg of vegetables, such as leeks, cabbages, onions, peas, and beans, together with eggs and scraps of meat.

For the poorest it could not at any time have been anything other than meagre fare. In years of poor harvests and food shortages their circumstances must have been infinitely worse. It was at these times of dearth that the divergence in the quality of living between rich and poor emerged at its starkest and most unbridgeable, for there seems to be distinct evidence of famine affecting parts of Wales more desperately than ever before. Bad harvests had always led to the gnawing pangs of hunger; late in the sixteenth century and early in the seventeenth they appeared to be bringing actual deaths from starvation in their train. In November 1597 Sir John Wynn wrote of an appalling corn shortage in Caernarfonshire and Merioneth, and accounted it literally a gift from God when a man-of-war laden with corn went aground in Anglesey. He was on tenterhooks lest its cargo should be carried away by force by other shipping and regarded the saving of it as being a matter 'of the greatest importance that ever happened in our or our fathers' time'. His evidence was still more poignant in 1623–4. In January 1623 he described the country as 'exceeding poor past belief'; by March and April, as the long famine-stricken winter dragged to its bitter end, he told how many 'were dying of hunger and the rest bore the impression of hunger in their faces'. Again in January 1624 he was obliged to report 'a great famine and a new sickness (especially in Wales) whereof many die'.[34] So dire was the extremity that prisoners had to be released from the gaols. Down in south Wales the Carmarthenshire author, William Vaughan, testified in *The Golden Fleece* in 1626 that during 'these last dear years 100 persons have yearly died in a parish . . . the most part for lack of food, fuel and raiment in which the poorer sort are in greater need'.[35] Such evidence suggests that those 'crises of subsistence' known to have affected parts of northern England at this time also reaped their deadly harvest in some parts of Wales too. Small wonder that the population, expanding for most of the sixteenth century but already slowing down markedly between 1600 and 1630, received a still sharper check in the years between 1630 and 1670. The shears of Fate had remorselessly intervened to cut off a large part of the surplus population and, inevitably, it was the hapless mass of the poorest who suffered most from famine and disease. At no point did the steadily expanding chasm between rich and poor appear more widely or cruelly obvious.

[34] *CWP*, pp. 35, 173, 175, 190.   [35] Vaughan, *Golden Fleece*, III, 13.

CHAPTER 18

EDUCATION AND CULTURE

ALL those trends towards the extension of education observable among the lay men and women of the fifteenth century were much strengthened during the century that followed. Literacy became more common and there was a livelier interest in acquiring manuscripts and books, greatly stimulated by the readier availability of printed volumes. Education admittedly suffered a distinct blow when monastic and mendicant orders were dissolved and chantries and guilds suppressed, but the need for teaching remained greater than ever. Leading gentry families continued to engage domestic chaplains and household bards to teach their own children and others; and a girl no less than a boy would be given a measure of education, being brought up at her book, needle, and other things befitting her station, including instrumental music and song.[1] Sir Rice Mansel in his will of 1558 stipulated that an 'honest and learned man' be found to teach his descendants 'and three of four of the aptest children' of his tenants.[2] Lewis Thomas, BA instructed George Owen's children and other pupils, while Thomas Pierson, chaplain to Sir Robert Harley and a fine scholar, prepared many youths for the universities. The Mostyns and the Wynns had their own chaplains and household bards, and Lady Lewis of Y Fan kept three tutors to teach her children Welsh, French, and Latin. We hear of a young curate come to remote Dolwyddelan to serve the cure and 'keep school in the parish' in 1625. Such clerics serving as schoolmasters had to be licensed by their bishop; and back in 1561 Bishop Thomas Davies of St Asaph had urged all good Christians to keep up the stipend formerly paid to the lady priest to maintain 'such schoolmasters as shall be thought meet by me'.[3]

There must have been a large number of parish, town, or private-venture schools up and down the land—more than has usually been realized, judging by the widespread degree of literacy existing among the minor gentry, yeomen, and burgesses. Men of this status would have found it cheaper and less burdensome to send their children to such schools. In Glamorgan alone there were schools of this kind at Cardiff, Llandaff, St Nicholas, Cowbridge (not Cowbridge Grammar School), Neath, Swansea, and Llantwit, according to Rice Merrick. Some of them were rudimentary,

---

[1] *CWP*, p. 151.   [2] *Cartae*, v, 2038, 2046.
[3] *CWP*, p. 155; D. R. Thomas, *St. Asaph*, i, 90.

makeshift affairs like the one at Denbigh kept by Alice Carter, who turned her shop into an improvised classroom in 1574. But others may well have been schools of more than average quality when kept by men of the calibre of Gervase Babington, later bishop of Llandaff, or Robert Gwyn, Catholic poet and martyr. One former pedagogue, at least, John Price, a Cambridge scholar, left a record of his disillusionment with private teaching, telling how his one-time 'wondrous great delight' had been changed into a view of it as a 'toilsome and cumbersome kind of life', of which he was glad to be shot.[4] How many more, one cannot help wondering, were similarly disenchanted?

There were, in addition, the old grammar schools associated with the cathedrals and some of the larger parishes. In the 1530s William Barlow was scathing in his remarks about poor provision in his diocese. He himself set up at a school at Brecon in 1541; and the grammar school at St Davids was placed on a sound footing in 1547 and proved good enough to provide John Perrot with his education. The school at St Asaph was reorganized in 1548, with a strong suggestion that it should be moved to Denbigh; but in 1614 it was still at St Asaph and was referred to as an excellent establishment, visited by the bishop once or twice a week.

From the middle decades of the sixteenth century, one of the most striking features of the cultural life of England and Wales was the much more general insistence by the laity on the need for academic education. What transformed the situation was the diminished emphasis on the previously dominant need for military expertise to be put at the service of king or overlord, or both, and the increased call for men appropriately trained in legal and administrative skills. As the Tudor monarchy and its governments expanded the scope of their activities, they needed more men who had had at least enough education effectively to shoulder the responsibility of public office and local administration and justice. The three qualities regarded as essential were loyalty to the Crown, ability, and education. As the gentry were given a constantly extended range of function and influence, their educational attainments needed to be adequate. Education became a status symbol for gentlemen and those who wished to be considered as gentlemen. Many new families were coming to the forefront and a convenient, fashionable, and practical way of setting the seal on their gentility was to give their sons a formal education. Welsh poets, who were quick to seize upon every new office acquired by their patrons, were equally prompt to emphasize the parallel importance of their educational attainments.

Furthermore, younger sons of gentry or men of burgess or yeoman stock who cherished ambitions of entering the public service or the professions

---

[4] NLW Bodwyryd Correspondence, No. 40.

had no hope of doing so without first climbing the rungs of the educational ladder. The Church had always needed many of its clergy to be extensively educated and now needed even more. But the law was the learned profession *par excellence* for Welshmen. 'If he would seek after worldly honour, the law is the only way', wrote Robert Wynn in 1611, whereas he added that what made clergymen 'so ill thought of' was that, 'being poor, they will run through fire and water for a benefice'.[5] Entry to the highest ranks of the legal profession called for a long and expensive training as well as native wit and eloquence. Medicine attracted far fewer recruits and offered more modest rewards; but it seemed to offer inviting enough prospects for men as gifted as Humphrey Llwyd, physician to the earl of Arundel, one of England's leading Renaissance figures, or Thomas Phaer, a Norwich man who settled comfortably in Cilgerran, Pembrokeshire. To be really successful in commerce, too, often required considerable education; and it is plainly evident how much importance successful merchants of Welsh origin like Thomas Myddelton, Humphrey Toy, or William Jones attached to education. Prosperous men of business, with a social conscience, frequently aspired to create for poorer boys wider and better possibilities for social advancement allied to religious instruction. It was undoubtedly these practical considerations of education as the avenue to office, influence, and affluence that were uppermost in determining ambitious youths and families to seek it.

Another impetus of a more distinctively cultural kind was added by the metamorphosis of the concept of a gentleman. Borne from Italy to other European countries, including Wales, on the wings of admiration and emulation, came the ideal of the Renaissance man; the all-rounder depicted in books like Castiglione's *Il Cortegiano*: the courtier, man of affairs, and soldier; scholar, man of letters, and connoisseur; as virtuous as he was brave; as supple, strong, and disciplined in mind as in body; as sensitive to the delights of the intellect as he was accomplished in public dealings; a just magistrate and a generous patron. Only a handful may have imbibed its appeal in full and even fewer came near to achieving it in practice. Yet it percolated to Wales and was influential in moulding the cultural and educational ethos of the country. Major Renaissance figures like the first and second earls of Pembroke, the earl of Arundel, or Sir Philip Sidney inspired many followers from Wales, literally and figuratively; men like Sir Edward Carne or Sir John Price of an earlier generation, or Humphrey Llwyd, Maurice Kyffin, the two Stradlings (Edward and John), John Herbert, John Salusbury, or George Owen, and many others later.

Inextricably linked with the migration to England and Wales of Renaissance ideas was the triumph of the printing-press, the most important single key to their success and permanence. In the printed book, burgeoning nationalism, the power of the monarchy, the influence of the middle classes in town and country, the rise of the vernacular languages, and the rapid spread of literacy, all found one of their most formative vehicles of expression. Welshmen were quick to perceive the influence and importance of books and, as book-buyers, authors, and publishers, were alert to take advantage of them. Sir John Price of Brecon had a very large collection of books and manuscripts, as did Sir Edward Stradling in his magnificent library at St Donat's. Surviving family correspondence reveals that, for many of the gentry, lists of old or new books to be bought were among the most frequent commissions entrusted to friends visiting London. William Brynkir was only one among many who gloated over the tempting second-hand book bargains he had picked up; for which he would not take 'three times as much as I paid for them'.[6] Men with intellectual tastes like John Wynn were at pains to help the scholars, Camden and Speed, publish their books, wherein they 'showed their worthiness and love of their country'.[7] They further appreciated the utilitarian advantage to themselves of books as guides to farming, medicine, law and legal practice, and the like.

Nor should the continuing significance of manuscript publication be overlooked in this golden age of copying and circulating manuscripts. Catholic recusants had little choice but to publish in manuscript form; other authors regarded the practice as more gentlemanly and élitist; and there were some who indulged their own interests and curiosity and shared them with fellow-devotees. Active circles of scholarly connoisseurs flourished in the Vale of Clwyd, Glamorgan, and Pembrokeshire. Inspired by the enthusiasm of men like William Salesbury, Edward Stradling, or George Owen, they met frequently and regularly exchanged writings and ideas.

As powerful as any of the stimuli to education was the impact of religion. The Reformation was a religion of conversion and a religion 'of the Book'. Wherever it took root, it not only tended to appeal to those who could read but also added greatly to their number. It stressed crucially the need and the ability to read the vernacular version of the Bible; a trigger which, as its adherents knew only too well, released the most dynamic reforming forces among the emergent middling groups in town and country. In addition, the reformers had supreme confidence in the power of religious education to overcome what they envisaged as three of the most dangerous moral failings of the age: ignorance, corruption (including insobriety and blasphemy), and idleness. Roman Catholic reformers were equally convinced that the highest function of the revival of learning was to make

[6] *CLP*, p. 120.   [7] *CWP*, p. 160.

religion more intelligible and meaningful to the mass of the population; an end most effectively achieved by using the vernacular and extending literacy.

It would be wrong to draw fine distinctions between any of these motives. In practice they tended to feed upon one another and merge into a single whole—the consciousness of a 'new learning', a social and educational awareness whose prime object was to produce a better-educated governing class, capable of setting a good example to their families, dependants, and servants, loyal and useful subjects to the Crown, its efficient servants, good Christians, and individuals of integrity, learning, taste, and discernment. Many, of course, had only confused notions of the theoretical ideal and fell badly short of it in practice. Yet, by the 1650s, John Lewis of Glasgrug could not unjustly claim that Wales had 'as able and knowing gentry as ever';[8] and not merely among its greater county families but among a large number of its minor gentry and smaller freeholders as well. There were many homes which might have merited Huw Machno's eloquent commendation of Cynfal, the little *plas* in Ardudwy, where the greatest of all Welsh prose writers, Morgan Llwyd, was born in 1619 and brought up:

> Llyfrau ar silffau sydd
> deg olwg gyda'i gilydd[9]

[Books there are on the shelves, of fair appearance all together.]

One of the outstanding features of educational provision during the period was the encouragement of endowed grammar schools already established during the Middle Ages and the foundation of many new ones to cater for the vastly enhanced demand. England, already well endowed, became even more plentifully supplied with grammar schools during these years; and well-known establishments like Westminster, Eton, Winchester, Shrewsbury, Oswestry, Bedford, St Alban's, and Worcester attracted the sons of leading Welsh landowners. Grammar schools in Wales were fewer in number and slower in being endowed; but a number of new ones were founded nevertheless. Some were the result of limited royal patronage and support, like Abergavenny (1543) or Carmarthen (1576); others of clerical endowment—Brecon (1541), Carmarthen (1543), Ruthin (1574), and Botwnog (1616). There were even more as the result of lay initiative— Bangor (1557), Presteigne (1565), Beaumaris (1602), Wrexham (1603), Cowbridge (1609), Llanrwst (1610), or Haverfordwest (1613). Noticeable among the lay-founded schools was the interest of leading merchants like John Beddows at Presteigne or Valentine Broughton at Wrexham.

The aims of these grammar schools may briefly be described as the

---

[8] *Evangeliographa* (London, 1656), p. 26.
[9] *Gweithiau Morgan Llwyd*, ed. J. H. Davies (2 vols. Bangor, 1908), p. xviii.

preparing of boys to occupy a station or career in life and the development of mind and character moulded by learning, religion, morality, and discipline; 'good nurture and civil manners'. Their curriculum was almost exclusively concerned with Latin grammar and literature (suitably censored to cut out immoral or pagan bits!) and a little Greek. This was the indispensable foundation for university education and entry into all the learned professions. Pupils were sternly discouraged from speaking Welsh, as they were in English schools from speaking English. Nor were they usually instructed in music as they often had been in medieval schools, an omission which may help to explain the withering of a once-flourishing condition of musicianship in Wales. The number of scholars in a school might range from 20 to 120, though even in the largest there would rarely be more than two teachers, the master and the usher. All the boys would be taught under the same roof and, as likely as not, in the same room, the youngest at the front and the oldest at the back. Boys might enter the school at any age between eight and sixteen and would spend five or six years there if they lasted the whole course. Discipline was strict and hours of work long—eight hours or more a day, beginning at 6.0 a.m., for six days a week with perhaps one afternoon free. Though books were far more common than they had been, lessons consisted to a large extent of tedious oral repetition and learning by rote. Perhaps, therefore, it was hardly surprising that the poet, Siôn Tudur, should amusingly describe how, in spite of the new suit, satchel, and books bought for him, he reacted to school with extreme distaste and played truant, resorting to robbing orchards and other mischievous tricks. There may well have been many other rebels like him! When the grammar school course was complete, boys were either put to apprenticeship or proceeded to the universities.

The number of Welsh students entering Oxford, Cambridge, and the Inns of Court grew prodigiously between 1540 and 1640, and especially during the latter half of the period. A recent study has traced 2,004 Welshmen at the universities during these years, as compared with only 420 during the whole of the Middle Ages.[10] Medieval records are, admittedly, much scrappier and more meagre than those for a later period; but the palpable contrast between the two sets of statistics appears to show an enormous increase in the number of students enrolled from Wales during the Tudor and Stuart era. A large proportion would still be clerics, themselves going to university in larger number; but the most striking change was the far higher proportion of young men intended for lay occupations. Oxford remained far more popular with Welshmen than Cambridge, recruiting 1,762 as compared with 242; and the proportion from south-west Wales, at

[10] W. P. Griffith, 'Welsh Students at Oxford, Cambridge and the Inns of Court' (Ph.D. Thesis, Bangor, 1981).

343 for Oxford as compared with 30 for Cambridge, was even higher.[11] This would suggest that Oxford, being nearer, was the more popular. Dr John Wynn of the Gwydir family left an endowment for three fellowships and six studentships at St John's College, Cambridge, which explains why a number of distinguished north Walians, William Morgan, Edmwnd Prys, and Archbishop John Williams among them, graduated from there. But Oxford, especially after the foundation of Jesus College by Hugh Price in 1571—not originally established exclusively for Welsh students, though it soon began to draw them in large numbers—remained the popular choice. The 'third university of the realm', as the Inns of Court were often described, also attracted during this period some 699 Welsh students (205 at least having previously graduated at university). The last years of the sixteenth century and first decades of the seventeenth saw a steep rise in their numbers. At Lincoln's Inn alone, some 90 Welshmen were admitted between 1570 and 1610, 64 of them between 1590 and 1610. In many instances, education in England or Wales was rounded off with a spell abroad. William Thomas and Siôn Dafydd Rhys both spent many years studying in Italy. Others indulged in an extensive period of travel, a kind of 'Grand Tour', as when Edward Stradling travelled widely in Italy with Thomas Hoby, or John Wynn's eldest son, John, toured extensively in France and Italy, dying in Lucca at an early age, poor man, in 1614.

Some criticisms have been expressed in recent years of the somewhat limited impact of university education and training at the Inns of Court on those who partook of it. Men who had never been there turned out to be magnificent scholars. Lord Herbert, no mean judge of intellectual attainment, testified that Edward Thelwall of Plas-y-ward 'acquired the exact knowledge of Greek, Latin, French, Italian and Spanish and all other learning' without going abroad or having the 'benefit of any universities'.[12] Nor can it be denied that there were often disturbing distractions for young students. Understandably anxious parents feared that their sons might pick up undesirable habits like drinking, smoking, gambling, or wenching, and be led astray by some of the wilder among their fellow-countrymen, described by one solicitous father as all too 'prone to be more idle and riotous than the English'![13] Yet it is hard to believe that undergraduates did not gain much from being exposed to new ideas and civilizing influences not only from those who taught them but also from their companions and their surroundings.

Just how much improvement had been effected in Wales by Charles I's reign, as a result of all these educational developments, is difficult to assess. The considerably increased number of clerics educated at grammar schools and universities must have done appreciable good. In Bangor, the

[11] H. A. Lloyd, *The Gentry of South-west Wales, 1540–1640* (Cardiff, 1968), pp. 194–5.
[12] *Autobiography*, ed. S. Lee (London, 1886), p. 20.   [13] *CLP*, p. 126.

only Welsh diocese for which fairly full figures of ordinations are available, there were four graduates ordained between 1560–9, as compared with forty-one between 1600 and 1609, though only about half of them were presented to livings in the diocese and it is not certain how many of these were resident. Still, since the clergy were the group most heavily involved in formal and informal instruction of their parishioners, it might be supposed that better education among them would have achieved positive educational and moral results among their flocks as well, had it not been that criticism of their efforts was still very prevalent in the early Stuart period. Pro rata, the laity who had been through schools and university increased in numbers more than the clergy. From their midst came a number of able scholars and active public figures. There is no question at all that the range and level of educational attainment among the gentry, major and minor, had been greatly raised and extended.

What is much more difficult to tell is how far down the social scale the process had permeated by the 1630s, when there appears to be a sharp conflict of testimony on this subject. Humphrey Llwyd's confident assertion of 1568 that 'there is no man so poor but for some space he setteth forth his children to school . . . few of the ruder sort . . . cannot read and write their own name and play on the harp after their manner' has often been quoted in support of the keenness of the Welsh for education and its spread among them.[14] Dr Geraint D. Owen has also adduced evidence of a pedlar woman being willing to spend threepence a term on her son's education and argues that the 'boon of literacy' was something to which even the 'members of this humble and despised class' aspired.[15] There is indeed considerable evidence by the early Stuart era that the ability to read and write was widespread among most merchants and burgesses, yeomen and substantial farmers. The author of *Car-wr y Cymry* (1631), commenting on the availability of the Bible of 1630 to the poor, spoke of those who could read their own language, 'of which everyone should be capable' [*yr hyn a ddylei pawb ei fedru*].[16] As against that, a very different picture emerges from other sources. George Owen strongly deplored the lack of schools and schoolmasters in his native Pembrokeshire and the backwardness of its youth in consequence. An English author of 1622 firmly placed the 'ignorant country' of Wales among the 'barbarous nations' along with Ireland and Virginia,[17] though mainly on account of its people's inability to read English. But Vicar Prichard's strictures on their inability to read their own language are very well-known and are confirmed, oddly enough, by the author of *Car-wr y Cymry*. Both he and the Vicar urged the heads of households to teach their whole household to

---

[14] *Breviary of Britayne (1573)*, pp. 60v–61.   [15] *Eliz. Wales*, p. 207.
[16] *Car-wr y Cymry*, ed. J. Ballinger (Cardiff, 1930), p. 4.
[17] John Brinsley, *A Consolation for Our Grammar Schools* (London, 1622), p. 4.

read; the author of *Car-wr* getting in a sly dig at the universal pride of Welshmen in their gentility by insisting that if they wished to be considered truly gentle [*yn wir foneddig*] they should dedicate themselves to reading God's Word. The reason for this apparent conflict of testimony may well lie in the difference of attitude between authors like Humphrey Llwyd, who had only the upper groups of freeborn Welshmen in mind, and others like Vicar Prichard, who were thinking of the whole population. Most of the former probably could read, whereas the mass of the people were still sorely ignorant. If we were to conclude that something of the order of 15 to 20 per cent of the population could read, that might be as reasonable an estimate as could be made at this stage.

The changes and developments of the sixteenth century left a profound impression on the cultural life of Wales. Among the most significant consequences was the impact of the Reformation on the visual arts. They now largely lost contact with the parish churches and parishioners and were confined mainly to embellishing the homes of the well-to-do. The work of all those sculptors, masons, woodcarvers, carpenters, glaziers, painters, jewellers, vestment-makers, and the like, previously so productively and profitably engaged on the beautifying of churches, was now deprived of its broader-based patronage, support, and contacts. Many of these craftsmen may admittedly have come from outside Wales, but some of the most gifted of them, like the woodcarvers, were undoubtedly local men. The close and fruitful connection between religion and music was also sadly weakened. Even though a reformer as 'way-out' and iconoclastic, in some respects, as William Barlow exhorted the clerics of his newly established college at Brecon in 1541 to continue with their singing and organ-music, the disappearance of chantry and guild song-schools and the curtailment of music in church services proved a severe blow. Music vanished from the curriculum of the grammar schools, except in the cathedral schools, and even there occupied a much smaller place than it had enjoyed. The steady stream of composers and musicians from Wales dwindled to a trickle, with only an occasional distinguished figure like Thomas Tomkins or John Bull—Welsh, in spite of his archetypally English name—to remind us of former glories. Song and harp music remained popular and widely cultivated, but systematic musical education had seriously declined.

The main focus of cultural activity was still literature. There had always been in Wales two broad strands of literary achievement—the native Welsh tradition, and also a non-Welsh, mainly Latin, literature. Latin still continued to be the lingua franca of the literati throughout Europe in the sixteenth century. Synonymous with learning [*dysg*], it was the passport to knowledge, the key to the professions. Many sixteenth- and seventeenth-century Welsh authors, yearning to reach an enlightened and learned European public, wrote in Latin. What was equally striking about the new age was that others wrote in European vernacular languages like French, Italian, and, above all, English. That so many of them should choose to write in English was not in the least surprising. The language had gained immensely in status and esteem in Tudor England, becoming firmly established as the language of the court, government, judicature, religion, literature, and aristocratic society. The closer contacts of every kind coming into existence between Welsh and English, the increased emphasis on the capacity to speak and read English, the relative ease with which it could be learnt, and the tendency of many Welshmen to go to England and into English-speaking towns in Wales to find advancement all contributed to the wider knowledge of the English tongue. English was, in addition, the language favoured in all the educational institutions open to ambitious Welshmen. The only conveniently available printing-presses were to be found in England; and there, too, was a swiftly growing public among whom an author might hope to sell his books and find acclaim and esteem. So that when Maurice Kyffin, friend of authors as famous as John Dee, Edmund Spenser, or William Camden, and widely travelled scholar and soldier, reflected ruefully, 'God knows it would have been much easier for me and more to my personal fame to have written such a work [his translation of Jewel's *Apologia*] in some language other than Welsh', he had good reason to be aware of the full implications of what he wrote.[18]

Welsh authors published many more books in other languages than in their own. The number of these works and the wide range of subjects they covered make it impossible to treat them other than in broad and superficial outline; but some indication of their nature should be given. A major category, in view of the great popularity of devotional texts among early printed works, predictably consisted of religious books. One of the earliest and most talented authors was Richard Whitford, bosom friend of Erasmus and Thomas More, who was responsible for some seven or eight books, which he felt impelled to print because of the alarm he experienced at the spread of heresy. The mounting fury of religious controversy inspired others to don gladiatorial armour and venture into the literary fray on both sides of the great debate. Early champions of the Catholic cause were Edward Powell, author of a Latin work, *Propugnaculum Summi Sacerdotii Evangelici . . .* (1523), which took the form of a dialogue between himself and the heresiarch, Martin Luther; and John Gwynedd, better known as a gifted musician but who published five books between 1536 and 1554 to confute the heresy of John Frith. Later in the period, the exceptionally gifted David Augustine Baker, master of the spiritual life, wrote a number of books, none of which was published before 1657, and also left six manuscript volumes on the history of his own order, the

---

[18] *Deffynniad Ffydd Eglwys Loegr*, ed. W. P. Williams (Bangor, 1908), p. ix.

Benedictines. As Protestantism gradually made headway in Wales it, too, produced its defenders. John Penry, most famous of Welsh sixteenth-century Puritans, moving all the way from Presbyterianism to a fully blown Separatist critique of the Church, remains of particular interest as the author of three searing pamphlets on the state of Wales in 1587–8. A more moderate Puritan, but far more successful author, was Lewis Bayly, author of the *Practice of Piety* (1611), which ran through no fewer than seventy-one editions between 1611 and 1792 and exercised a profound influence on individuals as different and as unexpected as John Bunyan and Count Zinzendorf. Gabriel Powel, a prodigy of learning whose promising career was cut off far too soon, published extensively between 1602 and 1609, defending the Anglican Church and refusing point-blank to countenance the use of the term 'Protestant' in relation to it.

Given the antiquity and popularity of the poetic tradition in Wales, along with the phenomenal upsurge of English poetry in the Tudor age, it was perhaps only natural that a number of English-language poets and poetasters should have emerged. Sir John Salusbury wrote a number of sonnets and love lyrics, which have only a limited literary merit but are interesting for the light they shed on the poetry of Shakespeare and other contemporaries.[19] Two much more brilliant poets of Welsh origins, who scaled the poetic heights and have remained in the front rank of English poets, were George Herbert, author of *The Temple* (1633) and Henry Vaughan the Silurist. Another poet, now much less well-known than either, but one of the most celebrated poets in the Europe of his day, was the Latin epigrammatist, John Owen, whose eleven books of epigrams were first collected together in 1624.

Two prose authors who gave evidence of the remarkable mastery over the English tongue won by some Welshmen were George Herbert's brother, Edward Lord Herbert of Chirbury, and James Howell. Lord Herbert wrote an unusually engaging if not always credible autobiography, never published in his lifetime, and a *History of Henry VIII*, also published posthumously. James Howell, historiographer royal, who was proud to remember his Welsh origins, claiming that the cask always flavoured of the liquor it first took in, was nevertheless one of the earliest writers to make a livelihood from English literature.[20] His literary power was exhibited at its best in his letters, three volumes out of four of which he wrote while a prisoner in the Fleet (1645–55).

The intense interest shown by many Welshmen in the history of Britain and the role of their own people in its unfolding gave birth, as might have been expected, to several books. All the more so when they felt compelled to defend Geoffrey of Monmouth's traditional account of the glorious

[19] Carleton Brown, *Poems by Sir John Salusbury and Robert Chester* (London, 1914).
[20] W. H. Vann, *Notes on the Writings of James Howell* (Baylor Univ. Press, Texas, 1924).

British past against the 'calumnies' of Polydore Vergil. Among the subtlest and most learned of those taking up the cudgels on Geoffrey's behalf were Sir John Price, whose *Historiae Britannicae Defensio* was published by his son in 1573, and John Lewis of Llynwene (d. 1616), whose *History of Great Britain* did not appear until 1729. History was in this age a greatly regarded study. It was believed to reveal God's providence in maintaining a people or a family, to confer wisdom upon an individual in determining his own course of action, and to establish the truth concerning past events. Sir Richard Bulkeley, no scholar, was nevertheless a great reader of histories. Most celebrated Welsh historian of the age was Dr David Powel, who took up the history at the point where Geoffrey of Monmouth left off and published his *Historie of Cambria now called Wales* in 1584.

Wales also produced a number of highly talented topographers and antiquaries. Foremost among them was Humphrey Llwyd, described by William Salesbury as 'the Welshman most universally seen in history and most singularly skilled in rare subtleties', friend and coadjutor of Ortelius, and responsible for a number of works in Latin and English.[21] Less well-known were the two Glamorgan scholars, Edward Stradling and Rice Merrick, and Caernarfonshire's John Wynn, whose *History of the Gwydir Family* remains a most valuable and lively source. Ablest and most versatile of them all was George Owen of Henllys: antiquary, historian, topographer, cartographer, geologist, patron of literature, and social commentator without equal in Tudor Wales. All these antiquarians were content, like many gentry authors, to let their works circulate in manuscript among the circles of scholarly friends and acquaintances which they inspired.

In keeping with the curiosity awakened in a whole spectrum of intellectual interests by the Renaissance, other writers broke new ground with books on various aspects of science. Lewis of Caerleon, physician to Henry VII and his mother, left a number of Latin medical works in manuscript. The accomplished Robert Record wrote on a variety of mathematical subjects and in *The Pathway to Knowledge* (1557) explained for the benefit of lay readers the nature of solar and lunar eclipses on the Copernican system, which he was one of the first to accept and publicize in this country. Towering above them all was the polymath, John Dee, born in London of Welsh parents, who wrote no fewer than seventy-nine works in Latin or English, most of which were never published, on a variety of scientific, mathematical, and astronomical topics. A notable exponent of the 'gloomy science' of economics was Lewis Roberts of Anglesey, author of *The Merchant's Mappe of Commerce* (1638), one of the first systematic treatises on the subject in English.

[21] G. Williams, *Religion, Language and Literature in Wales* (Cardiff, 1979), p. 188.

Finally, among the more individual and out-of-the-way Welsh writers were William Thomas and William Vaughan. Thomas lived in Italy for several years and was the first from this country to appreciate the significance of Machiavelli's political philosophy. He published some highly interesting books, including a defence of Henry VIII in Italian, *Il Pellegrino Inglese . . .* (1552), as well as a *Historie of Italie* (1549) and *Principal Rules of the Italian Grammar . . .* (1550). Vaughan produced in 1600 *The Golden Grove*, which provides a mass of information on the manners and devotions of the age. Between 1617 and 1619 he tried unsuccessfully to found a Welsh colony at Cambriol in Newfoundland but never lost his faith in colonization there. In 1626 he issued his *The Golden Fleece*, in which a series of characters presented bills of complaint in the Court of Apollo against the evils of the age and claimed that the golden fleece, the remedy to all ills, was to be found in Newfoundland, 'where we should perform miracles and return yearly into Great Britain a surer gain than Jason's Golden Fleece from Colochos'.[22]

In spite of these bubbling springs of enthusiasm for publishing in English and other languages and the diverse threats testing the Welsh language, native literature remained virile and responsive for much of the century between 1540 and 1640. It was given fresh pride and inspiration by notions first promulgated in this country by John Leland: that ancient Britain had been the cradle of men of learning and poets; its Druids, Bards, and Vates had left behind them, as their successors, the poets of Wales; and many early manuscripts containing their treasures of wisdom and literature had been lost or gone astray. This last suggestion prompted Welsh humanist scholars to urge upon their countrymen the need to bring their manuscripts out into the light of day. John Bale added further lustre to these myths of venerable and civilized origins by tracing the bards back to Bardus, a descendant of Samothes. Many contemporaries in England, as well as Wales, believed that the old British tongue was one of the seventy-two cardinal languages spoken at the diffusion following the fall of the Tower of Babel and transmitted down the centuries from the time of Gomer, whom Dr John Davies of Mallwyd, particularly, regarded as the father of the Welsh nation. It was Sir Philip Sidney's conviction of the incredibly ancient origins of Welsh literature that led this influential and munificent literary patron to comment that it was 'not more notable in soon beginning than in long continuing'.[23]

Many of the Welsh gentry, in spite of the new horizons and wider educational opportunities opening up before them, were for a long time loth to see their ancient British tongue die in their midst and for most of this period kept up their knowledge of it, some even sending their sons,

[22] *The Golden Fleece* (1626), III, 9–10, 80.
[23] J. Buxton, *Sir Philip Sidney and the English Renaissance* (London, 1954), p. 97.

when necessary, to Welsh families to learn it, as happened to Lord Herbert. They encouraged their English daughters-in-law, too, to acquire at least a smattering of it, if only to prevent them from being cheated by their servants! Bards figured in a number of leading households, and bardic instruction was maintained for most of the sixteenth century and persisted into the seventeenth, though on a less secure footing. The most eminent bardic teacher of Tudor times was Gruffudd Hiraethog, a pupil of Tudur Aled himself. He was a distinguished poet and a man whose passion for the Welsh language, broad erudition, quick intelligence, and eagerness to accept some of the key concepts of the New Learning won him the unqualified admiration of Wales's leading Renaissance scholar, William Salesbury. Gruffudd Hiraethog numbered among his own pupils the greatest poets of the second half of the century—Wiliam Llŷn, Simwnt Fychan, Wiliam Cynwal, Siôn Tudur, and Raff ap Robert—as well as gentlemen of the scholarly calibre of William Salesbury and Richard Davies.

If Welsh poetry after 1540 reached nothing like the same exalted level of excellence as in the century from 1435 to 1535, there was at least one master-poet whose work deserved to rank with that of the earlier great exponents of the poetic art. He was Wiliam Llŷn, acknowledged as *pencerdd* [chief of song] in the Caerwys Eisteddfod of 1567 at the early age of 33. He had only another thirteen years to live, unfortunately, but during that time he gave abundant evidence of flawless control over metres and *cynghanedd*, pregnant and aphoristic economy of style and diction, and vivid and unforgettable mastery of imagery and contrast. He also revealed the heroic Christian stoicism of his view of the world that sprang from a melancholy but profoundly reflective temperament. That he was, perhaps, the supreme elegist in the whole history of Welsh poetry was itself exquisitely appropriate, for he seemed to be sorrowing not only for the passing of friends and patrons but also to be intuitively grieving inconsolably at the sunset of a dying bardic order. In mourning the death of his friend, the poet Siôn Brwynog, whether he knew it or not, he tolled a knell for the whole course of traditional Welsh poetry moving slowly to its close:

Dydd brawd ar gerdd dafod aeth[24]

[Judgement Day has come to the art of poetry]

Though there may have been no more than one poet of the highest order, the general level of poetic output remained creditable and, in terms of the sheer quantity of verse produced, was distinctly impressive. There may well have been more poets than ever at this time, all churning out

---

[24] *W.Ll.*, p. 119.

verses to meet the demand from gentry families, who, in growing numbers, wished to have bards entertain them and applaud their superiority. Thus, at Christmas 1595, John Salusbury, descendant of many generations of patrons, having just succeeded in restoring his family's honour following its earlier eclipse as a result of the Babington Conspiracy and now a squire of the body, invited seven bards, four harpists, and two crowthers to Lleweni fittingly to celebrate his newly recovered status. Even a migrant from Wales like Theodore Price, in company with other exiled 'Cambro-Britons', joyfully welcomed the *cywyddau* addressed to him at his distant exile's home 'by the waters of Babylon'. New families, with no previous tradition of patronage, were on tiptoe to display the place in society they now occupied by commissioning from bards a public attestation of their status as gentry. In Gwent and Glamorgan, a poet of such moderate talent as Dafydd Benwyn, unworthy of comparison with earlier giants like Iorwerth Fynglwyd or Lewis Morgannwg, nevertheless enjoyed a most extensive circle of patrons, many of them of the 'first generation'.

There may well have been a danger that there were too many poets in relation to the number of patrons available. In an age when the authorities of central and local government were deeply troubled about the excessive numbers of vagrants and wanderers of all sorts already tramping the roads and scaring the wits out of town and parish officers, it was deemed wise to exercise a measure of formal restraint on those who were to be allowed to itinerate as bards. An *eisteddfod* was more than ever needed to distinguish between the genuine poets and the 'vagrant and idle persons naming themselves minstrels, rhymers and bards'. So a further assembly of poets was convened at Caerwys in 1567. The terms of its commission proclaimed that the unlicensed rhymesters had grown into an 'intolerable multitude within the principality of north Wales' and by their 'shameless disorders' constituted themselves a pestiferous nuisance to the gentry. Once again, therefore, the *eisteddfod*, held under the leadership of the Mostyn family and supporting gentry and men-of-letters, gave the authentic bards an opportunity of being officially recognized and licensed. All those who received a degree had the right to itinerate the gentry houses and be paid for their work; the rest were excluded.[25]

Nearly all the poetry emanating from the bards thus authorized continued to fall into the well-defined categories: poems of praise, elegies, begging poems, love poems, religious poems, poems of bardic controversy, and the rest. Inevitably, the main feature of classical *cynghanedd* verse was the praise-poetry directed to upper-class patrons. As the poets voiced the age-old conventions of idealized and exaggerated approval of the standard qualities, they were becoming increasingly stereotyped and predictable in

[25] G. Thomas, *Eisteddfodau Caerwys* (Cardiff, 1968).

the patterns of what they had to say and how they said it. For example, Owain Gwynedd, one of the better poets of mid-sixteenth century, had set a pattern, in which he ordinarily greeted his patron effusively, traced his long and (of course!) honourable lineage, enthusiastically described his hall and hospitality, applauded his wife's distinguished pedigree, went into detail about any particular merits—rarely any but the stock virtues—that characterized either or both of them, proclaimed faith in their future, and ended by invoking God's blessing.[26] This kind of poetry lasted well into the seventeenth century, when the remarkable Phylip family of Ardudwy contrived to produce four poets between c.1560 and 1677: Siôn Phylip (d. 1620), his brother Rhisiart (d. 1641), Siôn's son Gruffudd (d. 1666), and another son Phylip Siôn Phylip (d. c.1677). Both the latter were among the last of the trained professional bards. By that time, in a more settled age, there was usually far less emphasis on the patron's military prowess and greater concentration on his more peaceful attributes: godly living, virtuous behaviour as an officer of government, evenhanded administration of justice, and qualities of learning and education. There were also unmistakable indications of the changes overtaking society: appeals to the gentry not to spend so much time in England; veiled hints that English wives had little sympathy with poets; and gnawing anxieties at the decay of the language [*tranc yr iaith*]. Sadly enough, in a world which was fast abandoning the poets' time-honoured postulates and values, they seemed incapable of doing anything more than going through the customary motions of their outworn medieval art.[27]

Alongside the *cynghanedd* poetry flourished a mass of free-metre verse in the form of carols, *cwndidau*, and such like. Though they may have flourished earlier, they had almost never attained sufficient status to be recorded in writing. Now accorded much greater esteem and recognition, they were clearly widely enjoyed by those substantial and numerous social groups flourishing just below the rank of leading gentry and may have constituted the Welsh equivalent of 'popular' art. Writing early in the eighteenth century of the emergence of one of the most popular genres of this kind of poetry, Erasmus Saunders observed how his countrymen were 'naturally addicted to poetry; so some of the more skilful and knowing among them frequently composed a kind of divine hymns or songs'.[28] Some of the *cynghanedd* poets themselves were not above indulging in free-metre poetry as well; established bards like Siôn Tudur, gentlemen-poets such as Tomas Llywelyn of Rhegoes, and cleric-poets like Edmwnd

---

[26] R. Saer, 'Testun Beirniadol o Waith Owain Gwynedd' (MA Thesis, Aberystwyth, 1961).

[27] G. Thomas, 'Y Portread o Uchelwr Ym Marddoniaeth Gaeth y 17eg Ganrif', *YB*, VIII, 110–29.

[28] *A View of the State of Religion* . . . (Repr. Cardiff, 1949), p. 33.

Prys. Tomas ab Ieuan ap Rhys went as far as to use free-metre verse and not *cynghanedd* to praise some of his patrons. Their compositions were sufficiently well thought of to be copied into the manuscripts of the period. Llanover MS B 9, for instance, contains a large collection of *cwndidau* compiled and transcribed by Llywelyn Siôn, one of the most accomplished Welsh scribes. There were two broad classes of free poetry. One, inherited from the Middle Ages, consisted of established and recognized metres but composed without any formal *cynghanedd*, though they very often had strong echoes of *cynghanedd* [*clec y gynghanedd*]. The other resulted from the adoption into Welsh verse of metres popular in England and sung to well-known tunes. Composed on a wide variety of subjects, they were concerned in general with love, religion, and the state of society. Their message was hardly new: the pangs and pleasures of love and rejection; the heedless sinfulness of men and women, and their need to take Christian duties more seriously; and the extortionate rapacity of the rich and powerful. Their most striking characteristic, as compared with the aristocratic *cynghanedd* poetry, was their authors' greater freedom to sound a much more critical and irreverent note and thus to appeal to a socially broader and less élitist public. Outstandingly successful among them were two sets of verse that tend to stand out on their own—Edmwnd Prys's metrical psalms and the popular religious verses of Vicar Prichard. Alongside all this there existed yet another, simpler, genre of folk-verses, most of them anonymous, commemorating the season's activities, the weather, love, longing, folk-wisdom, and any other memorable events in folk-life. They survive because in their unsophisticated but sharp-edged mode of address they so frequently enable us to penetrate for once to 'the depth of longing, passionate yearnings and heartfelt sadness' of ordinary people.[29] Expression in all the free poetry was slacker and more diffuse than in the *cynghanedd* verse, and the language simpler, more debased, and full of dialect words and forms eschewed by the classical poets.

Symptomatic of all this literary activity and interest was the intense concern for manuscripts and manuscript-copying. The conviction that waiting to be uncovered was a large and ancient corpus of Welsh literature, nearly as old as the Latin and Greek classics and dating back all the way to Taliesin and possibly earlier, led to an eager search for manuscripts containing treasures of every kind. As early as 1547 Salesbury had besought his compatriots not to allow their manuscripts to lie unheeded, gathering dust and cobwebs, but to bring them to the attention of scholars. The works of poets and prose authors of every variety down the centuries were to be hunted out and diligently recopied. Many contemporary and near-contemporary compositions had also to be committed to manuscripts.

---

[29] T. H. Parry-Williams in *HWL*, p. 234; cf. also *OBWV*, pp. 90–3.

One copyist, Ieuan ap Wiliam ap Dafydd ab Einws of Powys, sadly aware of the slow progress of printing in Wales, complained that many of the kinds of texts he so painstakingly had to copy by hand were to be found in printed editions in England, whereas in Wales he and others like him had no option but to go on copying laboriously. Thanks to their conscientious labours, none the less, a great mass of literature was preserved that might otherwise have been lost for ever. Poets, professional scribes, and interested gentlemen all worked as copyists, though there was a good deal of overlapping between them. A number of sixteenth- and seventeenth-century poets, some of them quite secondary figures like Sils ap Siôn, copied out their own and other poets' work. There were professional scribes, too, such as Llywelyn Siôn or, most expert and industrious of them all, John Jones of Gellilyfdy, who spent several years in prison for debt but still managed to copy more than a hundred volumes of manuscripts in a beautiful and sophisticated hand. Finally, there were gentlemen, or clerics like Roger Morris of Coed-y-talwrn, or John Davies of Mallwyd, who copied vast quantities of materials himself and also hired scribes to transcribe others to be used in his grammar and dictionary. The keenest connoisseurs among the gentry built up splendid libraries of manuscripts, pre-eminent among them the superb collection assembled at Hengwrt near Dolgellau by Robert Vaughan (d. 1666), which included most of the important early manuscripts as well as a number of significant transcripts.

The zeal and urgency with which literature was being copied could not conceal the fact that, behind this apparently impressive façade, all was far from well with Welsh poetry. Indeed, the very frenzy to preserve it may well have been prompted by consciousness of its inner decay. Alarm bells had already been sounded by some of the most forward-looking Welsh intellectuals, critical of the introverted conservatism of the poets, the way in which their verse was ossifying into lifeless repetition, and their failure to find fresh sources of inspiration. Such critics, themselves deeply imbued with an awareness of the antiquity and excellence of native literature and genuinely respectful of the high quality of bardic training and knowledge, nevertheless wanted to reinvigorate and rejuvenate poetry's hardened arteries by injecting into them the elixir of Renaissance culture. Men like William Salesbury and Gruffudd Robert castigated the poets for their inveterate secrecy and urged them to throw open the portals of their art to the revivifying zephyrs of the new ideals.

Of all the critics the most trenchant was Edmwnd Prys who, unwearyingly earnest in his zest for change, conducted a marathon poetic controversy, lasting from 1580 to 1587 and running to fifty-four *cywyddau* and about 5,500 lines of poetry, with Wiliam Cynwal, a not unworthy champion of the old order. Prys's aim was to convince Cynwal and his fellows that the modes and criteria of the bardic establishment had been shown up as hopelessly antiquated and threadbare by the advent of the New Learning and the printed book. Steeped as Prys was in the classics, the Bible, and the Early Fathers, as well as Welsh literary culture, he laid about him with a will on two fronts. He pressed that literature should be primarily religious and moral in purpose; and he advocated that it should be learned and printed. He censured poets for their habitual dishonesty in pandering to the vanity of unworthy patrons, for the sake mainly of gain, and for clinging to exploded papist untruths and superstitions. He urged them to adopt the godly Christian muse, become men of learning at the universities, abandon the *cynghanedd* if need be, and publish their new-style poetry in printed books. Such a call for a transformed poet was a well-worn plea in Europe, virtually a cliché of the age in Italy, France, and England. Wiliam Cynwal's response was rather disappointingly limp and defensive. He could do little more than insist that his opponent was not a bard but a cleric, who had no right to meddle with another man's office. He had not been trained by a bardic teacher nor graduated as a poet and only someone who had done so had the right to practise as a poet.

Other poets from time to time acknowledged the point of some of the criticisms. Siôn Tudur composed a celebrated *cywydd* 'to denounce the bards' in which he berated his fellow-poets, in tones closely akin to those of Edmwnd Prys, for rendering indiscriminate praise:

> But base-born ploughman, now, we
> Poets turn into gentry.
> Give pedigrees to blazon
> Jack with praise the same as John[30]

Gentlemen like Thomas Prys or William Peilyn tried to introduce new themes, bringing a flavour of the devil-may-care adventure and camaraderie of free-booting on the high seas into their verse. Edmwnd Prys was also to score one of the outstanding successes of the age in his translations of the Psalms. But, by and large, the poets did not take up the challenge and missed the opportunity of accommodating Renaissance and Reformation learning, themes, and measures within Welsh verse. This, according to Wales's greatest literary historian, was the 'great disaster of our literature in the seventeenth and eighteenth centuries'. His verdict was not unjustified; yet in fairness to the poets it has to be questioned whether or not any attempt on their part to adjust to the views of their critics could have succeeded. Their patrons do not seem to have demanded or welcomed any new approach by the poets. Even if they had, the new kind of poetic training required would have been extraordinarily expensive in time and money when there were already dire complaints about the effects of inflation and the lack of generous patrons. Moreover, any new-style

[30] *HWL*, p. 221.

poetry would have had to be printed in books and not diffused by declamation or manuscript, and this raises the critical question: Did patrons and a literate book-buying public exist in Wales on a sufficient scale to sustain such a literature, or was Wales still economically too poor to be able to give birth to the wide range of printed books her most gifted sons had longed for?

For, quite apart from the failure of the poets to become 'men of the New Learning', there were other profoundly important reasons for the decline of their order. The age and conservatism of the *cynghanedd* literature alone may already have contributed irreversibly to the decay of a tradition which had probably explored almost every avenue open to it. Contemporary inflationary pressures and economic difficulties—mounting rapidly in the 1590s and the 1620s and 1630s—put a further tight squeeze on patrons and poets. The accustomed rewards, unless they kept pace with inflation, which seems decidedly improbable, would be insufficient to maintain poets and probably had crippling effects on bardic schools and apprenticeship. Such conditions led to the shrinking of poetic itineraries and frequent complaints in the poetry of 'miserly', grudging, and scarce patrons—animadversions not peculiar to Wales but commonly heard in England, Scotland, and Ireland also. Furthermore, the gradual anglicization of the gentry, for a variety of reasons, was bound to have a sadly detrimental effect on the status in their eyes of the language and the poets. Nor did competition from free-metre poetry, which had become so popular, do anything but take away from the acceptability of *cynghanedd* verse. Finally, the upper classes, traditionally mentors and patrons of the poetry, found themselves enticed by a growing range of counter-attractions on which to expend their resources and demonstrate their status, often at the expense of the poetry (above, pp. 422–8). An early Stuart poet, Morys Benwyn, greeting the Vaughans of Corsygedol, contrasted their generosity with the attitude of many less committed and more niggardly gentry and reflected downheartedly:

> Oer yw'r sâl ar yr oes hon,
> Oes heb urddas i'r beirddion.[31]

[Chill is the reward in this age, an age which offers no status to the poets.]

or Rhisiart Phylip, in a *cywydd* of 1627 to John Davies of Mallwyd, addressed the Welsh language thus:

> Come, tell me now, dear tongue of mine—
> Thy judgment still is rich and fine—
> Lives there a man who will avow
> Of all thy kin, he knows thee now.[32]

[31] A. Ll. Hughes, 'Rhai o Noddwyr y Beirdd yn Sir Feirionnydd', *Llên Cymru*, x (1969), 45.
[32] *HWL*, p. 221.

While the author of *The Three Antiquities of Britain* [*Tri Chof Ynys Prydain*] declared despairingly that 'all the great knowledge of the Bards, their credit and worth is altogether decayed and worn out, so that at this time they are extinguish[ed] amongst us / And the *Prydyddion* [poets] at this time likewise are of no estimation'.[33]

But if poetry failed to respond to the winds of sixteenth-century change, Welsh prose did accept the challenge and its subsequent success constituted the most vital development of the age in Welsh literature. Not that prose started from a particularly promising base. The precedents for authors in the form of earlier romances, laws, chronicles, and religious texts were limited and the prospects for the future bleak enough. Welsh prose faced a stern struggle to establish itself and was, for a long time, engaged in an arduous effort to find a 'standardized voice' for itself.[34] Yet it had fewer constraining shackles to throw off than Welsh poetry and could adapt to rapidly changing circumstances more easily. At least printed prose would not cut at the very roots of a professional littérateur's existence in the way that printed poetry would; and it was compatible with an author's 'amateur status'. Moreover, if the Reformation was, in the short run, to make any inroads on the mass of conservative belief and custom-bound ignorance, without, in the longer term, irreparably jeopardizing the native language and literature, there was an overriding case for a Welsh translation of the Bible, Prayer Book, and ancillary literature. There was, too, a strong element of utilitarian edification in the new ideas which lent itself more readily to expression in prose than poetry. Many humanists supposed that only as a result of extensive prose preparation in advance could poetry be induced to transform itself. Finally, it would almost certainly be easier to find patrons, publishers, and buyers for prose than poetry. Those associated with early prose works, whether authors like Maurice Kyffin or Oliver Thomas, wealthy merchant-patrons like Humphrey Toy or Thomas Myddelton, or publishers like Thomas Salusbury, were all noticeably puritannical in attitude. Sober didactic prose works were much more to their liking than flights of poetic fancy. Besides, there was much less danger of losing money on prose, and something akin to a captive market for it among clerics and serious-minded heads of households. Not surprisingly, therefore, most of the early printed books were translations into Welsh of established religious prose classics.

There was one other incentive driving men to aim at the publication of prose works in Welsh or relating to the Welsh language. This was the irresistible humanist desire to re-equip the ancient language of Britain so as to fit it for a deserving place alongside other European languages as a worthy medium for learning and scholarship; to enrich its vocabulary,

---

[33] NLW Llanstephan MS 144, fo. 16—in the hand of John Jones, Gellilyfdy.
[34] *Perl Mewn Adfyd*, p. xxxvii.

extend its figures of speech, embellish its modes of expression, and standardize its written form. Hence the importance attached to compiling dictionaries like those of William Salesbury (1547), Thomas Wiliems and John Davies of Mallwyd (1632), or of the publication of grammars by Gruffudd Robert (1567), Siôn Dafydd Rhys (1592), Henry Salesbury (1593), or John Davies (1621). Gruffudd Robert, Catholic exile, impeccable scholar, and superlative master of polished and urbane prose, was the first person ever to describe and analyse the Welsh language, in his grammar of 1567, and had as his object to show Welsh poets and writers that it was possible for them to attain to the same standards of literary elegance and opulence that he had seen on the Continent. Thomas Wiliems, some of whose work was incorporated in John Davies's Dictionary, avowed that his aim was to preserve the Welsh language for ever and 'to shame those Judases who desire to see the death of this polished tongue'.[35] John Davies's own Grammar represented the pinnacle of Welsh humanist achievement. To him must go most of the credit for paving the way for the excellence of the seventeenth and eighteenth centuries, the period in which emerged those authors generally regarded as the finest exemplars of Welsh prose-writing. Addressing Ben Jonson, James Howell described John Davies's feat as having been

> ... thus to tame
> A wild and wealthy language, and to frame
> Grammatic toils to curb her so that she
> Now speaks by rules and sings by prosody:
> Such is the strength of Art rough things to shape,
> And of rude commons rich Enclosures make.[36]

[35] G. J. Williams, 'The History of Welsh Scholarship', *Studia Celtica*, VIII–IX (1973–4), 201.
[36] *OBWV*, p. 99.

CHAPTER 19

IDENTITY AND DIASPORA

THROUGHOUT the centuries it was always the littérateurs who had chiefly created, shaped, fostered, preserved, and made articulate the national feeling of those who considered themselves to be *Cymry* (singular *Cymro* < *Combrogos*, meaning 'a man from the same country; fellow-countryman'). That term *Cymry* had originally been the name for the land (it later became *Cymru*) as well as the people who inhabited it.[1] Throughout the Middle Ages they thought of themselves as *Cymry* or *Brythoniaid* or *Brytaniaid*. They disliked the name 'Welsh', applied to them by the Saxons (< OE *Welise* from *Wealh*) because it meant 'foreigners', and who could blame them for resenting a word which designated them as aliens in their own land? Further back still, before the battle of Chester of AD 616, and for some time after, they considered all those Britons living in Cumbria and Strathclyde as belonging to the same people as themselves. This sense of solidarity shared by the *Cymry* who lived in Wales and their hatred of foreigners, especially those with whom they came into contact most often and from whom they had most to fear—the English—were, like similar patriotic sentiments associated with other peoples, given an idealized literary form by their poets and authors, some of whom, like Nennius, had written in Latin not Welsh. Their perception of nationality had originally been focused on the native ruling dynasties, furiously though these had frequently fought against each other as well as outsiders. It had crystallized in addition around Welsh law which, in spite of regional variations, was a folk law [*Volksrecht*] common to the whole of Wales, at once a 'mirror and a mould' of its legal and social institutions. It had also expressed itself in a distinctive ecclesiastical tradition, deeply cherished in the Middle Ages, as might have been expected.

By honoured custom, the literary men, exalted figures at court and in the counsels of rulers, had had a threefold obligation to fulfil as remembrancers: to preserve the history of kings and princes of their country; to guard its language and literature; and to record the genealogies of free men. Even when the last princes had been defeated and Welsh political independence extinguished, the poets and their gentry patrons had kept alive their heritage of a common lineage, history, ecclesiastical tradition, language,

[1] *GPC*, s.n. 'Cymro'; cf. R. R. Davies, *ante*, vol. II, ch. 1.

literature, culture, and sentiment. They continued to believe that the *Cymry* had a God-given right to maintain their own identity and rule their own land and people. Just where the frontiers of that land lay was very uncertain; for though on three sides the sea formed an unmistakable boundary, on the land side it was fluid and uncertain. Not only politically, by reason of the existence of Marcher lordships, but also because many people who spoke the language of the *Cymry*, or British tongue, patronized their literature, and regarded themselves in all essential aspects as descendants of the *Brythoniaid*, lived east of Offa's Dyke in districts like Erging or Ewias. As late as Edward Lhuyd's day, the language and 'the ancient British customs and names of men and places remain still for some space on the English side', even in towns such as Oswestry and Shrewsbury.[2] This common experience of identity found its most vivid and eloquent expression in Welsh literature, which during the Middle Ages had spilled freely into some areas long considered part of England.

In the fifteenth-century poetry, expressions of loyalty to the values of the *Cymry* and an equally intense prejudice against foreigners were very marked. In many other European countries of the time such national reactions were just as apparent. Not only had national feelings intensified, but the growth of a well-defined regional or local consciousness is also almost equally discernible. In a number of countries these emotions were given added force and wider circulation by the emergence of the printed book and the spread of literacy. Though none of the contemporary Welsh literature had as yet been printed, it was widely diffused orally and in manuscript. In it were to be found five closely related strands of central importance in the awareness of Welshness: concepts of lineage, history, religion, language, and literature.

Assumptions concerning lineage were embodied in a captivating, emotive, and indestructible myth about the origins of the Britons or *Cymry* as a people. Considerably older in outline than Geoffrey of Monmouth's work, the legend in its most finished and durable literary form owed an incalculable debt to his genius in purveying a detailed and colourful, if manufactured, saga of the mighty empire allegedly established in Britain by Brutus and his Trojan followers and the deeds of their descendants down to Cadwaladr (d. AD 664). Accepted as genuine history by most people in Europe, and nowhere more ecstatically received than in Wales, it enabled the free-born *Cymry* to conceive of themselves as the offspring of the oldest, most illustrious, and most authentic inhabitants of Britain, and those still having the best title to rule over the whole island. Intertwined with this concept was another which linked the lustrous and heroic past to an equally brilliant future: belief in the prophecy, reputedly delivered to

---

[2] *Camden's Wales*, p. 24.

the last British king, Cadwaladr, by an angel, that in the fullness of time God would bring forth a son of destiny [*mab darogan*] to lead the descendants of the ancient British (i.e., the *Cymry*) to victory over the Saxons. This charismatic figure would himself be a descendant of Cadwaladr who would restore the true ruling house to its ancient glory. The power of that prophecy to survive in Wales in spite of countless defeats and disappointments is an extraordinary phenomenon. Small wonder that Henry Tudor, claiming descent from Cadwaladr and born in Wales, when he came to the throne as Henry VII should be rapturously received. To many of his Welsh followers he could be presented as the long-promised deliverer and the vindicator of the hoary prophecies—not least because they so fervently wanted to believe him to be just that.

If the lineage and much of the history associated with it were just figments of the literary imagination, the Welsh nevertheless had an experience of actual history which was real and painful enough. Its leitmotif was the long and desperate struggle to defend their homeland against what they saw as the invariable hostility, treachery, and oppression of the *Saeson* (literally, 'Saxons'—they did not draw any obvious distinction between Saxons and Normans in this respect). In the process they had forfeited much of their territory, many of their native laws, and, eventually, their last vestiges of political independence. But they never yielded their pride in their ruling families nor their belief in the inherent right of those princely lines and their successors to hold authority in Wales. Early in the fifteenth century, they had unsuccessfully rebelled in support of Glyndŵr's claims to be their prince; he had been defeated but not forgotten. Many of their gentry, moreover, claimed descent from those earlier princes and stubbornly clung to the conviction that the right to jurisdiction within their localities belonged to them. Some of the freemen had also maintained the remnants of Welsh law in parts of Wales, even if it had been losing out heavily to English law since 1284. Closely bound up with the sense of history were two other strongly defined characteristics: an intense attachment to locality and a deeprooted antipathy to the foreigner. Any wider sense of belonging to the *Cymry* or *Brythoniaid* was firmly grounded in a grass-roots attachment to a local community, with all that that conveyed in terms of land, ruling families, laws, institutions, prerogatives, and culture. Men conceived a deep fidelity to a local *gwlad* [country, region]—Morgannwg, Brycheiniog, Ceredigion in the south; Môn, Arfon, Tegeingl in the north; or even to smaller units like Penllyn or Iâl, or Meisgyn or Cyfeiliog. The other face of that coin was mistrust of the outsider, and the tense, impassioned, and undying hatred of the *Saeson*. Out of innumerable examples of poetic hatred of the English, two only are here singled out: one from Dafydd Llwyd, the other from Tudur Aled. In the work of no fifteenth-century poet is anti-English prejudice more raw, virulent, all-pervading, almost pathological, than in that of Dafydd Llwyd.

> Tems a red, t'yma sy ris,
> O waed teulu plant Alis . . .
> Am waith Banbri daw dial,
> O daw ar fen ŷd o'r fal.
> Trwy Dal-arth, troed awel wen,
> Y trywenir plant Ronwen.[3]

[The Thames will run red with the blood of the children of Alice [i.e., the English] . . .
For the battle of Banbury we shall gain revenge, as surely as corn comes from the
harvest. Through Talgarth as the favourable breeze turns, the children of Rowena
[the English] will be pierced through'.]

It would be unwise, perhaps, to interpret the poem quite literally, but its
Anglophobia and yearning for vengeance are unmistakable. An interesting
feature of Dafydd Llwyd's poetry is the persistence of these passions even
after Henry VII's accession. A poet like Tudur Aled, too, who accepted
without demur the early Tudor establishment in Wales, nevertheless saw
Henry's victory as the successful culmination of a struggle that dated right
back to the earliest advent of the Saxons to Britain:

> Ymliw ag wyrion Rhonwen,
> Ymladd hwnt am y wledd hen,
> Can gyson ar y cŵn o Gent,
> Coffa 'wasel', cyffesent.[4]

[Struggling with the descendants of Rowena, fighting yonder for the old feast. Sing
constantly to the dogs of Kent to remember the 'wassail' that they confess. [This was
a reference to the 'night of the long knives' when the Saxons treacherously killed the
Welsh at a feast.]]

Religion, as might be anticipated, was another powerful element in the
self-consciousness of the Welsh as of other peoples in the Middle Ages.
Like the rest of the inhabitants of Christendom they had been subjected to
heavy religious indoctrination, no small part of which had been concerned
with the Old Testament's keynote vision of the special relationship existing
between God and His chosen people. The national pride of the *Cymry* was,
like that of others, closely linked to what they believed were their Christian
origins. Three aspects of the latter were singled out for special emphasis.
First, there was that signal proof of God's favour—early conversion to the
faith; either by Joseph of Arimathea or by Lucius son of Coel *c*.AD 180.
Neither account was historically accurate but both were sincerely believed.
Second, it had always been insisted that the Britons and their progeny had
never been seduced from the faith by heresy or infidelity; their loyalty had
always been beyond reproach or suspicion. Lastly, those to whom they
owed most for their Christianity were their own native saints, who were
still the most frequent subjects of praise and admiration in the religious

---

[3] *D.Ll.F.*, p. 34.   [4] *TA*, p. xlviii.

literature of the later Middle Ages. Their patron saint, Dewi Sant, had been for centuries one of the central focuses of their patriotism. Almost every parish had its own native patronal saint(s), often commemorated in its name and whose holy exploits were integrally woven into local memory and folklore. Deeply embedded in their minds was an ineradicable conviction that they were an elect people singled out by God to perform great deeds. The Lollard, Walter Brut, for instance, thought that it was their special mission to overthrow Antichrist, whom Brut tended to equate with the papacy.

Then there was their language. Ironically enough, it was English representatives at the Council of Constance early in the fifteenth century who described 'difference of language' as being 'by divine and human law the greatest and most authentic mark of a nation and the essence of it'.[5] But any Welshman of the age would have willingly assented to that proposition. He might well have gone further and maintained that his language was an extraordinarily ancient and distinctive one; the tongue spoken by his illustrious Brythonic forebears. As erudite a savant as John Dee, immensely proud of his Cymric antecedents, was at one with his compatriots in believing the language, the *Cambricalingua* as he called it, to be as ancient and worthy of respect and veneration as Hebrew or Latin. Furthermore, it was a language lovingly safeguarded and kept pure and unchanged by untold generations of poets. It was understood and appreciated in all parts of Wales, in spite of the intense localism of the country and the powerful impress of multifarious and widely differing dialects on the vocabulary and intonation of everyday speech.

This pride in language was inextricably linked with delight in literature. That literature was, indeed, an ancient one; as old as almost any vernacular literature in Europe and older than most. Leland and Bale were soon to give wider currency to the belief that it had come down from the Druids of ancient Britain. It had certainly been kept alive over many centuries by a professional order of littérateurs, in whose midst the poets had been primarily responsible for preserving and diffusing the distinctive consciousness of nationhood. The image of Welshness which they had projected had flourished because the most influential social groups in Wales had wanted it to survive and were prepared to extend their patronage to the poets in order to enable them to ensure its perpetuation. It was widely diffused among the free population; all those who considered themselves *boneddigion*. They formed an unusually large proportion of the population—perhaps nearly a half—and took an enormous pride in their ancestry and the duty they believed it imposed on them to behave in a way that they deemed worthy of their illustrious forebears.

---

[5] M. Aston, *The Fifteenth Century* (London, 1968), p. 41.

Such characteristics were not peculiar to Wales; *mutatis mutandis*, they were common among other European peoples. Origin myths of various kinds were potent and widespread. Since the Romans had claimed Trojan ancestry it was hardly surprising that other European peoples should seek to give their own origins the same five-star status; and France was another country where belief in the Trojan descent of their ancestors was similar to Welsh origin myths. Messianic prophecies, like those current in Wales, were commonly found elsewhere in Europe. In addition to the perennial Christian expectations of the second coming of Christ voiced at many points in time and space, there were influential secular myths foretelling the reappearance of Arthur, Charlemagne, Barbarossa, El Cid, and other comparable heroes. Again, the sense of being God's chosen people was nearly as common as Christian belief itself; and many countries had their own special saints and leaders—Hungary's Stephen, Ireland's Patrick, Spain's James, and the rest. Pride had been growing apace, also, in the vernacular languages and literatures, being given added impetus in the fifteenth century by the increase in lay literacy and the spread, first, of manuscripts and, later, of printed books. In the fifteenth and sixteenth centuries many countries would experience an intensified national awareness: Italy on account of the Renaissance; Portugal from the voyages of discovery; Spain with the completion of the *reconquista* and the creation of an overseas empire; Germany as a result of the Reformation; and England with the overthrow of the papacy and the defeat of Spain. There was hardly a people in western Europe that would not be deeply susceptible to those appeals so regularly uttered in that swiftly changing age that men and women should be 'worthy of their ancestors'.[6]

As far as Wales was concerned it could well appear on the face of things that the profound changes of the sixteenth century posed a devastating threat to some of the essential constituents of that sense of identity already outlined. There was first the challenge to its concept of lineage. The notions of Trojan descent and the many splendoured imperial story of early Britain depended heavily on Geoffrey's *Historia Regum Britanniae*. His credibility, however, came under searching and damaging scrutiny by Renaissance scholarship, especially that of Polydore Vergil. Polydore's basic criticism was hard to rebut: if there had been such a glorious and triumphant empire in early Britain, why had classical authors made no mention of it? Not only was Geoffrey's history attacked but the Tudor state cast a jaundicedly discouraging eye on those grandiloquent prophecies based on it that were so popular in Wales. Whatever impact they may have made on Henry VII, his Tudor successors clamped down with frowning disapproval on such vaticinations and also made little boast of their British descent.

[6] E. D. Marcu, *Sixteenth-century Nationalism* (New York, 1976), p. 20.

Again, although the Welsh had lost their independence with the death of their last princes and failed to revive it by Glyndŵr's rebellion, they had somehow managed to survive in a kind of twilight world without being completely absorbed into the kingdom of England and had even preserved some of their own institutions, including a few of the provisions of their own laws. But those Acts of 1536–43 seemed finally to have deleted the last lingering remnants of separate existence and institutions and wholly to have assimilated Wales into England. Apart from the Council in the Marches and the Court of Great Sessions, exceptions in form rather than substance, Wales had been assimilated, territorially, judicially, and administratively into England. When the imperial ambassador, Chapuys, reported to Charles V that Henry VIII had taken away from the Welsh their 'national laws, customs and privileges, which is the very thing they can endure least patiently', he was only commenting on what others also thought the Welsh would find unacceptable,[7] namely, the ultimate extinction, as it seemed, of their independent history. He was not alone in expecting and predicting that there would be trouble; all the more so when at the very same time great changes were also taking place in religion.

In the same decade as the Act of Union was passed, an even more dramatic revolution in religion was being pushed through to exclude papal jurisdiction and establish royal supremacy. In Edward VI's reign Protestant belief and worship were introduced by the Book of Common Prayer. English replaced Latin even in those parts of the realm where it was as unintelligible as Latin. In the eyes of conservative and indignant Welsh poets the people of Wales were forced to betray the faith and, for the first time in their history, to become heretics—and English heretics at that! Two crucially damaging indictments of the Reformation, which it took a long time to rebut, were first ventilated at this time. First, it was a new-fangled heresy having no basis in faith or history; and second, it was an English imposition, totally alien to the Welsh, being foisted on them by the insensitive diktat of a remote and unfeeling government.

The changes implemented by the Act of Union and the Reformation confronted the Welsh language with a direct challenge on the fronts of religion and politics. For the first time, English became insisted upon as the official language of all government and law, and only those who had an adequate knowledge of it would be allowed to hold public office. Additionally, the Act of Uniformity of 1549 had laid down that all forms of public worship must be conducted in English. There was no provision for a translation of the Prayer Book into the native tongue to be made available for Wales, Cornwall, Ireland, or the Isle of Man.

Any threats of this kind to the language were also, indirectly at least,

---

[7] *L. and P.*, VII, 1534.

likely to imperil the literature, when the people most affected by changes in religion and politics were its patrons. But in addition to the impact of politico-religious innovation, Welsh men-of-letters were also becoming increasingly conscious of another challenge being brought home to them all the more forcefully at this time—that of the Renaissance and the printed book. The Renaissance, as its name suggests, not only connoted the 'rebirth' of classical languages and literature, it also injected an immensely potent stimulus into the vernacular languages as well. It made exciting new demands on them, inviting them to become the media of civilized expression in printed books that would make them the equal of Latin and Greek. The key question for Welsh authors, as for those elsewhere, was, Could their language measure up to the contemporary Renaissance modes and criteria and could it meet the challenge of the printed book? Hitherto, theirs had been pre-eminently an oral literature. Could it adapt itself to the exigencies of the revolutionary new medium of communication, the printing-press? Could printed books flourish in a country lacking nearly all the normal social and cultural stimuli to new-style literature—its own court, capital city, university, wealthy aristocratic and clerical households, big centres of population, numerous professional men, literate merchants and artisans, and an extensive reading public? And one being increasingly absorbed into a state where all these encouragements worked in a direction away from Welsh?[8]

From the 1540s onwards, a tiny handful of Welsh scholars was painfully aware that their people stood at the crossroads. These men had a rarefied sense of peril and opportunity. The peril they envisaged was that the Welsh language and the cultural values associated with it might fail to adapt to the new age; that it might succumb to the same fate as Cornish and Breton (also descendants of the old British tongue) and become, in William Salesbury's words, 'full of corrupt speech and well-nigh completely lost',[9] i.e., a vulgar patois incapable of preserving, still less enriching, the treasured cultural and historical patrimony handed down from the past. The opportunity, on the other hand, was that the Welsh should rise to the challenge and give their inheritance a new lease of life. They should prove themselves worthy of their immortal predecessors—the familiar rallying-cry so often heard among other European peoples. It was William Salesbury who was more clearly apprised than anyone else of the dangers and the opportunities and who gave the successful lead. He not only urged upon his countrymen the need for a vigorous response, he also pioneered it in a number of different directions. It was he above all others who created an intellectual framework of Cymric awareness appropriate to a changing age.

[8] R. B. Jones, *The Old British Tongue: the Vernacular in Wales, 1540–1640* (Cardiff, 1970).
[9] 'Y Diarebion Camberaec', *Rhyddiaith Gymraeg* (Cardiff, 1954), p. 64.

In view of the profound and rapid changes of the sixteenth century and the danger they posed to the kind of self-awareness with which the Welsh had associated themselves for many centuries, it is astonishing that it should have survived as well as it did and that the Welsh were able to respond so successfully. This came about partly because the old sense of identity was firmly rooted and widely diffused; partly because the challenge was less drastic than might on the surface appear; but also because the response to it was, in the circumstances, extraordinarily resilient and perceptive.

Surveying the outcome in each of the five strands originally noted, we realize first that, in relation to lineage, penetrating as Polydore Vergil's criticisms were of Geoffrey's version of British history, they had only a limited impact on sixteenth-century opinion. Intriguingly enough, many English authors—Leland, Bale, Drayton, and Spenser[10] among them—repudiated Polydore Vergil's 'calumnies' indignantly. Welsh writers to a man, foreseeably perhaps, upheld Geoffrey's reputation and authority; and his version of history survived virtually intact among them for much of the Tudor and Stuart period. Some of them went further and proclaimed the Tudor dynasty as the consummation and vindication of the prophetic themes of the restoration of the rightful British kingship. What they confidently saw as a British or Welsh dynasty now ruled. They were even prepared to recognize James I—much to that antiquarian-minded monarch's delight—as a rightful successor to the Tudors.

Far from seeing Tudor policy as implying the extinction of the history of the Welsh, many influential contemporaries viewed it as serving to enlarge their history and extend their liberties. Salesbury, for example, applauded Henry VIII's 'excellent wisdom' in ensuring 'that there shall be no difference in laws and language between the Welsh and English'.[11] George Owen, most articulate of Welsh Tudor antiquarians, waxed lyrical about the 'joyful metamorphosis' of Wales as the result of Tudor rule, hailing Henry VII and Henry VIII as the 'deliverers' of the Welsh, who 'came to redress enormities and to establish good and wholesome laws among them and to give them magistrates of their own nation'.[12] The emphasis on 'magistrates of their own nation' pointed up two issues of great significance for the gentry of Wales. It showed, first, how they interpreted Tudor policy as the Crown's handing back of local authority over Wales to the Welsh—'self-government' in the sense in which the sixteenth century understood it. It also revealed how the gentry saw this as confirming, in the most public and indisputable fashion, the rights of the native families to

---

[10] Spenser devoted the tenth canto of the second book of the *Fairie Queene* to 'A chronicle of British Kings/ From Brutus to Uther's rayne,/ And rolls of Elfin Superior/ Till time of Gloriane.'

[11] *Dictionary* (1547), dedication.   [12] Owen, III, 37–8.

bear authority in their own localities—a point of which the sixteenth-century poets made much when praising their patrons by singling out for honourable mention all the offices they held under the Crown.

In relation to the King's religious policies, however, it was a very different story in the early days of the Reformation. Fears were more than once expressed during Henry VIII's reign and that of Edward VI that the Welsh might rise in revolt against innovations so uncongenial to them. Not until Elizabeth's reign was the Reformation convincingly and acceptably presented. The secret then lay in a dramatic historical reinterpretation of early British history and in the translation of Bible and Prayer Book. The former sought to show that the Reformation was a return to the Church as it had existed in its pristine purity in the days of the ancient Britons and not a new-fangled heresy; and that, far from being an alien Saxon imposition, it was true to the earliest and most authentically British sources of Christian belief. Even more influential was the translation of the Bible and the order of service. It served in Wales, as in a number of European countries, to bond the Reformation to primordial patriotic myths and instincts. This linking may have been decisive for the survival of the Welsh sense of identity. The whole weight of English state authority from Elizabeth's reign onwards was thrown in behind the Reformation. If national feeling in Wales had been opposed to the reformed church, then *ipso facto* it would have set itself in opposition to the State. The Welsh language might, as a result, have been proscribed; it would certainly have been reduced to a much more depressed and unhonoured status. As it was, however, the decision to make Welsh the medium of public worship in the state-sponsored church had far-reaching implications for the language and its literature as well as religion.

The effects on the public use of the language and esteem for it have already been noted (above, pp. 322–3, 330–1). The consequences for Welsh literature were no less momentous (above, pp. 449–50). Welsh had become the language of reformed religion and literature, and they, in turn, became the nursing mothers of an intensified patriotic sentiment.

That there had been a remarkably conscious, energetic, and successful response by a handful of reformers, scholars, and writers is undoubtedly true. That it was carried on into the eighteenth century and given a revivifying blood transfusion which transformed the prospects for the future cannot be denied.[13] That should not, however, preclude the recognition that the Welsh sense of identity was also largely preserved by the forces of inertia, i.e., because Wales, until the Industrial Revolution, continued to be a remote and thinly populated land inhabited mainly by small-scale stock-rearing peasants, whose way of life remained immune

---

[13] P. T. J. Morgan, *The Eighteenth-Century Renaissance* (Llandybïe, 1981).

from cultural dislocation and whose attitudes and values could be transmitted largely unchanged from one generation to another. That was not true of the upper classes, whose existence was much more open to extraneous influences. Among them the seeds of change had already been sown and were germinating vigorously in the century between 1536 and 1642, if not before. The resultant harvest became increasingly apparent in the seventeenth and eighteenth centuries.

However strongly Welshmen and others defended Galfridian history, in the long run it and the prophecies associated with it were bound to be wasting assets and increasingly discredited. Also gone was their former sense of being a subordinate, underprivileged people forced to defend themselves and their mountains under severe pressure from an oppressive neighbour, bigger, wealthier, and more powerful. In so far as the politically conscious among the Welsh felt their interests to be threatened now, it was the external Catholic enemies of the realm and their potential 'fifth column' of internal Catholic believers whom they feared most. Their loyalty had become increasingly identified with an idealized English monarchy dispensing authority and benefits, with its national erastian church and its institutions of government and law entrusting power to the ruling gentry. All these interests had been brought more and more to their notice and thrown into sharp relief when seeming to be at stake in the struggle with international Catholicism, in the course of which they had become completely integrated into mechanisms for the defence of the realm and on behalf of which they had had to make heavy sacrifices. There was no doubt that by the early seventeenth century they saw their future welfare as being inextricably linked with the destinies of the kingdom of England.

Many of the earlier historical bases of the difference between Welsh and English had therefore been eroded to the point of extinction as far as the gentry were concerned. The distinctive linguistic component of the difference between them at upper-class level had also been greatly diluted. English was firmly established in Wales as the language of law, government, administration, politics, education, and polite society. It dominated printed books, writing, and correspondence in an increasingly literate upper-class milieu. The incentives for wealthy, leisured, and educated people to learn and use English were many and powerful; those inducing them to retain their Welsh were few and weak. The process of gentry anglicization took some generations to complete, but carried with it grave consequences for cultural values as well as linguistic usage. It weakened beyond repair the connection between the gentry and the native literary culture. By the later half of the seventeenth century, the old bardic order, the group which more than any other had given shape, expression, and continuity to the former sense of Welsh identity, had become defunct. The

Welsh awareness would in future have to learn to live without the participation of the gentry; their eyes were fixed more and more on the wider life of the kingdom outside Wales.

The lure of employment, profit, interest, and adventure outside Wales was not something which emerged brand new in the Tudor era. It had drawn Welsh people to leave their native country in large numbers during the Middle Ages too. Long before Henry Tudor's victory on Bosworth Field they had found their way to court and aristocratic households, to London and other English cities, to Marcher lordships and English shires. But the Tudor's triumph, and his son's assimilation of Wales into England, had given their Welsh subjects greater encouragement and more freedom to migrate in markedly larger numbers. They were to play a part in the wider life of Tudor and early Stuart England out of all proportion to their numbers; a contribution which elicited approving comments from contemporaries on their willingness and capacity to serve monarch and commonwealth. That ardent patriot, George Owen, predictably wrote in glowing terms of how,

since the time of Henry VII and Henry VIII that we were emancipated, as it were, and made free to trade and traffic through England, the gentlemen and people in Wales have greatly increased in learning and civility . . . some prove to be learned men and good members in the Commonwealth of England and Wales; some worthy labourers in the Lord's vineyard; many of them have proved excellent in the Civil Laws, some in Physic, and other laudable studies.[14]

That was not to be attributed simply to parochial pride on Owen's part, for the most impeccable of English Elizabethan antiquaries, William Camden, also referred to the Welsh as having plentifully yielded 'martial captains, judicious civilians, skilful common lawyers, learned divines, complete courtiers and adventurous soldiers'.[15]

Owen and Camden had in mind the more dazzling Welsh luminaries, mainly the men of upper-class origin. What was just as significant, or more significant in terms of the numbers involved, even if far less known, was the vast outflux of men and women of humbler origin. This was not confined to the Welsh, nor is it something which can be attributed, as it usually is, solely, or even primarily, to some special relationship between the Welsh and the Tudors, created by Henry VII and reinforced by his son. It was part of a wider movement within the British Isles and was as apparent among the Irish and the Scots too. In fact, the 'diaspora' worked in reverse in prosperous south Pembrokeshire, where the Irish were attracted in such large numbers that George Owen believed that in the near future they were 'like to match the other inhabitants in number', there being some

---

[14] Owen, III, 56.
[15] W. J. Hughes, *Wales and the Welsh in English Literature* (Wrexham, 1924), p. 12.

'whole parishes inhabited by the Irish'.[16] To the north-eastern counties of Wales, likewise, there came many English between 1550 and 1670; no fewer than 700 families into Flintshire, 680 into Denbighshire, and 570 into Montgomeryshire, it is estimated.[17]

Some of the conditions leading to this kind of migration were common to many peoples in Europe. They lived in an age when the two most powerful social and economic forces were rapid inflation and population pressure, which tended to press more than ordinarily painfully on the more limited resources of poorer areas such as the Highland Zone of Britain. Those who, as a result, became footloose were attracted or pushed out to the growth-points of the economy in the Lowland Zone. Their more thriving agriculture, industry, and trade offered the best chances for impoverished farmers, craftsmen, labourers, even paupers and vagrants, and their sons and daughters, when forced to leave their homes by the pressure of too many hands to employ and too many mouths to feed. Girls from Montgomeryshire and other shires settled as maids in Chester and elsewhere, Welsh weavers moved to Berkshire, clothiers to Somerset, tanners to Shropshire, coopers to Suffolk, and some shopkeepers to Kent. Their social superiors—younger sons and daughters of gentry, lawyers, clergy, and yeomen—may have had somewhat more chance of choosing when and where they would go. But it was motives of money, honour, or duty, in that order, which impelled them to seek their fortune; and it was doubtless money, employment, or the bare hope of staying alive on the proceeds of begging or petty crime that inexorably drove their less fortunate brethren to go also. Moreover, the whole process was indirectly encouraged by the policies of the Tudor state. The more firmly it asserted its right to rule the outlying areas of the north and west, the more likely its subjects from the periphery were to take the path to the centre of political and economic gravity.

So Welsh men and women in large numbers left their own country to settle elsewhere. This diaspora is a huge and fascinating subject, the surface of which has barely been scratched and one which merits a volume to itself. Though Welsh names crop up all over the place in widely differing contexts only rarely can we begin, as yet, to quantify the numbers involved in a few aspects of the migration. The registers of schools, colleges, and Inns of Court shed much light on the numbers of Welsh recruited there (see pp. 434–5).[18] There are also a few figures relating to two major urban centres, Shrewsbury and Bristol. In a list of Shrewsbury shearmen of 1587, one-third out of 205 of them were patently Welsh by origin. Out of 1,426 apprentices registered in Bristol between 1532 and 1542 no fewer

---

[16] Owen, I, 41.
[17] Owen, *Trans. Cymmr.*, 1959, p. 102.
[18] Griffith, 'Welsh Students'.

than 174 of them—a few girls as well as boys—came from the counties of Wales.[19]

Some of those who arrived in England were apt to forget their Welshness and affect English modes and manners with a slavish readiness that made them an object of contempt and ridicule to Welsh authors. Gruffudd Robert, his own patriotic loyalty glowing bright and staunch at Milan for many years after 1559, dismissed them as men who, as soon as they saw the spires of Shrewsbury and heard an Englishman say 'Good morrow' promptly forgot all their Welsh. Yet the first earl of Pembroke was praised by Wiliam Llŷn for unrepentantly speaking Welsh at court, and even as late as 1642 there were large numbers who spoke Welsh in Hereford.[20] Many, probably most, of them remained unmistakably and unashamedly Welsh, like Richard Parry who, after nearly fifty years as a parson in Norfolk, proudly styled himself a 'Cambro-Briton' in his will of 1624. They welcomed other Welsh people to their midst and would, in the words of one of their number, 'steal opportunities to serve some friends' turns'. Having prospered abroad, not a few invested their gains in landed estates in Wales: the Myddeltons in Chirk, William Aubrey in Breconshire, and William Owen in Pembrokeshire. Others remembered their home districts with lavish bequests and endowments in their wills. Geoffrey Glyn of Doctors Commons founded Friars School Bangor; Hugh Myddelton left handsome silver cups to Denbigh and Ruthin; and William Jones of Monmouth provided his home town with a whole range of social institutions—grammar school, almshouses, a lectureship, and other charities.

These Welsh incomers seemed to their English hosts to be readily recognizable: the closest and most familiar of foreigners, and also the most distant and outlandish of provincials. Even when they conversed together in Welsh, everyone in England seemed to know who they were, and it has been suggested that the average Elizabethan playgoer would have a smattering of Welsh, just as his modern counterpart can be expected to know some French. Once the Welsh began speaking English, their pronunciation and usage of the language gave rise to idiosyncrasies so widely and easily recognizable as to become the clichés of regular satire. Although proverbially voluble and fluent in speech, the Welsh themselves had occasional misgivings about their command of English. One of the earl of Essex's captains, Thomas Madryn, apologized to him in 1598: 'If I have in any wise offended you, either in speaking false English or other wise in my simple manner of speech, I beseech you to consider that I am a Welshman'.[21] Even in a border market-town like Abergavenny, where

---

[19] D. Hollis, *Calendar of the Bristol Apprentice Book, 1532–1542* (Bristol Rec. Soc.), XIV (1949).
[20] *CSP Dom. 1641–3*, p. 399.   [21] *HMC Salisbury MSS*, VIII, 153.

English would have been more common than in most parts of Wales, the local Welsh inhabitant was said to have found it impossible to speak English 'without any corruption from his mother-tongue, which doth commonly infect our country, so that they cannot speak English but that they be discovered by their vicious pronunciation or idiotisms'.[22] For these speech foibles on their part, the Welsh were regularly twitted and satirized by English authors, who loved to tease them for the difficulty they had in enunciating consonants like b, d, or g, and the dreadful muddles they got into over the tenses of verbs and the uses of pronouns, especially their propensity for using 'she' and 'her' as all-purpose pronouns. One doggerel-writer could not resist ribbing the Welsh as much on account of their strange-sounding English as for their excessive delight in their descent from the Trojans:

> Pye Got, they bee all Shentlemen
> Was descended from Shoves none lyne, [Jove's own line]
> Parte humane and parte divine . . .
> And from Ffenus, that fayre Goddesse,
> And twenty other shentle poddies,
> Hector stoute and comely Paris,
> Arthur, Prutus, King of Ffayres.[23]

That verse is typical in tone of the treatment of the Welsh in Elizabethan and Jacobean literature. The stage and literary Welshman was a well-known stereotype, appearing over and over again endowed with his stock national traits. He was impulsive and eloquent by nature, warm-hearted but quick-tempered; he had a passionate sense of honour, and was fervently, almost aggressively, patriotic (much more so than either Scot or Irishman); he was inordinately proud of the history and lineage of his nation and his own as an individual; he was as addicted to pedigrees and genealogies as to toasted cheese, leeks, and *metheglin* [the Welsh mead]; and he held in deepest affection poetry and rhetoric, music and harps, and mountains and goats. It was not a profound or subtle thumb-nail sketch, but it did set out in high relief some instantly identifiable characteristics, and though it embodied a good deal of teasing and banter, it was usually presented in a good-humoured and affectionate way, in which the Welsh normally appeared in a distinctly more amiable light than either the Scots or Irish.[24]

To prepare themselves for their future, some of the Welsh first crossed Offa's Dyke to obtain education or training in England. Schools like Oswestry and Shrewsbury, set in border towns redolent with a Welsh

---

[22] *Memorials of Father Augustine Baker* . . . , ed. J. McCann and H. Connolly (Catholic Rec. Soc. Pubs.), XXXIII (1933), 56.
[23] BL Add. MSS 21,435; cf. Owen, *Eliz. Wales*, p. 14.
[24] J. O. Bartley, *Teague, Shenkin and Sawney* (Cork, 1954).

atmosphere, might have been expected to exert a strong pull, but other famous academies more distant—Westminster and Winchester—also attracted many pupils from Wales; Westminster because for sixty years its deans were Welshmen! Others went into service in great aristocratic households like that of the earl of Arundel, where Humphrey Llwyd served as a physician, or Lord Buckhurst, who recruited Maurice Kyffin. Many of the ill-starred Essex's boisterous and ambitious henchmen were Welsh, foremost among them his steward and *éminence grise*, Gelly Meyrick. The hopes of others lay in commerce, and for them the path to fame and fortune lay through an apprenticeship, preferably to a great London merchant, but failing that to a lesser figure in one of the provincial towns or cities. Richard Clough of Denbigh was first the apprentice and later the trusted deputy of Sir Thomas Gresham, whose fabulous success on the Continent he shared. But one of the most successful London-Welsh merchants was William Jones, who began his career as a mere porter. Yet, because 'his brains were better than his back', he 'made such a vent for Welsh cottons [in Hamburg] that what he found drugs at home he left dainties beyond the sea'.[25]

At court and in government the Welsh attained some key positions, as well as in all the learned professions and the highest business circles. A handful penetrated to the innermost corridors of the ruling élite. Henry Tudor himself, of course, was the supreme example of the local Welsh boy who made good, and his uncle, Jasper, was his most-trusted and best-rewarded adviser. Blanche Parry, a Welsh-speaking woman from Herefordshire, described by David Powel as a 'singular well-willer and furtherer of the weal public of Wales', was the Queen's first gentlewoman from 1565 until 1590. William Cecil, for forty years her most influential servant, was the grandson of a Welsh immigrant and never lost his soft spot for genealogies and other things Welsh. William Herbert, first earl of Pembroke, second son of a modest Monmouthshire squire, spoke Welsh more readily than English, and rose to be one of the foremost aristocrats and military commanders of his age. Sir John Perrot, reputedly Henry VIII's by-blow son by Mary Berkeley, was a tempestuous and choleric character of Shakespearian proportions, and was entrusted with high office in Ireland and made a member of the Privy Council in 1589.

In the next category of royal servants came those who, lacking aristocratic birth or connections, by their own talent and training achieved high office as leading civil servants and career diplomats. Sir Edward Carne served Henry VIII at Rome during the process for the annulment of his marriage to Catherine of Aragon, yet, paradoxically, ended up as her daughter Mary's ambassador to the papacy—the only independent English

[25] W. K. Jordan, *The Charities of London, 1480–1660* (London, 1960), p. 338.

representative then maintained abroad. William Thomas, clerk to Edward VI's Privy Council, also spent years in Italy immersing himself in a study of its arts, language, and history, and in the political philosophy of the subversive and alarming Machiavelli. Sir John Herbert, lawyer, linguist, and diplomat, rose to the rank of Second Secretary of State to Sir Robert Cecil. Most notable of them all was that last in a long line of gifted ecclesiastics-cum-statesmen, John Williams. A brilliant youth, early singled out for promotion, chaplain to Lord Chancellor Ellesmere by the time he was thirty, he was made Lord Keeper of the Great Seal, bishop of Lincoln at forty, and finally archbishop of York. It is interesting to recall in this context that in the seventeenth century the youthful Richard Baxter, son of an unimportant yeoman, was urged to make acquaintances at court and acquire some office as being the best hope of rising in the world.[26]

Lawyers, as Camden observed, proliferated among the Welsh. Theirs was a profession more than ordinarily attractive to men whose talent and ambition exceeded their birth and possessions. All Souls College was so full of Welsh lawyers in the sixteenth century as to lead to a justifiable suspicion of national log-rolling in the choice of fellows. When Queen Elizabeth visited Oxford in 1566 she was greeted by three leading Welsh civilians out of four chosen to debate in her honour: William Aubrey, formerly professor of Civil Law, Robert Loughor, then professor, and Hugh Lloyd, master of Winchester College. Aubrey, great-grandfather of John Aubrey the antiquarian, was associated with a whole series of major judgements in ecclesiastical, international, constitutional, and maritime law. David Williams, son of a yeoman, rose to become Justice of the King's Bench, and his most celebrated judgement was that of the *post-nati*, which determined the legal status of the Scottish subjects of James I after the union of the English and Scottish crowns.

Clerics also blossomed in the sun of royal patronage. As well as the many Welshmen appointed to Welsh bishoprics, some were elevated to English sees. Thomas Young, bishop of St Davids 1560–1, was translated to York and became President of the Council in the North, 1561–8. Richard Vaughan went from Bangor to Chester and thence to London. Gabriel Goodman was dean of Westminster from 1561 to 1601, and candidate, *proxime accessit*, for the episcopal bench on no fewer than seven occasions. His nephew, Godfrey, did, however, become bishop of Gloucester in 1625; and Thomas Howell achieved the melancholy distinction of being the last bishop to be consecrated for sixteen years when he became bishop of Bristol in 1644.

Particularly impressive was the record of Welsh merchants, some of whom became very well-known figures indeed. Morgan Wolfe of Chepstow

---

[26] *The Autobiography of Richard Baxter* (Everyman edn., 1925), p. 12.

was Henry VIII's goldsmith, and Thomas Howell, who died in Seville, is still commemorated in two schools which bear his name in Denbigh and Llandaff. Three of the most celebrated were the Myddelton brothers, Thomas, Hugh, and Robert. Thomas was a major backer of maritime companies, ended up as Lord Mayor of London, and planted his family at Chirk, while Hugh is chiefly remembered for his part in bringing a pure water supply to London. Among the great London philanthropists traced by Professor W. K. Jordan were nine Welshmen, together with a further twenty-three lesser ones.[27] Successful Welsh merchants were not found only in London. Every one of the major English border towns and cities had its quota, and there were colonies of them further east in towns like Stratford and Worcester, and many other places no doubt. Richard Owen or Thomas Jones in Shrewsbury, Henry Vaughan in Henry VII's Bristol and Thomas James a century later, were only a handful of the Welsh who made their mark in English provincial cities.

A number of others were bent on exchanging ideas rather than commodities. They were at the forefront of a wide range of scholarly and intellectual circles, and many sought a more extensive and permanent medium for their opinions in print. Leonard Cox, one of the numerous Welsh schoolmasters in England who provided Shakespeare with his proto-types of Sir Hugh Evans, was the author of the first English book of rhetoric designed as a school textbook. Robert Recorde of Tenby, successful physician, master of the Mint, and General Surveyor of the Mines, had more advanced scientifically minded pupils in his sights when he explained solar and lunar eclipses on the Copernican system, which he was the first to accept and publicize in this country. John Dee has good claims to have been the most versatile intellectual in Elizabethan England, possessing a private library of some 2,600 books and manuscripts. He is well-summed up in Lilly's verdict that he was 'Elizabeth's Intelligencer . . . a ready-witted man, quick of apprehension, . . . a perfect astronomer, a curious astrologer; to speak truth he was excellent in all kinds of learning'.[28] It has already been shown (see pp. 437–41) how a whole bevy of Welsh authors was responsible for a miscellany of scholarly and literary works written in a number of languages. Welshmen, indeed, had a profound concern for books and publishing. Thomas James was Bodley's first librarian; Richard Jones and Thomas Salusbury were well-known London printers; James Roberts, printer of the first quarto of *The Merchant of Venice*, included a Welsh motto on the title-page; and if John Penry was not Martin Marprelate, he played a central role in organizing the press on which the devastatingly successful satirical pamphlets were published.

In more martial exchanges Welsh soldiers and sailors have already been

[27] Jordan, *Charities London*, p. 313.
[28] R. Deacon, *John Dee* (London, 1968), p. 46.

seen to be active and venturesome. The nonpareil among Welsh soldiers was Roger Williams. Veteran of innumerable campaigns and well-known to generals of European stature like Henry of Navarre or Alexander of Parma, he wrote books on warfare which stamped him as a military analyst and historian of rare percipience, as well as a fighting man of unblemished courage and resource. In Stuart times Sir Charles Lloyd, having learned his military trade in the Netherlands, came home to serve the royalist cause as general-in-chief of engineers to Charles I. Sir Robert Mansel was the last great admiral of the Hawkins–Drake tradition, a sailor whose exploits in battle were decidedly worthier of commendation than his more dubious operations as Treasurer of the Navy between 1614 and 1618. Sir Thomas Button won fame as an explorer searching for the north-west passage, giving names like New North Wales and New South Wales, which he hoped—alas vainly!—would survive permanently. Tomos Prys of Plas Iolyn, the sailor and adventurer, who seems best-known to us on account of his partly autobiographical Welsh verse, encapsulated in his poems much of that flavour of recklessness, bravado, and camaraderie of the seagoing fraternity.

In spite of the active role of Welsh soldiers, sailors, and merchants, they could not be said to have played an outstanding part in the early discovery, exploitation, or settlement of the trans-Atlantic world, though they 'touched on its successive manifestations at many points, if peripherally. Welsh merchants, sailors and intellectuals in Bristol and London probably played a greater part than Welshmen in Wales'.[29] The most fascinating, if not the most successful, individual among the latter was William Vaughan of Llangyndeyrn. Despairing of the poverty and over-population he saw around him, he set his sights on colonizing in Newfoundland, but without success (above, p. 441). Welsh fishermen did rather better in fishing voyages off Newfoundland, and a few adventurers, mainly from Glamorgan and Monmouthshire, were attracted to the possibility of infiltrating into the Spanish zone in America and combining that with robbery.

Nearer home, Ireland in the reigns of Elizabeth and James offered alluring prospects of titles, estates, and wealth for ambitious settlers. Sir John Perrot took with him to Ireland a considerable following of 'Castle Welshmen'. Outstanding among the 'undertakers' in Munster was Sir William Herbert of St Julian's, Monmouthshire, who took out broad estates and settled at Castle Island. He was solicitous enough of the interests of the Irish to have arranged for parts of the Anglican service to be translated into their language and cherished plans to set up a college in their midst, but had to return home disappointed. The earl of Essex had many Welshmen in his entourage when he came to put down Tyrone's

[29] Quinn in Davies, *Welsh Society and Nationhood*, p. 106.

rebellion. Two of them stayed on to become leading landowners during James's reign and ultimately to acquire titles in the Irish peerage. Edward Blayney, a soldier from his youth with long experience in Continental warfare, was elevated first Lord Blayney in 1621; and John Vaughan of Golden Grove was created earl of Carbery. Along with these two, another member of the Irish Privy Council was a distinguished Welsh lawyer, William Jones of Castellmarch, who became Chief Justice of Ireland. Two Welsh clerics who found Irish episcopal promotions within their reach were Lewis Jones, made bishop of Killaloe, and Griffith Williams, formerly dean of Bangor, who became bishop of Ossory.

Surveying the overall impact made by the Welsh on the life of the kingdom, it is difficult not to be impressed by the phenomenal success achieved by many of them. This period served to open up opportunities to previously under-used Welsh talents on a scale not seen again until the spread of secondary and university education in the last century and this. Wales, said Ben Jonson in James I's reign, had long been 'a very garden and seed plot of honest minds and men. Whence hath the Crown . . . had better servitors, more liberal of their lives and fortunes?' The metaphor of a 'garden' or 'seed plot' came readily to mind at the sight of the flowering of such a profusion of able men and women. Many of those who made the most notable impression were those who might have been at a distinct disadvantage if they had stayed at home—younger sons of landed families, or gifted boys of modest birth and means. They were predictably the ones who would be most enthusiastic to avail themselves of the new avenues to advancement opened by better education, increased social mobility, the improved political and legal climate, and economic growth. They seized with alacrity those careers where talent and training counted for more than birth or influence. The age-long, innate Welsh respect for rhetoric and eloquence may explain why many were attracted to those callings where facility in the use of language was an asset—the Church, authorship, publishing, and above all, perhaps, the law. The swift progression of many in trade is less easily explicable; but it may be that they, like the Scots, coming from a poor mountain country, were accustomed to being frugal and thrifty and were well-used to having to drive a hard bargain. What all the successful migrants appear to have had in common was a keen ambition, reinforced by the bounding energy, will to succeed, and confidence of being a chosen people, which were typical of the age in which they lived. It was a combination of qualities which took some of their representatives to the top, or near it, in virtually every facet of contemporary achievement.

CHAPTER 20

THE EARLY STUART REGIME, 1603–1642

Two years before the death of Queen Elizabeth there were portents of the end of an era in Wales, when the two men with the greatest influence there—usually pitted one against the other—had passed from the scene. The second earl of Pembroke, President of the Council in the Marches, had like his father before him maintained close contacts with Wales, through his extensive family ties, his broad acres in the south-east, and his office as president. After his death in 1601 not only were his own family's links far weaker but the last of the great sixteenth-century Presidents of the Council with Welsh connections had gone. The earl of Essex, darling of so many of the more dashing younger spirits, the Queen's favourite, and once a towering figure at court, had also met his sad end in 1601. By virtue of his magnetic personality, adventurous career, and following in Wales, he had attracted to himself a powerful faction. Bent on bringing James's claims to the succession to a point of decision, he gathered around him a motley and not altogether compatible company, made up of youthful hotheads bored by Robert Cecil's cautious ways, Catholics who were pro-Stuart and anti-Spanish in their proclivities, Puritans who looked hopefully to James's Calvinist sympathies, and Welsh adventurers who aspired to benefit personally from the Scottish king's accession. The intended coup had failed, trailing many alarming reverberations in its wake. Fortunately for the King of Scots, Essex's rashness had done nothing to jeopardize his chances. James was still in close touch with Cecil, and even in clandestine contact with the Pope, in his efforts to ensure the succession. Eventually in 1603 Elizabeth died, evincing to the very end her mortal horror of naming a successor; but by this time there was no real alternative to the Stuart.

Too sharp a contrast between the era of Elizabeth and that of James should be avoided. Nor should it be supposed that severe and widening constitutional conflict between King and Parliament was implicit in the relationships between them from the start. James may have lacked much of Elizabeth's regal dignity and her experience of handling English politics and parliaments; but he was, nevertheless, a tried and highly successful king of Scotland. He was, in addition, a ruler who, in spite of his penchant for theorizing about kingly prerogatives, was in practice pragmatic, astute, good-humoured, and capable of compromise. He was by no means the inflexible or foolish monarch that it was once fashionable to depict. His relationships with his favourites were admittedly unwise; he allowed himself to slide too far under Buckingham's thumb; and his attempts simultaneously to champion the Protestant cause and keep the peace after 1618 were ill-advised. But, although relationships between him and his last parliaments deteriorated, there was no sign of an irreconcilable breach between King and Parliament when he died in 1625. There was, in fact, a much sharper contrast between his regime and that of his obstinate and untrustworthy successor than between his and that of Elizabeth.

James was cordially received in England and Wales. He recalled with unconcealed satisfaction how people had greeted him on his first arrival in England with 'sparkles of affection . . . sounds of joy . . . and a passionate longing and earnestness to meet and embrace their new sovereign' and he spoke with no less pleasure of how Welsh 'loyalty, faith and obedience' were equally well known to him.[1] In many respects James was very acceptable in Wales. As William Vaughan was later to write: 'I rejoice that the memorial of Offa's Dyke is extinguished with love and charity: that our green leeks, sometimes offensive to your dainty nostrils, are now tempered with your fragrant roses . . . God give us grace to dwell together without enmity, without detraction'.[2] The secret of the Tudors' success in their dealings with the Welsh had been the wish of both parties to seal the alliance between the instinctive, inherent fidelity to Welsh ideals of ancient loyalty and the newer attachment to the principles and institutions of authority and government associated with the Tudor monarchy. William Vaughan was therefore expressing a view widely current among his countrymen. James I, a descendant of Henry Tudor and appearing to have Elizabeth's blessing, was enthusiastically received in Wales, where the bonds of family and kindred still counted for much. He came as the upholder of the Tudor monarchy and regime, loyalty to whose key institutions was now so deeprooted among the Welsh. Although he was king of a foreign country, Scotland, he was far less objectionable than would have been a representative of Spain, whose friendship with the Irish papists and whose threat to the security of the Welsh coastline and the stability of the Protestant settlement had long been abhorrent. Moreover, a Spanish successor, in close touch with the most powerful Catholic monarchy in Europe, would have carried a much greater risk than James to that prospect of 'jobs for Welsh boys', which had been so agreeably available in state service, law, church, and aristocratic households. James's succession had been carefully prepared by Robert Cecil and others and was widely welcomed. The few odd traces of resentment there may have been had no real depth or staying power. At Newtown a man was alleged to have challenged James's proclamation with the scornful cry, 'Shall we have

---

[1] *Commons Journals*, I, 42.   [2] Dodd, *Wales through Ages*, II, 54.

a Scot for a king?' and some years later, in 1610, as influential a figure as Sir John Wynn was accused of having been reluctant to acknowledge James's succession.[3] But any such hesitations as there may have been were quickly swept aside and the new king entered into his inheritance without misgiving.

Some Catholics, however, quickly became disillusioned with the new king's attitude towards their co-religionists, especially his apparent determination to exact heavy fines from them. They plotted to seize his person and free him from the influence of his Protestant advisers. But although their leader, a Roman priest called Watson, was in touch with Morgan Clynnog, 'a cunning man in prophecies', and hoped for the support of 10,000 Catholics ready to rise in revolt in Wales, nothing came of his schemes. Nor did anything materialize from Guy Fawkes's attempts to organize yet another plan for an attack on Milford Haven. James's vacillations over his attitude towards recusants continued to encourage a mixture of hope and irritation on their part. In May 1605 there was turmoil in Herefordshire, in an old recusant stronghold on the borders of Wales, over the illegal Catholic burial of a young woman and a subsequent attack by armed men on representatives of the law. Although the government exploited to the full the anti-Catholic propaganda value of the *émeute*, it seems unlikely that it was part of some larger and more sinister conspiracy. A short while later, when the Gunpowder Plot failed, political Catholicism came to an inglorious end. By contrast with the many schemes and intrigues plotted during Elizabeth's reign for the assassination of the ruler, invasion of the country, and overthrow of the regime, that of James was singularly free of such conspiracies.

In other respects, James's reign appeared to be largely a continuation of his predecessor's. The King was keenly aware of Welsh loyalty and appreciative of it. True, he replaced the Welsh dragon with the Scottish unicorn in his coat of arms, but in other ways he gave Wales and Welshmen an honoured place in his government. He was quick to confer favours on the heirs to the Essex faction—Gelly Meyrick's son, Rowland, and his daughter Margaret and her husband, John Vaughan of Golden Grove, and Robert Vaughan of Llwydiarth, whom he knighted and rewarded with land. Again, the earl of Worcester, a stiff papist, was confirmed as Master of the Horse and later created Lord Privy Seal for his services in suppressing the Gunpowder Plot. Others to be honoured by him were the earl of Pembroke, Sir Thomas Parry, Sir Robert Mansel, Sir John Herbert, and Sir Richard Wynn. James was also delighted to welcome such greetings as that of William Herbert of Glamorgan to him as 'our second Brutus' or the perfervid support of Sir William Maurice of Clenennau for his title of

[3] PRO STAC 8/34/33.

'King of Great Britain'. James saw in particular how telling an argument the English assimilation of Wales could be in support of his own pet design for a union between Scotland, England, and Wales. He put the point explicitly to the members of his first Parliament, 'Do you not gain from the union with Wales and is not Scotland greater than Wales?' He was lavish in his praise for Welsh members who 'served for the country of Wales' and for the 'loyalty, faith and obedience' of their constituents. He indicated his gratitude for their reaction to him by removing any lingering 'mark of separation in point of freedom' between Welsh and English and by introducing 'Welsh speeches' into the investiture of his son as prince of Wales.[4]

Politically speaking, Wales gratefully welcomed the advent of James the royal peacemaker. Exhausted by the crippling and protracted burden of warfare spread over nearly twenty years after 1585 and bled white by the seemingly unending demands for men and money, the Welsh were greatly relieved by the conclusion of hostilities with Spain and the years of freedom from military and financial exactions which followed. Administratively, there were no significant changes in the structure of government and justice created during the sixteenth century, which was still monopolized by the leading county families. Surveillance of law and order and jurisdiction rested, as before, mainly in the hands of the Council in the Marches, though its Jacobean presidents, Lords Zouche and Eure, were no longer leading personalities with strong Welsh associations as Sidney or Pembroke had been. Opposition to the Council, emanating from some of the distinguished common lawyers who objected to the pretensions of the Council as a prerogative court, and still more from men like Sir Herbert Croft and Roger Owen, MPs for Herefordshire, who constituted themselves spokesmen for the English border counties, continued to rumble on menacingly.

James was himself a zealous defender of the Council, less on its own account than on the grounds of what he took to be two principles of overriding importance. The first was defence of his own royal prerogative, which he did not wish to see diminished in any particular; and the second was the importance of the precedent of Wales for achieving union with Scotland. He argued eloquently that England and Wales were held together by their common government 'in terms of love'. Any threat to the Council which had first done so much to bring them together might well have the effect of 'reviving the ancient enmity between these two peoples'. Moreover, it would have a bad effect on 'traffic and commerce' between the two countries if equal justice between Welsh and English were not readily available at Ludlow. As it was, the English sent yearly 'great herds

[4] A. H. Dodd, 'The Pattern of Politics in Stuart Wales', *Trans. Cymmr.*, 1948, p. 16.

of cattle' to be summered in Wales and bought there 'great store of cattle, sheep, wools, friezes, and cottons for exchange of corn, fruit, and merchandise of all sorts'. But if there were any significant weakening of the Council, this traffic 'must necessarily decay; and so both must return to their poverty, rudeness and disorder' of former times. Furthermore, James harboured darker fears of the potential rebelliousness of the Welsh who, 'being ever prone to riots and rebellions, do therefore need to be bridled with the strength of these shires'. Most dangerous of all, he contended, was that any disaffection in Wales might prove a 'manifest overture' to comparable troubles in the north of England.[5] The King's arguments in favour of the close and beneficial commercial and other contacts between Wales and England were warmly seconded by Francis Bacon, who recalled persuasively that one of the main objects of setting up the Council had been to make 'a better equality of commerce and intercourse' between the King's Welsh and English subjects.[6] Nor, in 1618, was James prepared to entertain any proposals by the Surveyor of Crown Lands in Wales under which Crown lands in south Wales were to be colonized after the Irish pattern, even though it had the approval of the President of the Council himself.

That the Council in the Marches was continuingly effective in curbing the excesses of even the most powerful gentry emerged in the relations between it and Sir John Wynn. Wynn had himself been a member of the Council and was one of the best-known and most forceful personalities in north Wales. Nevertheless, information was laid against him by the King's Attorney in 1615, at the instigation, it would seem, of Sir Richard Lewkenor, justice of Great Sessions and Wynn's sworn enemy, concerning 'several oppressions and violences', the proofs of which had been 'so apparent and the offences so foul and monstrous', viz., 'putting out whole families, some of them being young children and naked, by three o' clock in the morning'.[7] Sir John had at first obviously intended to brazen it out defiantly, but later changed his mind. The Council was induced to accept his surrender on the grounds that the voluntary submission of so great a gentleman 'so strongly allied in his country and so supported with so powerful friends in Court' would 'add more grace and lustre to the authority of the Lord President'.[8] It was a striking vindication of the Council's authority.

Wynn's own surviving correspondence and other records relating to the gentry indicate that they kept in touch with the political issues of the day. A growing number of them, having been educated at the Inns of Court, were thereby brought into contact with the law, lawsuits, and political developments in London. Other Welshmen, pursuing their careers as

[5] PRO SP16/19/53B.
[6] BL Add. MSS, 25, 244, fos. 5–8.
[7] PRO SP16/84/25.
[8] CWP, pp. 113–19, 121.

lawyers, minor Civil Servants, in commerce or other occupations in the capital, mostly tended to keep in regular touch with their relatives and friends back home and purveyed gossip and information about what was going on in London. Newsworthy events of James's reign, such as the committal of Sir Walter Ralegh, the Gunpowder Plot, the war in the Palatinate, or the death of Prince Henry, are all referred to in the Wynn Papers, for example. From time to time, also, Parliament was summoned and the Welsh constituencies duly sent up their members, who ordinarily received the opinions of their leading constituents beforehand and in due course circulated news and information on their return. A handful of Welsh members, such as Sir William Maurice, irrepressible in his enthusiasm for 'Great Britain', or Sir James Perrot, incorrigibly suspicious of the machinations of recusants, might draw attention to themselves in the Commons; but most of their colleagues were distinguished only by a resounding silence in the deliberations of the House. Politics were still almost entirely a matter of county personalities and issues. The few disputed elections of which we have any record—Cardigan Boroughs in 1604, the furiously fought Caernarfonshire contests of 1620–1, or the Radnorshire election of 1621—were all concerned with local struggles for power and pre-eminence and did not involve any serious issues of high political principle. In Caernarfonshire, John Griffiths of Llŷn headed a faction of western backwoodsmen to wrest the seat from Richard, son and heir of Sir John Wynn, who was incensed by their temerity. In Radnorshire, William Vaughan indicted James Price, member for the shire since 1592, in Star Chamber for intimidation, riot, and illegal hours of polling.

If the political life of James's reign was very much a continuation of the Elizabethan scene, so too was that of the Church. The Established Church, still thoroughly Calvinist in its theology, found a staunch and supportive ally in the King, who regarded it as one of the stoutest buttresses of his monarchical authority. Anglicanism, having been installed as the official creed of the populace since 1559, had by this time won a secure place in the affections of the people. Its liturgy, worship, and instruction, conducted in Welsh, had become increasingly familiar as the years passed by. They were considerably strengthened by a number of new translations of key works. In 1606, Edward James, a Glamorgan cleric inspired by William Morgan, published his admirable Welsh version of the Book of Homilies, which must have been a godsend to the many non-preaching incumbents of Wales and their congregations. In 1620 came the superb translation of the Authorized Version of the Bible and a new Prayer Book, the work of Bishop Richard Parry and Dr John Davies of Mallwyd, another of Morgan's protégés and the greatest Welsh scholar of the age, if not of all time. Shortly after, in 1621, appeared Edmwnd Prys's immensely popular metrical translation of the Psalms. At regular intervals, in 1607, 1612, 1618, and 1633, were published new editions of the highly esteemed *Llyfr Plygain* [Book of Matins]. Preaching in Welsh was warmly encouraged by Bishop Morgan in St Asaph and Bishop Bayly in Bangor, while, in the diocese of St Davids, Vicar Rhys Prichard's religious precepts expressed in homely, memorizable verse found a wide and willing audience. In each of the dioceses the number of graduate clergy continued to increase steadily.

For all that, the familiar earlier weaknesses continued to be evident. James was not as careful as Elizabeth had been to appoint Welshmen as bishops of the two southern sees, and English bishops like Francis Godwin of Llandaff, though admirable men, usually introduced a number of other strangers separated from most of their parishioners by the gulf of language. One or two of those chosen as bishops, notably Theophilus Field, who served at Llandaff and St Davids, were distinctly inferior in calibre. Even the Carmarthenshire man, Lewis Bayly, author of the universally admired *Practice of Piety*, was not entirely successful in his dealings with the laity of his diocese of Bangor. Impoverishment of the Church, on account of lay impropriations, continued to be general; and this led, in turn, to the customary abuses of pluralism and non-residence on the part of higher and lower clergy. Though preachers were more numerous than they had been, there continued to be far too few of them. The earnest Bishop Bayly's report of 1623 deplored the scarcity of preachers and the general dereliction of pastoral duties such as christening infants, visiting the sick, and even burying the dead. The clergy were also censured for celebrating clandestine marriages, condoning bigamy and adultery, and conniving at the abduction of heiresses. Moralists like Vicar Prichard and Robert Llwyd, vicar of Chirk, were deeply distressed at the universal tendency to frequent alehouses and indulge in Sunday games, dancing, and ballad-singing, all at the expense of church services. Superstitious practices, such as crossing one's self, or invoking the aid of the saints or the virtues of holy wells, and resorting to sorcerers, conjurors, or 'wise men', were still as widely practised as ever.

As for the recusants, initial hopes that James would favour Catholic aspirations were still-born; but though he was not as well disposed towards them as they had at first expected him to be, he was rather less harsh in his treatment of them than the Elizabethan regime had been. They remained a small, suspected, embattled minority; but they clung tenaciously to their faith and their numbers actually grew during his reign. In Flintshire, for example, the number of recusants reported to Great Sessions increased from 99 in 1606 to 153 in 1624, though part of the increase in numbers may be due to heightened vigilance on the part of the reporting authorities. The main centres of Catholic strength continued to be the counties of Flint and Denbigh in the north, and Monmouthshire and Glamorgan in the south.

The reputation of St Winifred's Well for sanctity and healing made it the most powerful drawing-card in north Wales—for many Catholics from outside as well as inside Wales; and they were sufficiently numerous and daring there to compel Bishop William Morgan to abandon Anglican services in the ruined well chapel. Monmouthshire, where the faithful enjoyed the protection of the earl of Worcester and the Morgans of Llantarnam, was their most formidable Welsh stronghold. The county was described by Lord Eure, President of the Council in the Marches, as being 'wholly divided almost into factions by reason of the number of those who, being addicted and misled with Popery, are so powerful . . . that few causes arise in the shire which is not a question betwixt the Protestant and the recusant'.[9] Strongly as Catholics continued to defend their position, an essential source of their former power was draining away, as fewer young men came forward to enter the priesthood. Whereas in Llandaff, strongest centre of Catholicism among Welsh dioceses, sixteen young men had become priests during Elizabeth's reign, only four did between 1603 and 1642. Without the continuing commitment of young priests, recusancy must necessarily wither.

Economic conditions during most of the Jacobean era were favourable. The harvests of its opening years were plentiful; indeed, between 1603 and 1620 only three poor harvests were recorded—in 1603, 1613, and 1617. As a result, food prices in England and Wales generally were more stable and in 1620 were only 10 per cent above what they had been in 1600. The long years of peace between 1604 and 1625 further helped the economy considerably by easing the onerous demands made during Elizabeth's last years for war-supplies. In the closing years of James's reign after 1620, however, the situation undoubtedly deteriorated sharply. During 1620–2 there was a severe slump in the cloth-making industry; and it was followed by the disastrous harvests of 1622 and 1623, which led to grave food-deficiencies and even crises of subsistence in parts of Wales. All these untoward events were occurring at a time when the situation in Europe, following the outbreak of the Thirty Years War in 1618, was becoming much more troubled and leading to an imminent risk of war. In such circumstances, it was not to be wondered at that relations between King and Parliament should be somewhat fraught during its sessions of 1621 and 1624, or that financial grievances relating to monopolies should be at the forefront of discussion as they had been in Elizabeth's last parliaments. Three such issues particularly affected Wales. The monopoly of sales of Welsh cloth enjoyed by Shrewsbury Drapers was quashed by Parliament in 1624, but this proved to be a hollow triumph for free trade since the Shrewsbury men were too powerful to be ousted. Nor did better success

---

[9] PRO SP16/48/163.

attend a similar effort to break the monopoly of Welsh butter resting in the hands of a syndicate of English speculators. As for the third issue, the import of Irish cattle, the Welsh were in this instance keen to restrict freedom of imports in order to protect their own near-monopoly interests, though a bill for the purpose failed to reach the statute book. Yet these and other frictions were weathered by James with little difficulty and, at the end of his reign, he was still on good terms with his subjects. If there were clouds on the horizon they were as yet little bigger than a man's hand and contemporaries would scarcely have discerned in them any portents of a major storm.

THE REIGN OF CHARLES I

Charles was patently different from his father in temperament and in his approach to the tasks of kingship. To the end, James, even when sick and ageing, showed considerably more political nous and judgement when dealing with Parliament than his son was ever to possess, and he exercised a more sensitive control of the art of knowing when to compromise and make concessions than Charles would reveal. The son theorized far less about the nature of monarchy than the father, but in practice was much more pig-headed in his determination to give effect to his prerogative and far more likely to rub up the wrong way the parliamentary representatives of the political nation. Unlike James he had moved away from Calvinism and was deeply and, from the point of view of many of his subjects, dangerously committed to an Arminian position. This, coupled with his marriage to an unconcealedly Catholic queen, would lead to profound and growing unease concerning what his ultimate aims in religion were. Even before James's death, Charles had come completely under Buckingham's domination and remained under the favourite's spell until the latter's assassination in 1628. The pair found themselves in an unenviable situation, faced with a belligerent Spain and soon by a hostile France as well; a diplomatic and military imbroglio not made any easier by their own inept handling of it. In a crisis calling for the utmost unity between King and Parliament, relations between them soon became severely strained.

Charles's first demands in Wales for men and money to meet the challenge of the Catholic powers were readily met. Fears of the threat of invasion by Spain and France elicited a willing enough response, though there were criticisms of Buckingham's policies. But early enthusiasm for the war soon began to evaporate and there was growing reluctance in a number of Welsh counties to raise the men, money, and ships required of them (see pp. 373–4). Much of the opposition in Parliament was inspired by the earl of Pembroke, who found agents in men like Robert Mansel and Charles Price of Pilleth eager enough to voice it in the Commons. There were mounting rumblings of discontent at the prospect of measures being taken without parliamentary sanction. Yet there were also unmistakable signs that the Welsh gentry were intensely sensitive to any threat to the Welsh coastline from the feared and hated Catholic powers—the *dynion duon* [black men] of Spain and the unpopular Irish—and were still prepared to respond to the Crown when it found itself in a crisis situation.

From 1629 to 1640 Charles was engaged in his period of personal rule. But too much can easily be made of this phenomenon. It was not unusual for a ruler to allow many years to pass without summoning a parliament, which public opinion accepted should only be called when a king found himself in exceptionally dire need of money or some other comparable emergency. Neither should it be supposed that these eleven years constituted a period of especially strong authoritarian rule: Charles had neither the personality nor the personnel for such a regimen. To some extent, indeed, Wales benefited from the personal rule, in so far as the country was free from musters for military service in Europe or Ireland, and also because the Welsh coast was singled out for heightened attention in an effort to reduce the operations of pirates. But in general this was a decade of stringencies. There were a number of bad harvests, causing high food prices and industrial depression and unemployment. Plague, too, was rampant in mid-Wales in 1636–7 and south Wales during 1639. These misfortunes forced Charles's government to concentrate on the problems of poverty, distress, famine, and disorder. In January 1631 the Privy Council issued its Book of Orders to the magistrates in every county in an effort to enforce the working of the poor law, the apprenticing of children, control of food supplies and prices, and other measures to relieve poverty as well as the punishment of offenders against the penal statutes. Municipal records show that brisk attempts were made in towns like Swansea and Haverfordwest to carry out these orders. But the truth is that not nearly enough investigation has so far been undertaken into the condition of the mass of the population at this time and we know far too little as yet to be able to generalize with confidence about the reactions of the Welsh shires to the years of personal rule.

Of the response of Wales to the exaction of Ship Money, Charles's main device for raising money in the 1630s, a good deal more is known. In origin, Ship Money was an ancient means of calling upon coastal towns to provide ships, or a cash equivalent, to defend the country in times of danger. From 1634 onwards, the King organized its collection on a county basis and it soon became clear that he intended to demand it every year, even though the country was at peace. Some Welshmen, like David Jenkins of Hensol, later to be a dyed-in-the-wool Royalist during the Civil Wars, objected in principle to the dubious legality of such impositions. But the first demand in 1634 was for the relatively modest sum of £2,000 for

Wales, which met with little opposition. It was the increase to £10,500 in 1636 and the annual regularity of the levy which provoked much greater resentment. The sheriff of Cardiganshire reported in 1637 that he had been unable to raise a penny, and his colleague in Pembrokeshire could not collect arrears 'in respect of men's poverty and not otherwise'.[10] As time went on, the tax became more and more unpopular and evoked resistance on constitutional grounds, as well as because of widespread poverty. This reached a pitch with the sixth and last levy which coincided with the calling-up of a large military force to fight the Scots Covenanters. Even so, reluctance to pay Ship Money was less pronounced in Wales than in most parts of the realm; and four Welsh counties—Anglesey, Glamorgan, Monmouthshire, and Radnorshire—were among the nine counties throughout the kingdom that paid the highest proportion of Ship Money.

Another reason for the exacerbation of ill-feeling between the King and his subjects—possibly, indeed, the most serious of all—was his support for Arminian opinion and sentiment in the Church. Soon after his accession, Charles and Buckingham openly revealed their encouragement of these doctrines, so intensely disliked and morbidly suspected of being designed to lead the English church back to the Roman fold. Between 1625 and 1629 Arminianism became firmly entrenched at court and its influence became no less apparent in the choice of bishops. William Laud himself, principal ecclesiastical champion of the tendency, had been bishop of St Davids from 1621 to 1627, though his concerns elsewhere led to his having little impact there. His friend and protégé, the Scot William Murray, was appointed bishop of Llandaff in 1627 and was succeeded there in 1639 by a still more devoted admirer of Laud, Morgan Owen. Another staunch Laudian, John Owen, had already been appointed to St Asaph in 1629, while the most loyal adherent of all, Roger Manwaring, already accused by John Pym in the House of Commons of endeavouring 'to destroy the King and Kingdom by his divinity',[11] went to St Davids in 1635. All these bishops were anxious to implement, within the limits of their powers, Arminian principles for improving the appearance of churches, restoring seemliness, dignity, and the 'beauty of holiness' to the services, and generally emphasizing the sacerdotal aspects of the Church and priesthood. It is not easy to tell how much effect their efforts had in the parishes nor how favourably they were received. But it may be more than a coincidence that Owen in St Asaph, Manwaring in St Davids, and William Murray in Llandaff, in particular, were faced with an increase in the number of recusants on the one hand, and on the other with the rise of Puritan separatists, few in number but overt, determined, and articulate.

There seems to have been something of an upsurge in recusant numbers

[10] CSP Dom., Chas. I, 366, 45.
[11] E. Yardley, Menevia Sacra (Arch. Camb. Supplement, 1927), p. 110.

during Charles's reign. The second Stuart ruler, a tolerant man, had a wife and a number of influential courtiers who were Roman Catholics. During his eleven years of personal rule, although he himself gave no sign of going over to the Roman Church, when he was freed from the necessity of having to placate a Puritanly minded lower House, something of the rigour may have gone out of the prosecution of recusants. The state papers of 1629 record that a concourse of some 1,400 to 1,600 devotees assembled at St Winifred's Well. Among them were two leading members of the nobility, Lord William Howard and the earl of Shrewsbury, together with a number of squires from the Wirral and 'divers others knights, ladies, gentlemen and gentlewomen of divers countries'.[12] In 1636 the chief justice of Chester gave the Privy Council a detailed account of the steps he had taken to try to put a stop to these pilgrimages: ensuring that justices of the peace closed down taverns where the recusants stayed; placing tavern-keepers under bonds to give an account of all who stayed with them; and keeping close watch every spring and summer when they were likely to congregate. There was some evidence of a small increase in Catholic numbers too. Glamorgan rose from an average of about twenty-five to forty-eight (1629) and forty-six (1636) and Carmarthenshire to nineteen in 1637. This small but perceptible rise in Catholic numbers and activities, together with the proclivities of King and Queen and some of their courtiers, gave rise to mounting opposition, some of which found expression in more aggressive Puritan opinions.

Puritanism had not made much headway in Wales during the sixteenth and early seventeenth centuries; not surprisingly, in view of the heavy weather being made by the Reformation in general. A few traces can be discerned of a moderate Puritanism which emerged in the shape of determined Protestant convictions, such as greater concern for preaching the Word or an emphasis on personal sanctity of life, and a hearty contempt for popery in all its forms. Welsh MPs, like the lawyer Sir Eubule Thelwall or the fiery Sir James Perrot, eloquently gave tongue to their strong anti-Catholic prejudices in the Commons. Some of the larger towns—Wrexham, where Sir William Meredith as early as 1603 had left £30 in his will for the purpose, Swansea, and Haverfordwest—paid for sermons delivered by Puritan or quasi-Puritan 'lecturers', who were invited to edify the townspeople on Sundays at times other than the usual service hours; and their citizens also began to show a taste for giving their children Old Testament names which had not been known previously. Preachers like the golden-voiced Robert Powell, vicar of Cadoxton-juxta-Neath from 1620 to c. 1640, of whom Vicar Prichard said he knew 'no church minister who had such care and regard to the interest of Christ', exercised considerable

---

[12] H. Foley, *Records of the English Province of the Society of Jesus* (London, 1827–9), IV, 534–5.

influence. Prichard himself, although throughout his life a devoted member of the Anglican Church, betrayed conspicuous sympathy with orthodox Church Puritanism. Similar tendencies are readily observable in a crop of prose works that were published in the early 1630s: the first cheap Welsh Bible, *Y Beibl Bach* of 1630, priced five shillings; Robert Llwyd's *Llwybr Hyffordd* (1630), a translation of Dent's *Plain Pathway to Heaven*; Rowland Vaughan's translation of *The Practice of Piety*, *Yr Ymarfer o Dduwioldeb* (1630); John Davies's *Llyfr y Resolusion* (1632); and the more unmistakably Puritan *Car-wr y Cymru* (1630 and 1631) of Oliver Thomas. All these publications may have emerged partly, at least, in answer to the growing Arminian tendencies of the time. Much of the cost of publishing them was borne by two wealthy merchants of Welsh origin, Thomas Myddelton and Rowland Heylin, both of whom had come under strong Puritan influence.

More positively linked to the reaction against Arminianism, however, was the rise in the 1630s of a more radical Puritanism, taken eventually to the point of open separation. A noticeable feature of this kind of Puritanism was that it was in those parts of Wales like the north-eastern border around Wrexham and Flintshire, or along the south Wales sea-coast, and above all in Monmouthshire that it showed itself. These were not only the areas that were nearest to England and most open to extraneous influences, but were also the ones in which Catholic recusancy was strongest, best-organized, most articulate, and most liable to evoke an equally positive and forthright Puritan response. The apostle of all the early Welsh Puritans of this sort was William Wroth, a Monmouthshire man, made rector of Llanfaches in that county in 1617, at James I's presentation. For nearly twenty years afterwards, by ardent preaching and personal holiness, he converted many from what a Puritan record described as 'their sinful courses in the world'.[13] Among his early associates were William Erbury of Cardiff and Walter Cradock of Monmouthshire. Not until 1634 did they run into serious difficulty with their diocesan. In that year Charles, under Laud's inspiration, issued instructions to every bishop to present an annual report to his metropolitan. Bishop Murray of Llandaff, in his reply of 1635, reported that Wroth was 'leading away many simple people' and that Erbury and Cradock had 'preached very schismatically and dangerously to the people'.[14] Cradock was now suspended and departed to Wrexham. There, he became curate to Robert Lloyd and enjoyed an exceptional reputation as a preacher for his 'wonderful faculty of coming down and bringing with him the things of God to the meanest of his auditors'.[15] But he spent only a year at Wrexham

---

[13] *DWB*, s.n. 'Wroth'.
[14] *The Works of . . . Archbishop William Laud* (Oxford, 1853), v, ii, 321, 329.
[15] G. F. Nuttall, *The Welsh Saints, 1640–1660* (Cardiff, 1957), pp. 21–2.

before leaving for the Puritan household of the Harleys at Brampton Bryan, where he was joined by his two brilliant young converts, Morgan Llwyd, greatest of all Welsh Puritan authors, and Vavasor Powell, later to be one of their most outstanding evangelists. In the mean time, articles had also been preferred against Wroth and Erbury in the Court of High Commission.

Further west, in that part of Glamorgan which lay within the diocese of St Davids, Bishop Manwaring reported that he had found it necessary to condemn Marmaduke Matthews, vicar of Penmaen, for 'preaching against the keeping of all holy days with divers other, as fond, of profane opinions'.[16] He, too, was threatened with proceedings in the Court of High Commission, but he emigrated in 1638 to New England, where he became a Puritan pastor. In the same year Erbury was forced to resign his Cardiff living, though he continued to live in the town, preaching to those who sympathized with him. Wroth is also said to have resigned his living; but there is no trace of this in the contemporary Institution Books. In November of the following year 1639, however, Wroth founded at Llanfaches the first Independent Church in Wales, where Cradock joined him as his assistant. This church at Llanfaches had almost certainly not broken irretrievably with the Church of England. Probably, like the churches of New England, it regarded itself as 'separated from the world, not the saints'. Nevertheless, it seemed to the hard core of devoted Puritans to be 'like Antioch', 'the mother church in that Gentile country' of south Wales.[17] It was to be joined by two similar churches before the outbreak of the Civil War—the one founded at Cardiff in 1642, with Erbury as its minister, and the other established in the Swansea area by Ambrose Mostyn, appointed lecturer in the Gower parish of Pennard by a committee set up by the Long Parliament to improve the state of religion. But this small group of hard-line Puritans were no more than an uninfluential handful when the Civil War broke out. Wales was no place for such convinced upholders of these radical religious ideals, who, almost to a man, fled to more congenial havens in England, leaving behind them the mass of their fellow-countrymen unmoved by sympathy for or understanding of their cause.

Throughout the years of personal rule, it had been essential for Charles to avoid the danger of warfare. At the first sign of any major emergency necessitating the summons of Parliament, much of the latent opposition to him was bound to burst into the open. The portents of such a crisis emerged in 1637–8 in Scotland, where Charles, because of his own inexperience of Scottish affairs, reinforced by his unbending and dogmatic approach, insisted upon trying to enforce a new prayer book on the totally

[16] *Laud's Works*, v, ii, 244–5.
[17] Thomas Richards, *A History of the Puritan Movement in Wales* (London, 1928), p. 28.

resistant subjects of his northern kingdom. The outcome was the Scottish National Covenant and the adoption of a rebellious posture on its part. In raising an army to suppress these rebels, Charles at first sought to levy 700 men from Wales; but in 1639 that figure was nearly doubled, only to fall back again to 600 when it was found that the Exchequer could not meet the expense of the larger force. While there was no actual fighting during the First Bishops' War, the military requirements of the Second Bishops' War were more exacting, and Wales was this time required to find 2,000 infantry—nearly twice as many as the most ambitious plan for 1639 and three times as many as were actually sent.

While preparations to raise these troops were proceeding, in July 1640 there occurred an episode which occasioned grave misgivings. The King wrote to the earl of Bridgwater as President of the Council in the Marches instructing him to charge the deputy-lieutenants of south Wales to place themselves at the disposal of the papist earl of Worcester, who had been entrusted with some unspecified 'secret service'. At the same time, Charles also directed the earl of Pembroke to require all his friends and tenants to obey Worcester's commands. The inference drawn by many was that the kingdom which Charles had it in mind to crush with a papist force under the command of Strafford and Worcester was England, not Scotland. By September the King's situation was so desperate that he summoned all the trained bands to the north. While they were away, Bridgwater was cast into profound gloom about the state of Wales, fearing that evil spirits had walked abroad there during the past year and that, in the absence of the trained bands, 'mischief' was bound to occur. Later, a Scots minister was to write to his brethren to inform them of the danger so narrowly averted that 'a combination of the Papists with Strafford's Irish army' was 'to have landed, not in Scotland, but in Wales, where the earl of Worcester, a firm head of the Popish faction, had commission to receive them'.[18] There was also supposed to have been an extension of their 'plot' to mid and north Wales, where Sir Percy Herbert of Montgomery was credited with making use of his powers as deputy-lieutenant to secure papist control of county magazine, bench, and granary.

By the autumn of 1640, with the collapse of the Scottish campaign, Charles was again obliged to summon Parliament. Already, earlier in the year, he had had to call the abortive Short Parliament; now, in November, the famous Long Parliament was to hold its first session. It was a Parliament in which most of the Lords and Commons were at first agreed in their opposition to the King. A number of Welsh members themselves initially joined in the chorus of criticism, especially in relation to the deeds of the two Laudian bishops, Roger Manwaring and Morgan Owen, and

18 Dodd, *Trans. Cymmr.*, 1948, p. 45.

recusants like the earl of Worcester and the Montgomeryshire Herberts. Most of all they opposed the alleged invasion plan in which Strafford and Worcester were supposed to be involved. Yet moves for the attainder of Strafford found a number of Welsh members to be luke-warm, even opposed, in their attitude. The truth was that, during 1641–2, the House, which had at the outset seemed so nearly united, was now dividing into two factions, as mutual suspicions deepened on both sides, leaving many teetering nervously between them. The King, who bitterly regretted yielding up Strafford to his enemies, and those who supported him were convinced that the hard-liners among the parliamentary leaders were bent on depriving him of some of the essential sinews of his sovereignty. His opponents, on the other hand, wanted to ensure the permanence of the constitutional gains they had already made since 1640 and were genuinely fearful for their own lives.

Even the outbreak of the Irish Rebellion in October 1641, and the panic it aroused concerning Anglesey and Milford Haven, were not enough to prevent the gradual coalescing of opinion in Wales behind the King during the spring and summer of 1642. The crux of the dispute was the army needed to put down the Irish rebels. In order to secure guarantees that this force would not be used against itself, Parliament insisted that command of the militia should be entrusted to its own nominees. Charles, for his part, regarded the choice of lords lieutenant as an essential attribute of his royal prerogative and refused to give in over the issue. The crunch came when Parliament proceeded to enforce its Militia Ordinance in the shires through its approved representatives. In most of the Welsh counties the authority of Parliament and its nominees was resisted, and gentlemen loyal to the King began to raise men and money on his behalf. Even before Charles had actually raised his standard, the leading gentry of Denbighshire and Flintshire had declared against the Ordinance and for the King. Anglesey and Caernarfonshire followed suit; down in south-east Wales the influence of the earl of Worcester was able to carry all before it; while in Carmarthenshire, the county's parliamentary lord lieutenant, the earl of Carbery, ironically enough, led his own shire and Cardiganshire and Pembrokeshire into the royal camp. The lines of battle were being drawn, and it was plainly apparent that most of Wales would throw its weight behind Charles I. It remains only to examine why most of Wales joined the royalist cause.

When discussing the causes of the Civil War, historians have tended to disagree about the relative importance of the long- and short-term reasons for it. There have been those who argue that the war was primarily the outcome of long-term trends: the change, over a hundred to a hundred and fifty years, in the balance of economic and social power, in favour of the gentry and merchant groups at the expense of the Crown and the aristocracy. Others have contended that the decisive causes are to be found in those short-term conflicts over constitutional, religious, and economic issues which emerged between the King and his subjects between 1624 and 1640. This division of opinion is not new but goes back to the seventeenth century. Observers like James Harington and Richard Baxter argued in favour of a long-term explanation. Baxter's analysis of a broad division between the King's supporters and those of Parliament remains very persuasive. He maintained that most of the knights and gentlemen in the counties, the majority of their tenants, and what he called the 'rabble' were for the King; while the smaller part of the gentry and most of the tradesmen, freeholders, and 'the middle sort of men', especially in the towns and shires which depended on cloth-making and other manufactures, were for Parliament. But another highly experienced and perceptive observer, Edward Hyde, earl of Clarendon, was convinced that there was no need to look beyond the events of Charles's reign for the fatal sources of division. The difference between the two kinds of explanation may not in fact be as great as it might at first appear to be. Though it was undoubtedly the dissensions of Charles's reign which precipitated the crisis which, had he been a wiser and more capable ruler, might have been averted altogether, it was the longer-term developments, and the interests thereby created, which in large measure determined the stand that men ultimately took. But it is equally important to remember that the decision on which side to fight, or whether to fight at all, was also shaped by that pressure of local interests and the influence of personalities which loomed so large in seventeenth-century politics.

As far as Wales was concerned there were good reasons why the Parliamentary cause should be relatively weak. The country was remote and the majority of its population insulated by the barriers of language from those constitutional and religious disagreements which convulsed the southern and eastern counties of England. Furthermore, its trading and manufacturing interests and its merchants and commercial groups were feeble and ill-developed in comparison with those of England; nor had the immensely powerful London commercial concerns, so dominant in the south-east, any great interest or influence in Wales. The intense Puritan convictions frequently associated with merchants and gentry engaged in those great commercial enterprises had made little impact in Wales. So shallowly rooted were they and so tender their growth that most leading Welsh Puritans had fled precipitately when war broke out. Yet it was the depth and fervour of Puritan principles, and the detestation that they bred of Arminianism, which in England gave many the steely resolution to resort to what they believed to be a holy war against the King. Not that it was Arminian beliefs that kept Wales loyal to Charles; they had had as little impact there as Puritanism, possibly even less.

On the other hand, there were many considerations which explained Welsh loyalty to the Crown when the moment of decision came. It had taken the Welsh gentry possessing decisive power in the counties a long, uphill struggle to secure their position of supremacy. For much of the century before the Act of Union they had been striving for, or exercising *de facto*, administrative authority and economic power locally. Their rule had been given statutory recognition by King and Parliament in 1536–43 and they had continued to fortify it ever since. Their now unchallenged power, influence, and prosperity in their own countryside were intimately associated in their minds with being *en rapport* with the existing order. Neither that nor the loyalty that they felt for a dynasty descended from the 'Welsh' Tudors had prevented them from criticizing on constitutional and financial grounds what the King had been doing in the 1630s, and their representatives had joined in the widespread chorus of condemnation in the early stages of the Long Parliament. But, in the last resort, most of them saw a threat to Charles's sovereignty as a threat to their own local supremacy. They now cherished a profound respect for the common law and Parliament as guaranteeing their own jurisdiction; witness the certainty of the men of Flintshire, for example, that they were 'thoroughly persuaded of the sincerity and constancy' of Charles's resolution to maintain the laws of the land, the privileges of Parliament, and the liberties of the subject. Most of them were no less convinced of the King's steadfastness as a defender of 'the true Protestant religion', as embodied in the Anglican Church, which upheld the authority delegated to him by God to rule his subjects and the latter's own right to rule their tenantry.[19] That church had by this time struck deep roots in their affection and respect by the dignified comeliness of its services. As Huw Morus had it:

> Ti a fuost gyfannedd, yn cynnal trefn santedd,
> Ac athro'r gwirionedd, cysonedd i sain.[20]

[Thou wast an habitation, upholding holy order; and teacher of the truth, constant in its message.]

They approved strongly of its erastian organization, which gave them a secure hold over its local destinies, buttressing their jurisdiction, and offering their younger sons and nephews an avenue of promotion. That minority among them still loyal to the Roman faith naturally saw in a Puritanly inspired Parliament and its adherents their most fanatical opponents; and the leading recusant figure, the earl of Worcester, was, not surprisingly, to be the King's stoutest as well as his richest supporter.

---

[19] J. R. Phillips, *Memoirs of the Civil Wars in Wales* (2 vols. London, 1874), II, 1–3.
[20] Thomas, *Wales 1485–1660*, p. 200.

Of course, royalist support, though in a clear majority, was not and could not be monolithic. In some counties there were pockets of Parliamentary adherents: Pembrokeshire, with Rowland Laugharne, John Poyer, Rice Powell, and Hugh Owen; and Denbighshire, with Thomas and William Myddelton, the Thelwalls, and Sir John Trevor, above all the rest. But in most counties there were at least a handful of determined Parliamentarians. Some were moved by Puritan convictions, some by local feuds and rivalries, a few were soldiers of fortune, and others were lesser landowners with an eye for the main chance. Not a few were swayed by the influence of powerful outside forces or individuals—the Myddeltons by their close connection with the City of London, the Pembrokeshire men by the influence of the third earl of Essex.

Yet it would be wrong not to acknowledge the deep reluctance with which many took up arms on both sides, or never took them up seriously at all. They were not unaware of the rapine, pillage, and devastation inflicted upon much of Europe in the course of the Thirty Years War, which had raged for a quarter of a century since 1618. As the Civil War in England and Wales proceeded they would become more and more convinced of its appalling effects, whereby 'the whole kingdom is, and shall be yet more, by the continuance thereof, unspeakably impoverished and plunged into all kinds of miseries',[21] as Griffith Williams, bishop of Ossory, lamented. From the beginning there was a deep-seated vein of neutralism, a desire to opt out or at least to limit the disastrous consequences as far as possible. A plea from the gentry of the south-west that the holding of Pembrokeshire by Parliamentary forces was objectionable, because it was 'an encouragement to invite foreign and rebellious forces to enter the said counties and ruin the same',[22] would have found increasing support in other Welsh counties as the conflict intensified. The ruling classes had no illusions that all the gains from which they and their kind had chiefly profited over the previous century were being placed in jeopardy. As for the mass of small farmers, labourers, and poor, their already unenviable lot was being even more drastically downgraded. Whatever remained of the prosperity of the years down to 1620 was fast being swallowed up in the maelstrom of internecine warfare. The wheel had come nearly full circle: Wales was being dragged back into the strife, bloodshed, and devastation of those disasters of the early fifteenth century with which we began.

[21] Thomas, *Wales 1485–1660*, p. 202.
[22] Phillips, *Civil Wars*, II, 120.

BIBLIOGRAPHY

THE list of sources given below should not be regarded as constituting anything like a comprehensive bibliography. To include all the material available on British history for the period, not to mention European history, would be quite impracticable. Attention has therefore been given primarily to items of specifically Welsh interest, though the final choice has had to mean the exclusion of a number of those. The most useful general bibliographies are E. B. Graves (ed.), *A Bibliography of English History to 1485* Oxford, (1975); C. Read (ed.), *Bibliography of British History: The Tudor Period, 1485–1603* (Oxford, 1959); M. F. Keeler (ed.), *Bibliography of British History: The Stuart Period, 1603–1714* (Oxford, 1970); D. J. Guth, *Late-Medieval England, 1377–1485* (Cambridge, 1976); M. Levine, *Tudor England, 1485–1603* (Cambridge, 1968); and J. S. Morrill, *Seventeenth-century Britain, 1603–1714* (Folkestone, 1980). The best check-list of current publications is the Royal Historical Society's *Annual Bibliography of British and Irish History* (London, 1975–). E. C. L. Mullins, *Texts and Calendars: An Analytical Guide* (London, 1958) is useful for serial publications.

The *Bibliography of the History of Wales* (Cardiff, 1962), with supplements in *BBCS*, XX (1963), XXII (1966), XXIII (1969), and XXIV (1972), is now out of date but still valuable. It has been replaced by P. H. Jones, *A Bibliography of the History of Wales* (Cardiff, 1989). Useful lists of current publications appear regularly in *Arch. Camb., Studia Celtica*, and *WHR*. The bibliographies in the relevant sections of *Bibliotheca Celtica* (Aberystwyth, 1909– ; new series, 1954–) should also be consulted. A helpful short guide to the sources of Welsh medieval history is R. I. Jack, *Medieval Wales* (London, 1972). A valuable bibliography on Welsh literary history is that by T. Parry and M. Morgan (eds.), *Llyfryddiaeth Llenyddiaeth Gymraeg* (Cardiff, 1976), with a supplement by G. O. Watts, *BBCS*, XXX (1982). A. E. Davis, *Welsh Language and Welsh Dissertations* (Cardiff, 1973) lists unpublished thesis material up to 1971. Lists of theses of historical interest have been contributed by D. L. Jones to *WHR* in June 1971, June 1974, June 1976, and June 1986.

The sections in the following bibliography have been deliberately restricted to a few broad categories. Many of the books listed might have been assigned to more than one section but have been included in the one deemed most appropriate.

A. MANUSCRIPT SOURCES

The three main manuscript repositories are the Public Record Office, the British Library, and the National Library of Wales.

The best introduction to the collections at the Public Record Office is M. S. Giuseppi, *Guide to the Contents of the Public Record Office* (2 vols. London, 1963). More detailed information is given in *Public Record Office Lists and Indexes* (55 vols.

London, 1892–1936). This series has been vastly enlarged by the publications of the List and Index Society (London, 1965–). See also H. Owen, *A Catalogue of Public Records relating to Pembrokeshire* (London, 1911–18). The collections at the Public Record Office are so vast and widely ranging that it would be impossible to list even the most important here; but some of the collections found most helpful in the writing of this volume were:

Chancery: Judicial Proceedings (C 1)
Duchy of Lancaster Records: Miscellaneous Books
Exchequer: Judicial Proceedings (E 112)
Exchequer: Proceedings of the Court of Augmentations (E 321)
Land Registry Records (LR 6)
Special Collections: Ministers Accounts (SC 6)
Star Chamber Proceedings (STAC 1–STAC 9)
State Papers Domestic (SP 1–SP 16)

A guide to the material of Welsh interest among the older manuscript collections of the British Library (formerly British Museum Library) will be found in E. Owen, *A Catalogue of the Manuscripts relating to Wales in the British Museum* (4 vols. London, 1900–22). See also the *Catalogue of Additions to Manuscripts in the British Museum* (London, 1843–); and H. Bell, 'The Welsh Manuscripts in the British Museum', *Trans. Cymm.*, 1936.

Very important collections exist in the National Library of Wales, especially manuscripts in the Welsh language. A guide to the basic Welsh-language collections was prepared by J. Gwenogvryn Evans, *Report on Manuscripts in the Welsh Language* (2 vols. in 7 parts. Hist. MSS Commission, 1898–1910). Most of the major collections at the Library are dealt with in catalogues and schedules kept in the Reading Room at Aberystwyth. Additionally, the Library lists its accessions in its Annual Reports and has added at regular intervals to its *Handlist of Manuscripts* (Aberystwyth, 1943–). Many important collections have been described and discussed in *NLWJ*, e.g., E. D. Jones, 'The Brogyntyn Welsh Manuscripts'; *NLWJ*, vi (1950). Among the collections found particularly useful in preparing this volume were the following:

Clenennau Letters and Papers
Great Sessions Records (see also *List of Records of the Principality of Wales* (PRO
    Lists and Indexes, London, 1914)
Llanstephan MSS
Mostyn MSS
Penrice and Margam Original Correspondence
Welsh Church Records
Wynn of Gwydir Papers

There are other important repositories of Welsh manuscripts, mostly situated in Wales. Some of the county record offices have published introductory guides to their collections. e.g., W. G. Baker, *Guide to the Monmouthshire Record Office* (Newport, 1959); M. Elsas, 'The Glamorgan Record Office', *Archives*, iii (1950); A. G. Veysey, *Guide to the Flintshire Record Office* (Flintshire County Council, 1974); and W. O. Williams, *Guide to the Carnarvonshire Record Office*

(Caernarvon, 1952). Annual Reports are also published by all the County Record Offices. Valuable collections are kept at all the following centres:

Cardiff Central Library
Clwyd Record Office (Hawarden)
Dyfed Record Office (Carmarthen)
Glamorgan Record Office (Cardiff)
Gwent Record Office (Newport)
Gwynedd Record Office (Caernarfon)
Oxford (Bodleian Library and Jesus College)
University College of North Wales (Bangor)
University College of Swansea

B. PRINTED SOURCES

Acts of the Privy Council (London, 1890–)
Bacon, F., *The History of the Reign of King Henry VII*, ed. F. L. Levy (New York, 1972)
Barddoniaeth Wiliam Llŷn, ed. J. C. Morrice (Bangor, 1908)
The Breviary of Britayne, trans. T. Twyne (London, 1573)
British Museum Catalogue of Printed Books (London, 1881–)
Calendar of Ancient Petitions relating to Wales, ed. W. Rees (Cardiff, 1975)
Calendar of Deeds and Documents: *Coleman, Crosswood and Hawarden Deeds* (Aberystwyth, 1921–31)
Calendar of Inquisitions Miscellaneous (London, 1916–)
Calendar of Letters relating to North Wales, ed. B. E. Howells (Cardiff, 1967)
Calendar of Papal Letters (London, 1894–)
Calendar of State Papers Domestic (London, 1856–)
    Foreign (London, 1861–)
    Ireland (London, 1860–)
    Spanish (London, 1862–)
    Venetian (London, 1864–)
Calendar of the Caernarvonshire Quarter Sessions Records, I, 1541–58, ed. W. O. Williams (Caernarfon, 1956)
Calendar of the Carew Manuscripts . . . (London, 1867–73)
Calendar of the Close Rolls (London, 1892–)
Calendar of the Patent Rolls (London, 1891–)
Calendar of the Register of the Council in the Marches of Wales, 1569–91, ed. R. Flenley (London, 1916)
Calendar of the Salusbury Correspondence, 1553–c. 1700, ed. W. J. Smith (Cardiff, 1954)
Calendar of the Wynn (of Gwydir) Papers, ed. J. Ballinger (Aberystwyth, 1926)
Camden's Wales (Carmarthen, 1984)
Car-wr y Cymry, ed. J. Ballinger (Cardiff, 1930)
Casgliad o Waith Ieuan Deulwyn, ed. Ifor Williams (Bangor, 1909)
Catalogue of Manuscripts relating to Wales in the British Museum, ed. E. Owen (1 vol. in 4. London, 1900–22)

Catalogue of Star Chamber Proceedings relating to Wales, ed. I ab O. Edwards (Cardiff, 1929)

Chronicon Ade de Usk, ed. E. Maunde Thompson (London, 1904)

Churchyard, T., *The Worthiness of Wales* (London, 1587; repr. 1876)

Clenennau Letters and Papers, ed. T. Jones Pierce (Aberystwyth, 1947)

Clynnog, Morys, *Athravaeth Gristnogawl* (1568; repr. London, 1880)

Collins, A. (ed.), *Letters and Memorials . . . by Sir Henry Sidney*, etc. (London, 1746)

Commynes, P., *Mémoires 1461–83*, ed. M. Jones (London, 1972)

Conran, A., *The Penguin Book of Welsh Verse* (Penguin Books, 1967)

Cywyddau Iolo Goch ac Eraill, ed. H. Lewis *et al.* (Cardiff, 1937)

Davies, Richard, *Funeral Sermon Preached on the Death of the Earl of Essex* (London, 1577), no pagination.

Detholiad o Waith Gruffudd ab Ieuan ap Llywelyn Fychan, ed. J. C. Morrice, (Bangor 1910)

Dodd, A. H., 'A Commendacion of Welshmen', *BBCS*, xix (1960–2), 235–49

Drych Cristianogawl . . . (1586)

Dwnn, Lewys, *Heraldic Visitations of Wales*, ed. S. R. Meyrick (2 vols. Llandovery, 1846)

Early Chancery Proceedings concerning Wales, ed. E. A. Lewis (Cardiff, 1937)

Ellis, H. (ed.), *Original Letters Illustrative of English History . . .* (11 vols. London, 1824–46)

The Episcopal Registers of St. Davids's, 1397–1518, ed. R. F. Issacson (3 vols. London, 1917–20)

Evans, J. X. (ed.), *The Works of Sir Roger Williams* (Oxford, 1972)

Exchequer Proceedings concerning Wales, ed. E. G. Jones (Cardiff, 1939)

Exchequer Proceedings concerning Wales in temp. James I, ed. T. I. J. Jones (Cardiff, 1955)

Fisher, J., *The Cefn Coch Manuscripts* (Bangor, 1899)

Foley, H., *Records of the English Province of the Society of Jesus* (7 vols. London, 1877–9)

Foxe, J., *Acts and Monuments*, ed. S. Catley (London, 1837–41)

Geiriadur Prifysgol Cymru (Cardiff, 1950–)

Gramadegau'r Penceirddiaid, ed. G. J. Williams and E. J. Jones (Cardiff, 1934)

Gwaith Dafydd ab Edmwnd, ed. Thomas Roberts (Bangor, 1914)

[Gwaith] *Dafydd ap Gwilym*, ed. Thomas Parry (Cardiff, 1952)

Gwaith Dafydd Llwyd o Fathafarn, ed. W. L. Richards (Cardiff, 1964)

Gwaith Guto'r Glyn, ed. I. Williams and J. Ll. Williams (Cardiff, 1939)

Gwaith Huw Cae Llwyd ac Eraill, ed. L. Harris (Cardiff, 1953)

Gwaith Hywel Swrdwal a'i Fab Ieuan, ed. J. C. Morrice (Bangor, 1908)

Gwaith Iorwerth Fynglwyd, ed. E. I. Rowlands (Cardiff, 1975)

Gwaith Lewys Glyn Cothi, ed. Gwallter Mechain and Ioan Tegid (2 vols. Oxford, 1837)

Gwaith Lewys Glyn Cothi, ed. E. D. Jones (Cardiff and Aberystwyth, 1953)

Gwaith Lewys Môn, ed. E. I. Rowlands (Cardiff, 1975)

Gwaith Rhys Brydydd a Rhisiart ap Rhys, ed. J. M. Williams and E. I. Rowlands (Cardiff, 1976)

Gwaith Siôn Tudur, ed. E. P. Roberts (2 vols. Bangor, 1978)

Gwaith Tudur Aled, ed. T. G. Jones (2 vols. Cardiff, 1926)

Gwaith Tudur Penllyn . . ., ed. T. Roberts (Cardiff, 1958)

Hall, E., *The Union of the Two Noble and Illustre Famelies York and Lancaster . . .*, ed. H. Ellis (London, 1809)

Hen Gwndidau, Carolau a Chywyddau, ed. L. J. Hopkin-James and T. C. Evans (Bangor, 1910)

Herbert, Lord. *An Autobiography*, ed. S. Lee (London, 1886)

Historical Collections of a Citizen of London in the Fifteenth Century, ed. J. Gairdner (Camden Soc., 1876)

Historical Manuscripts Commision: Reports on Manuscripts in the Welsh Language (London, 1898–1910)

    Salisbury Manuscripts (London, 1883–)

Hughes, G. H. *Hen Ragymadroddion, 1547–1648* (Cardiff, 1951)

Jones, E. G. (ed.), 'History of the Bulkeley Family', *AAST*, 1948

Kennedy, W. P. M. *Elizabethan Episcopal Administration* (Alcuin Club, 1925)

Kyffin, Maurice, *Deffynniad Ffydd Eglwys Loegr*, ed. W. P. Williams (Cardiff, 1908)

Laud, William, *Works* (Oxford, 1853)

Leland's Itinerary in Wales, ed. L. T. Smith (London, 1906)

Letters and Memorials of Cardinal Allen, ed. T. F. Knox (London, 1906)

Letters and Papers, Foreign and Domestic, of the Reign of Henry VIII . . ., ed. J. S. Brewer, J. Gairdner, and R. H. Brodie (23 vols. London, 1862–1932)

Letters and Papers Illustrative of the Reigns of Richard III and Henry VII, ed. J. Gairdner (2 vols. London, 1861–3)

Lewis, E. A., *The Welsh Port Books, 1558–1603* (London, 1927)

Lewys, Huw, *Perl Mewn Adfyd*, ed. W. J. Gruffydd (Cardiff, 1929)

Lewys Glyn Cothi (Detholiad), ed. E. D. Jones (Cardiff, 1984)

Lloyd Jenkins, D., *Cerddi Rhydd Cynnar* (Llandysul, 1931)

Mathew, D., 'Some Elizabethan Documents', *BBCS*, VI (1931–3)

The Merioneth Subsidy Roll, 1292–3, ed. K. Williams Jones (Cardiff, 1976)

Merrick, Rice, *A Booke of Glamorganshire Antiquities*, ed. B. Ll. James (Cardiff, 1984)

Myers, A. R., *English Historical Documents, 1327–1485* (London, 1969)

L'Œuvre poétique de Gutun Owain, ed. E. Bachellery (2 vols. Paris, 1950–1)

Owen, George, *Description of Pembrokeshire* (3 vols. London, 1906)

—— *A Taylor's Cussion*, ed. E. M. Pritchard (London, 1906)

Owen, H. (ed.), 'The Diary of Bulkeley of Dronwy, 1630–36', *AAST*, 1937

The Oxford Book of Welsh Verse, ed. T. Parry (London, 1962)

The Oxford Book of Welsh Verse in English, ed. G. Jones (London, 1977)

Paston Letters, ed. J. Gairdner (3 vols. London, 1872)

Pembrokeshire Life, 1572–1842, ed. B. E. Howells and K. A. Howells (Pembs. Record Soc., 1872)

Penry, John, *Three Treatises concerning Wales*, ed. D. Williams (Cardiff, 1960)

Pollard, A. F. *The Reign of Henry VII from Contemporary Sources* (3 vols. London, 1913–14)

Polydore Vergil, *Three Books of Polydore Vergil History . . .*, ed. H. Ellis (Camden Soc., 1844)

Powel, D. *The Historie of Cambria* (London, 1584)

Prichard, Rees, *Canwyll y Cymru*, ed. S. Hughes (London, 1672)

Proceedings and Ordinances of the Privy Council of England, ed. H. Nicolas (7 vols. London, 1834–7)

Pryce, A. I., *The Diocese of Bangor in the Sixteenth Century* (Bangor, 1923)

Pugh, T. B., *The Marcher Lordships of South Wales, 1415–1536* (Cardiff, 1963)

Records of the County Borough of Cardiff, ed. J. H. Matthews (6 vols. Cardiff, 1898–1911)

Records of the Court of Augmentations relating to Wales and Monmouthshire, ed. E. A. Lewis and J. C. Davies (Cardiff, 1954)

A Relation of the Island of England . . . about the Year 1500, trans. C. A. Sneyd (Camden Soc., 1847)

Rhyddiaith Gymraeg: I. Detholion o Lawysgrifau, 1488–1609, ed. T. H. Parry Williams (Cardiff, 1954); *II. Detholion o Lawysgrifau a Llyfrau Printiedig, 1547–1618*, ed. T. Jones (Cardiff, 1956)

Riley, H. T. (ed.), *Ingulph's Chronicle of the Abbey of Croyland* (London, 1854)

Robert, Gruffudd, *Gramadeg Cymraeg*, ed. G. J. Williams (Cardiff, 1939)

Rotuli Parliamentorum; ut et Petitiones, et Placita in Parliamento (7 vols. London, 1783–1832)

Royal and Historical Letters during the Reign of Henry IV, ed. F. C. Hingeston (London, 1860)

Rymer, T., *Foedera, Conventiones, Litterae, et Cuiuscunque Generis Acta Publica . . .* (20 vols. London, 1704–35)

Salesbury, William, *A Dictionary in Englishe and Welshe* (1547)

—— *Kynniver Llith a Ban*, ed. J. Fisher (Cardiff, 1931)

—— *Oll Synnwyr Pen Kembero Ygyd . . .* (1547)

Saunders, Erasmus, *A View of the State of Religion in the Diocese of St David's* (Repr. Cardiff, 1949)

Statutes of the Realm, (11 vols. London, 1810–28)

The Statutes of Wales, ed. I. Bowen (London, 1908)

Stradling, John, 'The Storie of the Lower Borowes of Merthyr Mawr', *SWMRS*, 1 (1932)

The Stradling Correspondence, ed. J. M. Traherne (London, 1840)

Survey of the Duchy of Lancaster Lordships in Wales, 1609–17, ed. W. Rees (Cardiff, 1953)

Testament Newydd 1567 (Repr. Caernarvon, 1850)

Three Chapters of Letters relating to the Suppression of English Monasteries, ed. T. Wright (Camden Soc., 1843)

Three Fifteenth-century Chronicles, ed. J. Gairdner (Camden Soc., 1880)

Tudur Economic Documents, ed. R. H. Tawney and E. Power (3 vols. London, 1924)

Valor Ecclesiasticus temp. Henr. VIII . . ., ed. J. Caley (6 vols. London, 1810–34)

Vaughan, W., *The Golden Fleece* (1626)

Williams, C. H., *English Historical Documents, 1485–1558* (London, 1967)

C. SECONDARY SOURCES

1. General Surveys of British History

Many of the following volumes have good bibliographies.

Ashton, R., *Reformation and Revolution, 1558–1660* (Paladin Books, 1984)
Aston, M., *The Fifteenth Century* (London, 1968)
Aylmer, G., *The Struggle for the Constitution* (London, 1968)
Black, J. B., *The Age of Elizabeth* (Oxford, 1936)
Coleman, D. C., *The Economy of England, 1450–1750* (Oxford, 1977)
Coward, B., *The Stuart Age* (London, 1980)
Davies, C. S. L., *Peace, Print and Protestantism, 1450–1558* (Paladin Books, 1977)
Davies, G., *The Earlier Stuarts* (London, 1959)
Donaldson, G. S., *Scotland: James V–James VII* (Edinburgh, 1965)
Du Boulay, F. R. H., *An Age of Ambition* (London, 1970)
Elton, G. R., *England under the Tudors* (London, 1974)
—— *Modern Historians on British History* (London, 1970)
—— *Reform and Reformation: England, 1509–1558* (London, 1977)
—— *The Tudor Constitution* (Cambridge, 1982)
Hill, C., *The Century of Revolution, 1603–1714* (London, 1961)
Jacob, E. F., *The Fifteenth Century* (Oxford, 1961)
Kenyon, J. P., *The Stuart Constitution* (Cambridge, 1966)
Lander, J. R., *Conflict and Stability in Fifteenth-century England* (London, 1977)
—— *Government and Community: England, 1450–1509* (London, 1980)
Mackie, J. D., *The Early Tudors* (Oxford, 1952)
Moody, T. W. *et al.* (eds.), *A New History of Ireland* (Oxford, 1984)
Russell, C., *The Crisis of Parliaments: English History, 1509–1660* (Oxford, 1971)
Smith, A. G. R., *The Emergence of a Nation State, 1529–1660* (London, 1984)
Smout, C., *A History of the Scottish People, 1560–1830* (London, 1969)
Thomson, J. A. F., *The Transformation of England, 1370–1529* (London, 1983)
Williams, P., *The Tudor Régime* (Oxford, 1979)
Wormald, J., *Court, Kirk and Community, 1470–1625* (London, 1981)

2 General Studies of Wales

Bebb, W. A., *Cyfnod y Tuduriaid* (Wrexham, 1939)
—— *Machlud yr Oesoedd Canol* (Swansea, 1951)
Bowen, E. G. (ed.), *Wales, a Physical, Historical and Regional Geography* (London, 1957)
Carter, H., *National Atlas of Wales* (Cardiff, 1980–)
—— *The Towns of Wales* (Cardiff, 1965)
Coupland, R., *Welsh and Scottish Nationalism* (London, 1954)
Davies, E. (ed.), *Celtic Studies in Wales* (Cardiff, 1963)
Davies, M., *Wales in Maps* (Cardiff, 1959)
Davies, R. R. *et al.* (eds.), *Welsh Society and Nationhood* (Cardiff, 1984)
Dictionary of Welsh Biography down to 1940 (London, 1959)
Dodd, A. H., *A History of Caernarvonshire, 1284–1900* (Caernarvon, 1968)
—— *Life in Wales* (London, 1972)
Edwards, O. M., *Wales* (London, 1901)

Emery, F. V., *The World's Landscapes: Wales* (London, 1969)

Evans, C. J. O., *Glamorgan: its History and Topography* (Cardiff, 1938)

—— *Monmouthshire: its History and Topography* (Cardiff, 1954)

Evans, G., *Land of my Fathers* (Swansea, 1974)

Fraser, D., *Wales in History: the Adventurers* (Cardiff, 1978)

Glamorgan County History: III Medieval Glamorgan, ed. T. B. Pugh (Cardiff 1971); *IV Early Modern Glamorgan*, ed. G. Williams (Cardiff, 1974)

Griffith, W. Ll., *The Welsh* (Penguin, 1950)

Humphreys, E., *The Taliesin Tradition* (London, 1983)

Jenkins, G. H., *Hanes Cymru yn y Cyfnod Modern Cynnar, 1536–1760* (Cardiff, 1983)

Jones, G. E., *Modern Wales: a Concise History, 1485–1979* (Cambridge, 1984)

Jones, R. B. (ed.), *Anatomy of Wales* (Peterston-super-Ely, 1972)

Lloyd, D. M. (ed.), *A Book of Wales* (London, 1953)

—— *The Historical Foundations of Welsh Nationalism* (Cardiff, 1954)

Lloyd, J. E. (ed.), *The History of Carmarthenshire* (2 vols. Cardiff, 1935–9)

Morgan, P. T. J., *Background to Wales* (Llandybïe, 1968)

Morgan, P. T. J. and D. Thomas (eds.), *Wales: the Shaping of a Nation* (Newton Abbot, 1984)

Morris, J., *The Matter of Wales* (Oxford, 1984)

Parry, T., *A History of Welsh Literature*, trans. H. I. Bell (Oxford, 1955)

Phillips, J., *A History of Pembrokeshire* (London, 1909)

Rees, J. F., *Studies in Welsh History* (Cardiff, 1965)

Rees, W., *An Historical Atlas of Wales* (Cardiff, 1966)

Rhys, J. and B. Jones, *The Welsh People* (London, 1906)

Richards, G. M., *Welsh Administrative and Territorial Units, Medieval and Modern* (Cardiff, 1969)

Richards, R., *Cymru'r Oesoedd Canol* (Wrexham, 1933)

Roberts, G., *Aspects of Welsh History* (Cardiff, 1969)

Roderick, A. J. (ed.), *Wales through the Ages* (2 vols. Llandybïe, 1959, 1961)

Stephens, M. (ed.), *The Oxford Companion to Welsh Literature* (Oxford, 1986)

Sylvester, D., *A History of Gwynedd* (Chichester, 1983)

—— *The Rural Landscape of the Welsh Borderland* (London, 1969)

Thomas, D. (ed.), *Wales: a New Study* (Newton Abbot, 1977)

Thomas, J. D. H., *A History of Wales, 1485–1660* (Cardiff, 1972)

Thomas, W. S. K., *Stuart Wales* (Llandysul, 1988)

—— *Tudor Wales* (Llandysul, 1983)

Williams, D., *Modern Wales* (London, 1977)

Williams, G., *Religion, Language and Nationality in Wales* (Cardiff, 1979)

Williams, G. A., *The Welsh in their History* (London, 1982)

—— *When Was Wales?* (London, 1985)

Williams, W. Ll., *The Making of Modern Wales* (London, 1919)

3. Political History

Bebb, W. A., *Y Deddfau Uno* (Caernarfon, 1937)

Bennett, M., *The Battle of Bosworth* (Gloucester, 1985)

Bindoff, S. T. (ed.), *History of Parliament: The Commons, 1509–1558* (London, 1982)

Bradley, A. G., *Owen Glyndwr* (London, 1901)

Carr, A. D., 'An Aristocracy in Decline: The Native Welsh Lords after the Edwardian Conquest', *WHR*, v (1970–1)

—— *Medieval Anglesey* (AAS, 1983)

—— 'Sir Lewis John—a Medieval London Welshman', *BBCS*, xxii (1966–8)

—— 'Welshmen and the Hundred Years War', *WHR*, iv (1968–9)

Charles, B. G., *George Owen of Henllys* (Aberystwyth, 1977)

Chrimes, S. B., *Henry VII* (London, 1972)

Chrimes, S. B. *et al.* (eds.), *Fifteenth-century England, 1399–1509* (Manchester, 1972)

—— —— 'The Landing Place of Henry of Richmond', *WHR*, ii (1964–5)

—— —— 'The Reign of Henry VII: Some Recent Contributions', *WHR*, x (1984–5)

Coward, B., *The Stanleys, Lords Stanley and Earls of Derby, 1385–1672* (Manchester, 1983)

Davies, D. J. G., *Owen Glyn Dŵr* (London, 1924)

Davies, R. R., 'Colonial Wales', *Past and Present*, 65 (1974)

—— *Lordship and Society in the March of Wales, 1282–1400* (Oxford, 1978)

—— 'Owain Glyn Dŵr and the Welsh Squirearchy', *Trans. Cymmr.*, 1968 (ii)

—— 'Race Relations in Post-Conquest Wales: Confrontation and Compromise', *Trans. Cymmr.*, 1974–5

Dodd, A. H., 'Caernarvonshire Elections to the Long Parliament', *BBCS*, xii (1946)

—— 'North Wales in the Essex Revolt in 1601', *EHR*, lix (1944)

—— 'The Pattern of Politics in Stuart Wales', *Trans. Cymmr.*, 1948

—— 'The Spanish Treason, Gunpowder Plot and the Catholic Refugees', *EHR*, liii (1938)

—— *Studies in Stuart Wales* (Cardiff, 1952)

—— 'Wales and the Second Bishops' War', *BBCS*, xii (1948)

—— 'Wales and the Stuart Succession', *Trans. Cymmr.*, 1937

—— 'Wales in the Parliaments of Charles I', *Trans. Cymmr.*, 1946–7

—— 'Wales's Parliamentary Apprenticeship, 1536–1625', *Trans. Cymmr.*, 1942

Eames, A., *Ships and Seamen of Anglesey* (Caernarfon, 1975)

Edwards, J. G., *The Principality of Wales, 1267–1967* (Denbigh, 1969)

Edwards, P. S., 'The Parliamentary Representation of the Welsh Boroughs in Mid Sixteenth Century', *BBCS*, xxvii (1978)

—— 'Cynrychiolaeth a Chynnen: Agweddau ar Hanes Seneddol a Chymdeithasol Sir Fôn yn yr 16eg Ganrif', *WHR*, x (1980)

Evans, H. T., *Wales and the Wars of the Roses* (Cambridge, 1915)

—— 'William Herbert, Earl of Pembroke', *Trans. Cymmr.*, 1909–10

Gillingham, J., *The Wars of the Roses* (London, 1981)

Goodman, A., *The Wars of the Roses* (London, 1981)

Grant, A., *Henry VII* (London, 1985)

Griffith, J. E., *Pedigrees of Caernarvonshire and Anglesey Familes* (Horncastle, 1914)

Griffiths, R. A., 'Gentlemen and Rebels in later Medieval Cardiganshire', *Ceredigion*, V (1964–5)

—— 'The Glyn Dŵr Rebellion through the Eyes of an Englishman', *BBCS* XXII (1966–8)

—— 'Gruffydd ap Nicholas and the Fall of the House of Lancaster', *WHR*, II (1964–5)

—— 'Gruffydd ap Nicholas and the Rise of the House of Dinefwr', *NLWJ*, XIII (1964)

—— *The Principality of Wales in the Later Middle Ages: I. South Wales, 1277–1536* (Cardiff, 1972)

—— *The Reign of Henry VI* (London, 1981)

—— 'The Rise of the Stradlings of St. Donat's', *Morgannwg*, VII (1963)

Griffiths, R. A. and R. S. Thomas, *The Making of the Tudor Dynasty* (Gloucester, 1985)

Gruenfelder, J. K., 'The Wynns of Gwydir and Parliamentary Elections in Wales, 1604–1610', *WHR*, IX (1976–7)

Holmes, G. A., *The Estates of the Higher Nobility in 14th-Century England* (1957)

Jones, E. D., *Beirdd y Bymthegfed Ganrif a'u Cefndir* (Aberystwyth, 1984)

Jones, E. G., 'Anglesey and Invasion', *AAST*, 1947

—— 'County Politics and Electioneering, 1558–1625', *Trans. Caerns. Hist. Soc.*, 1939

Jones, E. W., *Bosworth Field: A Welsh Retrospect* (Liverpool, 1984)

Jones, F., 'An Approach to Welsh Genealogy', *Trans. Cymmr.*, 1948

—— 'Sir Rhys ap Thomas and the Knights of St. John', *Carmarthen Antiquary*, II (1951)

Jones, G. E., *The Gentry and the Elizabethan State* (Swansea, 1977)

Jones, W. G., 'Welsh Nationalism and Henry Tudor', *Trans. Cymmr.*, 1916–17

Lewis, E. A., *The Medieval Boroughs of Snowdonia* (London, 1912)

Lloyd, H. A., 'Corruption and Sir John Trevor', *Trans Cymmr.*, 1974–5

—— 'The Essex Inheritance', *WHR*, VII (1974–5)

—— *The Gentry of South-West Wales, 1540–1640* (Cardiff, 1968)

Lloyd, J. E., *Owen Glendower* (Oxford, 1931)

Makinson, A., 'The Road to Bosworth Field', *History Today*, XIII (1963)

Mathew, D., *The Celtic Peoples and Renaissance Europe* (London, 1934)

—— 'Wales and England in the Early Seventeenth Century', *Trans. Cymmr.*, 1955

McGurk, J. J. N., 'A Survey of the Demands made on Welsh Shires . . . for the Irish War, 1594–1602', *Trans. Cymmr.*, 1983

Messham, J. E., 'The County of Flint and the Rebellion of Owain Glyndŵr . . .', *FHSP*, XXIII (1967–8)

Neale, J. E., *The Elizabethan House of Commons* (London, 1949)

—— 'Three Elizabethan Elections', *EHR*, XLVI (1931)

Owen, G. D., *Elizabethan Wales: the Social Scene* (London, 1962)

Owen, H. G., 'Family Politics in Elizabethan Merionethshire', *BBCS*, XVIII (1959)

Phillips, J. R., *The Civil War in Wales* (2 vols. London, 1874)

Probert, Y., 'Mathew Gough, 1390–1450', *Trans. Cymmr.*, 1961

Pugh, T. B., 'The Indenture for the Marches between Henry VII and Edward Stafford, Duke of Buckingham', *EHR*, LXXI (1956)

Pugh, T. B. and W. R. B. Robinson, 'Sessions in Eyre in a Marcher Lordship . . .', *SWMRS.*, IV (1957)

Rawcliffe, C., *The Staffords, Earls of Stafford and Dukes of Buckingham* (Cambridge, 1978)

Rees, W., *South Wales and the March, 1282–1415* (Oxford, 1924)

—— 'The Union of England and Wales', *Trans. Cymmr.*, 1937

Reeves, A. C., *The Lordship of Newport, 1317–1536* (Ann Arbor, Michigan, 1979)

—— *The Marcher Lordships* (Swansea, 1983)

Roberts, P. R., 'The Acts of Union and Wales', *Trans. Cymmr.*, 1974

—— 'A Breviat of the Effectes devised for Wales', *Camden Miscellany*, XXVI (1975)

—— 'The Union with England and the Identity of "Anglican" Wales', *TRHS*, XXII (1972)

Robinson, W. R. B., 'Early Tudor Policy Towards Wales', *BBCS*, XX–XXI (1962–6)

—— 'The Marcher Lords of Wales, 1525–31', *BBCS*, XXVI (1972–3)

—— 'The Welsh Estates of Charles, Earl of Worcester', *BBCS*, XXIV (1971)

Ross, C., *Edward IV* (London, 1974)

—— *Richard III* (London, 1981)

Rowse, A. L., *The England of Elizabeth* (London, 1951)

—— *The Expansion of Elizabethan England* (London, 1955)

Scattergood, V. J., *Politics and Poetry in the Fifteenth Century* (London, 1972)

Skeel, C. A. J., *The Council in the Marches of Wales* (London, 1903)

—— 'Wales under Henry VII' in *Tudor Studies*, ed. R. W. Seton-Watson, (London, 1924)

Smith, J. B., 'Crown and Community in the Principality of North Wales in the Reign of Henry VII', *WHR*, III (1966–7)

—— 'The Last Phase of the Glyndŵr Rebellion', *BBCS*, XXII (1966–8)

Somerville, R., *History of the Duchy of Lancaster: I. 1265–1603* (London, 1953)

Waters, W. H., *The Edwardian Settlement of North Wales in its Administrative and Legal Aspects* (Cardiff, 1935)

Wernham, R. B., *England Before the Armada* (London, 1966)

Williams, D., 'The Welsh Tudors', *History Today*, IV (1954)

Williams, E. R., *Some Studies in Elizabethan Wales* (Newton, 1924)

Williams, G., *Harri Tudur a Chymru: Henry Tudor and Wales* (Bilingual, Cardiff, 1985)

—— *Owen Glendower* (Oxford, 1966)

Williams, P., 'The Attack on the Council in the Marches, 1603–42', *Trans. Cymmr.*, 1961

—— *The Council in the Marches of Wales under Elizabeth I* (Cardiff, 1958)

—— 'The Welsh Borderland under Queen Elizabeth', *WHR*, I (1960)

Williams, W. Ll., 'The King's Court of Great Sessions', *Y Cymmr.* XXVI (1912)

—— 'The Union of England and Wales', *Trans. Cymm.*, 1907–8

—— 'A Welsh Insurrection', *Y Cymmr.*, XVI (1902)

Williams, W. T., 'Henry Richmond's Itinerary to Bosworth', *Y Cymmr.*, XXIX (1915)

4. Legal and Constitutional History

Ancient Laws and Institutes of Wales, ed. A. Owen (London, 1841)

Bellamy, J., *Crime and Public Order in England in the Later Middle Ages* (London, 1973)

Clive, R. H., *Documents connected with the History of Ludlow* (London, 1841)

Davies, R. R., 'The Law of the March', *WHR*, v (1970–1)

—— 'The Survival of the Blood Feud in Medieval Wales', *History*, LIV (1969)

—— 'The Twilight of Welsh Law', *History*, LI (1966)

Fox, K. O., 'An Edited Calendar of the First Brecknockshire Plea-roll . . .', *NLWJ*, XIV (1965–6)

Gunn, S. J., 'The Regime of Charles, Duke of Suffolk in North Wales', *WHR*, XII (1984–5)

Hearder, H. and H. R. Loyn (eds.), *British Government and Administration* (Cardiff, 1974)

Ives, E. W., 'Court and County Palatine in the Reign of Henry VIII: the Career of William Brereton of Malpas', *Trans. Hist. Soc. of Lancs. and Cheshire*, 123 (1972)

Jenkins, D., *Cyfraith Hywel* (Llandysul, 1974)

Jenkins, D. and M. Owen (eds.), *The Welsh Law of Women* (Cardiff, 1980)

Jones, F., *The Princes and Principality of Wales* (Cardiff, 1969)

Jones, J. G., 'Awdurdod Cyfreithiol a Gweinyddol Lleol yng Ngogledd Cymru yn y Cyfnod 1540–1640 yn ôl Tystiolaeth y Beirdd', *Llên Cymru*, XII (1973)

—— 'Caernarvonshire Administration: the Activities of the Justices of the Peace, 1603–40', *WHR*, v (1970–1)

Jones Pierce, T., *Medieval Welsh Society* (Cardiff, 1972)

Lewis, T. H., 'The Administration of Justice in the Welsh County in its Relations to Other Organs of Justice', *Trans. Cymm.*, 1943–4

Lowe, D. E., 'The Council of the Prince of Wales . . . during the Reign of Edward IV', *BBCS*, XXVII (1977–8)

Ormerod, G., *The History of the County Palatine and City of Chester* (3 vols. London, 1875–82)

Otway-Ruthven, A. J., 'The Constitutional Position of the Great Lordships of South Wales', *TRHS*, v, VIII (1958)

Owen, H. and J. B. Blakeway, *History of Shrewsbury* (2 vols. London, 1875–82)

Phillips, J. R. S., *The Justices of the Peace in Wales and Monmouthshire, 1541–1689* (Cardiff, 1975)

Rees, W., 'Gower and the March of Wales', *Arch. Camb.*, 1961

—— 'The Medieval Lordship of Brecon', *Trans. Cymm.*, 1915–16

—— *South Wales and the March, 1282–1415* (Oxford, 1924)

Sherrington, E. J., 'The Plea-rolls of the Courts of Great Sessions, 1541–1575', *NLWJ*, XIII (1963–4)

Slack, W. J., *The Lordship of Oswestry, 1393–1607* (Shrewsbury, 1951)

Wade-Evans, A. W., *Welsh Medieval Law* (Oxford, 1909)

Williams, P., 'The Star Chamber and the Council in the Marches of Wales, 1558–1603'. *BBCS*, XVI (1956)

Williams, W. R., *The History of the Great Sessions, 1542–1830* (Brecon, 1899)

—— *The Parliamentary History of Wales, 1541–1895* (Brecon, 1895)

Wright, T., *The History of Ludlow and its Neighbourhood* (London, 1852)

5. Social and Economic History

Agrarian History of England and Wales: IV. 1500–1640, ed. J. Thirsk (Cambridge, 1967)

Ariès, P., *The Hour of Our Death* (Peregrine Books, 1983)

Bartrum, P. C., *Welsh Genealogies A.D. 1400–1500* (10 vols. Aberystwyth, 1983)

Boon, G. C., *Cardiganshire Silver and the Aberystwyth Mint in Peace and War* (Cardiff, 1982)

—— *Welsh Tokens of the Seventeenth Century* (Cardiff, 1973)

Burke, P., *Popular Culture in Early Modern Europe* (London, 1978)

Carr, A. D., 'The Making of the Mostyns . . .', *Trans. Cymmr.*, 1979

—— 'The Mostyns of Mostyn', *FHSP*, 28 (1977–8)

Chambers, J. D., *Population, Economy and Society in Pre-industrial England* (Oxford, 1977)

Charles, B. G., 'Haverfordwest Accounts, 1563–1620', *NLWJ*, IX (1955–6)

Coleman, D. C., *The Economy of England, 1450–1750* (Oxford, 1977)

—— *Industry in Tudor and Stuart England* (London, 1975)

Colyer, R. J., *The Welsh Cattle Drovers* (Cardiff, 1976)

Cule, J. (ed.), *Wales and Medicine* (London, 1975)

Davies, D. J., *The Economic History of South Wales before 1800* (Cardiff, 1933)

Dodd, A. H., *A History of Wrexham* (Wrexham, 1957)

—— *Life in Elizabethan England* (London, 1961)

—— 'Mr. Myddelton, the Merchant of Tower St.', *Elizabethan Government and Society*, ed. S. T. Bindoff *et al.* (London, 1961)

Donald, M. B., *Elizabethan Copper: The History of the Company of Mines Royal 1568–1605* (London, 1955)

—— *Elizabethan Monopolies: The History of the Company of Mineral and Battery Works, 1565–1604* (London, 1961)

Emery, F. V., 'West Glamorgan Farming, c. 1580–1620', *NLWJ*, IX–X (1955–7)

Evans, B. M., 'The Commote of Cyfeiliog in the Late-Sixteenth Century', *Mont. Colls.*, IX (1967–8)

Fisher, F. J., (ed.), *Essays in the Economic and Social History of Tudor and Stuart England* (Cambridge, 1961)

Fox, C. and Lord Raglan, *Monmouthshire Houses . . . in the Fifteenth and Sixteenth Centuries* (3 vols. Cardiff, 1951–4)

Gough, J. W., *Sir Hugh Myddelton: Entrepreneur and Engineer* (Oxford, 1964)

—— *The Superlative Prodigal: A Life of Thomas Bushell* (Bristol, 1932)

Gresham, C., *Eifionydd* (Cardiff, 1973)

Griffiths, R. A. (ed.), *Boroughs of Medieval Wales* (Cardiff, 1978)

Gwyndaf, R., 'Sir Richard Clough', *TDHS*, XIX, XXII (1970–3)

Haslam, R., *Powys: The Buildings of Wales* (Penguin, 1979)

Hatcher, J., *Plague, Population and the English Economy, 1348–1530* (Cambridge, 1977)

—— *Rural Economy and Society in the Duchy of Cornwall, 1300–1500* (Cambridge, 1970)

Hilling, J. B., *The Historic Architecture of Wales* (Cardiff, 1977)

Holderness, B., *Pre-industrial English Economy and Society, 1500–1750* (London, 1976)

Hollingsworth, T. H., *Historical Demography* (London, 1969)

Hoskins, W. G., *The Age of Plunder* (London, 1976)

—— 'Harvest Fluctuations and English Economic History, 1480–1619', *Agric. Hist. Rev.*, 12 (1964)

—— 'Harvest Fluctuations and English Economic History, 1620–1759', *Agric. Hist. Rev.*, 16 (1968)

—— 'The Rebuilding of Rural England', *Past and Present*, 4 (1953)

Howells, B. E., 'The Elizabethan Squirearchy in Pembrokeshire', *Pembrokeshire Historian*, 1 (1959)

—— 'The Historical Demography of Wales: Some Notes on Sources', *The Local Historian*, x (1973))

—— 'Pembrokeshire Farming', *NLWJ*, IX (1955–6)

—— 'Social and Agrarian Change in Early Modern Cardiganshire', *Ceredigion*, VII (1974)

Howells, B. E. and J., 'Peasant Houses in Stuart Pembrokeshire', *NLWJ*, XXI (1980)

Hubbard, E., *Clwyd: The Buildings of Wales* (Penguin Books, 1986)

Jack, R. I., 'The Cloth Industry in Medieval Ruthin', *TDHS*, XII (1963)

—— 'The Cloth Industry in Medieval Wales', *WHR*, x (1979–80)

—— 'Fulling-mills in Wales and the March before 1547', *Arch. Camb.*, 1981

Jack, S. M., *Trade and Industry in Tudor and Stuart England* (London, 1987)

James, M., *Family, Lineage and Civil Society* (Oxford, 1974)

James, T., *Carmarthen: an Archaeological and Topographical Survey* (Carmarthen, 1980)

Jenkins, E. (ed.), *Neath and District: A Symposium* (Neath, 1974)

Jenkins, G. H., 'Popular Beliefs in Wales from the Restoration to the Methodist Revival', *BBCS*, XXVII (1977)

Jenkins, J. G., *Life and Tradition in Rural Wales* (London, 1976)

—— *The Welsh Woollen Industry* (Cardiff, 1969)

Jones, A. M., *The Rural Industries of England and Wales: IV. Wales* (Oxford, 1927)

Jones, D. C., 'The Bulkeleys of Beaumaris, 1440–1547', *AAST*, 1961

Jones, G. P., *Newyn a Haint yng Nghymru* (Caernarfon, 1963)

Jones, J. G., 'Priodoleddau Bonheddig yn Nheulu'r Wyniaid o Wedir', *Trans. Cymm.*, 1978

—— 'Syr John Wynn of Wedir: Ei Gymeriad a'i Gefndir', *THSC*, 36 (1975)

Jones, W. R., 'England against the Celtic Fringe', *Journ. World History*, XIII (1971)

Jordan, W. K., *The Charities of London, 1480–1660* (London, 1961)

—— *Philanthropy in England, 1480–1660* (London, 1959)

Lewis, E. A., 'A Contribution to the Commercial History of Medieval Wales, 1301–1547', *Y Cymmr.*, XXIV (1913)

—— 'The Decay of Tribalism in North Wales', *Trans. Cymm.*, 1902–3

—— 'The Development of Industry and Commerce in Wales during the Middle Ages', *TRHS*, XVII (1903)

Lewis, E. A., 'The Port Books of Cardigan in Elizabethan and Stuart Times', *Trans. Cards. Antiq. Soc.*, VII (1930).

—— 'The Toll-books of some North Pembrokeshire Fairs, 1509–1603', *BBCS*, VII (1934)

Linnard, W., *Welsh Woods and Forests: History and Utilization* (Cardiff, 1982)

Llewellin, W., 'Some Account of the Iron and Wire Works at Tintern', *Arch. Camb.*, 1863

—— 'Sussex Ironmasters in Glamorgan', *Arch. Camb.*, 1863

McGrath, P., *Merchants . . . in Seventeenth-Century Bristol* (Bristol, 1955)

Mendenhall, T. C., *The Shrewsbury Drapers and the Welsh Wool Trade in the XVI and XVII Centuries* (Oxford, 1953)

Nef, J. U., *The Rise of the British Coal Industry* (2 vols. London, 1932)

Outhwaite, R. B., *Inflation in Tudor and Early-Stuart England* (London, 1969)

Owen, L., 'The Population of Wales in the Sixteenth and Seventeenth Centuries', *Trans. Cymm.*, 1959

Owen, T. M., *Welsh Folk Customs* (Cardiff, 1968)

Palliser, D. M., *The Age of Elizabeth* (London, 1983)

Parry, B. R., 'Huw Nanney Hen (*c.* 1546–1623), Squire of Nannau', *JMHRS*, V (1965–8)

—— 'A Sixteenth-century Merioneth Ironworks', *JMHRS*, IV (1961–4)

Payne, F. G., *Yr Aradr Gymreig* (Cardiff, 1954)

Peate, I. C., *Y Crefftwr yng Nghymru* (Aberystwyth, 1933)

—— *Cymru a'i Phobl* (Cardiff, 1931)

—— *Tradition and Folk Life: A Welsh View* (London, 1972)

—— *The Welsh House* (Liverpool, 1946)

Phillips, D. R., *A History of the Vale of Neath* (Swansea, 1925)

Phillips, J., 'Glimpses of Elizabethan Pembrokeshire', *Arch. Camb.*, 1897, 1899, 1904

Ramsey, P. H., *The Price Revolution in Sixteenth-century England* (London, 1971)

RCAHM, *Inventories*

Flintshire (1912)	Pembrokeshire (1925)
Radnorshire (1913)	Anglesey (1937)
Denbighshire (1914)	Caernarvonshire (3 vols. 1956–64)
Carmarthenshire (1917)	Glamorgan (1976–)
Merioneth (1921)	

Rees, D. M., *Industrial Archaeology of Wales* (London, 1975)

—— *Mines, Mills and Furnaces* (Cardiff, 1969)

Rees, W., *Industry before the Industrial Revolution* (2 vols. Cardiff, 1968)

—— 'The port of Cardiff . . . 1606–1610' *SWMRS*, III (1954)

Roberts, P., *Y Cwtta Cyfarwydd*, ed. D.R. Thomas (London, 1883)

Robinson, D. M., *Cowbridge* (Glam./Gwent Archaeological Trust, 1980)

Robinson, W. R. B., 'Dr. Phaer's Report on the Harbours and Customs Administration of Wales', *BBCS*, XXIV (1972)

—— 'The Establishment of Royal Customs in Glamorgan and Monmouthshire under Elizabeth I', *BBCS*, XXIV (1970–1)

—— 'The First Subsidy Assessment of the Hundreds of Swansea and Llangyfelach', *WHR*, II (1964–5)

—— 'The Litigation of Edward, Earl of Worcester, concerning Gower', *BBCS*, XXII–XXIII (1966–70)

—— 'The *Valor Ecclesiasticus* of 1535 as Evidence of Agrarian Output', *BIHR*, 56 (1983)

Rosenthal, J., *The Estates and Finances of Richard Duke of York, 1441–60* (Lincoln, Nebr., 1968)

Schubert, H. R., *History of the British Iron and Steel Industry* (London, 1951)

Scott, W. R., *The Constitution and Finance . . . of Joint-stock Companies to 1770* (3 vols. Cambridge, 1911)

Skeel, C. A. J., 'The Cattle Trade between England and Wales from the Fifteenth Century to the Nineteenth', *TRHS*, iv, IX (1926)

—— 'The Welsh Woollen Industry in the Sixteenth and Seventeenth Centuries', *Arch. Camb.*, 1922

Smith, P., *Houses of the Welsh Countryside* (London, 1975)

Smith, W. J., 'The Salusburies as Maintainers of Murderers', *NLWJ*, VII (1951–2)

Soulsby, I., *The Towns of Wales* (Chichester, 1983)

Stone, L., *The Crisis of the Aristocracy, 1558–1641* (Oxford, 1965)

—— *Family, Sex and Marriage in England, 1500–1800* (Penguin, 1977)

Thomas, B. B., *Braslun o Hanes Economaidd Cymru* (Cardiff, 1941)

Thomas, C., 'Patterns and Processes of Estate Expansion in the Fifteenth and Sixteenth Centuries', *JMHRS*, VI (1969–72)

—— 'Place-name Studies and Agrarian Colonization', *WHR*, X (1984)

—— 'Social Organization and Rural Settlement in Medieval North Wales', *JMHRS*, VI (1969)

Thomas, K. V., *Religion and the Decline of Magic* (London, 1971)

Williams, D. T., *The Economic Development of Swansea and the Swansea District* (Cardiff, 1940)

Williams, E., *Traditional Farm Buildings in North-east Wales* (Cardiff, 1982)

Williams, J. G., 'Rhai Agweddau ar y Gymdeithas Gymreig yn yr Ail Ganrif ar Bymtheg', *Efrydiau Athronyddol*, XXX (1968)

Williams, M. I., 'Some Aspects of the Economic and Social Life of Glamorgan 1600–1800', *Morgannwg*, III (1959)

—— 'The Commercial History of Glamorgan', *NLWJ*, XI (1960)

—— 'A Further Contribution to the Commercial History of Glamorgan', *NLWJ*, XII (1961–2)

—— 'Some Aspects of the Economic and Social Life of Glamorgan 1600–1800', *Morgannwg*, III (1959)

Williams, W. O., 'The Anglesey Gentry as Businessmen in Tudor and Stuart Wales', *AAST*, 1948

—— 'The Social Order in Tudor Wales', *Trans. Cymm.*, 1967 (ii)

Wrightson, K., *English Society, 1580–1680* (London, 1982)

Wrigley, K. A. and R. S. Schofield, *The Population History of England, 1541 to 1871* (Cambridge, 1981)

Youings, J., *Sixteenth-century England* (Pelican Books, 1984)

6. Religious History

Ashton, C., *Bywyd ac Amserau yr Esgob William Morgan* (Treherbert, 1891)

Ballinger, J., *The Bible in Wales* (London, 1906)

Baskerville, G., *English Monks and the Suppression of the Monasteries* (London, 1949)

Bebb, W. A., *Machlud y Mynachlogydd* (Aberystwyth, 1937)

Bevan, W. L., *St. David's* (London, 1888)

Birch, W. de G., *A History of Margam Abbey* (London, 1897)

—— *A History of Neath Abbey* (London, 1902)

—— *Memorials of the See and Cathedral of Llandaff* (Neath, 1912)

Bossy, J., *The English Catholic Community, 1570–1850* (London, 1977)

Bowen, D. J., 'Englynion o Hiraeth am yr Hen Ffydd', *Efrydiau Catholig*, VI, 1954

Bowen, G., *Gwssanaeth y Gwŷr Newydd* (Cardiff, 1970)

Clark, S. and P. T. J. Morgan, 'Religion and Magic in Elizabethan Wales: Robert Holland's Dialogue on Witchcraft', *Journ. Eccles. Hist.*, 27 (1976)

Clarke, M. L., *Bangor Cathedral* (Cardiff, 1969)

Cleary, J. M., 'The Catholic Resistance in Wales, 1568–1678', *Blackfriars*, 38 (1951)

—— *A Checklist of Welsh Students in the Seminaries* (Cardiff, 1958)

Cohn, N., *The Pursuit of the Millennium* (London, 1957)

Cofrestri Plwyf Cymru: Welsh Parish Registers, ed. G. J. Williams and J. Watts-Williams (Aberystwyth, 1986)

Cross, F. L. (ed.), *The Oxford Dictionary of the Christian Church* (Oxford, 1957)

Davies, C. T. B., 'Y Cerddi i'r Tai Crefydd fel Ffynhonnell Hanes', *NLWJ*, XVIII (1974)

Davies, E. T., *The Story of the Church in Glamorgan, 560–1960* (London, 1962)

Dodd, A. H., 'The Reformation in Wales', *Welsh Church Congress Handbook* (1953)

Dickens, A. G., *The Reformation in England* (London, 1964)

Edwards, A. G., *Landmarks in the History of the Welsh Church* (London, 1914)

Ellis, T. P., *The Catholic Martyrs of Wales* (London, 1933)

—— *Welsh Benedictines of the Terror* (Newton, 1936)

Evans, A. L., *Margam Abbey* (Port Talbot, 1958)

Evans, A. O., *The Life and Work of Edmwnd Prys* (Carmarthen, 1923)

Fisher, J., *The Private Devotions of the Welsh* (Liverpool, 1898)

Gresham, C., *Medieval Stone Carving in North Wales* (Cardiff, 1968)

Griffiths, G. M., 'St. Asaph Episcopal Acts, 1536–1558', *JHSCW*, IX (1959)

Gruffydd, R. G., *Argraffwyr Cyntaf Cymru* (Cardiff, 1972)

—— 'Yny Lhyvyr Hwnn (1546): the Earliest Welsh Printed Book', *BBCS*, XXIII (1968–70)

Guide to the Parish Records of Clwyd, ed. A. G. Veysey (Clwyd County Council, 1984)

Hays, R. W., *The History of the Abbey of Aberconway, 1186–1537* (Cardiff, 1963)

Hill, C., 'Puritans and the "Dark Corners of the Land"', *TRHS*, v, XIII (1963)

Hirsch-Davies, J. E., *Catholicism in Medieval Wales* (London, 1916)

Hughes, H. and H. L. North, *The Old Churches of Snowdonia* (Bangor, 1924)

Huizinga, J. H., *The Waning of the Middle Ages* (London, 1950)

James, J. W., *A Church History of Wales* (Ilfracombe, 1945)

Jones, D. G., *Y Ficer Prichard a 'Canwyll y Cymry'* (Caernarfon, 1946)

Jones, E. G., *Cymru a'r Hen Ffydd* (Cardiff, 1951)

Jones, F., *The Holy Wells of Wales* (Cardiff, 1954)

Jones, G., *A Study of Three Welsh Religious Plays* (Privately printed, 1939)

Jones, G. H., *Celtic Britain and the Pilgrim Movement* (London, 1912)

Jones, J. G., 'Bishop William Morgan's Dispute with John Wynn of Gwydir', *JHSCW*, XXII (1972)

Jones, O. W. and D. G. Walker, *Links with the Past* (Llandybïe, 1974)

Jones, T., *Y Bibyl Ynghymraec* (Cardiff, 1943)

—— 'Pre-Reformation Welsh Versions of the Scriptures', *NLWJ*, IV (1946)

Jones, W. B. and E. A. Freeman, *The History and Antiquities of St. Davids's* (London, 856)

Knowles, D., *The Religious Orders in England* (3 vols. Cambridge, 1948–59)

Le Neve, J., *Fasti Ecclesiae Anglicanae, 300–1541: XI. The Welsh Dioceses*, ed. B. Jones (London, 1965)

Lewis, F. R., 'Racial Sympathies of Welsh Cistercians', *Trans. Cymm.*, 1938

Lewis, H., 'Darnau o'r Efengylau', *Y Cymm.*, XXXI (1921)

Lewis, H. E., 'Welsh Catholic Poetry of the Fifteenth Century', *Trans. Cymm.*, 1911–12

Lewis, M., *Stained Glass in North Wales up to 1850* (Altrincham, 1970)

Lewis, S., 'Damcaniaeth Eglwysig Brotestannaidd', *Efrydiau Catholig*, II (1947)

Lewis, T. H., 'Carmarthenshire and the Reformation', *Trans. Carms. Antiq. Soc.*, XIV (191–21)

Llyfr Gweddi Gyffredin 1567, ed. G. M. Richards and G. Williams (Cardiff, 1965)

Mathias, R., *Whitsun Riot* (London, 1963)

Mathias, W. A., 'William Salesbury a'i Gyfieithiadau', *Diwinyddiaeth* XVIII (1967)

McGinn, D., *John Penry and the Marprelate Controversy* (Rutgers UP, 1966)

Newell, E. J., *A History of the Welsh Church to the Dissolution of the Monasteries* (London, 1895)

—— *Llandaff* (London, 1902)

Nuttall, G. F., *The Welsh Saints, 1640–1660* (Cardiff, 1967)

O'Sullivan, J. F., *Cistercian Settlements in Wales and Monmouthshire, 1140–1540* (New York, 1947)

Owst, G. R., *Literature and the Pulpit in Medieval England* (Cambridge, 1933)

Pierce, W., *John Penry, His Life, Times and Writings* (London, 1923)

Price, G. V., *Valle Crucis Abbey* (Liverpool, 1952)

Rees, W., *The Order of St. John in Wales* (Cardiff, 1947)

Richards, T., *Cymru a'r Uchel Gomisiwn, 1633–40* (Liverpool, 1930)

—— *The Puritan Movement in Wales, 1639–1654* (London, 1920)

Roberts, B. F., *Gwassanaeth Meir* (Cardiff, 1961)

Roberts, E. P., 'Canu Wiliam Cynwal i'r Clerigwyr', *TDHS*, XIV (1965)

Roberts, G. J., *Yr Esgob William Morgan* (Denbigh, 1955)

Robinson, W. R. B., 'The Church in Gower before the Reformation', *Morgannwg*, XII (1968)

Seaborne, M. V. J., *The Reformation in Wales* (London, 1952)

Talbot, C. H., *Letters from the English Abbots to the Chapter of Cîteaux, 1442–1521* (Camden Society, 1967)

Thomas, D. A., *The Welsh Elizabethan Catholic Martyrs* (Cardiff, 1971)

Thomas, D. R., *The History of the Diocese of St. Asaph* (3 vols. Oswestry, 1908–13)

—— *The Life of Bishop Richard Davies and William Salesbury* (Oswestry, 1902)

Thomas, L., *The Reformation in the Old Diocese of Llandaff* (Cardiff, 1930)

Thomas, I., *Y Testament Newydd Cymraeg, 1551–1620* (Cardiff, 1976)

—— *William Salesbury a'i Destament* (Cardiff, 1967)

Walker, D. G. (ed.), *A History of the Church in Wales* (Penarth, 1976)

Williams, D. H., *The Welsh Cistercians* (2 vols. Caldey Island, Tenby, 1983–4)

—— *The Welsh Cistercians: Aspects of Their Economic History* (Pontypool, 1969)

Williams, G., 'Bishop William Morgan and the First Welsh Bible', *JMHRS*, VII (1976)

—— *Bywyd ac Amserau'r Esgob Richard Davies* (Cardiff, 1963)

—— *Grym Tafodau Tân* (Llandysul, 1984)

—— 'Religion and Welsh Literature in the Age of the Reformation', *Procs. of the British Academy*, LXIX (1983)

—— 'Wales and the Reign of Mary I', *WHR*, X (1980–1)

—— *The Welsh Church from Conquest to Reformation* (Cardiff, 1976)

—— *Welsh Reformation Essays* (Cardiff, 1967)

Williams, J. E. C., 'Medieval Welsh Religious Prose', *Procs. Inter. Congress of Celtic Studies 1963* (Cardiff, 1966)

Willis, B., *A Survey of the Cathedral Church of Bangor* (London, 1721)

—— *A Survey of the Cathedral Church of Llandaff* (London, 1719)

—— *A Survey of the Cathedral Church of St. Asaph* (2 vols. London, 1801)

Yardley, E., *Menevia Sacra* (*Arch. Camb.* Supplement, 1927)

7. Education and Culture

Bartley, J. O., *Teague, Shenkin and Sawney* (Cork, 1954)

Bell, D., *The Artist in Wales* (London, 1957)

Bell, H. I., *The Development of Welsh Poetry* (Oxford, 1936)

Bennett, H. S., *English Books and their Readers, 1475 to 1557* (Cambridge, 1952)

Bowen, D. J., 'Agweddau ar Ganu'r Unfed Ganrif ar Bymtheg', *Trans. Cymm.*, 1969

—— 'Ail Eisteddfod Caerwys', *Llên Cymru*, III (1954–5)

—— *Barddoniaeth yr Uchelwyr* (Cardiff, 1957)

—— 'Gruffudd Hiraethog ac Argyfwng Cerdd Dafod', *Llên Cymru*, II (1952–3)

—— *Gruffudd Hiraethog a'i Oes* (Cardiff, 1958)

Bowen, G. (ed.), *Y Traddodiad Rhyddiaith* (Llandysul, 1970)

Bromwich, R., *Trioedd Ynys Prydain. The Welsh Triads* (Cardiff, 1961)

Clancy, J. P., *The Earliest Welsh Poetry* (London, 1970)

—— *Medieval Welsh Lyrics* (London, 1965)

Crossley, F. H., 'Screens, Lofts and Stalls Situated in Wales and Monmouthshire' *Arch. Camb.*, XCVII–CVII (1943–58)

Crossley-Holland, P., *Music in Wales* (London, 1948)

Davies, C., *Rhagymadroddion a Chyflwyniadau Lladin, 1551–1632* (Cardiff, 1980)

—— *Writers of Wales: Latin Writers of the Renaissance* (Cardiff, 1981)

Davies, W. Ll., 'Phylipiaid Ardudwy', *Y Cymm.*, XLII (1932)

Denholm-Young, N., *Handwriting in England and Wales* (Cardiff, 1954)

Ellis, O., *Hanes y Delyn yng Nghymru* (Cardiff, 1980)

Emden, A. B., *A Biographical Register of the University of Cambridge to 1500* (Cambridge, 1963)

—— *A Biographical Register of the University of Oxford to 1500* (3 vols. Oxford, 1955–9)

Evans, E. V., 'Andrew Boorde and the Welsh People', *Y Cymm.*, XXIX (1919)

Fisher, J., *The Cefn Coch Manuscripts* (Bangor, 1899)

Gresham, C. A., *Medieval Stone Carving in North Wales* (Cardiff, 1968)

Griffiths, G. M., 'Educational Activity in the Diocese of St Asaph', *JHSCW*, III (1953)

Griffiths, M. E., *Early Vaticination in Welsh* (Cardiff, 1937)

Gruffydd, R. G., 'Humphrey Llwyd: Dyneiddiwr', *Efrydiau Athronyddol*, XXXIII (1970)

—— 'The Life of Dr. John Davies of Brecon', *Trans. Cymm.*, 1971

Gruffydd, R. G. (ed.), *Meistri'r Canrifoedd* (Cardiff, 1973)

Gruffydd, W. J., *Llenyddiaeth Cymru o 1450 hyd 1600* (Liverpool, 1922)

—— *Llenyddiaeth Cymru: Rhyddiaith o 1540 hyd 1660* (Wrexham, 1926)

Harries, F. J., *Shakespeare and the Welsh* (London, 1919)

—— *The Welsh Elizabethans* (Pontypridd, 1924)

Harrison, F. L., *Music in Medieval Britain* (London, 1967)

Hughes, G. H., 'Cefndir Meddwl yr Ail Ganrif ar Bymtheg', *Efrydiau Athronyddol*, XVIII (1955)

Jarman, A. O. H. and G. R. Hughes, *A Guide to Welsh Literature* (2 vols. Swansea, 1976, 1979)

Jones, E. D., *Beirdd y Bymthegfed Ganrif a'u Cefndir* (Aberystwyth, 1984)

—— 'The Brogyntyn Welsh Manuscripts', *NLWJ*, V–VIII (1948–53)

—— 'Some Fifteenth-century Poetry relating to Montgomeryshire', *Mont. Coll.*, LIII–LIV (1951–6)

Jones, J., *Cynfeirdd Llŷn, 1500–1800* (Pwllheli, 1905)

Jones, J. G., 'Diddordebau Wynniaid Gwedir', *Llên Cymru*, XI (1970)

Jones, J. H., 'John Owen: Cambro-Britannus', *Trans. Cymm.*, 1940

Jones, R. B., *The Old British Tongue: the Vernacular in Wales, 1540–1640* (Cardiff, 1970)

Jones, R. G., *Guto'r Glyn* (Market Drayton, 1976)

Jones, R. M., *I'r Arch* (Llandybïe, 1959)

Jones, R. M., *Highlights in Welsh Literature: Talks with a Prince* (Llandybïe, 1969)

Jones, T. G., 'Bardism and Romance', *Trans. Cymm.*, 1913–14

—— 'Cultural Bases: a Study of the Tudor Period in Wales', *Y Cymmr.*, XXXI (1921)

Kendrick, T. D., *British Antiquity* (London, 1950)

Ker, N. R., *The Medieval Libraries of Great Britain* (London, 1941)

—— 'Sir John Prise', *The Library*, V (1955)

Knight, L. S., 'Welsh Cathedral Schools to 1600 A.D.', *Y Cymmr.*, XXIX (1919)

—— *Welsh Independent Grammar Schools to 1600* (Newtown, 1926)

—— 'Welsh Schools from A.D. 1000 to A.D. 1600', *Arch. Camb.*, 1919

Lewis, S., *Braslun o Hanes Llenyddiaeth Gymraeg* (Cardiff, 1932)

Lloyd, H. W., 'Welsh Books Printed Abroad in the Sixteenth and Seventeenth Centuries', *Y Cymmr.*, IV (1881)

Lloyd, J. E., 'Powel's *Historie* (1584)', *Arch. Camb.*, 1943

Miller, E. J., 'Wales and the Tudor Drama', *Trans. Cymm.*, 1948

Morgan, T. J., 'Arddull yr Awdl a'r Cywydd', *Trans. Cymm.*, 1946–7

—— 'Rhagarweiniad i Ryddiaith Gymraeg', *Trans. Cymm.*, 1948

Morrice, J. C., *Wales in the Seventeenth Century* . . . (Bangor, 1918)

New Oxford Companion to Music, ed. D. Arnold (2 vols. Oxford, 1984)

Parry-Williams, T. H., *Canu Rhydd Cynnar* (Cardiff, 1932)

—— *Carolau Richard White* (Cardiff, 1931)

Rees, B., *Dulliau'r Canu Rhydd* (Cardiff, 1952)

Roberts, E., *Dafydd Llwyd o Fathafarn* (Caernarfon, 1981)

Roberts, E. P., 'The Renaissance in the Vale of Clwyd', *FHSP*, XV (1954–5)

—— 'Siôn Tudur', *Llên Cymru*, II (1952–3)

Rowan, E. (ed.), *Art in Wales, 2000 B.C.–1850 A.D.* (Cardiff, 1978)

Rowlands, E. I., *Poems of the Cywyddwyr: a Selection of Cywyddau, c. 1375–1525* (Dublin, 1976)

Steegman, J., *Portraits from Welsh Houses: I. Houses in North Wales* (Cardiff, 1957); II. *Houses in South Wales* (Cardiff, 1962)

Thomas, G., *Eisteddfodau Caerwys* (Cardiff, 1968)

Thomas, I., 'Cyfieithu'r Hen Destament i'r Gymraeg', *NLWJ* XXI (1980)

Ward, A. W. and A. R. Waller, *The Cambridge History of English Literature* (Cambridge, 1949)

Williams, G., *Dadeni, Diwygiad a Diwylliant Cymru* (Cardiff, 1964)

Williams, G. A., 'Golwg ar Ymryson Edmwnd Prys a Wiliam Cynwal', *YB*, VIII (1974)

Williams, G. J., *Agweddau ar Hanes Dysg Gymraeg* (Cardiff, 1969)

—— 'Traddodiad Llenyddol Dyffryn Clwyd', *TDHS*, I (1952)

—— *Traddodiad Llenyddol Morgannwg* (Cardiff, 1948)

Williams, I. M., 'Ysgolheictod Hanesyddol yr Unfed Ganrif ar Bymtheg', *Llên Cymru*, II (1952–3)

Williams, W. O., 'The Survival of the Welsh Language after the Union of England and Wales: The First Phase, 1536–1642', *WHR*, II (1964)

D. UNPUBLISHED THESES

Bowen, G., 'Llenyddiaeth Gatholig y Cymry (1559–1829)' (MA Liverpool, 1952–3)

Bowen, G., 'Rhyddiaith Reciwsantiaid Cymru' (Ph.D. Aberystwyth, 1978)

Bowen, D. J., 'Y Gymdeithas Gymreig yn Niwedd yr Oesoedd Canol fel yr Adlewyrchir Hi yn y Farddoniaeth Uchelwrol' (MA Aberystwyth, 1951)

Carr, A. D., 'The Mostyn Family and Estate, 1200–1642' (Ph.D. Bangor, 1976)

Cleary, J. M., 'Welsh Recusant Clergy' (MA Liverpool, 1965–6)

Cole, D. M., 'The Mansells of Oxwich and Margam, 1487–1631' (MA Birmingham, 1966)

Eames, A., 'Seapower and Welsh History, 1625–60' (MA Bangor, 1954)

Edwards, P. S., 'The Parliamentary Representation of Wales and Monmouthshire, 1542–1558' (Ph.D. Cambridge, 1971)

Evans, B. M., 'The Welsh Coal Trade during the Stuart Period, 1603–1709' (MA Aberystwyth, 1928)

Evans, P. C. C., 'Sir John Perrot' (MA Cardiff, 1940)

George, I., 'Syr Dafydd Trefor, ei Oes a'i Waith' (MA Cardiff, 1928)

Gray, M., 'The Dispersal of Crown Property in Monmouthshire, 1500–1603' (Ph.D. Cardiff, 1985)

Greenway, W., 'The Bishops and Chapter of St. David's, 1280–1407' (M.Litt. Cambridge, 1959)

Griffith, W. P., 'Welsh Students at Oxford, Cambridge and the Inns of Court' (Ph.D. Bangor, 1981)

Griffiths, R. A., 'Royal Government in the Southern Counties of the Principality of Wales, 1422–85' (Ph.D. Bristol, 1962)

Gruffydd, R. G., 'Religious Prose in Welsh from the Beginning of the Reign of Elizabeth to the Restoration' (D.Phil. Oxford, 1952–3)

Herbert, A., 'Public Order and Private Violence in Herefordshire, 1413–61' (MA Swansea, 1978)

Howells, B. E., 'Studies in the Social and Agrarian History of Medieval and Early Modern Pembrokeshire' (MA Aberystwyth, 1956)

Thomas, C., 'The Evolution of Rural Settlement and Land Tenure' (Ph.D. Aberystwyth, 1965)

Thomas, C. M., 'The First Civil War in Glamorgan, 1642–46' (MA Swansea, 1963)

Thomas, D. H., 'The Herberts of Raglan as Supporters of the House of York in the Second Half of the Fifteenth Century' (MA Cardiff, 1968)

Thomas, G. R., 'Sir Thomas Myddelton II, 1586–1666' (MA Bangor, 1968)

Thomas, R. S., 'The Political Career, Estates and "Connection" of Jasper Tudor . . .' (Ph.D. Swansea, 1971)

Thomas, W. S. K., 'The History of Swansea from the Accession of the Tudors to the Restoration', (Ph.D. Swansea, 1958)

Williams, G. A., 'Astudiaeth Destunol a Beirniadol o Ymryson Barddol Edmwnd Prys a William Cynwal' (Ph.D. Bangor, 1978)

Williams, I. M., 'Hanesyddiaeth yng Nghymru yn yr Unfed Ganrif ar Bymtheg' (MA Aberystwyth, 1951)

Williams, J. G., 'Sir John Vaughan, Chief Justice of Common Pleas, 1603–74' (MA Bangor, 1952)

Williams, J. M., 'The Works of Some Fifteenth-century Glamorgan Poets' (MA Cardiff, 1923)

INDEX